THE LANAHAN READINGS

in the

American Polity

SECOND EDITION

THE LANAHAN READINGS

in the

American Polity

SECOND EDITION

Ann G. Serow
Kingswood-Oxford School
Central Connecticut State University

Everett C. Ladd
The Roper Center for Public Opinion Research
University of Connecticut

LANAHAN PUBLISHERS, INC.

Baltimore

Printed in the United States of America.

The text of this book was composed in Bembo with display type set in Garamond.
Composition by Bytheway Publishing Services.
Manufacturing by Victor Graphics, Inc.

ISBN 0-9652687-7-2

LANAHAN PUBLISHERS, INC.
324 Hawthorne Road
Baltimore, MD 21210

2 3 4 5 6 7 8 9 0

To Our Students

CONTENTS

PART FOUR

Federalism

PART FIVE

Congress

PART SIX

The Presidency

PART SEVEN

The Executive Branch

PART EIGHT

The Judiciary

PART TEN

Interest Groups

PART ELEVEN

Voting and Elections

PART TWELVE

Political Parties

PART THIRTEEN

The Media

PART FOURTEEN

Civil Liberties and Civil Rights

PART SIXTEEN

Public Welfare

PART SEVENTEEN

America in the World

PREFACE

The first edition of *The LANAHAN READINGS in The American Polity* began a happy new collaboration of the editors with LANAHAN PUBLISHERS, INC., and Donald W. Fusting, who founded this new publishing company in 1995. For over a decade, we had worked closely and confidently with Don on two earlier versions of this book, *The American Polity Reader*, and we were pleased that the association would continue—in fact, quite pleased as it turned out: *The LANAHAN READINGS* was assigned in over two hundred schools.

Launching another new edition of an established volume is still a big step. What matters to students using the volume, however, is what's between the covers. Here, readers of the new second edition will find in large measure both fundamental continuity in basic design and big changes in specific readings.

There's good reason for continuity. This book is designed to help undergraduates who are taking the basic American government course better understand their country's political system by providing essential readings on American ideas, constitutional system, core political institutions, public opinion, political competition, and policy debates. All of these readings have in fact shown exceptional continuity over time because they reflect the views and values of a society that is strikingly similar now at the end of the twentieth century to what it was when the United States was founded in the late eighteenth century.

At first glance, this proposition might seem surprising. After all, in some regards the America we now inhabit differs greatly from that of George Washington, John Adams, and Thomas Jefferson. They traveled either on foot or, quite literally, by horsepower; we travel faster and more comfortably in automobiles and jet planes. They could communicate only face to face or through the written word; we have now gone beyond the telephone to the Internet. The average life expectancy in their day was thirty-three years; in ours, seventy-five—and so on is the process of change across so many of the physical dimensions of life.

But in social and political values, Americans in 1776 and now, in the twenty-first century, are similar people. That's true because America's founding brought the nation to modernity so abruptly and completely. It was a profound break from the aristocratic past that dominated European life—as indeed life in countries all around the world. The great French social commentator, Alexis de Tocqueville, grasped this fact more fully perhaps than anyone else and wrote what is still the most insightful book on American society, *Democracy in America* (Volume I, 1835 and Volume II, 1839). "The emigrants who colonized America at the beginning of the seventeenth century," Tocqueville wrote, "in some way separated the principle of democracy from all those other principles against which they contended when living in the heart of the old European societies, and transplanted that principle only on the shores of the New World." He did not study America, Tocqueville went on, "just to satisfy curiosity, however legitimate; I sought there lessons from which we might profit. . . . I accept that [democratic] revolution as an accomplished fact, or a fact that soon will be accomplished, and I selected of all the peoples experiencing it that nation in which it has come to the fullest and most peaceful completion. . . . I admit that I saw in America more than America; it was the shape of democracy itself which I sought, its inclinations, character, prejudices, and passions."

Now, over 160 years after Tocqueville wrote, America remains a democratic nation and an intensely individualist society—the latter encompassing much of what he understood when he used the term "democracy." This broad continuity in social values and social structure goes far to explain the institutional continuities we find in *The LANAHAN READINGS.*

The world of American politics keeps changing, nonetheless. Students need readings on the country's political institutions and its political competition that present the American polity in a fresh, contemporary form. So for the second edition of *The LANAHAN READINGS in The American Polity*, we have replaced about a third of the selections. Among the many new readings:

Seymour Martin Lipset in *American Exceptionalism* describes American individualism as a double-edged sword.

Robert Roberts and Marion Doss discuss scandals, ethics, and the ongoing "public integrity war."

David Brady and Craig Volden focus in on "supermajorities" to explain congressional gridlock.

Linda Killian looks at what happened to the Republican revolution in *The Freshmen.*

Irwin Gertzog reports on the status of women in Congress.

Maurilio Vigil examines the Congressional Hispanic Caucus.

In *Strangers Among Us*, Roberto Suro reveals the grassroots development of an Hispanic activist group.

Steven Epstein discusses the variety of gay and lesbian movements and their goals.

Charles Black interprets the Founders' carefully wrought basis for impeachment.

E. J. Dionne sets the stage for election 2000 by examining the courting of the "Anxious Middle" voters by the Democratic, Republican, and Reform Parties.

Larry Sabato and Glenn Simpson in *Dirty Little Secrets* and Stephen Ansolabehere and Shanto Iyengar in *Going Negative* reveal the negative campaign strategies that will likely show up during election 2000.

Minnesota Governor Jesse Ventura offers his own approach to winning elections.

Michael Lewis in *Trail Fever* and Howard Kurtz in *Spin Cycle* offer some insights on politicians and the media.

To guide readers through these and all other selections, a brief description of each article appears in brackets below its listing in the Table of Contents. To help orient students, we continue to provide brief introductions to each article. In doing so, we can offer some political, and occasionally, historical and cultural background to the selections. To help students further, we again continue the process of writing footnotes not to dredge up obscure and unnecessary information, but to make clear those words, phrases, and allusions that students need defined or explained in order to understand the particular reading.

As with the first edition, Ann Serow has written the *Instructor's Guide and Quiz Book*. This ancillary gives instructors an ample amount of questions with which to test their students on each of the readings, and also, some further ideas on how the selections can be used. For example, there are a number of readings that can be set up in a point-counterpoint arrangement for instructors who might want to include this approach in their classroom.

Returning to our opening comments, we have been engaged in this project for over a decade. We believe that the continuity of having the same team, author/editors and publishing editor, has helped keep the goals of the book in focus: This is a book for students of American government and the list of selections was made, and revised, for them.

They, too, have contributed heavily to the reader-making process by their in-class comments. The selections can truly be said to have been class-tested. For this, we again dedicate *The LANAHAN READINGS* to these willing and observant participants, our students.

AGS
ECL

THE LANAHAN READINGS

in the

American Polity

SECOND EDITION

PART ONE

American Ideology

I

ALEXIS DE TOCQUEVILLE

From *Democracy in America*

In May of 1831, a fancily-dressed, young French aristocrat arrived in the United States to begin his "scientific" study of a new social and political phenomenon, American democracy. After nine months of traveling across the new nation, interviewing numerous Americans from all walks of life, Alexis de Tocqueville returned to France to write Democracy in America, *the single best source with which to begin our exploration of American government and politics. Tocqueville saw the United States as a unique nation. From the start, Americans were all equal. Some were richer and others were poorer, but all who were not indentured or enslaved had an equal opportunity from the start. This clearly was not the case in any other nineteenth-century nation. To the young visitor, this idea of equality was America's identifying mark, a most cherished, if elusive, national virtue.*

AFTER THE BIRTH of a human being his early years are obscurely spent in the toils or pleasures of childhood. As he grows up the world receives him, when his manhood begins, and he enters into contact with his fellows. He is then studied for the first time, and it is imagined that the germ of the vices and the virtues of his maturer years is then formed.

This, if I am not mistaken, is a great error. We must begin higher up; we must watch the infant in his mother's arms; we must see the first images which the external world casts upon the dark mirror of his mind; the first occurrences which he witnesses; we must hear the first words which awaken the sleeping powers of thought, and stand by his earliest efforts, if we would understand the prejudices, the habits, and the passions which will rule his life. The entire man is, so to speak, to be seen in the cradle of the child.

The growth of nations presents something analogous to this: they all bear some marks of their origin; and the circumstances which accompanied their birth and contributed to their rise affect the whole term of their being.

If we were able to go back to the elements of states, and to examine the oldest monuments of their history, I doubt not that we should discover in them the primal cause of the prejudices, the habits, the ruling passions, and, in short, of all that constitutes what is called the national character: we should there find the explanation of certain customs which now seem at variance with the prevailing manners; of such laws as conflict with established principles; and of such incoherent opinions as are here and there to be met with in society, like those fragments of broken chains which we sometimes see hanging from the vault of an edifice, and supporting nothing. This might explain the destinies of certain nations which seem borne on by an unknown force to ends of which they themselves are ignorant. But hitherto facts have been wanting to researches of this kind: the spirit of inquiry has only come upon communities in their latter days; and when they at length contemplated their origin, time had already obscured it, or ignorance and pride adorned it with truth-concealing fables.

America is the only country in which it has been possible to witness the natural and tranquil growth of society, and where the influence exercised on the future condition of states by their origin is clearly distinguishable. . . .

America, consequently, exhibits in the broad light of day the phenomena which the ignorance or rudeness of earlier ages conceals from our researches. Near enough to the time when the states of America were founded, to be accurately acquainted with their elements, and sufficiently removed from that period to judge of some of their results, the men of our own day seem destined to see further than their predecessors into the series of human events. Providence has given us a torch which our forefathers did not possess, and has allowed us to discern fundamental causes in the history of the world which the obscurity of the past concealed from them.

If we carefully examine the social and political state of America, after having studied its history, we shall remain perfectly convinced that not an opinion, not a custom, not a law, I may even say not an event, is upon record which the origin of that people will not explain. The readers of this book will find the germ of all that is to follow in the present chapter, and the key to almost the whole work.

The emigrants who came at different periods to occupy the territory now covered by the American Union, differed from each other in many respects; their aim was not the same, and they governed themselves on different principles.

These men had, however, certain features in common, and they were all placed in an analogous situation. The tie of language is perhaps the strongest and the most durable that can unite mankind. All the emigrants spoke the same tongue; they were all offsets from the same people. Born in a country which had been agitated for centuries by the struggles of faction, and in which all parties had been obliged in their turn to place themselves under the protection of the laws, their political education had been perfected in this rude school, and they were more conversant with the notions of right, and the principles of true freedom, than the greater part of their European contemporaries. At the period of the first emigrations, the parish system, that fruitful germ of free institutions, was deeply rooted in the habits of the English; and with it the doctrine of the sovereignty of the people. . . .

Another remark, to which we shall hereafter have occasion to recur, is applicable not only to the English, but to . . . all the Europeans who successively established themselves in the New World. All these European colonies contained the elements, if not the development, of a complete democracy. Two causes led to this result. It may safely be advanced that on leaving the mother country the emigrants had in general no notion of superiority one over another. The happy and the powerful do not go into exile, and there are no surer guaranties of equality among men than poverty and misfortune. It happened, however, on several occasions, that persons of rank were driven to America by political and religious quarrels. Laws were made to establish a gradation of ranks; but it was soon found that the soil of America was opposed to a territorial aristocracy. To bring that refractory land into cultivation, the constant and interested exertions of the owner himself were necessary; and when the ground was prepared, its produce was found to be insufficient to enrich a master and a farmer at the same time. The land was then naturally broken up into small portions, which the proprietor cultivated for himself. Land is the basis of an aristocracy, which clings to the soil that supports it; for it is not by privileges alone, nor by birth, but by landed property handed down from generation to generation, that an aristocracy is constituted. A nation may present immense fortunes and extreme wretchedness; but unless those fortunes are territorial there is no true aristocracy, but simply the class of the rich and that of the poor. . . .

In virtue of the law of partible inheritance, the death of every proprietor brings about a kind of revolution in the property; not only do his possessions change hands, but their very nature is altered; since they are parcelled into shares, which become smaller and smaller at each division. This is the direct and, as it were, the physical effect of the law. It follows, then, that in countries where equality of inheritance is established by law, property, and especially landed property, must have a tendency to perpetual diminuation. . . .

. . . But the law of equal division exercises its influence not merely upon the property itself, but it affects the minds of the heirs, and brings their passions into play. These indirect consequences tend powerfully to the destruction of large fortunes, and especially of large domains. . . .

Great landed estates which have once been divided never come together again; for the small proprietor draws from his land a better revenue, in proportion, than the large owner does from his; and of course he sells it at a higher rate. The calculations of gain, therefore, which decide the rich man to sell his domain, will still more powerfully influence him against buying small estates to unite them into a large one.

What is called family-pride is often founded upon an illusion of self-love. A man wishes to perpetuate and immortalize himself, as it were, in his great-grandchildren. Where the *esprit de famille* ceases to act, individual selfishness comes into play. When the idea of family becomes vague, indeterminate, and uncertain, a man thinks of his present convenience; he provides for the establishment of his succeeding generation, and no more.

Either a man gives up the idea of perpetuating his family, or at any rate, he seeks to accomplish it by other means than that of a landed estate. . . .

I do not mean that there is any deficiency of wealthy individuals in the United States; I know of no country, indeed, where the love of money has taken stronger hold on the affections of men, and where a profounder contempt is expressed for the theory of the permanent equality of property. But wealth circulates with inconceivable rapidity, and experience shows that it is rare to find two succeeding generations in the full enjoyment of it. . . .

. . . The social condition of the Americans is eminently democratic; this was its character at the foundation of the Colonies, and it is still more strongly marked at the present day. . . .

America, then, exhibits in her social state an extraordinary phenomenon. Men are there seen on a greater equality in point of fortune and intellect, or, in other words, more equal in their strength, than in any other country of the world, or in any age of which history has preserved the remembrance.

The political consequences of such a social condition as this are easily deducible.

It is impossible to believe that equality will not eventually find its way into the political world as it does everywhere else. To conceive of men remaining for ever unequal upon a single point, yet equal on all others, is impossible; they must come in the end to be equal upon all. . . .

2

JAMES BRYCE

From *The American Commonwealth*

The Englishman James Bryce visited the United States in the 1880s, during the so-called Gilded Age. His topic in this excerpt is equality in America. Equality can be measured in several different ways, he says, by money, knowledge, position, and status. The first three measures of equality point up the obvious differences among the American people. But wealthy or poor, educated or not, highly-positioned or lowly, Bryce concludes, Americans regard one another as fundamentally equal as human beings. A fellow citizen may be more famous or more accomplished or more successful, "but it is not a reason for . . . treating him as if he were porcelain and yourself only earthenware." Is Bryce on target one hundred years later? What has happened to the idea of equality in America in the post-porcelain, post-earthenware age?

THE UNITED STATES are deemed all the world over to be preeminently the land of equality. This was the first feature which struck Europeans when they began, after the peace of 1815 had left them time to look beyond the Atlantic, to feel curious about the phenomena of a new society. This was the great theme of Tocqueville's description, and the starting point of his speculations; this has been the most constant boast of the Americans themselves, who have believed their liberty more complete than that of any other people, because equality has been more fully blended with it. Yet some philosophers say that equality is impossible, and others, who express themselves more precisely, insist that distinctions of rank are so inevitable, that however you try to expunge them, they are sure to reappear. Before we discuss this question, let us see in what senses the word is used.

First there is legal equality, including both what one may call passive or private equality, i.e. the equal possession of civil private rights by all inhabitants, and active or public equality, the equal possession by all of rights to a share in the government, such as the electoral franchise and eligibility to public office. Both kinds of political equality exist in America, in the amplest measure, and may be dismissed from the present discussion.

Next there is the equality of material conditions, that is, of wealth, and all that wealth gives; there is the equality of education and intelligence: there is the equality of social status or rank: and there is (what comes near to, but is not exactly the same as, this last) the equality of estimation, i.e. of the value which men set upon one another, whatever be the elements that come into this value, whether wealth, or education, or official rank, or social rank, or any other species of excellence. In how many and which of these senses of the word does equality exist in the United States?

Not as regards material conditions. Till about the middle of last century there were no great fortunes in America, few large fortunes, no poverty. Now there is some poverty (though only in a few places can it be called pauperism), many large fortunes, and a greater number of gigantic fortunes than in any other country in the world. . . .

As respects education, the profusion of superior as well as elementary schools tends to raise the mass to a somewhat higher point than in Europe, while the stimulus of life being keener and the habit of reading more general, the number of persons one finds on the same general level of brightness, keenness, and a superficially competent knowledge of common facts, whether in science, history, geography, or literature, is extremely large. This general level tends to rise. But the level of exceptional attainment in that still relatively small though increasing class who have studied at the best native universities or in Europe, and who pursue learning and science either as a profession or as a source of pleasure, rises faster than does the general level of the multitude, so that in this regard also it appears that equality has diminished and will diminish further.

So far we have been on comparatively smooth and easy ground. Equality of wealth is a concrete thing; equality of intellectual possession and resource is a thing which can be perceived and gauged. Of social equality, of distinctions of standing and estimation in private life, it is far more difficult to speak, and in what follows I speak with some hesitation.

One thing, and perhaps one thing only, may be asserted with confidence. There is no rank in America, that is to say, no external and recognized stamp, marking one man as entitled to any social privileges, or to deference and respect from others. No man is entitled to think himself better than his fellows, or to expect any exceptional consideration to be shown by them to him. Except in the national capital, there is no such thing as a recognized order of precedence, either on public occasions or at a private party, save that yielded to a few official persons, such as the governor and chief judges of a State within that State, as well as to the President and Vice-President, the Speaker of the House, the Federal senators, the judges of the Supreme Federal Court, and the members of the President's cabinet everywhere through the Union. In fact, the idea of a regular "rule of precedence" displeases the Americans. . . .

The fault which Americans are most frequently accused of is the worship of wealth. The amazing fuss which is made about very rich men, the descriptions of their doings, the speculation as to their intentions, the gossip about their private life, lend colour to the reproach. He who builds up a huge fortune, especially if he does it suddenly, is no doubt a sort of hero, because an enormous number of men have the same ambition. Having done best what millions are trying to do, he is discussed, admired, and envied in the same way as the captain of a cricket eleven is at an English school, or the stroke of the university boat at Oxford or Cambridge. If he be a great financier, or the owner of a great railroad or a great newspaper, he exercises vast power, and is therefore well worth courting by those who desire his help or would avert his enmity. Admitting all this, it may seem a paradox to observe that a millionaire has a better and easier social career open to him in England than in America. Nevertheless there is a sense in which this is true. In America, if his private character be bad, if he be mean, or openly immoral, or personally vulgar, or dishonest, the best society may keep its doors closed against him. In England great wealth, skilfully employed, will more readily force these doors to open. For in England great wealth can, by using the appropriate methods, practically buy rank from those who bestow it; or by obliging persons whose position enables them to command fashionable society, can induce them to stand sponsors for the upstart, and force him into society, a thing which no person in America has the power of doing. To effect such a stroke in England the rich man must of course have stopped short of positive frauds, that is, of such frauds as could be proved in court. But he may be still distrusted and disliked by the *élite* of the commercial world, he may be vulgar and ill-educated, and indeed have nothing to recommend him except his wealth and his willingness to spend it in providing amusement for fashionable people. All this will not prevent him from becoming a baronet, or possibly a peer, and thereby acquiring a position of assured dignity which he can transmit to his offspring. The existence of a system of artificial rank enables a stamp to be given to base metal in Europe which cannot be given in a thoroughly republican country. The feeling of the American public towards the very rich is, so far as a stranger can judge, one of curiosity and wonder rather than of respect. There is less snobbishness shown towards them than in England. They are admired as a famous runner or jockey is admired, and the talents they have shown, say, in railroad management or in finance, are felt to reflect lustre on the nation. But they do not necessarily receive either flattery or social deference, and sometimes, where it can be alleged that they have won their wealth as the leading spirits in monopolistic combinations, they are made targets for attack, though they may have done nothing more than what other business men have attempted, with less ability and less success.

The persons to whom official rank gives importance are very few indeed, being for the nation at large only about one hundred persons at the top of the Federal Government, and in each State less than a dozen of its highest State functionaries. For these State functionaries, indeed, the respect shown is extremely scanty, and much more official than personal. A high Federal officer, a senator, or justice of the Supreme Court, or cabinet minister, is conspicuous while he holds his place, and is of course a personage in any private society he may enter; but less so than a corresponding official would be in Europe. A simple member of the House of Representatives is nobody. Even men of the highest official rank do not give themselves airs on the score of their position. Long ago, in Washington, I was taken to be presented to the then head of the United States army, a great soldier whose fame all the world knows. We found him standing at a desk in a bare room in the War Department, at work with one clerk. While he was talking to us the door of the room was pushed open, and there appeared the figure of a Western sight-seer belonging to what Europeans would call the lower middle class, followed by his wife and sister, who were "doing" Washington. Perceiving that the room was occupied they began to retreat, but the Commander-in-chief called them back. "Walk-in, ladies," he said. 'You can look around. You won't disturb me; make yourselves at home." . . .

Perhaps the best way of explaining how some of the differences above mentioned, in wealth or official position or intellectual eminence, affect social equality is by reverting to what was called, a few pages back, equality of estimation—the idea which men form of other men as compared with themselves. It is in this that the real sense of equality comes out. In America men hold others to be at bottom exactly the same as themselves. If a man is enormously rich, or if he is a great orator, like Daniel Webster or Henry Ward Beecher, or a great soldier like Ulysses S. Grant, or a great writer like R. W. Emerson, or President, so much the better for him. He is an object of interest, perhaps of admiration, possibly even of reverence. But he is deemed to be still of the same flesh and blood as other men. The admiration felt for him may be a reason for going to see him and longing to shake hands with him, a longing frequent in America. But it is not a reason for bowing down to him, or addressing him in deferential terms, or treating him as if he were porcelain and yourself only earthenware.

3

LOUIS HARTZ

From *The Liberal Tradition in America*

Scholar Louis Hartz has used Alexis de Tocqueville's idea that Americans were "born equal" as a take-off point for his complicated philosophical analysis of the American political tradition. Citing the ideas of John Locke, Edmund Burke, and Jeremy Bentham, Hartz points to the many paradoxes evident in American thought: "pragmatism and absolutism, historicism and rationalism, optimism and pessimism, materialism and idealism, individualism and conformism." Underlying all these paradoxes is the ultimate one. Hartz argues that America, in many ways the most revolutionary nation in the world, never really had a revolution to attain the goal of equality. This paradox places the United States in a "strange relationship" with the nations that seek to emulate America's success.

THE ANALYSIS which this book contains is based on what might be called the storybook truth about American history: that America was settled by men who fled from the feudal and clerical oppressions of the Old World. If there is anything in this view, as old as the national folklore itself, then the outstanding thing about the American community in Western history ought to be the nonexistence of those oppressions, or since the reaction against them was in the broadest sense liberal, that the American community is a liberal community. We are confronted, as it were, with a kind of inverted Trotskyite law of combined development, America skipping the feudal stage of history as Russia presumably skipped the liberal stage. . . . One of the central characteristics of a nonfeudal society is that it lacks a genuine revolutionary tradition, the tradition which in Europe has been linked with the Puritan and French revolutions: that it is "born equal," as Tocqueville said. . . .

Surely, then, it is a remarkable force: this fixed, dogmatic liberalism of a liberal way of life. It is the secret root from which have sprung many of the most puzzling of American cultural phenomena. . . .

At bottom it is riddled with paradox. Here is a Lockian doctrine which in the West as a whole is the symbol of rationalism, yet in America the devotion to it has been so irrational that it has not even been recognized for what it is: liberalism. There has never been a "liberal movement" or a real "liberal party" in America: we have only had the American Way of Life, a nationalist articulation of Locke which usually does not know that Locke himself is involved; and we did not even get that until after the Civil War when the Whigs of the nation, deserting the Hamiltonian tradition, saw the capital that could be made out of it. This is why even critics who have noticed America's moral unity have usually missed its substance. Ironically, "liberalism" is a stranger in the land of its greatest realization and fulfillment. But this is not all. Here is a doctrine which everywhere in the West has been a glorious symbol of individual liberty, yet in America its compulsive power has been so great that it has posed a threat to liberty itself. Actually Locke has a hidden conformitarian germ to begin with, since natural law tells equal people equal things, but when this germ is fed by the explosive power of modern nationalism, it mushrooms into something pretty remarkable. One can reasonably wonder about the liberty one finds in Burke.

I believe that this is the basic ethical problem of a liberal society: not the danger of the majority which has been its conscious fear, but the danger of unanimity, which has slumbered unconsciously behind it: the "tyranny of opinion" that Tocqueville saw unfolding. . . . When Tocqueville wrote that the "great advantage" of the American lay in the fact that he did not have "to endure a democratic revolution," he advanced what was surely one of his most fundamental insights into American life. However, while many of his observations have been remembered but not followed up, this one has scarcely even been remembered. Perhaps it is because, fearing revolution in the present, we like to think of it in the past, and we are reluctant to concede that its romance has been missing from our lives. Perhaps it is because the plain evidence of the American revolution of 1776, especially the evidence of its social impact that our newer historians have collected, has made the comment of Tocqueville seem thoroughly enigmatic. But in the last analysis, of course, the question of its validity is a question of perspective. Tocqueville was writing with the great revolutions of Europe in mind, and from that point of view the outstanding thing about the American effort of 1776 was bound to be, not the freedom to which it led, but the established feudal structure it did not have to destroy. . . .

Thus the fact that the Americans did not have to endure a "democratic revolution" deeply conditioned their outlook on people elsewhere who did; and by helping to thwart the crusading spirit in them, it gave to the wild enthusiasms of Europe an appearance not only of analytic error but of unrequited love. Symbols of a world revolution, the Americans were not in truth world revolutionaries. There is no use complaining about the confusions implicit in this position, as Woodrow Wilson used to complain when he said that we had "no business" permitting the French to get the wrong impression about the American revolution. On both sides the reactions that arose were well-nigh inevitable. But one cannot help wondering about something else: the satisfying use to which our folklore has been able to put the incongruity of America's revolutionary role. For if the "contamination" that Jefferson feared, and that found its classic expression in Washington's Farewell Address, has been a part of the American myth, so has the "round the world" significance of the shots that were fired at Concord. We have been able to dream of ourselves as emancipators of the world at the very moment that we have withdrawn from it. We have been able to see ourselves as saviors at the very moment that we have been isolationists. Here, surely, is one of the great American luxuries that the twentieth century has destroyed. . . . When the Americans celebrated the uniqueness of their own society, they were on the track of a personal insight of the profoundest importance. For the nonfeudal world in which they lived shaped every aspect of their social thought: it gave them a frame of mind that cannot be found anywhere else in the eighteenth century, or in the wider history of modern revolutions. . . . The issue of history itself is deeply involved here. On this score, inevitably, the fact that the revolutionaries of 1776 had inherited the freest society in the world shaped their thinking in an intricate way. It gave them, in the first place, an appearance of outright conservatism. . . . The past had been good to the Americans, and they knew it. . . .

Actually, the form of America's traditionalism was one thing, its content quite another. Colonial history had not been the slow and glacial record of development that Bonald and Maistre loved to talk about.* On the contrary, since the first sailing of the *Mayflower*, it had been a story of new beginnings, daring enterprises, and explicitly stated principles—it breathed, in other words, the spirit of Bentham himself. The result was that the traditionalism of the Americans, like a pure freak of logic, often bore amazing marks of antihistorical rationalism. The clearest case of this undoubtedly is to be found in the revolutionary constitutions of 1776, which evoked, as Franklin reported, the "rapture" of European liberals everywhere. In America, of course, the concept of a written constitution, including many of the mechanical devices it embodied, was the end-product of a chain of historical experience that went back to the Mayflower

*Louis Bonald and Joseph de Maistre were prominent French conservative political theorists of the early nineteenth century. Both were inveterate enemies of the radical and rationalistic ideas associated with the French Revolution. They were leading figures in the European Reaction.—EDS.

Compact and the Plantation Covenants of the New England towns: it was the essence of political traditionalism. But in Europe just the reverse was true. The concept was the darling of the rationalists—a symbol of the emancipated mind at work. . . .

But how then are we to describe these baffling Americans? Were they rationalists or were they traditionalists? The truth is, they were neither, which is perhaps another way of saying that they were both. For the war between Burke and Bentham on the score of tradition, which made a great deal of sense in a society where men had lived in the shadow of feudal institutions, made comparatively little sense in a society where for years they had been creating new states, planning new settlements, and, as Jefferson said, literally building new lives.* In such a society a strange dialectic was fated to appear, which would somehow unite the antagonistic components of the European mind; the past became a continuous future, and the God of the traditionalists sanctioned the very arrogance of the men who defied Him.

This shattering of the time categories of Europe, this Hegelian-like revolution in historic perspective, goes far to explain one of the enduring secrets of the American character: a capacity to combine rock-ribbed traditionalism with high inventiveness, ancestor worship with ardent optimism. Most critics have seized upon one or the other of these aspects of the American mind, finding it impossible to conceive how both can go together. That is why the insight of Gunnar Myrdal is a very distinguished one when he writes: "America is . . . conservative. . . . But the principles conserved are liberal and some, indeed, are radical." Radicalism and conservatism have been twisted entirely out of shape by the liberal flow of American history. . . .

What I have been doing here is fairly evident: I have been interpreting the social thought of the American revolution in terms of the social goals *it did not need to achieve.* Given the usual approach, this may seem like a perverse inversion of the reasonable course of things; but in a world where the "canon and feudal law" are missing, how else are we to understand the philosophy of a liberal revolution? The remarkable thing about the "spirit of 1776," as we have seen, is not that it sought emancipation but that it sought it in a sober temper; not that it opposed power but that it opposed it ruthlessly and continuously; not that it looked forward to the

*Edmund Burke, an eighteenth-century English political theorist, is perhaps the most artful defender of tradition in the history of political theory. Jeremy Bentham, an English theorist of the late eighteenth and early nineteenth centuries, was as rationalistic as Burke was traditionalistic. While Burke generally saw virtues in inherited institutions, Bentham generally advocated their reform.—EDS.

future but that it worshiped the past as well. Even these perspectives, however, are only part of the story, misleading in themselves. The "free air" of American life, as John Jay once happily put it, penetrated to deeper levels of the American mind, twisting it in strange ways, producing a set of results fundamental to everything else in American thought. The clue to these results lies in the following fact: the Americans, though models to all the world of the middle class way of life, lacked the passionate middle class consciousness which saturated the liberal thought of Europe. . . .

But this is not all. If the position of the colonial Americans saved them from many of the class obsessions of Europe, it did something else as well: it inspired them with a peculiar sense of community that Europe had never known. . . . Amid the "free air" of American life, something new appeared: men began to be held together, not by the knowledge that they were different parts of a corporate whole, but by the knowledge that they were similar participants in a uniform way of life—by that "pleasing uniformity of decent competence" which Crèvecoeur loved so much. The Americans themselves were not unaware of this. When Peter Thacher proudly announced that "simplicity of manners" was the mark of the revolutionary colonists, what was he saying if not that the norms of a single class in Europe were enough to sustain virtually a whole society in America? Richard Hildreth, writing after the leveling impact of the Jacksonian revolution had made this point far more obvious, put his finger directly on it. He denounced feudal Europe, where "half a dozen different codes of morals," often in flagrant contradiction with one another, flourished "in the same community," and celebrated the fact that America was producing "one code, moral standard, by which the actions of all are to be judged. . . . " Hildreth knew that America was a marvelous mixture of many peoples and many religions, but he also knew that it was characterized by something more marvelous even than that: the power of the liberal norm to penetrate them all.

Now a sense of community based on a sense of uniformity is a deceptive thing. It looks individualistic, and in part it actually is. It cannot tolerate internal relationships of disparity, and hence can easily inspire the kind of advice that Professor Nettels once imagined a colonial farmer giving his son: "Remember that you are as good as any man—and also that you are no better." But in another sense it is profoundly anti-individualistic, because the common standard is its very essence, and deviations from that standard inspire it with an irrational fright. The man who is as good as his neighbors is in a tough spot when he confronts all of his neighbors combined. Thus William Graham Sumner looked at the other side of

Professor Nettels's colonial coin and did not like what he saw: "public opinion" was an "impervious mistress. . . . Mrs. Grundy held powerful sway and Gossip was her prime minister."

Here we have the "tyranny of the majority" that Tocqueville later described in American life; here too we have the deeper paradox out of which it was destined to appear. Freedom in the fullest sense implies both variety and equality. . . . At the bottom of the American experience of freedom, not in antagonism to it but as a constituent element of it, there has always lain the inarticulate premise of conformity. . . . American political thought, as we have seen, is a veritable maze of polar contradictions, winding in and out of each other hopelessly: pragmatism and absolutism, historicism and rationalism, optimism and pessimism, materialism and idealism, individualism and conformism. But, after all, the human mind works by polar contradictions; and when we have evolved an interpretation of it which leads cleanly in a single direction, we may be sure that we have missed a lot. The task of the cultural analyst is not to discover simplicity, or even to discover unity, for simplicity and unity do not exist, but to drive a wedge of rationality through the pathetic indecisions of social thought. In the American case that wedge is not hard to find. . . .

It is this business of destruction and creation which goes to the heart of the problem. For the point of departure of great revolutionary thought everywhere else in the world has been the effort to build a new society on the ruins of an old one, and this is an experience America has never had. We are reminded again of Tocqueville's statement: the Americans are "born equal."

That statement, especially in light of the strange relationship which the revolutionary Americans had with their admirers abroad, raises an obvious question. Can a people that is born equal ever understand peoples elsewhere that have become so? Can it ever lead them? . . . America's experience of being born equal has put it in a strange relationship to the rest of the world.

4

SEYMOUR MARTIN LIPSET

From *American Exceptionalism*

The first colony born of a revolution to become an independent nation, America has often been seen as an "outlier." In this reading, scholar Seymour Martin Lipset explores this idea, "American exceptionalism," in the context of the current decline in morals and civil society, the distrust of political leaders and institutions, and the data underlying Americans' support for the nation's creed. America's "individualism" can have both an "up" and a "down" side.

AMERICANS ONCE PROUDLY emphasized their uniqueness, their differences from the rest of the world, the vitality of their democracy, the growth potential of their economy. Some now worry that our best years as a nation are behind us. Americans distrust their leaders and institutions. The public opinion indicators of confidence in institutions are the lowest since polling on the subject began in the early sixties. These concerns suggest the need to look again at the country in comparative perspective, at the ways it differs from other economically developed nations. As I have frequently argued, it is impossible to understand a country without seeing how it varies from others. Those who know only one country know no country.

The idea of American exceptionalism has interested many outside the United States. One of the most important bodies of writing dealing with this country is referred to as the "foreign traveler" literature. These are articles and books written by visitors, largely European, dealing with the way in which America works as compared with their home country or area. Perhaps the best known and still most influential is Alexis de Tocqueville's *Democracy in America.* The French aristocrat came here in the 1830s to find out why the efforts at establishing democracy in his native country, starting with the French Revolution, had failed while the American Revolution had produced a stable democratic republic. The comparison, of course, was broader than just with France; no other European country with the partial exception of Great Britain was then a democracy. In his great book, Tocqueville is the first to refer to the United States as exceptional—that is, qualitatively different from all other countries.

He is, therefore, the initiator of the writings on American exceptionalism. . . .

When Tocqueville or other "foreign traveler" writers or social scientists have used the term "exceptional" to describe the United States, they have not meant, as some critics of the concept assume, that America is better than other countries or has a superior culture. Rather, they have simply been suggesting that it is qualitatively different, that it is an outlier. Exceptionalism is a double-edged concept. As I shall elaborate, we are the worst as well as the best, depending on which quality is being addressed.

The United States is exceptional in starting from a revolutionary event, in being "the first new nation," the first colony, other than Iceland, to become independent. It has defined its *raison d'être* ideologically. As historian Richard Hofstadter has noted, "It has been our fate as a nation not to have ideologies, but to be one." In saying this, Hofstadter reiterated Ralph Waldo Emerson's and Abraham Lincoln's emphases on the country's "political religion," alluding in effect to the former's statement that becoming American was a religious, that is, ideological act. The ex–Soviet Union apart, other countries define themselves by a common history as birthright communities, not by ideology.

The American Creed can be described in five terms: liberty, egalitarianism, individualism, populism, and laissez-faire. Egalitarianism, in its American meaning, as Tocqueville emphasized, involves equality of opportunity and respect, not of result or condition. These values reflect the absence of feudal structures, monarchies, and aristocracies. As a new society, the country lacked the emphasis on social hierarchy and status differences. . . .

The belief that the traditional values which underlie American exceptionalism will continue to determine American behavior at the end of the twentieth century has been challenged by those who call for a fundamental change in our national values to stop a moral decline. These critics do not see that what they find fault with is the dark side of American exceptionalism; developments which, like many of the positive features, derive from the country's organizing principles. These include rising crime rates, increased drug use, the dissolution of the traditional family, sexual promiscuity, and excessive litigiousness.

Public opinion data over the past thirty years reveal a consistently pessimistic outlook regarding the ethical stock of America. The Gallup organization has measured this sentiment in polls over three decades. Even in 1963, only 34 percent responded affirmatively to the question whether they were "satisfied with the honesty and standards of behavior of people in the country today?" while 59 percent were dissatisfied. In 1973, 22 percent were satisfied and 72 percent were not; by 1992, the gap widened to 20 percent and 78 percent. Americans have always yearned for the "good old days." Yet, as the statistics show, the trend over the past few decades is toward great pessimism about the country. People are more negative with regard to moral prospects than before. In mid-1994, three-quarters of Americans told pollsters that the country is in moral and spiritual decline. Over two-thirds believe it is seriously off track.

Though some of these social trends are recent and disturbing, others have surprisingly long-standing roots in American society. The critics have exaggerated many of the problems in the quest to demonstrate decay. There is, however, no denying that the impression of a change in basic values exists, and to dismiss public perception as somehow wrong or misinformed is to deny the reality of individual experience. The most forceful and well-intentioned attempts to address these perceptions have sought to hold the emphasis on individualism and competitiveness as being responsible for the rending of the nation's social and political fabric, and the corresponding decline in adherence to traditional norms. And to be sure . . . these values are significant forces in American culture, with wide spread impact on Americans' views of their social obligations.

American values are quite complex, particularly because of paradoxes within our culture that permit pernicious and beneficial social phenomena to arise simultaneously from the same basic beliefs. The American Creed is something of a double-edged sword: it fosters a high sense of personal responsibility, independent initiative, and voluntarism even as it also encourages self-serving behavior, atomism, and a disregard for communal good. More specifically, its emphasis on individualism threatens traditional forms of community morality, and thus has historically promoted a particularly virulent strain of greedy behavior. At the same time, it represents a tremendous asset, encouraging the self-reflection necessary for responsible judgment, for fostering the strength of voluntary communal and civic bonds, for principled opposition to wars, and for patriotism. . . .

The moral content of Americanism is only meaningful insofar as it is expressed within a social context, and that context is civil society. Commentaries, derived from Tocqueville, on the importance of civil associations permeate classically liberal (i.e., libertarian) treatments of democratic life, which argue that an idealized individualism is more attractive and more readily attainable than any idealized collectivism.

Central to this American conception of individualism is the importance of civil society and voluntary associations. Zbigniew Rau comments: "Civil society is an association of rational agents who decide for themselves whether to join it and how to act in it. . . . Therefore, the creation of and participation in civil society is caused by and further promotes the reassertion of its members as fully rational and moral agents." These associations—including churches, civic organizations, school boards, and philanthropic volunteer groups—are lifelong training grounds of citizenship and leadership, and create communication networks, conclusions Tocqueville drew from American practice. They strengthen moral bonds and facilitate the understanding of democracy.

But taking part in civil society does not simply mean belonging to collective entities and thereby embedding oneself within a social identity. Rather, it is a dynamic and sometimes problematic process of engagement between the individual and associations linked to interests and ideas. . . .

Although civil society, association life, is, as Tocqueville also noted, stronger here than elsewhere, the American data, much of which has been assembled by Robert Putnam, indicate that "civic engagement," to use his term, and political commitment have declined in the past three decades. He notes that "participation in many types of civic associations from religious groups to labor unions, from women's clubs to fraternal clubs and from neighborhood gatherings to bowling leagues has fallen off."

Most, but not all, of the available evidence bears out these generalizations. A Roper survey taken in August 1993 indicates that the percentage of people who have "attended a public meeting on town or school affairs" has dropped by more than a third, from 23 percent in 1973 to 16 percent in 1993. NORC data indicate that the proportion who attended a political rally or speech, who served on a committee, or who were officers of a club or organization also fell off over this twenty-year period. All told, those reporting involvement in at least one of six civic activities declined from 50 to 43 percent.

One of the most critical forms of community participation in the United States has been in parent-teacher associations (PTA), reflecting Americans' high commitment to education. Putnam reports a very significant drop-off in membership in the PTA from the 1960s to the present, from 12 million in 1964 to 5 million in 1982, though there is some indication that membership may have rebounded somewhat to 7 million in recent years. Survey data gathered by NORC from 1974 to 1993 indicate that fraternal organizations have experienced a steady decline.

There are some contradictory trends. As noted above, Gallup Polls find that the proportion of people indicating that they have volunteered for charitable, "social service," or "non-profit" organizations has doubled between 1977 and the 1990s. Ethnic organizations have increased their total membership in percentage terms. And Putnam reports a type of civic organization that has grown in membership in recent years, groups like the National Organization of Women, the Sierra Club, and the American Association of Retired People (AARP). The latter increased from 400,000 dues-paying members in 1960 to 33 million in 1993. But these Putnam sees as essentially checkbook organizations, which do not promote civic engagement. Their members pay dues, but rarely attend any meetings and seldom, if ever, knowingly encounter other members. They are not mechanisms for communication or the learning of politically relevant skills. In any case, looking at the international data, Putnam reaffirms the conclusion that Americans are "more trusting and civically engaged than most other people in the world."

Putnam discusses various possible causes for the falloff in activity, including the movement of women into the labor force, the decline in the size and stability of the family, and high rates of geographic mobility, and finds good reason to reject these hypotheses. He notes the importance of television in helping to individualize the use of leisure time and points to various time-budget studies documenting the steady increase in time devoted to television, which has "dwarfed all of the changes in the way Americans spend their days and nights." NORC finds that the percentage of the population who watch television for only an hour a day or less decreased from 37 in 1964, to 27 in 1978, to 22 in 1989, and then went up to 25 in 1993. Those looking at the tube for four hours or more a day climbed from 19 percent in 1964 to 28 percent in 1993. Conversely, the proportion reading newspapers every day fell from 73 percent in 1967 to 46 percent in 1993. Other technological developments have had similar effects. For example, the growth in the technology for listening to music—the cassette tape, compact disc, and the Walkman—has helped privatize Americans and reduced their interpersonal contacts outside work. . . .

Popular involvement in civil society apart, the evidence has been growing that all is not well with the American polity. Over the past three decades, opinion polls show that the citizenry is increasingly distrustful of its political leaders and institutions. When asked about their "confidence" in government, large majorities, here as in almost every country, report that they have "none," "little," or "a fair amount" of trust in the president and the legislative bodies. Those who are strongly positive are minorities, usually small ones.

The United States provides a striking example of this breakdown of respect for authority. Confidence in all United States institutions inquired about in the opinion surveys declined precipitously and steadily from the mid-1960s, though the greatest part of the fall occurred early in that decade. The Louis Harris Poll, which has investigated the subject since 1966, reported in 1994 the lowest level of confidence in government institutions ever. Those expressing a "great deal" of confidence in the executive branch of government constituted only 12 percent of a national sample in 1994, as compared to 24 percent in 1981, and 41 percent in 1966. Trust in Congress was even lower—8 percent in 1994, contrasted with 16 percent in 1981, and 42 percent in 1966. Daniel Yankelovich reports a drastic shift for the worse in response to the question, "How much of the time can you trust the government to do what's right?" In 1964, 76 percent said "always" or "most of the time." The proportion so answering fell to 44 percent in 1984, and then to an all-time low of 19 percent in 1994, a finding reported in the latest Luntz Poll for the Hudson Institute as well. . . .

Given the anger about politics in the United States, what accounts for the continued stability of the American system? Why do we not witness grievous forms of mass unrest? Why is the major protest movement, led by Ross Perot, basically centrist, even conservative with respect to economic and social policy? Part of the answer to the conundrum is that most Americans are not unhappy about their personal lives or prospects; if anything, the opposite is true. They still view the United States as a country that rewards personal integrity and hard work, as one that, government and politics apart, still works. The American Dream is still alive, even if the government and other institutions are seen as corrupt and inefficient. A 1994 survey-based study of "The American Dream" conducted for the Hudson Institute finds that over four-fifths, 81 percent, agree with the statement, "I am optimistic about my personal future," while about two-thirds, 64 percent are "optimistic about America's future." Three-quarters, 74 percent, agreed that "In America, if you work hard, you can be anything you want to be." And almost 72 percent felt that "As Americans, we can always find a way to solve our problems and get what we want." And not surprisingly, when asked to choose between "having the opportunity to succeed and having security from failing," over three-quarters, 76 percent opt for the former; only a fifth, 20 percent, prefer the security option.

Gallup polling for *Times-Mirror* in 1994 presents similar results. Over two-thirds, 67 percent, expect their financial situation to improve a lot or some; only 14 percent say it will get worse. Large majorities reject the statement that "Success in life is pretty much determined by forces outside our control." Most affirm the traditional American laissez-faire ideology, with its emphasis on individualism, with 88 percent agreeing with the statement, "I admire people who get rich by working hard," and 85 percent agreeing that "Poor people have become too dependent on government assistance programs." More significantly, perhaps, 78 percent endorse the view: "The strength of this country today is mostly based on the success of American business."

The American political system, though distrusted and ineffective in dealing with major social issues, is clearly not in danger. Most Americans remain highly patriotic and religious, believe they are living in the best society in the world, and think that their country and economy, in spite of problems, still offer them opportunity and economic security.

5

EVERETT CARLL LADD

From *The Ladd Report*

In his role as executive director of the Roper Center for Public Opinion Research at the University of Connecticut, Professor Everett Carll Ladd closely follows the data on many political and social aspects of America. Here he uses poll data to assess the popular thesis found in the work of Robert Putnam and other social scientists that citizens no longer take part in associations and groups as they once did but rather prefer to carry on private, individual-centered lives. Putnam termed this phenomenon "bowling alone." Ladd, however, finds the evidence quite contrary. While older groups may have lost membership, newer ones are thriving. Americans are more active than ever in joining together for civic, religious, and political goals. Ladd's example of the displacement of the PTA by other parent-teacher school organizations illustrates his interpretation of the richness of group activity in the United States and reveals how carefully data must be analyzed to arrive at valid conclusions.

THE UNITED STATES is an individualist democracy. "Let government do it" has never been our thing. We've counted on individuals doing it—by accepting responsibility for building and maintaining a good society.

Somewhat paradoxically, an individualist democracy is unusually dependent on harnessing collective or cooperative energies. Individual citizens can't manage a society—can't possibly address its manifold needs in any satisfactory fashion—through solitary labors. We must come together in associations large and small where we learn and practice *citizenship.*

Our ideal has been and remains an America of active civic and social organizations, churches, philanthropies, and voluntarism—not just to help concretely with a myriad of social needs and problems but, even more important, to sustain vibrant community life. That the "me" will become too insistent, at the expense of the "we," is a persistent American worry. And engaging citizens in civic affairs is the persistent American answer to how a narrowly self-serving individualism can best be avoided.

No one has ever thought it would be easy, though. A "collectivist" individualism built around community engagement can release enormous civic energy, but it asks a lot of millions of citizens. It's not surprising that many in each succeeding generation of Americans have worried that vigorous community participation through groups and charities and voluntary service is somehow losing ground. . . .

These worries are very much evident today. The U.S. economy is hugely successful, but isn't "community" suffering even amidst these burgeoning material resources? Aren't we too transfixed by what *I need*, to make *me* happy, at the expense of what *we need*, as in our family life, for real individual fulfillment? Aren't we losing the level of confidence and trust in one another that's essential to the health of our democracy? Aren't we retreating into private pursuits, or to use a metaphor that has resonated in recent years, aren't we now increasingly "bowling alone"?

Polls pick up the current angst. For example, surveys taken by ABC News and the *Washington Post* regularly ask respondents if they think "things in this country are generally going in the right direction, or . . . have gotten pretty seriously off on the wrong track?" Much of the time large majorities answer that we're heading the wrong way: 57 percent said this in late summer 1997, even though the economy was doing nicely, compared with just 39 percent who thought the country was moving in the right direction. The *Los Angeles Times* had asked this same question in a 1995 survey and got similar results—55 percent said we were off on the wrong track, only 35 percent that things were on the whole moving positively. What's most instructive, when the newspaper's pollsters followed up by asking those who had said the country was somehow going the wrong way rather than progressing why they felt this way, 50 percent talked about crime, family breakdown, and a weakening of religious commitments and standards (while just 19 percent mentioned anything to do with the economy).

Such concerns are often expressed in terms of our "social capital" account. The traditional reference to capital involves economics, of course. My dictionary defines the term as "the wealth, whether in money or property, owned or employed in business . . . "; and as "any form of wealth employed or capable of being employed in the production of more wealth." Drawing on this root, "social capital" encompasses any form of citizens' civic engagement employed or capable of being employed to address community needs and problems and, in general, to enhance community life. The Great Social Capital Debate addresses this question: Are we spending down our supply of social capital? Many think that the balance is now dangerously low and worry about the consequences.

Are we right to so worry? In the pages that follow I will argue that the answer is yes from one important perspective, but an emphatic no from another. Social capital *is* crucial, and it's undergoing some major changes of form. But at the same time, an extensive record shows that we're building up our supply of social capital, not depleting it. . . .

I was waiting in line for a cup of coffee at a gourmet coffee wagon near my office when a hand patted my back and a voice boomed out: "So what do you think about 'Bowling Alone'?"

It was a distinguished colleague, not in the social sciences, who had just finished reading commentary on Robert Putnam's work, in particular on the argument advanced in his famous article ["Bowling Alone"]. It wasn't exactly the spot for an extended seminar on America's "social capital." I replied briefly that while I agreed entirely with Putnam (and many others) that the health of the country's associational life and individual participation in civic affairs is of vital importance, I didn't think Putnam was right in claiming that the data show civic decline. "Well, I don't know about the data," my friend replied, "but what he has to say feels right to me, right here." At that he gently patted his abdomen.

The Ladd Report wasn't written primarily as a response to Robert Putnam. Though his essays have received enormous attention, "bowling alone" has seemed to many a powerfully evocative metaphor for a set of worries—diffuse but substantial—about the health of contemporary citizenship. My University of Connecticut colleague is hardly alone in feeling that America's participatory civic life has fallen into sad disrepair. Instead of the nation of joiners so often celebrated in the past, we are, in this view, fast becoming a nation of loners. "Bowling alone" has become the widely accepted shorthand for these concerns. I take issue with Robert Putnam's essay, but only as one among many voices making similar claims. . . .

America's associational life is extensive, diverse, and decentralized—which makes it hard to sort out trends. As I've struggled with the data, I've often felt like I'm drowning in a sea of anecdotes. There are so many different stories—and inevitably they don't all point in the same direction.

These difficulties acknowledged, the debate over the health of civic America should be resolved by systematic empirical determination. I believe . . . that, taken together, the available data provide a reasonably clear picture of trends in our civic engagement—and that the trends show it extending, not contracting, as it finds new forms and outlets. . . .

Theda Skocpol thinks that the idea of a vigorous citizenry addressing social needs and problems outside of government is simply "Tocqueville romanticism." It's possible, of course, to present civic engagement in sentimental and unrealistic terms, but Tocqueville didn't romanticize things. He did observe that the United States of his day displayed a level and vigor in associational activity surpassing anything in Europe. "Americans of all ages, all conditions, and all dispositions constantly form associations," he wrote. "They have not only commercial and manufacturing companies, in which all take part, but associations of a thousand other kinds, religious, moral, serious, futile, general or restricted, enormous or diminutive." He thought that one type of American association that he called "intellectual and moral" was especially important. The United States had lots of groups pursuing political and economic interests, but Europe, too, had experience with groups such as these. It was in its churches, of great denominational diversity, and other groups committed to social improvement that America stood out. . . .

Tocqueville saw political democracy growing out of experience acquired in the great variety of civil associations—many entirely nonpolitical. "The greater the multiplicity of small affairs, the more do men, even without knowing it, acquire facility in prosecuting great undertakings in common. Civil associations, therefore, facilitate political associations." An individualist democracy requires that many people be trained to participate and accept responsibility for social outcomes. Even when they entirely lack political objectives, then, small groups are a kind of school of democracy.

National political institutions, notably political parties, in their turn provide essential democratic education for narrowly based community organizations. The latter always run the risk of becoming too assertive of their own immediate objectives, too unwilling to compromise. Broad-based political parties teach people that they must join with many others of diverse views if they are to succeed in advancing general programs. "Thus political life makes the love and practice of association more general; it imparts a desire of union and teaches the means of combination to numbers of men who otherwise would have always lived apart. . . . "

Tocqueville's final major argument about Americans' civic engagement was that, somewhat paradoxically, it was spurred, not diminished, by the strength of their individualism. Unless ordinary citizens have an expansive sense of their rights and responsibilities, and are reasonably confident that their society is organized in a way that lets them really make a difference, they are unlikely to bestir themselves. Tocqueville concluded that individualist Americans believed they were obliged to make personal effort on behalf of social amelioration—and that their society was congenial to such efforts. Individuals *should* participate, and when they do *it works*.

Though individualism may become too narrowly self-serving, without a strong, self-confident individualism an expansive idea of citizenship is impossible. This citizen accepts partial ownership and responsibility for the health of his/her society—which can't be exercised passively. There is no need to introduce "romantic" or utopian standards. Tocqueville's argument is simply that active, voluntary participation by large segments of the populace is needed if individualist democracy is to work. . . .

As I will argue, civic engagement in America is high and in fact increasing. There is good reason for the trend: It is easier to be an engaged citizen in the Information Economy than in an Industrial Economy. Writing in the early 1970s, Daniel Bell described the emergence of the United States (and other economically advanced countries) into a broad new era. He contrasted this emergent "postindustrial" society with its predecessor, arguing that whereas "industrial society is the coordination of machines and men for the production of goods," postindustrial society is "organized around knowledge." The key developments defining postindustrialism, Bell concluded, are "the exponential growth and branching of science, the rise of a new intellectual technology, the creation of systematic research through R&D budgets, and . . . the codification of theoretical knowledge." The technological revolutions of the postindustrial age have also dramatically expanded wealth. Thus postindustrialism extends the resources for civic participation. It increases dramatically the proportion of the public given advanced educational skills and new communications tools. It frees broad segments of the populace from grinding physical toil. By extending material abundance, it widens the range of individual choice and invites millions to explore civic life in ways previously out of reach for them. . . .

One reason the idea of declining civic engagement has seemed plausible is easy to see: Many older groups have in fact lost ground. Robert Putnam notes that membership or participation is down significantly in Lions Clubs, Shriners, Jaycees, Elks, Masons, the League of Women Voters, the Federation of Women's Clubs, the PTA, labor unions . . . and bowling leagues. Of course, membership is down even more dramatically in the Grand Army of the Republic (GAR), easily the largest social/civic group in post–Civil War America; and in the Anti-Saloon League, an association which energized millions of Protestant Americans in towns across the country in an effort, for a time successful, to make prohibition the law of the land.

Granted, the factors that caused the demise of the GAR and the Anti-Saloon League predated by many decades the drop in Jaycees and Elks. But groups have always come and gone, for many reasons. Membership declines become worrisome only when they're widespread, or if limited, when the groups in retreat are highly important civically and aren't being satisfactorily replaced. If the PTA lost half its members and other parent-teacher associations did not fill the gap, or if the PTA's decline reflected a growing unwillingness of parents to join with others in support of school programs and improvements beyond what's good for Amy and Christopher, that would point to a troubling loss of social capital in at least one key area. But, is that the case?

We will see . . . that there has been in fact no loss of parental engagement in school affairs. And this reflects the general pattern. Important changes are occurring in group life—but not decline. Many civic groups in America are further decentralizing. "Devolution" has come to them far more forcefully than to government. In addition, lots of new groups have emerged, crowding out some of the players of earlier eras. Environmental organizations are one example of groups on the rise. Soccer leagues are another. Churches, long a primary part of the country's associational experience, continue to evolve in response to changing styles of religious expression and social needs. . . .

Of all of the assertions of a decline in civic participation made in recent years, one of the most troubling is that involving the National Congress of Parents and Teachers. Data provided by the organization's national headquarters in Chicago show that the number of parents in local chapters plunged from the early sixties through the early eighties. Membership reached a high of 12.1 million in 1962 and then began falling off, slowly at first but rapidly in the late 1960s and throughout the 1970s. It reached a modern-day low in 1981 of just 5.3 million—a drop in just twenty years of 6.8 million parents. . . . Since most of us agree with Robert Putnam that "parental involvement in the educational process represents a particularly productive form of social capital," the PTA's experience deserves examination.

A few factors immediately give pause to the idea that PTA's membership troubles reflect an erosion of social capital. For one thing, note what's happened since the early 1980s. PTA membership nationally has by no means regained anything approaching its high mark, but it has climbed by roughly 1.7 million (1982 to 1996). If the steep decline of the earlier years is a disheartening indicator of eroding social capital, then the substantial gains in recent years should be a heartening sign of recovery. More important, a number of national surveys showed parental involvement in school affairs high and, if anything, increasing over the span when PTAs were declining.

The real reason PTA membership fell off wasn't that parents stopped participating; *rather, they associated increasingly with groups other than the PTA*. That is, they substituted other groups for the same basic functions. This was a big deal for the PTA, and for those who believe that its lobbying efforts are important. But it has nothing to do with developments in civic America. Months after I began puzzling over the PTA story, I discussed it with Harry O'Neill of Roper Starch Worldwide. He noted that in the New Jersey community where he lived, the local parent-teacher groups had decided not to disband but to disaffiliate from the national PTA—largely to keep for local use the large portion of dues going to the national and state headquarters. When I related O'Neill's assessment to my wife, she reminded me that when she was an officer of our local Mansfield, Connecticut, PTA in the late sixties, the group voted to become independent—calling itself a parent-teacher organization, or PTO.

The PTA's loss in O'Neill's New Jersey hometown, and in Connecticut, certainly did not represent a lessening of parental involvement. But how typical, in fact, were parents' decisions in these two communities of what was happening across the United States? Highly so, it turns out. In the 1960s and 1970s, huge numbers of local parent-teacher groups disaffiliated from the national PTA. They then took on a great variety of different names, but a large majority became PTOs. . . .

. . . [B]y the mid-1990s, less than one-fourth of all public and private K–12 schools had PTA affiliates—ranging from lows of just 4 percent of schools in Massachusetts, 7 percent in Wyoming, 8 percent in Vermont, and 9 percent in Nebraska to highs of 48 percent in Virginia, 51 percent in Maryland, and 72 percent in Utah. On its face it was unlikely that in education-conscious Massachusetts only one school in twenty-five had a parent-teacher group. Something else had to be happening.

There's a political argument over the cause of the PTA's decline. Critics of the organization charge it with becoming a "lapdog of the teachers' unions." According to them, the National Education Association and the American Federation of Teachers have, in effect, taken over the PTA and shaped its political agenda. This has allegedly turned off large numbers of parents. It's clear that many prominent education activists are mad at the PTA for its stands on issues like vouchers and school choice—

which the PTA opposes vigorously. But for many parents, "controlling things ourselves right here in town" and keeping all the dues money for local use are probably more important factors leading them to disaffiliate.

How many of the schools without PTAs in fact have no parent-teacher organization at all, or at least none in which parents are much engaged? That was a hard question to answer because no one collects data on PTOs or other unaffiliated parent-teacher groups. We had to conduct our own survey. Covering all fifty states was not possible given our resources, but doing a careful study in a couple of states was. I picked Connecticut—my home state, the country's most affluent, and one with high education levels and a highly urban population. For the other state I picked Kansas, in the agricultural Midwest, which has a demographic profile sharply different from Connecticut's in income, educational background, ethnicity, and occupation. In both these states we drew a random 10 percent sample of all state-accredited private and public schools and contacted their principals' or superintendents' offices. We then conducted telephone interviews to find out what (if any) parent-teacher organizations operated in these schools. We received outstanding cooperation from local officials and completed interviews at more than 90 percent of the schools in our original samples.

We found that virtually all the schools had parent-teacher associations that officials said were active. These officials described concretely the work being done. Their descriptions of the activities belie any claim that we have entered an era of "schooling alone." In both states the preponderance of the parent-teacher groups aren't affiliated with the PTA (or for that matter, with any other body). By far the largest share of unaffiliates call themselves PTOs, but in Connecticut, with numerous Catholic schools, "Home and School Associations" are also common. In Kansas some groups call themselves "Parents in Education" and "Parent-Teacher Groups" (Tables 1 and 2).

"PTA" is still a shorthand reference for the entire range of parent-teacher organizations. In fact, the PTA isn't the primary association of parents and teachers any longer; it's now a minority player. But because "PTA" is still the widely accepted shorthand, we have had the confusing case of surveys showing enhanced levels of "PTA involvement" in school affairs, even though formal membership in the organization was declining, or holding at levels far below 1960s highs. Surveys taken by the Gallup Organization for Phi Delta Kappa found the proportion of parents of public school children saying they had attended "a PTA meeting" over the past school year up from 36 percent in 1983 to 49 percent in 1994. . . .

It's impossible to measure precisely the extent and variety of parents' engagement in school affairs—whether working with their own children individually or coming together with others in organized activity—to examine curriculum issues, complain about educational programs, or enhance the schools' social and recreational life. Still, it's striking that not one set of systematic data shows a decline in parental involvement, while many show increases. If there's an empirical case for the argument that America's social capital is eroding, the experience of parents and schools doesn't provide it. Instead, the PTO story makes the case for the existence of expansive, energetic local engagement. . . .

The American ideology is commonly described in terms of a far-reaching individualism, and while that's valid, unless carefully qualified it's also misleading. The drift and consequences of American individualism are collectivist, though certainly not of a state-centered variety. It's a collectivism of citizenship. The value of each individual's shareholding depends upon the beliefs and behavior of millions of others. A sense of ownership encourages us to make sweeping claims of our rights, and to accept responsibility for the nation's health—and yet in both areas to feel vulnerable. We Americans have been less inclined than our counterparts in other democracies to turn to government for answers—in part because we've sensed that only the quality of our shared citizenship, expressed through a vast array of self-formed and self-managed groups, can sustain the type of societal life to which we aspire. . . .

Shortcomings in citizens' performance are a recurring lament—and sometimes, it must be said, for good reason. . . .

Present-day worries about the depletion of vital social capital are the latest expression of this persistent American anxiety: that too many citizens—on whom the quality of our individualist democracy depends—may not be up to the job. Recessions and depressions have caused social pain and prompted national doubts, but it's the sense of broad moral decline or insufficiency that has really shaken us in every era. The triggering events this time around are well known and deeply disturbing: a surge in rates of violent crime and drug abuse; of illegitimacy, divorce, and single-parent households—and implicated in all these a corruption of their childhood for all too many kids. Some related developments, such as the widespread use of abortion to end unwanted pregnancies, are intensely controversial; many others, though, are uniformly regretted. All saw sharp increases in their incidence in the latter half of the 1960s and early 1970s; and while there has been some recent improvement, none have returned to their pre-1960 levels.

A great many analysts locate the roots of these developments in the

Table 1 · BUT IT'S NOT THAT PARENT-TEACHER GROUPS ARE IN DECLINE: IN CONNECTICUT, MOST PARENTS' GROUPS ACTIVE IN SCHOOLS AREN'T PTA-AFFILIATED

AUTHOR'S NOTE: Staff of the Roper Center reached a random sample of 115 K–8, state-accredited schools—public and private—in Connecticut. There are in all 1,066 such schools; we drew a random 10% sample. Principals' and superintendents' offices were then contacted for each selected school and asked what forms of parent-teacher organizations operated in their schools. What follows are the distributions given in these telephone interviews.

	N	%
PTA	26	23
All independent, nonaffiliated groups	87	76
PTO	54	47
Home and School Association*	13	11
PAC (Parents and Children)	2	2
Other	18	16
No formal group	1	1
Refused	1	1
Total *N* = 115		

*"Home and School Association" is the Catholic school equivalent of PTO. "Other" includes 18 organizations each found in only one of 18 schools. Examples—"Parent Activity Club," "Principal's Advisory Committee," "Parents' Association," "Parent Council," etc.

AND THESE PARENT-TEACHER GROUPS ARE ACTIVE: WHAT THEY DO

	N	%
In-School Volunteers		
General classroom and office help	68	59
Library volunteers	36	31
Computer room volunteers	18	16
Reading/literacy volunteers	10	9
Lunch room volunteers	9	8
Fund-Raising (book fairs, magazine drives, bake sales, fairs, etc.)	46	40
Field Trips	23	20
Social/Cultural/Charity Events and Activities (plays, dances, arts programs, concerts, environmental programs)	21	18
Senior Citizen Volunteers (senior literacy volunteers, grandparents' programs, retired people as classroom volunteers)	9	8

Note: Adds to more than 100% due to multiple responses.

Table 2 • IN KANSAS, THE STORY IS MUCH THE SAME

AUTHOR'S NOTE: Staff of the Roper Center reached a random sample of 81 K–8, state-accredited schools—public and private—in Kansas. There are in all 792 such schools; we drew a random 10% sample. Principals' and superintendents' offices were then contacted for each selected school and asked what forms of parent-teacher organizations operated in their schools. What follows are the distributions given in these telephone interviews.

	N	%
PTA	21	26
All independent, nonaffiliated groups	50	62
PTO	27	33
Home and School Association*	4	5
Site Council	4	5
Booster Club	2	2
Other	13	16
No formal group	8	10
Refused	2	2
Total *N* = 81		

*"Home and School Association" is the Catholic school equivalent of PTO. "Other" includes 13 organizations each found in only one of 13 schools. Examples—"Parents Always Support Schools," "Parents in Education," "Parent, Student, Teacher Organization," "Parent-Teacher Group," etc.

THE GROUPS ARE ACTIVE: WHAT THEY DO

	N	%
In-School Volunteers		
General classroom and office help	75	93
Library volunteers	13	16
Computer room volunteers	8	10
Reading/literacy volunteers	17	21
Lunch room volunteers	10	12
Fund-Raising (book fairs, magazine drives, bake sales, fairs, etc.)	44	54
Field Trips	32	40
Social/Cultural/Charity Events and Activities (plays, dances, arts programs, concerts, environmental programs)	43	53
Senior Citizen Volunteers (senior literacy volunteers, grandparents' programs, retired people as classroom volunteers)	3	4

Note: Adds to more than 100% due to multiple responses.

strong new currents that roiled our historic individualism in the quarter-century or so after World War II, leaving aspects of it altered. But here agreement breaks down. Some critics see contemporary individualism almost as the villain—as seriously, if not fatally, flawed. Robert Bellah and his colleagues argue, for example, that the self-imposed restraints that once tamed individualism in its biblical and republican forms have been weakened in today's "expressive" mutation, leaving a radically narrow and often destructive sense of individual autonomy. Mary Ann Glendon, writing from a public law perspective, believes that a narrow, unnecessarily exclusionist emphasis on individual rights has diminished the society's capacity to attend satisfactorily to *responsibilities*, as opposed to *entitlements*. She sees America as being "set apart from rights discourse in other liberal democracies by its starkness and simplicity, its prodigality in bestowing the rights label, its legalistic character, its exaggerated absoluteness, its hyperindividualism, its insularity, and its silence with respect to personal, civic, and collective responsibilities." . . .

Liberal individualism continues, however, to have strong defenders. Jeffrey Hayes and S. M. Lipset take issue with communitarians who argue "that norms of responsibility to the collective whole should somehow be 'emphasized' in order to 'counterbalance' the destructive tide of individualism and selfishness in modern America. But the scale is not out of whack. Social developments in America have always been wrought with complicated contradictions, successes and failures. The way to ensure that we avoid moral decay is not to alter the culture, but rather to illuminate the ways in which we can use the moral tools with which our individualistic culture provides us so that we can fix the social problems generated by the underside of individualism." I strongly agree.

If the public now showed signs of abandoning its historic inclination to join with others to meet common needs; if positive energy applied to social improvement were dissipating—leaving narrowly self-serving impulses, always present, ever more ascendant—we would in fact be facing a crisis of American citizenship. That's why it's so important for us to get the facts on social capital. The levels of engagement of individual citizens in associational activities documented here—involving millions of kids in the physical training, competition, and friendships of soccer leagues; enhancing and enjoying our natural environment; supporting school programs in almost every city and town; helping the elderly and the infirm; sustaining vigorous community religious life; etc.—clearly refute claims that individualism's "dark side" is becoming predominant.

There *is* a dark side. Tocqueville saw it more than a century and a half ago. Hayes and Lipset are right that the big contemporary challenge isn't between individualism and communitarianism, but rather between competing impulses that have always inhered in America's individualist philosophy. There isn't any viable alternative in the United States to a far-reaching individualism. The answer to its deficiencies can only be a more elevated sense of what individuals can accomplish when they accept the responsibilities of citizenship and work together more constructively.

There's no magic formula for achieving this, but surely we have lots of resources. The "nation of joiners, volunteers, and givers" idea isn't myth; the foundation built from past experience is pretty strong. What's more, present trends are encouraging. Contemporary socioeconomic developments are adding to the supply of civic resources. In today's postindustrial, knowledge-based economy, far more Americans than ever before are getting educations that help confer the skills needed for active participation. The old neighborhoods of tight physical propinquity are far less important than they used to be, but better systems of information exchange and transportation have created a great variety of new and more inclusive communities of social interaction. Greater affluence and freedom from harsh physical labor probably haven't made our lives any less stressful, but they do give more of us a chance to choose among forms of community engagement. . . .

Contemporary America hasn't dissipated the country's historic reserve of social capital. We really do have a chance to pass on to succeeding generations a richer supply than any predecessor enjoyed. And for all the hand-wringing, lots of Americans understand this. The record examined here hasn't been compiled by a public that's given up on the demands of citizenship.

6

CORNEL WEST

From *Race Matters*

The opening pages of Professor Cornel West's book tell an unforgettable story of the pervasiveness of racism in the United States. Think about it the next time you wait for a taxi. In an America that promises a chance for life, liberty, and the pursuit of happiness to all its citizens, "race matters," West contends. He challenges all Americans to change their thinking about race: the problems of African Americans are not their *problems but* American *problems. West identifies the issues that threaten to disrupt the fabric of the nation—economic, social, political, spiritual—and he suggests a broad outline for solutions. By the next century, will a taxi stop for Professor West?*

THIS PAST SEPTEMBER my wife, Elleni, and I made our biweekly trek to New York City from Princeton. I was in good spirits. My morning lecture on the first half of Plato's *Republic* in my European Cultural Studies course had gone well. And my afternoon lecture on W. E. B. Du Bois's *The Souls of Black Folk* in my Afro-American Cultural Studies course had left me exhausted yet exhilarated. Plato's powerful symbolism of Socrates' descent to the great port of Piraeus—the multicultural center of Greek trade and commerce and the stronghold of Athenian democracy—still rang in my ears. And Du Bois's prescient pronouncement—"The problem of the twentieth century is the problem of the color line"—haunted me. In a mysterious way, this classic twosome posed the most fundamental challenges to my basic aim in life: to speak the truth to power with love so that the quality of everyday life for ordinary people is enhanced and white supremacy is stripped of its authority and legitimacy. Plato's profound—yet unpersuasive—critique of Athenian democracy as inevitably corrupted by the ignorance and passions of the masses posed one challenge, and Du Bois's deep analysis of the intransigence of white supremacy in the American democratic experiment posed another.

As we approached Manhattan, my temperature rose, as it always does when I'm in a hurry near the Lincoln Tunnel. How rare it is that I miss the grinding gridlock—no matter the day or hour. But this time I drove right through and attributed my good luck to Elleni. As we entered the city, we pondered whether we would have enough time to stop at Sweetwater's (our favorite place to relax) after our appointments. I dropped my wife off for an appointment on 60th Street between Lexington and Park avenues. I left my car—a rather elegant one—in a safe parking lot and stood on the corner of 60th Street and Park Avenue to catch a taxi. I felt quite relaxed since I had an hour until my next engagement. At 5:00 P.M. I had to meet a photographer who would take the picture for the cover of this book on the roof of an apartment building in East Harlem on 115th Street and 1st Avenue. I waited and waited and waited. After the ninth taxi refused me, my blood began to boil. The tenth taxi refused me and stopped for a kind, well-dressed, smiling female fellow citizen of European descent. As she stepped in the cab, she said, "This is really ridiculous, is it not?"

Ugly racial memories of the past flashed through my mind. Years ago, while driving from New York to teach at Williams College, I was stopped on fake charges of trafficking cocaine. When I told the police officer I was a professor of religion, he replied "Yeh, and I'm the Flying Nun. Let's go, nigger!" I was stopped three times in my first ten days in Princeton for driving too slowly on a residential street with a speed limit of twenty-five miles per hour. (And my son, Clifton, already has similar memories at the tender age of fifteen.) Needless to say, these incidents are dwarfed by those like Rodney King's beating* or the abuse of black targets of the FBI's COINTELPRO† efforts in the 1960s and 1970s. Yet the memories cut like a merciless knife at my soul as I waited on that godforsaken corner. Finally I decided to take the subway. I walked three long avenues, arrived late, and had to catch my moral breath as I approached the white male photographer and white female cover designer. I chose not to dwell on this everyday experience of black New Yorkers. And we had a good time talking, posing, and taking pictures.

When I picked up Elleni, I told her of my hour spent on the corner, my tardy arrival, and the expertise and enthusiasm of the photographer and designer. We talked about our fantasy of moving to Addis Ababa, Ethiopia—her home and the site of the most pleasant event of my life. I toyed with the idea of attending the last day of the revival led by the Rev. Jeremiah Wright of Chicago at Rev. Wyatt T. Walker's Canaan Baptist Church of Christ in Harlem. But we settled for Sweetwater's. And the ugly memories faded in the face of soulful music, soulful food, and soulful folk.

As we rode back to Princeton, above the soothing black music of Van Harper's Quiet Storm on WBLS, 107.5 on the radio dial, we talked about what *race* matters have meant to the American past and of how much race *matters* in the American present. And I vowed to be more vigilant and virtuous in my efforts to meet the formidable challenges posed by Plato and Du Bois. For me, it is an urgent question of power and morality; for others, it is an everyday matter of life and death. . . .

What happened in Los Angeles in April of 1992 was neither a race riot

*In 1992, four Los Angeles policemen were charged in criminal court with using unnecessary force in the arrest of Rodney King, a black man whom they had stopped while he was driving.—EDS.

†COINTELPRO was the FBI's "counterintelligence program," conducted over decades but most active in the 1960s. FBI Director J. Edgar Hoover used COINTELPRO to investigate and harass Americans whose activities were considered by the bureau to be subversive: socialist and communist sympathizers; anti-Vietnam War protestors; and especially, black citizens active in the civil rights movement. The press was instrumental in uncovering COINTELPRO's secret machinations in the mid-1970s.—EDS.

nor a class rebellion.* Rather, this monumental upheaval was a multiracial, trans-class, and largely male display of justified social rage. For all its ugly, xenophobic resentment, its air of adolescent carnival, and its downright barbaric behavior, it signified the sense of powerlessness in American society. Glib attempts to reduce its meaning to the pathologies of the black underclass, the criminal actions of hoodlums, or the political revolt of the oppressed urban masses miss the mark. Of those arrested, only 36 percent were black, more than a third had full-time jobs, and most claimed to shun political affiliation. What we witnessed in Los Angeles was the consequence of a lethal linkage of economic decline, cultural decay, and political lethargy in American life. Race was the visible catalyst, not the underlying cause.

The meaning of the earthshaking events in Los Angeles is difficult to grasp because most of us remain trapped in the narrow framework of the dominant liberal and conservative views of race in America, which with its worn-out vocabulary leaves us intellectually debilitated, morally disempowered, and personally depressed. The astonishing disappearance of the event from public dialogue is testimony to just how painful and distressing a serious engagement with race is. Our truncated public discussions of race suppress the best of who and what we are as a people because they fail to confront the complexity of the issue in a candid and critical manner. The predictable pitting of liberals against conservatives, Great Society Democrats against self-help Republicans, reinforces intellectual parochialism and political paralysis.

The liberal notion that more government programs can solve racial problems is simplistic—precisely because it focuses *solely* on the economic dimension. And the conservative idea that what is needed is a change in the moral behavior of poor black urban dwellers (especially poor black men, who, they say, should stay married, support their children, and stop committing so much crime) highlights immoral actions while ignoring public responsibility for the immoral circumstances that haunt our fellow citizens.

The common denominator of these views of race is that each still sees black people as a "problem people," in the words of Dorothy I. Height, president of the National Council of Negro Women, rather than as fellow American citizens with problems. Her words echo the poignant "unasked question" of W. E. B. Du Bois, who, in *The Souls of Black Folk* (1903), wrote:

*Rioting occurred in Los Angeles after a jury, made up of white citizens, acquitted the policemen who had been accused in the beating of Rodney King.—EDS.

> They approach me in a half-hesitant sort of way, eye me curiously or compassionately, and then instead of saying directly, How does it feel to be a problem? they say, I know an excellent colored man in my town. . . . Do not these Southern outrages make your blood boil? At these I smile, or am interested, or reduce the boiling to a simmer, as the occasion may require. To the real question, How does it feel to be a problem? I answer seldom a word.

Nearly a century later, we confine discussions about race in America to the "problems" black people pose for whites rather than consider what this way of viewing black people reveals about us as a nation.

This paralyzing framework encourages liberals to relieve their guilty consciences by supporting public funds directed at "the problems"; but at the same time, reluctant to exercise principled criticism of black people, liberals deny them the freedom to err. Similarly, conservatives blame the "problems" on black people themselves—and thereby render black social misery invisible or unworthy of public attention.

Hence, for liberals, black people are to be "included" and "integrated" into "our" society and culture, while for conservatives they are to be "well behaved" and "worthy of acceptance" by "our" way of life. Both fail to see that the presence and predicaments of black people are neither additions to nor defections from American life, but rather *constitutive elements of that life.*

To engage in a serious discussion of race in America, we must begin not with the problems of black people but with the flaws of American society—flaws rooted in historic inequalities and longstanding cultural stereotypes. How we set up the terms for discussing racial issues shapes our perception and response to these issues. As long as black people are viewed as a "them," the burden falls on blacks to do all the "cultural" and "moral" work necessary for healthy race relations. The implication is that only certain Americans can define what it means to be American—and the rest must simply "fit in."

The emergence of strong black-nationalist sentiments among blacks, especially among young people, is a revolt against this sense of having to "fit in." The variety of black-nationalist ideologies, from the moderate views of Supreme Court Justice Clarence Thomas in his youth to those of Louis Farrakhan today, rest upon a fundamental truth: white America has been historically weak-willed in ensuring racial justice and has continued to resist fully accepting the humanity of blacks. As long as double standards and differential treatment abound—as long as the rap performer Ice-T is harshly condemned while former Los Angeles Police Chief Daryl F. Gates's antiblack comments are received in polite silence, as long as Dr.

Leonard Jeffries's anti-Semitic statements are met with vitriolic outrage while presidential candidate Patrick J. Buchanan's anti-Semitism receives a genteel response—black nationalisms will thrive.

Afrocentrism, a contemporary species of black nationalism, is a gallant yet misguided attempt to define an African identity in a white society perceived to be hostile. It is gallant because it puts black doings and sufferings, not white anxieties and fears, at the center of discussion. It is misguided because—out of fear of cultural hybridization and through silence on the issue of class, retrograde views on black women, gay men, and lesbians, and a reluctance to link race to the common good—it reinforces the narrow discussions about race.

To establish a new framework, we need to begin with a frank acknowledgment of the basic humanness and Americanness of each of us. And we must acknowledge that as a people—*E Pluribus Unum*—we are on a slippery slope toward economic strife, social turmoil, and cultural chaos. If we go down, we go down together. The Los Angeles upheaval forced us to see not only that we are not connected in ways we would like to be but also, in a more profound sense, that this failure to connect binds us even more tightly together. The paradox of race in America is that our common destiny is more pronounced and imperiled precisely when our divisions are deeper. The Civil War and its legacy speak loudly here. And our divisions are growing deeper. Today, eighty-six percent of white suburban Americans live in neighborhoods that are less than 1 percent black, meaning that the prospects for the country depend largely on how its cities fare in the hands of a suburban electorate. There is no escape from our interracial interdependence, yet enforced racial hierarchy dooms us as a nation to collective paranoia and hysteria—the unmaking of any democratic order.

The verdict in the Rodney King case which sparked the incidents in Los Angeles was perceived to be wrong by the vast majority of Americans. But whites have often failed to acknowledge the widespread mistreatment of black people, especially black men, by law enforcement agencies, which helped ignite the spark. The verdict was merely the occasion for deep-seated rage to come to the surface. This rage is fed by the "silent" depression ravaging the country—in which real weekly wages of all American workers since 1973 have declined nearly 20 percent, while at the same time wealth has been upwardly distributed.

The exodus of stable industrial jobs from urban centers to cheaper labor markets here and abroad, housing policies that have created "chocolate cities and vanilla suburbs" (to use the popular musical artist George Clinton's memorable phrase), white fear of black crime, and the urban influx of poor Spanish-speaking and Asian immigrants—all have helped erode the tax base of American cities just as the federal government has cut its supports and programs. The result is unemployment, hunger, homelessness, and sickness for millions.

And a pervasive spiritual impoverishment grows. The collapse of meaning in life—the eclipse of hope and absence of love of self and others, the breakdown of family and neighborhood bonds—leads to the social deracination and cultural denudement of urban dwellers, especially children. We have created rootless, dangling people with little link to the supportive networks—family, friends, school—that sustain some sense of purpose in life. We have witnessed the collapse of the spiritual communities that in the past helped Americans face despair, disease, and death and that transmit through the generations dignity and decency, excellence and elegance.

The result is lives of what we might call "random nows," of fortuitous and feeling moments preoccupied with "getting over"—with acquiring pleasure, property, and power by any means necessary. (This is not what Malcolm X meant by this famous phrase.) Post-modern culture is more and more a market culture dominated by gangster mentalities and self-destructive wantonness. This culture engulfs all of us—yet its impact on the disadvantaged is devastating, resulting in extreme violence in everyday life. Sexual violence against women and homicidal assaults by young black men on one another are only the most obvious signs of this empty quest for pleasure, property, and power.

Last, this rage is fueled by a political atmosphere in which images, not ideas, dominate, where politicians spend more time raising money than debating issues. The functions of parties have been displaced by public polls, and politicians behave less as thermostats that determine the climate of opinion than as thermometers registering the public mood. American politics has been rocked by an unleashing of greed among opportunistic public officials—who have followed the lead of their counterparts in the private sphere, where, as of 1989, 1 percent of the population owned 37 percent of the wealth and 10 percent of the population owned 86 percent of the wealth—leading to a profound cynicism and pessimism among the citizenry.

And given the way in which the Republican Party since 1968 has appealed to popular xenophobic images—playing the black, female, and homophobic cards to realign the electorate along race, sex, and sexual-orientation lines—it is no surprise that the notion that we are all part of one garment of destiny is discredited. Appeals to special interests rather than to public interests reinforce this polarization. The Los Angeles upheaval was an expression of utter fragmentation by a powerless citizenry that includes not just the poor but all of us.

What is to be done? How do we capture a new spirit and vision to meet the challenges of the post-industrial city, post-modern culture, and post-party politics?

First, we must admit that the most valuable sources for help, hope, and power consist of ourselves and our common history. As in the ages of Lincoln, Roosevelt, and King, we must look to new frameworks and languages to understand our multilayered crisis and overcome our deep malaise.

Second, we must focus our attention on the public square—the common good that undergirds our national and global destinies. The vitality of any public square ultimately depends on how much we *care* about the quality of our lives together. The neglect of our public infrastructure, for example—our water and sewage systems, bridges, tunnels, highways, subways, and streets—reflects not only our myopic economic policies, which impede productivity, but also the low priority we place on our common life.

The tragic plight of our children clearly reveals our deep disregard for public well-being. About one out of every five children in this country lives in poverty, including one out of every two black children and two out of every five Hispanic children. Most of our children—neglected by overburdened parents and bombarded by the market values of profit-hungry corporations—are ill-equipped to live lives of spiritual and cultural quality. Faced with these facts, how do we expect ever to constitute a vibrant society?

One essential step is some form of large-scale public intervention to ensure access to basic social goods—housing, food, health care, education, child care, and jobs. We must invigorate the common good with a mixture of government, business, and labor that does not follow any existing blueprint. After a period in which the private sphere has been sacralized and the public square gutted, the temptation is to make a fetish of the public square. We need to resist such dogmatic swings.

Last, the major challenge is to meet the need to generate new leadership. The paucity of courageous leaders—so apparent in the response to the events in Los Angeles—requires that we look beyond the same elites and voices that recycle the older frameworks. We need leaders—neither saints nor sparkling television personalities—who can situate themselves within a larger historical narrative of this country and our world, who can grasp the complex dynamics of our peoplehood and imagine a future grounded in the best of our past, yet who are attuned to the frightening obstacles that now perplex us. Our ideals of freedom, democracy, and equality must be invoked to invigorate all of us, especially the landless, propertyless, and luckless. Only a visionary leadership that can motivate "the better angels of our nature," as Lincoln said, and activate possibilities for a freer, more efficient, and stable America—only that leadership deserves cultivation and support.

This new leadership must be grounded in grass-roots organizing that highlights democratic accountability. Whoever *our* leaders will be as we approach the twenty-first century, their challenge will be to help Americans determine whether a genuine multiracial democracy can be created and sustained in an era of global economy and a moment of xenophobic frenzy.

Let us hope and pray that the vast intelligence, imagination, humor, and courage of Americans will not fail us. Either we learn a new language of empathy and compassion, or the fire this time will consume us all.*

7

MICHAEL KAMMEN

From *People of Paradox*

Thinking about the United States, its history, culture, and politics, as a paradox is one of the most useful ways to tie together all the themes and facts in American government. Historian Michael Kammen offers a sometimes-fanciful, sometimes-profound analysis of the many paradoxes that riddle American life. Citizens expect their leaders to be "Everyman and Superman," he perceptively observes. Kammen takes on the difficult issue of the American melting pot; he substitutes the metaphor of a "super-highway" to explain nicely the country and its people. He points out paradoxes in all aspects of American life, ending with a poetic vision of the super-highway, along the side of the road, at Thanksgiving. Many scholars and thinkers are quoted in Kammen's piece, but his top source opens the selection: "We have met the enemy and he is us," cartoon character Pogo recognizes.

We have met the enemy and he is us.

POGO

*In *The Fire Next Time* (1963), African-American writer James Baldwin quotes a black slave's prophecy, found in a song recreated from the Bible, "God gave Noah the rainbow sign, no more water, the fire next time!"—EDS.

. . . OUR INHERITANCE has indeed been bitter-sweet, and our difficulty in assessing it just now arises from the fact that American institutions have had too many uncritical lovers and too many unloving critics. We have managed to graft pride onto guilt—guilt over social injustice and abuses of power—and find that pride and guilt do not neutralize each other, but make many decisions seem questionable, motives suspect, and consciences troubled.

Perhaps so many American shibboleths seem to generate their very opposites because they are often half-truths rather than the wholesome verities we believe them to be. Perhaps we ought to recall Alice in Wonderland playing croquet against herself, "for this curious child was very fond of pretending to be two people. 'But it's no use now,' thought poor Alice, 'to pretend to be two people! Why, there's hardly enough of me left to make one respectable person!'" . . .

This dualistic state of mind may be found also in the domestic political values subscribed to by most Americans. We are comfortable believing in both majority rule and minority rights, in both consensus and freedom, federalism and centralization. It may be perfectly reasonable to support majority rule with reservations, or minority rights with certain other reservations. But this has not been our method. Rather, we have tended to hold contradictory ideas in suspension and ignore the intellectual and behavioral consequences of such "doublethink." . . .

Americans have managed to be both puritanical and hedonistic, idealistic and materialistic, peace-loving and war-mongering, isolationist and interventionist, conformist and individualist, consensus-minded and conflict-prone. "We recognize the American," wrote Gunnar Myrdal in 1944, "wherever we meet him, as a practical idealist." . . .

Americans expect their heroes to be Everyman and Superman simultaneously. I once overheard on an airplane the following fragment of conversation: "He has none of the virtues I respect, and none of the vices I admire." We cherish the humanity of our past leaders: George Washington's false teeth and whimsical orthography, Benjamin Franklin's lechery and cunning. The quintessential American hero wears both a halo *and* horns.

Because our society is so pluralistic, the American politician must be all things to all people. Dwight Eisenhower represented the most advanced industrial nation, but his chief appeal rested in a naive simplicity which recalled our pre-industrial past. Robert Frost once advised President Kennedy to be as much an Irishman as a Harvard man: "You have to have both the pragmatism and the idealism." The ambivalent American is ambitious and ambidextrous; but the appearance of ambidexterity—to some, at least—suggests the danger of double-dealing and deceit. The story is told of a U.S. senator meeting the press one Sunday afternoon. "How do you stand on conservation, Senator?" asked one panelist. The senator squirmed. "Well, I'll tell you," he said. "Some of my constituents are for conservation, and some of my constituents are against conservation, and I stand foresquare behind my constituents." . . .

Raymond Aron, the French sociologist, has remarked that a "dialectic of plurality and conformism lies at the core of American life, making for the originality of the social structure, and raising the most contradictory evaluations." Americans have repeatedly reaffirmed the social philosophy of individualism, even making it the basis of their political thought. Yet they have been a nation of joiners and have developed the largest associations and corporations the world has ever known. Nor has American respect for the abstract "individual" always guaranteed respect for particular persons.

There is a persistent tension between authoritarianism and individualism in American history. The genius of American institutions at their best has been to find a place and a use for both innovators and consolidators, rebellious dreamers and realistic adjudicators. "America has been built on a mixture of discipline and rebellion," writes Christopher Jencks, "but the balance between them has constantly shifted over the years." Our individualism, therefore, has been of a particular sort, a collective individualism. Individuality is not synonymous in the United States with singularity. When Americans develop an oddity they make a fad of it so that they may be comfortable among familiar oddities. Their unity, as Emerson wrote in his essay on the New England Reformers, "is only perfect when all the uniters are isolated."

How then can we adequately summarize the buried historical roots of our paradoxes, tensions, and biformities? The incongruities in American life are not merely fortuitous, and their stimuli appear from the very beginning. "America was always promises," as Archibald MacLeish has put it. "From the first voyage and the first ship there were promises." Many of these have gone unfulfilled—an endless source of ambiguity and equivocation. . . .

Above all other factors, however, the greatest source of dualisms in American life has been unstable pluralism in all its manifold forms: cultural, social, sequential, and political. *E pluribus unum* is a misbegotten motto because we have *not* become one out of many. The myth of the melting pot is precisely that: a myth. Moreover, our constitutional system seems to foster fragmentation of power while our economic-technological system seems to encourage consolidation of power. Thus the imperatives of pluralism under conditions of large-scale technology commonly conflict with principles and practices of constitutional democracy. . . .

It has been the impulse of our egalitarianism to make all men American and alike, but the thrust of our social order and intolerance to accentuate differences among groups. We have achieved expertise at both xenophobia and self-hate! At several stages of our history, population growth has outstripped institutional change. The result in many cases has been violence, vigilante movements, or economic unrest, all with the special coloration of unstable pluralism. Because there are significant variations in state laws regulating economic enterprise, taxation, and welfare payments, people and corporations move to tax-sheltered states and to those with the most generous welfare provisions. In this way mobility becomes a function of pluralism.

I do not argue that pluralism is a peculiarly American phenomenon. But I do believe that unstable pluralism on a scale of unprecedented proportion is especially American. . . .

There is a sense in which the super-highway is the most appropriate American metaphor. We have vast and anonymous numbers of people rushing individually (but simultaneously) in opposite directions. In between lies a no-man's-land, usually landscaped with a barrier of shrubs and trees, so that we cannot see the road to Elsewhere, but cannot easily turn back either. Indeed, the American experience in some spheres has moved from unity to diversity (e.g., denominationalism), while in other areas it has flowed in the opposite direction, from diversity to unity (e.g., political institutions). Along both roads we have paused from time to time in order to pay substantially for the privilege of traveling these thoroughfares.

There have always been Americans aware of unresolved contradictions between creed and reality, disturbed by the performance of their system and culture. Told how much liberty they enjoy, they feel less free; told how much equality they enjoy, they feel less equal; told how much progress they enjoy, their environment seems even more out of control. Most of all, told that they should be happy, they sense a steady growth in American unhappiness. Conflicts *between* Americans have been visible for a very long time, but most of us are just beginning to perceive the conflicts *within* us individually.

It is a consequence of some concern that our ambiguities often appear to the wider world as malicious hypocrisies. As when we vacillate, for example, between our missionary impulse and our isolationist instinct. From time to time we recognize that the needs of national security and the furtherance of national ideals may both be served by our vigorous but restrained participation in world affairs. At other times these two desiderata tug in opposite directions. However much we desperately want to be understood, we are too often misunderstood. . . .

Because of our ambivalent ambiance, we are frequently indecisive. "I cannot be a crusader," remarked Ralph McGill, "because I have been cursed all my life with the ability to see both sides." Our experience with polarities provides us with the potential for flexibility and diversity; yet too often it chills us into sheer inaction, or into contradictory appraisals of our own designs and historical development. Often we are willing to split the difference and seek consensus. "It is this intolerable paradox," James Reston writes, "of being caught between the unimaginable achievements of men when they cooperate for common goals, and their spectacular failures when they divide on how to achieve the simple decencies of life, that creates the present atmosphere of division and confusion." . . .

We have reached a moment in time when the national condition seems neither lifeless nor deathless. It's like the barren but sensuous serenity of the natural world in late autumn, before Thanksgiving, containing the promise of rebirth and the potential for resurrection. On bare branches whose leaves have fallen, buds bulge visibly in preparation for spring. Along the roadside, goldenrod stands sere and grizzled, and the leafless milkweed with its goosehead pods strews fluff and floss to every breeze, thereby seeding the countryside with frail fertility. The litter of autumn becomes the mulch, and then the humus, for roots and tender seeds. So it was, so it has been, and so it will be with the growth of American Civilization.

8

ROBERT BELLAH AND OTHERS

From *Habits of the Heart*

American ideology touches more than just government and politics. It also guides the nation's social, economic, religious, and cultural life. It is fitting, therefore, that an important comment on American ideology comes from the discipline of sociology. Robert Bellah and his colleagues borrow Alexis de Tocqueville's phrase "habits of the heart" to explore the place of individualism in American life. The authors concede that individualism is the single most important ingredient in the nation's values, illustrating it with the symbol of cowboy-heroes Shane and the Lone Ranger. But, they contend, individualism cannot exist without being balanced by a sense of community.

INDIVIDUALISM lies at the very core of American culture. Every one of the four traditions we have singled out is in a profound sense individualistic. There is a biblical individualism and a civic individualism as well as a utilitarian and an expressive individualism. Whatever the differences among the traditions and the consequent differences in their understandings of individualism, there are some things they all share, things that are basic to American identity. We believe in the dignity, indeed the sacredness, of the individual. Anything that would violate our right to think for ourselves, judge for ourselves, make our own decisions, live our lives as we see fit, is not only morally wrong, it is sacrilegious. Our highest and noblest aspirations, not only for ourselves, but for those we care about, for our society and for the world, are closely linked to our individualism. Yet, as we have been suggesting repeatedly in this book, some of our deepest problems both as individuals and as a society are also closely linked to our individualism. We do not argue that Americans should abandon individualism—that would mean for us to abandon our deepest identity. But individualism has come to mean so many things and to contain such contradictions and paradoxes that even to defend it requires that we analyze it critically, that we consider especially those tendencies that would destroy it from within. . . .

The question is whether an individualism in which the self has become the main form of reality can really be sustained. What is at issue is not simply whether self-contained individuals might withdraw from the public sphere to pursue purely private ends, but whether such individuals are capable of sustaining either a public *or* a private life. If this is the danger, perhaps only the civic and biblical forms of individualism—forms that see the individual in relation to a larger whole, a community and a tradition—are capable of sustaining genuine individuality and nurturing both public and private life. . . .

America is also the inventor of that most mythic individual hero, the cowboy, who again and again saves a society he can never completely fit into. The cowboy has a special talent—he can shoot straighter and faster than other men—and a special sense of justice. But these characteristics make him so unique that he can never fully belong to society. His destiny is to defend society without ever really joining it. He rides off alone into the sunset like Shane,* or like the Lone Ranger moves on accompanied only by his Indian companion. But the cowboy's importance is not that he is isolated or antisocial. Rather, his significance lies in his unique, individual virtue and special skill and it is because of those qualities that

*Shane is the gunfighter-hero of the 1953 western film *Shane.*—EDS.

society needs and welcomes him. Shane, after all, starts as a real outsider, but ends up with the gratitude of the community and the love of a woman and a boy. And while the Lone Ranger never settles down and marries the local schoolteacher, he always leaves with the affection and gratitude of the people he has helped. It is as if the myth says you can be a truly good person, worthy of admiration and love, only if you resist fully joining the group. But sometimes the tension leads to an irreparable break. Will Kane, the hero of *High Noon*, abandoned by the cowardly townspeople, saves them from an unrestrained killer, but then throws his sheriff's badge in the dust and goes off into the desert with his bride. One is left wondering where they will go, for there is no longer any link with any town. . . .

[T]he cowboy . . . tell[s] us something important about American individualism. The cowboy . . . can be valuable to society only because he is a completely autonomous individual who stands outside it. To serve society, one must be able to stand alone, not needing others, not depending on their judgment, and not submitting to their wishes. Yet this individualism is not selfishness. Indeed, it is a kind of heroic selflessness. One accepts the necessity of remaining alone in order to serve the values of the group. And this obligation to aloneness is an important key to the American moral imagination. Yet it is part of the profound ambiguity of the mythology of American individualism that its moral heroism is always just a step away from despair. . . .

. . . The inner tensions of American individualism add up to a classic case of ambivalence. We strongly assert the value of our self-reliance and autonomy. We deeply feel the emptiness of a life without sustaining social commitments. Yet we are hesitant to articulate our sense that we need one another as much as we need to stand alone, for fear that if we did we would lose our independence altogether. The tensions of our lives would be even greater if we did not, in fact, engage in practices that constantly limit the effects of an isolating individualism, even though we cannot articulate those practices nearly as well as we can the quest for autonomy. . . .

. . . It is now time to consider what a self that is not empty would be like—one that is constituted rather than unencumbered, one that has, let us admit it, encumbrances, but whose encumbrances make connection to others easier and more natural. Just as the empty self makes sense in a particular institutional context—that of the upward mobility of the middle-class individual who must leave home and church in order to succeed in an impersonal world of rationality and competition—so a constituted self makes sense in terms of another institutional context, what we would call, in the full sense of the world, community.

Communities, in the sense in which we are using the term, have a history—in an important sense they are constituted by their past—and for this reason we can speak of a real community as a "community of memory," one that does not forget its past. In order not to forget that past, a community is involved in retelling its story, its constitutive narrative, and in so doing, it offers examples of the men and women who have embodied and exemplified the meaning of the community. These stories of collective history and exemplary individuals are an important part of the tradition that is so central to a community of memory. . . .

Examples of such genuine communities are not hard to find in the United States. There are ethnic and racial communities, each with its own story and its own heroes and heroines. There are religious communities that recall and reenact their stories in the weekly and annual cycles of their ritual year, remembering the scriptural stories that tell them who they are and the saints and martyrs who define their identity. There is the national community, defined by its history and by the character of its representative leaders from [early colonist] John Winthrop to [civil rights leader] Martin Luther King, Jr. Americans identify with their national community partly because there is little else that we all share in common but also partly because America's history exemplifies aspirations widely shared throughout the world: the ideal of a free society, respecting all its citizens, however diverse, and allowing them all to fulfill themselves. Yet some Americans also remember the history of suffering inflicted and the gap between promise and realization, which has always been very great. At some times, neighborhoods, localities, and regions have been communities in America, but that has been hard to sustain in our restless and mobile society. Families can be communities, remembering their past, telling the children the stories of parents' and grandparents' lives, and sustaining hope for the future—though without the context of a larger community that sense of family is hard to maintain. Where history and hope are forgotten and community means only the gathering of the similar, community degenerates into lifestyle enclave. The temptation toward that transformation is endemic in America, though the transition is seldom complete.

People growing up in communities of memory not only hear the stories that tell how the community came to be, what its hopes and fears are, and how its ideals are exemplified in outstanding men and women; they also participate in the practices—ritual, aesthetic, ethical—that define the community as a way of life. We call these "practices of commitment" for they define the patterns of loyalty and obligation that keep the community alive. And if the language of the self-reliant individual is the first language of American moral life, the languages of tradition and commitment in communities of memory are "second languages" that most Americans know as well, and which they use when the language of the radically separate self does not seem adequate. . . . Sometimes Americans make a rather sharp dichotomy between private and public life. Viewing one's primary task as "finding oneself" in autonomous self-reliance, separating oneself not only from one's parents but also from those larger communities and traditions that constitute one's past, leads to the notion that it is in oneself, perhaps in relation to a few intimate others, that fulfillment is to be found. Individualism of this sort often implies a negative view of public life. The impersonal forces of the economic and political worlds are what the individual needs protection against. In this perspective, even occupation, which has been so central to the identity of Americans in the past, becomes instrumental—not a good in itself, but only a means to the attainment of a rich and satisfying private life. But on the basis of what we have seen in our observation of middle-class American life, it would seem that this quest for purely private fulfillment is illusory: it often ends in emptiness instead. On the other hand, we found many people . . . for whom private fulfillment and public involvement are not antithetical. These people evince an individualism that is not empty but is full of content drawn from an active identification with communities and traditions. Perhaps the notion that private life and public life are at odds is incorrect. Perhaps they are so deeply involved with each other that the impoverishment of one entails the impoverishment of the other. Parker Palmer is probably right when he says that "in a healthy society the private and the public are not mutually exclusive, not in competition with each other. They are, instead, two halves of a whole, two poles of a paradox. They work together dialectically, helping to create and nurture one another."

Certainly this dialectical relationship is clear where public life degenerates into violence and fear. One cannot live a rich private life in a state of siege, mistrusting all strangers and turning one's home into an armed camp. A minimum of public decency and civility is a precondition for a fulfilling private life. On the other hand, public involvement is often difficult and demanding. To engage successfully in the public world, one needs personal strength and the support of family and friends. A rewarding private life is one of the preconditions for a healthy public life.

For all their doubts about the public sphere, Americans are more engaged in voluntary associations and civic organizations than the citizens of most other industrial nations. In spite of all the difficulties, many Americans feel they must "get involved." In public life as in private, we can discern the habits of the heart that sustain individualism and commitment, as well as what makes them problematic. . . .

The communities of memory of which we have spoken are concerned in a variety of ways to give a qualitative meaning to the living of life, to time and space, to persons and groups. Religious communities, for example, do not experience time in the way the mass media present it—as a continuous flow of qualitatively meaningless sensations. The day, the week, the season, the year are punctuated by an alternation of the sacred and the profane. Prayer breaks into our daily life at the beginning of a meal, at the end of the day, at common worship, reminding us that our utilitarian pursuits are not the whole of life, that a fulfilled life is one in which God and neighbor are remembered first. Many of our religious traditions recognize the significance of silence as a way of breaking the incessant flow of sensations and opening our hearts to the wholeness of being. And our republican tradition, too, has ways of giving form to time, reminding us on particular dates of the great events of our past or of the heroes who helped to teach us what we are as a free people. Even our private family life takes on a shared rhythm with a Thanksgiving dinner or a Fourth of July picnic.

In short, we have never been, and still are not, a collection of private individuals who, except for a conscious contract to create a minimal government, have nothing in common. Our lives make sense in a thousand ways, most of which we are unaware of, because of traditions that are centuries, if not millennia, old. It is these traditions that help us to know that it does make a difference who we are and how we treat one another.

PART TWO

The Constitution and American Democracy

9

RICHARD HOFSTADTER

From *The American Political Tradition*

Richard Hofstadter, one of the nation's leading historians, explores the real thoughts and motivations behind the men whom all schoolchildren have been taught to revere as Founding Fathers. Hofstadter's classic work points out the ambivalence of those who wrote the Constitution: they viewed human beings as selfish and untrustworthy, yet they strongly believed in the importance of self-government. The founders' ambivalence toward democracy led them to design the political system the United States still lives with today, one in which each interest (or branch or layer of government or economic class or region . . .) would be checked and balanced by competing interests. Hofstadter goes on to interpret what the near-sacred idea of liberty meant to the founders. Liberty was not really related to democracy, he contends, but rather ensured the freedom to attain and enjoy private property. To make this idea clearer, test the author's thesis against the current political debate over health care, welfare, or tax reform.

. . . THE MEN who drew up the Constitution in Philadelphia during the summer of 1787 had a vivid Calvinistic sense of human evil and damnation and believed with Hobbes that men are selfish and contentious. They were men of affairs, merchants, lawyers, planter-businessmen, speculators, investors. Having seen human nature on display in the marketplace, the courtroom, the legislative chamber, and in every secret path and alleyway where wealth and power are courted, they felt they knew it in all its frailty. To them a human being was an atom of self-interest. They did not believe in man, but they did believe in the power of a good political constitution to control him.

This may be an abstract notion to ascribe to practical men, but it follows the language that the Fathers themselves used. General Knox, for example, wrote in disgust to Washington after the Shays Rebellion that Americans were, after all, "men—actual men possessing all the turbulent passions belonging to that animal." Throughout the secret discussions at the Constitutional Convention it was clear that this distrust of man was first and foremost a distrust of the common man and democratic rule. . . .

And yet there was another side to the picture. The Fathers were intellectual heirs of seventeenth-century English republicanism with its opposition to arbitrary rule and faith in popular sovereignty. If they feared the advance of democracy, they also had misgivings about turning to the extreme right. Having recently experienced a bitter revolutionary struggle with an external power beyond their control, they were in no mood to follow Hobbes to his conclusion that any kind of government must be accepted in order to avert the anarchy and terror of a state of nature. . . .

Unwilling to turn their backs on republicanism, the Fathers also wished to avoid violating the prejudices of the people. "Notwithstanding the oppression and injustice experienced among us from democracy," said George Mason, "the genius of the people is in favor of it, and the genius of the people must be consulted." Mason admitted "that we had been too democratic," but feared that "we should incautiously run into the opposite extreme." James Madison, who has quite rightfully been called the philosopher of the Constitution, told the delegates: "It seems indispensable that the mass of citizens should not be without a voice in making the laws which they are to obey, and in choosing the magistrates who are to administer them." James Wilson, the outstanding jurist of the age, later appointed to the Supreme Court by Washington, said again and again that the ultimate power of government must of necessity reside in the people. This the Fathers commonly accepted, for if government did not proceed from the people, from what other source could it legitimately come? To adopt any other premise not only would be inconsistent with everything they had said against British rule in the past but would open the gates to an extreme concentration of power in the future. . . .

If the masses were turbulent and unregenerate, and yet if government must be founded upon their suffrage and consent, what could a Constitution-maker do? One thing that the Fathers did not propose to do, because they thought it impossible, was to change the nature of man to conform with a more ideal system. They were inordinately confident that they knew what man always had been and what he always would be. The eighteenth-century mind had great faith in universals. . . .

. . . It was too much to expect that vice could be checked by virtue; the Fathers relied instead upon checking vice with vice. Madison once objected during the Convention that Gouverneur Morris was "forever inculcating the utter political depravity of men and the necessity of opposing one vice and interest to another vice and interest." And yet Madison himself in the *Federalist* number 51 later set forth an excellent statement of the same thesis:

> Ambition must be made to counteract ambition. . . . It may be a reflection on human nature that such devices should be necessary to control the abuses of government. But what is government itself, but the greatest of all reflections on human nature? If men were angels, no government would be necessary. . . . In framing a government which is to be administered by men over men, the great difficulty lies in this: you must first enable the government to control the governed; and in the next place oblige it to control itself.

. . . If, in a state that lacked constitutional balance, one class or one interest gained control, they believed, it would surely plunder all other interests. The Fathers, of course, were especially fearful that the poor would plunder the rich, but most of them would probably have admitted that the rich, unrestrained, would also plunder the poor. . . .

In practical form, therefore, the quest of the Fathers reduced primarily to a search for constitutional devices that would force various interests to check and control one another. Among those who favored the federal Constitution three such devices were distinguished.

The first of these was the advantage of a federated government in maintaining order against popular uprisings or majority rule. In a single state a faction might arise and take complete control by force; but if the states were bound in a federation, the central government could step in and prevent it. . . .

The second advantage of good constitutional government resided in the mechanism of representation itself. In a small direct democracy the unstable passions of the people would dominate lawmaking; but a representative government, as Madison said, would "refine and enlarge the public views by passing them through the medium of a chosen body of citizens." . . .

The third advantage of the government . . . [was that] each element should be given its own house of the legislature, and over both houses there should be set a capable, strong, and impartial executive armed with the veto power. This split assembly would contain within itself an organic check and would be capable of self-control under the governance of the executive. The whole system was to be capped by an independent judiciary. The inevitable tendency of the rich and the poor to plunder each other would be kept in hand. . . .

It is ironical that the Constitution, which Americans venerate so deeply, is based upon a political theory that at one crucial point stands in direct antithesis to the mainstream of American democratic faith. Modern American folklore assumes that democracy and liberty are all but identical, and when democratic writers take the trouble to make the distinction, they usually assume that democracy is necessary to liberty. But the Founding Fathers thought that the liberty with which they were most concerned was menaced by democracy. In their minds liberty was linked not to democracy but to property.

What did the Fathers mean by liberty? What did Jay mean when he spoke of "the charms of liberty"? Or Madison when he declared that to destroy liberty in order to destroy factions would be a remedy worse than the disease? Certainly the men who met at Philadelphia were not interested in extending liberty to those classes in America, the Negro slaves and the indentured servants, who were most in need of it, for slavery was recognized in the organic structure of the Constitution and indentured servitude was no concern of the Convention. Nor was the regard of the delegates for civil liberties any too tender. It was the opponents of the Constitution who were most active in demanding such vital liberties as freedom of religion, freedom of speech and press, jury trial, due process, and protection from "unreasonable searches and seizures." These guarantees had to be incorporated in the first ten amendments because the Convention neglected to put them in the original document. Turning to economic issues, it was not freedom of trade in the modern sense that the Fathers were striving for. Although they did not believe in impeding trade unnecessarily, they felt that failure to regulate it was one of the central weaknesses of the Articles of Confederation, and they stood closer to the mercantilists than to Adam Smith. Again, liberty to them did not mean free access to the nation's unappropriated wealth. At least fourteen of them were land speculators. They did not believe in the right of the squatter to occupy unused land, but rather in the right of the absentee owner or speculator to preempt it.

The liberties that the constitutionalists hoped to gain were chiefly negative. They wanted freedom from fiscal uncertainty and irregularities in the currency, from trade wars among the states, from economic discrimination by more powerful foreign governments, from attacks on the creditor class or on property, from popular insurrection. They aimed to create a government that would act as an honest broker among a variety of propertied interests, giving them all protection from their common enemies and preventing any one of them from becoming too powerful. The Convention was a fraternity of types of absentee ownership. All property should be permitted to have its proportionate voice in government. Individual property interests might have to be sacrificed at times, but only for the community of propertied interests. Freedom for property would result in liberty for men—perhaps not for all men, but at least for all worthy men. Because men have different faculties and abilities, the Fathers believed, they acquire different amounts of property. To protect property is only to protect men in the exercise of their natural faculties. Among the many liberties, therefore, freedom to hold and dispose [of] property is paramount. Democracy, unchecked rule by the masses, is sure to bring arbitrary redistribution of property, destroying the very essence of liberty. . . .

A cardinal tenet in the faith of the men who made the Constitution was the belief that democracy can never be more than a transitional stage in government, that it always evolves into either a tyranny (the rule of the rich demagogue who has patronized the mob) or an aristocracy (the original leaders of the democratic elements). . . .

What encouraged the Fathers about their own era, however, was the broad dispersion of landed property. The small land-owning farmers had been troublesome in recent years, but there was a general conviction that under a properly made Constitution a *modus vivendi* could be worked out with them. The possession of moderate plots of property presumably gave them a sufficient stake in society to be safe and responsible citizens under the restraints of balanced government. Influence in government would be proportionate to property: merchants and great landholders would be dominant, but small property-owners would have an independent and far from negligible voice. It was "politic as well as just," said Madison, "that the interests and rights of every class should be duly represented and understood in the public councils," and John Adams declared that there could be "no free government without a democratical branch in the constitution." . . .

. . . At the very beginning contemporary opponents of the Constitution foresaw an apocalyptic destruction of local government and popular institutions, while conservative Europeans of the old regime thought the young American Republic was a dangerous leftist experiment. Modern critical scholarship, which reached a high point in Charles A. Beard's *An Economic Interpretation of the Constitution of the United States*, started a new turn in the debate. The antagonism, long latent, between the philosophy of the Constitution and the philosophy of American democracy again came into the open. Professor Beard's work appeared in 1913 at the peak of the Progressive era, when the muckraking fever was still high; some readers tended to conclude from his findings that the Fathers were selfish reactionaries who do not deserve their high place in American esteem. Still more recently, other writers, inverting this logic, have used Beard's facts to praise the Fathers for their opposition to "democracy" and as an argument for returning again to the idea of a "republic."

In fact, the Fathers' image of themselves as moderate republicans standing between political extremes was quite accurate. They were impelled by class motives more than pietistic writers like to admit, but they were also controlled, as Professor Beard himself has recently emphasized, by a statesmanlike sense of moderation and a scrupulously republican philosophy. Any attempt, however, to tear their ideas out of the eighteenth-century context is sure to make them seem starkly reactionary. Consider, for example, the favorite maxim of John Jay: "The people who own the country ought to govern it." To the Fathers this was simply a swift axiomatic statement of the stake-in-society theory of political rights, a moderate conservative position under eighteenth-century conditions of property distribution in America. Under modern property relations this maxim demands a drastic restriction of the base of political power. A large portion of the modern middle class—and it is the strength of this class upon which balanced government depends—is propertyless; and the urban proletariat, which the Fathers so greatly feared, is almost one half the population. Further, the separation of ownership from control that has come with the corporation deprives Jay's maxim of twentieth-century meaning even for many propertied people. The six hundred thousand stockholders of the American Telephone & Telegraph Company not only do not acquire political power by virtue of their stock-ownership, but they do not even acquire economic power: they cannot control their own company.

From a humanistic standpoint there is a serious dilemma in the philosophy of the Fathers, which derives from their conception of man. They thought man was a creature of rapacious self-interest, and yet they wanted him to be free—free, in essence, to contend, to engage in an umpired strife, to use property to get property. They accepted the mercantile image of life as an eternal battleground, and assumed the Hobbesian war of each against all; they did not propose to put an end to this war, but merely to stabilize it and make it less murderous. They had no hope and they offered none for any ultimate organic change in the way men conduct themselves. The result was that while they thought self-interest the most dangerous and unbrookable quality of man, they necessarily underwrote it in trying to control it. . . .

10

JAMES MADISON

From *The Federalist 10*

This is the most important reading in an American government class. Along with its companion, Federalist 51 *(coming in the next section of the book), James Madison's* Federalist 10 *is the first and last word on U.S. government and politics. In it, he takes up the idea of "faction," by which he means any single group (especially the mob-like majority, but perhaps even a tiny minority) that tries to dominate the political process. Can faction be removed from politics? No, he admits, for a variety of reasons that deeply illuminate his assessment of the American people. But faction can be controlled by a republican (representative) system. Madison favored a large and diverse nation; if there were many groups, no one faction would ever be able to dominate. Signing these papers Publius, Madison, along with Alexander Hamilton and John Jay, wrote eighty-four essays collectively known as* The Federalist Papers, *which were published in several New York newspapers on behalf of the ratification of the new Constitution in 1787. James Madison's genius is revealed not only in the workable system of government he helped create for America, but also in his vision of the United States in the future, very much as it is today.*

No. 10: Madison

AMONG the numerous advantages promised by a well-constructed Union, none deserves to be more accurately developed than its tendency to break and control the violence of faction. The friend of popular governments never finds himself so much alarmed for their character and fate as when he contemplates their propensity to this dangerous vice. He will not fail, therefore, to set a due value on any plan which, without violating the principles to which he is attached, provides a proper cure for it. The instability, injustice, and confusion introduced into the public councils have, in truth, been the mortal diseases under which popular governments have everywhere perished, as they continue to be the favorite and fruitful topics from which the adversaries to liberty derive their most specious declamations. The valuable improvements made by the American constitutions on the popular models, both ancient and modern, cannot certainly be too much admired; but it would be an unwarrantable partiality to contend that they have as effectually obviated the danger on this side, as was wished and expected. Complaints are everywhere heard from our most considerate and virtuous citizens, equally the friends of public and private faith and of public and personal liberty, that our governments are too unstable, that the public good is disregarded in the conflicts of rival parties, and that measures are too often decided, not according to the rules of justice and the rights of the minor party, but by the superior force of an interested and overbearing majority. However anxiously we may wish that these complaints had no foundation, the evidence of known facts will not permit us to deny that they are in some degree true. It will be found, indeed, on a candid review of our situation, that some of the distresses under which we labor have been erroneously charged on the operation of our governments; but it will be found, at the same time, that other causes will not alone account for many of our heaviest misfortunes; and, particularly, for that prevailing and increasing distrust of public engagements and alarm for private rights which are echoed from one end of the continent to the other. These must be chiefly, if not wholly, effects of the unsteadiness and injustice with which a factious spirit has tainted our public administration.

By a faction I understand a number of citizens, whether amounting to a majority or minority of the whole, who are united and actuated by some common impulse of passion, or of interest, adverse to the rights of other citizens, or to the permanent and aggregate interests of the community.

There are two methods of curing the mischiefs of faction: the one, by removing its causes; the other, by controlling its effects.

There are again two methods of removing the causes of faction: the one, by destroying the liberty which is essential to its existence; the other, by giving to every citizen the same opinions, the same passions, and the same interests.

It could never be more truly said than of the first remedy that it was worse than the disease. Liberty is to faction what air is to fire, an aliment without which it instantly expires. But it could not be a less folly to abolish liberty, which is essential to political life, because it nourishes faction than it would be to wish the annihilation of air, which is essential to animal life, because it imparts to fire its destructive agency.

The second expedient is as impracticable as the first would be unwise. As long as the reason of man continues fallible, and he is at liberty to exercise it, different opinions will be formed. As long as the connection subsists between his reason and his self-love, his opinions and his passions will have a reciprocal influence on each other; and the former will be objects to which the latter will attach themselves. The diversity in the faculties of men, from which the rights of property originate, is not less an insuperable obstacle to a uniformity of interests. The protection of these faculties is the first object of government. From the protection of different and unequal faculties of acquiring property, the possession of different degrees and kinds of property immediately results; and from the influence of these on the sentiments and views of the respective proprietors ensues a division of the society into different interests and parties.

The latent causes of faction are thus sown in the nature of man; and we see them everywhere brought into different degrees of activity, according to the different circumstances of civil society. A zeal for different opinions concerning religion, concerning government, and many other points, as well of speculation as of practice; an attachment to different leaders ambitiously contending for pre-eminence and power; or to persons of other descriptions whose fortunes have been interesting to the human passions, have, in turn, divided mankind into parties, inflamed them with mutual animosity, and rendered them much more disposed to vex and oppress each other than to co-operate for their common good. So strong is this propensity of mankind to fall into mutual animosities that where no substantial occasion presents itself the most frivolous and fanciful distinctions have been sufficient to kindle their unfriendly passions and excite their most violent conflicts. But the most common and durable source of factions has been the various and unequal distribution of property. Those who hold and those who are without property have ever formed distinct interests in society. Those who are creditors, and those who are debtors, fall under a like discrimination. A landed interest, a manufacturing interest, a mercantile interest, a moneyed interest, with many lesser interests, grow up of necessity in civilized nations, and divide them into different classes, actuated by different sentiments and views. The regulation of these various and interfering interests forms the principal task of modern legislation and involves the spirit of party and faction in the necessary and ordinary operations of government.

No man is allowed to be a judge in his own cause, because his interest would certainly bias his judgment, and, not improbably, corrupt his integrity. With equal, nay with greater reason, a body of men are unfit to be both judges and parties at the same time; yet what are many of the most important acts of legislation but so many judicial determinations, not indeed concerning the rights of single persons, but concerning the rights of large bodies of citizens? And what are the different classes of legislators but advocates and parties to the causes which they determine?

Is a law proposed concerning private debts? It is a question to which the creditors are parties on one side and the debtors on the other. Justice ought to hold the balance between them. Yet the parties are, and must be, themselves the judges; and the most numerous party, or in other words, the most powerful faction must be expected to prevail. Shall domestic manufacturers be encouraged, and in what degree, by restrictions on foreign manufacturers? are questions which would be differently decided by the landed and the manufacturing classes, and probably by neither with a sole regard to justice and the public good. The apportionment of taxes on the various descriptions of property is an act which seems to require the most exact impartiality; yet there is, perhaps, no legislative act in which greater opportunity and temptation are given to a predominant party to trample on the rules of justice. Every shilling with which they overburden the inferior number is a shilling saved to their own pockets.

It is in vain to say that enlightened statesmen will be able to adjust these clashing interests and render them all subservient to the public good. Enlightened statesmen will not always be at the helm. Nor, in many cases, can such an adjustment be made at all without taking into view indirect and remote considerations, which will rarely prevail over the immediate interest which one party may find in disregarding the rights of another or the good of the whole.

The inference to which we are brought is that the *causes* of faction cannot be removed and that relief is only to be sought in the means of controlling its *effects*.

If a faction consists of less than a majority, relief is supplied by the republican principle, which enables the majority to defeat its sinister views by regular vote. It may clog the administration, it may convulse the society; but it will be unable to execute and mask its violence under the forms of the Constitution. When a majority is included in a faction, the form of popular government, on the other hand, enables it to sacrifice to its ruling passion or interest both the public good and the rights of other citizens. To secure the public good and private rights against the danger of such a faction, and at the same time to preserve the spirit and the form of popular government, is then the great object to which our inquiries are directed. Let me add that it is the great desideratum by which alone this form of government can be rescued from the opprobrium under which it has so long labored and be recommended to the esteem and adoption of mankind.

By what means is this object attainable? Evidently by one of two only. Either the existence of the same passion or interest in a majority at the same time must be prevented, or the majority, having such coexistent passion or interest, must be rendered, by their number and local situation, unable to concert and carry into effect schemes of oppression. If the impulse and the opportunity be suffered to coincide, we well know that neither moral nor religious motives can be relied on as an adequate control. They are not found to be such on the injustice and violence of individuals, and lose their efficacy in proportion to the number combined together, that is, in proportion as their efficacy becomes needful.

From this view of the subject it may be concluded that a pure democracy, by which I mean a society consisting of a small number of citizens, who assemble and administer the government in person, can admit of no cure for the mischiefs of faction. A common passion or interest will, in almost every case, be felt by a majority of the whole; a communication and concert results from the form of government itself; and there is nothing to check the inducements to sacrifice the weaker party or an obnoxious individual. Hence it is that such democracies have ever been spectacles of turbulence and contention; have ever been found incompatible with personal security or the rights of property; and have in general been as short in their lives as they have been violent in their deaths. Theoretic politicians, who have patronized this species of government, have erroneously supposed that by reducing mankind to a perfect equality in their political rights, they would at the same time be perfectly equalized and assimilated in their possessions, their opinions, and their passions.

A republic, by which I mean a government in which the scheme of representation takes place, opens a different prospect and promises the cure for which we are seeking. Let us examine the points in which it varies from pure democracy, and we shall comprehend both the nature of the cure and the efficacy which it must derive from the Union.

The two great points of difference between a democracy and a republic are: first, the delegation of the government, in the latter, to a small number of citizens elected by the rest; secondly, the greater number of citizens and greater sphere of country over which the latter may be extended.

The effect of the first difference is, on the one hand, to refine and enlarge the public views by passing them through the medium of a chosen body of citizens, whose wisdom may best discern the true interest of their country and whose patriotism and love of justice will be least likely to sacrifice it to temporary or partial considerations. Under such a regulation it may well happen that the public voice, pronounced by the representatives of the people, will be more consonant to the public good than if pronounced by the people themselves, convened for the purpose. On the other hand, the effect may be inverted. Men of factious tempers, of local prejudices, or of sinister designs, may, by intrigue, by corruption, or by other means, first obtain the suffrages, and then betray the interests of the people. The question resulting is, whether small or extensive republics are most favorable to the election of proper guardians of the public weal; and it is clearly decided in favor of the latter by two obvious considerations.

In the first place it is to be remarked that however small the republic may be the representatives must be raised to a certain number in order to guard against the cabals of a few; and that however large it may be they must be limited to a certain number in order to guard against the confusion of a multitude. Hence, the number of representatives in the two cases not being in proportion to that of the constituents, and being proportionally greatest in the small republic, it follows that if the proportion of fit characters be not less in the large than in the small republic, the former will present a greater option, and consequently a greater probability of a fit choice.

In the next place, as each representative will be chosen by a greater number of citizens in the large than in the small republic, it will be more difficult for unworthy candidates to practise with success the vicious arts by which elections are too often carried; and the suffrages of the people being more free, will be more likely to center on men who possess the most attractive merit and the most diffusive and established characters.

It must be confessed that in this, as in most other cases, there is a mean, on both sides of which inconveniencies will be found to lie. By enlarging too much the number of electors, you render the representative too little acquainted with all their local circumstances and lesser interests; as by reducing it too much, you render him unduly attached to these, and too little fit to comprehend and pursue great and national objects. The federal Constitution forms a happy combination in this respect; the great and aggregate interests being referred to the national, the local and particular to the State legislatures.

The other point of difference is the greater number of citizens and extent of territory which may be brought within the compass of republican than of democratic government; and it is this circumstance principally which renders factious combinations less to be dreaded in the former than in the latter. The smaller the society, the fewer probably will be the distinct parties and interests composing it; the fewer the distinct parties and interests, the more frequently will a majority be found of the same party; and the smaller the number of individuals composing a majority, and the smaller the compass within which they are placed, the more easily will they concert and execute their plans of oppression. Extend the sphere and you take in a greater variety of parties and interests; you make it less probable that a majority of the whole will have a common motive to invade the rights of other citizens; or if such a common motive exists, it will be more difficult for all who feel it to discover their own strength and to act in unison with each other. Besides other impediments, it may be remarked that, where there is a consciousness of unjust or dishonorable purposes, communication is always checked by distrust in proportion to the number whose concurrence is necessary.

Hence, it clearly appears that the same advantage which a republic has over a democracy in controlling the effects of faction is enjoyed by a large over a small republic—is enjoyed by the Union over the States composing it. Does this advantage consist in the substitution of representatives whose enlightened views and virtuous sentiments render them superior to local prejudices and to schemes of injustice? It will not be denied that the representation of the Union will be most likely to possess these requisite endowments. Does it consist in the greater security afforded by a greater variety of parties, against the event of any one party being able to outnumber and oppress the rest? In an equal degree does the increased variety of parties comprised within the Union increase this security? Does it, in fine, consist in the greater obstacles opposed to the concert and accomplishment of the secret wishes of an unjust and interested majority? Here again the extent of the Union gives it the most palpable advantage.

The influence of factious leaders may kindle a flame within their particular States but will be unable to spread a general conflagration through the other States. A religious sect may degenerate into a political faction in a part of the Confederacy; but the variety of sects dispersed over the entire face of it must secure the national councils against any danger from that source. A rage for paper money, for an abolition of debts, for an equal division of property, or for any other improper or wicked project, will be less apt to pervade the whole body of the Union than a particular member of it, in the same proportion as such a malady is more likely to taint a particular county or district than an entire State.

In the extent and proper structure of the Union, therefore, we behold a republican remedy for the diseases most incident to republican government. And according to the degree of pleasure and pride we feel in being republicans ought to be our zeal in cherishing the spirit and supporting the character of federalists.

Publius

II

MICHAEL KAMMEN

From *A Machine That Would Go of Itself*

Written at the time of the bicentennial of the United States Constitution, historian Michael Kammen's book is of interest to those seeking greater depth on the evolution of the nation's basic document. Kammen traces the shifts in thought about the Constitution's interpretation, from that of a "machine" that once put in motion would function steadily and unchangingly forever, to a more fluid and malleable plan. Particularly memorable is his analogy of a 1966 "Star Trek" episode, "The Omega Glory," in which we see Captain Kirk and the crew of the Enterprise *grappling with the same questions that we ask today about the Constitution.*

THE [metaphor], the notion of a constitution as some sort of machine or engine, had its origins in Newtonian science. Enlightened philosophers, such as David Hume, liked to contemplate the world with all of its components as a great machine. Perhaps it was inevitable, as politics came to be regarded as a science during the 1770s and '80s, that leading revolutionaries in the colonies would utilize the metaphor to suit their purposes. In 1774 Jefferson's *Summary View* mentioned "the great machine of government." . . .

Over the next one hundred years such imagery did not disappear. But neither did it notably increase; and hardly anyone expressed apprehension about the adverse implications of employing mechanistic metaphors. Occasionally an observer or enthusiast might call the Constitution "the best national machine that is now in existence" (1794); or, at the Golden Jubilee in 1839, John Quincy Adams could comment that "fifty years have passed away since the first impulse was given to the wheels of this political machine."

James Fenimore Cooper uttered one of the few expressions of concern couched in this language between 1787 and 1887. "The boldest violations of the Constitution are daily proposed by politicians in this country," he observed in 1848, "but they do not produce the fruits which might be expected, because the nation is so accustomed to work in the harness it has placed on itself, that nothing seems seriously to arrest the movement of the great national car." Although his metaphors are ridiculously muddled, the message is clear enough. Exactly forty years later James Russell Lowell articulated this same apprehension much more cogently in an address to the Reform Club of New York. The pertinent passage marks the apogee of the metaphor, and remains today as profound a warning as it was in 1888.

> After our Constitution got fairly into working order it really seemed as if we had invented a machine that would go of itself, and this begot a faith in our luck which even the civil war itself but momentarily disturbed. Circumstances continued favorable, and our prosperity went on increasing. I admire the splendid complacency of my countrymen, and find something exhilarating and inspiring in it. We are a nation which has *struck ile* [sic], but we are also a nation that is sure the well will never run dry. And this confidence in our luck with the absorption in material interests, generated by unparalleled opportunity, has in some respects made us neglectful of our political duties.

That statement epitomizes not merely the main historical theme of this book, but the homily that I hope to convey as well. Machine imagery lingered on for fifty years, casually used by legal scholars, journalists, civics textbooks, even great jurists like Holmes, and by Franklin D. Roosevelt in his first inaugural address. On occasion, during the 1920s and '30s especially, conservatives would declare that the apparatus, being more than adequate, should not be tampered with, whereas reformers insisted that "the machinery of government under which we live is hopelessly antiquated" (a word they loved) and therefore "should be overhauled."

In the quarter century that followed Lowell's 1888 lament, a cultural transition took place that leads us to the last of the major constitutional metaphors. We may exemplify it with brief extracts from three prominent justices: Holmes, who wrote in 1914 that "the provisions of the Constitution are not mathematical formulas . . . they are organic living institutions"; Cardozo, who observed in 1925 that "a Constitution has an organic life"; and Frankfurter, who declared in 1951 that "the Constitution is an organism."

Unlike the other analogies that have been discussed, which were not mutually exclusive, this shift was not merely deliberate but intellectually aggressive at times. The quarter century is punctuated by the declarations of two political scientists deeply involved in public affairs. At the close of the 1880s, A. Lawrence Lowell wrote that "a political system is not a mere machine which can be constructed on any desired plan. . . . It is far more than this. It is an organism . . . whose various parts act and react upon one another." In 1912, when Woodrow Wilson ran for the presidency, a key passage in his campaign statement, *The New Freedom*, elaborated upon Lowell's assertion. "The makers of our Federal Constitution," in Wilson's words, "constructed a government as they would have constructed an orrery,*—to display the laws of nature. Politics in their thought was a variety of mechanics. The Constitution was founded on the law of gravitation. The government was to exist and move by virtue of the efficacy of 'checks and balances.'"

Lowell and Wilson had obviously responded to the same current of cultural change; but they were not attempting to be intellectually trendy by explaining government in terms of evolutionary theory. The word-concept they both used in condemning a Newtonian notion of constitutionalism was "static." Wilson spelled out the implications: "Society is a living organism and must obey the laws of life, not of mechanics; it must develop. All that progressives ask or desire is permission—in an era when 'development,' 'evolution,' is the scientific word—to interpret the Constitution according to the Darwinian principle; all they ask is recognition of the fact that a nation is a living thing and not a machine." . . .

I would describe the basic pattern of American constitutionalism as one of *conflict within consensus*. At first glance, perhaps, we are more likely to notice the consensus. . . .

The volume of evidence is overwhelming that our constitutional conflicts have been consequential, and considerably more revealing than the consensual framework within which they operate. When Americans have been aware of the dynamic of conflict within consensus, most often they have regarded it as a normative pattern for a pluralistic polity. . . .

There is . . . a . . . closely linked aspect of American constitutionalism about which there has been no consensus: namely, whether our frame of government was meant to be fairly unchanging or flexible. Commentators are quick to quote Justice Holmes's "theory of our Constitution. It is an experiment, as all life is an experiment." Although much less familiar, and less eloquent, more Americans have probably shared this sentiment, written in 1936 by an uncommon common man, the chief clerk in the Vermont Department of Highways: "I regard the Constitution as of too much value to be experimented with."

The assumption that our Constitution is lapidary has a lineage that runs, among the justices, from Marshall and Taney to David J. Brewer and George Sutherland. It has been the dominant assumption for most of our history, and provided the basis for Walter Bagehot, Lord Bryce, and others to regard the U.S. Constitution as "rigid" by comparison with the British. The idea that adaptability was desirable emerged gradually during the mid-nineteenth century, appeared in some manuals aimed at

*An apparatus for representing the motions . . . of the planets. . . .

a popular audience by the 1880s, and achieved added respectability in 1906 when Justice Henry Billings Brown spoke at a dinner in his honor. The Constitution, he said, "should be liberally interpreted—interpreted as if it were intended as the foundation of a great nation, and not merely a temporary expedient for the united action of thirteen small States. . . . Like all written Constitutions, there is an underlying danger in its inflexibility." For about a generation that outlook slowly gained adherents, until the two contradictory views were essentially counterpoised in strength by the 1930s.

Meanwhile, a third position appeared during the early decades of the twentieth century—one that might be considered a compromise because it blended facets of the other two. This moderately conservative, evolutionary position was expressed in 1903 by James Ford Rhodes, a nationalistic businessman-turned-historian. The Constitution, in his mind, "is rigid in those matters which should not be submitted to the decision of a legislature or to a popular vote without checks which secure reflection and a chance for the sober second thought, [yet] it has proved flexible in its adaptation to the growth of the country." . . .

Admittedly, our strict constructionists have on occasion stretched the Constitution, as Jefferson did in 1803 to acquire the vast Louisiana Territory. Lincoln, Wilson, and FDR each stood accused of ignoring constitutional restraints; yet each one could honestly respond that, within the framework of a Constitution intended to be flexible in an emergency, his goal had been to preserve the Union, to win a war fought for noble goals, or to overcome the worst and most prolonged economic disaster in American history. In each instance their constitutional critics spoke out clearly, a national debate took place, and clarification of our constitutional values occurred. Sometimes that clarification has come from the Supreme Court; sometimes from a presidential election campaign; sometimes from a combination of the two; and sometimes by means of political compromise. Each mode of resolution is a necessary part of our democratic system. I am led to conclude that Americans have been more likely to read and understand their Constitution when it has been controversial, or when some group contended that it had been misused, than in those calmer moments when it has been widely venerated as an instrument for all time. . . .

During the later 1950s, Robert M. Hutchins and his colleagues at the Center for the Study of Democratic Institutions, located in Santa Barbara, California, began to discuss the desirability of far-reaching constitutional changes. In 1964, following a series of seminars modestly entitled "Drafting a New Constitution for the United States and the World,"

Hutchins invited Rexford G. Tugwell, once a member of FDR's "Brain Trust," to direct a reassessment of the Constitution. Tugwell accepted and spent two years conferring with hundreds of jurists, politicians, and scholars. . . .

During the 1970s the Center's primary concerns shifted away from constitutionalism; Tugwell's two major volumes (1974 and 1976) received little attention aside from scholarly journals. When Tugwell died in 1979 at the age of eighty-eight, the *New York Times*'s appreciative editorial did not even mention the revised constitution on which he labored for more than a decade. The *Times* apparently did not regard it as a fitting culmination for a distinguished career in scholarship and public service.

The negligible impact of this seasoned planner's constitutional vision provides a striking contrast with an extremely tradition-oriented interpolation of the U.S. Constitution in science fiction. One popular episode of the television series "Star Trek," written in 1966, received hundreds of reruns during the many years when Tugwell labored over his revision. Millions of Americans watched "The Omega Glory" and recognized its affirmation of the good old Constitution that continued to function even though space, time, and ignorance shrouded its meaning.

Reducing the saga to its ideological essence, Captain Kirk and the starship *Enterprise* land on a planet where the inhabitants are guided by a Prime Directive that must not be violated. Those inhabitants are called Yangs (presumably the descendants of colonizers once known as Yanks), and possess "a worn parchment document" that is "the greatest of holies." Kirk and his crew encounter a bizarre political situation that is not so very different from the one criticized by James Russell Lowell in 1888. The Yangs worship "freedom" but do not understand what it means. Through the ages it has become a ritualized "worship word." The Yangs believe that their ancestors must have been very superior people; they swear an oath to abide by all regulations in the Prime Directive; and they can recite the opening lines of the Prime Directive, but "without meaning."

Following a primitive court scene, complete with jury, it becomes clear that institutions of justice are amazingly resilient—capable of enduring even though their rationale has suffered badly from neglect and amnesia. At the culmination Captain Kirk informs the Yangs that they revere a sacred document without understanding what it is all about. Kirk faces Cloud William, chief of the Yangs, and explains the meaning of the Prime Directive's preamble. Enlightenment then occurs and the great question—is the Prime Directive still operative, and does it apply to this planet?—

achieves a satisfactory resolution. To use the language of yesteryear, "constitutional morality" would surely be restored.

Unlike Rexford Tugwell's new constitution, which kept "emerging" for so long that after a while no one cared, "Star Trek" had a constitutional homily with a happy ending. Americans like happy endings. Hence many younger Americans can still narrate "The Omega Glory" (Old Glory? Ultimate Glory?) flawlessly. How much of the homily got through, however, is another matter. . . .

Ultimately, however, for better and for worse, it is ideological conflict that most meaningfully calls attention to the Constitution. We are then reminded that all Americans do not agree about the most appropriate division of authority: federalism tilting toward states' rights or federalism leaning toward national authority? We are then reminded that we still have broad and strict constructionists, followers of Hamilton and followers of Madison. And we are then reminded that we have had two complementary but divergent modes of constitutional interpretation: a tradition of conflict within consensus. . . .

It is instructive to recall that the founders did not expect their instrument of government to achieve utopia: "merely" national cohesion, political stability, economic growth, and individual liberty. Despite abundant setbacks and imperfections, much of that agenda has been fulfilled for a great many Americans. During the past generation social justice got explicitly added to the agenda as a high priority, and the American Constitution, interpreted by the Supreme Court, was adapted accordingly. For a society to progress toward social justice within a constitutional framework, even by trial and error, is a considerable undertaking. To do so in good faith, more often than not, is equally commendable. If from time to time we require the assistance of gadflies, what flourishing political culture does not? Senator Lowell P. Weicker of Connecticut, for example, has played that role rather well on occasion. As he thundered in 1981, during debate over a legislative amendment to endorse organized prayer in public schools: "To my amazement, any time the word constitutionalism comes up it's looked upon as a threat. A threat! It shouldn't be; it's what holds us all together."

That has been true more often than not. Perhaps those who feel threatened by constitutionalism do not fully understand it. People frequently feel threatened by the unfamiliar. Perhaps it has not been fully understood because it has not been adequately explained. Perhaps it has perplexed us because aspects of its meaning have changed over time. Back in 1786 Benjamin Rush believed it "possible to convert men into republican machines. This must be done if we expect them to perform their parts properly in the great machine of the government of the state." His contemporaries not only took Rush at his word, but regarded the conversion of men into republican machines as a national imperative. . . .

More than a century later, Woodrow Wilson presented a piece of wisdom that tacked the other way. Call it constitutional revisionism if you like. He declared that if the real government of the United States "had, in fact, been a machine governed by mechanically automatic balances, it would have had no history; but it was not, and its history has been rich with the influences and personalities of the men who have conducted it and made it a living reality." Walter Lippmann chose to quote that sentence in 1913 when he wrote *A Preface to Politics*. But he promptly added that "only by violating the very spirit of the constitution have we been able to preserve the letter of it." What Lippmann had in mind was the role played by that palpable reality the Progressives called "invisible government": political parties, interest groups, trade unions, and so on.

Lippmann's remark was not meant to be as cynical as it might sound. It reflects the Progressive desire to be realistic and tough-minded. It also reflects the fact that Americans have been profoundly ambivalent in their feelings about government. Then, too, it reflects the discovery by three overlapping generations of Americans—represented by James Russell Lowell, Wilson, and Lippmann—that the U.S. Constitution is not, and was not meant to be, a machine that would go of itself.

Above all, Lippmann wanted to build upon his excerpt from Wilson and establish the point that there has been more to the story of constitutionalism in American culture than the history of the Constitution itself. The latter is a cherished charter of institutions and a declaration of protections. The former, constitutionalism, embodies a set of values, a range of options, and a means of resolving conflicts within a framework of consensus. It has supplied stability and continuity to a degree the framers could barely have imagined.

12

C. WRIGHT MILLS

From *The Power Elite*

C. Wright Mills's book The Power Elite *stands as a classic in political science. In it he offers one answer to the question "Who rules America?" A three-part elite rules, he believes, composed of corporate, political, and military leaders. These sectors of American life are connected, creating an "interlocking" power structure with highly centralized decision-making. Mills considers a conspiracy theory to account for the power elite's control, but rejects it for something much more frightening. Average Americans are like "trusting children" who rely on the power elite to run things smoothly and well. Today, approaching a new century, not quite forty years after Mills wrote, his ideas seem a bit ultra-dramatic and overstated. Still, Mills offers a warning about power in America that is timeless, one that many people believe is true.*

THE POWERS of ordinary men are circumscribed by the everyday worlds in which they live, yet even in these rounds of job, family, and neighborhood they often seem driven by forces they can neither understand nor govern. "Great changes" are beyond their control, but affect their conduct and outlook none the less. The very framework of modern society confines them to projects not their own, but from every side, such changes now press upon the men and women of the mass society, who accordingly feel that they are without purpose in an epoch in which they are without power.

But not all men are in this sense ordinary. As the means of information and of power are centralized, some men come to occupy positions in American society from which they can look down upon, so to speak, and by their decisions mightily affect, the everyday worlds of ordinary men and women. They are not made by their jobs; they set up and break down jobs for thousands of others; they are not confined by simple family responsibilities; they can escape. They may live in many hotels and houses, but they are bound by no one community. They need not merely "meet the demands of the day and hour"; in some part, they create these demands, and cause others to meet them. Whether or not they profess their power, their technical and political experience of it far transcends that of the underlying population. What Jacob Burckhardt said of "great men," most Americans might well say of their elite: "They are all that we are not."

The power elite is composed of men whose positions enable them to transcend the ordinary environments of ordinary men and women; they are in positions to make decisions having major consequences. Whether they do or do not make such decisions is less important than the fact that they do occupy such pivotal positions: their failure to act, their failure to make decisions, is itself an act that is often of greater consequence than the decisions they do make. For they are in command of the major hierarchies and organizations of modern society. They rule the big corporations. They run the machinery of the state and claim its prerogatives. They direct the military establishment. They occupy the strategic command posts of the social structure, in which are now centered the effective means of the power and the wealth and the celebrity which they enjoy.

The power elite are not solitary rulers. Advisers and consultants, spokesmen and opinion-makers are often the captains of their higher thought and decision. Immediately below the elite are the professional politicians of the middle levels of power, in the Congress and in the pressure groups, as well as among the new and old upper classes of town and city and region. Mingling with them, in curious ways which we shall explore, are those professional celebrities who live by being continually displayed but are never, so long as they remain celebrities, displayed enough. If such celebrities are not at the head of any dominating hierarchy, they do often have the power to distract the attention of the public or afford sensations to the masses, or, more directly, to gain the ear of those who do occupy positions of direct power. More or less unattached, as critics of morality and technicians of power, as spokesmen of God and creators of mass sensibility, such celebrities and consultants are part of the immediate scene in which the drama of the elite is enacted. But that drama itself is centered in the command posts of the major institutional hierarchies.

The truth about the nature and the power of the elite is not some secret which men of affairs know but will not tell. Such men hold quite various theories about their own roles in the sequence of event and decision. Often they are uncertain about their roles, and even more often they allow their fears and their hopes to affect their assessment of their own power. No matter how great their actual power, they tend to be less acutely aware of it than of the resistances of others to its use. Moreover, most American men of affairs have learned well the rhetoric of public relations, in some cases even to the point of using it when they are alone, and thus coming to believe it. The personal awareness of the actors is only one of the several sources one must examine in order to understand the higher circles. Yet many who believe that there is no elite, or at any rate none of any consequence, rest their argument upon what men of affairs believe about themselves, or at least assert in public.

There is, however, another view: those who feel, even if vaguely, that a compact and powerful elite of great importance does now prevail in America often base that feeling upon the historical trend of our time. They have felt, for example, the domination of the military event, and from this they infer that generals and admirals, as well as other men of decision influenced by them, must be enormously powerful. They hear that the Congress has again abdicated to a handful of men decisions clearly related to the issue of war or peace. They know that the bomb was dropped over Japan in the name of the United States of America, although they were at no time consulted about the matter. They feel that they live in a time of big decisions; they know that they are not making any. Accordingly, as they consider the present as history, they infer that at its center, making decisions or failing to make them, there must be an elite of power.

On the one hand, those who share this feeling about big historical events assume that there is an elite and that its power is great. On the other hand, those who listen carefully to the reports of men apparently involved in the great decisions often do not believe that there is an elite whose powers are of decisive consequence.

Both views must be taken into account, but neither is adequate. The way to understand the power of the American elite lies neither solely in recognizing the historic scale of events nor in accepting the personal awareness reported by men of apparent decision. Behind such men and behind the events of history, linking the two, are the major institutions of modern society. These hierarchies of state and corporation and army constitute the means of power; as such they are now of a consequence not before equaled in human history—and at their summits, there are now those command posts of modern society which offer us the sociological key to an understanding of the role of the higher circles in America.

Within American society, major national power now resides in the economic, the political, and the military domains. Other institutions seem off to the side of modern history, and, on occasion, duly subordinated to these. No family is as directly powerful in national affairs as any major corporation; no church is as directly powerful in the external biographies of young men in America today as the military establishment; no college is as powerful in the shaping of momentous events as the National Security

Council. Religious, educational, and family institutions are not autonomous centers of national power; on the contrary, these decentralized areas are increasingly shaped by the big three, in which developments of decisive and immediate consequence now occur.

Families and churches and schools adapt to modern life; governments and armies and corporations shape it; and, as they do so, they turn these lesser institutions into means for their ends. Religious institutions provide chaplains to the armed forces where they are used as a means of increasing the effectiveness of its morale to kill. Schools select and train men for their jobs in corporations and their specialized tasks in the armed forces. The extended family has, of course, long been broken up by the industrial revolution, and now the son and the father are removed from the family, by compulsion if need be, whenever the army of the state sends out the call. And the symbols of all these lesser institutions are used to legitimate the power and the decisions of the big three.

The life-fate of the modern individual depends not only upon the family into which he was born or which he enters by marriage, but increasingly upon the corporation in which he spends the most alert hours of his best years; not only upon the school where he is educated as a child and adolescent, but also upon the state which touches him throughout his life; not only upon the church in which on occasion he hears the word of God, but also upon the army in which he is disciplined.

If the centralized state could not rely upon the inculcation of nationalist loyalties in public and private schools, its leaders would promptly seek to modify the decentralized educational system. If the bankruptcy rate among the top five hundred corporations were as high as the general divorce rate among the thirty-seven million married couples, there would be economic catastrophe on an international scale. If members of armies gave to them no more of their lives than do believers to the churches to which they belong, there would be a military crisis.

Within each of the big three, the typical institutional unit has become enlarged, has become administrative, and, in the power of its decisions, has become centralized. Behind these developments there is a fabulous technology, for as institutions, they have incorporated this technology and guide it, even as it shapes and paces their developments.

The economy—once a great scatter of small productive units in autonomous balance—has become dominated by two or three hundred giant corporations, administratively and politically interrelated, which together hold the keys to economic decisions.

The political order, once a decentralized set of several dozen states with a weak spinal cord, has become a centralized, executive establishment which has taken up into itself many powers previously scattered, and now enters into each and every crany of the social structure.

The military order, once a slim establishment in a context of distrust fed by state militia, has become the largest and most expensive feature of government, and, although well versed in smiling public relations, now has all the grim and clumsy efficiency of a sprawling bureaucratic domain.

In each of these institutional areas, the means of power at the disposal of decision makers have increased enormously; their central executive powers have been enhanced; within each of them modern administrative routines have been elaborated and tightened up.

As each of these domains becomes enlarged and centralized, the consequences of its activities become greater, and its traffic with the others increases. The decisions of a handful of corporations bear upon military and political as well as upon economic developments around the world. The decisions of the military establishment rest upon and grievously affect political life as well as the very level of economic activity. The decisions made within the political domain determine economic activities and military programs. There is no longer, on the one hand, an economy, and, on the other hand, a political order containing a military establishment unimportant to politics and to money-making. There is a political economy linked, in a thousand ways, with military institutions and decisions. On each side of the world-split running through central Europe and around the Asiatic rimlands, there is an ever-increasing interlocking of economic, military, and political structures. If there is government intervention in the corporate economy, so is there corporate intervention in the governmental process. In the structural sense, this triangle of power is the source of the interlocking directorate that is most important for the historical structure of the present.

The fact of the interlocking is clearly revealed at each of the points of crisis of modern capitalist society—slump, war, and boom. In each, men of decision are led to an awareness of the interdependence of the major institutional orders. In the nineteenth century, when the scale of all institutions was smaller, their liberal integration was achieved in the automatic economy, by an autonomous play of market forces, and in the automatic political domain, by the bargain and the vote. It was then assumed that out of the imbalance and friction that followed the limited decisions then possible a new equilibrium would in due course emerge. That can no longer be assumed, and it is not assumed by the men at the top of each of the three dominant hierarchies.

For given the scope of their consequences, decisions—and indecisions—in any one of these ramify into the others, and hence top decisions tend either to become co-ordinated or to lead to a commanding indecision. It has not always been like this. When numerous small entrepreneurs made up the economy, for example, many of them could fail and the consequences still remain local; political and military authorities did not intervene. But now, given political expectations and military commitments, can they afford to allow key units of the private corporate economy to break down in slump? Increasingly, they do intervene in economic affairs, and as they do so, the controlling decisions in each order are inspected by agents of the other two, and economic, military, and political structures are interlocked.

At the pinnacle of each of the three enlarged and centralized domains, there have arisen those higher circles which make up the economic, the political, and the military elites. At the top of the economy, among the corporate rich, there are the chief executives; at the top of the political order, the members of the political directorate; at the top of the military establishment, the elite of soldier-statesmen clustered in and around the Joint Chiefs of Staff and the upper echelon. As each of these domains has coincided with the others, as decisions tend to become total in their consequence, the leading men in each of the three domains of power—the warlords, the corporation chieftains, the political directorate—tend to come together, to form the power elite of America. . . .

The conception of the power elite and of its unity rests upon the corresponding developments and the coincidence of interests among economic, political, and military organizations. It also rests upon the similarity of origin and outlook, and the social and personal intermingling of the top circles from each of these dominant hierarchies. This conjunction of institutional and psychological forces, in turn, is revealed by the heavy personnel traffic within and between the big three institutional orders, as well as by the rise of go-betweens as in the high-level lobbying. The conception of the power elite, accordingly, does *not* rest upon the assumption that American history since the origins of World War II must be understood as a secret plot, or as a great and co-ordinated conspiracy of the members of this elite. The conception rests upon quite impersonal grounds.

There is, however, little doubt that the American power elite—which contains, we are told, some of "the greatest organizers in the world"—has also planned and has plotted. The rise of the elite, as we have already made clear, was not and could not have been caused by a plot; and the tenability of the conception does not rest upon the existence of any secret or any publicly known organization. But, once the conjunction of structural trend and of the personal will to utilize it gave rise to the power elite, then plans and programs did occur to its members and indeed it is not possible to interpret many events and official policies of the fifth epoch without reference to the power elite. "There is a great difference," Richard Hofstadter has remarked, "between locating conspiracies *in* history and saying that history *is*, in effect, a conspiracy . . . "

The structural trends of institutions become defined as opportunities by those who occupy their command posts. Once such opportunities are recognized, men may avail themselves of them. Certain types of men from each of the dominant institutional areas, more far-sighted than others, have actively promoted the liaison before it took its truly modern shape. They have often done so for reasons not shared by their partners, although not objected to by them either; and often the outcome of their liaison has had consequences which none of them foresaw, much less shaped, and which only later in the course of development came under explicit control. Only after it was well under way did most of its members find themselves part of it and become gladdened, although sometimes also worried, by this fact. But once the co-ordination is a going concern, new men come readily into it and assume its existence without question.

So far as explicit organization—conspiratorial or not—is concerned, the power elite, by its very nature, is more likely to use existing organizations, working within and between them, than to set up explicit organizations whose membership is strictly limited to its own members. But if there is no machinery in existence to ensure, for example, that military and political factors will be balanced in decisions made, they will invent such machinery and use it, as with the National Security Council. Moreover, in a formally democratic polity, the aims and the powers of the various elements of this elite are further supported by an aspect of the permanent war economy: the assumption that the security of the nation supposedly rests upon great secrecy of plan and intent. Many higher events that would reveal the working of the power elite can be withheld from public knowledge under the guise of secrecy. With the wide secrecy covering their operations and decisions, the power elite can mask their intentions, operations, and further consolidation. Any secrecy that is imposed upon those in positions to observe high decision-makers clearly works for and not against the operations of the power elite.

There is accordingly reason to suspect—but by the nature of the case, no proof—that the power elite is not altogether "surfaced." There is nothing hidden about it, although its activities are not publicized. As an elite, it is not organized, although its members often know one another, seem quite naturally to work together, and share many organizations in common. There is nothing conspiratorial about it, although its decisions are often publicly unknown and its mode of operation manipulative rather than explicit.

It is not that the elite "believe in" a compact elite behind the scenes and a mass down below. It is not put in that language. It is just that the people are of necessity confused and must, like trusting children, place all the new world of foreign policy and strategy and executive action in the hands of experts. It is just that everyone knows somebody has got to run the show, and that somebody usually does. Others do not really care anyway, and besides, they do not know how. So the gap between the two types gets wider.

13

RICHARD ZWEIGENHAFT AND G. WILLIAM DOMHOFF

From *Diversity in the Power Elite*

In the previous excerpt, C. Wright Mills presented his interpretation of who holds power in America: a small elite. Mills wrote his classic book decades ago. Richard Zweigenhaft and G. William Domhoff revisit Mills's thesis by examining the composition of today's power elite—assuming, of course, that there is such an elite. The authors offer a fascinating account of Jews, women, blacks, Latinos, Asian Americans, and gay men and lesbians in the elite, including many personal stories of powerful individuals. The excerpt here looks at corporate women and African-American men in the military. Yes, the elite looks different today, but no, it is not really so different than when Mills wrote.

INJUSTICES BASED ON race, gender, ethnicity, and sexual orientation have been the most emotional and contested issues in American society since the end of the 1960s, far exceeding concerns with social class, and rivaled only by conflicts about abortion. These issues are now subsumed under the umbrella terms *diversity* and *multiculturalism*, and they have been written about extensively from the perspectives of both the aggrieved and those at the middle and lower levels of the social ladder who resist any changes.

. . . [W]e look at multiculturalism from a new angle: we examine its impact on the small group at the top of American society that we call the power elite—those who own and manage large banks and corporations, finance the political campaigns of conservative Democrats and virtually all Republicans at the state and national levels, and serve in government as appointed officials and military leaders. We ask whether the decades of pressure from civil rights groups, feminists, and gay and lesbian rights activists has resulted in a more culturally diverse power elite. If it has, what effects has this new diversity had on the functioning of the power elite and on its relation to the rest of society? . . .

According to many commentators, the higher circles in the United States had indeed become multicultural by the late 1980s and early 1990s. Some went even further, saying that the old power elite had been pushed aside entirely. The demise of the "old" power elite was the theme of such books as Nelson Aldrich's *Old Money* and Robert Christopher's *Crashing the Gates*, the latter emphasizing the rise of ethnic minorities. There have also been wide-eyed articles in mainstream magazines, such as one in the late 1980s in *U.S. News and World Report* entitled "The New American Establishment," which celebrated a new diversity at the top, claiming that "new kinds of men and women" have "taken control of institutions that influence important aspects of American life." School and club ties are no longer important, the article announced; the new role of women was highlighted with a picture of some of the "wise women" who had joined the "wise men" who dominated the old establishment.

Then, in July 1995, *Newsweek* ran a cover story on "The Rise of the Overclass," featuring a gallery of one hundred high-tech, media, and Wall Street stars, women as well as men, minorities as well as whites, who supposedly come from all rungs of the social ladder. The term *overclass* was relatively new, but the argument—that the power elite was dead, superseded by a diverse meritocratic elite—was not. . . .

Since the 1870s the refrain about the new diversity of the governing circles has been closely intertwined with a staple of American culture created by Horatio Alger Jr., whose name has become synonymous with upward mobility in America. Born in 1832 to a patrician family—Alger's father was a Harvard graduate, a Unitarian minister, and a Massachusetts state senator—Alger graduated from Harvard at the age of nineteen. There followed a series of unsuccessful efforts to establish himself in various careers. Finally, in 1864 Alger was hired as a Unitarian minister in Brewster, Massachusetts. Fifteen months later, he was dismissed from this position for homosexual acts with boys in the congregation.

Alger returned to New York, where he soon began to spend a great deal of time at the Newsboys' Lodging House, founded in 1853 for footloose youngsters between the ages of twelve and sixteen and home to many youths who had been mustered out of the Union Army after serving as drummer boys. At the Newsboys' Lodging House Alger found his literary niche and his subsequent claim to fame: writing books in which poor boys make good. His books sold by the hundreds of thousands in the last third of the nineteenth century, and by 1910 they were enjoying annual sales of more than one million in paperback.

The deck is not stacked against the poor, according to Horatio Alger. When they simply show a bit of gumption, work hard, and thereby catch a break or two, they can become part of the American elite. The persistence of this theme, reinforced by the annual Horatio Alger Awards to such well-known personalities as Ronald Reagan, Bob Hope, and Billy Graham (who might not have been so eager to accept them if they had known of Alger's shadowed past), suggests that we may be dealing once again with a cultural myth. In its early versions, of course, the story concerned the great opportunities available for poor white boys willing to work their way to the top. More recently, the story has featured black Horatio Algers who started in the ghetto, Latino Horatio Algers who started in the barrio, Asian-American Horatio Algers whose parents were immigrants, and female Horatio Algers who seem to have no class backgrounds—all of whom now sit on the boards of the country's largest corporations.

But is any of this true? Can anecdotes and self-serving autobiographical accounts about diversity, meritocracy, and upward social mobility survive a more systematic analysis? Have very many women and previously excluded minorities made it to the top? Has class lost its importance in shaping life chances?

. . . [W]e address these and related questions within the framework provided by the iconoclastic sociologist C. Wright Mills in his hard-hitting classic *The Power Elite*, published in 1956 when the media were in the midst of what Mills called the Great American Celebration. In spite of the Depression of the 1930s, Americans had pulled together to win World War II, and the country was both prosperous at home and influential abroad. Most of all, according to enthusiasts, the United States had become a relatively classless and pluralistic society, where power belonged to the people through their political parties and public opinion. Some groups certainly had more power than others, but no group or class had too much. The New Deal and World War II had forever transformed the corporate-based power structure of earlier decades.

Mills challenged this celebration of pluralism by studying the social backgrounds and career paths of the people who occupied the highest positions in what he saw as the three major institutional hierarchies in postwar America—the corporations, the executive branch of the federal government, and the military. He found that almost all the members of this leadership group, which he called the power elite, were white Christian males who came from "at most, the upper third of the income and occupational pyramids," despite the many Horatio Algeresque claims to the contrary. . . .

The power elite depicted by C. Wright Mills was, without doubt, an exclusively male preserve. On the opening page of *The Power Elite*—a book with no preface, no introduction, no acknowledgments, just a direct plunge into the opening chapter—Mills stated clearly that "the power elite is composed of men whose positions enable them to transcend the ordinary environments of ordinary men and women." Although there were some women in the corporate, political, and military worlds, very few were in or near the higher circles that constituted the power elite. Are they there now? If so, how substantial and how visible is their presence? When did they arrive, and how did they get there? What are their future prospects? . . .

In 1990, Elizabeth Dole, then secretary of labor, initiated a department-level investigation into the question of whether or not there was a "glass ceiling" blocking women and minorities from the highest ranks of U.S. corporations. When the report was issued by the Federal Glass Ceiling Commission in 1995, comments by the white male managers who had been interviewed and surveyed supported the earlier claims that upper management was willing to accept women and minorities only if they were not too different. As one manager explained, "What's important is comfort, chemistry, relationships, and collaborations. That's what makes a shop work. When we find minorities and women who think like we do, we snatch them up."

Terry Miyamoto, an Asian-American labor relations executive at U.S. West, Inc., a telecommunications company that ranked number 62 on the Fortune 500 list in 1995, uses the term "comfort zone" to make the same point about "chemistry" and reducing "uncertainty": "You need to build relationships," she said, "and you need to be pretty savvy. And for a woman or a person of color at this company, you have to put in more effort to get into this comfort zone."

Much has been made of the fact that men have traditionally been socialized to play competitive team sports and women have not. In *The Managerial Woman*, Margaret Hennig and Anne Jardim argue that the experience of having participated in competitive team sports has provided men with many advantages in the corporate world. Playing on sports teams teaches boys such things as how to develop their individual skills in the context of helping the team to win, how to develop cooperative goal-oriented relationships with teammates, how to focus on winning, and how to deal with losing. "The experience of most little girls," they wrote, "has no parallel." Although the opportunities for young women to participate in competitive sports have increased dramatically in recent years, including team sports like basketball and soccer, few such opportunities were available when most women now in higher management in U.S. corporations were young.

Just as football is often identified as the classic competitive and aggressive team sport that prepares men for the rough and tumble (and hierarchical) world of the corporation, an individual sport—golf—is the more convivial but still competitive game that allows boys to play together, shoot the breeze, and do business. As Marcia Chambers shows in *The Unplayable Lie*, the golf course, and especially the country club, can be as segregated by sex as the football field. Few clubs bar women, but some clubs do not allow women to vote, sit on their governing boards, or play golf on weekend mornings.

Many women managers are convinced that their careers suffer because of discrimination against them by golf clubs. In a study of executives who manage "corporate-government affairs," Denise Benoit Scott found that the women in such positions "share meals with staff members and other government relations officials but never play golf." In contrast, men in such positions "play golf with a broad range of people in business and government, including legislators and top corporate executives." As one of the women she interviewed put it: "I wish I played golf. I think golf is the key. If you want to make it, you have to play golf."

Similarly, when the editors of *Executive Female* magazine surveyed the top fifty women in line-management positions (in sales, marketing, production, and general management with a direct impact on the company's bottom line), they asked them why more women had not made it to the "upper reaches of corporate America." The most frequently identified problem was the "comfort factor"—that the men atop their corporations wanted others around them with whom they were comfortable, and that generally meant other men similar to themselves. One of the other most frequently identified problems, not unrelated to the comfort factor, was the exclusion from "the social networks—the clubs, the golf course—where the informal networking that is so important to moving up the ladder often takes place."

Based on the interviews they conducted for *Members of the Club*, Dawn-Marie Driscoll and Carol Goldberg also conclude that there is an important connection between golf and business. Both Driscoll and

Goldberg have held directorships on major corporate boards. They establish their insider status at the beginning of their book: "We are both insiders. We always have been and probably always will be." In a section entitled "The Link That Counts," they explain how they came to realize the importance of golf: "We heard so many stories about golf that we began to pay more attention to the interaction between golf and business. We realized the importance of golf had been right in front of our eyes all the time, but because neither of us played golf, we had missed it as an issue for executive women. But golf is central to many business circles."

A few months before Bill Clinton was elected president, his future secretary of energy had some pertinent comments about the importance of fitting into corporate culture and the relevance of playing golf. "Without losing your own personality," said Hazel O'Leary, then an executive vice president at Northern States Power in Minnesota, "it's important to be part of the prevailing corporate culture. At this company, it's golf. I've resisted learning to play golf all my life, but I finally had to admit I was missing something that way." She took up golf.

There is evidence that the golf anxiety expressed by women executives has its counterpart in the attitudes held by male executives: in its 1995 report, the Federal Glass Ceiling Commission found that many white male executives "fretted" that minorities and women did not know how to play golf.

Whether or not playing golf is necessary to fit in, it is clear that women who make it into the corporate elite must assimilate sufficiently into the predominantly male culture to make it into the comfort zone. . . .

. . . [W]e told of Midshipman Leonard Kaplan's being "sent to Coventry"—which meant that no one spoke to him during his entire four years at the Naval Academy. Benjamin O. Davis Jr., the first black to graduate from the U.S. Military Academy in the twentieth century, had a parallel experience during his four years at that institution. After he had been at West Point for a short time, there was a knock on his door announcing a meeting in the basement in ten minutes. Davis painfully recalls that meeting and its long-term effects in the autobiography he wrote almost sixty years later:

> As I approached the assembly where the meeting was in progress, I heard someone ask, "What are we going to do about the nigger?" I realized then that the meeting was about me, and I was not supposed to attend. I turned on my heel and double-timed back to my room.
>
> From that meeting on, the cadets who roomed across the hall, who had been friendly earlier, no longer spoke to me. In fact, no one spoke to me except in

the line of duty. Apparently, certain upperclass cadets had determined that I was getting along too well at the Academy to suit them, and they were going to enforce an old West Point tradition—"silencing"—with the object of making my life so unhappy that I would resign. Silencing had been applied in the past to certain cadets who were considered to have violated the honor code and refused to resign. In my case there was no question of such a violation; I was to be silenced solely because cadets did not want blacks at West Point. Their only purpose was to freeze me out.

Except for the recognition ceremony at the end of plebe year, I was silenced for the entire four years of my stay at the Academy.

Davis stuck it out at West Point and graduated near the top of his class. Even after graduation in 1936, his classmates (among them William Westmoreland, from a wealthy textile family in South Carolina) continued their silent treatment of him for years. In fact, for the next fifteen years, as his assignments took him to different locations in the United States and around the world, not only did his classmates continue to give him the silent treatment, but they and their wives also shunned Davis's wife. . . .

Still, a retired black general has become one of the best-known and most admired Americans. It was a major breakthrough in 1989 when Colin Powell was named chairman of the Joint Chiefs of Staff. And, indeed, Powell's ascendance to the top of the military hierarchy has had as much impact for civilians as for soldiers. According to Moskos and Butler, "the elevation of Colin Luther Powell to the chairmanship of the Joint Chiefs of Staff in 1989 was an epic event in American race relations, whose significance has yet to be fully realized."

Powell's parents were both Jamaican immigrants, a fact he makes much of. . . . While a student at the City College of New York, Powell joined ROTC, and when he graduated in 1958, he was commissioned as a second lieutenant. Powell has emphasized that he "found himself" in ROTC: "Suddenly everything clicked. . . . I had found something I was good at. . . . For the first time, in the military I always knew exactly what was expected of me." Equally important, the military had become a place where blacks could do well. "I had an intuitive sense that this was a career which was beginning to open up for blacks," says Powell. "You could not name, in those days, another profession where black men routinely told white men what to do and how to do it."

Powell rose through the ranks. He served as a junior officer in Vietnam, then held a series of command and staff jobs. In 1972 he became a White House Fellow; noting that race worked to his advantage in this appointment, he said to a friend, "I was lucky to be born black." Four years later, Jimmy Carter appointed Clifford Alexander as secretary of the army, and the number of black generals tripled while Alexander held that position. "My method was simple," Alexander revealed. "I just told everyone that I would not sign the goddam promotion list unless it was fair." In 1979, at the age of forty-two, Colin Powell achieved the rank of general. By 1987 he had become national security adviser under Reagan, and in 1989, under Bush, he became the first black—and the youngest man ever—to be chairman of the Joint Chiefs of Staff. After the Gulf War, polls consistently indicated that Powell was among the most admired people in America. . . .

The power elite has been strengthened because diversity has been achieved primarily by the selection of women and minorities who share the prevailing perspectives and values of those already in power. The power elite is not "multicultural" in any full sense of the concept, but only in terms of ethnic or racial origins. This process has been helped along by those who have called for the inclusion of women and minorities without any consideration of criteria other than sex, race, or ethnicity. Because the demand was strictly for a woman on the Supreme Court, President Reagan could comply by choosing a conservative upper-class corporate lawyer, Sandra Day O'Connor. When pressure mounted to have more black justices, President Bush could respond by appointing Clarence Thomas, a conservative black Republican with a law degree from Yale University. It is yet another irony that appointments like these served to undercut the liberal social movements that caused them to happen.

It is not surprising, therefore, that when we look at the business practices of the women and minorities who have risen to the top of the corporate world, we find that their perspectives and values do not differ markedly from those of their white male counterparts. When Linda Wachner, one of the few women to become CEO of a *Fortune*-level company, the Warnaco Group, concluded that one of Warnaco's many holdings, the Hathaway Shirt Company, was unprofitable, she decided to stop making Hathaway shirts and to sell or close down the factory. It did not matter to Wachner that Hathaway, which started making shirts in 1837, was one of the oldest companies in Maine, that almost all of the five hundred employees at the factory were working-class women, or even that the workers had given up a pay raise to hire consultants to teach them to work more effectively and, as a result, had doubled their productivity. The bottom-line issue was that the company was considered unprofitable, and the average wage of the Hathaway workers, $7.50 an hour, was thought to be too high. (In 1995 Wachner was paid $10 million in salary and stock, and Warnaco had a net income of $46.5 million.) We did need to do the right thing for the company and the stockholders," explained Wachner.

Nor did ethnic background matter to Thomas Fuentes, a senior vice president at a consulting firm in Orange County, California, a director of Fleetwood Enterprises, and chairman of the Orange County Republican Party. Fuentes targeted fellow Latinos who happened to be Democrats when he sent uniformed security guards to twenty polling places in 1988 "carrying signs in Spanish and English warning people not to vote if they were not U.S. citizens." The security firm ended up paying $60,000 in damages when it lost a lawsuit stemming from this intimidation.

We also recall that the Fanjuls, the Cuban-American sugar barons, have had no problem ignoring labor laws in dealing with their migrant labor force, and that the Sakioka family illegally gave short-handled hoes to its migrant farm workers. These people were acting as employers, not as members of ethnic groups. That is, members of the power elite of both genders and all ethnicities have practiced class politics, making it possible for the power structure to weather the challenge created by the social movements that began in the 1960s.

Those who challenged Christian white male homogeneity in the power structure during the 1960s not only sought to create civil rights and new job opportunities for men and women who had previously been mistreated, important though these goals were. They also hoped that new perspectives in the boardrooms and the halls of government would bring greater openness throughout the society. The idea was both to diversify the power elite and to shift some of its power to previously excluded groups and social classes. The social movements of the 1960s were strikingly successful in increasing the individual rights and freedoms available to all Americans, especially African Americans. As we have shown, they also created pressures that led to openings at the top for individuals from groups that had previously been excluded.

But as the concerns of social movements, political leaders, and the courts came to focus more and more on individual rights, the emphasis on social class and "distributive justice" was lost. The age-old American commitment to individualism, reinforced at every turn by members of the power elite, won out over the commitment to greater equality of income and wealth that had been one strand of New Deal liberalism and a major emphasis of left-wing activists in the 1960s.

We therefore have to conclude on the basis of our findings that the diversification of the power elite did not generate any changes in an underlying class system in which the top 1 percent have 45.6 percent of all financial wealth, the next 19 percent have 46.7 percent, and the bottom 80 percent have 7.8 percent. The values of liberal individualism embedded in the Declaration of Independence, the Bill of Rights, and the civic culture were renewed by vigorous and courageous activists, but despite their efforts the class structure remains a major obstacle to individual fulfillment for the overwhelming majority of Americans. This fact is more than an irony. It is a dilemma. It combines with the dilemma of race to create a nation that celebrates equal opportunity but is, in reality, a bastion of class privilege and conservatism.

14

ROBERT DAHL

From *Who Governs?* and from *A Preface to Democratic Theory*

In any city in the United States—like New Haven, Connecticut—as in the entire nation, political power is no longer in the hands of a few people as it once was early in American history. Nor is power spread evenly among all citizens. Influential political theorist Robert Dahl presents here the classic statement of pluralism: the dispersion of power among many groups of people. Dahl differentiates the "political stratum," made up of interested and involved citizens, from the "apolitical stratum," those who do not take an active part in government. These two segments of society are vastly different in their degree of involvement, yet they are closely tied together in many ways in a pluralist system. At least in theory, anyone can enter the political stratum where numerous interest groups compete and bargain for their goals. Public policy is made by "the steady appeasement of relatively small groups." Because of this "strange hybrid," Dahl contends, pluralism is the best way to describe how power is distributed in America.

IN A POLITICAL SYSTEM where nearly every adult may vote but where knowledge, wealth, social position, access to officials, and other resources are unequally distributed, who actually governs?

The question has been asked, I imagine, wherever popular government has developed and intelligent citizens have reached the stage of critical self-consciousness concerning their society. It must have been put many times in Athens even before it was posed by Plato and Aristotle.

The question is peculiarly relevant to the United States and to Americans. In the first place, Americans espouse democratic beliefs with a fervency and a unanimity that have been a regular source of astonishment to foreign observers . . . [such as] Tocqueville and Bryce. . . .

In the course of the past two centuries, New Haven has gradually changed from oligarchy to pluralism. Accompanying and probably causing this change—one might properly call it a revolution—appears to be a profound alteration in the way political resources are distributed among the citizens of New Haven. This silent socioeconomic revolution has not substituted equality for inequality so much as it has involved a shift from cumulative inequalities in political resources—to use an expression introduced a moment ago—to noncumulative or dispersed inequalities. This point will grow clearer as we proceed. . . .

In the political system of the patrician oligarchy, political resources were marked by a cumulative inequality: when one individual was much better off than another in one resource, such as wealth, he was usually better off in almost every other resource—social standing, legitimacy, control over religious and educational institutions, knowledge, office. In the political system of today, inequalities in political resources remain, but they tend to be *noncumulative*. The political system of New Haven, then, is one of *dispersed inequalities*. . . .

Within a century a political system dominated by one cohesive set of leaders had given way to a system dominated by many different sets of leaders, each having access to a different combination of political resources. It was, in short, a pluralist system. If the pluralist system was very far from being an oligarchy, it was also a long way from achieving the goal of political equality advocated by the philosophers of democracy and incorporated into the creed of democracy and equality practically every American professes to uphold.

An elite no longer rules New Haven. But in the strict democratic sense, the disappearance of elite rule has not led to the emergence of rule by the people. Who, then, rules in a pluralist democracy? . . .

One of the difficulties that confronts anyone who attempts to answer the question, "Who rules in a pluralist democracy?" is the ambiguous relationship of leaders to citizens.

Viewed from one position, leaders are enormously influential—so influential that if they are seen only in this perspective they might well be considered a kind of ruling elite. Viewed from another position, however, many influential leaders seem to be captives of their constituents. Like the blind men with the elephant, different analysts have meticulously examined different aspects of the body politic and arrived at radically different conclusions. To some, a pluralistic democracy with dispersed inequalities is all head and no body; to others it is all body and no head. . . .

Two additional factors help to account for this obscurity. First, among all the persons who influence a decision, some do so more directly than others in the sense that they are closer to the stage where concrete alternatives are initiated or vetoed in an explicit and immediate way. Indirect influence might be very great but comparatively difficult to observe and weigh. Yet to ignore indirect influence in analysis of the distribution of influence would be to exclude what might well prove to be a highly significant process of control in a pluralistic democracy.

Second, the relationship between leaders and citizens in a pluralistic democracy is frequently reciprocal: leaders influence the decisions of constituents, but the decisions of leaders are also determined in part by what they think are, will be, or have been the preferences of their constituents. Ordinarily it is much easier to observe and describe the distribution of influence in a political system where the flow of influence is strongly in one direction (an asymmetrical or unilateral system, as it is sometimes called) than in a system marked by strong reciprocal relations. In a political system with competitive elections, such as New Haven's, it is not unreasonable to expect that relationships between leaders and constituents would normally be reciprocal. . . .

In New Haven, as in other political systems, a small stratum of individuals is much more highly involved in political thought, discussion, and action than the rest of the population. These citizens constitute the political stratum.

Members of this stratum live in a political subculture that is partly but not wholly shared by the great majority of citizens. Just as artists and intellectuals are the principal bearers of the artistic, literary, and scientific skills of a society, so the members of the political stratum are the main bearers of political skills. If intellectuals were to vanish overnight, a society would be reduced to artistic, literary, and scientific poverty. If the political stratum were destroyed, the previous political institutions of the society would temporarily stop functioning. In both cases, the speed with which the loss could be overcome would depend on the extent to which the elementary knowledge and basic attitudes of the elite had been diffused. In an open society with widespread education and training in civic attitudes, many citizens hitherto in the apolitical strata could doubtless step into roles that had been filled by members of the political stratum. However, sharp discontinuities and important changes in the operation of the political system almost certainly would occur.

In New Haven, as in the United States, and indeed perhaps in all pluralistic democracies, differences in the subcultures of the political and the apolitical strata are marked, particularly at the extremes. In the political stratum, politics is highly salient; among the apolitical strata, it is remote. In the political stratum, individuals tend to be rather calculating in their choice of strategies; members of the political stratum are, in a sense, relatively rational political beings. In the apolitical strata, people are notably less calculating; their political choices are more strongly influenced by inertia, habit, unexamined loyalties, personal attachments, emotions, transient impulses. In the political stratum, an individual's political beliefs tend to fall into patterns that have a relatively high degree of coherence and internal consistency; in the apolitical strata, political orientations are disorganized, disconnected, and unideological. In the political stratum, information about politics and the issues of the day is extensive; the apolitical strata are poorly informed. Individuals in the political stratum tend to participate rather actively in politics; in the apolitical strata citizens rarely go beyond voting and many do not even vote. Individuals in the political stratum exert a good deal of steady, direct, and active influence on government policy; in fact some individuals have a quite extraordinary amount of influence. Individuals in the apolitical strata, on the other hand, have much less direct or active influence on policies.

Communication within the political stratum tends to be rapid and extensive. Members of the stratum read many of the same newspapers and magazines; in New Haven, for example, they are likely to read the *New York Times* or the *Herald Tribune*, and *Time* or *Newsweek*. Much information also passes by word of mouth. The political strata of different communities and regions are linked in a national network of communications. Even in small towns, one or two members of the local political stratum usually are in touch with members of a state organization, and certain members of the political stratum of a state or any large city maintain relations with members of organizations in other states and cities, or with national figures. Moreover, many channels of communication not designed specifically for political purposes—trade associations, professional associations, and labor organizations, for example—serve as a part of the network of the political stratum.

In many pluralistic systems, however, the political stratum is far from being a closed or static group. In the United States the political stratum does not constitute a homogeneous class with well-defined class interests. In New Haven, in fact, the political stratum is easily penetrated by anyone whose interests and concerns attract him to the distinctive political culture of the stratum. It is easily penetrated because (among other reasons) elections and competitive parties give politicians a powerful motive for expanding their coalitions and increasing their electoral followings.

In an open pluralistic system, where movement into the political stratum is easy, the stratum embodies many of the most widely shared values and goals in the society. If popular values are strongly pragmatic, then the political stratum is likely to be pragmatic; if popular values prescribe reverence toward the past, then the political stratum probably shares that reverence; if popular values are oriented toward material gain and personal advancement, then the political stratum probably reflects these values; if popular values are particularly favorable to political, social, or economic equality, then the political stratum is likely to emphasize equality. The apolitical strata can be said to "govern" as much through the sharing of common values and goals with members of the political stratum as by other means. However, if it were not for elections and competitive parties, this sharing would—other things remaining the same—rapidly decline.

Not only is the political stratum in New Haven not a closed group, but its "members" are far from united in their orientations and strategies. There are many lines of cleavage. . . .

Because of the ease with which the political stratum can be penetrated, whenever dissatisfaction builds up in some segment of the electorate party politicians will probably learn of the discontent and calculate whether it might be converted into a political issue with an electoral payoff. If a party politician sees no payoff, his interest is likely to be small; if he foresees an adverse effect, he will avoid the issue if he can. As a result, there is usually some conflict in the political stratum between intellectuals, experts, and others who formulate issues, and the party politicians themselves, for the first group often demands attention to issues in which the politicians see no profit and possibly even electoral damage.

The independence, penetrability, and heterogeneity of the various segments of the political stratum all but guarantee that any dissatisfied group will find spokesmen in the political stratum, but to have a spokesman does not insure that the group's problems will be solved by political action. Politicians may not see how they can gain by taking a position on an issue; action by government may seem to be wholly inappropriate; policies intended to cope with dissatisfaction may be blocked; solutions may be improperly designed; indeed, politicians may even find it politically profitable to maintain a shaky coalition by keeping tension and discontent alive and deflecting attention to irrelevant "solutions" or alternative issues. . . .

. . . In devising strategies for building coalitions and allocating rewards, one must take into account a large number of different categories of citizens. It would be dangerous to formulate strategies on the assumption that most or all citizens can be divided into two or three categories, for a successful political coalition necessarily rests upon a multiplicity of groups and categories. . . .*

. . . I defined the "normal" American political process as one in which there is a high probability that an active and legitimate group in the population can make itself heard effectively at some crucial stage in the process of decision. To be "heard" covers a wide range of activities, and I do not intend to define the word rigorously. Clearly, it does not mean that every group has equal control over the outcome.

In American politics, as in all other societies, control over decisions is unevenly distributed; neither individuals nor groups are political equals. When I say that a group is heard "effectively" I mean more than the simple fact that it makes a noise; I mean that one or more officials are not only ready to listen to the noise, but expect to suffer in some significant way if they do not placate the group, its leaders, or its most vociferous members. To satisfy the group may require one or more of a great variety of actions by the responsive leader: pressure for substantive policies, appointments, graft, respect, expression of the appropriate emotions, or the right combination of reciprocal noises.

Thus the making of governmental decisions is not a majestic march of great majorities united upon certain matters of basic policy. It is the steady appeasement of relatively small groups. . . .

To be sure, reformers with a tidy sense of order dislike it. Foreign observers, even sympathetic ones, are often astonished and confounded by it. Many Americans are frequently dismayed by its paradoxes; indeed, few Americans who look upon our political process attentively can fail, at times, to feel deep frustration and angry resentment with a system that on the surface has so little order and so much chaos.

For it is a markedly decentralized system. Decisions are made by endless bargaining; perhaps in no other national political system in the world is bargaining so basic a component of the political process. In an age when the efficiencies of hierarchy have been re-emphasized on every continent, no doubt the normal American political system is something of an anomaly, if not, indeed, at times an anachronism. For as a means

*At this point, the excerpt from *Who Governs?* ends, and *A Preface to Democratic Theory* begins.—EDS.

to highly integrated, consistent decisions in some important areas—foreign policy, for example—it often appears to operate in a creaking fashion verging on total collapse.

Yet we should not be too quick in our appraisal, for where its vices stand out, its virtues are concealed to the hasty eye. Luckily the normal system has the virtues of its vices. With all its defects, it does nonetheless provide a high probability that any active and legitimate group will make itself heard effectively at some stage in the process of decision. This is no mean thing in a political system.

It is not a static system. The normal American system has evolved, and by evolving it has survived. It has evolved and survived from aristocracy to mass democracy, through slavery, civil war, the tentative uneasy reconciliation of North and South, the repression of Negroes and their halting liberation; through two great wars of worldwide scope, mobilization, far-flung military enterprise, and return to hazardous peace; through numerous periods of economic instability and one prolonged depression with mass unemployment, farm "holidays," veterans' marches, tear gas, and even bullets; through two periods of postwar cynicism, demagogic excesses, invasions of traditional liberties, and the groping, awkward, often savage, attempt to cope with problems of subversion, fear, and civil tension.

Probably this strange hybrid, the normal American political system, is not for export to others. But so long as the social prerequisites of democracy are substantially intact in this country, it appears to be a relatively efficient system for reinforcing agreement, encouraging moderation, and maintaining social peace in a restless and immoderate people operating a gigantic, powerful, diversified, and incredibly complex society.

This is no negligible contribution, then, that Americans have made to the arts of government—and to that branch, which of all the arts of politics is the most difficult, the art of democratic government.

15

ROBERT ROBERTS AND MARION DOSS

From *From Watergate to Whitewater*

The scandals that dominated the news from 1997 through 1999, during President Bill Clinton's second term, are really part of a bigger trend in American politics. Robert Roberts and Marion Doss call it the "public integrity war." A vast ideological divide between "movement conservatives" and "new progressives" has resulted in bitter political conflict that takes the form of ethics accusations. The authors assess Clinton's handling of the warfare that he found himself caught up in. The future? "The public integrity war will only end when we stop viewing political opponents as mortal enemies."

ON MAY 28, 1996, a Little Rock, Arkansas, Federal Court jury convicted Arkansas Governor Jim Guy Tucker and Susan and James McDougal on multiple fraud charges. The Whitewater investigation, at that moment, ceased being a political witch-hunt. Prior to the verdict, the Clinton White House and supporters of President Clinton had conducted an all-out campaign to discredit the independent counsel investigation of Kenneth Starr. The convictions gave Kenneth Starr a new mandate to pursue his Whitewater investigation.

The *Washington Post*, on February 6, 1995, published an opinion piece by Meg Greenfield entitled "Right and Wrong in Washington: Why Do Our Officials Need Specialists to Tell the Difference?" Greenfield, editor of the *Washington Post* editorial page and long-time Washington observer, reminded Washington that "having all those ethics boards is not the same as having ethics." Greenfield wondered why Washington public officials had become so dependent upon ethics specialists to distinguish between right and wrong. "What has been reached in our age is the idea of ethics not as an intrinsic and understood and codifiable aspect of human behavior, but rather as one of many highly technical side concerns."

Greenfield argued that Washington had lost its moral compass. No one seemed any longer to understand the difference between right and wrong. "What we once were assumed to know ourselves if we affected to be upstanding people, and could always count on parents, pastors and cops to call briskly to our attention [if] we didn't . . . is now believed to be beyond our own power of comprehension."

[We] attempt . . . to explain how this situation has come to pass. Today's public integrity war is the result of growing divisions over the appropriate role of government in American society. Critics of big government, on one side of the political spectrum, see public corruption scandals as evidence of the moral bankruptcy of big government. Supporters of big government, on the other hand, see these scandals as the result of special interests exercising too much power in the political system. Both critics and supporters of government have come to regard ethics scandals as support for their visions of the role of government in American society.

The roots of the modern public integrity war can be traced back to colonial times and to the struggle for independence. Throughout much of American history there has been a struggle between those advocating a greater role for government and those fearful that a larger government will lead to tyranny and oppression. Watergate, however, ushered in a new phase of this struggle. Movement conservatives and new progressives turned to public integrity attacks as a means of persuading Americans to join their political movements. Likewise, new progressive and movement conservative supporters have come to view attacks on their leaders as attacks on their movements. Neither movement can afford to throw overboard a leader who strays from the straight and narrow.

[We] also argue . . . that Bill Clinton's political survival ironically can be traced directly to the public integrity war. Despite nearly four years of allegations of impropriety on the part of Bill Clinton and Hillary Rodham Clinton, and numerous other high-level Clinton administration officials, Bill Clinton's political base has remained loyal. A decade earlier, supporters of Ronald Reagan reacted in much the same way with respect to attacks leveled against members of that administration.

. . . [F]inally, [we] argue . . . that as long as movement conservatives and new progressives battle for political power, the public integrity war will continue to intensify. Innocent public servants will find themselves targets of unjustified attacks. Unethical public servants will find it possible to characterize themselves as martyrs in the public integrity war. This integrity war has made it next to impossible for the public to distinguish between villains and victims. . . .

Throughout American history, presidents and members of their administrations have faced allegations of improper and illegal conduct. After the Second World War, the growing power of movement conservatives and new progressives guaranteed that allegations of improper conduct by high-level public officials would receive much closer scrutiny.

The term *movement conservatives* refers to those people who argue that big government constitutes the most serious problem facing the nation. Movement conservatives blame the growth of the administrative state for destroying individual initiative, for putting in place policies and programs hostile to traditional American families, and for attempting to limit the role of religion in American society.

New progressives, on the other side of the political aisle, argue that powerful special interests exert far too much control over the political process. They feel that average Americans need a government to stand up for their interests and make a difference in their lives. The industrial revolution, according to this line of reasoning, changed the nation forever.

The country ceased being a Jeffersonian agrarian nation of small towns and farmers. Powerful private interests acquired the ability to control the political process through legal or illegal means. Government, more often than not, did the bidding of special interests rather than acting in the public interest.

. . . [What] follow[s] tell[s] the story of how fighting corruption in government evolved from an attempt to rid government of bad individuals into an ideological battle for the hearts of the American people. New progressives have seen ethics reform as a way to prevent powerful special interests from rolling back progressive measures. Movement conservatives have viewed ethics reform as a way to equate corruption with big government, leading to demands to dismantle the welfare state. Each side believes it holds the moral high ground. Each believes that the vision and values of its foe threaten the very foundation of the nation. Neither movement understands that the issue of ethics in government simply is not great enough to sway voters to shift their allegiance. . . .

Blaming the media for the public integrity war has become a growth industry. The public integrity war, it must be remembered, started long before the 1960s or the Watergate scandal. However, media coverage of political ethics has played a major role in making it next to impossible for public officials to lead public and private lives. Much of the unhappiness over the selection of leaders comes from the impression that few political figures of our day have the same personal qualities of earlier leaders. The problem may be that we simply know much more about the lives of our prospective leaders before we decide to entrust them with tremendous responsibilities.

No practical way exists to get the genie back inside the bottle. Even if the traditional media outlets agreed to implement a code of conduct for reporting allegations of impropriety, the proliferation of other media forms means that any allegation will ultimately make its way to the public. New progressives and movement conservatives show little inclination to stop trying to portray one another as leading the nation to ruin.

Therefore, media coverage of the public integrity war has played into the hands of both the new progressives and the movement conservatives. New progressives believe that if the media focus on the power of special interests, the electorate will eventually see the light and place new progressives in positions of authority. Movement conservatives, on the other hand, believe extensive media coverage of waste, fraud and abuse in public programs will inevitably convince the public that too much government actually makes things worse.

Print and broadcast journalists have done a remarkable job covering the battles of the public integrity war. One can only estimate the number of words written and spoken on the subject of ethics since the resignation of Richard Nixon in August 1973. Many journalists believe that by focusing on ethics in government, public confidence in government will ultimately be restored. Unfortunately, this has not happened and is unlikely to happen.

After years of struggling with allegations, investigations and reports, the public appears ready to put such stories in perspective. The 1992 election of Bill Clinton and the subsequent Whitewater investigation provide strong evidence that ethics allegations have lost their potency as political weapons. Because mudslinging has become such a common feature of American politics, the public pays little attention to new allegations of improper conduct by public figures. . . .

The Clinton presidency will go down as one of the more unusual in American history. Few observers in 1991 gave William Jefferson Clinton, governor of a poor southern state, any chance of winning the 1992 Democratic nomination, let alone the presidency. Few pundits, following the mid-term congressional election in 1994, gave him any chance of winning reelection. But by the beginning of May 1996, Clinton held a twenty-point lead over Republican challenger Bob Dole.

Political observers search to explain why Bill Clinton has faced such strong criticism throughout his presidency. It has become clear that Clinton failed to understand how the public integrity war has ended any hope of privacy for a president or his family. For reasons impossible to understand, Clinton and his closest associates apparently believed that, once the campaign ended, the character issues that almost destroyed his candidacy would be forgotten. However, the new rules of public integrity warfare require full investigation of even the smallest allegation of wrongdoing. It may take historians and political scientists decades to determine why the Clinton camp believed that he was above the rules. This miscalculation has cost them dearly.

In the end, House Speaker Newt Gingrich and his contingent of movement conservatives saved Clinton from political oblivion. Gingrich had misread the 1994 election results as a mandate to dismantle the administrative state. But many Americans had second thoughts about his "revolution" when it became clear that he honestly intended to codify his reform agenda. As Americans compared Clinton with Gingrich, Clinton's standing rose.

But in retrospect, Clinton had taken a tremendous risk when he first decided to run for president. Since Watergate, experienced pols inside the Washington beltway understood that public figures no longer were permitted any personal secrets. If there were any skeletons in the Clinton closet, they surely would be uncovered during a national election. Either Clinton's staff underestimated the difficulty of keeping embarrassing stories out of the mainstream media, or they believed swing voters cared much more about the economy than about any possible flaws in his character.

Clinton survived, in large measure, because public integrity allegations had lost much of their impact on the electorate. The public has come to expect character attacks on public officials. No practical way exists for the electorate to distinguish between legitimate criticism and attacks motivated by partisan politics or ideology. . . .

Clinton apparently took a calculated risk that the public had tired of the public integrity war. He read America much better than most political experts and pundits. Even after the Democratic Party suffered its worst defeat in forty years, he sensed that a majority of Americans would reject the fine print of the Contract with America. Clinton understood that, while character mattered, issues and ideology mattered more. . . .

In the aftermath of the Watergate scandal, it appeared that Watergate-inspired reforms might help repair the damage done to public trust in government. But growing divisions over the role of government quickly shattered this dream. The public integrity war has profoundly changed the character of American politics and government. A constant barrage of allegations has made it next to impossible for most Americans to distinguish between legitimate charges of improper conduct and those motivated by ideology. Forty-nine percent of eligible voters—the lowest figure since 1924—turned out to vote in the 1996 presidential election.

The public integrity war has helped to transform the political landscape into a battlefield where honesty in government is simply another political issue. The day after the 1996 presidential election, the *Washington Post* ran a front-page story entitled "Clashing Coalitions Produce Split in Government Power: 2 Constituencies in Opposition Ideologically, Demographically." The Republican coalition, "more male-dominated, more pessimistic, more Protestant, more conservative and more likely to own a gun," placed a much higher priority on honesty in government than did members of the Democratic coalition, who are "more apt to be female, Catholic, single," and "ideologically moderate to liberal." Members of the clashing coalitions, in fact, regard the role of government not the integrity of public officials as their primary concern. . . .

Throughout the modern public integrity war, proposals for massive political reform have followed each new series of scandals. Almost simultaneous with the swearing in of William Jefferson Clinton for a second term as president of the United States, Speaker of the House Newt

Gingrich accepted a reprimand from the House and a $300,000 penalty for violating House ethics rules related to using tax exempt donations to fund a television course. Despite the prospect of a number of ongoing ethics investigations related to Whitewater, Paula Corbin Jones and questionable fund-raising efforts by the Democratic National Committee during the 1996 presidential campaign, President Clinton embarked upon a campaign [to] cast himself as the mediator between the clashing coalitions: "We need a new government for a new century humble enough not to try to solve all our problems for us, but strong enough to give us the tools to solve our problems ourselves." The conciliatory tone did nothing to slow the ongoing ethics investigations.

Although numerous public officials have found their lives turned upside down by the public integrity war, the American public has turned out [to] be the greatest loser. Sadly, a large percentage of the public has come to accept apparent unethical behavior by public officials as the rule rather than the exception. The restoration of public trust in government will take much more than the passage of a new campaign finance law or the tightening of existing ethics laws and rules. It will take a realization that neither movement conservatives nor new progressives have much hope of forcing each other into an unconditional surrender.

The vast majority of public servants work hard and strive to comply with the numerous ethics regulations spawned by the public integrity wars. Ethics rules and regulations, however, play a small role in the moral development of public servants. Too many public servants . . . have learned to rationalize questionable conduct as necessary to prevent "evil forces" from taking or remaining in power.

The public integrity war is not a story of saints and sinners. It is a story of how easily the passion for policies and programs can cloud one's judgement. Congress can do little to legislate the end to the public integrity war. New presidential directives on government ethics will only complicate the problem. The public integrity war will only end when we stop viewing political opponents as mortal enemies. Only then will we regain the ability to distinguish between individuals who have truly violated the public trust and those individuals simply caught up in the battles of the public integrity war.

PART THREE

Separation of Powers

16

JAMES MADISON

From *The Federalist* 51

In Federalist *10, an earlier selection, one of the Constitution's designers, James Madison, explained his fear of "faction"—any single group that tries to dominate the political process—and why faction cannot be removed from politics. Madison's solution was to accept factions, but control them.* Federalist *10 offered a republican (representative) government and a large, diverse nation with many factions as effective controls. In No. 51 he continues, citing the structural features that characterize American government. Power will be separated among different departments, or branches, of government, independent from one another. Then, power will be divided between the national and state levels, a system called federalism. Madison's philosophy for government is here in this essay too: "Ambition must be made to counteract ambition." Don't miss that paragraph, since it contains warnings that resonate across the centuries.*

No. 51: Madison

TO WHAT EXPEDIENT, then, shall we finally resort, for maintaining in practice the necessary partition of power among the several departments as laid down in the Constitution? The only answer that can be given is that as all these exterior provisions are found to be inadequate the defect must be supplied, by so contriving the interior structure of the government as that its several constituent parts may, by their mutual relations, be the means of keeping each other in their proper places. Without presuming to undertake a full development of this important idea I will hazard a few general observations which may perhaps place it in a clearer light, and enable us to form a more correct judgment of the principles and structure of the government planned by the convention.

In order to lay a due foundation for that separate and distinct exercise of the different powers of government, which to a certain extent is admitted on all hands to be essential to the preservation of liberty, it is evident that each department should have a will of its own; and consequently should be so constituted that the members of each should have as little agency as possible in the appointment of the members of the others. Were this principle rigorously adhered to, it would require that all the appointments for the supreme executive, legislative, and judiciary magistracies should be drawn from the same fountain of authority, the people, through channels having no communication whatever with one another. Perhaps such a plan of constructing the several departments would be less difficult in practice than it may in contemplation appear. Some difficulties, however, and some additional expense would attend the execution of it. Some deviations, therefore, from the principle must be admitted. In the constitution of the judiciary department in particular, it might be inexpedient to insist rigorously on the principle: first, because peculiar qualifications being essential in the members, the primary consideration ought to be to select that mode of choice which best secures these qualifications; second, because the permanent tenure by which the appointments are held in that department must soon destroy all sense of dependence on the authority conferring them.

It is equally evident that the members of each department should be as little dependent as possible on those of the others for the emoluments annexed to their offices. Were the executive magistrate, or the judges, not independent of the legislature in this particular, their independence in every other would be merely nominal.

But the great security against a gradual concentration of the several powers in the same department consists in giving to those who administer each department the necessary constitutional means and personal motives to resist encroachments of the others. The provision for defense must in this, as in all other cases, be made commensurate to the danger of attack. Ambition must be made to counteract ambition. The interest of the man must be connected with the constitutional rights of the place. It may be a reflection on human nature that such devices should be necessary to control the abuses of government. But what is government itself but the greatest of all reflections on human nature? If men were angels, no government would be necessary. If angels were to govern men, neither external nor internal controls on government would be necessary. In framing a government which is to be administered by men over men, the great difficulty lies in this: you must first enable the government to control the governed; and in the next place oblige it to control itself. A dependence on the people is, no doubt, the primary control on the government; but experience has taught mankind the necessity of auxiliary precautions.

This policy of supplying, by opposite and rival interests, the defect of better motives, might be traced through the whole system of human affairs, private as well as public. We see it particularly displayed in all the subordinate distributions of power, where the constant aim is to divide and arrange the several offices in such a manner as that each may be a check on the other—that the private interest of every individual may be a sentinel over the public rights. These inventions of prudence cannot be less requisite in the distribution of the supreme powers of the State.

But it is not possible to give to each department an equal power of self-defense. In republican government, the legislative authority necessarily predominates. The remedy for this inconveniency is to divide the legislature into different branches; and to render them, by different modes of election and different principles of action, as little connected with each other as the nature of their common functions and their common dependence on the society will admit. It may even be necessary to guard against dangerous encroachments by still further precautions. As the weight of the legislative authority requires that it should be thus divided, the weakness of the executive may require, on the other hand, that it should be fortified. An absolute negative on the legislature appears, at first view, to be the natural defense with which the executive magistrate should be armed. But perhaps it would be neither altogether safe nor alone sufficient. On ordinary occasions it might not be exerted with the requisite firmness, and on extraordinary occasions it might be perfidiously abused. May not this defect of an absolute negative be supplied by some qualified connection between this weaker department and the weaker branch of the stronger department, by which the latter may be led to support the constitutional rights of the former, without being too much detached from the rights of its own department?

If the principles on which these observations are founded be just, as I persuade myself they are, and they be applied as a criterion to the several State constitutions, and to the federal Constitution, it will be found that if the latter does not perfectly correspond with them, the former are infinitely less able to bear such a test.

There are, moreover, two considerations particularly applicable to the federal system of America, which place that system in a very interesting point of view.

First. In a single republic, all the power surrendered by the people is submitted to the administration of a single government; and the usurpations are guarded against by a division of the government into distinct and separate departments. In the compound republic of America, the power surrendered by the people is first divided between two distinct governments, and then the portion allotted to each subdivided among distinct and separate departments. Hence a double security arises to the rights of the people. The different governments will control each other, at the same time that each will be controlled by itself.

Second. It is of great importance in a republic not only to guard the society against the oppression of its rulers, but to guard one part of the society against the injustice of the other part. Different interests necessarily exist in different classes of citizens. If a majority be united by a common interest, the rights of the minority will be insecure. There are but two methods of providing against this evil: the one by creating a will in the community independent of the majority—that is, of the society itself; the other, by comprehending in the society so many separate descriptions of citizens as will render an unjust combination of a majority of the whole very improbable, if not impracticable. The first method prevails in all governments possessing an hereditary or self-appointed authority. This, at best, is but a precarious security; because a power independent of the society may as well espouse the unjust views of the major as the rightful interests of the minor party, and may possibly be turned against both parties. The second method will be exemplified in the federal republic of the United States. Whilst all authority in it will be derived from and dependent on the society, the society itself will be broken into so many parts, interests and classes of citizens, that the rights of individuals, or of the minority, will be in little danger from interested combinations of the majority. In a free government the security for civil rights must be the same as that for religious rights. It consists in the one case in the multiplicity of interests, and in the other in the multiplicity of sects. The degree of security in both cases will depend on the number of interests and sects; and this may be presumed to depend on the extent of country and number of people comprehended under the same government. This view of the subject must particularly recommend a proper federal system to all the sincere and considerate friends of republican government, since it shows that in exact proportion as the territory of the Union may be formed into more circumscribed Confederacies, or States, oppressive combinations of a majority will be facilitated; the best security, under the republican forms, for the rights of every class of citizen, will be diminished; and consequently the stability and independence of some member of the government, the only other security, must be proportionally increased. Justice is the end of government. It is the end of civil society. It ever has been and ever will be pursued until it be obtained, or until liberty be lost in the pursuit. In a society under the forms of which the stronger faction can readily unite and oppress the weaker, anarchy may as truly be said to reign as in a state of nature, where the weaker individual is not secured against the violence of the stronger; and as, in the latter state, even the stronger individuals are prompted, by the uncertainty of their condition, to submit to a government which may protect the weak as well as themselves; so, in the former state, will the more powerful factions or parties be gradually induced, by a like motive, to wish for a government which will protect all parties, the weaker as well as the more powerful. It can be little doubted that if the State of Rhode Island was separated from the Confederacy and left to itself, the insecurity of rights under the popular form of government within such narrow limits would be displayed by such reiterated oppressions of factious majorities that some power altogether independent of the people would soon be called for by the voice of the very factions whose misrule had proved the necessity of it. In the extended republic of the United States, and among the great variety of interests, parties, and sects which it embraces, a coalition of a majority of the whole society could seldom take place on any other principles than those of justice and the general good; whilst there being thus less danger to a minor from the will of a major party, there must be less pretext, also, to provide for the security of the former, by introducing into the government a will not dependent on the latter, or, in other words, a will independent of the society itself. It is no less certain than it is important, notwithstanding the contrary opinions which have been entertained, that the larger the society, provided it lie within a practicable sphere, the more duly capable it will be of self-government. And happily for the *republican cause*, the practicable sphere may be carried to a very great extent by a judicious modification and mixture of the *federal principle*. *Publius*

17

WOODROW WILSON

From *Congressional Government*

Before becoming president of the United States, Woodrow Wilson was governor of New Jersey. Previously, he had been the president of Princeton University and, earlier still, a professor of political science. In his 1885 doctoral writings, Wilson criticizes the fragmentation of power and lack of clear accountability in the American structure of government. The dilution of the national government's authority by state governments excites Wilson's ire, too. He sympathizes with the president's position because of its weakness relative to Congress at the time. Wilson's strongest negative judgment is saved for congressional committees, which he considered major impediments to getting the nation's business accomplished efficiently. Wilson the political scientist makes a good case against the gridlock inherent in the framers' separation of powers design. One wonders whether the beleaguered President Wilson re-read his own scholarly treatise in 1919, at the end of World

War I, when Senator Henry Cabot Lodge led the Foreign Relations Committee in blocking the passage of the Versailles Treaty based on Wilson's Fourteen Points and containing his League of Nations.

I KNOW OF few things harder to state clearly and within reasonable compass than just how the nation keeps control of policy in spite of these hide-and-seek vagaries of authority. Indeed, it is doubtful if it does keep control through all the roundabout paths which legislative and executive responsibility are permitted to take. It must follow Congress somewhat blindly; Congress is known to obey without altogether understanding its Committees: and the Committees must consign the execution of their plans to officials who have opportunities not a few to hoodwink them. At the end of these blind processes is it probable that the ultimate authority, the people, is quite clear in its mind as to what has been done or what may be done another time? Take, for example, financial policy,—a very fair example, because, as I have shown, the legislative stages of financial policy are more talked about than any other congressional business, though for that reason an extreme example. If, after appropriations and adjustments of taxation have been tardily and in much tribulation of scheming and argument agreed upon by the House, the imperative suggestions and stubborn insistence of the Senate confuse matters till hardly the Conference Committees themselves know clearly what the outcome of the disagreements has been; and if, when these compromise measures are launched as laws, the method of their execution is beyond the view of the Houses, in the semi-privacy of the departments, how is the comprehension—not to speak of the will—of the people to keep any sort of hold upon the course of affairs? There are no screws of responsibility which they can turn upon the consciences or upon the official thumbs of the congressional Committees principally concerned. Congressional Committees are nothing to the nation; they are only pieces of the interior mechanism of Congress. To Congress they stand or fall. And, since Congress itself can scarcely be sure of having its own way with them, the constituencies are manifestly unlikely to be able to govern them. As for the departments, the people can hardly do more in drilling them to unquestioning obedience and docile efficiency than Congress can. Congress is, and must be, in these matters the nation's eyes and voice. If it cannot see what goes wrong and cannot get itself heeded when it commands, the nation likewise is both blind and dumb.

This, plainly put, is the practical result of the piecing of authority,

the cutting of it up into small bits, which is contrived in our constitutional system. Each branch of the government is fitted out with a small section of responsibility, whose limited opportunities afford to the conscience of each many easy escapes. Every suspected culprit may shift the responsibility upon his fellows. Is Congress rated for corrupt or imperfect or foolish legislation? It may urge that it has to follow hastily its Committees or do nothing at all but talk; how can it help it if a stupid Committee leads it unawares into unjust or fatuous enterprises? Does administration blunder and run itself into all sorts of straits? The Secretaries hasten to plead the unreasonable or unwise commands of Congress, and Congress falls to blaming the Secretaries. The Secretaries aver that the whole mischief might have been avoided if they had only been allowed to suggest the proper measures; and the men who framed the existing measures in their turn avow their despair of good government so long as they must intrust all their plans to the bungling incompetence of men who are appointed by and responsible to somebody else. How is the schoolmaster, the nation, to know which boy needs the whipping?

Moreover, it is impossible to deny that this division of authority and concealment of responsibility are calculated to subject the government to a very distressing paralysis in moments of emergency. There are few, if any, important steps that can be taken by any one branch of the government without the consent or coöperation of some other branch. Congress must act through the President and his Cabinet; the President and his Cabinet must wait upon the will of Congress. There is no one supreme, ultimate head—whether magistrate or representative body—which can decide at once and with conclusive authority what shall be done at those times when some decision there must be, and that immediately. Of course this lack is of a sort to be felt at all times, in seasons of tranquil rounds of business as well as at moments of sharp crisis; but in times of sudden exigency it might prove fatal,—fatal either in breaking down the system or in failing to meet the emergency. Policy cannot be either prompt or straightforward when it must serve many masters. It must either equivocate, or hesitate, or fail altogether. It may set out with clear purpose from Congress, but get waylaid or maimed by the Executive.

If there be one principle clearer than another, it is this: that in any business, whether of government or of mere merchandising, *somebody must be trusted*, in order that when things go wrong it may be quite plain who should be punished. In order to drive trade at the speed and with the success you desire, you must confide without suspicion in your chief clerk, giving him the power to ruin you, because you thereby furnish him with a motive for serving you. His reputation, his own honor or disgrace, all his own commercial prospects, hang upon your success. And human nature is much the same in government as in the dry-goods trade. *Power and strict accountability for its use* are the essential constituents of good government. A sense of highest responsibility, a dignifying and elevating sense of being trusted, together with a consciousness of being in an official station so conspicuous that no faithful discharge of duty can go unacknowledged and unrewarded, and no breach of trust undiscovered and unpunished,—these are the influences, the only influences, which foster practical, energetic, and trustworthy statesmanship. The best rulers are always those to whom great power is entrusted in such a manner as to make them feel that they will surely be abundantly honored and recompensed for a just and patriotic use of it, and to make them know that nothing can shield them from full retribution for every abuse of it.

It is, therefore, manifestly a radical defect in our federal system that it parcels out power and confuses responsibility as it does. The main purpose of the Convention of 1787 seems to have been to accomplish this grievous mistake. The "literary theory" of checks and balances is simply a consistent account of what our constitution-makers tried to do; and those checks and balances have proved mischievous just to the extent to which they have succeeded in establishing themselves as realities. It is quite safe to say that were it possible to call together again the members of that wonderful Convention to view the work of their hands in the light of the century that has tested it, they would be the first to admit that the only fruit of dividing power had been to make it irresponsible. . . .

It was something more than natural that the Convention of 1787 should desire to erect a Congress which would not be subservient and an executive which could not be despotic. And it was equally to have been expected that they should regard an absolute separation of these two great branches of the system as the only effectual means for the accomplishment of that much desired end. It was impossible that they could believe that executive and legislature could be brought into close relations of cooperation and mutual confidence without being tempted, nay, even bidden, to collude. How could either maintain its independence of action unless each were to have the guaranty of the Constitution that its own domain should be absolutely safe from invasion, its own prerogatives absolutely free from challenge? "They shrank from placing sovereign power anywhere. They feared that it would generate tyranny; George III had been a tyrant to them, and come what might they would not make a George III." They would conquer, by dividing, the power they so much feared to see in any single hand. . . .

The natural, the inevitable tendency of every system of self-government like our own and the British is to exalt the representative body, the people's parliament, to a position of absolute supremacy. . . . Our Constitution, like every other constitution which puts the authority to make laws and the duty of controlling the public expenditure into the hands of a popular assembly, practically sets that assembly to rule the affairs of the nation as supreme overlord. But, by separating it entirely from its executive agencies, it deprives it of the opportunity and means for making its authority complete and convenient. The constitutional machinery is left of such a pattern that other forces less than that of Congress may cross and compete with Congress, though they are too small to overcome or long offset it; and the result is simply an unpleasant, wearing friction which, with other adjustments, more felicitous and equally safe, might readily be avoided. . . .

The dangers of this serious imperfection in our governmental machinery have not been clearly demonstrated in our experience hitherto; but now their delayed fulfillment seems to be close at hand. The plain tendency is towards a centralization of all the greater powers of government in the hands of the federal authorities, and towards the practical confirmation of those prerogatives of supreme overlordship which Congress has been gradually arrogating to itself. The central government is constantly becoming stronger and more active, and Congress is establishing itself as the one sovereign authority in that government. In constitutional theory and in the broader features of past practice, ours has been what Mr. Bagehot has called a "composite" government.* Besides state and federal authorities to dispute as to sovereignty, there have been within the federal system itself rival and irreconcilable powers. But gradually the strong are overcoming the weak. If the signs of the times are to be credited, we are fast approaching an adjustment of sovereignty quite as "simple" as need be. Congress is not only to retain the authority it already possesses, but is to be brought again and again face to face with still greater demands upon its energy, its wisdom, and its conscience, is to have ever-widening duties and responsibilities thrust upon it, without being granted a moment's opportunity to look back from the plough to which it has set its hands.

The sphere and influence of national administration and national legislation are widening rapidly. Our populations are growing at such a rate that one's reckoning staggers at counting the possible millions that may have a home and a work on this continent ere fifty more years shall

*Walter Bagehot (1826–1877), British economist, political theorist, and journalist, wrote *The English Constitution*, a book that had great influence on the young Woodrow Wilson. The idealized picture of the virtues of the British polity that informs *Congressional Government* is straight out of Bagehot.—Eds.

have filled their short span. The East will not always be the centre of national life. The South is fast accumulating wealth, and will faster recover influence. The West has already achieved a greatness which no man can gainsay, and has in store a power of future growth which no man can estimate. Whether these sections are to be harmonious or dissentient depends almost entirely upon the methods and policy of the federal government. If that government be not careful to keep within its own proper sphere and prudent to square its policy by rules of national welfare, sectional lines must and will be known; citizens of one part of the country may look with jealousy and even with hatred upon their fellow-citizens of another part; and faction must tear and dissension distract a country which Providence would bless, but which man may curse. The government of a country so vast and various must be strong, prompt, wieldy, and efficient. Its strength must consist in the certainty and uniformity of its purposes, in its accord with national sentiment, in its unhesitating action, and in its honest aims. It must be steadied and approved by open administration diligently obedient to the more permanent judgments of public opinion; and its only active agency, its representative chambers, must be equipped with something besides abundant powers of legislation.

As at present constituted, the federal government lacks strength because its powers are divided, lacks promptness because its authorities are multiplied, lacks wieldiness because its processes are roundabout, lacks efficiency because its responsibility is indistinct and its action without competent direction. It is a government in which every officer may talk about every other officer's duty without having to render strict account for not doing his own, and in which the masters are held in check and offered contradiction by the servants. Mr. Lowell has called it "government by declamation." Talk is not sobered by any necessity imposed upon those who utter it to suit their actions to their words. There is no day of reckoning for words spoken. The speakers of a congressional majority may, without risk of incurring ridicule or discredit, condemn what their own Committees are doing; and the spokesmen of a minority may urge what contrary courses they please with a well-grounded assurance that what they say will be forgotten before they can be called upon to put it into practice. Nobody stands sponsor for the policy of the government. A dozen men originate it; a dozen compromises twist and alter it; a dozen offices whose names are scarcely known outside of Washington put it into execution. . . .

An intelligent observer of our politics has declared that there is in the United States "a class, including thousands and tens of thousands of the best men in the country, who think it possible to enjoy the fruits of good government without working for them." Every one who has seen beyond the outside of our American life must recognize the truth of this; to explain it is to state the sum of all the most valid criticisms of congressional government. Public opinion has no easy vehicle for its judgments, no quick channels for its action. Nothing about the system is direct and simple. Authority is perplexingly subdivided and distributed, and responsibility has to be hunted down in out-of-the-way corners. So that the sum of the whole matter is that the means of working for the fruits of good government are not readily to be found. The average citizen may be excused for esteeming government at best but a haphazard affair, upon which his vote and all of his influence can have but little effect. How is his choice of a representative in Congress to affect the policy of the country as regards the questions in which he is most interested, if the man for whom he votes has no chance of getting on the Standing Committee which has virtual charge of those questions? How is it to make any difference who is chosen President? Has the President any very great authority in matters of vital policy? It seems almost a thing of despair to get any assurance that any vote he may cast will even in an infinitesimal degree affect the essential courses of administration. There are so many cooks mixing their ingredients in the national broth that it seems hopeless, this thing of changing one cook at a time.

The charm of our constitutional ideal has now been long enough wound up to enable sober men who do not believe in political witchcraft to judge what it has accomplished, and is likely still to accomplish, without further winding. The Constitution is not honored by blind worship. The more open-eyed we become, as a nation, to its defects, and the prompter we grow in applying with the unhesitating courage of conviction all thoroughly-tested or well-considered expedients necessary to make self-government among us a straightforward thing of simple method, single, unstinted power, and clear responsibility, the nearer will we approach to the sound sense and practical genius of the great and honorable statesmen of 1787. And the first step towards emancipation from the timidity and false pride which have led us to seek to thrive despite the defects of our national system rather than seem to deny its perfection is a fearless criticism of that system. When we shall have examined all its parts without sentiment, and gauged all its functions by the standards of practical common sense, we shall have established anew our right to the claim of political sagacity; and it will remain only to act intelligently upon what our opened eyes have seen in order to prove again the justice of our claim to political genius.

18

JAMES STERLING YOUNG

From *The Washington Community: 1800–1828*

Numerous books and articles have been written about the early years of American government, right after the Constitution was ratified. It seems that scholars have left nothing uncovered in their exploration of that crucial era. But historian James Young succeeds in finding a most unusual angle, one that has great significance for students of American government. He relates the physical living arrangements in early Washington to the separation of powers embodied in the Constitution. Young describes the swamp that delineated parts of the town. He recounts stories about the boardinghouses where legislators lived and sometimes argued vehemently. Young's depiction of House and Senate floor activity can certainly match today's C-SPAN for excitement. Early Washington, D.C., established a clear precedent for the future: many interests were represented, but cooperation was minimal. As Young observes, "Some government!"

DESOLATE IN SURROUNDING, derogatory in self-image, the governmental community was also distinctive for the extraordinary manner in which the personnel chose to situate themselves in Washington—the social formations into which they deployed on the terrain. The settlement pattern of a community is, in a sense, the signature that its social organization inscribes upon the landscape, defining the groups of major importance in the life of the community and suggesting the relationships among them. In the case of the early Washington community that signature is very clear.

The members did not, in their residential arrangements, disperse uniformly or at random over the wide tract of the intended city. Nor did they draw together at any single place. The governmental community rather inscribed itself upon the terrain as a series of distinct subcommunities, separated by a considerable distance, with stretches of empty land between them. Each was clustered around one of the widely separated public buildings; each was a self-contained social and economic entity. The personnel of the governmental community segregated themselves, in short, into distinct groups, and formed a society of "we's" and "they's." . . .

From data gathered in an 1801 survey, listing the location of houses completed and under construction in the capital, it is possible to reconstruct the settlement pattern of the early governmental community with reasonable accuracy. . . .

Members of the different branches of government chose to situate themselves close by the respective centers of power with which they were affiliated, seeking their primary associations in extra-official life among their fellow branch members.

Despite its relative civilization, old Georgetown attracted few members of government as residents, and most of those who stayed there moved as soon as they could find quarters in Washington, nearer to their places of work. . . .

At the opposite end of the city, about five miles from Georgetown, near the Capitol but separated from it by a dense swamp, was the village of the armed forces. . . .

. . . Commercialization failing, the environs became the site of the congressional burying ground, a poorhouse, and a penitentiary with an arsenal "near, much too near" it, thus associating by coresidence the men and matériel of war with the dead, the indigent, and the incorrigible. The settlement was generally shunned by civilian members of the government as a place to live, and high-ranking military and naval officers also forsook it eventually to take up residence in the executive sector.

The chief centers of activity were the village community of the executives and the village community of the legislators, lying "one mile and a half and seventeen perches" apart as the crow flies, on the "great heath" bisected by the River Tiber.

Senators and Representatives lived in the shadow of the Capitol itself, most of them in knots of dwellings but a moment's walk from their place of meeting. . . .

The knolltop settlement of legislators was a complete and self-contained village community from beginning to end of the Jeffersonian era. Neither work nor diversion, nor consumer needs, nor religious needs required them to set foot outside it. Eight boardinghouses, a tailor, a shoemaker, a washerwoman, a grocery store, and an oyster house served the congressional settlement in 1801. Within three years a notary, an ironmonger, a saddle maker, several more tailors and bootmakers, a liquor store, bookstores, stables, bakery, and taverns had been added. In twenty years' time the settlement had increased to more than two thousand people and the Capitol was nearly surrounded by brick houses "three stories high, and decent, without being in the least elegant," where the lawmakers lodged during the session. An itinerant barber served the community, shuttling between the scattered villages of the capital on horseback, and a nearby bathhouse catered to congressional clientele. Legislators with families could send their children to school on the Hill. The members had their own congressional library and their own post office, dispatching and receiving mail—which was distributed on the floor of the Senate and the House daily—without leaving the Hill. Page boys, doorkeepers, sergeants-at-arms, and other ancillary personnel for Congress were supplied from the permanent population of Capitol Hill—mainly the boardinghouse proprietors and their families. . . . The settlement pattern of early Washington clearly reveals a community structure paralleling the constitutional structure of government itself. The "separation of powers" became a separation of persons, and each of the branches of government became a self-contained, segregated social system within the larger governmental establishment. Legislators with legislators, executives with executives, judges with judges, the members gathered together in their extra-official as well as in their official activities, and in their community associations deepened, rather than bridged, the group cleavages prescribed by the Constitution.

Why did the rulers make this highly contrived, unconventional legal structure into their community structure at Washington? . . . A key factor contributing to social segregation by branch affiliation is suggested by the consistency between such behavior and community attitudes about power and politicians. In the absence of any extrinsic forces compelling the rulers to segregate in community life, patterned avoidance between executives, legislators, and judges indicates that they felt a stronger sense of identification with their constitutional roles than with other more partisan roles they may have had in the community. Social segregation on the basis of branch affiliation suggests, in other words, that the rulers generally considered themselves executives, legislators, or judges first, and politicians or party members second. Such a preference for nonpartisan, constitutionally sanctioned roles fully accords with, and tends to confirm the authenticity of, the members' disparaging image of politicians. Their decided preference for associating with fellow branch members in extraofficial life is also precisely the sort of social behavior that was foreshadowed by the attitudes they held concerning power. Power-holders acculturated to antipower values would, it was predicted, be attracted toward behaviors and associations which were sanctioned by the Constitution. By subdividing into separate societies of executives, legislators, and judges, the rulers could not have more literally translated constitutional principles of organization into social realities nor afforded themselves greater security from reproach in this aspect of their community life at Washington. When one sees, moreover, the remarkable consistency between the organizational precepts of the Constitution of 1787 and the community plan of 1791, on the one hand, and, on the other hand, the actual community structure of the governing politicians from 1800 to 1828, one must presume a consistency also in the attitudes from which these principles of organization originally derived, namely, attitudes of mistrust toward political power.

Whatever the underlying causes, here was a community of powerholders who preferred and who sanctioned, in their extraofficial life, a structural configuration that had been designed explicitly to check power. Here was a community of rulers who chose, among all the alternatives of social organization open to them, precisely the one most prejudicial to their capacity to rule. . . . Power made a community of cultural strangers. And power, shared, was hardly a thing to bind strangers together.

To achieve political accord among men of such disparate interests and different acculturation would not have been an easy task even under the most auspicious circumstances. For those gathered to govern on Capitol Hill in the Jeffersonian era, the circumstances were anything but auspicious.

To the political cleavages inherent in any representative assembly were added the deeper social tensions that are generated when men of widely diverging beliefs and behaviors are thrust upon each other in everyday living. Close-quarters living gave rise to personal animus even between "men whose natural interests and stand in society are in many respects similar. . . . The more I know of [two New England Senators] the more I am impressed with the idea how unsuited they are ever to co-operate," commented a fellow lodger; "never were two substances more completely adapted to make each other explode." As social intimacy bared the depth of their behavioral differences, tolerance among men from different regions was strained to the breaking point. Political coexistence with the South and the frontier states was hard enough for New Englanders to accept. Social coexistence was insufferable with slaveholders "accustomed to speak in the tone of masters" and with frontiersmen having "a license of tongue incident to a wild and uncultivated state of society. With men of such states of mind and temperament," a Massachusetts delegate protested, "men educated in . . . New England . . . could have little pleasure in intercourse, less in controversy, and of course no sympathy." Close scrutiny of their New England neighbors in power could convince southerners, in their turn, that there was "not one [who] possesses the slightest tie of common interest or of common feeling with us," planters and gentlemen cast among men "who raised 'beef and pork, and butter and cheese, and potatoes and cabbages'" and carried on "a paltry trade in potash and codfish." Cultural antipathies, crowded barracks, poor rations, and separation from families left at home combined to make tempers wear thin as the winters wore on, leading to sporadic eruptions of violence. In a sudden affray at the table in Miss Shields's boardinghouse, Randolph, "pouring out a glass of wine, dashed it in Alston's face. Alston sent a decanter at his head in return, and these and similar missiles continued to fly to and fro, until there was much destruction of glass ware." The chambers of the Capitol themselves witnessed more than one scuffle, and, though it was not yet the custom for legislators to arm themselves when legislating, pistols at twenty paces cracked more than once in the woods outside the Capitol.

To those who would seek political agreement in an atmosphere of social tensions, the rules of proceeding in Congress offered no aid at all. On the contrary, contentiousness was encouraged by Senate and House rules which gave higher precedence to raising questions than to deciding them and which guaranteed almost total freedom from restraint to the idiosyncratic protagonist. . . . "Political hostilities are waged with great vigour," commented another observer, "yet both in attack and defence there is evidently an entire want both of discipline and organization. There is no concert, no division of duties, no compromise of opinion. . . . Any general system of effective co-operation is impossible."

The result was a scene of confusion daily on the floor of House and Senate that bore no resemblance to the deliberative processes of either the town meeting or the parliamentary assemblies of the Old World. Congress at work was Hyde Park* set down in the lobby of a busy hotel—hortatory outcry in milling throngs, all wearing hats as if just arrived or on the verge of departure, variously attired in the fashions of faraway places. Comings and goings were continual—to the rostrum to see the clerk, to the anterooms to meet friends, to the Speaker's chair in a sudden surge to hear the results of a vote, to the firesides for hasty caucuses and strategy-planning sessions. Some gave audience to the speaker of the moment; some sat at their desks reading or catching up on correspondence; some stood chatting with lady friends, invited on the floor; others dozed, feet propped high. Page boys weaved through the crowd, "little Mercuries" bearing messages, pitchers of water for parched throats, bundles of documents, calling out members' names, distributing mail just arrived on the stagecoach. Quills scratched, bond crackled as knuckles rapped the sand off wet ink, countless newspapers rustled. Desk drawers banged, feet

*Hyde Park, in London, has a corner reserved for those in the public who wish to stand up in front of the crowd and offer their views on various issues. At any moment of the day, Hyde Park is filled with raucous, boisterous argument on every subject under the sun.—Eds.

shuffled in a sea of documents strewn on the floor. Bird dogs fresh from the hunt bounded in with their masters, yapping accompaniment to contenders for attention, contenders for power. Some government! . . .

What emerges from a community study of Capitol Hill is, therefore, a social system which gave probably greater sanction and encouragement to constituency-oriented behavior than any institutional norms or organizational features of the modern Congress. . . . Constituency-oriented behavior, in other words, justified the possession of power in a context of personal and national values which seems to have demanded justification for the possession of power. . . .

As a system for the effective representation of citizen interests the social system of Capitol Hill has probably never been surpassed in the history of republican government. But a fragmented social system of small blocs, more anarchic than cohesive, seems hardly to meet the minimal requirements for a viable system of managing social conflict, for performing "the regulation of . . . various and interfering interests" which the author of *The Federalist*, No. 10 acknowledged to be "the principal task of modern legislation." Far from serving as an institution for the management of conflict, the little democracy on the Hill seems more likely to have acted as a source of conflict in the polity. An ironic and provocative judgment is thus suggested by the community record of Capitol Hill: at a time when citizen interest in national government was at its lowest point in history the power-holders on the Potomac fashioned a system of surpassing excellence for representing the people and grossly deficient in the means for governing the people.

19

DAVID BRADY AND CRAIG VOLDEN

From *Revolving Gridlock*

Political scientists David Brady and Craig Volden offer a complex but fascinating analysis of gridlock, the failure of the Congress and the president to be able to achieve major changes in policy. Gridlock can occur not only when there is divided government—when the presidency and the Congress are controlled by different political parties—but also, surprisingly, when the president and the legislature are of the same party. The reason for this, Brady and Volden argue, is that the real cause of gridlock lies with "supermajorities," the number of senators needed to end a filibuster (three-fifths) and the number of legislators needed to override a presidential veto (two-thirds of each chamber). In other words, a party's simple majority status is not enough to ensure control. This excerpt is difficult to grasp with a quick reading, so go slowly. It also demands some basic knowledge of the workings of the legislative process.

AS THE 103RD CONGRESS (1993–1994) ground to a close, political columnists, television commentators, Senators and Representatives, as well as the President, bemoaned the lack of progress on health care, campaign finance reform, and environmental legislation. "The worst Congress in over fifty years" and "gridlock dominates" proclaimed newspaper headlines and stories. The election of a Democratic President and Democratic majorities in the House and Senate in 1992 had heralded the end of both divided government and policy gridlock. The Democratic campaign of 1992 had featured gridlock as an issue, and the early passage of family leave and the reconciliation budget was trumpeted as the end of policy gridlock. Yet by January 1994 the story began to shift, as health care and other legislation was deeply mired in the congressional labyrinth. Political scientists, columnists, Washington insiders, and other observers began to characterize the 103rd Congress as overtly partisan and controlled by "special interests"; the filibuster in the Senate was seen as largely responsible for the lack of legislative action. By early October both parties were pointing fingers, trying to interpret the inaction in ways that forwarded their own electoral purposes. Democrats, including the President, blamed Republicans for the gridlock; whereas Republicans, sensing victory in the 1994 elections, tried to make President Clinton the issue and thus the election a referendum on his performance. Congress as an institution was held in ever lower esteem, and the turnover of the 1994 elections brought in the first Republican Congress in forty years.

The newly elected Republican majority in Congress pushed through some of the reforms defined by their Contract with America—ending unfunded mandates, enacting a line-item veto, and, in the House, passing a balanced budget amendment. By April, Congress enjoyed its highest approval ratings in over twenty years, Speaker Newt Gingrich was riding high in the opinion polls, and Americans saw Republicans as the party of action, fully capable of balancing the budget. Yet within seven months all this had changed. Congress's approval rating had shrunk to about 20 percent; Speaker Gingrich's approval rating had fallen to 30 percent; President Clinton's popularity was over 50 percent for the first time in more than a year; and the government was operating on a continuing resolution (after a seven-day shutdown) while the President and the Republican Congress negotiated a new budget deal that was far to the left of the one originally passed by Congress.

What accounts for the "failure" of unified government in the 103rd Congress to break gridlock? Why, given a mandate in the 104th Congress, couldn't the Republicans have their way on policy? In the following . . . we shall attempt to define gridlock and to explain why gridlock characterized both the unified government of the 103rd Congress and the divided government of the 104th. The explanation will not focus on the role of special interests, political parties, or the media, and it does not rely heavily on presidential leadership. This is not to say that these variables don't play a role in making public policy—clearly they do. Nevertheless, our explanation for gridlock focuses on two primary factors: (1) the preferences of members of Congress regarding particular policies, and (2) supermajority institutions—the Senate filibuster and the presidential veto. . . .

The idea is really quite straightforward. When considering the U.S. Congress, instead of thinking of which party is in control, think of the members as arrayed from left to right—liberal to conservative. The further left a member is positioned, the more that member favors increased government activity on health care, the environment, education, and so on. The further right one moves, the more the members favor less government activity on health care, the environment, and education; these members thus favor lower taxes. Given this ordering of preferences, what does it take to achieve a policy change? . . .

Because in some legislation a minority of members can block a majority, the gridlock region (the range of status quo policies that is nearly impossible to change) can be sizable. Consider the filibuster as allowed by Rule XXII in the Senate. That rule, roughly, allows forty-one determined Senators to dominate floor activity so as to prohibit a bare majority from enacting its legislation. Such supermajoritarian institutions are common in state legislatures and in many foreign legislatures. The idea is that in some matters 50 percent is not enough to make fundamental changes, so rules requiring a supermajority are used. . . .

. . . [H]ow many voters are needed to move the policy—one-half (a simple majority), three-fifths (to break a filibuster), or two-thirds (to override a veto)—determines policy. Thus if the preferences of key members of Congress remain similar from one administration to the next, the party of the President won't tell us much about policy results. In addition to the distribution of preferences, supermajority institutional rules, specifically the Senate filibuster and the presidential veto (or threat to veto), also affect policy. . . .

The first institutional feature of note is the filibuster. The Senate has always been known for its slow and deliberate consideration of issues. In particular, a Senator, once given the floor, can continue to speak for extended periods of time. When a Senator's right to hold the floor indefinitely is utilized to slow or stop the advancement of a bill, the action is commonly referred to as a filibuster. The filibuster gained particular notoriety during the passage of civil rights bills in the 1950s and 1960s. In one instance, Strom Thurmond of South Carolina, speaking out against civil rights legislation, held the floor for twenty-four hours and eighteen minutes. Obviously, filibusters could keep the Senate from acting on important legislation. As a result, the Senate has over time adopted rules limiting the use of the filibuster. Of great significance is Senate Rule XXII, allowing for a cloture vote to end debate. To invoke cloture, sixty Senators must agree that the issue has been sufficiently discussed and that the Senate should continue on with its business, often leading to a vote on the bill being filibustered. The cloture rule thus limits the power of any small group of Senators who wish to talk an issue to death. But it still allows a minority to have significant power over an issue. If forty-one Senators wish to kill a bill through a filibuster, they can do so by voting against cloture. This institutional feature thus can have a great impact on policy outcomes. . . .

It should not be assumed that this model rests on the *observance* of filibusters and vetoes. The mere *threat* of a veto or a filibuster is often enough to kill a bill or to force it to be altered so as to override a veto or to gain sufficient votes for cloture. Successful vetoes and filibusters might actually be quite rare. Because time and effort are scarce commodities in Congress, it would be easier for the majority and the leadership to abandon a bill early on than to lose it to a filibuster or veto. However, in some circumstances politicians may wish to go down swinging. Opponents can raise the issue of repeated sustained vetoes, such as those in the Bush presidency, as an example of the President and his party causing gridlock. And Democrats could claim that the repeated filibusters by Bob Dole and other conservatives in the 103rd Congress were "obstructionist." Of course, on the other side of the coin, during the 1994 elections Republicans effectively claimed that the Democrats were poor at policymaking, unable to pass major legislation even with control of Congress and the presidency. . . .

. . . Our argument was that it is not parties that cause gridlock; rather, it is preferences of the members of the House and Senate in combination with supermajoritarian institutions like Senate Rule XXII that cause gridlock. . . .

If the preferences of key members of Congress essentially drive policies, what further conclusions can we draw? The first is that the President's powers are generally overrated by some scholars and the media, and that Congress ultimately determines policy results. Gridlock objectively means that neither conservative nor liberal Presidents can pull or push policy far away from where Congress wants it. Unified government gridlock simply means that policy change will be held back by the filibuster . . . , rather than by the members needed to override a veto. In short, in order to get any kind of legislation from budgets to civil rights acts passed, Republican Presidents are forced to move their proposals to the left whereas Democratic Presidents must move theirs right. Second, since policy is maintained within a narrow band controlled by moderate Democrats and Republicans, gridlock occurs under both unified and divided government. Third, the key to understanding what will happen to today's proposed policies is [:] . . . If they are to pass, policy proposals must be modified to accommodate these key members. . . .

In addition, not only is there a lack of consensus in the Congress, there is a lack of consensus among the public about what should be done. "The budget should be balanced while taxes are cut and expenses increased" is a classic example of the American public's contradictory views on policy. It is hard to determine whether voters are inherently unrealistic or whether they have been induced to be unrealistic. Consider the budget problem. The public (a majority of respondents in various surveys) believes that we can reduce taxes, increase expenditures (in different areas, depending on the respondent's particulars), and have a balanced budget all at the same time. One view drawn from such results is that the public is uninformed, irrational, and/or unrealistic. A counter to this would be: What should we expect from a public that has for decades been told that solving the budget problem will be painless? From Jimmy Carter's energy crises as "the moral equivalent of war" to Walter Mondale's pledge to raise taxes, to George Bush breaking his opposing pledge of "no new taxes," politicians who admitted that pain was involved in problem solving have not fared well at the polls. Politicians from LBJ (with his Great Society) to Ronald Reagan (with his Morning in America) who focused on the positive have done much better at the polls. In short, politicians often tell the public that problems can be solved without pain. Whether right or wrong, the 1996 campaign for the presidency took Social Security and Medicare off the table as policy areas vulnerable to change. Both parties' candidates spent considerable time assuring citizens that they were better able to protect these entitlements than their opponents. President Clinton had a real advantage over Dole on this issue, forcing Dole to claim time and again that Medicare would be safe under him. After twenty years of being told that budget problems can be solved without cutting middle-class entitlements or raising middle-class taxes, the public may well have begun to believe it. . . .

. . . We believe . . . that an inability to override vetoes or end filibusters is a further testimony to the lack of policy consensus in the United States.

This is not to say that we are not troubled by policy gridlock. . . . The revolving gridlock theory predicts that often the majority view is tempered by the need to secure supermajorities, and by the complexity of the issues. Where the will of the majority is continually thwarted by diverse preferences and supermajority institutions, the public may turn to elections to align politicians' preferences. But when politicians are already representing diverse district preferences, gridlock continues. Gridlock thus represents a lack of policy consensus regarding the difficult decisions we ask our representatives to make. Whether caused by complex issues or supermajority institutions, the political wrangling and subsequent inability to break gridlock leaves the public feeling dissatisfied.

The predicament of contemporary politics in America could be relieved by lowering public expectations about what the government is able to achieve, given the diversity of views held by Americans and the complexity of the problems with which the country is faced.

PART FOUR

Federalism

20

JAMES MADISON

From *The Federalist* Nos. 39 and 46

Ratification of the Constitution in 1787 required delicate and persuasive diplomacy. The Articles of Confederation, flawed as they were in allowing virtually no centralized governmental power, did give each state the near-total independence valued after their experiences as English colonies. The proponents of the new Constitution had to convince the states to adopt a new structure of government that would strengthen national power. In Nos. 39 and 46, Madison first discusses the importance of representative government. Then he turns to the "bold and radical innovation" that both divided and shared power between the national government and the state governments—what we today call federalism. The approval of the Constitution was to be by the people of the states, and once in operation, the government would be both national and federal. But, Madison explained, the American people would be the ultimate repository of power. State governments would always claim the citizenry's top loyalty, unless the people chose otherwise. Publius argued successfully in the great American tradition of compromise; there was something for everyone in the Constitution.

No. 39: Madison

. . . THE FIRST QUESTION that offers itself is whether the general form and aspect of the government be strictly republican. It is evident that no other form would be reconcilable with the genius of the people of America; with the fundamental principles of the Revolution; or with that honorable determination which animates every votary of freedom to rest all our political experiments on the capacity of mankind for self-government. If the plan of the convention, therefore, be found to depart from the republican character, its advocates must abandon it as no longer defensible.

What, then, are the distinctive characters of the republican form? . . .

If we resort for a criterion to the different principles on which different forms of government are established, we may define a republic to be, or at least may bestow that name on, a government which derives all its powers directly or indirectly from the great body of the people, and is administered by persons holding their offices during pleasure for a limited period, or during good behavior. It is *essential* to such a government that it be derived from the great body of the society, not from an inconsiderable proportion or a favored class of it; otherwise a handful of tyrannical nobles, exercising their oppressions by a delegation of their powers, might aspire to the rank of republicans and claim for their government the honorable title of republic. It is *sufficient* for such a government that the persons administering it be appointed, either directly or indirectly, by the people; and that they hold their appointments by either of the tenures just specified; otherwise every government in the United States, as well as every other popular government that has been or can be well organized or well executed, would be degraded from the republican character. According to the constitution of every State in the Union, some or other of the officers of government are appointed indirectly only by the people. According to most of them, the chief magistrate himself is so appointed. And according to one, this mode of appointment is extended to one of the co-ordinate branches of the legislature. According to all the constitutions, also, the tenure of the highest offices is extended to a definite period, and in many instances, both within the legislative and executive departments, to a period of years. According to the provisions of most of the constitutions, again, as well as according to the most respectable and received opinions on the subject, the members of the judiciary department are to retain their offices by the firm tenure of good behavior. . . .

"But it was not sufficient," say the adversaries of the proposed Constitution, "for the convention to adhere to the republican form. They ought with equal care to have preserved the *federal* form, which regards the Union as a *Confederacy* of sovereign states; instead of which they have framed a *national* government, which regards the Union as a *consolidation* of the States." And it is asked by what authority this bold and radical innovation was undertaken? . . .

First.—In order to ascertain the real character of the government, it may be considered in relation to the foundation on which it is to be established; to the sources from which its ordinary powers are to be drawn; to the operation of those powers; to the extent of them; and to the authority by which future changes in the government are to be introduced.

On examining the first relation, it appears, on one hand, that the Constitution is to be founded on the assent and ratification of the people of America, given by deputies elected for the special purpose; but, on the other, that this assent and ratification is to be given by the people, not as individuals composing one entire nation, but as composing the distinct and independent States to which they respectively belong. It is to be the assent and ratification of the several States, derived from the supreme authority in each State—the authority of the people themselves. The act, therefore, establishing the Constitution will not be a *national* but a *federal* act.

That it will be a federal and not a national act, as these terms are understood by the objectors—the act of the people, as forming so many independent States, not as forming one aggregate nation—is obvious from this single consideration: that it is to result neither from the decision of a *majority* of the people of the Union, nor from that of a *majority* of the States. It must result from the *unanimous* assent of the several States that are parties to it, differing not otherwise from their ordinary dissent than in its being expressed, not by the legislative authority, but by that of the people themselves. . . . Each State, in ratifying the Constitution, is considered as a sovereign body independent of all others, and only to be bound by its own voluntary act. In this relation, then, the new Constitution will, if established, be a *federal* and not a *national* constitution.

The next relation is to the sources from which the ordinary powers of government are to be derived. The House of Representatives will derive its powers from the people of America; and the people will be represented in the same proportion and on the same principle as they are in the legislature of a particular State. So far the government is *national*, not *federal*. The Senate, on the other hand, will derive its powers from the States as political and coequal societies; and these will be represented on the principle of equality in the Senate, as they now are in the existing Congress. So far the government is *federal*, not *national*. The executive power will be derived from a very compound source. The immediate election of the President is to be made by the States in their political characters. The votes allotted to them are in a compound ratio, which considers them partly as distinct and coequal societies, partly as unequal members of the same society. . . . From this aspect of the government it appears to be of a mixed character, presenting at least as many *federal* as *national* features. . . . The idea of a national government involves in it not only an authority over the individual citizens, but an indefinite supremacy over all persons and things, so far as they are objects of lawful government. Among a people consolidated into one nation, this supremacy is completely vested in the national legislature. Among communities united for particular purposes, it is vested partly in the general and partly in the municipal legislatures. In the former case, all local authorities are subordinate to the supreme; and may be controlled, directed, or abolished by it at pleasure. In the latter, the local or municipal authorities form distinct and independent portions of the supremacy, no more subject, within their respective spheres, to the general authority than the general authority is subject to them, within its own sphere. In this relation, then, the proposed government cannot be deemed a *national* one; since its jurisdiction extends to certain enumerated objects only, and leaves to the several States a residuary and inviolable sovereignty over all other objects. . . .

If we try the Constitution by its last relation to the authority by which amendments are to be made, we find it neither wholly *national* nor wholly *federal.* Were it wholly national, the supreme and ultimate authority would reside in the *majority* of the people of the Union; and this authority would be competent at all times, like that of a majority of every national society to alter or abolish its established government. Were it wholly federal, on the other hand, the concurrence of each State in the Union would be essential to every alteration that would be binding on all. The mode provided by the plan of the convention is not founded on either of these principles. In requiring more than a majority, and particularly in computing the proportion by *States,* not by *citizens,* it departs from the national and advances towards the *federal* character; in rendering the concurrence of less than the whole number of States sufficient, it loses again the *federal* and partakes of the *national* character.

The proposed Constitution, therefore, even when tested by the rules laid down by its antagonists, is, in strictness, neither a national nor a federal Constitution, but a composition of both. In its foundation it is federal, not national; in the sources from which the ordinary powers of the government are drawn, it is partly federal and partly national; in the operation of these powers, it is national, not federal; in the extent of them, again, it is federal, not national; and, finally in the authoritative mode of introducing amendments, it is neither wholly federal nor wholly national.

Publius

No. 46: Madison

. . . I proceed to inquire whether the federal government or the State governments will have the advantage with regard to the predilection and support of the people. Notwithstanding the different modes in which they are appointed, we must consider both of them as substantially dependent on the great body of the citizens of the United States. I assume this position here as it respects the first, reserving the proofs for another place. The federal and State governments are in fact but different agents and trustees of the people, constituted with different powers and designed for different purposes. The adversaries of the Constitution seem to have lost sight of the people altogether in their reasonings on this subject; and to have viewed these different establishments not only as mutual rivals and enemies, but as uncontrolled by any common superior in their efforts to usurp the authorities of each other. These gentlemen must here be reminded of their error. They must be told that the ultimate authority, wherever the derivative may be found, resides in the people alone, and that it will not depend merely on the comparative ambition or address of the different governments whether either, or which of them, will be able to enlarge its sphere of jurisdiction at the expense of the other. Truth, no less than decency, requires that the event in every case should be supposed to depend on the sentiments and sanction of their common constituents. . . .

Many considerations, besides those suggested on a former occasion, seem to place it beyond doubt that the first and most natural attachment of the people will be to the governments of their respective States. . . .

If . . . the people should in future become more partial to the federal than to the State governments, the change can only result from such manifest and irresistible proofs of a better administration as will overcome all their antecedent propensities. And in that case, the people ought not surely to be precluded from giving most of their confidence where they may discover it to be most due; but even in that case the State governments could have little to apprehend, because it is only within a certain sphere that the federal power can, in the nature of things, be advantageously administered.

Publius

21

DANIEL ELAZAR

From *American Federalism*

American government has been based on a system of federalism since the Constitution was ratified. Yet, over two centuries, change and flexibility have marked American federalism; the national and state governments have shared power in different ways, to different degrees, with different roles. In the mid-1990s, for example, there is much talk in Washington about moving more governmental programs and policy decisions back to the state level, away from central government edicts. Professor Daniel Elazar offers a classic piece on federalism in which he defends the importance of state governments, even at a time when the national government seemed to dominate. Elazar points to the innovative ideas developed at the state level. He recognizes the states' importance as managers of government programs. Elazar is right on target for today, viewing American federalism as an ever-changing "partnership" between Washington, D.C., and the state capitals.

THE SYSTEM of state-federal relations . . . is not the neat system often pictured in the textbooks. If that neat system of separate governments performing separate functions in something akin to isolation is used as the model of what federalism should be to enable the states to maintain their integrity as political systems, then the states are in great difficulty indeed. If, however, the states have found ways to function as integral political systems—civil societies, if you will—within the somewhat chaotic system of intergovernmental sharing that exists, then they are, as the saying goes, in a different ball game. . . . We have tried to show that the states are indeed in a different ball game and as players in that game are not doing badly at all. Viewed from the perspective of that ball game, the strength and vitality of the states—and the strength and vitality of the American system as a whole—must be assessed by different standards from those commonly used.

In the first place, the states exist. This point is no less significant for its simplicity. The fact that the states survive as going concerns (as distinct from sets of historical boundaries used for the administration of centrally directed programs) after thirty-five years of depression, global war, and then cold war, which have all functioned to reduce the domestic freedom necessary to preserve noncentralized government, is in itself testimony to their vitality as political institutions. . . . Every day, in many ways, the states are actively contributing to the achievement of American goals and to the continuing efforts to define those goals.

Consequently, it is a mistake to think that national adoption of goals shared by an overwhelming majority of the states is simply centralization. To believe that is to deny the operation of the dynamics of history within a federal system. Any assessment of the states' position in the federal union must be made against a background of continuous social change. It is no more reasonable to assume that the states have lost power vis-à-vis the federal government since 1789 because they can no longer maintain established churches than it is to believe that white men are no longer as free as they were in that year because they can no longer own slaves. An apparent loss of freedom in one sphere may be more than made up by gains in another. Massachusetts exercises more power over its economy today than its governors ever hoped to exercise over its churches five generations ago. National values change by popular consensus and *all* governments must adapt themselves to those changes. The success of the states is that they have been able to adapt themselves well.

Part of the states' adaptation has been manifested in their efforts to improve their institutional capabilities to handle the new tasks they have assumed. In the twentieth century, there has been an extensive and continuing reorganization of state governments leading to increased executive responsibility, greater central budgetary control, and growing expertise of state personnel (whose numbers are also increasing). . . .

There has also been a great and continuing increase in the states' supervision of the functions carried out in their local subdivisions. The states' role in this respect has grown as fast as or faster than that of the federal government and is often exercised more stringently, a possibility enhanced by the constitutionally unitary character of the states. The states' supervision has been increased through the provision of technical aid to their localities, through financial grants, and through control of the power to raise (or authorize the raising of) revenue for all subdivisions.

In all this, though, there remains one major unsolved problem, whose importance cannot be overemphasized: that of the metropolitan areas. By and large, the states have been unwilling or unable to do enough to meet metropolitan problems, particularly governmental ones. Here, too, some states have better records than others but none have been able to deal with metropolitan problems comprehensively and thoroughly. It is becoming increasingly clear that—whatever their successes in the past—the future role of the states will be determined by their ability to come to grips with those problems.

A fourth factor that adds to the strength and vitality of the states is the manner in which state revenues and expenditures have been expanding since the end of World War II. . . .

Still a fifth factor is the continuing role of the states as primary managers of great programs and as important innovators in the governmental realm. Both management and innovation in education, for example, continue to be primary state responsibilities in which outside aid is used to support locally initiated ideas.

Even in areas of apparent state deficiencies, many states pursue innovative policies. Much publicity has been generated in recent years that reflects upon police procedures in certain states; yet effective actions to eliminate the death penalty have been confined to the state level. The states have also been active in developing means for releasing persons accused of crimes on their own recognizance when they cannot afford to post bail, thus reducing the imprisonment of people not yet convicted of criminal activity.

Because the states are political systems able to direct the utilization of the resources sent their way, federal grants have served as a stimulus to the development of state capabilities and, hence, have helped enhance their strength and vitality. Federal grants have helped the states in a positive way by broadening the programs they can offer their citizens and strengthening state administration of those programs. Conversely, the grants have prevented centralization of those programs and have given the states the ability to maintain their position despite the centralizing tendencies of the times.

For this reason, and because the concerns of American politics are universal ones, there is relatively little basic conflict between the federal government and the states or even between their respective interests. Most of the conflicts connected with federal-state relations are of two kinds: (1) conflicts between interests that use the federal versus state argument as a means to legitimize their demands or (2) low-level conflicts over the best way to handle specific cooperative activities. There are cases, of course, when interests representing real differences are able to align themselves with different levels of government to create serious federal-state conflict. The civil rights question in its southern manifestation is today's example of that kind of situation.

Finally, the noncentralized character of American politics has served to strengthen the states. Noncentralization makes possible intergovernment cooperation without the concomitant weakening of the smaller partners by giving those partners significant ways in which to preserve their integrity. This is because a noncentralized system functions to a great extent through bargaining and negotiation. Since its components are relatively equal in their freedom to act, it can utilize only a few of the hierarchical powers available in centralized systems. In essence, its general government can only use those powers set forth in the fundamental compact between the partners as necessary to the maintenance of the system as a whole. Stated baldly, congressional authorization of new federal programs is frequently no more than a license allowing federal authorities to begin negotiations with the states and localities. . . .

In the last analysis, the states remain viable entities in a federal system that has every tendency toward centralization present in all strong governments. They remain viable because they exist as civil societies with political systems of their own. They maintain that existence because the American political tradition and the Constitution embodying it give the states an important place in the overall fabric of American civil society. The tradition and the Constitution remain viable because neither Capitol Hill nor the fifty state houses have alone been able to serve all the variegated interests on the American scene that compete equally well without working in partnership.

The states remain vital political systems for larger reasons as well as immediate ones, reasons that are often passed over unnoticed in the public's concern with day-to-day problems of government. These larger reasons are not new; though they have changed in certain details, they remain essentially the same as in the early days of the Union.

The states remain important in a continental nation as reflectors of sectional and regional differences that are enhanced by the growing social and economic complexity of every part of the country, even as the older cultural differences may be diminished by modern communications. They remain important as experimenters and innovators over a wider range of fields than ever before, simply because government at every level in the United States has been expanding. The role of the states as recruiters of political participants and trainers of political leaders has in no way been diminished, particularly since the number of political offices of every kind seems to be increasing at least in proportion to population growth.

In at least two ways, traditional roles of the states have been enhanced by recent trends. They have become even more active promoters and administrators of public services than ever before. In part, this is simply because governments are doing more than they had in the past, but it is also because they provide ways to increase governmental activity while maintaining noncentralized government. By handling important programs at a level that can be reached by many people, the contribute to the maintenance of a traditional interest of democratic politics, namely, the maximization of local control over the political and administrative decision-makers whose actions affect the lives of every citizen in ever-increasing ways.

As the population of the nation increases, the states become increasingly able to manage major governmental activities with the competence and expertise demanded by the metropolitan–technological frontier. At the same time, the federal government becomes further removed from popular pressures simply by virtue of the increased size of the population it must serve. The states may well be on their way to becoming the most "manageable" civil societies in the nation. Their size and scale remain comprehensible to people even as they are enabled to do more things better.

In sum, the virtue of the federal system lies in its ability to develop and maintain mechanisms vital to the perpetuation of the unique combination of governmental strength, political flexibility, and individual liberty, which has been the central concern of American politics. The American people are known to appreciate their political tradition and the Constitution. Most important, they seem to appreciate the partnership, too, in some unreasoned way, and have learned to use all its elements to reasonably satisfy their claims on government.

22

DAVID OSBORNE

From *Laboratories of Democracy*

Earlier in the twentieth century, Supreme Court Justice Louis Brandeis called state governments "laboratories of democracy." States were where new policy ideas were first developed and tried out. Yet, after President Franklin Roosevelt's New Deal in the 1930s, state governments hardly seemed to be where the action was in government. A strong national government dominated American politics—until recently. Public policy specialist David Osborne looks at the way reinvigorated state governments have taken the lead in developing innovative ideas today. In this excerpt, he focuses on former Arizona governor—later Clinton administration Interior secretary—Bruce Babbitt, who transformed Arizona's old politics-as-usual state government into a modern, forward-looking one. Osborne's book is the prelude to Reinventing Government, *which carries further his idea of a "new paradigm" for "entrepreneurial" government.*

FRANKLIN ROOSEVELT once said of the New Deal, "Practically all the things we've done in the federal government are like things Al Smith did as governor of New York." There was surprising honesty in Roosevelt's remark, though he might have credited other states as well. Many of FDR's initiatives—including unemployment compensation, massive public works programs, deposit insurance, and social security—were modeled on successful state programs. The groundwork for much of the New Deal social agenda was laid in the states during the Progressive Era.

A similar process is under way today, particularly in the economic arena. The 1980s have been a decade of enormous innovation at the state level. For those unfamiliar with state politics—and given the media's relentless focus on Washington, that includes most Americans—the specifics are often startling. While the Reagan administration was denouncing government intervention in the marketplace, governors of both parties were embracing an unprecedented role as economic activists. Over the past decade, they have created well over 100 public investment funds, to make loans to and investments in businesses. Half the states have set up public venture capital funds; others have invested public money in the creation of private financial institutions. At least 40 states have created programs to stimulate technological innovation, which now number at least 200. Dozens of states have overhauled their public education systems. Tripartite business-labor-government boards have sprung up, often with the purpose of financing local committees dedicated to restructuring labor-management relations. A few states have even launched cooperative efforts with management and labor to revitalize regional industries.

Why this sudden burst of innovation at the state level? Just 25 years ago, state governments were widely regarded as the enemies of change, their resistance symbolized by George Wallace in the schoolhouse door.* The answer has to do with the profound and wrenching economic transition the United States has experienced over the past two decades. In the 1980s, a fundamentally new economy has been born. With it has come a series of new problems, new opportunities, and new challenges. In the states, government has responded.

The notion that America has left the industrial era behind is now commonplace. Some call the new age the "postindustrial era," some the "information age," others the "era of human capital." But most agree that the fundamental organization of the American and international economies that prevailed for three decades after World War II has changed. The United States has evolved from an industrial economy built upon assembly-line manufacturing in large, stable firms to a rapidly changing, knowledge-intensive economy built upon technological innovation.

The most obvious symptoms of this transition are idle factories, dislocated workers, and depressed manufacturing regions. Less obvious are the problems that inhibit our ability to innovate: a poorly educated and trained work force; adversarial relations between labor and management; inadequate supplies of risk capital; and corporate institutions that lag behind their foreign competitors in the speed with which they commercialize the fruits of their research, adopt new production technologies, and exploit foreign markets.

Jimmy Carter was elected just as the public began to sense that something had gone wrong with the American economy. Like other national politicians of his day, he only dimly perceived the emerging realities of the new economy. Ronald Reagan owed his election to the deepening

*George Wallace was the governor of Alabama in 1963, when the federal government forced the state to integrate its schools following the Supreme Court's 1954 *Brown v. Board of Education* decision. President Kennedy mobilized the Alabama National Guard, despite the governor's defiance of the desegregation decree. Governor Wallace gave a speech against desegregation at the schoolhouse door before the guard ushered African-American students into the building.—EDS.

economic crisis, but his solution was to reach back to the free-market myths of the preindustrial era. He had the luxury to do so because he governed an enormously diverse nation, in which rapid growth along both coasts balanced the pain experienced in the industrial and agricultural heartland.

Most governors have not had that luxury. When unemployment approached 13 percent in Massachusetts, or 15 percent in Pennsylvania, or 18 percent in Michigan, governors had to respond. They could not afford to wait for the next recovery, or to evoke the nostrums of free-market theory.

The same dynamic occurred during the last great economic transformation: the birth of our industrial economy. The Progressive movement, which originated at the state and local level, grew up in response to the new problems created by rapid industrialization: the explosion of the cities, the emergence of massive corporate trusts, the growth of urban political machines, the exploitation of industrial labor.* Many Progressive reforms introduced in the cities or states were gradually institutionalized at the federal level—culminating in the New Deal.

This reality led Supreme Court Justice Louis Brandeis to coin his famous phrase, "laboratories of democracy." One of America's leading Progressive activists during the early decades of the twentieth century, Brandeis viewed the states as laboratories in which the Progressives could experiment with new solutions to social and economic problems. Those that worked could be applied nationally; those that failed could be discarded.

Brandeis's phrase captured the peculiar, pragmatic genius of the federal system. As one approach to government—one political paradigm—wears thin, its successor is molded in the states, piece by piece. The process has little to do with ideology and everything to do with trial-and-error, seat-of-the-pants pragmatism. Part of the beauty, as Brandeis pointed out, is that new ideas can be tested on a limited scale—to see if they work, and to see if they sell—before they are imposed on the entire nation.

Today, at both the state and local levels, we are in the midst of a new progressive era. Just as the state and local Progressivism of Brandeis's day

*Progressivism was a movement that developed during the first two decades of the twentieth century advocating reform at all levels of government. Well-known as progressives were Governor Robert La Follette of Wisconsin and President Theodore Roosevelt, who ran as a Progressive in the 1912 presidential election. Progressives wanted to clean up urban government, throw out party bosses, and place more power in the hands of ordinary voters through referendum and the direct primary. In journalism, the Muckrakers uncovered political corruption, exploitative working conditions, corporate greed, and consumer abuse as targets for Progressive reform.—EDS.

foreshadowed the New Deal, the state and local experimentation of the 1980s may foreshadow a new national agenda. . . .

Life in Arizona is something few Americans raised east of the Mississippi would recognize. Two-thirds of all state residents were born elsewhere. Half arrived in the last fifteen years. Every fall a third of the students in the typical Phoenix school district are new. In 1986, *61* new shopping centers were completed or under way in the Phoenix metropolitan area.

In the mid-1980s, Phoenix was the nation's fastest growing city; Arizona one of its fastest growing states. At the current pace, the Phoenix area will double its population of 1.9 million—nearly half the state total—within 15 years. Every year this mushrooming metropolis—an endless expanse of one-story, suburban-style homes and shopping centers—gobbles up thousands of acres of desert in a race for the horizon. At 400 square miles, it now covers more ground than New York City.

This explosive growth has transformed a dusty, sparsely populated frontier state into a land of the modern, Sunbelt metropolis. Arizona was the last of the contiguous 48 states to join the union, in 1912. By 1940, it had only 500,000 people, spread out in small, desert towns and over vast Indian reservations. Phoenix had only 65,000 people. But World War II brought military bases and defense plants, and the postwar boom brought air conditioning and air travel. Suddenly Arizona's location and climate were advantages, rather than disadvantages. The defense contractors, aerospace companies, and electronics manufacturers poured in, bringing an army of young engineers and technicians with their wives and their children. This was the Eisenhower generation—raised during the depression, hardened by World War II, anxious for the security of a job, a home, and a future for their children. With their crew cuts and their conservatism, they transformed Arizona from a sleepy, almost southern Democratic state into a bastion of Sunbelt Republicanism.

Before the Republican takeover in the 1950s, the farmers, the mining companies, and the bankers had run the state. Copper, cotton, and cattle were king. "It used to be that there were five or six men who would sit around a luncheon table at the old Arizona Club and pretty much decide on how things were going to be," says Jack Pfister, general manager of the Salt River Project, the state's largest water and power utility. "Some legislators were said to wear a copper collar."

At first, the new suburban middle class did not change this arrangement a great deal. Real estate developers, the new millionaires on the block, joined the club. But even as the Republicans cemented their control in the 1960s, rural legislators held onto the reins of seniority—and thus power. State government was tiny, the governor a figurehead. And the new suburbanites embraced the frontier ethos in which the old Arizona had taken such pride. Ignoring the fact that without major government investments—in military bases, defense plants, and dams—Arizona would still be a rural backwater, they believed their newfound prosperity was the product of untrammeled free enterprise. Beginning in 1952, they voted Republican in every presidential election. They had little truck with Washington. In the 1950s, Arizona declined to participate in the federal Interstate Highway System; in the 1960s, it turned down medicaid. As local people still say with a hint of pride, Arizona is the last preserve of the lone gun slinger.

The combination of explosive growth and a frontier mentality created problems very different from those encountered by the other states profiled in this book. "In the East, you have old cities, old infrastructure, and a fight for economic survival," says Republican Senator Anne Lindemann. "Here, we're trying to control the growth as best we can."

This process was not without its lessons for the rest of the nation, however. Because Arizona is a desert, with a fragile ecosystem, its rapid growth threw into sharp relief the most serious environmental problems of the postindustrial era—particularly those involving water and toxic chemicals. And because the political climate makes public resources so scarce, the struggle to cope with the social problems created by a modern economy stimulated a degree of creativity rarely seen in a conservative state.

The task of dragging Arizona into the modern era fell to Bruce Babbitt, who by the time he left office in 1987 had changed the very nature of the governorship. A lanky, scholarly type whose habitual slouch and thoughtful manner hide an enormous drive, Babbitt looks like a cross between Donald Sutherland and Tom Poston. He has sandy hair, a lined face that has begun to sag with the wear of 14 years in politics, and large, pale eyes that bulge out from behind his eyebrows when he scowls. In a small group, when he is in his natural, analytic mode, Babbitt can be brilliant. On a dais, when he tries to sound like a politician, his body stiffens, his eyes bulge, and he does a good imitation of Don Knotts.

Despite his weakness as a public speaker, Babbitt captivated the Arizona electorate. He was elected in 1978 with 52 percent of the vote, re-elected four years later, during a recession, with 62 percent. Summing up the Babbitt years, the *Arizona Republic*, a conservative newspaper, called him the "take-charge governor." "He is without a doubt the smartest, quickest elected official I have ever met," an environmental activist told me, in a comment echoed by many others. "Babbitt plays it on the precipice," added a state senator. "He is constantly pushing this state forward, and he has an uncanny ability to pull it off." . . .

Traditionally, the governor's office in Arizona had been extremely weak. Arizona was perhaps the only state in the union in which a governor would consider the ambassadorship to Argentina a step up. State government was run by a small group of senior legislators and their staffs, who brought out the governor for ceremonial occasions. The notion that a governor might try to set an agenda for the state, or dare to veto a bill, never crossed most politicians' minds.

Babbitt immediately set out to change that. Six weeks into his term he vetoed two bills on the same day—then timed his veto message for the evening news, knocking the wind out of a planned override. The legislature reacted with shock. "Our idea of an activist governor was one who met with us once a month to seek our advice," said Alfredo Gutierrez. "This guy called us daily to tell us what he wanted to do."

Babbitt vetoed 21 bills in 1979, 30 more over the next two years. His total of 114 vetoes in nine years was more than double the record set by Arizona's first governor, who served for 13 years. "My business friends used to complain that we had a weak governor," says Jack Pfister. "After Babbitt was in there about two or three years, you never heard anybody complain about that again. What he demonstrated was that it was more the individual than the structure of the office itself." . . .

In Arizona, the economic problem has been too much growth, not too little. Ever since Motorola built an R&D center for military electronics in Phoenix in 1948, high-tech manufacturers have flocked to the state. They have been lured—many of them from nearby California—by the cheap land, the cheap labor, and the desert climate, all of which make Arizona perfect for manufacturing precision electronics. As time passed, the only problems they experienced arose from the state's failure to keep up with their growth.

The most pressing problem, aside from water, was the higher education system. Arizona State University, the major school in the Phoenix area, was known for big-time sports and big-time parties. *Playboy* once named it the nation's number one party school. Its engineering and business schools were second rate. As the high-tech industries boomed, they began having trouble recruiting engineers—many of whom wanted to update their education every three to five years to remain on top of their fields—because of the poor reputation of ASU's engineering school. In 1978, industry leaders created an advisory committee to work with the school and took their case to the governor.

Babbitt stole their thunder. His friend Pat Haggerty, the founder and then chairman of Texas Instruments, had convinced him that sustained high-tech growth depended upon top-quality higher education and research institutions. He interrupted the committee presentation, told them about Haggerty, and instructed them to think big. "I'm not interested in being behind short-term or small-time budget increases," he said. "Come back to me with a sweeping multiyear program, and I'll support you."

The advisory committee drew up a five-year plan calling for $32 million in new investments in the engineering school—from industry, from the federal government, and from the state. (As it worked out, industry raised $18.5 million, the federal government contributed about $8 million, and the state provided about $28 million.) With both the governor and the business community pushing the package, the legislature embraced it. Between 1979 and 1984, the College of Engineering and Applied Science built a 120,000-square-foot Engineering Research Center, installed $15 million worth of new equipment, hired 65 new faculty, moved from $1 million a year in research to $9.4 million, and set up a continuing education program that included televised classes beamed right into local plants and offices. In 1984, the National Academy of Sciences ranked ASU's Mechanical Engineering and Electrical Engineering departments second and third in the nation, respectively, in improvement over the previous five years.

In July 1985, the advisory committee and the engineering school adopted a second five-year plan. This one called for $62 million in new money, split among industry, the federal government, and the state. The goal was to move the school into the top ten in the nation.

ASU also launched a university research park. It decided to allow professors to own their own companies, to spend 20 percent of their time working in industry, and to keep a portion of the patent rights on their discoveries. The Babbitt administration played a role in both developments. Babbitt also pushed through a new Disease Control Research Commission, to fund medical research.

Throughout this period, Babbitt worked hard to convince the public that investment in its universities was critical. "In earlier, less complex times, universities were nice to have but not essential to economic growth," he said in a 1983 speech to a high-technology symposium he organized. "When Arizona's first great industry, copper, developed in the late nineteenth century, the main ingredient for success was a strong back and a lot of courage in the face of drought. Then came tourism; its principal ingredients were sunshine and hospitality.

"Now, in 1983, high technology is our growth industry, and the essential resource to sustain high technology cannot be mined from the hills or grown in our soil or derived from hospitality. The main ingredient of the new high-technology evolution is education, in the form of well-educated citizens with strong scientific and technical skills. . . . Universities and colleges are now an economic asset as important to our economic future as copper ore, farms, banks, factories, and airlines." . . .

If traditional liberalism was the thesis and Reagan conservatism was its antithesis, the developments in America's state capitols offer the glimmerings of a new synthesis—a paradigm that may foreshadow the *next* realignment of American politics, as progressivism foreshadowed New Deal liberalism. The thesis, in its purist form, viewed the private sector as the problem and government as the solution. The antithesis, again in its extreme form, viewed government as the problem and the private sector as the solution. The synthesis redefines the nature of both the problem and its solution. It defines the problem as our changing role in the international marketplace. It defines the solution as new roles for and new relationships between our national institutions—public sector and private, labor and management, education and business. The fundamental goal is no longer to create—or eliminate—government programs; it is to use government to change the nature of the marketplace. To boil it down to a slogan, if the thesis was government as solution and the antithesis was government as problem, the synthesis is government as partner.

The new paradigm can be described as a series of interdependent assumptions about political reality, which together form a coherent way of thinking about our problems. The first assumption is that economic growth must be our major priority, but that it can be combined with equity, environmental protection, and other social goals. Whereas interest-group liberals put their social goals first, and Reagan conservatives put growth first, many governors are beginning to understand that in the new economy, growth *requires* equity and environmental protection.

Second, and perhaps most important, the new breed of governor assumes that the real solutions lie in changing the structure of the marketplace. By the late 1960s, many liberals had come to view the market as the problem; often they saw government as a way to overcome or replace the market. If the market would not build low-income housing, government would. If the market would not bring capital into Appalachia, government would. Reagan conservatives, in contrast, wanted government out of the marketplace—a logical contradiction, given that government sets the rules that allow the marketplace to operate. Today both Democratic and Republican governors understand that the market is far more powerful than government—that government cannot "overcome" or "replace" it. But they also understand that government *shapes* the market. To solve problems, they change the rules of the marketplace, or they use government to channel the market in new directions.

A related assumption has to do with attitudes toward government bureaucracies. Today's governors search for nonbureaucratic solutions to problems; if reshaping the marketplace will not suffice, they turn to third-sector organizations. They believe that many of the large, centralized government programs created in the past—medicaid, medicare, welfare, housing programs—have been inefficient and wasteful (often because government had to buy off the private sector, as in the case of medicare and medicaid). . . .

The fourth assumption is that in the newly competitive global economy, our governments have in a sense bumped up against their fiscal limits. Every governor portrayed in this book has taken great pains to make it clear to the electorate that he is not a big spender. . . .

The fifth assumption flows from the fiscal climate: if public resources are relatively scarce, they must be *invested*, not merely spent. Interest-group liberals responded to many problems, as Ronald Reagan likes to say, by "throwing money at them." If people were poor, the solution was higher welfare grants, more food stamps, greater housing subsidies. Reagan and his followers responded to the same problems by taking money away. The failure of both approaches has created a deep ambivalence within the American public, and a desire for a third path. When public opinion polls ask voters if welfare spending should be increased, they overwhelmingly say no. When polls ask if we have a responsibility to improve the plight of the poor, they overwhelmingly say yes. This seeming contradiction actually has a compelling logic: voters want solutions, but not the ones the two parties have traditionally offered.

The governors are gradually working out new ways to address these problems, by investing in the capacities of poor people and poor communities. "I think the American people don't want to simply break with our commitment to improve the lives of the poor; they don't want to throw all that away," says Art Hamilton, the black minority leader of the Arizona House. "But they don't want to have to pay for all the Great Society madness. People don't believe that the welfare system is designed to put itself out of business; that's what bothers a lot of the people I talk to. If the system were designed to lift people from where they are to where their potential can take them, I think people would gladly support that system." . . .

The new paradigm also involves new assumptions about the proper roles of federal, state, and local governments. The New Deal was a time in which America finally accepted bigness: big business, big labor, and big government. An economy dominated by large, stable, mass-production industries required large, centralized institutions in all three areas. Today, however, our economy is decentralizing. Mass production is moving offshore, and smaller, more automated, more flexible manufacturing operations are thriving in the United States. In the service sector small businesses are proliferating, and in both sectors the entrepreneurial process is accelerating. In 1985, seven times as many new businesses were formed as in 1950. . . .

If current state trends do foreshadow national politics, these principles—growth with equity, a focus on market solutions, a search for non-bureaucratic methods, fiscal moderation, investment rather than spending, redistribution of opportunity rather than outcomes, and a new federalism—provide a rough outline of the next political paradigm.

23

United States v. Lopez

In 1995, the Supreme Court took a dramatic step in reinterpreting federalism, the division of power between the national government and the state governments. Federalism has been interpreted and reinterpreted a number of times in U.S. history. Mostly, since the late 1930s, the national government's powers have been expanded. In 1990, the Gun-Free School Zones Act—a federal law prohibiting the possession of a firearm within a school zone—became law. Two years later, a senior in a Texas high school was accused of violating the act by bringing a gun to school and thereby engaging in a form of interstate commerce. According to the act, the federal government was authorized to prosecute the student under its power to regulate interstate commerce. In a 5–4 decision, the Court ruled that bringing a gun to school was not an act that came under the federal government's interstate commerce powers; the guns-in-school issue belonged at the state and local level. Writing the majority opinion, Chief Justice William Rehnquist mentioned his reliance on the Constitution's "enumerated" powers as a guide to what the national government may control, in contrast to the many other powers left for the states.

United States v. Lopez
115 S. Ct. 1624 (1995)

Chief Justice REHNQUIST delivered the opinion of the Court.

In the Gun-Free School Zones Act of 1990, Congress made it a federal offense "for any individual knowingly to possess a firearm at a place that the individual knows, or has reasonable cause to believe, is a school zone." . . . The Act neither regulates a commercial activity nor contains a requirement that the possession be connected in any way to interstate commerce. We hold that the Act exceeds the authority of Congress "to regulate Commerce . . . among the several States. . . . " U.S. Const., Art. I, § 8, cl. 3.

On March 10, 1992, respondent, who was then a 12th-grade student, arrived at Edison High School in San Antonio, Texas, carrying a concealed .38 caliber handgun and five bullets. Acting upon an anonymous tip, school authorities confronted respondent, who admitted that he was carrying the weapon. He was arrested and charged under Texas law with firearm possession on school premises. . . . The next day, the state charges were dismissed after federal agents charged respondent by complaint with violating the Gun-Free School Zones Act of 1990. 18 U.S.C. § 922(q). . . .

We start with first principles. The Constitution creates a Federal Government of enumerated powers. See U.S. Const., Art. I., § 8. As James Madison wrote, "the powers delegated by the proposed Constitution to the federal government are few and defined. Those which are to remain in the State governments are numerous and indefinite." . . .

The Constitution delegates to Congress the power "to regulate Commerce with foreign Nations, and among the several States, and with the Indian Tribes." U.S. Const., Art. I, § 8, cl. 3. The Court, through Chief Justice Marshall, first defined the nature of Congress' commerce power in *Gibbons v. Ogden*. . . .

. . . In [*NLRB v.*] *Jones & Laughlin Steel*, the Court warned that the scope of the interstate commerce power "must be considered in the light of our dual system of government and may not be extended so as to embrace effects upon interstate commerce so indirect and remote that to embrace them, in view of our complex society, would effectually obliterate the distinction between what is national and what is local and create a completely centralized government." . . . Since that time, the Court has heeded that warning and undertaken to decide whether a rational basis existed for concluding that a regulated activity sufficiently affected interstate commerce. . . .

. . . We conclude, consistent with the great weight of our case law, that the proper test requires an analysis of whether the regulated activity "substantially affects" interstate commerce.

We now turn to consider the power of Congress, in the light of this framework, to enact § 922(q). The first two categories of authority may be quickly disposed of: § 922(q) is not a regulation of the use of the channels of interstate commerce, nor is it an attempt to prohibit the interstate transportation of a commodity through the channels of commerce; nor can § 922(q) be justified as a regulation by which Congress has sought to protect an instrumentality of interstate commerce or a thing in interstate commerce. Thus, if § 922(q) is to be sustained, it must be under the third category as a regulation of an activity that substantially affects interstate commerce.

First, we have upheld a wide variety of congressional Acts regulating intrastate economic activity where we have concluded that the activity substantially affected interstate commerce. Examples include the regulation of intrastate coal mining . . . restaurants utilizing substantial interstate supplies . . . inns and hotels catering to interstate guests . . . and production and consumption of home-grown wheat. . . . These examples are by no means exhaustive, but the pattern is clear. Where economic activity substantially affects interstate commerce, legislation regulating that activity will be sustained. . . .

Section 922(q) is a criminal statute that by its terms has nothing to do with "commerce" or any sort of economic enterprise, however broadly one might define those terms. Section 922 (q) is not an essential part of a larger regulation of economic activity, in which the regulatory scheme could be undercut unless the intrastate activity were regulated. It cannot, therefore, be sustained under our cases upholding regulations of activities that arise out of or are connected with a commercial transaction, which viewed in the aggregate, substantially affects interstate commerce. . . .

Although as part of our independent evaluation of constitutionality under the Commerce Clause we of course consider legislative findings, and indeed even congressional committee findings, regarding effect on interstate commerce . . . the Government concedes that "neither the statute nor its legislative history contains express congressional findings regarding the effects upon interstate commerce of gun possession in a school zone." . . .

The Government's essential contention, *in fine*, is that we may determine here that § 922(q) is valid because possession of a firearm in a local school zone does indeed substantially affect interstate commerce. . . . The Government argues that possession of a firearm in a school zone may result in violent crime and that violent crime can be expected to affect the functioning of the national economy in two ways. First, the costs of violent crime are substantial. . . . Second, violent crime reduces the willingness of individuals to travel to areas within the country that are perceived to be unsafe. . . . The Government also argues that the presence of guns in schools poses a substantial threat to the educational process by threatening the learning environment. A handicapped educational process, in turn, will result in a less productive citizenry. That, in turn, would have an adverse effect on the Nation's economic well-being. As a result, the Government argues that Congress could rationally have concluded that § 922(q) substantially affects interstate commerce.

We pause to consider the implications of the Government's arguments. The Government admits, under its "cost of crime" reasoning, that Congress could regulate not only all violent crime, but all activities that might lead to violent crime, regardless of how tenuously they relate to interstate commerce. . . . Similarly, under the Government's "national productivity" reasoning, Congress could regulate any activity that it found was related to the economic productivity of individual citizens: family law (including marriage, divorce, and child custody), for example. Under the theories that the Government presents in support of § 922(q), it is difficult to perceive any limitation on federal power, even in areas such as criminal law enforcement or education where States historically have been sovereign. Thus, if we were to accept the Government's arguments, we are hard-pressed to posit any activity by an individual that Congress is without power to regulate. . . .

For instance, if Congress can, pursuant to its Commerce Clause power, regulate activities that adversely affect the learning environment, then *a fortiori*, it also can regulate the educational process directly. Congress could determine that a school's curriculum has a "significant" effect on the extent of classroom learning. As a result, Congress could mandate a federal curriculum for local elementary and secondary schools because what is taught in local schools has a significant "effect on classroom learning," . . . and that, in turn, has a substantial effect on interstate commerce. . . .

. . . We do not doubt that Congress has authority under the Commerce Clause to regulate numerous commercial activities that substantially affect interstate commerce and also affect the educational process. That authority, though broad, does not include the authority to regulate each and every aspect of local schools. . . .

To uphold the Government's contentions here, we would have to pile inference upon inference in a manner that would bid fair to convert congressional authority under the Commerce Clause to a general police power of the sort retained by the States. Admittedly, some of our prior cases have taken long steps down that road, giving great deference to congressional action. . . . The broad language in these opinions has suggested the possibility of additional expansion, but we decline here to proceed any further. To do so would require us to conclude that the Constitution's enumeration of powers does not presuppose something not enumerated . . . and that there never will be a distinction between what is truly national and what is truly local. . . . This we are unwilling to do.

For the foregoing reasons the judgment of the Court of Appeals is *Affirmed.*

24

TOMMY THOMPSON

From *Power to the People*

The 1990s have shown a continual shift of power from the federal government to the states and local communities. Republican governor of Wisconsin, Tommy Thompson, remarks on this shift, as well as recounting the frustrations of the past federal setup and the challenges of the states' newfound power. As one example, Governor Thompson discusses the politics of welfare and the practicalities of bringing about Wisconsin's new welfare reform, W2 (Wisconsin Works).

"YOU HAVE two ears and one mouth. Use them in that proportion and you'll do just fine."

It was one of my father's favorite instructions to me, my sister, and my two brothers, the sort of "Midwestern intellect" I heard often while growing up in the small farming community of Elroy, Wisconsin. It is good advice for anyone, but especially for politicians. I have been the governor of Wisconsin for ten years, and I have always tried to follow that common-sense rule. Now, I'm trying to get Washington to do the same.

Like most Americans, my experience with the federal government has not been particularly pleasant. It is very hard to get Washington to listen. The federal bureaucracy seems impervious to ordinary citizens and governors alike. And yet, it appears to be everywhere, touching more of our everyday lives. Having dealt with Washington on numerous issues over the past decade, I can easily understand why many Americans are fed up with a government they view as increasingly unresponsive, wasteful, and inefficient at solving problems. I'm convinced most government officials in Washington actually have two mouths and one ear.

Since 1986, I have trudged regularly to the nation's capital, asking for more flexibility to make specific changes in federal programs affecting my state. Usually I was met with indifference. I'd have to schedule appointments weeks in advance, only to have a congressman say no to my request for more state-level authority. Even some congressmen from Wisconsin were not that eager to return more decision-making back home. And in most other congressional offices I was treated much like any other supplicant asking for something with very little to offer in return. "Governor who?" the earnest young staffers asked. It was as though Congress couldn't quite figure out how I or forty-nine other governors were relevant to their decision-making.

Asking Washington to give up any amount of control is not a pleasant undertaking. Having dealt with three different presidential administrations, I know the procedure all too well. It essentially means getting down on bended knee and kissing the rings of appointed bureaucrats who have the power to decide whether a governor—duly elected by the citizens of an entire state—can be trusted to change federal programs that clearly are failing. And it has mattered very little whether Democrats or Republicans were in charge. A capital city that runs on the political philosophy of "I can run your life better than you can" naturally fosters a certain arrogance among its inhabitants, regardless of political party. I felt as though Washington had actual contempt for those who didn't live and work inside the Beltway.

But Washington is starting to listen. Now when I visit Capitol Hill, members of Congress actually come out of their offices to greet me. "Tommy, how are you? Good to see you. Have any new ideas?" they ask. And these are just the Democrats.

The American political landscape is beginning to change. After nearly a century of consolidating more and more power in Washington, Congress appears genuinely interested in devolving power back to states and local communities. I know this for sure because on January 12, 1995, I was testifying before the Senate Labor Committee on the need to overhaul federal job-training programs. As Senator Edward Kennedy began his opening remarks before my testimony, I was bracing for a few partisan shots to the chin.

Instead, the senior senator from Massachusetts said, "I just want to say that we have heard great things about your training program, and that Wisconsin is really one of the outstanding states in terms of these programs. I know from the people whom I respect the most in my state that they have a very high regard for what you have done in Wisconsin. So we are looking forward to hearing from you."

"Great things . . . outstanding . . . looking forward to hearing from" me. I was temporarily speechless. But for the next hour or so we had a cordial, informative discussion about the importance of giving states more flexibility in running job-training programs. . . .

It is time for Washington—its politicians and bureaucrats—to realize they are not paragons of virtue: the states have innovative ideas that work. It is time for them to acknowledge that a one-size-fits-all brand of government handed down from Washington doesn't work today and will not work to meet the challenges of the next century.

America's last major political reform, the Progressive movement, started a century ago in the Republican Party of Wisconsin. It spread first across the Midwest and then many of its ideas were adopted and adapted by Republicans and Democrats. Today, governors—some in the very same states that launched the first Progressive movement—are succeeding with a new wave of innovative reforms and asking Washington to return power and authority to the states. For good reason.

In many ways, what's happening today at the state level is strikingly similar to the grassroots Progressive movement of a century ago. In fact, those today who call for the devolution of power from Washington back to the states are voicing a prominent theme of the early Progressives. Wisconsin Progressive Robert La Follette and his contemporaries strongly believed the states were America's laboratories of democracy. Woodrow Wilson, an early Progressive, warned as governor of New Jersey, "I suspect that the people of the United States understand their own interests better than any group of men in the confines of the country understand them. I don't want a smug lot of experts to sit down behind closed doors in Washington and play providence to me."

After nearly a century of increasing federal authority, this central issue has again risen to the surface of today's political debate. Can people be trusted to govern themselves at the state and local level, or do we need Washington to impose its mandates on all of us?

As we answer that question, America's laboratories of democracy are demonstrating new successes, solving problems where Washington has failed. Successful innovations at the state level are occurring when many of us are sick and tired of the partisan squabbling and arrogance that dominates the federal government. It's no coincidence. People today are trying to work things out closer to home. . . .

In late 1993, as I approached another election, Wisconsin welfare rolls had declined more than those of any other state—down by 19 percent since we first started the reforms in 1987. During the same period, welfare rolls had shot up by 30 percent nationally. We had dropped from the eighth highest state in the nation in percentage of people on welfare to thirty-first. This was too much for Democrats in the state legislature. Although several conservative Democrats had supported many of my reforms, the official posture of the more liberal Democrat leaders had been to criticize and try to block or dismantle many of them. They were beginning to understand that they were on the wrong end of the issue. Welfare reform was working in Wisconsin, and the people supported it.

Walter Kunicki, the Democrat speaker of the assembly, was thinking about running against me in 1994. He had seen Bill Clinton take the issue away from Republicans on the national level, and he wanted to pull a fast one on me. Kunicki said we had tried a lot of pilot projects here and there, but Governor Thompson was really just tinkering around the edges. If the governor were really serious about welfare reform, Kunicki said, he would support legislation to end it completely. Kunicki proposed abolishing welfare completely in Wisconsin. He didn't propose an alternative, he just said we should abolish it by 1999. It was hollow, just like Bill Clinton's promise to "end welfare as we know it."

Even so, it was a bold political strategy. Replacing the entire AFDC [Aid to Families with Dependent Children] system and coming up with a completely new alternative to welfare would be a huge task. It was a radical idea, and he was convinced I would veto it, which would hand the Democrats bragging rights on welfare reform in the next election.

Jerry Whitburn, whose leadership had helped guide us to the next level of reform over the past three years, was skeptical. This was a blatantly political move by the Democrats, and it should be vetoed. Maybe he was right. As the secretary of the department that would have to do most of the work, he knew what he was talking about. But I couldn't stop thinking, "This is a golden opportunity. How can the Democrats be so dumb to give me this chance to completely replace welfare?"

The bill passed both houses of the legislature, with the final vote occurring late on a Tuesday night. At seven-thirty the next morning, my senior staff met for our regular breakfast meeting. Jerry remained cool to the idea. I put down my fork and said, "Jerry, I'm going to sign it." And I later raised the ante—we moved up the timetable to end welfare by 1997.

The Democrats never even scored the political points they were after. I won the election in 1994, and for the first time since I had come to office, Republicans won both houses of the state legislature.

Despite his earlier reservations, Jerry enthusiastically threw himself into the project. He immediately put together a team of experts in DHSS [Department of Housing and Social Services] to design the replacement—as we had done with Work Not Welfare. After eight years of implementing reforms, this was a group of people who knew more about changing welfare than anyone in the nation. He put together a bipartisan group of legislative leaders and a group of business and community-based leaders to work with us on the project.

We also enlisted the help of the Hudson Institute, a respected national think tank based in Indianapolis. In 1994, I met with Hudson Institute president Les Lenkowsky to discuss my goals for the alternative to welfare. I said I wanted a program built around work. I wanted to end the cash benefit premise of welfare and replace it with a real-world concept: pay for performance. Everyone would have to work, and only work would pay. I described it as a new contract in which government and low-income families have concomitant responsibilities. Government would agree to provide child care, health care, and other assistance for a limited time to help people find and keep a job. In return, people must be willing to take personal responsibility for themselves and their families. They have to get up in the morning, get the kids fed and off to school or day care, and get themselves to a job, just like ordinary hardworking Americans. . . .

In early 1995, Massachusetts Governor William Weld hired Jerry Whitburn away from me. Before he left to run Massachusetts's welfare programs, Jerry presented me with a name that Jim Malone of DHSS had come up with for the program we were developing to replace welfare. It was W2—Wisconsin Works. We were going to replace the welfare check with a paycheck—something we had talked about when I first hired him as DHSS secretary in 1991.

No other state was in a position to do this. No other state had comparable experience in the field, experimenting, discovering what works. In many ways, all we had to do was put the pieces together. Washington was fighting over whether it should give states the authority to run welfare, Clinton had vetoed the welfare reform bill passed by the new Republican Congress, but we were moving ahead without them. Really, the building blocks for W2 were what our laboratory of ideas had discovered over the past eight years. From the WEJT [Wisconsin Employment and Job Training] program I had expanded in 1987, we learned that people move faster when you require them to do something, either training or work. From the JOBS program that grew out of WEJT, we learned that the transition to work was faster still when you add an actual work requirement instead of just training. From Work First, we learned that many people don't even need the first welfare check when you help them look at other options as soon as they come in to apply. And from Work Not Welfare, we learned that people achieve self-sufficiency fastest when you combine an immediate work requirement with a time limit, which instills a sense of urgency, and encourages saving that government check for when they really need it.

We decided that W2 should focus on moving people into private sector jobs as soon as possible. That meant an immediate full-time work requirement and time limits, but it also meant community-based partnerships with private employers. So we expanded the model we had set up in Work Not Welfare to create Community Steering Committees comprising local businesses, charities, and civic groups to coordinate job placement for people. And since W2 would be a jobs program rather than a cash benefit program, we decided to eliminate our welfare department and shift responsibility for W2 to our new jobs department. Building on lessons from Work First and Work Not Welfare, we replaced "economic support" workers with financial planners and employment specialists. Welfare workers who had been spending 80 percent of their time doing paperwork would now spend 90 percent of their time working directly with people who need help.

We also knew that W2 would cost more money up front. The welfare reforms we had implemented since 1987 had reduced Wisconsin welfare rolls by 36 percent. As a result, taxpayers were saving $19 million each and every month. Our reforms have saved the state and federal government nearly $1 billion since 1987. Yet to achieve those savings, I had invested more money on the front end. To help people make the transition from welfare to work, we invested more money in child care, health care, transportation, and caseworkers who would work with people one-on-one. Child care expenditures alone increased by more than 300 percent, from $13 million in 1987 to $56 million in 1995. If W2 would require everyone to work immediately, we were going to have to expand child care funding even more substantially. And we knew from our other experiments that providing up to twelve months of child care and health insurance after people had left welfare to work helped them get off welfare and stay off. That would mean even more money. Yet I wanted to make W2 as close to the real world as possible, so we developed a provision that would require W2 participants to co-pay for these benefits as they began earning money.

As we began to develop a concrete, comprehensive replacement to welfare that reflected the lessons we had learned from welfare reform, we confronted an issue that dooms many government programs. How could we construct a program that achieves what we believe will work without making it so rigid that it cannot adjust to the realities of helping people with different needs and abilities? The last thing I wanted to do was replace one bureaucracy with another. We wanted to place people in private sector jobs, but we knew that some individuals would not be able to be placed in private sector jobs right away. There was no model in place to base this on—we had to use the experience we had gained over the previous eight years.

We decided that we needed to create different levels of jobs—levels that would reflect the "readiness levels" most people fit into when they showed up at the welfare office. At the same time, however, I didn't want to create a make-work program of government-funded jobs. It was essential to me that we build in incentives for people to move up the ladder to private employment as soon as possible. So we created three levels of subsidized employment. The lowest level paid the least, the next level paid more, and the final level paid the most, but none of them paid as much as a private sector job.

To further encourage people to move up the ladder and into unsubsidized jobs in the private sector, we limited the amount of time anyone could be in a subsidized job. Again, we put two-year time limits on each category of subsidized jobs, although an individual cannot spend two years in each of the three levels. We established an overall limit of five years on a person's eligibility for W2. Individuals can use the five years of help all at once or pieces at a time when they need it, but after using a total of five years of services, they are no longer eligible for assistance. This is a combination of the "ticking clock" and "savings account" approach we had tried with Work Not Welfare.

Our premise in establishing job levels for W2 was that everyone is capable of performing some kind of work. The highest level of subsidized employment we called trial jobs. After private sector jobs, this is the level we would require most recipients to start with, based on our experience running the statewide JOBS program and other reforms. Trial jobs are for people who have good attitudes toward work but aren't immediately employable, usually because they have very little experience holding down a job. W2 will place them in a private sector job and provide a subsidy to the employer. When they gain enough work experience, W2 will help them find an unsubsidized job, with the same employer if possible.

The middle rung of the job ladder is community service jobs. These are for a limited number of people whose poor work habits and skills make them unemployable with a private firm, even with a subsidy. They will be provided government-funded jobs in the community to gain basic work skills. The lowest level is transitional jobs, for people who have serious impediments to work. In addition to work, transitional jobs include services such as vocational rehabilitation and drug and alcohol treatment, to further prepare participants for work.

In addition to the work requirements, we incorporated elements of earlier reforms that had worked. We incorporated school attendance requirements from Learnfare, child support enforcement from Children First, and parental and family responsibility provisions—such as no additional pay for having more children—from PFR. After more than a year of work putting the program together, I introduced it to the now-Republican controlled state legislature in 1995. On April 25, 1996, I signed W2 into law . . .

People, ordinary people, have a hard time being heard over the massive machinery of Washington—the grinding bureaucracy, the din of special interests, the partisan squabbling, and the clamor of the "inspectors"—the media. Sometimes, I think it really makes people who work in Washington hard of hearing.

I've learned that it is not so hard to listen when you are campaigning for elected office. Not only are you out there constantly shaking hands, you have pollsters and political advisers who can tell you exactly what percent of the population wants this or that. You can be responsive merely by talking about things—until you are elected. Then you are accountable, or you are supposed to be accountable, for getting things done. That is one thing Bill Clinton doesn't seem to understand—the difference between campaigning and governing. It is one thing to make promises that sound good to people and quite another to actually get them done.

Making it happen, making government truly effective, boils down to commitment and leadership. It means sticking with your ideas even when you're fighting an uphill battle, or taking a battering in the press. And when you think you've changed things, it means realizing that you're only part-way there. I hope [Wisconsin's experience] will encourage people to expect more of themselves and of their states. I hope it will encourage more governors and legislators to try different things. Wisconsin's experience shows that when you have a good idea and the courage to stick with it—even if it's not politically popular at the time—you can change government for the better. . . .

PART FIVE

Congress

25

DAVID MAYHEW

From *Congress: The Electoral Connection*

Congressional scholar David Mayhew admits from the start that his explanation for the motivation of members of Congress is one-dimensional: they are "single-minded seekers of reelection." While Mayhew's thesis is intentionally narrow and his examples a bit out-of-date (none of the members cited in the excerpt is still in the House), reelection remains a primary motivator for congressional behavior. To attain reelection, representatives use three strategies. They advertise, so that their names are well-known. They claim credit for goodies that flow to their districts. And they take positions on political issues. Mayhew's theme, illustrated with amusing examples, may seem cynical, but it is doubtlessly realistic. Perhaps his analysis should have been fair warning to members of Congress about the public's growing disillusionment with the national legislature.

... I SHALL CONJURE UP a vision of United States congressmen as single-minded seekers of reelection, see what kinds of activity that goal implies, and then speculate about how congressmen so motivated are likely to go about building and sustaining legislative institutions and making policy. . . .

I find an emphasis on the reelection goal attractive for a number of reasons. First, I think it fits political reality rather well. Second, it puts the spotlight directly on men rather than on parties and pressure groups, which in the past have often entered discussions of American politics as analytic phantoms. Third, I think politics is best studied as a struggle among men to gain and maintain power and the consequences of that struggle. Fourth—and perhaps most important—the reelection quest establishes an accountability relationship with an electorate, and any serious thinking about democratic theory has to give a central place to the question of accountability. . . .

Whether they are safe or marginal, cautious or audacious, congressmen must constantly engage in activities related to reelection. There will be differences in emphasis, but all members share the root need to do things—indeed, to do things day in and day out during their terms. The next step here is to present a typology, a short list of the *kinds* of activities congressmen find it electorally useful to engage in. . . .

One activity is *advertising*, defined here as any effort to disseminate one's name among constituents in such a fashion as to create a favorable image but in messages having little or no issue content. A successful congressman builds what amounts to a brand name, which may have a generalized electoral value for other politicians in the same family. The personal qualities to emphasize are experience, knowledge, responsiveness, concern, sincerity, independence, and the like. Just getting one's name across is difficult enough; only about half the electorate, if asked, can supply their House members' names. It helps a congressman to be known. "In the main, recognition carries a positive valence; to be perceived at all is to be perceived favorably." A vital advantage enjoyed by House incumbents is that they are much better known among voters than their November challengers. They are better known because they spend a great deal of time, energy, and money trying to make themselves better known. There are standard routines—frequent visits to the constituency, nonpolitical speeches to home audiences, the sending out of infant care booklets and letters of condolence and congratulation. . . .

Some routines are less standard. Congressman George E. Shipley (D., Ill.) claims to have met personally about half his constituents (i.e. some 200,000 people). For over twenty years Congressman Charles C. Diggs, Jr. (D., Mich.) has run a radio program featuring himself as a "combination disc jockey–commentator and minister." Congressman Daniel J. Flood (D., Pa.) is "famous for appearing unannounced and often uninvited at wedding anniversaries and other events." Anniversaries and other events aside, congressional advertising is done largely at public expense. Use of the franking privilege has mushroomed in recent years; in early 1973 one estimate predicted that House and Senate members would send out about 476 million pieces of mail in the year 1974, at a public cost of $38.1 million—or about 900,000 pieces per member with a subsidy of $70,000 per member. By far the heaviest mailroom traffic comes in Octobers of even-numbered years. There are some differences between House and Senate members in the ways they go about getting their names across. House members are free to blanket their constituencies with mailings for all boxholders; senators are not. But senators find it easier to appear on national television—for example, in short reaction statements on the nightly news shows. Advertising is a staple congressional activity, and there is no end to it. For each member there are always new voters to be apprised of his worthiness and old voters to be reminded of it.

A second activity may be called *credit claiming*, defined here as acting so as to generate a belief in a relevant political actor (or actors) that one is personally responsible for causing the government, or some unit thereof, to do something that the actor (or actors) considers desirable. The political logic of this, from the congressman's point of view, is that an actor who believes that a member can make pleasing things happen will no doubt wish to keep him in office so that he can make pleasing things happen in the future. The emphasis here is on individual accomplishment (rather than, say, party or governmental accomplishment) and on the congressman as doer (rather than as, say, expounder of constituency views). Credit claiming is highly important to congressmen, with the consequence that much of congressional life is a relentless search for opportunities to engage in it.

Where can credit be found? . . . For the average congressman the staple way of doing this is to traffic in what may be called "particularized benefits." . . .

In sheer volume the bulk of particularized benefits come under the heading of "casework"—the thousands of favors congressional offices perform for supplicants in ways that normally do not require legislative action. High school students ask for essay materials, soldiers for emergency leaves, pensioners for location of missing checks, local governments for grant information, and on and on. Each office has skilled professionals who can play the bureaucracy like an organ—pushing the right pedals to produce the desired effects. But many benefits require new legislation, or at least they require important allocative decisions on matters covered by existent legislation. Here the congressman fills the traditional role of supplier of goods to the home district. It is a believable role; when a member claims credit for a benefit on the order of a dam, he may well receive it. Shiny construction projects seem especially useful. . . .

The third activity congressmen engage in may be called *position taking*, defined here as the public enunciation of a judgmental statement on anything likely to be of interest to political actors. The statement may take the form of a roll call vote. The most important classes of judgmental statements are those prescribing American governmental ends (a vote cast against the war; a statement that "the war should be ended immediately") or governmental means (a statement that "the way to end the war is to take it to the United Nations"). . . .

The ways in which positions can be registered are numerous and often imaginative. There are floor addresses ranging from weighty orations to mass-produced "nationality day statements." There are speeches before home groups, television appearances, letters, newsletters, press releases, ghostwritten books, *Playboy* articles, even interviews with political scientists. . . . Outside the roll call process the congressman is usually able to tailor his positions to suit his audiences. . . .

. . . On a controversial issue a Capitol Hill office normally prepares two form letters to send out to constituent letter writers—one for the pros and one (not directly contradictory) for the antis. Handling discrete audiences in person requires simple agility, a talent well demonstrated in this selection from a Nader profile*:

"You may find this difficult to understand," said Democrat Edward R. Roybal, the Mexican-American representative from California's thirtieth district, "but sometimes I wind up making a patriotic speech one afternoon and later on that same day an anti-war speech. In the patriotic speech I speak of past wars but I also speak of the need to prevent more wars. My positions are not inconsistent; I just approach different people differently." Roybal went on to depict the diversity of crowds he speaks to: one afternoon he is surrounded by balding men wearing Veterans' caps and holding American flags; a few hours later he speaks to a crowd of Chicano youths, angry over American involvement in Vietnam. Such a diverse constituency, Roybal believes, calls for different methods of expressing one's convictions.

Indeed it does.

26

RICHARD FENNO

From *Home Style*

Stated simply, political scientist Richard Fenno had a wonderful idea for a book. Instead of studying members of Congress at work in Washington, D.C., on the House floor, legislating, he researched them in what has always seemed their most obscure, out-of-the-spotlight moments. At home, in their districts, very little was known about legislators until Fenno's work. He opens with the psychological concept of "presentation of self," a technique designed to "win trust" from constituents. Fenno makes mention of the important "delegate" and "trustee" models of representation. Legislators do not explain every detail of their policy positions to the voters, rather, they want voters to trust them enough to allow them "voting leeway" back in Washington.

---

*Ralph Nader is a public-interest activist who has dedicated himself to protecting the American people against both governmental and private industry wrong-doing. One of Nader's best known campaigns came in the 1960s against General Motors, whose Chevrolet Corvair, Nader claimed, was "unsafe at any speed." In the 1996 presidential election, he ran as a third-party candidate.—EDS.

MOST HOUSE MEMBERS spend a substantial proportion of their working lives "at home." Even those in our low frequency category return to their districts more often than we would have guessed. Over half of that group go home more than once a month. What, then, do representatives do there? Much of what they do is captured by Erving Goffman's idea of *the presentation of self.* That is, they place themselves in "the immediate physical presence" of others and then "make a presentation of themselves to others." Goffman writes about the ordinary encounters between people "in everyday life." But, the dramaturgical analogues he uses fit the political world, too. Politicians, like actors, speak to and act before audiences from whom they must draw both support and legitimacy. Without support and legitimacy, there is no political relationship.

In all his encounters, says Goffman, the performer will seek to control the response of others to him by expressing himself in ways that leave the correct impressions of himself with others. His expressions will be of two sorts—"the expressions that he gives and the expression that he gives off." The first are mostly verbal; the second are mostly nonverbal. Goffman is particularly interested in the second kind of expression—"the more theatrical and contextual kind"—because he believes that the performer is more likely to be judged by others according to the nonverbal than the verbal elements of his presentation of self. Those who must do the judging, Goffman says, will think that the verbal expressions are more controllable and manipulable by the performer. And they will, therefore, read his nonverbal "signs" as a check on the reliability of his verbal "signs." Basic to this reasoning is the idea that, of necessity, every presentation has a largely "promissory character" to it. Those who listen to and watch the presentation cannot be sure what the relationship between themselves and the performer really is. So the relationship must be sustained, on the part of those watching, by inference. They "must accept the individual on faith." In this process of acceptance, they will rely heavily on the inferences they draw from his nonverbal expressions—the expressions "given off."

Goffman does not talk about politicians; but politicians know what Goffman is talking about. The response they seek from others is political support. And the impressions they try to foster are those that will engender political support. House member politicians believe that a great deal of their support is won by the kind of individual self they present to others, i.e., to their constituents. More than most other people, they consciously try to manipulate it. Certainly, they believe that what they say, their verbal expression, is an integral part of their "self." But, with Goffman, they place special emphasis on the nonverbal, "contextual" aspects of their presentation. At the least, the nonverbal elements must be consistent with the verbal ones. At the most, the expressions "given off" will become the basis for constituent judgment. Like Goffman, members of Congress are willing to emphasize the latter because, with him, they believe that their constituents will apply a heavier discount to what they say than to how they say it or to how they act in the context in which they say it. In the members' own language, constituents want to judge you "as a person." The comment I have heard most often during my travels is: "he's a good man" or "she's a good woman," unembossed by qualifiers of any sort. Constituents, say House members, want to "size you up" or "get the feel of you" "as a person," or "as a human being." And the largest part of what House members mean when they say "as a person" is what Goffman means by expressions "given off." Largely from expressions given off comes the judgment: "he's a good man," "she's a good woman."

So members of Congress go home to present themselves as a person and to win the accolade: "he's a good man," "she's a good woman." With Goffman, they know there is a "promissory character" to their presentation. And their object is to present themselves as a person in such a way that the inferences drawn by those watching will be supportive. The representatives' word for these supportive inferences is *trust*. It is a word they use a great deal. When a constituent trusts a House member, the constituent is saying something like this: "I am willing to put myself in your hands temporarily; I know you will have opportunities to hurt me, although I may not know when those opportunities occur; I assume—and I will continue to assume until it is proven otherwise—that you will not hurt me; for the time being, then, I'm not going to worry about your behavior." The ultimate response House members seek is political support. But the instrumental response they seek is trust. The presentation of self—that which is given in words and given off as a person—will be calculated to win trust. "If people like you and trust you as individual," members often say, "they will vote for you." So trust becomes central to the representative-constituent relationship. For their part, constituents must rely on trust. They must "accept on faith" that the congressman is what he says he is and will do what he says he will do. House members, for their part, are quite happy to emphasize trust. It helps to allay the uncertainties they feel about their relationship with their supportive constituencies. If members are uncertain as to how to work for support directly, they can always work indirectly to win a degree of personal trust that will increase the likelihood of support or decrease the likelihood of opposition.

Trust is, however, a fragile relationship. It is not an overnight or a one-time thing. It is hard to win; and it must be constantly renewed and rewon. "Trust," said one member, "is a cumulative thing, a totality thing. . . . You do a little here and a little there." So it takes an enormous amount of time to build and to maintain constituent trust. That is what House members believe. And that is why they spend so much of their working time at home. Much of what I have observed in my travels can be explained as a continuous and continuing effort to win (for new members) and to hold (for old members) the trust of supportive constituencies. Most of the communication I have heard and seen is not overtly political at all. It is, rather, part of a ceaseless effort to reenforce the underpinnings of trust in the congressman or the congresswoman as a person. Viewed from this perspective, the archetypical constituent question is not "What have you done for me lately?" but "How have you looked to me lately?" In sum, House members make a strategic calculation that helps us understand why they go home so much. *Presentation of self enhances trust; enhancing trust takes time; therefore, presentation of self takes time.* . . .

Explaining Washington activity, as said at the outset, includes justifying that activity to one's constituents. The pursuit of power, for example, is sometimes justified with the argument that the representative accumulates power not for himself but for his constituents. In justifying their policy decisions, representatives sometimes claim that their policy decisions follow not what they want but what their constituents want. Recall the member who justified his decision not to support his own highway bill with the comment, "I'm not here to vote my own convictions. I'm here to represent my people." Similarly, the member who decided to yield to his constituent's wishes on gun control said, "I rationalize it by saying that I owe it to my constituents if they feel that strongly about it." But this is not a justification all members use. The independent, issue-oriented Judiciary Committee member mentioned earlier commented (privately) with heavy sarcasm,

> All some House members are interested in is "the folks." They think "the folks" are the second coming. They would no longer do anything to displease "the folks" than they would fly. They spend all their time trying to find out what "the folks" want. I imagine if they get five letters on one side and five letters on the other side, they die.

An alternative justification, of course, is that the representative's policy decisions are based on what he thinks is good public policy, regardless of what his constituents want. As the Judiciary Committee member told his constituents often, "If I were sitting where you are, I think what I would want is to elect a man to Congress who will exercise his best judgment on the facts when he has them all." At a large community college gathering in the heart of his district, a member who was supporting President Nixon's Vietnam policy was asked, "If a majority of your constituents signed a petition asking you to vote for a date to end the war, would you vote for it?" He answered,

> It's hard for me to imagine a majority of my constituents agreeing on anything. But if it did happen, then no, I would not vote for it. I would still have to use my own judgment—especially where the security of the country is involved. You can express opinions. I have to make the decision. If you disagree with my decisions, you have the power every two years to vote me out of office. I listen to you, believe me. But, in the end, I have to use my judgment as to what is in your best interests.

He then proceeded to describe his views on the substantive question.

To political scientists, these two kinds of policy justification are very familiar. One is a "delegate" justification, the other a "trustee" justification. The two persist side by side because the set of constituent attitudes on which each depends also exist side by side. Voters, that is, believe that members of Congress should follow constituents' wishes; and voters also believe that members of Congress should use their own best judgment. They want their representatives, it has been said, to be "common people of uncommon judgment." Most probably, though we do not know, voters want delegate behavior on matters most precious to them and trustee behavior on all others. Nonetheless, both kinds of justification are acceptable as a general proposition. Both are legitimate, and in explaining their Washington activity members are seeking to legitimate that activity. They use delegate and trustee justifications because both are legitimating concepts.

If, when they are deciding how to vote, House members think in terms of delegates and trustees, it is because they are thinking about the terms in which they will explain (i.e., justify or legitimate) that vote back home if the need to do so arises. If members never had to legitimate any of their policy decisions back home, they would stop altogether talking in delegate or trustee language. . . .

Members elaborate the linkage between presentation and explanation this way: There are at most only a very few policy issues on which representatives are constrained in their voting by the views of their reelection constituencies. They may not *feel* constrained, if they agree with those views. But that is beside the point; they are constrained nevertheless. On the vast majority of votes, however, representatives can do as they wish—provided only that they can, when they need to, explain their votes to the satisfaction of interested constituents. The ability to get explanations accepted at home is, then, the essential underpinning of a member's voting leeway in Washington.

So the question arises: How can representatives increase the likelihood that their explanations will be accepted at home? And the answer House members give is: They can win and hold constituent trust. The more your various constituencies trust you, members reason, the less likely they are to require an explanation of your votes and the more likely they are to accept your explanation when they do ask for it. The winning of trust, we have said earlier, depends largely on the presentation of self. Presentation of self, then, not only helps win votes at election time. It also makes voting in Washington easier. So members of Congress make a strategic calculation: *Presentation of self enhances trust; trust enhances the acceptability of explanations; the acceptability of explanations enhances voting leeway; therefore, presentation of self-enhances voting leeway. . . .*

The traditional focus of political scientists on the policy aspects of representation is probably related to the traditional focus on activity in the legislature. So long as concentration is on what happens in Washington, it is natural that policymaking will be thought of as the main activity of the legislature and representation will be evaluated in policy terms. To paraphrase Woodrow Wilson, it has been our view that Congress in Washington is Congress at work, while Congress at home is Congress on exhibition. The extrapolicy aspects of representational relationships have tended to be dismissed as symbolic—as somehow less substantial than the relationship embodied in a roll call vote in Washington—because what goes on at home has not been observed. For lack of observation, political scientists have tended to downgrade home activity as mere errand running or fence mending, as activity that takes the representative away from the important things—that is, making public policy in Washington. As one small example, the "Tuesday to Thursday Club" of House members who go home for long weekends—have always been criticized out of hand, on the assumption, presumably, that going home and doing things there was, ipso facto, bad. But no serious inquiry was ever undertaken into what they did there or what consequences—other than their obvious dereliction of duty—their home activity might have had. Home activity has been overlooked and denigrated and so, therefore, have those extra policy aspects of representation which can only be studied at home.

Predictably, the home activities described in this book will be regarded by some readers as further evidence that members of Congress spend too little of their time "on the job"—that is, in Washington, making policy. However, I hope readers will take from the book a different view—a view that values both Washington and home activity. Further, I hope readers will entertain the view that Washington and home activities may even be mutually supportive. Time spent at home can be time spent in developing leeway for activity undertaken in Washington. And that leeway in Washington should be more valued than the sheer number of contact hours spent there. If that should happen, we might then ask House members not to justify their time spent at home, but rather to justify their use of the leeway they have gained therefrom—during the legislative process in Washington. It may well be that a congressman's behavior in Washington is crucially influenced by the pattern of support he has developed at home, and by the allocational, presentational, and explanatory styles he displays there. To put the point most strongly, perhaps we can never understand his Washington activity without also understanding his perception of his various constituencies and the home style he uses to cultivate their support. . . .

27

IRWIN GERTZOG

From *Congressional Women*

Over the past twenty years, there has been a significant increase in the number of women elected to the House of Representatives. So is the House still seen as a "male institution"? In this piece, Irwin Gertzog compares the perceptions of the 1978 congresswomen with those of their 1993 counterparts. Incorporating some very telling quotes, Gertzog reveals what has changed and what has not changed at the House.

INTERVIEWS WITH THIRTY-THREE female Representatives, twelve male Representatives, and ten staff members during the 103rd Congress revealed both continuities and changes in the level of congresswomen's integration into the House. The most important continuity is that the House was still perceived as a "male institution" by almost all respondents. The most important changes were a product of the marked increase of women in the House and of the more liberated social orientations of the men with whom they were serving. . . .

Among the forty-five members interviewed, forty-one affirmed the "male" character of the House. Some justifications for this characterization were related to those offered earlier. The House was male because such amenities as toilets, the gym, and the swimming pool were less accessible to women. It was male because elevator operators, Capitol Hill police, and parking lot attendants could not bring themselves to treat congresswomen as House members, and because repeated slights, though often trivial, had a cumulative effect. It was male because the daily schedule, which often called for evening sessions, and the foreshortened weekly schedule were inconvenient for female members whose household, spousal, and child care concerns competed with their legislative responsibilities. These schedules, said one congresswoman, are determined by "male leaders who believe that members have wives" to take care of their families. A few first-term congresswomen mentioned the small number of female Representatives to explain House "maleness." However much they were impressed by gains following the 1992 election, they found 11 percent female membership little different from the 4 percent present in 1978.

Most respondents adopted variations on that theme, however, offering explanations that were heard less often in 1978, when the painfully small size of the female contingent obscured other fundamental disparities. The House was male, they said, because there were no women among top leaders of either party; because none chaired a standing committee; because no more than one token woman was ordinarily appointed to fill vacancies on Boards and Commissions; and because women were often denied recognition for legislative successes by committee chairs who became principal sponsors of the measures at the eleventh hour, only after women had done the spade work necessary to place them on the agenda. "Look at the photographs taken at bill-signing ceremonies," said one senior congresswoman. "The figures in the foreground are committee chairmen, with the women who were instrumental in passing the bill either relegated to the background or absent."

A large majority of 1993 respondents alluded to the "male culture of the House" to explain the chamber's gender imbalances, just as so many Representatives had in 1978. One congresswoman noted:

> Most men are more comfortable dealing with other men than they are with women, and they prefer to work with one another. There is a congeniality among men that does not include women and a congeniality among women that excludes men. Differences between us extend beyond "comfort levels" to the issues each group thinks are important.

From the point of view of some congresswomen, the difference was reflected in the way men and women defined themselves as human beings. "Being a congressman is central to most males' sense of self," said one first-term, female Representative. "Congresswomen," she continued, "define themselves as much by their family and kids as where they happen to work, and I am more excited when my daughter calls me 'mommy' than when someone else calls me 'the honorable.'"

These gender differences affected the day-to-day interactions female and male House members had with one another. Inasmuch as many older, influential congressmen continued to be uncomfortable with women and were disinclined to work with them, the relationships they established with female lawmakers were strained, perfunctory, and unproductive. Several congresswomen described interactions with male Representatives during which they were not taken seriously, "half-listened to," or advised, through body language, that they "didn't know what they were talking about." Two anecdotes, one told by a first-term congresswoman, the other by a veteran, highlight the difficulties female members encounter. The newcomer allowed that women have not been completely ignored, as was once the case, but they are sometimes treated with subtle disdain. She said:

> Men are not comfortable with us. In the cloak room, for example, a first-term woman will say "hello" to a congressman and he will be polite and say "hello," but soon dismiss her. But when that same congressman is greeted by a first-term male, he will be outgoing and friendly, sustaining the conversation. I understand that women have not spent much time in the cloak room, but I will make it a point to go there as often as possible in the future.

The second woman described a set of circumstances occurring repeatedly in subcommittee deliberations.

> The men have louder voices and they talk over you, more interested in what they have to say than what you have to contribute. At some point you will make what you think is a worthwhile point, but no one will acknowledge it. It's as if you hadn't opened your mouth. Ten minutes later the same observation will be made by a male, and the others will say "what a good idea" as if they had never heard it before. We will just have to shout and be more aggressive.

The cloak room was singled out by many congresswomen as a vivid expression of the institution's "male" identity.

The more overt forms of discrimination described in 1978 continued into the 1990s, although with less frequency. Among the four forms detailed by Kirkpatrick and observed in the House in 1978, three—linguistic discrimination, overprotective or flirtatious behavior, and insulting remarks—were mentioned by members of the 103rd Congress. Their occurrence, while unusual, was not rare.

Male members occasionally referred to the "gentlemen of the House" and employed other locutions suggesting an all-male chamber. Some were accused of using women's first names during committee sessions while referring to congressmen by title and surname. Early in her first term, Californian Maxine Waters stopped a subcommittee meeting dead in its tracks when the chair, Representative Joseph Gaydos, called her "Maxine," after using formal titles when calling upon males. The African-American congresswoman described the encounter as follows:

> I'd never met the man before in my life, and he turned to me and said "Maxine." I stopped right in the middle of that committee meeting and said "Just a minute. What are the rules around here? We must be consistent. If he's Congressman Barton, then I'm Congresswoman Waters."

This fractious exchange is a reflection of what might be a more deeply rooted division in the House. . . . Nevertheless, it is an example of discriminatory linguistic conventions that continue to be employed, even if heard less often than was once the case. By the 1990s, male members were more likely to use such terms as "Madam Chairwoman" when referring to a female presiding officer, and "my colleague," and "the member from California," terms they would use as a matter of course when referring to male members.

Patronizing behavior, described so vividly by earlier congresswomen, had also survived, even if manifested less frequently. Most male members, particularly junior congressmen, had had experience enough with professional women to treat them as colleagues. Such terms as "dear" or "young lady," let alone "honey," as they were once applied to congresswomen were infrequently uttered, although Marjorie Margolies-Mezvinsky describes an incident during which a committee chair responded to a congresswoman's request for the floor by saying "Well, young lady, what would you want?" At the same time, exaggerated politeness and condescension continued to be exhibited on Capitol Hill. One congressman told a first-term female colleague how "pleasing" all the new women were and how "they certainly brightened up the place." "The subtext of his remark," she said later, "was why else were we elected except to be pleasing and brighten up the place." And a young Democratic congresswoman publicly condemned unwanted sexual attention she had received from a male Representative. She said: "A colleague of mine complimented me on my appearance and then said he was going to chase me around the House floor. Because he was not my boss I was not intimidated, but I was offended and I was embarrassed."

The corps of unreconstructed congressmen who, in 1978, were described as "macho SOBs," whose image of female colleagues did not extend beyond prevailing stereotypes, who were flagrantly insensitive to public issues central to women's concerns and who were scornful of almost any professional activity in which women engaged, was also present in 1993, albeit diminished in size. Representatives recalled a dozen or more instances when they were embarrassed by the behavior of mostly senior congressmen toward women. These men were described as "insensitive," "vulgar," "insulting" or "sexist." One congressman recalled the committee chairman who appeared at orientation session for newly elected members and spent the afternoon "leering" at the congresswomen and commenting with coarse humor on their "good looks" and "nice bodies." According to this informant, nothing was said or done about the situation because no one wanted to tangle with a committee chairman.

Another informant described the strikingly insensitive behavior of a senior Democrat following a roll call vote. The vote was on an amendment to allow Medicaid funds to pay for mammograms annually—a preferred schedule for older women—rather than biennially, as had been stipulated in the original measure. When the amendment was defeated, a disappointed congresswoman was approached by a male opponent in the debate. In a sorry attempt at humor, he said "All is not lost. Poor women can still have one breast tested this year, the other breast tested next year."

The difficulty some men had in taking women professionals seriously was reflected in the comment of a highly respected Republican congressman to a National Public Television audience. He remarked that after the 1992 election "There are so many women in Congress now that it looks like a mall." Realizing that not everyone present appreciated his comment, he quickly denied authorship of the "joke," stating lamely that it did not originate with him, and adding "I am just repeating what other members of Congress are saying." . . .

Some of the incidents revealed a resistant, deeply rooted male chauvinism, even misogyny, among a small group of mostly senior males. Although almost all knew enough to avoid flagrantly sexist remarks, unusual events sometimes stripped away a fragile veneer of civility. One such event was the 1991 Clarence Thomas confirmation hearings before the Senate Judiciary Committee at which Anita Hill testified. Feelings about race, sexuality, ideology, and party advantage conjoined to raise emotions to extraordinary heights. After watching the televised hearings with a group of male Republicans, one of their colleagues reported that he was appalled by the blatantly sexist remarks made by men he believed were "above those kind of comments." "If a woman were present they would not have talked that way," he said. "The vulgar remarks about Anita Hill's sexuality shocked me. I had no idea that these men had such retrograde attitudes, and maybe it took the atmosphere of the Thomas hearings to trigger gutter values that they are usually able to mask."

Virtually all congresswomen interviewed in 1993 knew that some of their male colleagues were "beyond redemption," but, like most of their 1970s predecessors, they could not be bothered thinking about them as obstacles to their legislative effectiveness. One third-term woman observed that even talking about these men in an interview was unproductive—a waste of time because it means "we are not talking about issues that are really important." And a female Republican remarked:

> So much of life is reflected in the personal attitudes that you bring to a situation. I have tried to think positively and not let obstacles of this kind stand in my way. I want to establish a reputation as a hard-working, knowledgeable, conscientious, problem-solving, substantive person. I can't change the attitudes of some of these men but neither can I let these attitudes affect what I do. . . .

The most visible change affecting female integration into the House in 1993 was their increase from twenty-eight in the 102nd Congress to forty-seven in the 103rd. Other, related changes were sparked by the unprecedented increase.

The large turnover in House members in 1992 left a correspondingly large number of vacancies on coveted standing committees and on influential party instrumentalities. Democratic and Republican leaders had little choice but to fill many of these vacancies with women. Some informants said these leaders went out of their way to showcase female members. They were sensitive to the arrival of twenty-four new women, said some, and fearful that they would lose partisan advantage if they gave inadequate attention to female members' concerns. Such highly valued committees as Appropriations and Energy and Commerce were staffed with unprecedented numbers of women. So were party policy committees and the Whip networks. Veteran women capitalized on the high turnover and the seniority system, vaulting five or more positions up their committee ladders, poised to become senior and ranking members of key subcommittees. They now had unprecedented access to influential House-Senate conference committees. And this was just the beginning of an advantageous positioning process. Said one senior male Democrat, "No amount of male chauvinism can hold back a woman who occupies a top subcommittee position and who works hard at her job. She is an integral part of the process whether people like it or not."

Increased numbers were particularly helpful for Democratic women. Twenty-one first-term Democrats joined fifteen female party holdovers to produce a critical mass of votes which could, if cast as a unit on selected issues, hold the balance of power. Female ubiquity was especially apparent among the sixty-four Democratic first-termers, one-third of whom were women. The latter used their clout to help elect African-American Eva Clayton of North Carolina President of the Democratic class for the first session of the 103rd Congress.

The augmented numbers would not have produced as much change if the new women were not as experienced or as talented as they were. With most having served in state legislatures and on city or county councils, the female class of 1993 had already built reputations as able lawmakers, and as creative, caring public servants. They were capable, confident women, prepared to work hard, take their lumps and, said one senior congresswoman, "They do not say 'poor me' when they fail to achieve their goals." Official Washington could not ignore these "agents of change." The electorate had sent them to Washington to purge government of waste and corruption and they were conscious of their mandate. Floridian Tillie Fowler and Utah's Karen Shepherd became co-leaders of their respective parties' efforts to reform the House. In the meantime, the new congresswomen drew strength from their numbers and from highly visible, conscious attempts by the Clinton administration to appoint women to key executive branch positions. As one senior Republican put it, "women were now being judged by their dialectical more than their decorative contributions to government."

But the "decorative" was not being ignored. To punctuate their presence, congresswomen dressed in bright, feminine colors, and the pinks and reds and oranges and orchids and apricots and fuchsias accentuated the drabness of dark-suited congressmen when President Clinton came to the House for a televised speech to a joint session of Congress. Said one congresswoman: "We didn't necessarily plan it that way but each of us decided independently that we were going to make a visual statement and we wanted tens of millions of people to see that this was a start of a new era for the representation of women." Twenty-two of the twenty-four new women joined the Congressional Caucus for Women's Issues soon after they arrived. Caucus members and non-members, Democrats and Republicans, entered into an unprecedented network of mentoring relationships, with their conviviality occasionally crossing party lines. Said one senior Republican woman, "Can you imagine Democratic and Republican men arranging to break bread with one another?"

Whereas the partisan division between males was largely unbridgeable in the 103rd Congress, the social orientations of female and male Representatives were converging. This development was hastened by the wholesale replacement of older by younger men in the 1992 election. One second-term Democrat remarked on the shift in attitudes toward women held by recently elected congressmen. He said:

> My generation has been trained differently. We have become accustomed to dealing with women in professional situations. We have come to accept basic premises of the women's movement. Consequently, the proliferation of women in Congress poses no adjustment problems for us.

And several Representatives detected greater circumspection by senior congressmen in relationships established with congresswomen. Said one, "a few members of the old guard have concluded that the political liabilities of insensitivity are prohibitive."

Changes associated with increased numbers, with assignments to more valued committees, with more comprehensive networking and mentoring relationships among women, with women's greater visibility, and with new cohorts of socially aware male colleagues all had a profound effect on the level of female integration into the House. Whereas informants in 1978 frequently referred to women's exclusion from formal and informal House groups, few did so in 1993. . . .

Turnover and generational change among congressmen diminished even if it did not end the open, raw hostility exhibited by some males toward congresswomen. Many of the new men were hypersensitive to the feelings of female colleagues, and contemporary congresswomen recalled fewer examples of unconscious sexism than had their predecessors. Male behavior changed markedly after the Clarence Thomas hearings. The Navy's apologies following vulgar depictions of Congresswoman Pat Schroeder in skits produced in the wake of the Tailhook scandal also had an impact. And references which gratuitously called attention to gender differences among members, once common, became occasional. . . .

. . . The Clinton administration made women's concerns an integral part of the national agenda and feminist constituencies were better mobilized than they had been. Furthermore, many congressmen felt comfortable sponsoring feminist legislation, and congresswomen were emboldened by their numbers to determine priorities in terms of their own experience. As one senior Democratic congressman said, "For the first time it is possible to be a feminist and a 'House insider' at the same time."

28

MAURILIO VIGIL

From *Hispanics in Congress*

The 1990 census recorded a dramatic increase in the number of Americans who categorize themselves as Hispanic. Census 2000 will likely reveal the same. Along with this population growth will come congressional elections producing many new Hispanic members of the House of Representatives. Maurilio Vigil looks at the past, present, and future of Hispanics in Congress, emphasizing their organizing group, the Congressional Hispanic Caucus (CHC). The CHC has much potential for success. But it may be limited in effectiveness, Vigil notes, by the vast differences among Hispanics, who include Mexican Americans, Puerto Ricans, Cubans, and others, all across the country, each group often holding different partisan and issue positions.

TODAY'S CONGRESS WOULD, no doubt, seem alien to the authors of the Constitution, for it has evolved and changed in ways that differ markedly from that body which first convened in New York on April 1, 1789. Nevertheless, the basic structure of Congress continues to operate in much the same way as the framers planned it.

One of the basic elements of Congress that has remained true is the idea or concept that a representative should reflect the people he/she represents. In 1789, Anti-Federalist Robert Yates said that "the term, representative, implies that a person chosen for this purpose should resemble those who appoint them" and also that "for an assembly to be a true likeness of the people of any country, they must be considerably numerous." Yates went on to point out that the United States, albeit young at the time, was made up of a number of classes of people and that to have proper representation of them, all groups should have the opportunity of choosing their best informed to represent them. John Adams echoed this sentiment when he said that a representative legislature "should be an exact portrait, in miniature, of the people at large." Whether Adams' and Yates' views can be seen as a reflection of the founding fathers' perception of the ideal "representative" or of the ideal "Congress," they do show that the founders appreciated the value of diversity among representatives in the American Congress.

While the founders espoused diversity, it was of course meant in the narrowest of terms, for women and Blacks were absent from the early Congresses due to legal impediments.

Still, one of the most important features of the American Congress is that it has been made up of individuals who are as diverse as the people they represent. Hispanics are an ethnic minority who were never formally denied membership in the U.S. Congress. It may come as some surprise that Hispanics have been represented in the American Congress as early as the 1820s and almost continuously since the 1850s.

If the U.S. Congress of today were an "exact portrait in miniature of the people at large" of Adams' conception, there would be thirty Hispanics in the U.S. House of Representatives and seven in the U.S. Senate.

The 103rd Congress, which convened in January, 1993, welcomed the largest class of Hispanic Congresspersons in history. Eight new Hispanic members entered the U.S. House of Representatives and their overall number increased from ten to seventeen. Counting the two nonvoting members from Puerto Rico (Carlos Romero-Barcelo) and the Virgin Islands (Ron de Lugo), Hispanics number nineteen in the House, the largest delegation of Hispanics ever. Nevertheless, Hispanics, who constitute 9 percent of the United States population, are still underrepresented in the U.S. House with 4.4 percent of the membership. Hispanics have not been represented in the U.S. Senate since the defeat of Senator Joseph M. Montoya in 1976.

The span of time between 1822, when the first Hispanic, Joseph Marion Hernández, took his seat in Congress and January, 1993, when the record number of Hispanics were present, is but a small footnote in the history of the United States Congress, but it is a major chapter in the history of the Hispanic people in the United States. That chapter not only reflects the evolution and development of Hispanics in American society, but also relates a record of distinguished service among a number of Hispanics who emerged from modest backgrounds to the highest centers of political power in the greatest democracy on earth. . . .

In addition to the normal patterns of interaction among members of Congress such as partisanship and state delegations, Congress has developed various policy groups that provide opportunity for interpersonal contact among select congresspersons who have some other characteristic and policy interests in common. The first ethnic group to form a policy group were Blacks, who formed the Congressional Black Caucus (CBC) in 1969.

The Congressional Hispanic Caucus (CHC) was organized in December, 1976 by the five Hispanics then serving in the U.S. House of Representatives. Why the CHC had not been formed earlier remains a mystery, since most of the original members had been in Congress since the 1960s. Perhaps it was the formation and early success of the Black Caucus and the prompting of Herman Badillo, who entered Congress in 1970, that caused Hispanics to form their own caucus. The objectives of the caucus were to advance the interests of Hispanics through public policies and to enhance public awareness of Hispanic issues and problems. It was envisioned a bipartisan group of Congressmen with a common commitment to develop a united Congressional effort on behalf of Hispanic Americans.

The stated purposes of the Caucus were "to monitor legislation and other government activity that affects Hispanics" and "to develop programs and other activities that would increase opportunities for Hispanics to participate in and contribute to the American political system." Most importantly, the CHC was founded in order "to reverse the national pattern of neglect, exclusion and indifference suffered for decades by Spanish-speaking citizens of the U.S.," and to fulfill the need for the development of "a national policy on the Spanish-speaking". . . .

In 1993, as indicated before, seven new Hispanics entered the 103rd Congress bringing the total number of Hispanics to seventeen and all but two, Henry Gonzalez of Texas, and Matthew Martinez of California, became active in the CHC. José Serrano was selected as chairperson and the increased numbers promised to revitalize the Caucus. Almost immediately, the cohesiveness of the larger Caucus was tested as Congress debated the North American Free Trade Agreement (NAFTA)*, an issue of great importance to Hispanic Americans. Beyond the generic issues of expanded trade, business development and jobs, some analysts viewed NAFTA as a policy that would, if approved, bring the United States closer to the Hispanic countries of Latin America. On the other hand, if it was rejected it would create a wider barrier between the United States and those countries. NAFTA thus presented the CHC, if it could act as a unified bloc, with the opportunity of being at the vanguard of one of the most important American policy decisions relating to the Hispanic world. CHC unity was particularly important after it became apparent that the Congressional Black Caucus was overwhelmingly opposed to the accord.

*The North American Free Trade Agreement (NAFTA) treaty took effect on January 1, 1994. Debate in the country and in Congress during 1993 revealed the sharp divisions of opinion on NAFTA. Its purpose was to eliminate all trade restrictions among the United States, Canada, and Mexico. The treaty was supported by so-called free traders. Opponents of NAFTA believed that American workers would lose jobs to lower-wage Mexican laborers.—EDS.

After one of the most dramatic and bitter congressional battles of the 103rd Congress, NAFTA was approved. The CHC, like the Democratic majority in the House, was bitterly divided over the issue. Nine of the Hispanics supported NAFTA and eight opposed it. In fact, the issue split the Hispanics along regional and ethnic sub-group lines as the nine supporters of the measure were Mexican-Americans from the southwestern states and the opponents included the two Puerto Ricans from New York, the three Cubans from Florida and New Jersey and a Mexican-American from Chicago. Henry Gonzales (Texas) and Marty Martinez (California) were the only Mexican-Americans from the southwest who opposed it.

The fact that Congressman Bill Richardson, a former chairperson of the CHC and a Deputy Majority Whip in the House, was one of the two "point men" who orchestrated the successful vote in support of the Clinton administration, helped sway some of his Hispanic colleagues, but did not convert the others. The various reasons given for Hispanic Congressional opposition to NAFTA again reflected the diversity of the CHC. Democratic Congresspersons from Illinois, New York and New Jersey represent urban industrial centers with large working class populations who could be adversely affected by the loss of unskilled jobs. Indeed, the most intensive opposition to NAFTA came from organized labor. Cuban-American Congressmen opposed NAFTA because of their unhappiness with Mexican immigration policy. The Puerto Rican congresspersons were also concerned that NAFTA would weaken the United States' 936 program which gives U.S. companies tax breaks as inducements to invest in Puerto Rico. The division within the CHC caused by the NAFTA could have future consequences for unity as well, as Mexican-American congresspersons, bitter over the negative vote of their colleagues could retaliate in such future votes as expansion of tax breaks for corporations doing business in Puerto Rico or economic assistance and trade with Cuba if relations are normalized between the U.S. and that country. . . .

Still some progress has been made by the Caucus in laying the basis for a collective national leadership of Hispanics. A permanent CHC staff is in place and has begun to perform a variety of services for member Congressmen and Hispanics. This staff will likely push for greater cooperation among Hispanic Congressmen and their staffs. A method of financing CHC activities has been established with the annual banquet held during Hispanic Heritage week in September. A CHC institute to coordinate the Caucus educational programs and other activities has been created and the CHC has gained visibility among Hispanic organizations and is recognized for its policy-making orientations in Washington. Moreover, the CHC Washington staff and the CHC Institute have begun to serve as a clearinghouse for collecting and disseminating information on Hispanics. It also provides information on educational scholarships and fellowship programs for Hispanics.

The additional Hispanic Congresspersons who joined the CHC in the 103rd Congress did offer some prospect for the revitalization of the Caucus. The increased numbers made the Caucus "more visible and [it] will have a louder voice" as new member Frank Tejeda pointed out. Certainly the diversification of the Caucus (both geographically and by cultural group) with new members from Illinois (Gutíerrez), New Jersey (Menéndez), New York (Serrano and Velásquez), Florida (Ros-Lehtinen and Díaz-Bolart) and Arizona (Pastor) as well as the new members from California and Texas provided a greater ideological and regional mix that more accurately reflects the diversity of America's Hispanic population.

Until 1990, most Hispanics in Congress were Mexican-Americans from the Southwest. Today they include Mexican-Americans from the Southwest and Midwest, Puerto Ricans from New York and Cubans from Florida and New Jersey.

The ideological and partisan division of the Caucus will continue to be evident, with the Republicans from Florida (Ros-Lehtinen and Díaz-Balart) and Texas (Bonilla) more clearly juxtaposed to the remaining Caucus members who are liberal to moderate Democrats. And, not all Hispanic Congressmen are members of the Caucus. Henry Gonzales from Texas and Matthew "Marty" Martinez continue to boycott the Caucus in the 104th Congress. Nevertheless, as Solomon Ortiz (D. Texas) said, "there will be some issues that divide us, but there are more issues like education, housing and jobs that unite us." The new Chairman of the Caucus, José Serrano from New York, although a liberal Democrat, promised in 1993 to "lead the Caucus by consensus . . . on very emotional issues that we disagree on, we just won't go into them in the Caucus." . . .

The inability of the CHC to present a united front on a variety of issues deprives it of a very important strategic tool. The voting power of the Caucus, because of its small size in members, is insignificant, except in very close roll-call votes. Rather, unity is important because of its potential influence on the other 418 Congressmen, some of whom have sizable Hispanic constituencies or who may be sensitive to Hispanic concerns.

It is unlikely that all the members of the Hispanic Caucus will achieve consensus on all or even the most important issues to Hispanics. It is more likely that the different personalities, partisanship and political ideologies, constituency interests and personal agendas of the individual members, will undermine the unity of the Hispanic Caucus. However, the extent to which the individual members can rise above these differences and come together, on the basis of common, cultural, linguistic and surname characteristics, will determine the collective future of Hispanics in American politics. . . .

If the progress achieved by Hispanics in the past two decades is any indication, the prospects for Hispanics in the Congresses of the future appear bright. The advances of the 1980s and 1990s can be attributed to a combination of factors including continued Hispanic migration to the United States; the continued concentration of Hispanics in urban areas of industrial and sunbelt states; the passage and implementation of the 1965 Voting Rights Act and in particular, the amendments of 1975 and 1982; the effect of favorable court decisions which have enabled or even mandated the creation of minority-majority districts; the continued activism of Hispanic leaders and organizations which have lobbied for the creation of Hispanic-majority districts; and perhaps most importantly, the willingness of Hispanic voters to register and vote for their own Hispanic candidate when the opportunity presents itself.

Still, Hispanics remain underrepresented in Congress, and as was the case in 1992, their Congressional gains were far short of what they could have been, given their population increases. Only a more concerted effort by Hispanic leaders and organizations will assure that Hispanics secure their fair share of representation in the future.

29

PAUL STAROBIN

Pork: A Time-Honored Tradition Lives On

Journalist Paul Starobin's look at congressional "pork" updates a classic subject. Pork, a project that a representative can secure for her or his district, has been a central part of congressional politics from the start. In times past, pork was easier to notice—edifices like canals, highways, bridges—as well as less controversial. The United States needed these infrastructure improvements, and the money was available for a generous pork barrel. Today, pork carries a different connotation. Starobin lists the new forms that pork takes in the "post-industrial" era. Modern pork projects don't look like those of the past. And the pork barrel, while as popular as always, isn't nearly as deep as it once was. Legislators are under pressure to cut, not spend, and pork is a perfect target. But what is pork? Some other district's waste-treatment plant.

POLITICAL PORK. Since the first Congress convened two centuries ago, lawmakers have ladled it out to home constituencies in the form of cash for roads, bridges and sundry other civic projects. It is a safe bet that the distribution of such largess will continue for at least as long into the future.*

Pork-barrel politics, in fact, is as much a part of the congressional scene as the two parties or the rules of courtesy for floor debate. . . .

And yet pork-barrel politics always has stirred controversy. Critics dislike seeing raw politics guiding decisions on the distribution of federal money for parochial needs. They say disinterested experts, if possible, should guide that money flow.

And fiscal conservatives wonder how Congress will ever get a handle on the federal budget with so many lawmakers grabbing so forcefully for pork-barrel funds. "Let's change the system so we don't have so much porking," says James C. Miller III, director of the White House Office of Management and Budget (OMB). Miller says he gets complaints on the order of one a day from congressional members taking issue with OMB suggestions that particular "pork" items in the budget are wasteful.

But pork has its unabashed defenders. How, these people ask, can lawmakers ignore the legitimate demands of their constituents? When a highway needs to be built or a waterway constructed, the home folks quite naturally look to their congressional representative for help. Failure to respond amounts to political suicide.

"I've really always been a defender of pork-barreling because that's what I think people elect us for," says Rep. Douglas H. Bosco, D-Calif.

Moreover, many accept pork as a staple of the legislative process, lubricating the squeaky wheels of Congress by giving members a personal stake in major bills. . . .

Not only does the flow of pork continue pretty much unabated, it

*The interesting, little-known, and ignominious origin of the term "pork barrel" comes from early in American history, when a barrel of salt pork was given to slaves as a reward for their work. The slaves had to compete among themselves to get their piece of the handout.—EDS.

seems to be spreading to areas that traditionally haven't been subject to pork-barrel competition. Pork traditionally was identified with public-works projects such as roads, bridges, dams and harbors. But, as the economy and country have changed, lawmakers have shifted their appetites to what might be called "post-industrial" pork. Some examples:

• *Green Pork.* During the 1960s and 1970s, when dam-builders fought epic struggles with environmentalists, "pork-barrel" projects stereotypically meant bulldozers and concrete. But many of today's projects are more likely to draw praise than blame from environmentalists. The list includes sewer projects, waste-site cleanups, solar energy laboratories, pollution-control research, parks and park improvements and fish hatcheries, to name a few. . . .

• *Academic Pork.* Almost no federal funds for construction of university research facilities are being appropriated these days, except for special projects sponsored by lawmakers for campuses back home. Many of the sponsors sit on the Appropriations committees, from which they are well positioned to channel such funds. . . .

• *Defense Pork.* While the distribution of pork in the form of defense contracts and location of military installations certainly isn't new, there's no question that Reagan's military buildup has expanded opportunities for lawmakers to practice pork-barrel politics. . . .

This spread of the pork-barrel system to new areas raises a question: What exactly is pork? Reaching a definition isn't easy. Many people consider it wasteful spending that flows to a particular state or district and is sought to please the folks back home.

But what is wasteful? One man's boondoggle is another man's civic pride. Perhaps the most sensible definition is that which a member seeks for his own state or district but would not seek for anyone else's constituency.

Thus, pork goes to the heart of the age-old tension between a lawmaker's twin roles as representative of a particular area and member of a national legislative body. In the former capacity, the task is to promote the local interest; in the latter it is to weigh the national interest. . . .

Like other fraternities, the system has a code of behavior and a pecking order. It commands loyalty and serves the purpose of dividing up federal money that presumably has to go somewhere, of helping re-elect incumbents and of keeping the wheels of legislation turning. . . .

When applied with skill, pork can act as a lubricant to smooth passage of complex legislation. At the same time, when local benefits are distributed for merely "strategic" purposes, it can lead to waste. . . .

Just about everyone agrees that the budget crunch has made the competition to get pet projects in spending legislation more intense. Demand for such items has not shrunk nearly as much as the pool of available funds.

30

JOHN ELLWOOD AND ERIC PATASHNIK

In Praise of Pork

Pork-barrel spending is high on Americans' list of gripes against Congress. "Asparagus research and mink reproduction" typify the wasteful spending that seems to enrich congressional districts and states while bankrupting the nation. John Ellwood and Eric Patashnik take a different view. Pork is not the real cause of the nation's budget crisis, they feel. In fact, pork projects may be just what members of the House and Senate need to be able to satisfy constituents in order to summon the courage to vote for real, significant, painful budget cuts.

IN A WHITE HOUSE address . . . [in] March [1992], President Bush challenged Congress to cut $5.7 billion of pork barrel projects to help reduce the deficit.* Among the projects Bush proposed eliminating were such congressional favorites as funding for asparagus research, mink reproduction, and local parking garages. The examples he cited would be funny, said the President, "if the effect weren't so serious." . . .

Such episodes are a regular occurrence in Washington. Indeed, since the first Congress convened in 1789 and debated whether to build a lighthouse to protect the Chesapeake Bay, legislators of both parties have attempted to deliver federal funds back home for capital improvements and other projects, while presidents have tried to excise pork from the congressional diet. . . .

In recent years, public outrage over government waste has run high.

*The "pork-barrel" refers to congressional spending on projects that bring money and jobs to particular districts throughout America, thereby aiding legislators in their reelection bids. The interesting, little-known, and ignominious origin of the term "pork barrel" comes from early in American history, when a barrel of salt pork was given to slaves as a reward for their work. The slaves had to compete among themselves to get their piece of the handout.—EDS.

Many observers see pork barrel spending not only as a symbol of an out-of-control Congress but as a leading cause of the nation's worsening budget deficit. To cite one prominent example, *Washington Post* editor Brian Kelly claims in his recent book, *Adventures in Porkland: Why Washington Can't Stop Spending Your Money*, that the 1992 federal budget alone contains $97 billion of pork projects so entirely without merit that they could be "lopped out" without affecting the "welfare of the nation."

Kelly's claims are surely overblown. For example, he includes the lower prices that consumers would pay if certain price supports were withdrawn, even though these savings (while certainly desirable) would for the most part not show up in the government's ledgers. Yet reductions in pork barrel spending have also been advocated by those who acknowledge that pork, properly measured, comprises only a tiny fraction of total federal outlays. For example, Kansas Democrat Jim Slattery, who led the battle in the House in 1991 against using $500,000 in federal funds to turn Lawrence Welk's birthplace into a shrine, told *Common Cause Magazine*, "it's important from the standpoint of restoring public confidence in Congress to show we are prepared to stop wasteful spending," even if the cuts are only symbolic. In a similar vein, a recent *Newsweek* cover story, while conceding that "cutting out the most extreme forms of pork wouldn't eliminate the federal deficit," emphasizes that doing so "would demonstrate that Washington has the political will to reform its profligate ways."

The premise of these statements is that the first thing anyone—whether an individual consumer or the United States government—trying to save money should cut out is the fluff. As *Time* magazine rhetorically asks: "when Congress is struggling without much success to reduce the federal budget deficit, the question naturally arises: is pork *really* necessary?"

Our answer is yes. We believe in pork not because every new dam or overpass deserves to be funded, nor because we consider pork an appropriate instrument of fiscal policy (there are more efficient ways of stimulating a $5 trillion economy). Rather, we think that pork, doled out strategically, can help to sweeten an otherwise unpalatable piece of legislation.

No bill tastes so bitter to the average member of Congress as one that raises taxes or cuts popular programs. Any credible deficit-reduction package will almost certainly have to do both. In exchange for an increase in pork barrel spending, however, members of Congress just might be willing to bite the bullet and make the politically difficult decisions that will be required if the federal deficit is ever to be brought under control.

In a perfect world it would not be necessary to bribe elected officials to perform their jobs well. But, as James Madison pointed out two centuries ago in *Federalist* 51, men are not angels and we do not live in a perfect world. The object of government is therefore not to suppress the imperfections of human nature, which would be futile, but rather to harness the pursuit of self-interest to public ends.

Unfortunately, in the debate over how to reduce the deficit, Madison's advice has all too often gone ignored. Indeed, if there is anything the major budget-reform proposals of the last decade (Gramm-Rudman, the balanced-budget amendment, an entitlement cap*) have in common, it is that in seeking to impose artificial limits on government spending without offering anything in return, they work against the electoral interests of congressmen instead of with them—which is why these reforms have been so vigorously resisted.

No reasonable observer would argue that pork barrel spending has always been employed as a force for good or that there are no pork projects what would have been better left unbuilt. But singling out pork as the culprit for our fiscal troubles directs attention away from the largest sources of budgetary growth and contributes to the illusion that the budget can be balanced simply by eliminating waste and abuse. While proposals to achieve a pork-free budget are not without superficial appeal, they risk depriving leaders trying to enact real deficit-reduction measures of one of the most effective coalition-building tools at their disposal.

In order to appreciate why congressmen are so enamored of pork it is helpful to understand exactly what pork is. But defining pork is not as easy as it sounds. According to *Congressional Quarterly,* pork is usually considered to be "wasteful" spending that flows to a particular state or district in order to please voters back home. Like beauty, however, waste is in the eye of the beholder. As University of Michigan budget expert Edward M. Gramlich puts it, "one guy's pork is another guy's red meat." To a district plagued by double-digit unemployment, a new highway project is a sound investment, regardless of local transportation needs.

Some scholars simply define pork as any program that is economically inefficient—that is, any program whose total costs exceed its total benefits. But this definition tars with the same brush both real pork and programs that, while inefficient, can be justified on grounds of distributional equity or in which geographic legislative influence is small or nonexistent.

*Many attempts have been made in past years to lower the deficit. In 1985, the Gramm-Rudman-Hollings law set dollar-limit goals for deficit reduction, to be followed by automatic percentage cuts; however, many programs were exempted. A 1995 balanced-budget amendment passed the House, but failed to get two-thirds of the Senate's approval. Entitlement caps would seek to limit the total amount the federal government could pay out in programs such as Medicare, Medicaid, Social Security, and food stamps.—EDS.

A more promising approach is suggested by political scientist David Mayhew in his 1974 book, *Congress: The Electoral Connection*. According to Mayhew, congressional life consists largely of "a relentless search" for ways of claiming credit for making good things happen back home and thereby increasing the likelihood of remaining in office. Because there are 535 congressmen and not one, each individual congressman must try to "peel off pieces of governmental accomplishment for which he can believably generate a sense of responsibility." For most congressmen, the easiest way of doing this is to supply goods to their home districts.

From this perspective, the ideal pork barrel project has three key properties. First, benefits are conferred on a specific geographical constituency small enough to allow a single congressman to be recognized as the benefactor. Second, benefits are given out in such a fashion as to lead constituents to believe that the congressman had a hand in the allocation. Third, costs resulting from the project are widely diffused or otherwise obscured from taxpayer notice.

Political pork, then, offers a congressman's constituents an array of benefits at little apparent cost. Because pork projects are easily distinguished by voters from the ordinary outputs of government, they provide an incumbent with the opportunity to portray himself as a "prime mover" who deserves to be reelected. When a congressman attends a ribbon-cutting ceremony for a shiny new building in his district, every voter can *see* that he is accomplishing something in Washington. . . .

"It's outrageous that you've got to have such political payoffs to get Congress to do the nation's business," says James Miller, OMB director under Ronald Reagan. Miller's outrage is understandable but ultimately unproductive. Human nature and the electoral imperative being what they are, the pork barrel is here to stay.

But if pork is a permanent part of the political landscape, it is incumbent upon leaders to ensure that taxpayers get something for their money. Our most effective presidents have been those who have linked the distribution of pork to the achievement of critical national objectives. When Franklin Roosevelt discovered he could not develop an atomic bomb without the support of Tennessee Senator Kenneth McKellar, chairman of the Appropriations Committee, he readily agreed to locate the bomb facility in Oak Ridge. By contrast, our least effective presidents—Jimmy Carter comes to mind—have either given away plum projects for nothing or waged hopeless battles against pork, squandering scarce political capital and weakening their ability to govern in the process.

The real value of pork projects ultimately lies in their ability to induce rational legislators into taking electorally risky actions for the sake of the public good. Over the last ten years, as the discretionary part of the budget has shrunk, congressmen have had fewer and fewer opportunities to claim credit for directly aiding their constituents. As Brookings scholar R. Kent Weaver has argued, in an era of scarcity and difficult political choices, many legislators gave up on trying to accomplish anything positive, focusing their energies instead on blame avoidance. The result has been the creation of a political climate in which elected officials now believe the only way they can bring the nation back to fiscal health is to injure their own electoral chances. This cannot be good for the future of the republic.

Politics got us into the deficit mess, however, and only politics can get us out. According to both government and private estimates, annual deficits will soar after the mid-1990s, and could exceed $600 billion in 2002 if the economy performs poorly. Virtually every prominent mainstream economist agrees that reducing the deficit significantly will require Congress to do what it has been strenuously trying to avoid for more than a decade—rein in spending for Social Security, Medicare, and other popular, middle-class entitlement programs. Tax increases may also be necessary. From the vantage point of the average legislator, the risk of electoral retribution seems enormous.

If reductions in popular programs and increases in taxes are required to put our national economic house back in order, the strategic use of pork to obtain the support of key legislators for these measures will be crucial. . . .

. . . [T]he president should ignore the advice of fiscal puritans who would completely exorcise pork from the body politic. Favoring legislators with small gifts for their districts in order to achieve great things for the nation is an act not of sin but of statesmanship. To be sure, determining how much pork is needed and to which members it should be distributed is difficult. Rather than asking elected officials to become selfless angels, however, we would ask of them only that they be smart politicians. We suspect Madison would agree that the latter request has a far better chance of being favorably received.

31

DAVID PRICE

From *The Congressional Experience*

From a political science classroom at Duke University in Durham, North Carolina, to the U.S. House of Representatives, David Price describes his background, his decision to run for office, and his concerns for the future of the Congress. Price reveals his typical daily schedule as a representative. He discusses his distaste for "Congress-bashing," the favorite pastime of members of the Congress. Price condemns the "hot-button attack politics" campaigning style that has pushed issues aside and created a negative cynical tone in American politics.

In November 1994, Rep. David Price (D–NC) lost his seat in the House of Representatives to his Republican challenger. Then in November, 1996, Price won back his seat.

ON NOVEMBER 4, 1986, I was elected to the U.S. House of Representatives from the Fourth District of North Carolina, a five-county area that includes the cites of Raleigh, Chapel Hill, and Asheboro. Many thoughts crowded in on me on election night, but one of the most vivid was of that spring evening in 1959 when I had first set foot in the part of North Carolina I was now to represent. At the time, I was a student at Mars Hill, a junior college in the North Carolina mountains a few miles from my home in the small town of Erwin, Tennessee. I had taken an eight-hour bus ride from Mars Hill to Chapel Hill to be interviewed for a Morehead Scholarship, a generous award that subsequently made it possible for me to attend the University of North Carolina (UNC). I was awed by the university and nervous about the interview; thinking back on some of the answers I gave the next morning ("Would you say Cecil Rhodes was an imperialist?" "I believe so"), I still marvel that I won the scholarship. But I did, and the next two years were among the most formative and exciting of my life.

I went north in 1961 to divinity school and eventually to graduate school and a faculty appointment in political science at Yale University. But the idea of returning to the Raleigh-Durham-Chapel Hill area of North Carolina exerted a continuing tug on me, particularly as I decided on a teaching career and thought about where I would like to put down personal and academic roots. Fortunately, my wife, Lisa, also found the idea agreeable, despite her budding political career as a member of New Haven's Board of Aldermen. Therefore, when I received an offer to join the political science faculty at Duke University and also to help launch the university's Institute of Policy Sciences and Public Affairs, I jumped at the opportunity. In mid-1973, we moved with our two children—Karen, three, and Michael, one—to Chapel Hill. Though we were delighted with the community and the job and saw the move as a long-term one, I would have been incredulous at the suggestion that within fourteen years I would represent the district in Congress. . . .

Among some voters—and occasionally among congressional colleagues—my academic background has represented a barrier to be overcome. But usually it has not. My district, it is claimed, has the highest number of Ph.D.'s per capita of any comparable area in the country. Certainly, with eleven institutions of higher education and the kind of people who work in the Research Triangle Park, I have some remarkably literate constituents. I sometimes reflect ambivalently on this as I contemplate the piles of well-reasoned letters on every conceivable issue that come into my office. Yet the electoral advantages are considerable. During my first campaign, we polled to test public reactions to my academic affiliation and background, expecting to downplay them in the campaign. Instead, we found highly positive associations and ended up running a television ad that featured me in the classroom! . . .

Becoming a member of the House shakes up not only family life but also the roles and routines associated with one's previous career. I took a special interest, naturally, in [political scientist Richard] Fenno's* interview with a freshman senator who had been a college professor. "Life in the Senate," he said, "is the antithesis of academic life." I would not put it quite that way: Such a view seems both to exaggerate the orderliness and tranquility of modern academic life and to underestimate the extent to which one can impose a modicum of order on life in the Congress. Still, few jobs present as many diverse and competing demands as does service in Congress.

Consider, for example, my schedule for two rather typical days in the spring of 1991, reprinted here without change except for the deletion of

*Richard Fenno's most well-known book is his 1978 *Home Style*. It represented a whole new way to study Congress. He followed certain representatives as they returned home, to their districts, to meet with constituents. Fenno found that members of Congress try to build "trust" among the voters so that more "leeway" exists for members in their congressional voting. Much of Fenno's work involved interviewing and observing members of Congress as individuals, to gain insight into their behavior as elected officials.—EDS.

some personal names and the addition of a few explanatory notes. By this time, I had moved to the Appropriations Committee from the three committees on which I sat during my first term, so the hearing schedule was less demanding; nonetheless, the Agriculture Appropriations Subcommittee held hearings on each of these two days. I also testified on a North Carolina environmental matter before a subcommittee of which I was not a member. The Budget Study Group and the Mainstream Forum, two of the informal organizations with which I am affiliated, held meetings, and the Prayer Breakfast, an informal fellowship group, met, as usual, on Thursday morning. I had several scheduled media interviews and probably a number of unscheduled press calls as well. There were a number of party meetings and activities: The Democratic Caucus met to discuss the pending budget resolution; a whip's task force was organized to mobilize Democrats behind the resolution; the caucus held a "party effectiveness" luncheon open to all members to discuss a major pending issue; and I participated in a caucus-organized set of one-minute speeches at the beginning of the House session. The other items are self-explanatory—meetings with North Carolina groups on issues of concern, talks to student groups, and various receptions that substituted for dinner or at least provided enough sustenance to take me through the evening of editing letters and reading in my office. And of course, the schedule does not capture the numerous trips to the House floor for votes, the phone calls, and the staff conferences scattered throughout every day.

These schedules list only events I actually attended; they also reflect the rules of thumb by which my staff and I keep life from getting even more hectic. In general, I talk with groups about pending legislation only when there is a North Carolina connection; most Washington groups are well aware that their delegations need to include at least one representative from the district. I also generally skip receptions at the end of the day unless constituents are to be there or a colleague has asked me to attend.

This sheer busyness in Washington and at home as well surpasses what almost all members have experienced in their previous careers and requires specific survival techniques. Most important, you must set priorities—separate those matters in which you want to invest considerable time and energy from those you wish to handle perfunctorily or not deal with personally at all. Confronted with three simultaneous subcommittee hearings, a member often has a choice: pop in on each of the three for fifteen minutes or choose one and remain long enough to learn and contribute something. It is also essential to delegate a great deal to staff and to develop a good mutual understanding within the office as to when the member's personal direction and attention are required. But there are no manage-

Typical Member's Daily Schedule in Washington

	Wednesday, April 10, 1991
8:00 A.M.	Budget Study Group—Chairman Leon Panetta, Budget Committee, room 340 Cannon Building
8:45 A.M.	Mainstream Forum Meeting, room 2344 Rayburn Building
9:15 A.M.	Meeting with Consulting Engineers Council of N.C. from Raleigh about various issues of concern
9:45 A.M.	Meet with N.C. Soybean Assn. representatives re: agriculture appropriations projects
10:15 A.M.	WCHL radio interview (by phone)
10:30 A.M.	Tape weekly radio show—budget
11:00 A.M.	Meet with former student, now an author, about intellectual property issue
1:00 P.M.	Agriculture Subcommittee Hearing—Budget Overview and General Agriculture Outlook, room 2362 Rayburn Building
2:30 P.M.	Meeting with Chairman Bill Ford and southern Democrats re: HR-5, Striker Replacement Bill, possible amendments
3:15 P.M.	Meet with Close-Up students from district on steps of Capitol for photo and discussions
3:45 P.M.	Meet with Duke professor re: energy research programs
4:30 P.M.	Meet with constituent of Kurdish background re: situation in Iraq
5:30–7:00 P.M.	Reception—Sponsored by National Assn. of Home Builders, honoring new president Mark Tipton from Raleigh, H-328 Capitol
6:00–8:00 P.M.	Reception—Honoring retiring Rep. Bill Gray, Washington Court Hotel
6:00–8:00 P.M.	Reception–Sponsored by Firefighters Assn., room B-339 Rayburn Building
6:00–8:00 P.M.	Reception—American Financial Services Assn., Gold Room
	Thursday, April 11, 1991
8:00 A.M.	Prayer Breakfast—Rep. Charles Taylor to speak, room H-130 Capitol
9:00 A.M.	Whip meeting, room H-324 Capitol
10:00 A.M.	Democratic Caucus Meeting, Hall of the House, re: budget
10:25 A.M.	UNISYS reps. in office (staff, DP meets briefly)
10:30 A.M.	Firefighters from Raleigh re: Hatch Act Reform, Manufacturer's Presumptive Liability, etc.

TYPICAL MEMBER'S DAILY SCHEDULE IN WASHINGTON (*continued*)

11:00 A.M.	American Business Council of the Gulf Countries re: rebuilding the Gulf, improving competitiveness in Gulf market
11:15 A.M.	Whip Task Force meeting re: Budget Resolution, room H-114 Capitol
12:00 P.M.	Speech—One Minute on House floor re: budget
12:30 P.M.	Party Effectiveness Lunch—re: banking reform, room H-324 Capitol
1:00 P.M.	Agriculture Subcommittee Hearing—Inspector General Overview and the Office of the General Counsel, room 2362 Rayburn Building
3:00 P.M.	Testify at Oceanography Subcommittee Hearing re: naval vessel waste disposal on N.C. Outer Banks, room 1334 Longworth Building
3:30 P.M.	Speak to Duke public policy students re: operations of Congress, room 188 Russell Building
5:00 P.M.	Interview with Matthew Cross, WUNC stringer re: offshore drilling
6:45 P.M.	Depart National Airport for Raleigh-Durham

ment techniques on earth that could make a representative's life totally predictable or controllable or that could convert a congressional office into a tidy bureaucracy. A member (or aide) who requires that kind of control—who cannot tolerate, for example, being diverted to talk to a visiting school class or to hear out a visiting delegation of homebuilders or social workers—is simply in the wrong line of work.

. . . Former Congressman Bob Eckhardt (D–Texas) suggested that every member of Congress performs three functions: lawmaker, ombudsman, and educator. This last function, as I have shown, may be closely related to the first: Lawmakers who wish to do more than simply defer to the strongest and best-organized interests on a certain matter must give some attention to explaining their actions and educating their constituents, helping them place the issue in broader perspective or perhaps activating alternative bases of support. And the extent to which a member is willing and able to undertake such explanations is ethically as well as politically significant.

Here, I turn to another facet of the legislators' educative role: their portrayal of Congress itself. On traveling with House members around their districts, Richard Fenno noted that the greatest surprise for him was the extent to which each one "polished his or her individual reputation at the expense of the institutional reputation of Congress":

> In explaining what he was doing in Washington, every one of the eighteen House members took the opportunity to picture himself as different from, and better than, most of his fellow members in Congress. No one availed himself of the opportunity to educate his constituents about Congress as an institution—not in any way that would "hurt a little." To the contrary, the members' process of differentiating themselves from the Congress as a whole only served, directly or indirectly, to downgrade the Congress.

This was in the mid-1970s, and every indication is that such tactics have become even more prevalent as Congress-bashing by advocacy groups and in the media has intensified. "We have to differentiate me from the rest of those bandits down there in Congress," Fenno heard a member say to a campaign strategy group. "'They are awful, but our guy is wonderful'—that's the message we have to get across."

So much for the traditional norm of institutional patriotism! Opinion polls regularly reveal that public officials in general and Congress in particular rank low in public esteem, an evaluation reinforced by the recent spate of ethics charges in both houses but rooted much more deeply in our country's history and political culture. Every indication is that we members reinforce such an assessment by distancing ourselves from any responsibility for the institution's functioning. And we are phenomenally successful at it, matching a 30 percent approval rate for Congress with a 95+ percent reelection rate for ourselves.

My point is not that a member should defend Congress, right or wrong. I understand very well the disadvantages of being put on the defensive about Congress's ethical problems—pointing out that only a small number of members are involved, for example, or that Ethics Committee proceedings are generally bipartisan and fair—although I believe many of these defenses have merit. Rather, I am speaking of a more general tendency to trash the institution. It is often tempting—but I believe, also deceptive and irresponsible—to pose as the quintessential outsider, carping at accommodations that have been reached on a given issue as though problems could simply be ignored, cost-free solutions devised, or the painful necessities of compromise avoided. Responsible legislators will communicate to their constituencies not only the assembly's failings but also what it is fair and reasonable to expect, what accommodations they would be well advised to accept, and so forth. In the past, institutional patriotism has too often taken an uncritical form, assuming that whatever the process produces must be acceptable. But self-righteous, anti-institutional posturing is no better. The moral quixotism to which reelection-minded legislators are increasingly prone too often serves to rationalize their own nonproductive legislative roles and to perpetuate public misperceptions of the criteria one can reasonably apply to legislative performance.

Therefore, although it may be politically profitable to "run *for* Congress by running *against* Congress," the implications for the institution's effectiveness and legitimacy are ominous. As Fenno concluded, "The strategy is ubiquitous, addictive, cost-free, and foolproof. . . . In the short run, everybody plays and nearly everybody wins. Yet the institution bleeds from 435 separate cuts. In the long run, therefore, somebody may lose. . . . Congress may lack public support at the very time when the public needs Congress the most." . . .

My job keeps me very busy and flying, as they say, "close to the ground"—attending to myriad details in dealing with constituents, tracking appropriations, and all the rest. I sometimes feel that I had a better overview of the current state of American politics and even of certain broad policy questions before I was elected than I do now. I have, however, been in a position to observe some alarming trends in our politics and to develop strong convictions about our need to reverse them. I will therefore conclude with a few thoughts on the ominous gap that has opened up between campaigning and governing. . . . It is in the nature of political campaigns to polarize and to oversimplify, but the negative attacks and distortions have increased markedly. And the link between what candidates say in their campaign advertisements and the decisions they make once in office has become more and more tenuous. . . .

This trend has been reinforced by the new technology of campaign advertising and fund-raising; thirty-second television ads and direct mail financial solicitations, for example, put a premium on hard-hitting, oversimplified appeals and the pushing of symbolic hot buttons. The trend has also been both cause and effect of the modern emergence of cultural and value questions, like abortion, race, patriotism, and alternative lifestyles, that lend themselves to symbolic appeals. Republican candidates in particular have found in these issues a promising means of diverting voters' attention from economic and quality-of-life concerns and of driving divisive wedges in the Democratic coalition.

The growing gap between campaigning and governing also bespeaks a certain public alienation and cynicism. Voters complain about the nastiness and irrelevance of campaign advertising, and my campaigns have demonstrated that such tactics can effectively be turned against an opponent. But voters who find little to encourage or inspire them in politics are nonetheless tempted to vote in anger or in protest, inclinations that modern campaign advertising exploits very effectively. As E. J. Dionne suggested, the decline of the "politics of remedy"—that is, politics that attempts "to solve problems and resolve disputes"—seems to have created a vicious cycle:

> Campaigns have become negative in large part because of a sharp decline in popular faith in government. To appeal to an increasingly alienated electorate, candidates and their political consultants have adopted a cynical stance which, they believe with good reason, plays into popular cynicism about politics and thus wins them votes. But cynical campaigns do not resolve issues. They do not lead to "remedies." Therefore, problems get worse, the electorate becomes *more* cynical—and so does the advertising.

Responsibility for our descent into attack politics, increasingly divorced from the major problems faced by the American people, is widely shared—by journalists, interest groups, campaign consultants, and the viewing, voting public. Members of Congress are hardly helpless—or blameless—before these trends. For one thing, our defensiveness in the face of tough votes is often exaggerated; members frequently underestimate their ability to deflect attacks or to deal effectively with hostile charges. All of us feel occasionally that "I'd rather vote against this than to have to explain it," but we should worry if we find ourselves taking this way out too often or on matters of genuine consequence. It is our *job* to interpret and explain difficult decisions, and with sufficient effort, we can usually do so successfully.

We also have some choices about the kind of campaigns we run. By making campaign tactics themselves an issue, we can heighten public awareness of and resistance to distorted and manipulative appeals. Above all, we can tighten the link between what we say in our own campaigns and what we have done and intend to do in office. This is not a plea for dull campaigns; on the contrary, it is our duty to arouse people's concern and anger about areas of neglect, to convince them that we can do better, to inspire them to contribute to the solution. Most people believe that politics and politicians ought to have something constructive to offer in the realms of education, housing, health care, economic development, environmental protection, and other areas of tangible concern. Our task is to get to work on these major challenges in both campaigning *and* governing in a credible way that inspires confidence and enthusiasm. As that happens, hot-button attack politics will increasingly be seen as the sham that it is.

32

LINDA KILLIAN

From *The Freshmen*

When the Republican Party won a majority in the Congress in 1994, many political analysts focused on the leaders, such as Speaker of the House Newt Gingrich. He had engineered the electoral victory and assumed Americans had given him and his "freshmen" a mandate for big changes. Linda Killian looks at 1994 from the bottom up by interviewing Republican freshmen who came to Congress in 1994. Many errors were made during the 104th Congress, Killian finds. The freshmen, especially the "True Believers," were responsible for some of them; Speaker Gingrich, for others. Their biggest mistake was not listening to an American public who did not want immediate, radical change, but rather bipartisan congressional compromise.

I BEGAN WORK on this [subject] shortly after the Republican freshmen arrived in Washington. The election of 1994 and the Republican takeover of Congress were certainly historic. . . . But what I found more interesting than the GOP leaders, who were already well known and receiving plenty of attention, were the party's new House members. They were the ones who in large measure made the 104th Congress different from any that had come before.

Most of the 73 Republicans elected to the House for the first time in 1994 were citizen legislators who saw themselves as temporary emissaries sent by the voters to Washington on a mission. They were brash, irrepressible, and passionately committed to the cause of balancing the budget and shrinking the size of the federal government. The freshmen were a new breed, different from the men and women who had preceded them to Congress. They were not polished, cookie-cutter politicians. They were quirky and plainspoken.

I wanted to discover who these freshmen were—how they thought, what was important to them, and what they wanted to accomplish—to understand and to explain them both as politicians and as people. . . .

They were the self-described revolutionaries, the peasants with pitchforks who were not outside but inside the castle walls. They came to Washington to shake things up. They disdained compromise and prided themselves on their purity. They were going to slice and dice the federal budget no matter how much it hurt. In the beginning they ran around like kids who had taken over the classroom.

Largely because of their number and the historic nature of the 1994 election, the freshmen roared into town believing only they knew the truth of what was best for the country. They dismissed anyone who had the temerity to disagree with them, and they believed they had a mandate from the voters for their agenda.

One of the biggest mistakes the freshmen made was in misreading their mandate. It's true that no Republican incumbent lost in 1994. That undoubtedly said something about the mood of the voters and their dissatisfaction with the way Clinton and the Democrats had been running the country. But many of the freshmen won election by just a few thousand votes. The election of 1994 had been decisive in its unanimity but narrow in its margins. The Republicans did not have the sweeping mandate for change they thought they did.

What happened to the Republican revolution is that it never existed in the first place except in the minds of Newt Gingrich and the freshmen. *Webster's* defines "revolution" as a "complete, radical change" or "the overthrow of a government, form of government or social system by those governed." It's doubtful that any "revolution" could be effected by a single U.S. congressional election. But that's not what Americans voted for in 1994 anyway. The American people were not looking for a revolution, just some much-needed change. But the freshmen tried to give them a revolution anyway. Using the word "revolution" to describe what they were trying to do put the freshmen at a disadvantage right from the start.

The Republicans raised the bar of expectations too high to jump over. Revolutions are not meant to happen in a democracy like ours. The dramas of the 104th Congress perfectly illustrated the brilliance of the framers of the Constitution and the system of governance they created. The House, with its two-year terms, was expected to "ever be subject to precipitancy, changeability, and excess."

The freshmen would have done well to follow the advice of Oliver Ellsworth, a delegate to the Constitutional Convention from Connecticut, who urged, "Let not too much be attempted; by which all may be lost." And as delegate Edmund Randolph, the governor of Virginia, declared, the purpose of the Senate is "to restrain, if possible, the fury of democracy." The Senate served exactly that function in the 104th Congress, to the agitation of the impatient freshmen.

The Republicans scared people with their zeal and their unwillingness to hear any voice but their own. People thought they wanted to go too fast. They had not adequately explained what they were trying to do, and they had not convinced people it was the right thing.

Voters did want a balanced federal budget and smaller, more accountable, more sensible, less intrusive government. The freshmen were asking the right questions about our government, but they didn't always offer the right answers. In cutting the federal budget, the Republicans didn't apply the ax fairly. Yes, Americans were concerned about welfare, did not want it to become a way of life for people. But Americans are not mean-spirited; they did not want children to go hungry or elderly immigrants who came to this country legally years ago to be denied health care. The Republicans made budget cuts that disproportionately affected the poor while not doing enough to reduce corporate welfare, wasteful defense spending, and other pork programs.

An analysis by the Center on Budget and Policy Priorities conducted at the end of the 104th Congress found that more than 93 percent of the budget reductions in entitlements came from programs that affected low-income people, although those programs accounted for less than a quarter of total expenditures for entitlement programs, including Medicare and Social Security. When it came to discretionary spending, more than a third of the cuts made by the 104th Congress came from programs for the poor, although they accounted for less than a quarter of overall spending on nondefense discretionary programs. To be fair, many of the freshmen did push for such cuts but were outvoted by senior members of their own party and Democrats who wanted to protect programs important to constituencies and lobbyists that mattered to them.

The freshmen also made a mistake in trying to impose their social agenda on the Congress, which drew opposition not only from the Democrats but divided their own party. Although the hard-core, conservative supporters of the freshmen fervently endorsed their social agenda. most Americans did not believe the ban on assault weapons should be lifted, environmental regulations should be rolled back, or the abortion debate should be revisited at every opportunity.

And the Republicans made a number of tactical mistakes. They tried to ignore for too long the president and his veto power, even when they did not have enough votes to override that veto. The freshmen can be excused for not immediately realizing the dangers they faced in forcing a standoff with Clinton without a veto-proof majority, but their leaders should have known better.

The two words that best describe the way the Republicans functioned for most of the 104th Congress are "centralization" and "anarchy." Power was too centralized in [House Speaker] Gingrich, who was making key decisions and taking action on his own without discussing them with the Republican conference. And when his freshman troops thought they hadn't been adequately informed or disagreed with his actions, anarchy would often ensue.

The Republicans' biggest mistake was shutting down the government, which made them look petty and immature. They deflected attention away from what they were fighting for and handed Clinton a club to use against them. The government shutdown was a turning point and a low from which they never fully recovered. The shutdown, combined with all of their grandstanding in the first year, diminished many of their achievements. If you judge the 104th Congress against past Congresses, it was extremely productive and significant. Judged only by their own early rhetoric and goals, the Republicans didn't get most of what they were seeking.

Much of what the 104th Congress accomplished came at the end of the session, after the freshmen had learned how to govern, which meant they had learned how to compromise with the Democrats. Their constituents said they wanted it done, so they passed a minimum wage increase, even though many said privately they did not agree with it. They passed health insurance and welfare reform, which Americans also said they wanted. One could argue that at that point they became very much like the people they had replaced, part of the system. But had they not changed strategy in the spring and summer of 1996, it's a safe bet a great many more of the freshmen would not have been reelected and the Republicans could have lost the majority. By compromising to get a few things done, they lived to fight another day.

The Republican 104th Congress did make hard choices, helping to reduce the size of the deficit and beginning to control the rate of growth in government spending. The Republicans set in place a program to phase out agricultural subsidies even though many of them came from rural, farming districts. They passed the line-item veto, prevented unfunded federal mandates from being passed on to local and state governments, and reformed Congress by adopting a gift ban, revising the rules on lobbying, and requiring Congress to obey the laws it passed for everyone else. The congressional reform measures in particular never would have happened without the freshmen. They deserve credit for those things.

Clinton may have demonized the freshmen as extremists, but deep down he knew they were on to something. And so he stole their message. In many respects during the campaign he hewed to the freshman message more closely than did Dole. Clinton signed on to welfare reform, a balanced budget, smaller government, and a tax cut. The Democrats had no real message of their own. They had no vision of what they would do if they took Congress back. They simply said they were not the extremist Republicans.

It is no coincidence that Bill Clinton won decisive margins of victory in the same districts that reelected the freshmen. The voters believed that with a Republican Congress and Bill Clinton in the White House, they would get more or less what they wanted—that the Republican Congress and the Democratic president would moderate each other, pulling both toward the middle.

Many of the freshmen were inspired to run for office by Clinton, by the tax increase and big-government approach of his first two years. Many voters also thought Clinton was going too far to the left. And though the 1994 election looked like a repudiation of his administration, the Clinton presidency started to become a success only when he stood up to the freshmen during the government shutdown, when voters thought the Republicans were moving too far to the right. Clinton took the freshmen on, but he also got their message. He stood before the country and acknowledged that the era of big government was over. Likewise, the freshmen won the most approval from the public when they started working with the president to pass legislation.

Americans didn't want the federal government dismantled. They just wanted it to work better, to do what it is supposed to do. Government can't do everything, but it must do some things, and in many cases it can do them better than it's doing them now. That's what people elect politicians to do: to make government work better and to find solutions to national problems.

The freshmen and the 104th Congress expended most of their energy trying to balance the budget but left many serious problems unaddressed. What to do about the long-term future of Medicare and Social Security remains a significant national problem that must be dealt with on a bipartisan basis. This is a job too hard for one party to do alone. Congress must also address our largely failing public education system and the problems of our inner cities along with the lack of jobs for urban minorities, which has contributed to the problems of crime and drugs. And the failure of the freshmen and the 104th Congress to deal with campaign finance reform resulted in an election in 1996 that exemplified the worst excesses ever of the existing campaign financing system and its soft money loopholes. . . .

The most important contribution the freshmen and the Republicans made in 1994 and through the 104th Congress was to change the national debate and the national agenda. Suddenly it was no longer a matter of whether the budget would be balanced but when. Their efforts were fundamental in changing the way we view government and its role in our lives as we head into the 21st century. Rather than believing government can address any problem through the creation of yet another program, Americans now see the limits of government and of what we can afford. What the freshmen produced was not a revolution but an evolution, in thinking.

The election of the freshmen and the Republican House majority did signal the biggest change in American government in half a century. Whether it will be a lasting change is not yet clear.

To what extent have the freshmen reshaped American politics? They have certainly made it more popular to tell the truth. The freshmen were willing to tell it like it is. Even many people who didn't agree with them respected their candor and commitment. But did they permanently change Congress? They weren't able to eliminate anything big, like a cabinet department. And because of the closeness of the 1996 election, pressures were mounting before their second term began to push Congress back to the old way of doing things.

The freshmen realized about halfway through their first year in Congress that what they wanted to do was going to take longer than two years to accomplish. And in their reelection campaigns the freshmen asked the voters to let them finish the job they started. Having won reelection, they were a little older, a little wiser, and a lot more politically savvy. And while they may have derided the way Congress does its business when they arrived, they grudgingly learned respect for the power of the system's checks and balances.

When the freshmen returned to Washington shortly after the 1996 election for some organizational meetings, they seemed to be experiencing a strange mixture of euphoria, exhaustion, and disappointment. "I went up to my colleagues and started hugging them. 'It's great to have you back,' I told them. We really went through something. It's been a truly remarkable experience. We've been waging a political war and for two years there's been a siege mentality," Joe Scarborough told me.

They were back. And the ones who survived were both different and curiously the same. Many of the freshmen were never revolutionaries, just Republican politicians who happened to get elected in 1994. But after the 1996 election, a core group of about two dozen True Believers remained, united by the goals of reducing government spending and balancing the budget. Having been called Nazis, fascists, and radicals for two years, some of the freshmen were ready to give up the fight, but others were more determined than ever. "We won the idea war," Sam Brownback told me. "If we hadn't yelled so hard we wouldn't have gotten as far as we did. You have to give the war cry."

After the election many of the freshmen were feeling rather used by Gingrich. "We were the shock troops," said John Shadegg. The Republicans should have picked three or four things and pushed all the way to get them done rather than trying for everything and then caving in, he said. Their leaders should have known better. "Somebody should have been the adult. Somebody should have known you can't do it all at once." . . .

The 105th Congress began at a snail's pace compared to the 104th. After being sworn in, the members immediately left town for two weeks and were in session for only two more days in January.

And there were other differences that made this session of Congress look far more like traditional past Congresses than like the 104th. Since Gingrich seemed to have his hands full managing his image restoration, he had less time for top-down management of legislation. That meant committee chairs had more autonomy and bills were moving through the committee system as they had before the 104th Congress.

And the new GOP members elected in 1996 were a pale imitation of the previous freshman class. They were older and more moderate and had more traditional political experience than the class of '94. "They don't have the fervor we had. . . . I see the reform aspect of our agenda getting blunted pretty bad," [Congressman] Hilleary told me. There was also a lot less lockstep unity among the Republicans; party leaders were having trouble holding their troops together. Since their margin was so small, the defection of just a handful of Republicans could doom a piece of legislation. Not that the 105th Congress actually seemed to be doing that much.

They had managed to win reelection and to hold the majority, but they were acting like losers instead of winners. Feeling that they had been beaten over the head on Medicare and some other issues by the Democrats and the labor unions, the Republicans seemed unwilling to attempt anything too difficult or ambitious in the 105th Congress. The 1996 election had "scared the bejesus" out of the GOP moderates, according to one member. Their ranks had been thinned, especially in the Northeast. In Massachusetts two moderates had been defeated, leaving the state's 12-member congressional delegation without a single Republican.

From the very beginning of the 105th Congress, the moderates made it clear they planned to assert themselves and would not be forced into voting for things they didn't agree with for the good of party unity. "They feared for their political lives, and they told the Speaker to back off," as one member put it. This just exacerbated the already existing tensions between the GOP moderates and the conservatives.

The most conservative of the former freshmen figured there was strength in numbers and they needed to stick together, so a dozen of the True Believers decided to get offices on the same floor of one of the House office buildings. That way they could be near each other for late-night plotting sessions. A couple of hallways on the fourth floor of the Cannon House Office Building became their clubhouse. The list of former freshmen with offices on the floor read like a who's who of the class malcontents: Mark Souder, John Shadegg, Steve Largent, Tom Coburn, Mark Neumann, and John Hostettler. Altogether, 16 of the Republican freshmen of 1994 located their offices there—more than one-quarter of those who remained in the House.

Hilleary kept his office on the first floor of Cannon. But he had become part of the group of rebels. He was no longer the good soldier who saluted smartly and followed orders. Hilleary thought the True Believers' core, conservative principles and goals were being ignored and something had to be done about it.

Part of the reason for all the tiptoeing around was that Gingrich was badly wounded and no longer dealing from a position of strength but from one of weakness. The True Believers had lost confidence in his judgment, his management, and his ability to continue to pursue their conservative agenda. Gingrich was clearly not a man of moderation. He always seemed to be overreacting. First he overreacted in the 104th Congress by trying to go too far; now he was overcompensating and seemed afraid to do anything. "The Newt Gingrich that was the fire-eater changed into Newt Gingrich the compromiser," [Congressman] Salmon remarked.

The Republicans were suffering from a severe loss of momentum. The heady early days of the 104th Congress seemed like a distant memory. . . .

The freshmen of 1994 knew that their legacy was tenuous. It would depend not only on the congressional election of 1998 but the presidential contest of 2000. What happened in the first year of the 105th Congress made it clear that the achievements of the 104th Congress could easily be reversed, especially if the Republicans lost control of the House and failed to recapture the presidency. As Graham told me, "We could be a footnote, or we could be fundamental change. That's not decided yet."

PART SIX

The Presidency

33

RICHARD NEUSTADT

From *Presidential Power and the Modern Presidents*

From this often-read book comes the classic concept of presidential power as "the power to persuade." Richard Neustadt observed the essence of presidential power when working in the executive branch during Franklin Roosevelt's term as president. He stayed to serve under President Truman. It is said that President Kennedy brought Presidential Power *with him to the White House, and Neustadt worked briefly for JFK. The first half of the excerpt, in which he shows how presidents' well-developed personal characteristics permit successful persuasive abilities, comes from the book's first edition. The excerpt's closing pages reflect Neustadt's recent musings on the nation, on world affairs, and on the challenges presidents face.*

IN THE EARLY summer of 1952, before the heat of the campaign, President [Harry] Truman used to contemplate the problems of the general-become-President should [Dwight David] Eisenhower win the forthcoming election. "He'll sit here," Truman would remark (tapping his desk for emphasis), "and he'll say, 'Do this! Do that!' *And nothing will happen*. Poor Ike—it won't be a bit like the Army. He'll find it very frustrating."

Eisenhower evidently found it so. "In the face of the continuing dissidence and disunity, the President sometimes simply exploded with exasperation," wrote Robert Donovan in comment on the early months of Eisenhower's first term. "What was the use, he demanded to know, of his trying to lead the Republican Party. . . . " And this reaction was not limited to early months alone, or to his party only. "The President still feels," an Eisenhower aide remarked to me in 1958, "that when he's decided something, that *ought* to be the end of it . . . and when it bounces back undone or done wrong, he tends to react with shocked surprise."

Truman knew whereof he spoke. With "resignation" in the place of "shocked surprise," the aide's description would have fitted Truman. The former senator may have been less shocked than the former general, but he was no less subjected to that painful and repetitive experience: "Do this, do that, and nothing will happen." Long before he came to talk of Eisenhower he had put his own experience in other words: "I sit here all day trying to persuade people to do the things they ought to have sense enough to do without my persuading them. . . . That's all the powers of the President amount to."

In these words of a President, spoken on the job, one finds the essence of the problem now before us: "powers" are no guarantee of power; clerkship is no guarantee of leadership. The President of the United States has an extraordinary range of formal powers, of authority in statute law and in the Constitution. Here is testimony that despite his "powers" he does not obtain results by giving orders—or not, at any rate, merely by giving orders. He also has extraordinary status, ex officio, according to the customs of our government and politics. Here is testimony that despite his status he does not get action without argument. Presidential power is the power to persuade. . . .

The limits on command suggest the structure of our government. The Constitutional Convention of 1787 is supposed to have created a government of "separated powers." It did nothing of the sort. Rather, it created a government of separated institutions *sharing* powers. "I am part of the legislative process," Eisenhower often said in 1959 as a reminder of his veto. Congress, the dispenser of authority and funds, is no less part of the administrative process. Federalism adds another set of separated institutions. The Bill of Rights adds others. Many public purposes can only be achieved by voluntary acts of private institutions; the press, for one, in Douglass Cater's phrase, is a "fourth branch of government." And with the coming of alliances abroad, the separate institutions of a London, or a Bonn, share in the making of American public policy.

What the Constitution separates our political parties do not combine. The parties are themselves composed of separated organizations sharing public authority. The authority consists of nominating powers. Our national parties are confederations of state and local party institutions, with a headquarters that represents the White House, more or less, if the party has a President in office. These confederacies manage presidential nominations. All other public offices depend upon electorates confined within the states. All other nominations are controlled within the states. The President and congressmen who bear one party's label are divided by dependence upon different sets of voters. The differences are sharpest at the stage of nomination. The White House has too small a share in nominating congressmen, and Congress has too little weight in nominating presidents for party to erase their constitutional separation. Party links are stronger than is frequently supposed, but nominating processes assure the separation.

The separateness of institutions and the sharing of authority prescribe the terms on which a President persuades. When one man shares authority with another, but does not gain or lose his job upon the other's whim, his willingness to act upon the urging of the other turns on whether he conceives the action right for him. The essence of a President's persuasive task is to convince such men that what the White House wants of them is what they ought to do for their sake and on their authority. (Sex matters not at all; for *man* read *woman*.)

Persuasive power, thus defined, amounts to more than charm or reasoned argument. These have their uses for a President, but these are not the whole of his resources. For the individuals he would induce to do what he wants done on their own responsibility will need or fear some acts by him on his responsibility. If they share his authority, he has some share in theirs. Presidential "powers" may be inconclusive when a President commands, but always remain relevant as he persuades. The status and authority inherent in his office reinforce his logic and his charm. . . .

A President's authority and status give him great advantages in dealing with the men he would persuade. Each "power" is a vantage point for him in the degree that other men have use for his authority. From the veto to appointments, from publicity to budgeting, and so down a long list, the White House now controls the most encompassing array of vantage points in the American political system. With hardly an exception, those who share in governing this country are aware that at some time, in some degree, the doing of *their* jobs, the furthering of *their* ambitions, may depend upon the President of the United States. Their need for presidential action, or their fear of it, is bound to be recurrent if not actually continuous. Their need or fear is his advantage.

A President's advantages are greater than mere listing of his "powers" might suggest. Those with whom he deals must deal with him until the last day of his term. Because they have continuing relationships with him, his future, while it lasts, supports his present influence. Even though there is no need or fear of him today, what he could do tomorrow may supply today's advantage. Continuing relationships may convert any "power," any aspect of his status, into vantage points in almost any case. When he induces other people to do what he wants done, a President can trade on their dependence now and later.

The President's advantages are checked by the advantages of others. Continuing relationships will pull in both directions. These are relationships of mutual dependence. A President depends upon the persons whom he would persuade; he has to reckon with his need or fear of them. They too will possess status, or authority, or both, else they would be of little use to him. Their vantage points confront his own; their power tempers his. . . .

The power to persuade is the power to bargain. Status and authority yield bargaining advantages. But in a government of "separated institutions sharing powers," they yield them to all sides. With the array of vantage points at his disposal, a President may be far more persuasive than his logic or his charm could make him. But outcomes are not guaranteed by his advantages. There remain the counter pressures those whom he would influence can bring to bear on him from vantage points at their disposal. Command has limited utility; persuasion becomes give-and-take. It is well that the White House holds the vantage points it does. In such a business any President may need them all—and more. . . .

When a President confronts divergent policy advisers, disputing experts, conflicting data, and uncertain outlooks, yet must choose, there plainly *are* some other things he can do for himself besides consulting his own power stakes. But there is a proviso—provided he has done that first and keeps clear in his mind how much his prospects may depend on his authority, how much on reputation, how much on public standing. In the world Reagan inhabited where reputation and prestige are far more intertwined than they had been in Truman's time, or even LBJ's, this proviso is no easy test of presidential expertise. It calls for a good ear and a fine eye. . . .

But when a President turns to others, regardless of the mode, he is dependent on their knowledge, judgment, and good will. If he turns essentially to one, alone, he puts a heavy burden on that other's knowledge. If he chooses not to read or hear details, he puts an even greater burden on the other's judgment. If he consents, besides, to secrecy from everyone whose task in life is to protect his flanks, he courts deep trouble. Good will should not be stretched beyond endurance. In a system characterized by separated institutions sharing powers, where presidential interests will diverge in some degree from those of almost everybody else, that suggests not stretching very far. . . .

Personally, I prefer Presidents . . . more skeptical than trustful, more curious than committed, more nearly Roosevelts than Reagans. I think the former energize our governmental system better and bring out its defects less than do the latter. Reagan's years did not persuade me otherwise, in spite of his appeal on other scores. Every scandal in his wake, for instance, must owe something to the narrow range of his convictions and the breadth of his incuriosity, along with all that trust. A President cannot abolish bad behavior, but he sets a tone, and if he is alert to possibilities he can set traps, and with them limits. Reagan's tone, apparently, was heard by all too many as "enrich yourselves," while those few traps deregulation spared appear to have been sprung and left unbaited for the most part. But this book has not been written to expound my personal preferences. Rather it endeavors to expose the problem for a President of either sort who seeks to buttress prospects for his future influence while making present choices—"looking toward tomorrow from today," as I wrote at the start. For me that remains a crucial enterprise. It is not, of course, the only thing a President should put his mind to, but it is the subject to which I have put my own throughout this book. It remains crucial, in my view, not simply for the purposes of Presidents, but also for the products of the system, whether effective policy, or flawed or none. Thus it becomes crucial for us all.

We now stand on the threshold of a time in which those separated institutions, Congress and the President, share powers fully and uncomfortably across the board of policy, both foreign and domestic. From the 1940s through the 1960s—"midcentury" in this book's terms—Congress, having been embarrassed at Pearl Harbor by the isolationism it displayed beforehand, gave successive Presidents more scope in defense budgeting and in the conduct of diplomacy toward Europe and Japan than was the norm between the two world wars. Once the Cold War had gotten under way, and then been largely militarized after Korea, that scope widened. With the onset of the missile age it deepened. Should nuclear war impend, the President became the system's final arbiter. Thus I characterized JFK against the background of the Cuban missile crisis. But by 1975 the denouement of Watergate and that of Vietnam, eight months apart, had put a period to what remained of congressional reticence left over from Pearl Harbor. And the closing of the Cold War, now in sight though by no means achieved, promises an end to nuclear danger as between the Soviet Union and the United States. Threats of nuclear attack could well remain, from Third World dictators or terrorists, but not destruction of the Northern Hemisphere. So in the realm of military preparations—even, indeed, covert actions—the congressional role waxes as the Cold War wanes, returning toward normality as understood in Franklin Roosevelt's first two terms.

In a multipolar world, crisscrossed by transnational relations, with economic and environmental issues paramount, and issues of security reshaped on regional lines, our Presidents will less and less have reason to seek solace in foreign relations from the piled-up frustrations of home affairs. Their foreign frustrations will be piled high too.

Since FDR in wartime, every President including Bush has found the role of superpower sovereign beguiling: personal responsibility at once direct and high, issues at once gripping and arcane, opposite numbers frequently intriguing and well-mannered, acclaim by foreign audiences echoing well at home, foreign travel relatively glamorous, compared with home, interest groups less clamorous, excepting special cases, authority always stronger, Congress often tamer. But the distinctions lessen—compare Bush's time with Nixon's to say nothing of Eisenhower's—and we should expect that they will lessen further. Telecommunications, trade, aid, banking and stock markets combined with AIDS and birth control and hunger, topped off by toxic waste and global warming—these are not the stuff of which the Congress of Vienna* was made, much less the summits of yore. Moreover, Europeans ten years hence, as well as Japanese, may not resemble much the relatively acquiescent "middle powers" we grew used to in the 1960s and 1970s. Cooperating with them may come to seem to Presidents no easier than cooperating with Congress. Our friends abroad will see it quite the other way around: How are they to cooperate with our peculiar mix of separated institutions sharing powers? Theirs are ordered governments, ours a rat race. Complaints of us by others in these terms are nothing new. They have been rife throughout this century. But by the next, some of the chief complainants may have fewer needs of us, while ours of them grow relatively greater, than at any other time since World War II. In that case foreign policy could cease to be a source of pleasure for a President. By the same token, he or she would have to do abroad as on the Hill and in Peoria: Check carefully the possible effects of present choices on prospective reputation and prestige—thinking of other governments and publics quite as hard as those at home. It is not just our accustomed NATO and Pacific allies who may force the pace here, but the Soviet Union, if it holds together, and potentially great powers—China, India, perhaps Brazil—as well as our neighbors, north and south.

From the multicentered, interdependent world now coming into being, environmentally endangered as it is, Presidents may look back on the Cold War as an era of stability, authority, and glamour. They may yearn for the simplicity they see in retrospect, and also for the solace. Too bad. The job of being President is tougher when incumbents have to struggle for effective influence in foreign and domestic spheres at once, with their command of nuclear forces losing immediate relevance, and the American

*After the 1814 defeat of the French leader Napoleon by Russia, Prussia, Austria, and Britain, these great powers met in Vienna, Austria, to ensure that the future of Europe would be peaceful. At the Congress of Vienna, they created a "balance of power" system so that no single European nation could dominate the continent.—EDS.

economy shorn of its former clout. There are, however, compensations, one in particular. If we outlive the Cold War,* the personal responsibility attached to nuclear weapons should become less burdensome for Presidents themselves, while contemplation of their mere humanity becomes less haunting for the rest of us. To me that seems a fair exchange.

34

ARTHUR SCHLESINGER

From *The Imperial Presidency*

Historian Arthur Schlesinger coined one of the most famous and often-quoted political phrases, used not just in academe but in the real world of government too. The demise of Richard Nixon, because of the Watergate scandal, inspired Schlesinger to look back in U.S. history to locate the roots of the tremendous power that the executive had accumulated. His observations led him to develop the idea of an "imperial Presidency," with all the connotations that phrase carries. The author believes that the imperial presidency initially evolved for a clear and identifiable reason; it then grew due to other secondary factors. Certain presidents—Roosevelt and especially Kennedy—garner praise from Schlesinger for their judicious use of imperial powers. Other presidents he condemns. Schlesinger's discussion of Richard Nixon, the ultimate imperial president as well as its destroyer, is a frank and unvarnished critique of the man who turned the imperial presidency homeward, against the American people. Schlesinger concludes with an intriguing theory of presidential power.

IN THE LAST YEARS presidential primacy, so indispensable to the political order, has turned into presidential supremacy. The constitutional Presidency—as events so apparently disparate as the Indochina War and the Watergate affair showed—has become the imperial Presidency and threatens to be the revolutionary Presidency.

This book . . . deals essentially with the shift in the *constitutional* bal-

*The Cold War refers to the hostility that existed between the United States and the Soviet Union from the end of World War II until recent times. The Cold War involved many forms of hostility: democracy versus communism; America's NATO allies versus the Soviet Union's Warsaw Pact military partners; the threat of nuclear war; economic competition; the dividing of Third World nations into pro-U.S. and pro-Soviet camps. With the demise of communism in Eastern Europe and the disintegration of the Soviet Union, the Cold War era has ended.—EDS.

ance—with, that is, the appropriation by the Presidency, and particularly by the contemporary Presidency, of powers reserved by the Constitution and by long historical practice to Congress.

This process of appropriation took place in both foreign and domestic affairs. Especially in the twentieth century, the circumstances of an increasingly perilous world as well as of an increasingly interdependent economy and society seemed to compel a larger concentration of authority in the Presidency. It must be said that historians and political scientists, this writer among them, contributed to the rise of the presidential mystique. But the imperial Presidency received its decisive impetus, I believe, from foreign policy; above all, from the capture by the Presidency of the most vital of national decisions, the decision to go to war.

This book consequently devotes special attention to the history of the war-making power. The assumption of that power by the Presidency was gradual and usually under the demand or pretext of emergency. It was as much a matter of congressional abdication as of presidential usurpation. . . .

The imperial Presidency was essentially the creation of foreign policy. A combination of doctrines and emotions—belief in permanent and universal crisis, fear of communism, faith in the duty and the right of the United States to intervene swiftly in every part of the world—had brought about the unprecedented centralization of decisions over war and peace in the Presidency. With this there came an unprecedented exclusion of the rest of the executive branch, of Congress, of the press and of public opinion in general from these decisions. Prolonged war in Vietnam strengthened the tendencies toward both centralization and exclusion. So the imperial Presidency grew at the expense of the constitutional order. Like the cowbird, it hatched its own eggs and pushed the others out of the nest. And, as it overwhelmed the traditional separation of powers in foreign affairs, it began to aspire toward an equivalent centralization of power in the domestic polity.

. . . We saw in the case of Franklin D. Roosevelt and the New Deal that extraordinary power flowing into the Presidency to meet domestic problems by no means enlarged presidential authority in foreign affairs. But we also saw in the case of FDR and the Second World War and Harry S. Truman and the steel seizure that extraordinary power flowing into the Presidency to meet international problems could easily encourage Presidents to extend their unilateral claims at home. . . . Twenty years later, the spillover effect from Vietnam coincided with indigenous developments that were quite separately carrying new power to the Presidency.

For domestic as well as for international reasons, the imperial Presidency was sinking roots deep into the national society itself.

One such development was the decay of the traditional party system. . . . For much of American history the party has been the ultimate vehicle of political expression. Voters inherited their politics as they did their religion. . . . By the 1970s ticket-splitting had become common. Independent voting was spreading everywhere, especially among the young. Never had party loyalties been so weak, party affiliations so fluid, party organizations so irrelevant.

Many factors contributed to the decline of parties. The old political organizations had lost many of their functions. The waning of immigration, for example, had deprived the city machine of its classical clientele. The rise of civil service had cut off the machine's patronage. The New Deal had taken over the machine's social welfare role. Above all, the electronic revolution was drastically modifying the political environment. Two electronic devices had a particularly devastating impact on the traditional structure of politics—television and the computer. . . .

As the parties wasted away, the Presidency stood out in solitary majesty as the central focus of political emotion, the ever more potent symbol of national community. . . .

At the same time, the economic changes of the twentieth century had conferred vast new powers not just on the national government but more particularly on the Presidency. . . .

. . . The managed economy, in short, offered new forms of unilateral power to the President who was bold enough to take action on his own. . . .

. . . The imperial presidency, born in the 1940s and 1950s to save the outer world from perdition, thus began in the 1960s and 1970s to find nurture at home. Foreign policy had given the President the command of peace and war. Now the decay of the parties left him in command of the political scene, and the Keynesian revelation placed him in command of the economy. At this extraordinary historical moment, when foreign and domestic lines of force converged, much depended on whether the occupant of the White House was moved to ride the new tendencies of power or to resist them.

For the American Presidency was a peculiarly personal institution. It remained, of course, an agency of government, subject to unvarying demands and duties no matter who was President. But, more than most agencies of government, it changed shape, intensity and ethos according to the man in charge. . . . The management of the great foreign policy crisis of the Kennedy years—the Soviet attempt to install nuclear missiles in Cuba—came as if in proof of the proposition that the nuclear age left no alternative to unilateral presidential decision. . . .

. . . Time was short, because something had to be done before the bases became operational. Secrecy was imperative. Kennedy took the decision into his own hands, but it is to be noted that he did not make it in imperial solitude. The celebrated Executive Committee became a forum for exceedingly vigorous and intensive debate. Major alternatives received strong, even vehement, expression. Though there was no legislative consultation, there was most effective executive consultation. . . . But, even in retrospect, the missile crisis seems an emergency so acute in its nature and so peculiar in its structure that it did in fact require unilateral executive decision.

Yet this very acuteness and peculiarity disabled Kennedy's action in October 1962 as a precedent for future Presidents in situations less acute and less peculiar. For the missile crisis was unique in the postwar years in that it *really* combined all those pressures of threat, secrecy and time that the foreign policy establishment had claimed as characteristic of decisions in the nuclear age. Where the threat was less grave, the need for secrecy less urgent, the time for debate less restricted—i.e., in all other cases—the argument for independent and unilateral presidential action was notably less compelling.

Alas, Kennedy's action, which should have been celebrated as an exception, was instead enshrined as a rule. This was in great part because it so beautifully fulfilled both the romantic ideal of the strong President and the prophecy of split-second presidential decision in the nuclear age. The very brilliance of Kennedy's performance appeared to vindicate the idea that the President must take unto himself the final judgments of war and peace. The missile crisis, I believe, was superbly handled, and could not have been handled so well in any other way. But one of its legacies was the imperial conception of the Presidency that brought the republic so low in Vietnam. . . .

. . . Johnson talked to, even if he too seldom listened to, an endless stream of members of Congress and the press. He unquestionably denied himself reality for a long time, especially when it came to Vietnam. But in the end reality broke through, forcing him to accept unpleasant truths he did not wish to hear. Johnson's personality was far closer than Truman's to imperial specifications. But the fit was by no means perfect. . . .

Every President reconstructs the Presidency to meet his own psychological needs. Nixon displayed more monarchical yearnings than any of his predecessors. He plainly reveled in the ritual of the office, only regretting that it could not be more elaborate. What previous President, for example, would have dreamed of ceremonial trumpets or of putting the White House security force in costumes to rival the Guards at Buckingham Palace? Public ridicule stopped this. But Nixon saw no problem about using federal money, under the pretext of national security, to adorn his California and Florida estates with redwood fences, golf carts, heaters and wind screens for the swimming pool, beach cabanas, roof tiling, carpets, furniture, trees and shrubbery. . . . Nixon's fatal error was to institute within the White House itself a centralization even more total than that he contemplated for the executive branch. He rarely saw most of his so-called personal assistants. If an aide telephoned the President on a domestic matter, his call was switched to Haldeman's office.* If he sent the President a memorandum, Haldeman decided whether or not the President would see it. "Rather than the President telling someone to do something," Haldeman explained in 1971, "I'll tell the guy. If he wants to find out something from somebody, I'll do it."

Presidents like Roosevelt and Kennedy understood that, if the man at the top confined himself to a single information system, he became the prisoner of that system. Therefore they pitted sources of their own against the information delivered to them through official channels. They understood that contention was an indispensable means of government. But Nixon, instead of exposing himself to the chastening influence of debate, organized the executive branch and the White House in order to shield himself as far as humanly possible from direct question or challenge—i.e., from reality. . . .

As one examined the impressive range of Nixon's initiatives—from his appropriation of the war-making power to his interpretation of the appointing power, from his unilateral determination of social priorities to his unilateral abolition of statutory programs, from his attack on legislative privilege to his enlargement of executive privilege, from his theory of impoundment to his theory of the pocket veto, from his calculated disparagement of the cabinet and his calculated discrediting of the press to his carefully organized concentration of federal management in the White House—from all this a larger design ineluctably emerged. It was hard to know whether Nixon, whose style was banality, understood consciously where he was heading. He was not a man given to political philosophizing. But he was heading toward a new balance of constitutional powers, an

*Robert Haldeman headed Richard Nixon's White House staff. He was a stern gatekeeper (the president wished it so) before his resignation in the face of the exploding Watergate scandals during the spring of 1973. He was subsequently convicted of criminal charges and imprisoned for his role in Watergate.—EDS.

audacious and imaginative reconstruction of the American Constitution. He did indeed contemplate, as he said in 1971 State of the Union message, a New American Revolution. But the essence of this revolution was not, as he said at the time, power to the people. The essence was power to the Presidency. . . . His purpose was probably more unconscious than conscious; and his revolution took direction and color not just from the external circumstances pressing new powers on the Presidency but from the needs and drives of his own agitated psyche. This was the fatal flaw in the revolutionary design. For everywhere he looked he saw around him hideous threats to the national security—threats that, even though he would not describe them to Congress or the people, kept his White House in constant uproar and warranted in his own mind a clandestine presidential response of spectacular and historic illegality. If his public actions led toward a scheme of presidential supremacy under a considerably debilitated Constitution, his private obsessions pushed him toward the view that the Presidency could set itself, at will, *above* the Constitution. It was this theory that led straight to Watergate. . . .

Secrecy seemed to promise government three inestimable advantages: the power to withhold, the power to leak and the power to lie. . . .

The power to withhold held out the hope of denying the public the knowledge that would make possible an independent judgment on executive policy. The mystique of inside information—"if you only knew what we know"—was a most effective way to defend the national-security monopoly and prevent democratic control of foreign policy. . . .

The power to leak meant the power to tell the people what it served the government's purpose that they should know. . . .

The power to withhold and the power to leak led on inexorably to the power to lie. The secrecy system instilled in the executive branch the idea that foreign policy was no one's business save its own, and uncontrolled secrecy made it easy for lying to become routine. It was in this spirit that the Eisenhower administration concealed the CIA operations it was mounting against governments around the world. It was in this spirit that the Kennedy administration stealthily sent the Cuban brigade to the Bay of Pigs* and stealthily enlarged American involvement in Vietnam. It was in this spirit that the Johnson administration Americanized the Vietnam War, misrepresenting one episode after another to Congress and the peo-

*In 1961, President John F. Kennedy accepted responsibility for the disaster at the Bay of Pigs in Cuba. Over a thousand Cuban exiles, trained by the U.S. Central Intelligence Agency (CIA), tried to land in Cuba to overthrow the communist government of Fidel Castro. The invasion was a complete failure, forcing Kennedy to reassess his foreign policy approach, especially toward Latin America.—EDS.

ple—Tonkin Gulf, the first American ground force commitment, the bombing of North Vietnam, My Lai and the rest.*

The longer the secrecy system dominated government, the more government assumed the *right* to lie. . . .

God, it has been well said, looks after drunks, children and the United States of America. However, given the number, the brazen presumption and the clownish ineptitude of the conspirators, if it had not been Watergate, it would surely have been something else. For Watergate was a symptom, not a cause. Nixon's supporters complained that his critics were blowing up a petty incident out of all proportion to its importance. No doubt a burglary at Democratic headquarters was trivial next to a mission to Peking. But Watergate's importance was not simply in itself. Its importance was in the way it brought to the surface, symbolized and made politically accessible the great question posed by the Nixon administration in every sector—the question of presidential power. The unwarranted and unprecedented expansion of presidential power, because it ran through the whole Nixon system, was bound, if repressed at one point, to break out at another. This, not Watergate, was the central issue. . . . Watergate did stop the revolutionary Presidency in its tracks. It blew away the mystique of the mandate and reinvigorated the constitutional separation of powers. If the independent judiciary, the free press, Congress and the executive agencies could not really claim too much credit as institutions for work performed within them by brave individuals, nonetheless they all drew new confidence as institutions from the exercise of power they had forgotten they possessed. The result could only be to brace and strengthen the inner balance of American democracy. . . .

If the Nixon White House escaped the legal consequences of its illegal behavior, why would future Presidents and their associates not suppose themselves entitled to do what the Nixon White House had done? Only condign punishment would restore popular faith in the Presidency and

*The Tonkin Gulf incident involved two alleged attacks on American ships in the waters off the coast of Vietnam in 1964. President Lyndon Johnson may have exaggerated the extent of the attacks to gain support for widening the war. In response to the incident, the Senate voted 88 to 2 and the House of Representatives 416 to 0 to allow the president significant latitude in the use of American forces in Vietnam. No formal declaration of war was ever made concerning Vietnam, but the Gulf of Tonkin Resolution became the executive branch's "blank check" to expand the conflict. The 1968 My Lai massacre was a turning point in American public opinion concerning the Vietnam War. U.S. soldiers killed over a hundred Vietnamese villagers. One lieutenant was tried and convicted for the slaughter that had happened because of the inability of American troops to distinguish between enemy soldiers and civilians. Some Americans believed that those higher up in the military, not just Lieutenant William Calley, should have been prosecuted for the massacre.—EDS.

deter future Presidents from illegal conduct—so long, at least, as Watergate remained a vivid memory. We have noted that corruption appears to visit the White House in fifty-year cycles. This suggests that exposure and retribution inoculate the Presidency against its latent criminal impulses for about half a century. Around the year 2023 the American people would be well advised to go on the alert and start nailing down everything in sight.

35

THOMAS CRONIN AND MICHAEL GENOVESE

From *The Paradoxes of the American Presidency*

The United States as a nation of paradoxes is a theme frequently used to explain the contradictions found throughout American life. In an earlier selection (#7), Michael Kammen called Americans "people of paradox." Here, political scientists Thomas Cronin and Michael Genovese use the concept of paradox to explore the many images that citizens hold of their president. Each image they describe is accompanied by a contrary image. For example, Cronin and Genovese note, the president is supposed to be an average person just like us, while simultaneously being outstanding and extraordinary. With such paradoxical expectations of a president, is it any wonder that Americans judge the executive so harshly?

THE MIND SEARCHES FOR answers to the complexities of life. We often gravitate toward simple explanations for the world's mysteries. This is a natural way to try and make sense out of a world that seems to defy understanding. We are uncomfortable with contradictions so we reduce reality to understandable simplifications. And yet, contradictions and clashing expectations are part of life. "No aspect of society, no habit, custom, movement, development, is without cross-currents," says historian Barbara Tuchman. "Starving peasants in hovels live alongside prosperous landlords in featherbeds. Children are neglected and children are loved." In life we are confronted with paradoxes for which we seek meaning. The same is true for the American presidency. We admire presidential power, yet fear it. We yearn for the heroic, yet are also inherently suspicious of it. We demand dynamic leadership, yet grant only limited powers to the president. We want presidents to be dispassionate analysts and listeners, yet they must also be decisive. We are impressed with presidents who have great self-confidence, yet we dislike arrogance and respect those who express reasonable self-doubt.

How then are we to make sense of the presidency? This complex, multidimensional, even contradictory institution is vital to the American system of government. The physical and political laws that seem to constrain one president, liberate another. What proves successful in one, leads to failure in another. Rather than seeking one unifying theory of presidential politics that answers all our questions, we believe that the American presidency might be better understood as a series of paradoxes, clashing expectations and contradictions.

Leaders live with contradictions. Presidents, more than most people, learn to take advantage of contrary or divergent forces. Leadership situations commonly require successive displays of contrasting characteristics. Living with, even embracing, contradictions is a sign of political and personal maturity.

The effective leader understands the presence of opposites. The aware leader, much like a first-rate conductor, knows when to bring in various sections, knows when and how to turn the volume up and down, and learns how to balance opposing sections to achieve desired results. Effective presidents learn how to manage these contradictions and give meaning and purpose to confusing and often clashing expectations. The novelist F. Scott Fitzgerald once suggested that, "The test of a first-rate intelligence is the ability to hold two opposed ideas in the mind at the same time." Casey Stengel, long-time New York Yankee manager and occasional (if accidental) Zen philosopher, captured the essence of the paradox when he noted, "Good pitching will always stop good hitting, and vice versa."

Our expectations of, and demands on, the president are frequently so contradictory as to invite two-faced behavior by our presidents. Presidential powers are often not as great as many of us believe, and the president gets unjustly condemned as ineffective. Or a president will overreach or resort to unfair play while trying to live up to our demands.

The Constitution is of little help. The founders purposely left the presidency imprecisely defined. This was due in part to their fears of both the monarchy and the masses, and in part to their hopes that future presidents would create a more powerful office than the framers were able to do at the time. They knew that at times the president would have to move swiftly and effectively, yet they went to considerable lengths to avoid enumerating specific powers and duties in order to calm the then widespread fear of monarchy. After all, the nation had just fought a war against executive tyranny. Thus the paradox of the invention of the presidency: To get the presidency approved in 1787 and 1788, the framers had to leave several silences and ambiguities for fear of portraying the office as an overly centralized leadership institution. Yet when we need central leadership we turn to the president and read into Article II of the Constitution various prerogatives or inherent powers that allow the president to perform as an effective national leader.

Today the informal and symbolic powers of the presidency account for as much as the formal, stated ones. Presidential powers expand and contract in response to varying situational and technological changes. The powers of the presidency are thus interpreted so differently that they sometimes seem to be those of different offices. In some ways the modern presidency has virtually unlimited authority for almost anything its occupant chooses to do with it. In other ways, a president seems hopelessly ensnarled in a web of checks and balances.

Presidents and presidential candidates must constantly balance conflicting demands, cross pressures, and contradictions. It is characteristic of the American mind to hold contradictory ideas without bothering to resolve the conflicts between them. Perhaps some contradictions are best left unresolved, especially as ours is an imperfect world and our political system is a complicated one, held together by countless compromises. We may not be able to resolve many of these clashing expectations. Some of the inconsistencies in our judgments about presidents doubtless stem from the many ironies and paradoxes of the human condition. While difficult, at the least we should develop a better understanding of what it is we ask of our presidents, thereby increasing our sensitivity to the limits and possibilities of what a president can achieve. This might free presidents to lead and administer more effectively in those critical times when the nation has no choice but to turn to them. Whether we like it or not, the vitality of our democracy depends in large measure upon the sensitive interaction of presidential leadership with an understanding public willing to listen and willing to provide support. Carefully planned innovation is nearly impossible without the kind of leadership a competent and fair-minded president can provide.

The following are some of the paradoxes of the presidency. Some are cases of confused expectations. Some are cases of wanting one kind of presidential behavior at one time, and another kind later. Still others stem from the contradiction inherent in the concept of democratic leadership, which on the surface at least, appears to set up "democratic" and "leadership" as warring concepts. Whatever the source, each has implications for presidential performance and for how Americans judge presidential success and failure. . . .

Paradox #1. Americans demand powerful, popular presidential leadership that solves the nation's problems. Yet we are inherently suspicious of strong centralized leadership and especially the abuse of power and therefore we place significant limits on the president's powers.

We admire power but fear it. We love to unload responsibilities on our leaders, yet we intensely dislike being bossed around. We expect impressive leadership from presidents, and we simultaneously impose constitutional, cultural, and political restrictions on them. These restrictions often prevent presidents from living up to our expectations. . . .

Presidents are supposed to follow the laws and respect the constitutional procedures that were designed to restrict their power, yet still they must be powerful and effective when action is needed. For example, we approve of presidential military initiatives and covert operations when they work out well, but we criticize presidents and insist they work more closely with Congress when the initiatives fail. We recognize the need for secrecy in certain government actions, but we resent being deceived and left in the dark—again, especially when things go wrong, as in Reagan's Iranian arms sale diversions to the Contras.

Although we sometimes do not approve of the way a president acts, we often approve of the end results. Thus Lincoln is often criticized for acting outside the limits of the Constitution, but at the same time he is forgiven due to the obvious necessity for him to violate certain constitutional principles in order to preserve the Union. FDR was often flagrantly deceptive and manipulative not only of his political opponents but also of his staff and allies. FDR even relished pushing people around and toying with them. But leadership effectiveness in the end often comes down to whether a person acts in terms of the highest interests of the nation. Most historians conclude Lincoln and Roosevelt were responsible in the use of presidential power, to preserve the Union, to fight the depression and nazism. Historians also conclude that Nixon was wrong for acting beyond the law in pursuit of personal power. . . .

Paradox #2. We yearn for the democratic "common person" and also for the uncommon, charismatic, heroic, visionary performance.

We want our presidents to be like us, but better than us. We like to think America is the land where the common sense of the common person reigns. Nourished on a diet of Frank Capra's "common-man-as-hero" movies, and the literary celebration of the average citizen by authors such as Emerson, Whitman, and Thoreau, we prize the common touch. The plain-speaking Harry Truman, the up-from-the-log-cabin "man or woman of the people," is enticing. Few of us, however, settle for anything but the best; we want presidents to succeed and we hunger for brilliant, uncommon, and semiregal performances from presidents. . . .

It is said the American people crave to be governed by a president who is greater than anyone else yet not better than themselves. We are inconsistent; we want our president to be one of the folks yet also something special. If presidents get too special, however, they get criticized and roasted. If they try to be too folksy, people get bored. We cherish the myth that anyone can grow up to be president, that there are no barriers and no elite qualifications, but we don't want someone who is too ordinary. Would-be presidents have to prove their special qualifications—their excellence, their stamina, and their capacity for uncommon leadership. Fellow commoner, Truman, rose to the demands of the job and became an apparently gifted decision maker, or so his admirers would have us believe.

In 1976 Governor Jimmy Carter seemed to grasp this conflict and he ran as local, down-home, farm-boy-next-door makes good. The image of the peanut farmer turned gifted governor contributed greatly to Carter's success as a national candidate and he used it with consummate skill. Early in his presidential bid, Carter enjoyed introducing himself as peanut farmer *and* nuclear physicist, once again suggesting he was down to earth but cerebral as well.

Ronald Reagan illustrated another aspect of this paradox. He was a representative all-American—small-town, midwestern, and also a rich celebrity of stage, screen, and television. He boasted of having been a Democrat, yet campaigned as a Republican. A veritable Mr. Smith goes to Washington, he also had uncommon star quality. Bill Clinton liked us to view him as both a Rhodes scholar and an ordinary saxophone-playing member of the high school band from Hope, Arkansas; as a John Kennedy and even an Elvis figure; and also as just another jogger who would stop by for a Big Mac on the way home from a run in the neighborhood. . . .

Paradox #3. We want a decent, just, caring, and compassionate president, yet we admire a cunning, guileful, and, on occasions that warrant it, even a ruthless, manipulative president.

There is always a fine line between boldness and recklessness, between strong self-confidence and what the Greeks called "hubris," between dogged determination and pigheaded stubbornness. Opinion polls indicate people want a just, decent, and intellectually honest individual as our chief executive. Almost as strongly, however, the public also demands the quality of toughness.

We may admire modesty, humility, and a sense of proportion, but most of our great leaders have been vain and crafty. After all, you don't get to the White House by being a wallflower. Most have aggressively sought power and were rarely preoccupied with metaphysical inquiry or ethical considerations.

Franklin Roosevelt's biographers, while emphasizing his compassion for the average American, also agree he was vain, devious, and manipulative and had a passion for secrecy. These, they note, are often the standard weaknesses of great leaders. Significant social and political advances are made by those with drive, ambition, and a certain amount of brash, irrational self-confidence. . . .

Perhaps Dwight Eisenhower reconciled these clashing expectations better than recent presidents. Blessed with a wonderfully seductive, benign smile and a reserved, calming disposition, he was also the disciplined, strong, no-nonsense five-star general with all the medals and victories to go along with it. His ultimate resource as president was this reconciliation of decency and proven toughness, likability alongside demonstrated valor. Some of his biographers suggest his success was at least partly due to his uncanny ability to appear guileless to the public yet act with ample cunning in private. . . .

One of the ironies of the American presidency is that those characteristics we condemn in one president, we look for in another. Thus a supporter of Jimmy Carter's once suggested that Sunday school teacher Carter wasn't "rotten enough," "a wheeler-dealer," "an s.o.b."—precisely the virtues (if they can be called that) that Lyndon Johnson was most criticized for a decade earlier. President Clinton was viewed as both a gifted Southern Baptist–style preacher by some of his followers and a man who was character challenged, by opponents. . . .

Paradox #4. We admire the "above politics" nonpartisan or bipartisan approach, yet the presidency is perhaps the most political office in the American system, a system in which we need a creative entrepreneurial master politician.

The public yearns for a statesman in the White House, for a George Washington or a second "era of good feelings"—anything that might prevent partisanship or politics as usual in the White House. Former French President Charles de Gaulle once said, "I'm neither of the left nor of the right nor of the center, but above." In fact, however, the job of president demands that the officeholder be a gifted political broker, ever attentive to changing political moods and coalitions. . . .

Presidents are often expected to be above politics in some respects while being highly political in others. Presidents are never supposed to act with their eyes on the next election, yet their power position demands they must. They are neither supposed to favor any particular group or party nor wheel and deal and twist too many arms. That's politics and that's bad! Instead, a president is supposed to be "president of all the people," above politics. A president is also asked to lead a party, to help fellow party members get elected or reelected, to deal firmly with party barons, interest group chieftains, and congressional political brokers. His ability to gain legislative victories depends on his skills at party leadership and on the size of his party's congressional membership. Jimmy Carter once lamented that "It's very difficult for someone to serve in this office and meet the difficult issues in a proper and courageous way and still maintain a combination of interest-group approval that will provide a clear majority at election time."

To take the president out of politics is to assume, incorrectly, that a president will be generally right and the public generally wrong, that a president must be protected from the push and shove of political pressures. But what president has always been right? Over the years, public opinion has usually been as sober a guide as anything else on the political waterfront. And, lest we forget, having a president constrained and informed by public opinion is what democracy is all about.

The fallacy of antipolitics presidencies is that only one view of the national interest is tenable, and a president may pursue that view only by ignoring political conflict and pressure. Politics, properly conceived, is the art of accommodating the diversity and variety of public opinion to meet public goals. Politics is the task of building durable coalitions and majorities. It isn't always pretty. "The process isn't immaculate and cannot always be kid-gloved. A president and his men must reward loyalty and punish opposition; it is the only way." . . .

Paradox #5. We want a president who can unify us, yet the job requires taking firm stands, making unpopular or controversial decisions that necessarily upset and divide us.

Closely related to paradox #4, paradox #5 holds that we ask the president to be a national unifier and a *harmonizer* while at the same time the job requires priority setting and *advocacy* leadership. The tasks are near opposites. . . .

Our nation is one of the few in the world that calls on its chief executive to serve as its symbolic, ceremonial head of state *and* as its political head of government. Elsewhere, these tasks are spread around. In some nations there is a monarch and a prime minister; in others there are three visible national leaders—a head of state, a premier, and a powerful party chief.

In the absence of an alternative office or institution, we demand that our president act as a unifying force in our lives. Perhaps it all began with George Washington, who so artfully performed this function. At least for a while he truly was above politics, a unique symbol of our new nation. He was a healer, a unifier, and an extraordinary man for several seasons. Today we ask no less of our presidents than that they should do as Washington did, and more.

We have designed a presidential job description, however, that often forces our contemporary presidents to act as national dividers. Presidents must necessarily divide when they act as the leaders of their political parties, when they set priorities to the advantage of certain goals and groups at the expense of others, when they forge and lead political coalitions, when they move out ahead of public opinion and assume the role of national educators, when they choose one set of advisers over another. A president, as a creative executive leader, cannot help but offend certain interests. When Franklin Roosevelt was running for a second term, some garment workers unfolded a great sign that said, "We love him for the enemies he has made." Such is the fate of a president on an everyday basis; if presidents choose to use power they will lose the goodwill of those who preferred inaction. . . .

Paradox #6. We expect our presidents to provide bold, visionary, innovative, *programmatic* leadership and at the same time to *pragmatically* respond to the will of public opinion majorities; that is to say, we expect presidents to lead and to follow, to exercise "democratic leadership."

We want both pragmatic and programmatic leadership. We want principled leadership and flexible, adaptable leaders. *Lead us*, but also *listen to us.*

Most people can be led only where they want to go. "Authentic leadership," wrote James MacGregor Burns, "is a collective process." It emerges from a sensitivity or appreciation of the motives and goals of both followers and leaders. The test of leadership, according to Burns, "is the realization of intended, real change that meets people's enduring needs." Thus a key function of leadership is "to engage followers, not merely to activate them, to commingle needs and aspirations and goals in a common enterprise, and in the process to make better citizens of both leaders and followers."

We want our presidents to offer leadership, to be architects of the future and to offer visions, plans, and goals. At the same time we want them to stay in close touch with the sentiments of the people. We want a certain amount of innovation, but we resist being led too far in any one direction.

We expect vigorous, innovative leadership when crises occur. Once a crisis is past, however, we frequently treat presidents as if we didn't need or want them around. We do expect presidents to provide us with bold, creative, and forceful initiatives "to move us ahead," but we resist radical new ideas and changes and usually embrace "new" initiatives only after they have achieved some consensus.

Most of our presidents have been conservatives or at best "pragmatic liberals." They have seldom ventured much beyond the crowd. They have followed public opinion rather than shaped it. John F. Kennedy, the author of the much-acclaimed *Profiles in Courage*, was often criticized for presenting more profile than courage. He avoided political risks where possible. Kennedy was fond of pointing out that he had barely won election in 1960 and that great innovations should not be forced on the public by a leader with such a slender mandate. President Kennedy is often credited with encouraging widespread public participation in politics, but he repeatedly reminded Americans that caution is needed, that the important issues are complicated, technical, and best left to the administrative and political experts. Seldom did Kennedy attempt to change the political context in which he operated. Instead he resisted, "the new form of politics emerging with the civil rights movement: mass action, argument on social fundamentals, appeals to considerations of justice and morality. Moving the American political system in such a direction would necessarily have been long range, requiring arduous educational work and promising substantial political risk."

Kennedy, the pragmatist, shied away from such an unpragmatic undertaking. . . .

Paradox #7. Americans want powerful, self-confident presidential leadership. Yet we are inherently suspicious of leaders who are arrogant, infallible, and above criticism.

We unquestionably cherish our three branches of government with their checks and balances and theories of dispersed and separated powers. We want our presidents to be successful and to share their power with their cabinets, Congress, and other "responsible" national leaders. In theory, we oppose the concentration of power, we dislike secrecy, and we resent depending on any one person to provide all of our leadership.

But Americans also yearn for dynamic, aggressive presidents—even if they do cut some corners. We celebrate the gutsy presidents who make a practice of manipulating and pushing Congress. We perceive the great presidents to be those who stretched their legal authority and dominated the other branches of government. It is still Jefferson, Jackson, Lincoln, and the Roosevelts who get top billing. Whatever may have been the framers' intentions for the three branches, most experts now agree that most of the time, especially in crises, our system works best when the presidency is strong and when we have a self-confident, assertive president.

There is, of course, a fine line between confidence and arrogance, between firmness and inflexibility. We want presidents who are not afraid to exert their will, but at what point does this become antidemocratic, even authoritarian? . . .

Paradox #8. What it takes to become president may not be what is needed to govern the nation.

To win a presidential election takes ambition, money, luck, and masterful public relations strategies. It requires the formation of an electoral coalition. To govern a democracy requires much more. It requires the formation of a *governing* coalition, and the ability to compromise and bargain.

"People who win primaries may become good presidents—but 'it ain't necessarily so'" wrote columnist David Broder. "Organizing well is important in governing just as it is in winning primaries. But the Nixon years should teach us that good advance men do not necessarily make trustworthy White House aides. Establishing a government is a little more complicated than having the motorcade run on time."

Ambition (in heavy doses) and stiff-necked determination are essential for a presidential candidate, yet too much of either can be dangerous. A candidate must be bold and energetic, but in excess these characteristics can produce a cold, frenetic candidate. To win the presidency obviously requires a single-mindedness, yet our presidents must also have a sense of proportion, be well-rounded, have a sense of humor, be able to take a joke, and have hobbies and interests outside the realm of politics.

To win the presidency many of our candidates (Lincoln, Kennedy, and Clinton come to mind) had to pose as being more progressive or even populist than they actually felt; to be effective in the job they are compelled to appear more cautious and conservative than they often want to be. One of Carter's political strategists said, "Jimmy campaigned liberal but governed conservative." And as Bill Clinton pointed out toward the end of his first year in office, "We've all become Eisenhower Republicans." . . .

We often also want both a "fresh face," an outsider, as a presidential candidate *and* a seasoned, mature, experienced veteran who knows the corridors of power and the back alleyways of Washington. That's why Colin Powell fascinated so many people. Frustration with past presidential performances leads us to turn to a "fresh new face" uncorrupted by Washington's politics and its "buddy system" (Carter, Reagan, Clinton).

But inexperience, especially in foreign affairs, has sometimes led to blunders by the outsiders. . . .

Paradox #9. The presidency is sometimes too strong, yet other times too weak.

Presidents are granted wide latitude in dealing with events abroad. At times, presidents can act unilaterally, without the express consent of Congress. While the constitutional grounds for such action may be dubious, the climate of expectations allows presidents to act decisively abroad. This being the case, the public comes to think the president can do the same at home. But this is usually not the case. A clashing expectation is built into the presidency when strength in some areas is matched with weakness in other areas.

It often seems that our presidency is *always too strong* and *always too weak.* Always too powerful given our worst fears of tyranny and our ideals of a "government by the people." Always too strong, as well, because it now possesses the capacity to wage nuclear war (a capacity that doesn't permit much in the way of checks and balances and deliberative, participatory government). But always too weak when we remember nuclear proliferation, the rising national debt, the budget deficit, lingering discrimination, poverty, and the clutch of other fundamental problems yet to be solved.

The presidency is always too strong when we dislike the incumbent. Its limitations are bemoaned, however, when we believe the incumbent is striving valiantly to serve the public interest as we define it. The Johnson presidency vividly captured this paradox: many who believed he was too strong in Vietnam also believed he was too weak to wage his War on Poverty. Others believed just the opposite. . . .

Ultimately, being paradoxical does not make the presidency incomprehensible. Can we rid the presidency of all paradoxes? We couldn't, even if we wanted to do so. And anyway, what is wrong with some ambiguity? It is in embracing the paradoxical nature of the American presidency that we may be able to arrive at understanding. And with understanding may come enlightened or constructive criticism. This is the basis for citizen democracy.

36

CRAIG RIMMERMAN

From *The Rise of the Plebiscitary Presidency*

Scholars who examine American presidents look not only at individuals who have held the position but also at trends that mark different interpretations of the office. Here, Professor Craig Rimmerman builds on Theodore Lowi's concept of the "plebiscitary presidency," in which the president seeks to govern through the direct support of the American people. Likewise, citizens view the plebiscitary presidency as the focal point of government activity. Rimmerman believes this view to be vastly different from the Constitution's intent. He traces changes in the executive's power through several phases, mentioning the contributions of prominent scholars to an understanding of the presidency. From Presidents Roosevelt to Bush and to candidate Perot, Rimmerman asks his readers to consider carefully the consequences of such an exalted and unrealistic vision of presidential power.

THE CONSTITUTIONAL framers would undoubtedly be disturbed by the shift to the presidentially centered government that characterizes the modern era. Their fear of monarchy led them to reject the concept of executive popular leadership. Instead, they assumed that the legislative branch would occupy the central policymaking role and would be held more easily accountable through republican government.

Congress has failed, however, to adhere to the framers' intentions and has abdicated its policymaking responsibility. The legislature, with support from the Supreme Court, has been all too willing to promote the illusion of presidential governance by providing the executive with new sources of power, including a highly developed administrative apparatus, and by delegating authority for policy implementation to the executive through vague legislative statutes. . . .

The president-centered government of the modern, plebiscitary era draws much of its power and legitimacy from the popular support of the citizenry, support that is grounded in the development of the rhetorical presidency and the exalted role of the presidency in the American political culture. Theodore Lowi is surely on target when he identifies "the refocusing of mass expectations upon the presidency" as a key problem of presidential governance since Franklin Delano Roosevelt and as a problem associated with the rise of the plebiscitary presidency.

The plebiscitary presidency is characterized by the following: presidential power and legitimacy emanates from citizen support as measured through public opinion polls; in the absence of coherent political parties, presidents forge a direct link to the masses through television; and structural barriers associated with the Madisonian governmental framework make it difficult for presidents to deliver on their policy promises to the citizenry. The framers of the Constitution would hardly have approved of these developments, for they had no intention of establishing a popularly elected monarch. Moreover, the nature of the governmental framework that they created actually prevents occupants of the Oval Office from meeting the heightened citizen expectations associated with the plebiscitary presidency in terms of concrete public policy, especially in the domestic policy arena. This has become particularly clear in the modern era as presidents confront a more fragmented and independent legislature, a decline in the importance of the political party as a governing and coalition-building device, an increase in the power of interest groups and political action committees that foster policy fragmentation, and a bureaucracy that resists centralized coordination. . . .

Throughout much of the nineteenth century, a passive president in domestic policymaking was deemed both acceptable and desirable. Congress took the lead in formulating public policy initiatives and expressed outright hostility toward presidential suggestions that particular legislation should be introduced. In fact, early in the nineteenth century it was commonly believed that the president should not exercise the veto to express policy preferences. The president's primary responsibility was to faithfully execute the laws passed by Congress. For the occupants of the Oval Office in the traditional period, the Constitution imposed "strict limitations on what a President could do." The constitutional separation of powers was taken seriously by all parties, and the prevailing view regarding the proper role of government was "the best government governed least." As opposed to the presidential government of the modern period, the traditional era was characterized by congressional leadership in the policy process.

In the foreign policy arena, however, the president did establish himself through the war-making power. Yet even here the president was restrained when compared to the occupants of the Oval Office in the twentieth century. A prevailing view in the nineteenth century was that the president should avoid involvement with foreign nations, although negotiation with foreign countries was occasionally required. The first president to travel abroad on behalf of the United States was Theodore Roosevelt. Prior to the twentieth century, some members of Congress even argued that the president lacked the necessary legal authority to travel in this manner.

Presidential speechmaking also reflected the largely symbolic chief-of-state roles played by presidents in the traditional era. Jeffrey Tulis's content analysis of presidential speeches reveals that presidents rarely gave the kind of official popular speeches that characterize speech-making in the modern era. When speeches were given, they were considered "unofficial," and they rarely contained policy pronouncements. Tulis concludes that William McKinley's rhetoric was representative of the century as a whole: "Expressions of greeting, inculcations of patriotic sentiment, attempts at building 'harmony' among the regions of the country, and very general, principled statements of policy, usually expressed in terms of the policy's consistency with that president's understanding of republicanism." Virtually all presidents of the time adhered to the same kind of presidential speechmaking. The only exception was Andrew Johnson, who attempted to rally support for his policies in Congress through the use of fiery demagoguery. Johnson's "improper" rhetoric fueled his impeachment charge; yet it is this same kind of rhetoric that today is accepted as "proper" presidential rhetoric.

The reserved role played by the president in the nineteenth century was clearly in keeping with the intention of the constitutional framers. . . .

. . . Yet as the United States headed into its second full century, this situation was to change, as congressional government began to yield to the presidentially centered form of governance that has characterized the modern period.

Students of the presidency have identified a number of factors that have led to the development of the modern, personal, plebiscitary presidency as we know it today. The personal presidency is "an office of tremendous personal power drawn from the people—directly through Congress and the Supreme Court—and based on the new democratic theory that the presidency with all powers is the necessary condition for governing a large, democratic nation. Its development is rooted in changes in presidential rhetoric, the efforts of the progressive reformers of the early twentieth century, the Great Depression and Franklin Delano Roosevelt's New Deal, the role of Congress in granting the executive considerable discretionary power, and Supreme Court decisions throughout the twentieth century that have legitimated the central role that the president should play in the domestic and foreign policy arenas. . . .

Presidential scholars have contributed to the presidentially centered government and the accompanying citizen expectations of presidential performance that characterize the development of presidential power since Franklin Roosevelt. The "cult of the presidency," "textbook presidency," or "savior model" was developed in response to FDR's leadership during the Great Depression, and it prevailed through the presidency of John F. Kennedy. Underlying this "cult" or model approach is a firm commitment to the presidency as a strong office and to the desirability of this condition for the political system as a whole. Political science texts written during this period concluded approvingly that the presidency was growing larger, while gaining more responsibilities and resources. The use of laudatory labels, such as "the Wilson years," "the Roosevelt revolution," "the Eisenhower period," and "the Kennedy Camelot years" also fostered the cult of the presidency and reinforced the notion that the president is the key figure in the American political system. . . .

Perhaps no other work contributed more to the development of this approach that Richard Neustadt's *Presidential Power*, which was first published in 1960. Representing a sharp break with the legalistic and constitutional approach that had dominated presidential scholarship up until that time, *Presidential Power* reinforced the notion that strong presidential leadership should be linked to good government. Neustadt eschewed strict legalistic interpretations of presidential power and instead conceived of power in the following way: "'Power' I defined as personal influence on governmental action. This I distinguished sharply—a novel distinction then—from formal powers vested in the Presidency." For Neustadt, the Franklin Delano Roosevelt activist presidency was the ideal model for presidential leadership and the exercise of power. Future presidents, according to Neustadt, should be evaluated on the basis of how well they achieved the standards set by Roosevelt. Like presidential scholars of his time and many since, Neustadt rejected the framers' view that the Congress should be the chief policymaking branch and that the president should be constrained by numerous checks and balances. Instead, Neustadt spoke of "separated institutions sharing powers."

As Neustadt and other scholars embraced a presidentially centered form of government, they failed to recognize the consequences of imposing a new interpretation of the political order on a governmental framework rooted in Madisonian principles. One such consequence has been that as presidents attempt to meet the heightened expectations associated with the modern presidency, they are sometimes driven to assert presidential prerogative powers in ways that threaten both constitutional and democratic principles. The Johnson and Nixon presidencies, in particular, provided empirical evidence to support this concern. In response, presidential scholars embraced a new model for evaluating presidential power: "the imperial presidency."

Concerns about excessive presidential power were articulated in light of Lyndon Johnson's legislative victories in the 1960s, Johnson's and Nixon's decisionmaking in the Vietnam War, the Nixon/Kissinger Cambodian debacle, and the Nixon presidency's disgrace in the wake of Watergate.* Presidential scholars began to question whether presidential strength would necessarily lead to the promotion of the general welfare. Scholars spoke of the pathological presidency, reinforcing many of the constitutional framers' fears regarding the consequences of concentrating excessive powers in the executive.

Writing in this vein and responding to presidential excesses in the conduct of the Vietnam War and the Watergate scandal, Arthur Schlesinger, Jr., developed the concept of the "imperial presidency." Schlesinger recognized that the system of checks and balances needed vigorous action by one of the three branches if the stalemate built into the system was to be overcome. Schlesinger believed that the presidency was best equipped to fill this role. Rather than rejecting centralized presidential power per se, he spoke of presidential abuses: "In the last years presidential primacy, so indispensable to the political order, has turned into presidential supremacy. The constitutional Presidency—as events so apparently disparate as the Indochina War and the Watergate affair showed—has become the imperial Presidency and threatens to be the revolutionary Presidency." Schlesinger placed much of the blame for the imperial presidency on presidential excesses in foreign policy. . . . Truman, Kennedy, Johnson, and Nixon interpreted the Constitution to permit the president to commit American combat troops unilaterally, and the prolonged Vietnam War encouraged foreign policy centralization and the use of secrecy. The imperial presidency, or "the presidency as satan model," can also be applied to the Nixon administration's domestic activities, including wiretapping, the use of impoundments, executive branch reorganization for political purposes, and expansive interpretations of executive privilege.

Schlesinger's analysis is an important contribution to the study of presidential power because it recognizes the limitations imposed by the framers and the potentially negative consequences of the plebiscitary presidency. . . .

The plebiscitary presidency has been a key source of presidential

*Set in motion by strong presidents, these three episodes—the prolonging of the war in Vietnam, the bombing of Vietnam's neutral neighbor, Cambodia, and a presidential administration's heavy involvement in and coverup of the burglary of the Democratic Party's Watergate Hotel–based election headquarters—all greatly divided the nation.—EDS.

power since 1933. For presidents such as Ford and Carter, however, the heightened expectations associated with the personal, plebiscitary presidency have also led to citizen unhappiness and characterizations of presidential failure. The Carter presidency, in particular, reinforced elements of the plebiscitary presidency. As a "trustee" president, Jimmy Carter reinforced the notion that as the elected representative of all the people, "the president must act as the counterforce to special interests" and provide the leadership necessary in setting the policy agenda and introducing "comprehensive policy proposals." Charles Jones makes a persuasive case that Carter's vision of the trustee presidency was anathema to a Congress that had just passed a series of reforms designed to tame the imperial Nixon presidency. When Carter tried to introduce unpopular energy conservation policies and cut back "unnecessary dams and water projects" because they represented the "worst examples of the pork-barrel," he challenged Congress and the American people to reject politics as usual. In this sense, he was displaying a style of presidential leadership unseen in recent years, one that reinforced the plebiscitary presidency while at the same time challenging some of the assumptions on which it is based. Unlike his immediate predecessors and successors, Carter at least tried to heighten the level of dialogue around resource scarcity concerns. He soon learned, however, that his unwillingness to cultivate congressional support for his policies and his call for a shared sacrifice on the part of the American people undermined the plebiscitary foundations of the modern presidency. His 1980 presidential challenger understood Carter's problems quite well and was determined not to repeat them. Ronald Reagan's campaign and governing strategies accepted and extended the plebiscitary presidency. This helps to account for his victories in both 1980 and 1984. . . .

In the American political system, presidents perform two roles that in other countries are often filled by separate individuals. As head of the nation, the president is required to play a unifying role of the kind played by monarchs in Britain, Norway, and the Netherlands or by presidents in France, Germany, and Austria. In addition, presidents serve as political leaders, "a post held in these other nations by a prime minister or chancellor." This dual role virtually guarantees that American presidents will occupy the central political and cultural role as the chief spokesperson for the American way of life. Political scientists, historians, and journalists have all reinforced and popularized the view that the presidency is an office of overwhelming symbolic importance.

Only recently have political scientists begun to challenge this perspective and discuss the negative consequences of such hero worship in a country that purports to adhere to democratic principles. Barbara Hinckley captures these issues well in her recent analysis:

> It is the magic of symbolism to create illusion. But illusion has costs that must be considered by journalists, teachers of politics, and future presidents. Is the nation best served by carrying on the symbolism or by challenging it? Should the two contradictory pictures, in a kind of schizophrenic fashion, be carried on together? If so, what line should be drawn and what accommodation made between the two? The questions are compounded by the peculiar openness of the office to changing interpretations. By definition, all institutions are shaped by the expectations of relevant actors. The presidency is particularly susceptible to such influence.

As we have seen in our study of the Reagan and Bush presidencies, presidents attempt to build on their symbolic importance to enhance their public opinion ratings and to extend the plebiscitary presidency. The upshot of this activity over the past sixty years is that the public equates the president with the nation and the values associated with American exceptionalism. A president, such as Jimmy Carter, who attempts to challenge traditional elements of presidential symbolism and demystify the trappings of the White House, is treated with disdain by the public, the press, and to a certain extent by political scientists. . . .

This book suggests that Presidents Reagan and Bush turned to foreign policy when they encountered difficulties in translating their domestic campaign promises into concrete public policy and in meeting the demands of the plebiscitary presidency. Presidents who are caught between citizens' expectations and the constraints of the Madisonian policymaking process* look to the foreign policy arena in an effort to promote the values associated with American exceptionalism.

Any of the examples discussed . . . provide ample opportunity to explore these themes. The Iran-Contra affair,† in particular, raises compelling questions regarding presidential power in the foreign policy arena. In light of the aggrandizement of presidential power that characterized the Vietnam War period and Watergate and the resulting congressional response, it is important to ask students why a president and/or his staff would employ some of the same strategies in dealing with Congress, the media, and the American people. The role of covert activities in a democracy also deserves considerable attention.

*James Madison's plan for American government limits each branch by checking and balancing the power of one branch against another.—EDS.

†During President Reagan's administration, members of his National Security Council (NSC) were charged with secretly selling arms to Iran in order to fund anti-communist Nicaraguan Contra activities.—EDS.

If scholars of the presidency are truly concerned with developing a pedagogy and presidential evaluation scheme rooted in critical education for citizenship, then their students must be asked to consider why so little questioning generally occurs regarding the role of the president in committing American troops to war. The Persian Gulf war was a case in point.* It begged for serious discussion, reflection, debate, and questioning about the Bush administration's foreign policy decisionmaking. Some argued that those who dissented from the president's foreign policy strategy were un-American and unpatriotic and were trying to undermine the troops who were already in the Middle East. In fact, if citizens fail to question a president's decisionmaking, then they are giving the president virtually unchecked power to do what he wants with their lives. The failure to question a president abdicates all of the principles of a meaningful and effective democracy and embraces the dictates of an authoritarian and totalitarian regime. This is, of course, the logical consequence of the plebiscitary presidency.

Alexis de Tocqueville spoke of a blind and unreflective patriotism that characterized the American citizenry during the nineteenth century. He would surely see evidence of such patriotism in America today. There is little doubt that such patriotism can be connected to the relationship of the citizenry to the state and the office of the presidency. No modern president can expect to succeed without the support of the public. Yet this support must be grounded in a firm rejection of the unrealistic notion of presidential power. Citizens who respond to the presidency in a highly personalized and reverential manner are likely to be disappointed by presidential performance and are also likely to embrace political passivity and acquiescence in the face of presidential power. In the words of Benjamin Barber, "democratic politics thus becomes a matter of what leaders do, something that citizens watch rather than something they do." As this book has pointed out, Ronald Reagan and George Bush heightened these expectations even further by using techniques that emphasize the plebiscitary, personal character of the modern presidency. Ross Perot's 1992 presidential campaign was firmly rooted in plebiscitary principles. His proposals for nation-wide town meetings and an electronic democracy scheme reflected support for government by plebiscite. To Perot, running

*The Persian Gulf War occurred within a two-month period in early 1991. Backed by House and Senate resolutions of support—not an actual declaration of war—President Bush sent U.S. troops to the Persian Gulf as part of a multination coalition to force Iraqi President Saddam Hussein's military out of Kuwait. The United States experienced quick and dramatic success, with CNN's coverage bringing the war directly to Americans daily. Years later, questions remained about the long-term effectiveness of the military strikes in weakening the Iraqi threat.—EDS.

as an outsider, anti-establishment candidate, such a plan was desperately needed to challenge the gridlock growing out of the Madisonian policy process and two party system. His proposals also enabled him to emphasize his own leadership abilities and claim that he had the necessary leadership and entrepreneurial abilities to break governmental paralysis. In doing so, Perot reinforced the direct line between the presidency and the American people. Any course on the presidency should examine Perot's government-by-plebiscite proposals and the broader implications of his apparent willingness to bypass the congressional policy process and the two party system. The amount of attention and popularity that Perot's campaign garnered in a short period of time suggests once again that the plebiscitary presidency is an important explanatory construct. It also encourages political scientists to study, with renewed vigor, the relationship between the presidency and the citizenry.

For many students, the presidency is the personification of democratic politics and, as a result, monopolizes "the public space." This view impedes the development of the meaningful and effective participation needed by citizens as they attempt to control decisions that affect the quality and direction of their lives. Presidential scholars have been developing a more realistic understanding of the changing sources of presidential power and how individual presidents have used these powers through the years. We would also do well to consider Murray Edelman's claim that "leadership is an expression of the inadequate power of followers in their everyday lives." This is particularly important as we begin to evaluate the Bush presidency. It is also the first step toward challenging the plebiscitary presidency and achieving a more realistic and successful presidency, one that is grounded in principles of democratic accountability and the development of citizenship.

37

CHARLES BLACK

From *Impeachment: A Handbook*

There was a time, not that long ago, in American political history when textbook writers would tell us abstractly about the impeachment process. They would always use as an example the 1868 impeachment of President Andrew Johnson. They had to: It was the only *example. But the past twenty-five years or so have brought two more examples: In 1974, a House of Representatives committee drew up "Articles of Impeachment" against President Richard M. Nixon for his alleged role in the Watergate scandal. In 1999, the House of Representatives voted to impeach President William Jefferson Clinton for several offenses, among them, allegedly lying to a federal grand jury about his relationship with former White House intern Monica Lewinsky. President Nixon resigned from office before the House could take up a vote; the Senate voted against removing President Clinton from office. In this selection, noted constitutional scholar Charles Black offers us a sober and practical approach to understanding and debating the impeachments of two presidents and the near impeachment of another.*

. . . [A] PRESIDENT MAY, in the words of the Constitution, "be removed from Office on Impeachment for, and Conviction of, Treason, Bribery, or other high Crimes and Misdemeanors."

The presidency is a prime symbol of our national unity. The election of the president (with his alternate, the vice-president) is the only political act that we perform together as a nation; voting in the presidential election is certainly the political choice most significant to the American people, and most closely attended to by them. No matter, then, can be of higher political importance than our considering whether, in any given instance, this act of choice is to be undone, and the chosen president dismissed from office in disgrace. Everyone must shrink from this most drastic of measures.

Yet the Framers of our Constitution very clearly envisaged the occasional necessity of this awful step, and laid down a procedure and standards for its being taken. Their actions on this matter were, as the records of their debates show, very carefully considered. As is true, however, of most other parts of their Constitution, they put in place only a very general framework, leaving it to the future to fill in details, and leaving many questions open to honest difference of opinion. . . .

This [presentation] is for the citizen. What part ought the citizen to play in the process of impeachment and removal? My own answer would be that, for the most part, our attitude as to any impeachment ought to be that of vigilant waiting. The impeachment process, whether "judicial," "nonjudicial," "criminal," or "noncriminal," resembles the judicial criminal procedure in that it is confided by the Constitution to responsible tribunals—the House of Representatives and the Senate—and in that these bodies are duty-bound to act on their own views of the law and the facts, as free as may be of partisan political motives and pressures. In this process, a snow of telegrams ought to play no part.

At the same time we cannot, and perhaps ought not try to, keep ourselves free of opinions concerning the process; such views inevitably form themselves as one tries to follow and understand what is going on. In their formation, we ought to try to take the same stance of principled political neutrality that we hope to see taken by the House and the Senate as they go about their work. This is not easy, particularly as to questions that have no certain answers; it is always tempting to resolve such questions in favor of the immediate political result that is palatable to us, for one never can definitely be proved wrong, and so one is free to allow one's prejudices to assume the guise of reason. The best way to combat this tendency is to ask ourselves whether we would have answered the same question the same way if it came up with respect to a president toward whom we felt oppositely from the way we feel toward the president threatened with removal.

One further point: it is the cardinal principle at least of American constitutional interpretation that the Constitution is to be interpreted so as to be workable and reasonable. This principle does not collide with respect for the "intent of the Framers," because their transcendent intent was to build just such a Constitution. American constitutional law, as expounded by judges and others, is full of instances of the application of this principle. Applying it to doubtful questions regarding impeachment, [here] for the laity, I shall give chief emphasis to arguments of a practical cast. Such arguments do not have the fine savor of ancient learning, but they are the ones that usually do prevail in our constitutional law, particularly when it is at its admired best; and they have the advantage that laymen can understand them—in itself not an inconsiderable merit when one is dealing with a constitution meant for all. . . .

The procedures of the House of Representatives and of the Senate are highly technical, but most of this technicality is irrelevant to essential understanding. Let us consider in broad outline the processes of impeachment and removal.

Strictly speaking, "impeachment" means "accusation" or "charge." The House of Representatives has, under the Constitution, the "sole Power of Impeachment"—that is to say, the power to bring *charges* of the commission of one or more impeachable offenses. These charges are conventionally called "Articles of Impeachment." The House "impeaches" by simple majority vote of those present.

The Senate "tries" all impeachments—it determines, on evidence presented, whether the charge in each Article of Impeachment is true, and whether, if the charge is true, the acts that are proven constitute an impeachable offense. Such an affirmative finding is called a "conviction" on the Article of Impeachment being voted upon. A two-thirds majority of the senators present is necessary for conviction. . . .

We come now to the heart of the matter. What offenses are impeachable? The constitutional categories are "Treason, Bribery, and other high Crimes and Misdemeanors."

"Treason" Here we are on smooth ground. The Constitution narrowly defines "treason," in Article III:

> Treason against the United States shall consist only in levying War against them, or in adhering to their Enemies, giving them Aid and Comfort.

There is, in short, no reason to think the word means anything other than this in the impeachment passage. . . .

"Bribery" The first point to be made here is that bribery may mean the *taking* as well as the *giving* of a bribe. At the Constitutional Convention, [Governor] Morris gave the instance of Charles II, who "was bribed by Louis XIV."

As to both the taking and giving of bribes, several cases that have lately been in the spotlight remind us that the *states of mind* of giver and of recipient are all-important. There is nothing wrong with receiving a campaign contribution from dairy interests; there is nothing wrong in raising the price-support on milk. The question is as to the connection between the two events. An old English judge said that "The Devil himself knoweth not the heart of a man." But courts have to try, and continually do try, to work out the truth about intents and motives, for these are often (in bribery cases as elsewhere) of the very essence of the charge.

Is it "bribery" (or attempted "bribery") to suggest to a federal judge, engaged in trying a case crucial to the executive branch, that the directorship of the Federal Bureau of Investigation might be available? It is not wrong to offer a good district judge an important job. Almost all district judges, almost always, have government cases pending before them, in some number. Again, it is *motive* or *intent* that is crucial and that is hard to prove. . . .

"Other high Crimes and Misdemeanors" This is the third, catchall phrase in the formula designating impeachable offenses. The reader will hardly need to be told that it must generate, and has generated, great difficulties of interpretation. Some definite things can be said about its extent, but we will be left with an area of considerable vagueness. Let us take the definite things first.

It would be well to start with the one and only discussion of the phrase at the 1787 Constitutional Convention The day was September 8, 1787, just nine days before the Constitution was signed and transmitted for the adherence of the states. The impeachment provision, as reported out by the last of the convention committees (except the final one charged only with polishing the style of the Constitution), listed "treason and bribery" as the only grounds for impeachment and removal. The colloquy we need to look at was brief, taking perhaps five minutes:

> The clause referring to the Senate, the trial of impeachments agst. the President, for Treason & bribery, was taken up.
>
> Col. Mason. Why is the provision restrained to Treason & bribery only? Treason as defined in the Constitution will not reach many great and dangerous offences. Hastings is not guilty of Treason. Attempts to subvert the Constitution may not be Treason as above defined—As bills of attainder which have saved the British Constitution are forbidden, it is the more necessary to extend: the power of impeachments. He movd. to add after "bribery" "or maladministration". Mr. Gerry seconded him—
>
> Mr Madison So vague a term will be equivalent to a tenure during pleasure of the Senate.
>
> Mr Govr Morris, it will not be put in force & can do no harm—An election of every four years will prevent maladministration.
>
> Col. Mason withdrew "maladministration" & substitutes "other high crimes & misdemeanors" ⟨agst. the State"⟩
>
> On the question thus altered
>
> N. H—ay. Mas. ay—Ct. ay. (N. J. no) Pa no. Del. no. Md ay. Va. ay. N. C. ay. S. C. ay. Geo. ay. [Ayes—8; noes—3.]

This is by far the most important piece of evidence on the original intention with regard to the "other high Crimes and Misdemeanors" phrase. It is true that the proceedings of the Convention were secret (a fact, like the fact that the Supreme Court deliberates in deep secrecy, not often mentioned by those who would have us think that secrecy in public affairs is always wrong). But the men present were representative of their time, and their understanding, at the moment when the crucial language was under closest examination, tells us a great deal about its meaning.

It is interesting first that this passage quite definitely establishes that "maladministration" was distinctly *rejected* as a ground for impeachment. The conscious and deliberate character of this rejection is accentuated by the fact that a good many state constitutions of the time did have "maladministration" as an impeachment ground. This does not mean that a given act may not be an instance *both* of "maladministration" *and* of "high crime" or "misdemeanor." It does mean that not *all* acts of "maladministration" are covered by the phrase actually accepted. This follows inevitably from Madison's ready acceptance of the phraseology now in the text; if "maladministration" was too "vague" for him, and "high Crimes and Misdemeanors" included all "maladministration," then he would surely have objected to the phrase actually accepted, as being even "vaguer" than the one rejected.

On the other hand, Mason's ready substitution of "high Crimes and Misdemeanors" indicates that *he* thought (and no voice was raised in doubt) that this new phrase would satisfactorily cover "many great and dangerous offences" not reached by the words "treason" and "bribery"; its coverage was understood to be broad.

The whole colloquy just quoted seems to support the view that "high Crimes and Misdemeanors" ought to be conceived as offenses having about them some flavor of criminality. Mere "maladministration" was not to be enough for impeachment. This line may be a hard one to follow, but it is the line that the Framers quite clearly intended to draw, and we will have to try to follow it as best we can.

Several other things are to be noted about this colloquy of September 8, 1787. Madison's *reason* for objecting to "maladministration" as a ground was that the inclusion of this phrase would result in the president's holding his office "during pleasure of the Senate." In other words, if mere inefficient administration, or administration that did not accord with Congress's view of good policy, were enough for impeachment and removal, without any flavor of criminality or distinct wrongdoing, impeachment and removal would take on the character of a British parliamentary vote of "no confidence." The September 8 colloquy makes it very plain that this was not wanted, and certainly the phrase "high Crimes and Misdemeanors," whatever its vagueness at the edges, seems absolutely to forbid the removal of a president on the grounds that Congress does not on the whole think his administration of public affairs is good. This distinction may not be easy to draw in every case, but there are vast areas in which it is very clear. And it is perhaps the most important distinction of all, because it tells us—and Congress—that whatever may be the grounds for impeachment and removal, dislike of a president's policy is definitely not one of them, and ought to play *no* part in the decision on impeachment. There is every reason to think that most congressmen and senators are aware of this. . . .

The Relation between Impeachable Offenses and Ordinary Crimes "Treason" and "bribery" are crimes, whether committed by the president or by anyone else. Is the meaning of the phrase "high Crimes and Misdemeanors" limited to ordinary crimes? Can a president lawfully be impeached and removed *only* for conduct which would also be punishable crime for anybody?

Some have contended for this interpretation. It would be easeful to be able to adopt it, because the vague phrase "high Crimes and Misdemeanors" would thus be lent all the precision of the statute book; agonized attempts properly to limit it, while at the same time leaving it properly ample scope, would be avoided. But I cannot think it remotely possible that this interpretation is right.

Suppose a president were to move to Saudi Arabia, so he could have four wives, and were to propose to conduct the office of the presidency by mail and wireless from there. This would not be a crime, provided his passport were in order. Is it possible that such gross and wanton neglect of duty could not be grounds for impeachment and removal?

Suppose a president were to announce that he would under no circumstances appoint any Roman Catholic to office and were rigorously to stick to this plan. I am not sure that this conduct would be punishable as crime, though it would clearly violate the constitutional provision that "no religious test" may ever be required for holding federal office. I cannot believe that it would make any difference whether this conduct was criminal for general purposes; it would clearly be a gross and anticonstitutional abuse of power, going to the life of our national unity, and it would be absurd to think that a president might not properly be removed for it.

Suppose a president were to announce and follow a policy of granting full pardons, in advance of indictment or trial, to all federal agents or police who killed anybody in line of duty, in the District of Columbia, whatever the circumstances and however unnecessary the killing. This would not be a crime, and probably could not be made a crime under the Constitution. But could anybody doubt that such conduct would be impeachable?

These extreme examples test the overall validity of the proposition that impeachable offenses must be ordinary indictable crimes as well, and I think the proposition fails the test. But the rather extravagant character of the illustrations makes another point: most *actual* presidential misdeeds, of a seriousness sufficient to warrant impeachment, are likely to be ordinary crimes as well. It is somewhat strange, indeed, that the question here being examined has assumed such prominence in our days, because most of the wrongful acts that have been seriously charged against an incumbent president are regular crimes—bribery, obstruction of justice, income-tax fraud, and so on—so that, as to these offenses, the issue under discussion here need not arise.

One important exception may be warlike activity. It seems quite possible that military action, unauthorized by Congress and concealed from Congress, might at some point constitute such a murderous and insensate abuse of the commander-in-chief power as to amount to a "high Crime" or "Misdemeanor" for impeachment purposes, though not criminal in the ordinary sense. But . . . precedents of the distant and recent past make it hard to establish knowing wrongfulness in most such cases. And the question, specifically, whether the long-secret 1973 Cambodian bombing could amount to an impeachable offense is complicated by the fact that, on its being revealed, Congress, by postponing until August 15, 1973, the deadline for its ending, would seem to have come close to ratifying it. One is sailing very close to the wind when one says, "You may do it till August 15, but it is an impeachable offense."

To resume the main line of thought here, I would conclude that the limitation of impeachable offenses to those offenses made generally criminal by statute is unwarranted—even absurd. But it remains true that the House of Representatives and the Senate must feel more comfortable when dealing with conduct clearly criminal in the ordinary sense, for as one gets further from that area it becomes progressively more difficult to be certain, as to any particular offense, that it is impeachable.

To turn the coin around, it would be comforting to our desire for certainty to be able to conclude, at least, that all regular crimes are impeachable offenses. But a moment's reflection would show that this, too, would produce absurdities. Suppose a president transported a woman across a state line or even (so the Mann Act reads) from one point to another within the District of Columbia, for what is quaintly called an "immoral purpose." . . . Or suppose the president actively assisted a young White House intern in concealing the latter's possession of three ounces of marijuana—thus himself becoming guilty of "obstruction of justice." Or suppose, to take a real instance, that the presidential ladies' wearing of the Saudi Arabian jewels technically constituted a criminal "conversion" and that the president could be shown to have been an "accomplice." Would it not be preposterous to think that any of this is what the Framers meant when they referred to "Treason, Bribery, and other high Crimes and Misdemeanors," or that any sensible constitutional plan would make a president removable on such grounds?

An Affirmative Approach to the Meaning of "high Crimes and Misdemeanors"

At this point, I think, we have to have recourse to an old and quite sensible rule of legal construction. This rule has, expectably, a Latin name, *"eiusdem generis."* This phrase means "of the same kind," and what the rule *eiusdem generis* says is that, when a general word occurs after a number of specific words, the meaning of the general word ought often to be limited to the *kind* or *class* of things within which the specific words fall. Thus if I said, "Bring me some ice cream, or some candy, or something else good," I would think you had understood me well if you brought me a piece of good angel food cake, I would boggle a little, perhaps, if you brought me a good baked potato, and I would think you crazy or stupid or willful if you brought me a good book of sermons or a good bicycle tire pump.

Like all "rules" of interpretation, this one is not applicable everywhere. But it seems quite naturally to apply to the phrase "Treason, Bribery, or other high Crimes and Misdemeanors," and could help us toward identifying *both* those ordinary crimes which ought also to be looked upon as impeachable offenses, and those serious misdeeds, *not* ordinary crimes, which ought to be looked on as impeachable offenses, though not criminal in the ordinary sense.

The catch in applying this *eiusdem generis* rule is the difficulty (sometimes) of correctly pinning down the "kind" to which the specific items belong. In the present case, however, the "kind" to which "treason" and "bribery" belong is rather readily identifiable. They are offenses (1) which are extremely serious, (2) which in some way corrupt or subvert the political and governmental process, and (3) which are plainly wrong in themselves to a person of honor, or to a good citizen, regardless of words on the statute books.

Now this all may sound unbearably abstract, but this line of thought could solve many problems. Take the string of imagined cases used above to show the absurdity of limiting impeachable offenses to ordinary crimes—the examples of a president's migrating to Saudi Arabia, or of his excluding Roman Catholics from appointment to office, or of his systematically pardoning all government police who kill anybody under any circumstances. Is it not the fact that these are serious assaults on the integrity of the processes of government, obviously wrong to any man of normal good sense, that makes us feel certain they must be impeachable offenses? On the other hand, take the common crimes that I gave as examples of criminal offenses which we would probably not think impeachable—transporting a woman for "immoral purposes," or easing things a bit for [staff] in trouble. If you agree with me that these offenses ought not to be held impeachable, is that not because they are not (as treason and bribery are) serious offenses against the nation or its governmental and political processes, obviously wrong, in themselves, to any person of honor?

Let us test the power of this kind of thought by applying it to a far from fanciful set of facts. Suppose a president were shown by convincing evidence to have used the federal tax system consistently and massively as a means of harassing and punishing his political opponents. As far as I know, this conduct is not criminal in the ordinary sense. But does such gross misuse of what is supposed to be a politically neutral arm of government not tend seriously to undermine and corrupt the political order? Is it not obviously wrong, to any man of ordinary honor? If these questions are answered "yes," then this offense, as lawyers might say, is *eiusdem generis*, of the same kind, with treason and bribery. If it *is* a crime under statute, then it is the kind of ordinary crime that ought to be held impeachable. If it is *not* a crime under statute, then it is the kind of offense which ought to be held impeachable, though not criminal in the ordinary sense. In both cases, this is because such an offense is, in the relevant ways, of the same kind as treason and bribery.

This rule will not work all the way; rules of interpretation rarely do. But the one obvious exception may be more apparent than real. Many common crimes—willful murder, for example—though not subversive of government or political order, might be so serious as to make a president simply unviable as a national leader; I cannot think that a president who had committed murder could not be removed by impeachment. But the underlying reason remains much the same; such crimes would so stain a president as to make his continuance in office dangerous to public order. Indeed, it may be this *prospective* tainting of the presidency that caused even treason and bribery to be made impeachable. So far as *punishment* goes, we could punish a traitorous or corrupt president after his term expired; we *remove* him principally because we fear he will do it again, or because a traitor or the taker of a bribe is not thinkable as a national leader.

Now this has been a long pull, but we have our hands on a good first approximation to a rational definition of an impeachable "high Crime or Misdemeanor." Omitting qualifications, and recognizing that the definition is only an approximation, I think we can say that "high Crimes and Misdemeanors," in the constitutional sense, ought to be held to be those offenses which are rather obviously wrong, whether or not "criminal," and which so seriously threaten the order of political society as to make pestilent and dangerous the continuance in power of their perpetrator. The fact that such an act is also criminal helps, even if it is not essential, because a general societal view of wrongness, and sometimes of seriousness, is, in such a case, publicly and authoritatively recorded.

The phrase "high Crimes and Misdemeanors" carries another connotation—that of *distinctness of offense.* It seems that a charge of high crime or high misdemeanor ought to be a charge of a definite act or acts, each of which in itself satisfies the above requirements. General lowness and shabbiness ought not to be enough. The people take some chances when they elect a man to the presidency, and I think this is one of them. . . .

PART SEVEN

The Executive Branch

38

HUGH HECLO

From *A Government of Strangers*

To understand Hugh Heclo's intricate analysis of power inside the executive branch, students of American government must first know who the players are. Presidents select a small number (a few thousand) of high-level people to head the executive branch agencies. Among those appointments are cabinet secretaries, undersecretaries, assistant secretaries, and the like. The rest of those who work in the executive branch are civil servants, chosen for government jobs by merit exams, and they remain in government service for many years, even decades. They are the bureaucrats who provide continuity. Appointees come and go—as do presidents—but bureaucrats remain. Heclo identifies the often-unseen tension between a president's appointees and the bureaucrats. Be sure to pay particular attention to his discussion of the "iron triangle," one of the most interesting yet invisible forces in American government.

EVERY NEW ADMINISTRATION gives fresh impetus to an age-old struggle between change and continuity, between political leadership and bureaucratic power. Bureaucrats have a legitimate interest in maintaining the integrity of government programs and organizations. Political executives are supposed to have a broader responsibility: to guide rather than merely reflect the sum of special interests at work in the executive branch.

The search for effective political leadership in a bureaucracy of responsible career officials has become extraordinarily difficult in Washington. In every new crop of political appointees, some will have had government experience and a few will have worked together, but when it comes to group commitment to political leadership in the executive branch they constitute a government of strangers. And yet the fact remains that whether the President relies mainly on his White House aides or on his cabinet officials, someone is supposed to be mastering the bureaucracy "out there." For the President, his appointees, and high-ranking bureaucrats, the struggle to control the bureaucracy is usually a leap into the dark.

Despite a host of management and organization studies, Washington exposés and critiques of bureaucracy, very little information is available about the working world and everyday conduct of the top people in government. Even less is known about the operational lessons that could be drawn from their experiences. Congress is widely thought to have lost power to the executive branch, but congressional rather than executive behavior remains a major preoccupation in political research. Observers acknowledge that no president can cope with more than a tiny fraction of the decisionmaking in government, yet we know far more about a president's daily social errands than about the way vital public business is conducted by hundreds of political appointees and several thousand top bureaucrats who take executive actions in the name of the United States government—which is to say, in the name of us all. . . .

If popular impressions are any guide, few job titles are more suspect than "politician" and "bureaucrat." Periodic polls have shown that while most parents might want their offspring to become president, they dislike the notion of their becoming politicians. No pollster has dared to ask Americans what they would think of their children growing up to become Washington bureaucrats.

Yet in many ways the American form of government depends not only on a supply of able politicians and bureaucrats, but even more on a successful interaction between these two unpopular groups. . . .

. . . The administrative machinery in Washington represents a number of fragmented power centers rather than a set of subordinate units under the President. As many observers have noted, the cracks of fragmentation are not random but run along a number of well-established functional specialties and program interests that link particular government bureaus, congressional committees, and interest groups. People in the White House are aware of these subgovernments but have no obvious control over them. They seem to persist regardless of government reorganizations or, perhaps more to the point, they are able to prevent the reorganizations that displease them. In coping with these Washington subgovernments, the real lines of defense and accommodation are out in the departments, with their mundane operations of personnel actions, program approval, budget requests, regulation writing, and all the rest. These are the unglamorous tools with which political leaders in the agencies either help create a broader approach to the conduct of the public's business or acquiesce to the prevailing interest in business as usual. . . .

. . . Political executives who try to exercise leadership within government may encounter intense opposition that they can neither avoid nor reconcile. At such times some agency officials may try to undermine the efforts of political executives. Any number of reasons—some deplorable, some commendable—lie behind such bureaucratic opposition. Executive politics involves people, and certain individuals simply dislike each other and resort to personal vendettas. Many, however, sincerely believe in their bureau's purpose and feel they must protect its jurisdiction, programs, and budget at all costs. Others feel they have an obligation to "blow the whistle" as best they can when confronted with evidence of what they regard as improper conduct. In all these cases the result is likely to strike a political executive as bureaucratic subversion. To the officials, it is a question of higher loyalty, whether to one's self-interests, organization, or conscience.

The structure of most bureaucratic sabotage has been characterized as an "iron triangle" uniting a particular government bureau, its relevant interest group, and congressional supporters. The aims may be as narrow as individual profiteering and empire-building. Or they may be as magnanimous as "public interest" lobbies, reformist bureaucrats, and congressional crusaders all claiming somewhat incongruously to represent the unrepresented. There are alliances with fully developed shapes (e.g., the congressional sponsors of a program, the bureaucrats executing it, and its private clients or suppliers) and those made up of only a few diverse lines (e.g., a civil servant looking forward to post-retirement prospects with a particular lobby association or a congressman unconcerned about a bureaucrat's policy aims but aware that his specific favors can help win reelection). Some bureaucratic entrepreneurs initiate their own outside contacts; others have been pushed into becoming involved in outside alliances by former political appointees.

The common features of these subgovernments are enduring mutual interests across the executive and legislative branches and between the public and private sectors. However high-minded the ultimate purpose, the immediate aim of each alliance is to become "self-sustaining in control of power in its own sphere." The longer an agency's tradition of independence, the greater the political controversy surrounding its subject matter, and the more it is allied with outside groups, the more a new appointee can expect sub rosa opposition to develop to any proposed changes. If political leadership in the executive branch is to be more than the accidental sum of these alliances and if political representation is to be less arbitrary than the demands of any group that claims to speak for the unrepresented, then some conflict seems inevitable between higher political leaders and the subgovernments operating within their sphere.

Often sabotage is unrecognizable because of the virtually invisible ways civil servants can act in bad faith toward political executives. In addition to the bureaucracy's power of withholding needed information and services, there are other means. Like a long-married couple, bureaucrats and those in their networks can often communicate with a minimum of words: "If congressional staffs I trust call up and ask me, I might tell them. But I can also tell them I don't agree with the secretary by offering just technical information and not associating myself with the policy."

An official who does not want to risk direct dealings with Congress can encourage a private interest group to go to the agency's important appropriations and legislative committees, as one political executive discovered: "When we tried to downgrade the . . . bureau, its head was opposed, and he had a friend in a lobby group. After they got together rumblings started from the appropriations committee. I asked [the committee chairman] if he had a problem with this reorganization, and he said, 'No, you have the problem because if you touch that bureau I'll cut your job out of the budget.'" An experienced bureaucrat may not be able to make the decision, but he can try to arrange things to create the reaction he wants. "A colleague of mine," said a supergrade,* "keeps a file on field offices that can be abolished and their political sensitivity. Depending on who's pressing for cuts, he'll pull out those that are politically the worst for that particular configuration." The everyday relationships between people with specialized interests can shade effortlessly into subversion: "You know what it's like," said a bureau chief. "You've known each other and will have a drink complaining about what's happening and work up some little strategy of your own to do something about it." Or bureaucrats can work to get their way simply by not trying to know what is happening. One assistant secretary reported how his career subordinates agreed there might be mismanagement in the regional offices, "but they also said they didn't know what these offices were doing and so there wasn't enough information to justify doing what I wanted." Ignorance may not be bliss, but it can be security.

Political appointees can sometimes encounter much more vigorous forms of sabotage. These range from minor needling to massive retaliation. Since information is a prime strategic resource in Washington, the passing of unauthorized messages outside channels often approaches an art form. There are routine leaks to build credit and keep channels open for when they might be needed, positive leaks to promote something, negative leaks to discredit a person or policy, and counterleaks. There is even the daring reverse leak, an unauthorized release of information apparently for one reason but actually accomplishing the opposite.†

There is no lack of examples in every administration. A political

*Though not an official title, a "supergrade" would be a government civil servant in the upper levels of the bureaucracy.—EDS.

†One recent example involved a presidential assistant rather than a bureaucrat. While jockeying with another staff member, the assistant leaked a disclosure of his own impending removal from the West Wing. The opponent, who obviously stood the most to gain from

executive may discover that an agency subordinate "has gone to Congress and actually written the rider to the legislation that nullified the changes we wanted." A saboteur confided that "no one ever found it was [a division chief] who prepared the list showing which lobbyist was to contact which senator with what kind of argument." Still another official reported he had "seen appointees kept waiting in the outer office while their subordinate bureau officials were in private meetings with the congressional staff members." But waiting lines lack finesse. The telephone can be used with more delicacy, particularly after office hours: "The night before the hearings [a bureaucrat] fed the questions to the committee staff and then the agency witnesses spent the next two days having to reveal the information or duck the questions and catch hell." A young staff civil servant described how his superior operated:

> I used to sit in [the bureau chief's] office after 6 P.M. when all the important business got done. He'd call up a senator and say, "Tom, you know this program that you and I got through a while back? Well, there's no crisis, but here are some things I'd like to talk to you about." He'd hang up and get on the phone to [a House committee chairman] and say, "I've been talking with Tom about this issue, and I'd like to bring you in on it." Hell, you'd find [the bureau chief] had bills almost drafted before anybody else in the executive branch had ever heard about them.

Encountering such situations, a public executive becomes acutely aware that experience as a private manager provides scant guidance. As one corporate executive with a six-figure salary said, "The end-runs and preselling were incredible. To find an equivalent you'd have to imagine some of your division managers going to the executive board or a major stockholder behind your back." Learning to deal with sabotage is a function of an executive's political leadership, not his private management expertise.

How do political executives try to deal with bureaucratic sabotage? . . . One approach is simply to ignore bureaucratic sabotage. Since the damage that may be done can easily cripple an executive's aims, diminish his reputation, and threaten his circles of confidence, those adopting this strategy can be presumed to have abdicated any attempt at political leadership in the Washington bureaucracy.

A second approach, especially favored by forceful managers, is to try to root out the leakers and prevent any recurrence. But political executives

---

the story, was naturally asked to confirm or deny the report. Since he was not yet strong enough to accomplish such a removal, the opponent had to deny responsibility for the leak and its accuracy, thereby inadvertently strengthening the position of the presidential assistant who first leaked the story.

usually discover that this straightforward approach has considerable disadvantages. For one thing, it is extremely time-consuming and difficult to actually investigate acts of subversion and pin down blame. For another thing, there are few effective sanctions to prevent recurrences. Moreover, a search for the guilty party can easily displace more positive efforts and leadership initiatives an executive needs to make in dealing with the bureaucracy. Even if it were possible, trying to censor bureaucratic contacts would probably restrict the informal help these outside relationships provide, as well as the harm they do. And in the end any serious sabotage will probably be buttressed by some mandate from Congress; punishing the saboteurs can be seen as an assault on legislative prerogatives and thus invite even sterner retribution. It is circumstances such as these that led an experienced undersecretary to conclude:

> Of course you can't be a patsy, but by and large you've got to recognize that leaks and end-runs are going to happen. You can spend all your time at trying to find out who's doing it, and if you do, then what? [One of my colleagues] actually tried to stop some of his bureaucrats from accepting phone calls from the press. They did stop accepting the calls, but they sure as hell returned them quickly. In this town there are going to be people running behind your back, and there's not much you can do to stop it.

However, while academics write about the iron triangle as if it were an immutable force, prudent political executives recognize that although they cannot stop bureaucratic sabotage, neither are they helpless against it. They can use personnel sanctions where misconduct can be clearly proven. But far more important, they can work to counteract sabotage with their own efforts—strengthening their outside contacts, extending their own lines of information and competitive analysis, finding new points of countertension. In general, experienced political executives try to use all their means of self-help and working relations so as to reshape the iron triangles into more plastic polygons.

To deal with sabotage, wise political appointees try to render it more obvious:

> I make it clear that all the information and papers are supposed to move through me. It increases your work load tremendously, and maybe you don't understand everything you see, but everyone knows I'm supposed to be in on things and that they are accepting risks by acting otherwise.

They try to counteract unwanted messages with their own accounts to the press and others. The more the agency's boat is leaking, "the more you go out and work the pumps. You can't plug all the leaks, but you can make sure to get your side of the story out."

Political executives also make use of timing to deal with sabotage:

> I put in a one-year fudge factor for an important change. That's because I know people are going to be doing end-runs to Congress. This year lets congressmen blow off steam, and for another thing it shows me where the sensitive spots are so l can get busy trying to work out some compromises—you know, things that can serve the congressmen's interest as well as mine.

Substantial results can be achieved by bringing new forces into play, dealing not with just one alliance but creating tests of strengths among the triangles:

> It's like when officials were getting together with the unions and state administrators to get at some committee chairman. I hustled out to line up governors and show the congressmen that state administrators weren't speaking for all of state government.

Washington offers more opportunities to search for allies than is suggested by any simple image of political executives on one side and bureaucratic opponents on the other. Political appointees may be "back-doored" by other appointees, higher bureaucrats by lower bureaucrats. Fights may be extended to involve some appointees and bureaucrats versus others. As the leader of one faction put it, "Often a guy preselling things on the Hill is hurting people elsewhere, making it tougher for them to get money and approval and straining their relations. I use this fact to get allies."

A political executive who works hard at outside contacts will discover what subversives may learn too late: that many groups are fickle allies of the bureaucracy. This has seemed especially true as Congress has increased its own bureaucracy of uncoordinated staffs. A veteran bureaucrat described the risks run by would-be saboteurs:

> Everybody you might talk to weighs the value of the issue to them against the value of keeping you alive for the next time. I've seen [a congressman] ruin many a good civil servant by getting a relationship going with him and then dropping him to score points off the agency brass. Now, too, there are more Hill staffers running around telling appointees, "Hey, these guys from your department said this and that. How about it?" Then the appointee will go back to the agency and raise hell for the bureaucrat.

Thus the political executives' own positive efforts are the necessary—if not always a sufficient—condition for combating sabotage. Since some bureaucratic subversion is an ever-present possibility and since punishment is difficult, the government executives' real choice is to build and use their political relationships or forfeit most other strategic resources for leadership.

39

JOSEPH CALIFANO

From *Governing America*

While nearly twenty years have passed since the events related by former secretary of HEW (Health, Education and Welfare, now Health and Human Services), Joseph Califano, his personal account of life as part of President Jimmy Carter's administration remains fresh. Califano gives an insider's view of the transition period after Carter's election, before he took office. Staff problems that would later haunt Carter were already apparent. Califano observed how dramatically "Carter's face was graying and aging" over the course of his term, a phenomenon that all Americans could see. Conflict with Senator Ted Kennedy, the American hostages in Iran, and high inflation all contributed. Califano then chronicles his famous anti-smoking campaign that was eventually abandoned in the face of outside pressure. On the last page, Califano gives readers a rare and touching glimpse into a revealing moment. Take careful note of the Rose Garden, the peregrine falcon reference, and the way a president dismisses a cabinet member he had appointed with the advice and consent of the Senate.

MY FIRST impressions of Jimmy Carter's presidential style came at Sea Island, Georgia, during his initial meetings with the Cabinet over the 1976 Christmas holidays. The Cabinet stayed at the Cloister, a luxury resort; the Carters at the nearby Musgrove Plantation of R. J. Reynolds Tobacco heir Smith Bagley on St. Simons Island ten minutes away. During those early days, I was struck by the ostentatiously nonpresidential ambience of both the new President and his associates. Carter brandished informalities and religion. He slouched in a sweater and jeans, spoke softly, constantly appearing to defer to comments by members of the new Cabinet, especially Cyrus Vance. He prayed before meals, exuded fundamentalist intensity, invoked the name of God frequently. In each of our rooms when we arrived at the Cloister was a small book of religious poems written by LaBelle Lance, the wife of his friend Bert, who had been named Director of the Office of Management and Budget. I attributed much of this to Carter's born-again Baptist beliefs, and suppressed my Northeastern Catholic discomfort at such public displays of fundamentalist religion.

Again and again he stressed "ethics" and the importance of avoiding conflicts of interest. He wanted us publicly to reveal information about our holdings and earnings, to set up blind trusts over which we had no control. Carter put his White House counsel Robert Lipshutz in charge. I proposed Stanford Ross, a friend and personal attorney, as my blind trustee. Lipshutz checked with Carter and told me that Ross was too close; I had to get someone independent. I, therefore, asked a casual acquaintance, Republican Peter Peterson, Chairman of Lehman Brothers Kuhn Loeb, who had been Secretary of Commerce in the Nixon administration, to be my blind trustee. When Carter ultimately selected his intimate friend and advisor Charles Kirbo to be his, I began to suspect that much of what was going on was for public consumption.

The odor of naïveté perfumed those two days off the coast of Georgia. The new President evidenced little sense of what Washington was like or of the complexities of governing. Except for Stuart Eizenstat, who had been a junior aide under Johnson and had worked on Hubert Humphrey's 1968 presidential campaign, and Jack Watson, who had conducted a wide-ranging transition study, Carter's staff seemed naïve to a fault and appeared to believe the anti-Washington rhetoric that had carried Carter to the White House.

In the meetings, Carter spoke sincerely of his desire to use his presidency "for good," to restore the confidence of the people in their government, to "give them an administration as good as they are," to fulfill his campaign commitments, and to "maintain a close and intimate relationship with the voters." Hamilton Jordan worked at being the country boy from Georgia, wearing work boots, affecting boredom during much of the discussions. Jody Powell was disingenuously deferential, calling each Cabinet member Mister or Madame Secretary. Watson, the only Carter staffer with whom I had discussed organizing the government, was subdued, giving some validity to news reports that he was having his wings clipped by Jordan; Eizenstat was quiet and serious. As I sat at the meetings, I thought that Watson and Eizenstat would have to provide Carter his substantive staff advice. Bert Lance, who had been Carter's Georgia Highway Commissioner and banker, was charming, but displayed neither the personality, depth, nor motivation required to be OMB Director, and the others close to the President evidenced little interest in governing. . . .

Carter disliked the political aspects of the personnel process. At a Cabinet meeting early in the administration, he complained about the Congress, expressing his "disgust," particularly about House members. "I try to talk to them about substantive problems, like the energy program, and all they want to talk about is whether or not they can get their buddies appointed to some regional job in HUD [Housing and Urban Development] or HEW [Health, Education and Welfare]." His attitude infuriated some key House members. . . .

Carter's disdain of the political aspects of the appointment process sharply contrasted with the enthusiasm of Lyndon Johnson, who truly enjoyed this political give-and-take with the Congress. To him, the politics of personnel appointments were a key part of governing. He would ponder moves with the concentration of a chess master. He was interested in talent, but where he could combine that with a vote on a bill or a commitment to fund a program, he would. Indeed, Johnson would often tell a candidate he had already selected in his own mind to get some senators, congressmen, and interest groups to support his or her appointment. When the candidate did, Johnson would announce the selection, calling the supporters to say he had appointed their person. Months later, when the appointee took some action (often at Johnson's direction) that offended a group that supported him, he would say, "Hell, he's your man. You told me to appoint him." . . .

From the moment Edward M. Kennedy began questioning me about health policy during my confirmation hearing before the Senate Labor and Public Welfare Committee, I knew that national health insurance was going to be a major issue for him, for Carter, and for me. . . . I thought about Lyndon Johnson and Robert Kennedy, and about the inevitable problem any Democratic President would have with the last Kennedy brother in the Senate.

Carter's personality is very different from Johnson's. Carter is inner-directed, more like Nixon in his shyness and desire to be alone. Johnson was consumingly extroverted. He wanted company from the moment he rose in the morning until he fell asleep reading memos and talking to an aide with a masseur kneading his back. But Carter nurtured the same resentment of the liberal, Eastern establishment as Johnson, and no person could suffer the exhausting indignities of running for President without a monumental ego and enormous self-confidence, however disguised by the image-makers who told him to carry his own suitcase.

I knew how Johnson had felt about Robert Kennedy and how some of his feelings had spilled over on Ted Kennedy near the end of his presidency in late 1968. Carter was not immune to the same feelings. I thought it was only a matter of time before Carter and Edward Kennedy became a redux of Johnson and Robert Kennedy. Only this time, I thought, national health insurance will be a crucial issue, and Califano will be the rope for the tug of war. . . .

The political chances for Carter and Kennedy to agree on a national health plan were never good, given Kennedy's ambition, his tenacious staff, and the media's great interest in reading presidential aspirations into the slightest movement of a potential challenger. Moreover, Carter was going to be as combative as Kennedy. He suspected that Kennedy might be his opponent for the 1980 nomination. Annoyed once by a Kennedy comment that he was "indefinite and imprecise on the critical issues" during the 1976 campaign, Carter remarked privately, "I'm glad I don't have to depend on Kennedy or people like that to put me in office. I don't have to kiss his ass." . . .

That June 1 meeting lasted more than two hours. Carter opened by noting that he found "a paradox, an anomaly" in his situation. "I have already made a number of commitments—during my campaign and subsequently to the UAW [United Auto Workers] and to Senator Kennedy. At the same time, there appears to be no significant additional money for health care available in the budget in the next few years and I will not do anything to undermine my current effort to control inflation."

As he spoke, it struck me forcibly how Carter's face was graying and aging. What a toll this job takes on a human being, I thought. And meetings like this told why. He had a tough decision to make. "I am inclined to do what I've done in the past, to tell the American people the truth and lay out the problem." He talked about health system problems and concluded, "I don't believe a comprehensive program can possibly be passed this year. It is unlikely even next year. But there are some important advantages to be gained by discussing the problem and the issue openly." . . .

"It is ridiculous to think about endorsing a bill like Kennedy's. I am not going to destroy my credibility on inflation and budgetary matters. I intend to be honest and responsible with the American people." Carter did "not simply view this as a matter of accommodating particular political pressure groups." It was more "a question of what we get for different expenditures." He urged me to get on with drafting the principles and observed as he rose to leave the Cabinet Room, "We are still in a quandary as to how to proceed."

For the first time, I felt that Carter might abandon his commitment to a comprehensive plan, and with it the chance to achieve significant reform of the health system. The larger responsibilities of the presidency—to fight inflation particularly, but also as party leader to Democratic House members running for re-election in a conservative year—were weighing heavily on him. Unlike Kennedy, the President had to be an advocate of more than a single cause, however worthy. . . .

When I was designated Secretary, I had never thought about smoking as a serious health issue, within my responsibility (although I had quit smoking on October 21, 1975). When President-elect Carter told me at St. Simons Island in December 1976 that he wanted to move forcefully in the area of preventive care, I began to read and question experts about such programs. Invariably, they suggested a major anti-smoking campaign as a critical element of any such effort. . . .

Most of Washington closed down during the Christmas holidays, but not the Tobacco Institute. Institute lobbyists made several attempts to obtain a copy of my speech announcing the anti-smoking program. . . .

Tobacco politics is a hardball game. At my invitation, Pennsylvania Democratic Congressman Fred Rooney's wife, Evie Rooney, who quit smoking during the same Smokenders session I attended, sat on the stage during my speech. When a Tobacco Institute lobbyist saw her, he told her husband that he would never get another dollar from the industry. Rooney, who had received campaign contributions of several thousand dollars from tobacco interests over many years, got no contribution for his losing 1978 campaign. Governor Jim Hunt of North Carolina said that I should travel to his state to meet with some farmers to learn what tobacco meant to the state; North Carolina Democratic Congressman Charlie Rose said, "We're going to have to educate Mr. Califano with a two-by-four, not a trip." . . .

The political fallout from the anti-smoking effort was intense. The tobacco industry financed bumper stickers announcing "Califano is Dangerous to My Health," and there were highway billboards saying, "Califano Blows Smoke." The White House staff judged the program politically too dangerous. As always when criticizing a member of the Cabinet, the White House staff spoke anonymously, charging I had mounted the campaign without getting "political clearance" or "thinking through the political details." A "high-ranking White House aide" said "With all the problems Carter has in North Carolina [a reference to the court order to desegregate its higher education system that HEW was enforcing], he doesn't need an anti-smoking campaign." . . .

In early August 1978, Carter made his second of three trips to North Carolina in six months. He visited a tobacco warehouse in Wilson and spoke at a Democratic Party rally. At first the President kidded the audience about me: "I had planned today to bring Joe Califano with me, but he decided not to come. He discovered that not only is North Carolina the number-one tobacco-producing state, but that you produce more bricks than anyone in the nation as well." The crowd responded with applause mixed with laughter. "Joe Califano did encourage me to come though.

He said it was time for the White House staff to start smoking something regular," an allusion to rumors of pot smoking by some members of the President's staff. The crowd loved it. The President then told the audience his family had grown tobacco in North Carolina before moving to Georgia to grow peanuts. The health program the President described, however, was hardly HEW's. As he put it, we would conduct a research plan "to make the smoking of tobacco even more safe than it is today."

When the normally mild-mannered Surgeon General Julius Richmond heard that, he immediately called me. "This is terrible. The President is either terribly ill-informed or cynically political about this." These were strong words from the most soft-spoken member of the HEW team. I told him there was nothing we could do at the moment without further embarrassing the President. . . .

The new report of the Surgeon General on Smoking and Health was scheduled for release on Thursday, January 11, 1979. The massive, three-inch-thick book concluded that the case against cigarette smoking was "overwhelming." Indeed, the accumulation of evidence against cigarette smoking was so devastating, and the interest of government as the largest purchaser of health care so profound, that I decided to mount new and more extensive education efforts around its release. . . .

On the eve of the report's release, Jody Powell called me from National Airport in Washington. "I'm headed for North Carolina to do a Democratic fundraiser tonight. Is there anything to bring me up to date on?"

"My God," I exclaimed, and told him about the release of the Surgeon General's report and the media blitz that was coming. "I don't know what you can do," I concluded.

"Smoke," Powell replied. "I'll just smoke like hell when I'm down there." . . .

For the President, there was one unfortunate aspect of the television coverage. After reporting the case against cigarette smoking, the three networks showed footage of Carter amidst the tobacco leaves in the Wilson, North Carolina, warehouse, talking about making smoking "even more safe." After viewing the broadcasts, Vice-President Mondale, who never lost his wry sense of humor, called me. "Jeez," he said, "those guys in the White House really have it positioned—the President's for cancer and you're for health." . . .

The anti-smoking campaign generated more political opposition than any other effort I undertook at HEW. House Speaker Tip O'Neill told me in late 1978, "You're driving the tobacco people crazy. These guys are vicious. They're out to destroy you." In April 1979, Ted Kennedy told me, "You've got to get out of the Cabinet before the election. The President can't run in North Carolina with you at HEW. He's going to have to get rid of you." . . .

The early months of the Carter administration were charged with hope and expectation, but the anticipated political honeymoon never took shape and the innocence of Carter and his closest aides about governing and Washington provided cause for misgivings. The new President did wade into some tough problems—energy, SALT II, the Panama Canal Treaties, the Middle East, the Third World, welfare and tax reform—and at first his willingness to take them on was itself enough, a refreshing change from the laid-back presidency of Gerald Ford.

Carter also seemed determined to change the ambience of the federal government: to reorganize the bureaucracy more efficiently, reduce paperwork, eliminate irritating and unnecessary regulations, make those who sign regulations read every word of them, get rid of perks such as cars and chauffeurs. He intended to honor all his campaign commitments and the White House staff compiled a book dubbed "Promises, Promises" to keep them on the front burner.

Carter was bent on mastering every detail, and as his reading load increased, he and Rosalynn took a speed reading course on Tuesday nights at the White House and invited any interested members of the Cabinet to join them. Lyndon Johnson would have said, "Put a welfare reform program together that gives poor people some money and encourages people to work and keep their families together," and left all but the key policy and political judgments to his staff. Carter read hundreds of pages of material on welfare programs and did almost everything but draft the legislation. He displayed the same fervor for total immersion in energy, the African subcontinent, tax reform, and SALT II. In addition to being President, he was, as an HEW staffer remarked after one of my welfare reform briefings, the highest paid assistant secretary for planning that ever put a reform proposal together. . . .

As his first year in office ended, Carter was in trouble as both executive and leader. His administration lacked cohesion. The Office of Management and Budget and its new Director, James McIntyre, floundered along a conservative course while Eizenstat and the Domestic Policy Council steered toward a liberal one. Zbigniew Brzezinski sniped at Cyrus Vance in the press, and Jordan and Powell continued to cut up several Cabinet members anonymously, Mike Blumenthal being their favorite target. Most Cabinet officers and department heads tried to read what Carter wanted and sought to serve him and his administration, each in his own way. Excepting Stu Eizenstat and Jack Watson, they had little respect for the

Carter staff and no clear sense of where the President was leading them. At the same time, there was a real decline in public confidence. You could measure it not only by polls, but every time we left Washington people were anxious to tell us about it. Political leaders around the country had begun to ridicule the "governor from Georgia." "The job is too big for him," was what most business and labor leaders told us.

Things were even worse on Capitol Hill. House Speaker Tip O'Neill had been insulted by the arrogance of the Georgians in the early days. Ineptness in handling appointments and making announcements, in introducing and pushing legislation had alienated many key Democrats. The administration's initiatives were failing. . . .

The administration's situation continued to sour, Cabinet officers began to question the value of the weekly meetings, and self-interested leaks and internecine back-biting increased. The President gave the first indication of a desire to do something at a Cabinet meeting on April 10, 1978. He wanted the Cabinet to come to Camp David the next weekend to "think long-range about problems among ourselves, to express criticism freely about the relationship between the White House and your own departments." At last, Carter seemed ready to acknowledge a serious problem in Cabinet–White House staff relations. The number of articles—based on anonymous White House sources—critical of the Cabinet had continued to accumulate. . . .

The senior White House staff arrived at Camp David early on Sunday afternoon, April 16. . . .

Carter paused before turning to internal difficulties. "The problems that we do have I attribute primarily to the White House. Some leaks from the White House are inexcusable—derogatory remarks about Mike [Blumenthal] or Pat [Harris] or Brock [Adams]. If I could find one who did it, I would kick his ass out of the White House." I was incredulous. By now I suspected he had ordered or at least condoned much of it. My God, there is some Elmer Gantry in this born-again President, I thought. Carter then turned briefly to self-criticism. "We have a lack of Washington experience. We need to learn more. . . .

Carter then turned to Hamilton Jordan, who replied, "The mood of the country is passive and nonpartisan. Americans want better government, not more government. That is why Carter was elected. The people do not want more programs." He said there was "no party loyalty, no discipline within the Congress." The administration was dealing with 535 members, and thirty or forty interest groups within the Congress itself, as well as "dozens and dozens" of other pressure groups. "We are not tough; we are not in charge; we are not managing the mechanisms of government.

If this persists for three or four months, it will be irreversible. The worse thing is for [the Congress] to lose respect for us as politicians. We do not know how to use our resources politically—no rewards, no retributions. We need a system for doing better." He described himself "as basically an optimist," but said, "We must move in the next four or five months or we cannot govern. We need successes." . . .

Carter, looking suddenly tired, said he felt "like the referee between the Cabinet and the White House staff." At his meeting with the White House staff the day before, many "statements and insinuations were made that the Cabinet goes behind our back. Ninety percent of those could be resolved by thrashing issues out." He said we did not know Jody and Ham well enough, that we should meet with them on a Saturday morning. I wondered if he knew that Jordan never returned phone calls from most of us. Carter went on in a monotone, "If Ham or Stu or Jack calls on my behalf, take their word as coming directly from me. You have been overly reluctant to respond when the White House staff calls you." . . .

But the respite was brief. On May 22, New York Senator Moynihan expressed the opinion that unless Carter acted quickly to take charge, he would soon find "that he's governing by the sufferance of" Senator Edward Kennedy. And the next day, five House Democrats started their own "Dump Carter–Draft Kennedy" movement. Kennedy refused to unequivocally take himself out of the presidential race.

During May and the first days of June, the Congress defeated Carter's proposals for Rhodesian sanctions, gasoline rationing, and decontrol of oil prices. Despite what then seemed like a bravado claim that he would "whip Kennedy's ass" in a fight for the Democratic nomination, Carter was beginning to reveal his own discouragement publicly. . . .

At 10:30 A.M., the special Cabinet meeting for "principals only" began, with Hamilton Jordan as the only non-Cabinet member present, sitting in Mondale's chair across the table from the President. Mondale was on the road, pumping for the SALT Treaty and traveling abroad, trying to get as far away as possible from what was coming.*

It was to be the most intense Cabinet meeting of the Carter administration. The Washington press corps had begun the race to discover who would go. Rumors tumbled over one another, but my name was appearing on every list. Carter entered smiling; but his smile did not soften the taut lines on his face. He took his chair with its slightly higher back. Nixon had introduced that more formal chair as a symbol of the change from

*SALT stands for Strategic Arms Limitation Treaty. The 1979 SALT treaty, the Carter Administration's major effort to achieve an understanding with the Soviet Union on nuclear weapons, was not ratified by the Senate.—EDS.

Johnson, who had sat in a reclining, high-back desk chair. Ford had replaced Nixon's with a chair the same size as all the others. Carter had brought back the Nixon chair.

The President began softly. "I have deliberately excluded most of you from my life for the past couple of weeks." He said he had "wanted to get away from you and from Washington." He felt an obligation to reassess his presidency, to have "serious private talks about my role as President." His words were pessimistic, his voice somber. It was as close to quiet desperation as I had ever seen him. There has been "a lot of effort wasted on misdirections," he said. "My government is not leading the country. The people have lost confidence in me, in the Congress, in themselves, and in this nation." He talked of the "alarming deterioration in attitude of people toward their country." Then a tone of teeth-gritted determination came into his voice. He had held a host of meetings with all kinds of groups from all across the country. He had asked them about his Cabinet and his staff. The comments about his Cabinet were "serious and condemnatory. I was told, they are not working for you, but for themselves." He said that he had "repeatedly been told" that there was disloyalty "among some Cabinet members," that many had been the source of leaks that had hurt him. With a studied expression of hurt on his face, Carter allowed that he had given "great loyalty" to his Cabinet and had "great appreciation" for their sacrifice and service.

He paused. "I have decided to change my lifestyle, and my calendar. I have one and one-half years left as President, and I don't deserve to be re-elected if I can't do a better job. I intend to run for office and I intend to be re-elected." To get ready for this effort over the next eighteen months, personnel changes would be made in the Cabinet and the White House staff. "I will make the changes over the course of next week." He intended to change the administration's "way of doing business" as well as the "identity of key members of the administration." He complained that "some Cabinet officers do not have support among their constituents." . . .

Then the President opened the meeting. Blumenthal spoke briefly about "the difference between arguing for a point of view and disloyalty." Carter hardly listened. Pat Harris said, "We can move government forward by putting phones in the White House staff offices and the staff using them." She complained that her calls were never returned by White House aides. She said it was important to "fight fiercely for our point of view," that it was not "disloyal to disagree with the White House staff, provided one supports the administration when the decision is made."

U.N. Ambassador Andrew Young began to speak, echoing Harris's concern. The President's face reddened. He interrupted Young: "You have repeatedly embarrassed the administration. I was told this again and again at Camp David. . . . You have caused embarrassment to me by calling Britain the most racist country in history . . . saying Cuban troops in Angola were a stabilizing influence . . . saying there are hundreds of political prisoners in the United States."

Usually, Carter was uncomfortable when Cabinet members argued back to him, but now his voice and eyes were so angry that by the time he had ended his attack on Young, he had killed any other meaningful comment. He turned to Jordan.

Jordan admitted that after two and a half years "I have no relationship with many of you." He said the Cabinet had to be "more accountable, better disciplined," that we had to "resolve the little problems and not send them to the President." The redness of anger faded from Carter's face and he looked like a proud father as Jordan continued: The medium-sized problems would come to him for decision; McIntyre and Eizenstat would be involved in domestic issues, Brzezinski in foreign policy. The White House staff would "work as an organization, not as a democracy," he said. "The personnel changes will be made quickly, and the discipline will be imposed immediately, including over leaks."

Carter added an admonition to complete the personnel evaluation forms promptly, to get them back within a few days, and he left the room. Jordan distributed the personnel evaluation forms—so patently amateurish and preposterous that the expressions on several Cabinet members' faces were open-mouthed. I could think only of what a disaster Carter was headed for. . . .

The following morning, July 18, I had a quiet breakfast with my friend and former law partner Edward Bennett Williams at the Metropolitan Club in Washington. Sitting virtually alone in the vast dining room on the fourth floor, I talked about the possibility that Carter might fire me.

"I can't believe it," Williams said. "It doesn't make any sense."

I still thought it was a possibility: "I can't believe any President would let his staff put this stuff out to the press unless he had blessed it, or at a minimum they knew that I was on the way out."

Williams then said, leaning across the table, "It would be the best damn thing that could happen to you. The guy is through and it will give you a way to get out. You ought to hope he fires you. You may not be that lucky."

At noon, I went to Woodlawn in Baltimore to celebrate the anniversary of my reorganization of Medicare and Medicaid into the Health Care

Financing Administration. When I got back, Susanna McBee, who had been named to succeed Eileen Shanahan as Assistant Secretary for Public Affairs at HEW, told me that Pat Harris had been to see Carter, but that no word of what occurred had leaked. Heineman reported that OMB and Domestic Policy staff aides were suggesting me to their bosses as Secretary of Energy.

I was preparing for my testimony the next morning on the administration's Higher Education Act proposals when the President called me at 5:19 P.M. "Joe, how are you doing?" he asked softly.

"Fine, Mr. President," I responded.

"Can you come over here this afternoon?"

"Any time," I said. The President asked me to come right away.

I was prepared for whichever decision Carter reached, although I did not really think he would accept my resignation, despite all the published evidence to the contrary, because we always seemed to have gotten along well.

I walked into Nell Yates's office, between the Cabinet Room and the Oval Office. She had been Jack Valenti's secretary when I first met her on the LBJ staff. We chatted aimlessly as I watched the President in the Rose Garden through the French doors. He was looking up at the trees at some birds. As he came through the French doors, he said, "I think I may have seen one of Cec's peregrine falcons." He was referring to the birds that Interior Secretary Andrus had saved and brought to Washington.

Carter ushered me through the Oval Office into his small study. He sat behind his desk, and I sat on a couch to the right against the wall. In his desk chair, the President was perched slightly higher than me, as I sank into the soft-cushioned white couch.

"I have decided to accept your resignation," he said through a nervous smile.

40

JAMES Q. WILSON

From *Bureaucracy*

In an era when government inefficiency is under a barrage of continual criticism, James Q. Wilson's observations on governmental bureaucracy are particularly relevant. A much-quoted authority in the field, Wilson opens with New York developer Donald Trump's Central Park skating rink success. The story illustrates that, yes, private enterprise may be able to do a job more efficiently, but government cannot necessarily be criticized for its admitted inefficiency. Because of the special demands and conditions placed on government, public bureaucracies cannot and should not place efficiency as their top priority. As Wilson aptly states we make "tradeoffs," and they are ones that generally deliver quite effectively. This selection is important to think about in a time of increasing pressure on state and local governments to privatize services: trash collection, maintenance, maybe prisons, possibly even schools.

ON THE MORNING OF MAY 22, 1986, Donald Trump, the New York real estate developer, called one of his executives, Anthony Gliedman, into his office. They discussed the inability of the City of New York, despite six years of effort and the expenditure of nearly $13 million, to rebuild the ice-skating rink in Central Park. On May 28 Trump offered to take over the rink reconstruction, promising to do the job in less than six months. A week later Mayor Edward Koch accepted the offer and shortly thereafter the city appropriated $3 million on the understanding that Trump would have to pay for any cost overruns out of his own pocket. On October 28, the renovation was complete, over a month ahead of schedule and about $750,000 under budget. Two weeks later, skaters were using it.

For many readers it is obvious that private enterprise is more efficient than are public bureaucracies, and so they would file this story away as simply another illustration of what everyone already knows. But for other readers it is not so obvious what this story means; to them, business is greedy and unless watched like a hawk will fob off shoddy or overpriced goods on the American public, as when it sells the government $435 hammers and $3,000 coffeepots. Trump may have done a good job in this instance, but perhaps there is something about skating rinks or New York City government that gave him a comparative advantage; in any event, no larger lessons should be drawn from it.

Some lessons can be drawn, however, if one looks closely at the incentives and constraints facing Trump and the Department of Parks and Recreation. It becomes apparent that there is not one "bureaucracy problem" but several, and the solution to each in some degree is incompatible with the solution to every other. First there is the problem of accountability—getting agencies to serve agreed-upon goals. Second there is the problem of equity—treating all citizens fairly, which usually means treating them alike on the basis of clear rules known in advance. Third there is the problem of responsiveness—reacting reasonably to the special needs and circumstances of particular people. Fourth there is the problem of efficiency—obtaining the greatest output for a given level of resources. Finally there is the problem of fiscal integrity—assuring that public funds are spent prudently for public purposes. Donald Trump and Mayor Koch were situated differently with respect to most of these matters.

Accountability

The Mayor wanted the old skating rink refurbished, but he also wanted to minimize the cost of the fuel needed to operate the rink (the first effort to rebuild it occurred right after the Arab oil embargo and the attendant increase in energy prices*). Trying to achieve both goals led city hall to select a new refrigeration system that as it turned out would not work properly. Trump came on the scene when only one goal dominated: get the rink rebuilt. He felt free to select the most reliable refrigeration system without worrying too much about energy costs.

Equity

The Parks and Recreation Department was required by law to give every contractor an equal chance to do the job. This meant it had to put every part of the job out to bid and to accept the lowest without much regard to the reputation or prior performance of the lowest bidder. Moreover, state law forbade city agencies from hiring a general contractor and letting him select the subcontractors; in fact, the law forbade the city from even discussing the project in advance with a general contractor who might later bid on it—that would have been collusion. Trump, by contrast, was free to locate the rink builder with the best reputation and give him the job.

Fiscal Integrity

To reduce the chance of corruption or sweetheart deals the law required Parks and Recreation to furnish complete, detailed plans to every contractor bidding on the job; any changes after that would require renegotiating the contract. No such law constrained Trump; he was free

*The Arab oil embargo occurred in 1973 as a response to American support for Israel during the October War against Egypt and Syria. The Organization of Petroleum Exporting Countries (OPEC) stopped selling oil to the United States and raised all oil prices worldwide. Long gas lines and the federal 55-miles-per-hour highway speed limit resulted. Eventually, conservation of oil resources became an important part of American life.—EDS.

to give incomplete plans to his chosen contractor, hold him accountable for building a satisfactory rink, but allow him to work out the details as he went along.

Efficiency

When the Parks and Recreation Department spent over six years and $13 million and still could not reopen the rink, there was public criticism but no city official lost money. When Trump accepted a contract to do it, any cost overruns or delays would have come out of his pocket and any savings could have gone into his pocket (in this case, Trump agreed not to take a profit on the job).

Gliedman summarized the differences neatly: "The problem with government is that government can't say, 'yes' . . . there is nobody in government that can do that. There are fifteen or twenty people who have to agree. Government has to be slower. It has to safeguard the process." . . .

The government can't say "yes." In other words, the government is constrained. Where do the constraints come from? From us.

Herbert Kaufman has explained red tape as being of our own making: "Every restraint and requirement originates in somebody's demand for it." Applied to the Central Park skating rink Kaufman's insight reminds us that civil-service reformers demanded that no city official benefit personally from building a project; that contractors demanded that all be given an equal chance to bid on every job; and that fiscal watchdogs demanded that all contract specifications be as detailed as possible. For each demand a procedure was established; viewed from the outside, those procedures are called red tape. To enforce each procedure a manager was appointed; those managers are called bureaucrats. No organized group demanded that all skating rinks be rebuilt as quickly as possible, no procedure existed to enforce that demand, and no manager was appointed to enforce it. The political process can more easily enforce compliance with constraints than the attainment of goals.

When we denounce bureaucracy for being inefficient we are saying something that is half true. Efficiency is a ratio of valued resources used to valued outputs produced. The smaller that ratio the more efficient the production. If the valued output is a rebuilt skating rink, then whatever process uses the fewest dollars or the least time to produce a satisfactory rink is the most efficient process. By this test Trump was more efficient than the Parks and Recreation Department.

But that is too narrow a view of the matter. The economic definition of efficiency (efficiency in the small, so to speak) assumes that there is only one valued output, the new rink. But government has many valued outputs, including a reputation for integrity, the confidence of the people, and the support of important interest groups. When we complain about skating rinks not being built on time we speak as if all we cared about were skating rinks. But when we complain that contracts were awarded without competitive bidding or in a way that allowed bureaucrats to line their pockets we acknowledge that we care about many things besides skating rinks; we care about the contextual goals—the constraints—that we want government to observe. A government that is slow to build rinks but is honest and accountable in its actions and properly responsive to worthy constituencies may be a very efficient government, *if* we measure efficiency in the large by taking into account *all* of the valued outputs.

Calling a government agency efficient when it is slow, cumbersome, and costly may seem perverse. But that is only because we lack any objective way for deciding how much money or time should be devoted to maintaining honest behavior, producing a fair allocation of benefits, and generating popular support as well as to achieving the main goal of the project. If we could measure these things, and if we agreed as to their value, then we would be in a position to judge the true efficiency of a government agency and decide when it is taking too much time or spending too much money achieving all that we expect of it. But we cannot measure these things nor do we agree about their relative importance, and so government always will appear to be inefficient compared to organizations that have fewer goals.

Put simply, the only way to decide whether an agency is truly inefficient is to decide which of the constraints affecting its action ought to be ignored or discounted. In fact that is what most debates about agency behavior are all about. In fighting crime are the police handcuffed? In educating children are teachers tied down by rules? In launching a space shuttle are we too concerned with safety? In building a dam do we worry excessively about endangered species? In running the Postal Service is it important to have many post offices close to where people live? In the case of the skating rink, was the requirement of competitive bidding for each contract on the basis of detailed specifications a reasonable one? Probably not. But if it were abandoned, the gain (the swifter completion of the rink) would have to be balanced against the costs (complaints from contractors who might lose business and the chance of collusion and corruption in some future projects).

Even allowing for all of these constraints, government agencies may still be inefficient. Indeed, given the fact that bureaucrats cannot (for the most part) benefit monetarily from their agencies' achievements, it would be surprising if they were not inefficient. Efficiency, in the large or the small, doesn't pay. . . .

Inefficiency is not the only bureaucratic problem nor is it even the most important. A perfectly efficient agency could be a monstrous one, swiftly denying us our liberties, economically inflicting injustices, and competently expropriating our wealth. People complain about bureaucracy as often because it is unfair or unreasonable as because it is slow or cumbersome.

Arbitrary rule refers to officials acting without legal authority, or with that authority in a way that offends our sense of justice. Justice means, first, that we require the government to treat people equally on the basis of clear rules known in advance: If Becky and Bob both are driving sixty miles per hour in a thirty-mile-per-hour zone and the police give a ticket to Bob, we believe they also should give a ticket to Becky. Second, we believe that justice obliges the government to take into account the special needs and circumstances of individuals: If Becky is speeding because she is on her way to the hospital to give birth to a child and Bob is speeding for the fun of it, we may feel that the police should ticket Bob but not Becky. Justice in the first sense means fairness, in the second it means responsiveness. Obviously, fairness and responsiveness often are in conflict.

The checks and balances of the American constitutional system reflect our desire to reduce the arbitrariness of official rule. That desire is based squarely on the premise that inefficiency is a small price to pay for freedom and responsiveness. Congressional oversight, judicial review, interest-group participation, media investigations, and formalized procedures all are intended to check administrative discretion. It is not hyperbole to say that the constitutional order is animated by the desire to make the government "inefficient."

This creates two great tradeoffs. First, adding constraints reduces the efficiency with which the main goal of an agency can be attained but increases the chances that the agency will act in a nonarbitrary manner. Efficient police departments would seek out criminals without reading them their rights, allowing them to call their attorneys, or releasing them in response to a writ of habeas corpus. An efficient building department would issue construction permits on demand without insisting that the applicant first show that the proposed building meets fire, safety, sanitation, geological, and earthquake standards.

The second great tradeoff is between nonarbitrary governance defined as treating people equally and such governance defined as treating each case on its merits. We want the government to be both fair and responsive, but the more rules we impose to insure fairness (that is, to treat all people alike) the harder we make it for the government to be responsive (that is, to take into account the special needs and circumstances of a particular case).

The way our government manages these tradeoffs reflects both our political culture as well as the rivalries of our governing institutions. Both tend toward the same end: We define claims as rights, impose general rules to insure equal treatment, lament (but do nothing about) the resulting inefficiencies, and respond to revelations about unresponsiveness by adopting new rules intended to guarantee that special circumstances will be handled with special care (rarely bothering to reconcile the rules that require responsiveness with those that require equality). And we do all this out of the best of motives: a desire to be both just and benevolent. Justice inclines us to treat people equally, benevolence to treat them differently; both inclinations are expressed in rules, though in fact only justice can be. It is this futile desire to have a rule for every circumstance that led Herbert Kaufman to explain "how compassion spawns red tape." . . .

In the meantime we live in a country that despite its baffling array of rules and regulations and the insatiable desire of some people to use government to rationalize society still makes it possible to get drinkable water instantly, put through a telephone call in seconds, deliver a letter in a day, and obtain a passport in a week. Our Social Security checks arrive on time. Some state prisons, and most of the federal ones, are reasonably decent and humane institutions. The great majority of Americans, cursing all the while, pay their taxes. One can stand on the deck of an aircraft carrier during night flight operations and watch two thousand nineteen-year-old boys faultlessly operate one of the most complex organizational systems ever created. There are not many places where all this happens. It is astonishing it can be made to happen at all.

41

DAVID OSBORNE AND TED GAEBLER

From *Reinventing Government*

The bureaucratic rules surrounding the Defense Department's Sicilian bowling alley exemplify the inefficiency, waste, and absurdity often present in government regulations today. Critics David Osborne and Ted Gaebler want Americans to "reinvent government," to make it responsive to the needs of Americans in the twenty-first century. With financial resources tight and the effectiveness of government programs under attack, Osborne and Gaebler suggest a model for entrepreneurial government, as they term it. Their ideas have been widely acclaimed by public officials, but are less easily applied.

WE HAVE CHOSEN an audacious title for this book. We know that cynicism about government runs deep within the American soul. We all have our favorite epithets: "It's close enough for government work." "Feeding at the public trough." "I'm from the government and I'm here to help." "My friend doesn't work; she has a job with the government."

Our governments are in deep trouble today. This book is for those who are disturbed by that reality. It is for those who care about government—because they work in government, or work with government, or study government, or simply want their governments to be more effective. It is for those who know something is wrong, but are not sure just what it is; for those who have glimpsed a better way, but are not sure just how to bring it to life; for those who have launched successful experiments, but have watched those in power ignore them; for those who have a sense of where government needs to go, but are not quite sure how to get there. It is for the seekers.

If ever there were a time for seekers, this is it. The millennium approaches, and change is all around us. Eastern Europe is free; the Soviet empire is dissolving; the cold war is over. Western Europe is moving toward economic union. Asia is the new center of global economic power. From Poland to South Africa, democracy is on the march.

The idea of reinventing government may seem audacious to those who see government as something fixed, something that does not change. But in fact governments constantly change. At one time, government armories manufactured weapons, and no one would have considered letting private businesses do something so important. Today, no one would think of letting government do it.

At one time, no one expected government to take care of the poor; the welfare state did not exist until Bismarck created the first one in the 1870s.* Today, not only do most governments in the developed world take care of the poor, they pay for health care and retirement pensions for every citizen.

At one time, no one expected governments to fight fires. Today, no government would be without a fire department. In fact, huge controversies erupt when a government so much as contracts with a private company to fight fires.

At one time, governments were active investors in the private economy, routinely seeding new businesses with loans and grants and equity investments. The federal government actually gave 9.3 percent of all land in the continental United States to the railroads, as an inducement to build a transcontinental system. Today, no one would dream of such a thing.

We last "reinvented" our governments during the early decades of the twentieth century, roughly from 1900 through 1940. We did so, during the Progressive Era and the New Deal, to cope with the emergence of a new industrial economy, which created vast new problems and vast new opportunities in American life. Today, the world of government is once again in great flux. The emergence of a postindustrial, knowledge-based, global economy has undermined old realities throughout the world, creating wonderful opportunities and frightening problems. Governments large and small, American and foreign, federal, state, and local, have begun to respond.

Our purpose in writing this book is twofold: to take a snapshot of governments that have begun this journey and to provide a map to those who want to come along. When Columbus set off 500 years ago to find a new route to bring spices back from the Orient, he accidentally bumped into a New World. He and the explorers who followed him—Amerigo Vespucci and Sir Francis Drake and Hernando de Soto—all found different pieces of this New World. But it was up to the map makers to gather all

*In the 1870s and 1880s, German Chancellor Otto von Bismarck instituted a series of laws designed to provide some financial security for German workers. Germany established a sickness fund that included limited medical coverage, along with accident benefits for disabled workers and pensions for retired laborers. Government, employers, and employees all contributed.—EDS.

these seemingly unrelated bits of information and piece together a coherent map of the newly discovered continents.

In similar fashion, those who are today reinventing government originally set off to solve a problem, plug a deficit, or skirt a bureaucracy. But they too have bumped into a new world. Almost without knowing it, they have begun to invent a radically different way of doing business in the public sector. Just as Columbus never knew he had come upon a new continent, many of today's pioneers—from governors to city managers, teachers to social workers—do not understand the global significance of what they are doing. Each has touched a part of the new world; each has a view of one or two peninsulas or bays. But it will take others to gather all this information and piece together a coherent map of the new model they are creating. . . .

We are, of course, responsible for the ultimate shape of the map we have drawn. As such, we feel a responsibility to make explicit the underlying beliefs that have driven us to write this book—and that have no doubt animated its conclusions.

First, we believe deeply in government. We do not look at government as a necessary evil. All civilized societies have some form of government. Government is the mechanism we use to make communal decisions: where to build a highway, what to do about homeless people, what kind of education to provide for our children. It is the way we provide services that benefit all our people: national defense, environmental protection, police protection, highways, dams, water systems. It is the way we solve collective problems. Think of the problems facing American society today: drug use; crime; poverty; homelessness; illiteracy; toxic waste; the specter of global warming; the exploding cost of medical care. How will we solve these problems? By acting collectively. How do we act collectively? Through government.

Second, we believe that civilized society cannot function effectively *without* effective *government—something that is all too rare today.* We believe that industrial-era governments, with their large, centralized bureaucracies and standardized, "one-size-fits-all" services, are not up to the challenges of a rapidly changing information society and knowledge-based economy.

Third, we believe that the people *who work in government are not the problem; the* systems *in which they work are the problem.* We write not to berate public employees, but to give them hope. At times it may sound as if we are engaged in bureaucrat-bashing, but our intention is to bash *bureaucracies*, not bureaucrats. We have known thousands of civil servants through the years, and most—although certainly not all—have been responsible, talented, dedicated people, trapped in archaic systems that frustrate their creativity and sap their energy. We believe these systems can be changed, to liberate the enormous energies of public servants—and to heighten their ability to serve the public.

Fourth, we believe that neither traditional liberalism nor traditional conservatism has much relevance to the problems our governments face today. We will not solve our problems by spending more or spending less, by creating new public bureaucracies or by "privatizing" existing bureaucracies. At some times and in some places, we do need to spend more or spend less, create new programs or privatize public functions. But to make our governments effective again we must *reinvent* them.

Finally, we believe deeply in equity—in equal opportunity for all Americans. Some of the ideas we express in this book may strike readers as inequitable. When we talk about making public schools compete, for instance, some fear that the result would be an even less equitable education system than we have today. But we believe there are ways to use choice and competition to *increase* the equity in our school system. And we believe passionately that increased equity is not only right and just, but critical to our success as a nation. In today's global marketplace, America cannot compete effectively if it wastes 25 percent of its human resources.

We use the phrase *entrepreneurial government* to describe the new model we see emerging across America. . . .

Bob Stone works in America's archetypal bureaucracy, the Department of Defense. As deputy assistant secretary of defense for installations, he has at least theoretical authority over 600 bases and facilities, which house 4.5 million people and consume $100 billion a year. Soon after he was promoted to the job, in 1981, Stone visited an air base in Sicily. "We have 2,000 airmen there, and they're out in the middle of nowhere," he says:

> No families, no towns. They are an hour and a half drive over a horrible mountain road from a Sicilian city of 20,000—and when you get there there's not much to do. So most of our bases have bowling alleys, and we built a bowling alley at this base. I visited them two or three weeks after the bowling center opened. They took me in and they started showing me plans—they're going to take out this wall and add six more lanes over there. I thought, "Gee, you've been open for a couple of weeks, and you're going to tear the place apart and expand it? Why is that?"
>
> "Well," they told me, "there's this rule that says, if you have 2,000 troops, you're allowed to construct eight lanes." [You can get a waiver to build more—but only after you can prove you need them.] I got the book and that *is* what it

says: 1,000 troops, four lanes; 2,000 troops, eight lanes. And it's true if you're in the wilds of Sicily, with no families, or in the northern part of Greenland, where you can't even go outdoors for most of the year.

The rule book Stone refers to covered 400 pages. The rules governing the operation of military housing covered 800 pages. Personnel rules for civilian employees covered another 8,800 pages. "My guess is that *a third* of the defense budget goes into the friction of following bad regulations—doing work that doesn't have to be done," Stone says. Engineers in New Mexico write reports to convince people in Washington that their roofs leak. Soldiers trek halfway across their bases to the base chemist when the shelf life of a can of spray paint expires, to have it certified for another year. The Department of Defense (DOD) pays extra for special paint, but because it takes longer to establish its specifications than it takes companies to improve their paint, DOD employees pay a premium for paint that is inferior to paint available at their local store.

"This kind of rule has two costs," Stone says. "One is, we've got people wasting time. But the biggest cost—and the reason I say it's a third of the defense budget—is it's a message broadcast to everybody that works around this stuff that it's a crazy outfit. 'You're dumb. We don't trust you. Don't try to apply your common sense.'"

Stone cut the rules governing military base construction from 400 pages down to 4, those governing housing from 800 to 40. Then he decided to go farther. In an experiment straight out of *In Search of Excellence*, he decided to turn one base, called a Model Installation, free from these rules and regulations. If the commander would commit to radically improving his installation, Stone would do his best to get any rules that were standing in his way waived. The principle was simple: let the base commander run the base his way, rather than Washington's way. A corollary was also important: if he saved money in the process, he didn't have to give it back. He could keep it to spend on whatever he felt was most important.

Forty commanders volunteered for the experiment. In the first two years, they submitted more than 8,000 requests for waivers or changes in regulations. Stone can tell stories about them for hours. In the air force, for instance, airmen use complex electronic test kits to check Minuteman missiles. When a kit fails, they sent it to Hill Air Force Base in Utah for repair. Meanwhile, the missile is put off alert—typically for 10 days. An airman at Whiteman Air Force Base got approval to fix the test kits himself—and suddenly Whiteman didn't have a Minuteman missile off alert for more than three hours.

Throughout Defense, people buy by the book. Stone holds up a simple steam trap, which costs $100. "When it leaks," he says, "it leaks $50 a week worth of steam. The lesson is, when it leaks, replace it quick. But it takes us a year to replace it, because we have a system that wants to make sure we get the very best buy on this $100 item, and maybe by waiting a year we can buy the item for $2 less. In the meantime, we've lost $3,000 worth of steam." Under the Model Installations program, commanders requested authority to buy things on their own. An entire army command requested permission to let craftsmen decide for themselves when spray paint cans should be thrown away, rather than taking them to the base chemist. Five air force bases received permission to manage their own construction, rather than paying the Corps of Engineers to do it. Shaken by the threat of competition, the corps adopted a new goal: to be "leaders in customer care."

The Model Installations experiment was so successful that in March 1986, Deputy Secretary of Defense William Howard Taft IV directed that it be applied to all defense installations. Stone and his staff then developed a budget experiment modeled on Visalia's system. Normal installation budgets, first drawn up *three years in advance*, include hundreds of specific line items. The Unified Budget Test allowed commanders to ignore the line items and shift resources as needs changed.

In its first year, the test revealed that 7 to 10 percent of the funding locked into line items was in the wrong account, and that when commanders could move it around, they could significantly increase the performance of their troops. The army compared the results at its two participating bases with normal bases and concluded that in just one year, the Unified Budget increased performance by 3 percent. The long-term impact would no doubt be greater. According to Stone and his colleagues, "Senior leaders in the Services have estimated that if all the unnecessary constraints on their money were removed, they could accomplish their missions with up to 10 percent less money." But in a $100 billion installations budget, even 3 percent is $3 billion. . . .

Over the past five years, as we have journeyed through the landscape of governmental change, we have sought constantly to understand the underlying trends. We have asked ourselves: What do these innovative, entrepreneurial organizations have in common? What incentives have they changed, to create such different behavior? What have they done which, if other governments did the same, would make entrepreneurship the norm and bureaucracy the exception?

The common threads were not hard to find. Most entrepreneurial governments promote *competition* between service providers. They *empower* citizens by pushing control out of the bureaucracy, into the community. They measure the performance of their agencies, focusing not on inputs but on *outcomes*. They are driven by their goals—their *missions*—not by their rules and regulations. They redefine their clients as *customers* and offer them choices—between schools, between training programs, between housing options. They *prevent* problems before they emerge, rather than simply offering services afterward. They put their energies into *earning* money, not simply spending it. They *decentralize* authority, embracing participatory management. They prefer *market* mechanisms to bureaucratic mechanisms. And they focus not simply on providing public services, but on *catalyzing* all sectors—public, private, and voluntary—into action to solve their community's problems.

We believe that these ten principles, which we describe at length in the next ten chapters, are the fundamental principles behind this new form of government we see emerging: the spokes that hold together this new wheel. Together they form a coherent whole, a new model of government. They will not solve all of our problems. But if the experience of organizations that have embraced them is any guide, they will solve the major problems we experience with bureaucratic government. . . .

Most of our leaders still tell us that there are only two ways out of our repeated public crises: we can raise taxes, or we can cut spending. For almost two decades, we have asked for a third choice. We do not want less education, fewer roads, less health care. Nor do we want higher taxes. We want better education, better roads, and better health care, for the same tax dollar.

Unfortunately, we do not know how to get what we want. Most of our leaders assume that the only way to cut spending is to eliminate programs, agencies, and employees. Ronald Reagan talked as if we could simply go into the bureaucracy with a scalpel and cut out pockets of waste, fraud, and abuse.

But waste in government does not come tied up in neat packages. It is marbled throughout our bureaucracies. It is embedded in the very way we do business. It is employees on idle, working at half speed—or barely working at all. It is people working hard at tasks that aren't worth doing, following regulations that should never have been written, filling out forms that should never have been printed. It is the *$100 billion* a year that Bob Stone estimates the Department of Defense wastes with its foolish overregulation.

Waste in government is staggering, but we cannot get at it by wading through budgets and cutting line items. As one observer put it, our governments are like fat people who must lose weight. They need to eat less and exercise more; instead, when money is tight they cut off a few fingers and toes.

To melt the fat, we must change the basic incentives that drive our governments. We must turn bureaucratic institutions into entrepreneurial institutions, ready to kill off obsolete initiatives, willing to do more with less, eager to absorb new ideas.

The lessons are there: our more entrepreneurial governments have shown us the way. Yet few of our leaders are listening. Too busy climbing the rungs to their next office, they don't have time to stop and look anew. So they remain trapped in old ways of looking at our problems, blind to solutions that lie right in front of them. This is perhaps our greatest stumbling block: the power of outdated ideas. As the great economist John Maynard Keynes once noted, the difficulty lies not so much in developing new ideas as in escaping from old ones.

The old ideas still embraced by most public leaders and political reporters assume that the important question is *how much* government we have—not *what kind* of government. Most of our leaders take the old model as a given, and either advocate more of it (liberal Democrats), or less of it (Reagan Republicans), or less of one program but more of another (moderates of both parties).

But our fundamental problem today is not too much government or too little government. We have debated that issue endlessly since the tax revolt of 1978, and it has not solved our problems. Our fundamental problem is that we have *the wrong kind of government.* We do not need more government or less government, we need *better* government. To be more precise, we need better *governance.*

PART EIGHT

The Judiciary

42

ALEXANDER HAMILTON

From *The Federalist* 78

The 1787 Federalist Papers *have been quoted extensively in earlier sections of this book. The most famous selections belong to James Madison, writing about separation of powers and federalism.* The Federalist *actually had three authors: Madison, Alexander Hamilton, and John Jay. In No. 78, Hamilton expounded on the judicial branch. He makes a strong case for an independent judiciary, separate from the legislative and executive branches. He discusses the lifetime appointment of federal judges. Hamilton was a strong proponent of the courts' power, and as such, he believed that the Supreme Court should have the right to declare an act of Congress unconstitutional. This enormous power, termed judicial review, is explained and justified here by Hamilton, although it was not explicitly stated in the Constitution. In 1803, Chief Justice John Marshall established the precedent for the Supreme Court's use of judicial review in the landmark* Marbury v. Madison *case. The year after Marshall's decision, Alexander Hamilton was killed in a duel with Vice-President Aaron Burr.*

No. 78: Hamilton

WE PROCEED now to an examination of the judiciary department of the proposed government. . . .

Whoever attentively considers the different departments of power must perceive that, in a government in which they are separated from each other, the judiciary, from the nature of its functions, will always be the least dangerous to the political rights of the Constitution; because it will be least in a capacity to annoy or injure them. The executive not only dispenses the honors but holds the sword of the community. The legislature not only commands the purse but prescribes the rules by which the duties and rights of every citizen are to be regulated. The judiciary, on the contrary, has no influence over either the sword or the purse; no direction either of the strength or of the wealth of the society, and can take no active resolution whatever. It may truly be said to have neither FORCE nor WILL but merely judgment; and must ultimately depend upon the aid of the executive arm even for the efficacy of its judgments.

This simple view of the matter suggests several important consequences. It proves incontestably that the judiciary is beyond comparison the weakest of the three departments of power;* that it can never attack with success either of the other two; and that all possible care is requisite to enable it to defend itself against their attacks. It equally proves that though individual oppression may now and then proceed from the courts of justice, the general liberty of the people can never be endangered from that quarter; I mean so long as the judiciary remains truly distinct from both the legislature and the executive. For I agree that "there is no liberty if the power of judging be not separated from the legislative and executive powers."† And it proves, in the last place, that as liberty can have nothing to fear from the judiciary alone, but would have everything to fear from its union with either of the other departments; that as all the effects of such a union must ensue from a dependence of the former on the latter, notwithstanding a nominal and apparent separation; that as, from the natural feebleness of the judiciary, it is in continual jeopardy of being overpowered, awed, or influenced by its co-ordinate branches; and that as nothing can contribute so much to its firmness and independence as permanency in office, this quality may therefore be justly regarded as an indispensable ingredient in its constitution, and, in a great measure, as the citadel of the public justice and the public security.

The complete independence of the courts of justice is peculiarly essential in a limited Constitution. By a limited Constitution, I understand one which contains certain specified exceptions to the legislative authority; such, for instance, as that it shall pass no bills of attainder, no *ex post facto* laws, and the like. Limitations of this kind can be preserved in practice no other way than through the medium of courts of justice, whose duty it must be to declare all acts contrary to the manifest tenor of the Constitution void. Without this, all the reservations of particular rights or privileges would amount to nothing.

Some perplexity respecting the rights of the courts to pronounce legislative acts void, because contrary to the Constitution, has arisen from an imagination that the doctrine would imply a superiority of the judiciary to the legislative power. It is urged that the authority which can declare the acts of another void must necessarily be superior to the one whose acts may be declared void. As this doctrine is of great importance in all the American constitutions, a brief discussion of the grounds on which it rests cannot be unacceptable.

There is no position which depends on clearer principles than that

*The celebrated Montesquieu, speaking of them, says: "Of the three powers above mentioned, the JUDICIARY is next to nothing."—*Spirit of Laws*, Vol. I, page 186.
†*Idem*, page 181.

every act of a delegated authority, contrary to the tenor of the commission under which it is exercised, is void. No legislative act, therefore, contrary to the Constitution, can be valid. To deny this would be to affirm that the deputy is greater than his principal; that the servant is above his master; that the representatives of the people are superior to the people themselves; that men acting by virtue of powers may do not only what their powers do not authorize, but what they forbid.

If it be said that the legislative body are themselves the constitutional judges of their own powers and that the construction they put upon them is conclusive upon the other departments it may be answered that this cannot be the natural presumption where it is not to be collected from any particular provisions in the Constitution. It is not otherwise to be supposed that the Constitution could intend to enable the representatives of the people to substitute their *will* to that of their constituents. It is far more rational to suppose that the courts were designed to be an intermediate body between the people and the legislature in order, among other things, to keep the latter within the limits assigned to their authority. The interpretation of the laws is the proper and peculiar province of the courts. A constitution is, in fact, and must be regarded by the judges as, a fundamental law. It therefore belongs to them to ascertain its meaning as well as the meaning of any particular act proceeding from the legislative body. If there should happen to be an irreconcilable variance between the two, that which has the superior obligation and validity ought, of course, to be preferred; or, in other words, the Constitution ought to be preferred to the statute, the intention of the people to the intention of their agents.

Nor does this conclusion by any means suppose a superiority of the judicial to the legislative power. It only supposes that the power of the people is superior to both, and that where the will of the legislature, declared in its statutes, stands in opposition to that of the people, declared in the Constitution, the judges ought to be governed by the latter rather than the former. They ought to regulate their decisions by the fundamental laws rather than by those which are not fundamental. . . .

If, then, the courts of justice are to be considered as the bulwarks of a limited Constitution against legislative encroachments, this consideration will afford a strong argument for the permanent tenure of judicial offices, since nothing will contribute so much as this to that independent spirit in the judges which must be essential to the faithful performance of so arduous a duty.

This independence of the judges is equally requisite to guard the Constitution and the rights of individuals from the effects of those ill humors which the arts of designing men, or the influence of particular conjunctures, sometimes disseminate among the people themselves, and which, though they speedily give place to better information, and more deliberate reflection, have a tendency, in the meantime, to occasion dangerous innovations in the government, and serious oppressions of the minor party in the community. Though I trust the friends of the proposed Constitution will never concur with its enemies in questioning that fundamental principle of republican government which admits the right of the people to alter or abolish the established Constitution whenever they find it inconsistent with their happiness; yet it is not to be inferred from this principle that the representatives of the people, whenever a momentary inclination happens to lay hold of a majority of their constituents incompatible with the provisions in the existing Constitution would, on that account, be justifiable in a violation of those provisions; or that the courts would be under a greater obligation to connive at infractions in this shape than when they had proceeded wholly from the cabals of the representative body. Until the people have, by some solemn and authoritative act, annulled or changed the established form, it is binding upon themselves collectively, as well as individually; and no presumption, or even knowledge of their sentiments, can warrant their representatives in a departure from it prior to such an act. But it is easy to see that it would require an uncommon portion of fortitude in the judges to do their duty as faithful guardians of the Constitution, where legislative invasions of it had been instigated by the major voice of the community.

But it is not with a view to infractions of the Constitution only that the independence of the judges may be an essential safeguard against the effects of occasional ill humors in the society. These sometimes extend no farther than to the injury of the private rights of particular classes of citizens, by unjust and partial laws. Here also the firmness of the judicial magistracy is of vast importance in mitigating the severity and confining the operation of such laws. It not only serves to moderate the immediate mischiefs of those which may have been passed but it operates as a check upon the legislative body in passing them; who, perceiving that obstacles to the success of an iniquitous intention are to be expected from the scruples of the courts, are in a manner compelled, by the very motives of the injustice they meditate, to qualify their attempts. This is a circumstance calculated to have more influence upon the character of our governments than but few may be aware of. The benefits of the integrity and moderation of the judiciary have already been felt in more States than one; and though they may have displeased those whose sinister expectations they may have disappointed, they must have commanded the esteem and applause of all the virtuous and disinterested. Considerate men of every description ought to prize whatever will tend to beget or fortify that temper in the courts; as no man can be sure that he may not be tomorrow the victim of a spirit of injustice, by which he may be a gainer today. And every man must now feel that the inevitable tendency of such a spirit is to sap the foundations of public and private confidence and to introduce in its stead universal distrust and distress. . . .

Publius

43

EUGENE ROSTOW

The Democratic Character of Judicial Review

Written nearly half a century ago, this classic article by legal scholar Eugene Rostow remains the most important analysis written on the theory behind the Supreme Court's power. Judicial review, the ability of the Court to declare an act of Congress or the executive or a state law unconstitutional, may seem on the surface to be "antidemocratic." A handful of lifetime appointees determine the meaning of the Constitution and whether a law passed by Congress and signed by the president is valid. In precise terms and using complex reasoning, Rostow defends the Supreme Court's use of judicial review as being the essence of the American democratic system. In his words, "The political proposition underlying the survival of the power is that there are some phases of American life which should be beyond the reach of any majority, save by constitutional amendment." Rostow's argument is based on what is meant by a democracy. To add a bit to Rostow's explanation, the United States is a "polity" in which the majority rules with protections guaranteed for individuals and minorities. The judiciary ensures that the minority is protected from "tyranny of the majority." Notice the title of this reader.

THE IDEA that judicial review is undemocratic is not an academic issue of political philosophy. Like most abstractions, it has far-reaching practical consequences. I suspect that for some judges it is the mainspring of decision, inducing them in many cases to uphold legislative and executive action which would otherwise have been condemned. Particularly in the multiple opinions of recent years, the Supreme Court's self-searching often boils down to a debate within the bosoms of the Justices over the appropriateness of judicial review itself.

The attack on judicial review as undemocratic rests on the premise that the Constitution should be allowed to grow without a judicial check. The proponents of this view would have the Constitution mean what the President, the Congress, and the state legislatures say it means. . . .

It is a grave oversimplification to contend that no society can be democratic unless its legislature has sovereign powers. The social quality of democracy cannot be defined by so rigid a formula. Government and politics are after all the arms, not the end, of social life. The purpose of the Constitution is to assure the people a free and democratic society. The final aim of that society is as much freedom as possible for the individual human being. The Constitution provides society with a mechanism of government fully competent to its task, but by no means universal in its powers. The power to govern is parcelled out between the states and the nation and is further divided among the three main branches of all governmental units. By custom as well as constitutional practice, many vital aspects of community life are beyond the direct reach of government—for example, religion, the press, and, until recently at any rate, many phases of educational and cultural activity. The separation of powers under the Constitution serves the end of democracy in society by limiting the roles of the several branches of government and protecting the citizen, and the various parts of the state itself, against encroachments from any source. The root idea of the Constitution is that man can be free because the state is not.

The power of constitutional review, to be exercised by some part of the government, is implicit in the conception of a written constitution delegating limited powers. A written constitution would promote discord rather than order in society if there were no accepted authority to construe it, at the least in cases of conflicting action by different branches of government or of constitutionally unauthorized governmental action against individuals. The limitation and separation of powers, if they are to survive, require a procedure for independent mediation and construction to reconcile the inevitable disputes over the boundaries of constitutional power which arise in the process of government. . . .

So far as the American Constitution is concerned, there can be little real doubt that the courts were intended from the beginning to have the power they have exercised. The Federalist Papers are unequivocal; the Debates as clear as debates normally are. The power of judicial review was commonly exercised by the courts of the states, and the people were accustomed to judicial construction of the authority derived from colonial charters. Constitutional interpretation by the courts, Hamilton said, does not

> by any means suppose a superiority of the judicial to the legislative power. It only supposes that the power of the people is superior to both; and that where the will of the legislature, declared in its statutes, stands in opposition to that of the people, declared in the Constitution, the judges ought to be governed by the latter rather than the former. They ought to regulate their decisions by the fundamental laws, rather than by those which are not fundamental.

Hamilton's statement is sometimes criticized as a verbal legalism. But it has an advantage too. For much of the discussion has complicated the problem without clarifying it. Both judges and their critics have wrapped themselves so successfully in the difficulties of particular cases that they have been able to evade the ultimate issue posed in the Federalist Papers.

Whether another method of enforcing the Constitution could have been devised, the short answer is that no such method has developed. The argument over the constitutionality of judicial review has long since been settled by history. The power and duty of the Supreme Court to declare statutes or executive action unconstitutional in appropriate cases is part of the living Constitution. "The course of constitutional history," Mr. Justice Frankfurter recently remarked, has cast responsibilities upon the Supreme Court which it would be "stultification" for it to evade. The Court's power has been exercised differently at different times: sometimes with reckless and doctrinaire enthusiasm; sometimes with great deference to the status and responsibilities of other branches of the government; sometimes with a degree of weakness and timidity that comes close to the betrayal of trust. But the power exists, as an integral part of the process of American government. The Court has the duty of interpreting the Constitution in many of its most important aspects, and especially in those which concern the relations of the individual and the state. The political proposition underlying the survival of the power is that there are some phases of American life which should be beyond the reach of any majority, save by constitutional amendment. In Mr. Justice Jackson's phrase, "One's right to life, liberty, and property, to free speech, a free press, freedom of worship and assembly, and other fundamental rights may not be submitted to vote; they depend on the outcome of no elections." Whether or not this was the intention of the Founding Fathers, the unwritten Constitution is unmistakable.

If one may use a personal definition of the crucial word, this way of policing the Constitution is not undemocratic. True, it employs appointed officials, to whom large powers are irrevocably delegated. But democracies need not elect all the officers who exercise crucial authority in the name of the voters. Admirals and generals can win or lose wars in the exercise of their discretion. The independence of judges in the administration of justice has been the pride of communities which aspire to be free. Members of the Federal Reserve Board have the lawful power to plunge the country into depression or inflation. The list could readily be extended. Government by referendum or town meeting is not the only possible form of democracy. The task of democracy is not to have the people vote directly on every issue, but to assure their ultimate responsibility for the acts of their representatives, elected or appointed. For judges deciding ordinary litigation, the ultimate responsibility of the electorate has a special meaning. It is a responsibility for the quality of the judges and for the substance of their instructions, never a responsibility for their decisions in particular cases. It is hardly characteristic of law in democratic society to encourage bills of attainder, or to allow appeals from the courts in particular cases to legislatures or to mobs. Where the judges are carrying out the function of constitutional review, the final responsibility of the people is appropriately guaranteed by the provisions for amending the Constitution itself, and by the benign influence of time, which changes the personnel of courts. Given the possibility of constitutional amendment, there is nothing undemocratic in having responsible and independent judges act as important constitutional mediators. Within the narrow limits of their capacity to act, their great task is to help maintain a pluralist equilibrium in society. They can do much to keep it from being dominated by the states or the Federal Government, by Congress or the President, by the purse or the sword.

In the execution of this crucial but delicate function, constitutional review by the judiciary has an advantage thoroughly recognized in both theory and practice. The power of the courts, however final, can only be asserted in the course of litigation. Advisory opinions are forbidden, and reefs of self-limitation have grown up around the doctrine that the courts will determine constitutional questions only in cases of actual controversy, when no lesser ground of decision is available, and when the complaining party would be directly and personally injured by the assertion of the power deemed unconstitutional. Thus the check of judicial review upon the elected branches of government must be a mild one, limited not only by the detachment, integrity, and good sense of the Justices, but by the structural boundaries implicit in the fact that the power is entrusted to the courts. Judicial review is inherently adapted to preserving broad and flexible lines of constitutional growth, not to operating as a continuously active factor in legislative or executive decisions. . . .

Democracy is a slippery term. I shall make no effort at a formal definition here. . . . But it would be scholastic pedantry to define democracy in such a way as to deny the title of "democrat" to Jefferson, Madison,

Lincoln, Brandeis, and others who have found the American constitutional system, including its tradition of judicial review, well adapted to the needs of a free society. As Mr. Justice Brandeis said,

> the doctrine of the separation of powers was adopted by the Convention of 1787, not to promote efficiency but to preclude the exercise of arbitrary power. The purpose was, not to avoid friction, but, by means of the inevitable friction incident to the distribution of governmental powers among three departments, to save the people from autocracy.

It is error to insist that no society is democratic unless it has a government of unlimited powers, and that no government is democratic unless its legislature had unlimited powers. Constitutional review by an independent judiciary is a tool of proven use in the American quest for an open society of widely dispersed powers. In a vast country, of mixed population, with widely different regional problems, such an organization of society is the surest base for the hopes of democracy.

44

DAVID O'BRIEN

From *Storm Center*

Professor David O'Brien's fine book on the Supreme Court touches on many landmark cases in constitutional law. Few are more important than Brown v. Board of Education of Topeka, Kansas. *Today's students of American government often take* Brown *for granted, since they've lived with the Court's ruling their whole lives; thus they may forget the dramatic events surrounding the 1954 decision. In this excerpt O'Brien revisits the first* Brown *case, as well as* Brown II, *exploring the delicate relationship between the Court and public opinion. He then goes back to President Franklin Roosevelt's infamous 1937 "court-packing" scheme to illustrate another aspect of the impact of public opinion on the judiciary. Unlike the citizenry's direct and immediate reaction to Congress and the president, the communication of views between the public and the judiciary is less easy to measure, O'Brien acknowledges. Yet the Supreme Court lies, as it should, at the heart of the process that resolves the nation's monumental political issues.*

"WHY DOES the Supreme Court pass the school desegregation case?" asked one of Chief Justice Vinson's law clerks in 1952. *Brown v.*

Board of Education of Topeka, Kansas had arrived on the Court's docket in 1951, but it was carried over for oral argument the next term and then consolidated with four other cases and reargued in December 1953. The landmark ruling did not come down until May 17, 1954. "Well," Justice Frankfurter explained, "we're holding it for the election"—1952 was a presidential election year. "You're holding it for the election?" The clerk persisted in disbelief. "I thought the Supreme Court was supposed to decide cases without regard to elections." "When you have a major social political issue of this magnitude," timing and public reactions are important considerations, and, Frankfurter continued, "we do not think this is the time to decide it." Similarly, Tom Clark has recalled that the Court awaited, over Douglas's dissent, additional cases from the District of Columbia and other regions, so as "to get a national coverage, rather than a sectional one." Such political considerations are by no means unique. "We often delay adjudication. It's not a question of evading at all," Clark concluded. "It's just the practicalities of life—common sense."

Denied the power of the sword or the purse, the Court must cultivate its institutional prestige. The power of the Court lies in the pervasiveness of its rulings and ultimately rests with other political institutions and public opinion. As an independent force, the Court has no chance to resolve great issues of public policy. *Dred Scott v. Sandford* (1857) and *Brown v. Board of Education* (1954) illustrate the limitations of Supreme Court policy-making. The "great folly," as Senator Henry Cabot Lodge characterized *Dred Scott*, was not the Court's interpretation of the Constitution or the unpersuasive moral position that blacks were not persons under the Constitution. Rather, "the attempt of the Court to settle the slavery question by judicial decision was simple madness." . . . A hundred years later, political struggles within the country and, notably, presidential and congressional leadership in enforcing the Court's school desegregation ruling saved the moral appeal of *Brown* from becoming another "great folly."

Because the Court's decisions are not self-executing, public reactions inevitably weigh on the minds of the justices. . . .

. . . Opposition to the school desegregation ruling in *Brown* led to bitter, sometimes violent confrontations. In Little Rock, Arkansas, Governor Orval Faubus encouraged disobedience by southern segregationists. The federal National Guard had to be called out to maintain order. The school board in Little Rock unsuccessfully pleaded, in *Cooper v. Aaron* (1958), for the Court's postponement of the implementation of *Brown's* mandate. In the midst of the controversy, Frankfurter worried that Chief Justice Warren's attitude had become "more like that of a fighting politician than that of a judicial statesman." In such confrontations between the Court and the country, "the transcending issue," Frankfurter reminded the brethren, remains that of preserving "the Supreme Court as the authoritative organ of what the Constitution requires." When the justices move too far or too fast in their interpretation of the Constitution, they threaten public acceptance of the Court's legitimacy.

The political struggles of the Court (and among the justices) continue after the writing of opinions and final votes. Announcements of decisions trigger diverse reactions from the media, interest groups, lower courts, Congress, the President, and the general public. Their reactions may enhance or thwart compliance and reinforce or undermine the Court's prestige. Opinion days thus may reveal something of the political struggles that might otherwise remain hidden within the marble temple. They may also mark the beginning of larger political struggles for influence in the country. . . .

When deciding major issues of public law and policy, justices must consider strategies for getting public acceptance of their rulings. When striking down the doctrine of "separate but equal" facilities in 1954 in *Brown v. Board of Education (Brown I)*, for instance, the Warren Court waited a year before issuing, in *Brown II*, its mandate for "all deliberate speed" in ending racial segregation in public education.

Resistance to the social policy announced in *Brown I* was expected. A rigid timetable for desegregation would only intensify opposition. During oral arguments on *Brown II*, devoted to the question of what kind of decree the Court should issue to enforce *Brown*, Warren confronted the hard fact of southern resistance. The attorney for South Carolina, S. Emory Rogers, pressed for an open-ended decree—one that would not specify when and how desegregation should take place. He boldly proclaimed

> Mr. Chief Justice, to say we will conform depends on the decree handed down. I am frank to tell you, right now [in] our district I do not think that we will send—[that] the white people of the district will send their children to the Negro schools. It would be unfair to tell the Court that we are going to do that. I do not think it is. But I do think that something can be worked out. We hope so.

"It is not a question of attitude," Warren shot back, "it is a question of conforming to the decree." Their heated exchange continued as follows:

CHIEF JUSTICE WARREN: But you are not willing to say here that there would be an honest attempt to conform to this decree, if we did leave it to the district court [to implement]?

MR. ROGERS: No, I am not. Let us get the word "honest" out of there.
CHIEF JUSTICE WARREN: No, leave it in.
MR. ROGERS: No, because I would have to tell you that right now we would not conform—we would not send our white children to the negro schools. . . .

Agreement emerged that the Court should issue a short opinion-decree. In a memorandum, Warren summarized the main points of agreement. The opinion should simply state that *Brown I* held radically segregated public schools to be unconstitutional. *Brown II* should acknowledge that the ruling creates various administrative problems, but emphasize that "local school authorities have the primary responsibility for assessing and solving these problems; [and] the courts will have to consider these problems in determining whether the efforts of local school authorities" are in good-faith compliance. . . .

Enforcement and implementation required the cooperation and coordination of all three branches. Little progress could be made, as Assistant Attorney General Pollack has explained, "where historically there had been slavery and a long tradition of discrimination [until] all three branches of the federal government [could] be lined up in support of a movement forward or a requirement for change." The election of Nixon in 1968 then brought changes both in the policies of the executive branch and in the composition of the Court. The simplicity and flexibility of *Brown*, moreover, invited evasion. It produced a continuing struggle over measures, such as gerrymandering school district lines and busing in the 1970s and 1980s, because the mandate itself had evolved from one of ending segregation to one of securing integration in public schools. . . .

"By itself," the political scientist Robert Dahl observed, "the Court is almost powerless to affect the course of national policy." *Brown* dramatically altered the course of American life, but it also reflected the justices' awareness that their decisions are not self-executing. The rulings [in] *Brown* . . . were unanimous but ambiguous. The ambiguity in the desegregation rulings . . . was the price of achieving unanimity. Unanimity appeared necessary if the Court was to preserve its institutional prestige while pursuing revolutionary change in social policy. Justices sacrificed their own policy preferences for more precise guidelines, while the Court tolerated lengthy delays in recognition of the costs of open defiance and the pressures of public opinion. . . .

Public opinion serves to curb the Court when it threatens to go too far or too fast in its rulings. The Court has usually been in step with major political movements, except during transitional periods or critical elections. It would nevertheless be wrong to conclude, along with Peter Finley Dunne's fictional Mr. Dooley, that "th' supreme court follows th' iliction returns." To be sure, the battle over FDR's "Court-packing" plan and the Court's "switch-in-time-that-saved-nine" in 1937 gives that impression. Public opinion supported the New Deal, but turned against FDR after his landslide reelection in 1936 when he proposed to "pack the Court" by increasing its size from nine to fifteen. In a series of five-to-four and six-to-three decisions in 1935–1936, the Court had struck down virtually every important measure of FDR's New Deal program. But in the spring of 1937, while the Senate Judiciary Committee considered FDR's proposal, the Court abruptly handed down three five-to-four rulings upholding major pieces of New Deal legislation. Shortly afterward, FDR's close personal friend and soon-to-be nominee for the Court, Felix Frankfurter, wrote Justice Stone confessing that he was "not wholly happy in thinking that Mr. Dooley should, in the course of history turn out to have been one of the most distinguished legal philosophers." Frankfurter, of course, knew that justices do not simply follow the election returns. The influence of public opinion is more subtle and complex.

Life in the marble temple is not immune from shifts in public opinion. . . . The justices, however, deny being directly influenced by public opinion. The Court's prestige rests on preserving the public's view that justices base their decisions on interpretations of the law, rather than on their personal policy preferences. Yet, complete indifference to public opinion would be the height of judicial arrogance. . . .

"The powers exercised by this Court are inherently oligarchic," Frankfurter once observed when pointing out that "[t]he Court is not saved from being oligarchic because it professes to act in the service of humane ends." Judicial review is antidemocratic. But the Court's power stems from its duty to give authoritative meaning to the Constitution, and rests with the persuasive forces of reason, institutional prestige, the cooperation of other political institutions, and, ultimately, public opinion. The country, in a sense, saves the justices from being an oligarchy by curbing the Court when it goes too far or too fast with its policy-making. Violent opposition and resistance, however, threaten not merely the Court's prestige but the very idea of a government under law.

Some Court watchers, and occasionally even the justices, warn of "an imperial judiciary" and a "government by the judiciary." For much of the Court's history, though, the work of the justices has not involved major issues of public policy. In most areas of public law and policy, the fact that the Court decides an issue is more important than what it decides. Relatively few of the many issues of domestic and foreign policy that arise in government reach the Court. When the Court does decide major questions of public policy, it does so by bringing political controversies within the language, structure, and spirit of the Constitution. By deciding only immediate cases, the Court infuses constitutional meaning into the resolution of the larger surrounding political controversies. But by itself the Court cannot lay those controversies to rest.

The Court can profoundly influence American life. As a guardian of the Constitution, the Court sometimes invites controversy by challenging majoritarian sentiments to respect the rights of minorities and the principles of a representative democracy. The Court's influence is usually more subtle and indirect, varying over time and from one policy issue to another. In the end, the Court's influence on American life cannot be measured precisely, because its policy-making is inextricably bound up with that of other political institutions. Major confrontations in constitutional politics, like those over school desegregation, school prayer, and abortion, are determined as much by what is possible in a system of free government and in a pluralistic society as by what the Court says about the meaning of the Constitution. At its best, the Court appeals to the country to respect the substantive value choices of human dignity and self-governance embedded in our written Constitution.

45

PETER IRONS

From *Brennan vs. Rehnquist*

The U.S. Supreme Court today is different than it was when President Franklin Roosevelt called the justices "Nine Old Men." The Court's membership now includes justices who are black, female, and young, and they come from different regions, religions, and socioeconomic backgrounds. Yet the fundamental issues faced by the Court have not changed. Legal scholar Peter Irons examines a primary philosophical battle on the Supreme Court: individual and minority rights protected by an active judicial branch versus majority power, expressed by strong legislative and executive branches, with the Court exercising judicial restraint. The battle is never better illustrated, Irons feels, than in the contrast between former Justice William J. Brennan and Chief Justice William H. Rehnquist.

WILLIAM J. BRENNAN, JR., and William H. Rehnquist served together on the United States Supreme Court between 1972 and 1990.

During these eighteen years, they headed the Court's liberal and conservative wings, and lobbied for the votes of moderate justices. They provided intellectual and political leadership to contending sides in a battle over the Constitution that affected the lives of every American. The two justices brought divergent judicial philosophies to the Court, rooted in different values and views about the relations of individuals and the state. Each won major victories, but neither won a final triumph. . . . Setting aside unanimous decisions, Brennan and Rehnquist agreed in only 273 of 1,815 case in which one or more justices dissented, just 15 percent of the Court's divided decisions over a span of almost two decades. This was the lowest rate of agreement of any pair of justices over those years. And they disagreed in virtually every case that raised important constitutional issues.

Brennan and Rehnquist are almost totally opposite in background, philosophy, and judicial voting. During their years together, they battled over the Constitution, each trying to rally the Court's moderates to his side. The stakes were high—questions of abortion, affirmative action, capital punishment, and other controversial issues hung in the balance. . . .

This book perceives the Supreme Court as a political institution, and constitutional litigation as a form of politics. These are hardly radical—or recent—notions. "Scarcely any political question arises in the United States," Alexis de Tocqueville observed in 1835, "that is not resolved, sooner or later, into a judicial question." The Court's first major decision, *Marbury v. Madison* in 1803, drew the justices into an intensely political conflict among all three branches of the federal government. Chief Justice John Marshall did not shrink from this dispute. "It is emphatically the province and duty of the judicial department," he wrote, "to say what the law is." His opinion established the Court as the ultimate arbiter of political disputes the other branches could not resolve.

The Supreme Court remains embroiled in political disputes. . . .

There is little question that William Brennan brought with him to the Supreme Court bench a well-formed constitutional philosophy. Shaped in childhood and sharpened by law practice and judicial experience, it can be capsulized in one word: dignity. . . .

The Due Process clauses of the Constitution, added by the Fifth and Fourteenth amendments, were designed to limit governmental authority by protecting the "life, liberty, or property" of Americans from arbitrary official action. As Brennan put it, "Due process required fidelity to a more basic and more subtle principle: the essential dignity and worth of each individual." The Constitution required officials "to treat citizens not as subjects but as fellow human beings." Brennan added that "due process asks whether government has treated someone fairly, whether individual dignity has been honored, whether the worth of an individual has been acknowledged." Officials cannot answer these questions "solely by pointing to rational action taken according to standard rules. They must plumb their conduct more deeply, seeking answers in the more complex equations of human nature and experience." . . .

Another central theme of Brennan's judicial philosophy is that "due process" is a concept whose meaning is not static, frozen by the Framers in 1787, but one that changes over time, as society changes. The Framers did not intend, he argued, to impose on judges an inflexible definition of "a clause that reflects a principle as elusive as human dignity." . . .

The notion that the meaning of "due process" shifts over time imposes a burden on judges who share this approach to the Constitution. Placed by history within a "given age," Brennan said, judges "must draw on our own experience as inhabitants of that age, and our own sense of the uneven fabric of social life. We cannot delude ourselves that the Constitution takes the form of a theorem whose axioms need mere logical deduction." . . .

. . . [There is] another important theme of Brennan's jurisprudence. "The view that all matters of substantive policy should be resolved through the majoritarian process," he says, "has appeal under some circumstances, but I think ultimately it will not do." What the principle of majority rule cannot do, Brennan argues, is "to rectify claims of minority right that arise as a response to the outcomes of that very majoritarian process." When those outcomes—in voting booths and legislative chambers—display prejudice against the "outsiders" in American society, the Constitution requires judicial intervention. In Brennan's view, judges have the power and, in appropriate cases, the duty to displace majority rule when it violates the rights of minorities. "Faith in democracy is one thing," he says, "blind faith quite another." The Constitution was designed to place fundamental rights "beyond the reach of temporary political majorities."

This defense of minority rights does not lead Justice Brennan to advocate replacing what he calls legislative "imperialism" with an equivalent judicial imperialism. The Constitution does not empower judges to impose their own personal values on its provisions. But it does require them to speak, individually and collectively, for American society as a whole. "When Justices interpret the Constitution," Brennan says, "they speak for their community, not for themselves alone." This statement, of course, begs the question of how any justice can determine which "community" is relevant to the decision of a case. Some communities are delimited by geography as local, state, or national; others are defined as ethnic, religious, or racial. And the nation can be considered a "community" as a whole. Beyond these questions are those of public opinion and personal sentiment. No justice has ever proposed that the Court rely on public opinion polls in deciding controversial cases. And no justice has suggested that personal views are superior to the Constitution's demand for impersonal judging.

Justice Brennan does not evade these hard questions. He acknowledges that judges must make "substantive value choices" when they interpret constitutional provisions and that they "must accept the ambiguity inherent in the effort to apply them to modern circumstances." Justices, he says, "read the Constitution in the only way that we can: as twentieth-century Americans." He adds these words: "We look to the history of the time of framing and to the intervening history of interpretation. But the ultimate question must be: What do the words of the text mean in our time? For the genius of the Constitution rests not in any static meaning it might have had in a world that is dead and gone, but in the adaptability of its great principles to cope with current problems and current needs."

Brennan agrees that allowing unelected judges to reverse the decisions of elected lawmakers goes against the grain of democratic government. "These are important, recurrent worries," he admits. But he does not shrink from advocating "an active judiciary" as a counterweight to "legislative irresponsibility." He cites as examples of "panic" by majorities the prosecution of those who criticized American involvement in both world wars. Judges failed in each case to protect the victims of wartime hysteria, and the results "are among the least proud moments in the Court's history."

In summary, Justice Brennan's judicial philosophy begins with his deep religious faith in the "dignity" of every person, moves to the principle that government exists to serve the needs of individuals and to protect their dignity, and ends with the notion that the meaning of the Constitution must change as society changes. Judges speak for a community that is diverse and disputatious, and they must step in to prevent majorities, permanent or temporary, from trampling on the rights of minorities. The foundation of Brennan's jurisprudence is his view of the Constitution as "a living, evolving document that must be read anew" by each generation. . . .

William Rehnquist came to the bench with a clear, consistent political and legal philosophy, but without a judicial record that would show his philosophy in action. It took only a few years of votes and opinions to provide evidence that his judicial philosophy followed the path of his earlier positions. Speaking at the University of Texas Law School in 1976, he outlined his views in a speech entitled "The Notion of a Living Constitution." Of all his speeches, articles, and opinions, this address presents Rehnquist's jurisprudence in its most developed form.

In many ways, his Texas speech was simply an expanded version of the views expressed in Rehnquist's 1948 letter to the *Stanford Daily,* in which he argued that "one personal conviction is no better than another" and rejected "the implication that humanitarianism is desirable" as a moral value. His speech explicitly adopted the position of legal positivism, the notion that the legislative will is supreme and that the content of laws is not a proper concern of judges. If legislators follow the rules, they are constrained only by the explicit commands of the Constitution. The most extreme form of legal positivism—approached in the civil law system of continental Europe—does not allow for judicial review of legislation. The American form of positivism—articulated most forcefully by Robert Bork—gives judges an independent but limited role in reviewing laws, constrained by precedent and the constitutional text. In both systems, judges are expected to show deference to the legislative will. . . .

Rehnquist admitted that "in exercising the very delicate responsibility of judicial review," judges had authority to strike down laws they "find to violate some provision of the Constitution." But he took a narrow view of this authority. The concept of judicial review, he said, "has basically antidemocratic and antimajoritarian facets that require some justification" in a system based on majority rule. The idea of a "living Constitution" struck Rehnquist as a negation of "the nature of political value judgments in a democratic society." He agreed that constitutional safeguards for individual liberty "take on a generalized moral rightness or goodness." But this goodness has no source outside the premise of majority rule, no basis in any "morality" that relies on personal conscience. Constitutional protections "assume a general social acceptance," Rehnquist asserted, "neither because of any intrinsic worth nor because of any unique origins in someone's idea of natural justice but instead simply because they have been incorporated in a constitution by the people."

The major theme of Rehnquist's speech was that political majorities are entitled to enact "positive law" and to impose their moral views on minorities. Laws "take on a form of moral goodness because they have been enacted into positive law," he argued. One complement of legal positivism is moral relativism, the notion that no moral value is inherently superior to another. Rehnquist took this position as a college student and stuck by it as a justice. "There is no conceivable way," he told his Texas audience, "in which I can logically demonstrate to you that the judgments of my conscience are superior to the judgments of your conscience, and vice versa." The "goodness" of any value is decided in the voting booth. . . .

This record shows that Rehnquist is a principled political conservative. But is he also, as he describes himself, a judicial conservative? His philosophy of deference to legislative acts is not, by itself, either liberal or conservative. Laws can be "liberal" by granting rights to minorities, or "conservative" by placing burdens on them. For example, a legislature can pass laws that protect homosexuals from discrimination, or laws that make homosexual behavior a crime. However, in consistently voting to uphold criminal convictions, to deny First Amendment claims, and to reject the claims of racial minorities and women, Rehnquist has taken a "conservative" position on the political issues raised in these cases. He is equally *not* a conservative in the sense of displaying the respect for precedent shown by those who profess "judicial restraint" as a principle. . . .

The jurisprudence of Justice Rehnquist does, in fact, distinguish him from *all* of his colleagues since he joined the Court. None has voted more consistently to uphold governmental actions, legislative and executive. And none has voted more consistently against the claims of dissenters and minorities. His "deference" principle stands in stark contrast to the "dignity" value of Justice Brennan. Their competing visions of the Constitution are rooted in historic struggles over American law and politics. . . .

Supreme Court justices are placed on the bench by elected officials who owe their positions to the electorate. How we vote in elections for senators and presidents will affect the outcome of the Court's decisions in years and decades to come. This is an awesome power, one that every American should ponder before entering the voting booth. Justices Brennan and Rehnquist have offered persuasive arguments on either side of a continuing constitutional debate. But in the end, the decision is ours.

46

JAMES SIMON

From *The Center Holds*

The millennium U.S. Supreme Court is characterized here by James Simon as delicately but firmly in the center of American political ideology. Simon sketches out for readers the composition of the Court, first mentioning the conservative justices favored by Presidents Reagan and Bush: Chief Justice Rehnquist, Justice O'Connor, Justice Scalia, Justice Kennedy, Justice Souter, and Justice Thomas. To give insight into the confirmation process during the Clinton years, Simon describes in some detail the hearings held for Justices Ginsburg and Breyer. At the end of the 1990s, the Supreme Court sits with its centrist judges very much the deciding votes. Students of American politics, however, should anticipate the dramatic change that may come to the Court when veterans such as Chief Justice Rehnquist and Justice Stevens decide to retire. Will the center hold?

THIS IS THE STORY of a conservative judicial revolution that failed. It was led by the chief justice of the United States, William H. Rehnquist, and actively encouraged by two conservative Republican presidents, Ronald Reagan and George Bush. They hoped to reverse the liberal legacy of the Warren Court and its successor, the Burger Court, which had given the broadest scope in the nation's history to the civil rights and civil liberties protections of the Bill of Rights and the Fourteenth Amendment. With five Court appointments, and an aggressive litigation strategy developed by their Justice Department attorneys, Reagan and Bush had good reason to think they would succeed.

The numbers alone strongly suggested that the Supreme Court of the United States of the late 1980s and early '90s would take a radical turn to the right in all crucial areas of civil rights and liberties. By 1988, after the confirmation of Reagan's third appointee, Anthony M. Kennedy, Chief Justice Rehnquist operated with a working conservative majority: Rehnquist himself, the three Reagan appointees—Sandra Day O'Connor, Antonin E. Scalia, and Kennedy—and Byron R. White, a conservative holdover from the Warren and Burger Courts. Bush's appointments of David H. Souter and Clarence Thomas put the finishing touches on what conservatives inside, and outside, the Administration expected to be a solid majority that would steer the Court safely to the right into the next century.

But predicting the Court's direction has always been a hazardous business. In part, this is because the life-tenured justices often find a voice independent of their presidential sponsors once they are securely ensconced on the Court. That independence is encouraged by the Court's internal decision-making process itself. . . . A justice's firm vote in private conference may change as a result of a colleague's argument put forward in conversation, internal memorandum or draft opinion. That happened many times in the cases discussed [here]. In most instances, the center held largely because liberal justices were able to attract support from their more moderate brethren who refused to join the ideologically committed conservatives on the right wing of the Court. . . .

Leading the conservative charge in all of the cases was Chief Justice Rehnquist, who was appointed to the Court by President Richard M. Nixon in 1971 and quickly earned the reputation as the most outspoken conservative on the Court in more than a quarter of a century. As associate justice and later as chief justice, he consistently supported government regulations of individual liberties and rejected the civil rights claims of racial minorities.

His most reliable supporter among pre-Reagan appointees was Byron White, who had been named to the Court by President John F. Kennedy in 1962. White owed his appointment, in part, to his effectiveness as Robert Kennedy's deputy attorney general in enforcing the nation's civil rights laws with stern, understated authority. On the Court, White retained his sternness but little of the Kennedy Administration's liberal spirit. Instead, he wrote sharp dissents to many of the Warren and Burger Courts' most expansive libertarian decisions.

President Reagan's first appointee, Sandra Day O'Connor, had been a law school classmate of Rehnquist's at Stanford. Although not as rigidly conservative in her ideology as Rehnquist, O'Connor frequently supported government regulation of civil liberties, was openly critical of *Roe v. Wade* and opposed liberal interpretations of federal laws and the Fourteenth Amendment that provided broad legal remedies to racial minorities.

Antonin Scalia, appointed to the Court by Reagan the same day in 1986 that Rehnquist was elevated to the chief justiceship, championed a strong conservative ideology that matched well with Rehnquist's. With supreme confidence in his ability to defend his views, Scalia was eager to take on all comers in the privacy of the justices' conferences, in open court and in his uncompromising judicial opinions.

The Reagan Administration was confident that it had provided Chief Justice Rehnquist with the crucial fifth vote for his conservative majority with the appointment of Judge Anthony Kennedy of the U.S. Court of Appeals for the Ninth Circuit. Kennedy's name had surfaced after the bruising, unsuccessful confirmation fight over Judge Robert Bork. Although he was no ideologue, Kennedy exhibited a steady, cautious conservative record as a federal appeals judge. . . .

. . . President Bush appeared to solidify the conservative majority with two appointments. Little was known about his first appointee, David Souter, who had toiled quietly on the trial and state appellate courts in

New Hampshire. The same could not be said for Bush's second appointee, Clarence Thomas, whose aggressively conservative political pronouncements while chairman of the Equal Employment Opportunity Commission in the 1980s had endeared him to both Reagan and Bush.

. . . Justices Ruth Bader Ginsburg and Stephen G. Breyer, named to the Court by President Bill Clinton, became the first appointees by a Democratic president in a quarter century, interrupting a succession of ten Republican-appointed justices. Although it is too early to predict exactly where Ginsburg and Breyer will fit in ideologically, their prior records of moderation as federal appeals court judges virtually assure the denouement of the conservatives' revolution. . . .

Judge Ruth Bader Ginsburg of the U.S. Court of Appeals for the District of Columbia dressed immaculately for the formal occasion of her Senate Judiciary Committee hearings in July 1993, wearing a bright blue suit and an elegant brooch and earrings. As a woman nominated to the Court to succeed retiring Justice Byron White, Ginsburg was still something of a novelty, since only once before in the Court's 203-year history had a president appointed a member of her sex. But the more significant fact about the nomination was that Ginsburg, a former Columbia Law School professor and pioneering women's rights advocate, was the first Supreme Court nominee appointed by a Democratic president in a generation; it had been twenty-six years since President Johnson had nominated Thurgood Marshall.

The Ginsburg nomination interrupted the steady succession of appointments by four Republican presidents, from Richard Nixon's appointment of Chief Justice Warren Burger in 1969 to George Bush's nomination of Clarence Thomas twenty-two years later. More important, the Ginsburg appointment promised to contain the most serious threats to civil rights and liberties by the conservatives on the Rehnquist Court.

Comparing Judge Ginsburg to Justice Sandra Day O'Connor, the first woman to serve on the Court, was natural, but the more relevant professional comparison was to the last Democratic nominee, Thurgood Marshall. Ginsburg and Marshall were linked by their unique accomplishments as lawyers: Marshall would always be remembered as the great advocate of the civil rights movement, and Judge Ginsburg was justifiably admired as the lawyer who used the courts to force recognition of women's constitutional rights under the Equal Protection Clause.

After President Bill Clinton had stumbled through an awkward weekend of indecision in mid-June 1993, his nomination of Ginsburg allowed the entire nation to heave a collective sigh of relief. Ginsburg possessed the attributes of an excellent Court nominee—penetrating intellect, broad experience in the law, a calm, deliberate judicial temperament—and none of the prickly ideological thorns that had often transformed the Senate Caucus Room, where recent confirmation hearings had been held, into a political briar patch.

One political cartoon depicting the Ginsburg hearings had balloons floating festively above the senators, who sported conical party hats and displayed a large welcome sign: CONGRATULATIONS RUTH GINSBURG! And, indeed, the committee members, Republicans as well as Democrats, greeted the nominee with celebratory enthusiasm. The expanded committee of eighteen senators practically fell over one another in their rush to praise Judge Ginsburg; their laudatory prepared statements alone consumed a full two hours.

When she finally was allowed to read her own prepared statement, Judge Ginsburg, a small, sixty-year-old woman, who wore oversized glasses and her hair tightly brushed back in a bun, delivered the Brooklyn version of Clarence Thomas's Pin Point Remembrances—an affecting, personal trip backward in time to thank those who had helped her along the way to professional achievement. "Neither of my parents had the means to attend college, but both taught me to love learning, to care about people, and to work hard for whatever I wanted or believed in," Judge Ginsburg told the committee members. "Their parents had the foresight to leave the old country when Jewish ancestry and faith meant exposure to pogroms and denigration of one's human worth. What has become of me could happen only in America. . . . "

In her statement, Judge Ginsburg selected her judicial heroes carefully, quoting Judge Learned Hand, as well as Justices Holmes and Cardozo. All three practiced, and counseled their colleagues to exercise, judicial restraint. "Justice is not to be taken by storm," Judge Ginsburg said, quoting Cardozo. "She is to be wooed by slow advances." The nominee made the theme of judicial caution her own. "My approach, I believe, is neither liberal nor conservative," Ginsburg told the committee. "Rather, it is rooted in the place of the judiciary in our democratic society. The Constitution's preamble speaks first of 'we the people' and then of their elected representatives. The judiciary is third in line, and it is placed apart from the political fray so that its members can judge fairly, impartially, in accordance with the law and without fear about the animosity of any appreciate group."

At the end of her opening statement, Ginsburg invited the committee members to judge her on the basis of her professional record of thirty-four years—briefs, lectures, articles and opinions—an invitation, in fact and spirit, that contrasted starkly with the previous Court nominee, Judge

Clarence Thomas. Thomas did not encourage the Judiciary Committee to judge him on his written record; indeed, he disavowed much of it. There was a second, equally instructive, difference between the confirmation hearings of Ginsburg and Thomas. Judge Ginsburg built her answers to committee members' questions organically, from basic premises to general conclusions—in contrast to Judge Thomas, whose prepackaged responses seemed calculated to pass the committee's examination with the minimum amount of intellectual effort.

In the electronic age of punchy soundbites, Judge Ginsburg preferred serious discourse. Her answers were punctuated with long pauses, not, it was immediately obvious, because she could not think of an appropriate response, but because she could—and for this she demanded time to carefully organize her thoughts before she spoke.

Ginsburg was the first Court nominee, for example, to provide the Senate Judiciary Committee with a comprehensive analysis of her views on *Roe v. Wade.* She had ruminated publicly about an alternative to the *Roe* analysis, suggesting that both the Court and the nation might have been better served by a more cautious ruling. Ginsburg nonetheless gave her firm endorsement to a woman's constitutional right to an abortion, rooted either in the Due Process Clause or Equal Protection Clause of the Fourteenth Amendment (both of which she happily analyzed for the senators).

By the end of her three days of testimony, Ginsburg had provided the committee and the full Senate with a sound framework by which to evaluate her judicial qualifications and approach to the Court's work. Judge Ginsburg received 99 Senate votes for confirmation, 47 more than the previous nominee, Clarence Thomas. Ginsburg's lopsided Senate vote and her overwhelmingly positive public approval ratings suggested that her appointment traversed the nation's political spectrum.

Almost exactly a year after the Ginsburg confirmation hearings, President Clinton's second nominee to the Court, Chief Judge Stephen Breyer of the U.S. Court of Appeals for the First Circuit, sat at the same witness table before the Senate Judiciary Committee. Breyer, who had been nominated to replace the retiring Justice Harry Blackmun, had come tantalizingly close to making his appearance before the committee a year earlier. President Clinton, in a widely publicized invitation, had asked Breyer at that time to come to the White House to be interviewed as a possible successor to Justice Byron White. At the last moment, however, Clinton chose Judge Ruth Bader Ginsburg, not Breyer.

When Breyer finally faced the committee in July 1994, he appeared eager to demonstrate that the president had chosen well in nominating him. Breyer's gaunt, ascetic appearance concealed a warm and ingratiating personality. He spoke proudly of his maternal grandparents' immigration to the United States from Eastern Europe. And he credited his mother for profoundly influencing his values and aspirations. "She was the one who made absolutely clear to me in no uncertain terms that whatever intellectual ability I might have means nothing and won't mean anything unless I can work with other people and use whatever talents I have to help them," he told the committee. Breyer's mother had advised him not to spend too much time with books, and the nominee conceded that she was right. "I mean, my ideas about people do not come from libraries," he said.

Breyer could afford to emphasize his interpersonal skills since his outstanding academic record and professional accomplishments needed little elaboration. An honors graduate of the Harvard Law School, Breyer had clerked for Supreme Court Justice Arthur Goldberg, taught law at Harvard and served as chief counsel for the Senate Judiciary Committee before his appointment to the federal appeals court. His reputation on the U.S. Court of Appeals for the First Circuit was that of a lucid thinker and writer whose philosophy was not easily categorized—though he tended to lean slightly to the liberal side of center, a description that also fit Ruth Bader Ginsburg. And like Ginsburg, Breyer also reveled in the judge's craft, analyzing a legal problem exhaustively to arrive at what he considered to be a fair solution.

At his confirmation hearings, Breyer exhibited a child's enthusiasm in explaining the technical aspects of a judicial decision; he rapturously recited the details, for example, of a seventy-two-year-old property rights decision by Justice Oliver Wendell Holmes, Jr. He also quoted Holmes's famous aphorism that law reflects not so much logic as history and experience. The law, Breyer said, had a single basic purpose: to help Americans "live together productively, harmoniously and in freedom."

The nominee carefully sidestepped a discussion of specific constitutional issues that might come before the Court. Breyer nonetheless affirmed that a woman's right to an abortion was the law (but would not speculate on what state regulations of abortion would be constitutional). He also spoke openly about the wall of separation between church and state, Jefferson's metaphor that had been attacked by Rehnquist Court conservatives.

And though he rarely missed an opportunity to please his interrogators, Breyer was not always easily led by a senator's suggested conclusion. The ranking Republican member of the committee, Senator Orrin Hatch, invited the nominee to agree with him that a judge's role was limited to applying the law. "Of course, that is true," Breyer replied, but it wasn't always so clear what the law is in the "vast, open areas" in which the Supreme Court was required to judge. Since there were usually good arguments on both sides of important policy issues, the Court's job, Breyer suggested, was "to find the correct solution, the helpful solution consistent with the underlying human purpose." By implication, Breyer signaled that he would not bring to the Court an overarching ideology with ready answers to the most protracted constitutional problems.

Breyer's testimony satisfied Senator Hatch and an overwhelming majority of his colleagues, who confirmed the nominee for a seat on the Supreme Court.

If Ginsburg's and Breyer's extensive records on the federal appeals courts are a reliable guide to their future Court performances, there will be no special pleadings to their colleagues. Rather, Justices Ginsburg and Breyer will put forward their positions with fastidious regard for the legal contours of their arguments and arrive at narrow results that will reflect their own judicial caution. In that approach, they closely resemble another centrist on the Court, Justice David Souter.

At their confirmation hearings, all three—Souter, Ginsburg and Breyer—spoke admiringly of Justices Holmes; they admitted that their judicial model reflected their own interest in the labor-intensive craft of judging. Souter, Ginsburg and Breyer pride themselves on their technical abilities to break down a constitutional problem into its smallest component parts. They honor the Court's precedents, not in the abstract, but as a basis for building continuity into the law. And yet they are willing to act, however cautiously, in response to the changing demands of law in a dynamic society.

Justices Ginsburg and Breyer, like Souter, approach the writing of their opinions as an artist constructs a collage—with careful regard for the materials at hand but also with a desire to bring their unique experience and sensibilities to the project. As no two artists will produce the same collage, Souter, Ginsburg and Breyer will not always agree on the correct constitutional perspective. Souter's constitutional values are essentially conservative. Ginsburg and Breyer bring libertarian instincts to the Court—they have viewed the law from an outsider's perspective, Ginsburg as a woman and both Ginsburg and Breyer as Jews.

The final word on the Court of the 1990s has not, of course, been written. We know that either President Clinton or his successor in office will round out the Court appointments for this century, and, further, that no one can accurately predict where any single case will lead any of the sitting or future justices. But even if we accept these qualifications, there remains the unmistakable conclusion that the Ginsburg and Breyer appointments mark a critical turning point for the Rehnquist Court. Justices Ginsburg and Breyer have solidified the moderate center of this Court, and neither pressure from the right wing—Rehnquist, Scalia and Thomas—nor any later appointments are likely to undercut the prevailing judicial ethos of moderation.

By design, the Rehnquist Court has heard progressively fewer cases, and in many of their recent decisions the language of the Court majorities has tended to be more technical and less sweeping than in the past. But even if future Court majorities harbor less aggressive ambitions than the liberal activists on the Warren Court of the 1960s or the conservative activists on the Rehnquist Court, the results will be historic. For the centrists will reaffirm, in their restrained fashion, Madison's belief that an independent judiciary should stand as "an impenetrable bulwark" of liberty and strike down as unconstitutional any acts by the legislative and executive branches that violate the Bill of Rights. If that seems to be a tepid result, consider the alternative.

Had George Bush been reelected president in 1992, he would have had the opportunity to replace Justices White and Blackmun on the Court. If he modeled his second-term appointments on his last nominee, Clarence Thomas, Bush would have been able to accomplish what Chief Justice Rehnquist and his fellow conservative activists on the Court almost succeeded in doing without the help of a second Bush Administration: a wholesale reordering of the Court's constitutional priorities.

For those who value the civil rights and liberties protections guaranteed by the decisions of the modern Supreme Court spanning more than three decades, it was a very close call.

PART NINE

Public Opinion

47

JAMES BRYCE

From *The American Commonwealth*

In James Bryce's massive study of the United States, no topic is treated in more adulatory a way than public opinion. It is a little more than one hundred years after the distinguished British visitor's unabashed praise of the American people, whom he saw "freely and constantly reading, talking, and judging of public affairs with a view to voting thereon." Was Bryce writing about the United States when he described a nation that is "patient, tolerant, reasonable, and . . . more likely to be unembittered and unvexed by class divisions"? Perhaps America has not yet quite reached the point Bryce anticipated; maybe Bryce was right, and the United States today is too critical of itself; or, maybe Bryce was wrong.

OF ALL the experiments which America has made, this is that which best deserves study, for her solution of the problem differs from all previous solutions, and she has shown more boldness in trusting public opinion, in recognizing and giving effect to it, than has yet been shown elsewhere. Towering over Presidents and State governors, over Congress and State legislatures, over conventions and the vast machinery of party, public opinion stands out, in the United States, as the great source of power, the master of servants who tremble before it. . . .

In the United States public opinion is the opinion of the whole nation, with little distinction of social classes. The politicians, including the members of Congress and of State legislatures, are, perhaps not (as Americans sometimes insinuate) below, yet certainly not above the average level of their constituents. They find no difficulty in keeping touch with outside opinion. Washington or Albany may corrupt them, but not in the way of modifying their political ideas. They do not aspire to the function of forming opinion. They are like the Eastern slave who says "I hear and obey." Nor is there any one class or set of men, or any one "social layer," which more than another originates ideas and builds up political doctrine for the mass. The opinion of the nation is the resultant of the views, not of a number of classes, but of a multitude of individuals, diverse, no doubt, from one another, but, for the purposes of politics far less diverse than if they were members of groups defined by social rank or by property.

The consequences are noteworthy. One is, that statesmen cannot, as in Europe, declare any sentiment which they find telling on their friends or their opponents in politics to be confined to the rich, or to those occupied with government, and to be opposed to the general sentiment of the people. In America you cannot appeal from the classes to the masses. What the employer thinks, his workmen think. What the wholesale merchant feels, the retail storekeeper feels, and the poorer customers feel. Divisions of opinion are vertical and not horizontal. Obviously this makes opinion more easily ascertained, while increasing its force as a governing power, and gives the people, that is to say, all classes in the community, a clearer and stronger consciousness of being the rulers of their country than European peoples have. Every man knows that he is himself a part of the government, bound by duty as well as by self-interest to devote part of his time and thoughts to it. He may neglect this duty, but he admits it to be a duty. . . .

. . . The government is his own, and he individually responsible for its conduct. . . . The Americans are an educated people. . . . They know the constitution of their own country, they follow public affairs, they join in local government and learn from it how government must be carried on, and in particular how discussion must be conducted in meetings, and its results tested at elections. . . .

That the education of the masses is nevertheless a superficial education goes without saying. It is sufficient to enable them to think they know something about the great problems of politics: insufficient to show them how little they know. The public elementary school gives everybody the key to knowledge in making reading and writing familiar, but it has not time to teach him how to use the key. . . . This observation, however, is not so much a reproach to the schools, . . . as a tribute to the height of the ideal which the American conception of popular rule sets up. . . . For the functions of the citizen are not . . . confined to the choosing of legislators, who are then left to settle issues of policy and select executive rulers. The American citizen is virtually one of the governors of the republic. Issues are decided and rulers selected by the direct popular vote. Elections are so frequent that to do his duty at them a citizen ought to be constantly watching public affairs with a full comprehension of the principles involved in them, and a judgment of the candidates derived from a criticism of their arguments as well as a recollection of their past careers. As has been said, the instruction received in the common schools and from the newspapers, and supposed to be developed by the practice of primaries and conventions, while it makes the voter deem himself capable of governing, does not completely fit him to weigh the real merits of statesmen, to discern the true grounds on which questions ought to be decided, to note the drift of events and discover the direction in which parties are being carried. He is like a sailor who knows the spars and ropes of the ship and is expert in working her, but is ignorant of geography and navigation; who can perceive that some of the officers are smart and others dull, but cannot judge which of them is qualified to use the sextant or will best keep his head during a hurricane. . . .

The frame of the American government has assumed and trusted to the activity of public opinion, not only as the power which must correct and remove the difficulties due to the restrictions imposed on each department, and to possible collisions between them, but as the influence which must supply the defects incidental to a system which works entirely by the machinery of popular elections. Under a system of elections one man's vote is as good as another, the vicious and ignorant have as much weight as the wise and good. A system of elections might be imagined which would provide no security for due deliberation or full discussion, a system which, while democratic in name, recognizing no privilege, and referring everything to the vote of the majority, would in practice be hasty, violent, tyrannical. It is with such a possible democracy that one has to contrast the rule of public opinion as it exists in the United States. Opinion declares itself legally through elections. But opinion is at work at other times also, and has other methods of declaring itself. It secures full discussion of issues of policy and of the characters of men. It suffers nothing to be concealed. It listens patiently to all the arguments that are addressed to it. Eloquence, education, wisdom, the authority derived from experience and high character, tell upon it in the long run, and have, perhaps not always their due influence, but yet a great and growing influence. Thus a democracy governing itself through a constantly active public opinion, and not solely by its intermittent mechanism of elections, tends to become patient, tolerant, reasonable, and is more likely to be unembittered and unvexed by class divisions.

It is the existence of such a public opinion as this, the practice of freely and constantly reading, talking, and judging of public affairs with a view to voting thereon, rather than the mere possession of political rights, that gives to popular government that educative and stimulative power which is so frequently claimed as its highest merit.

48

WALTER LIPPMANN

From *The Phantom Public*

Walter Lippmann was a prominent American journalist who wrote during the first half of the twentieth century. In his much-read book on public opinion, The Phantom Public, *Lippmann took a hard and realistic look at the role played by the American people in government decision-making. His conclusions were startlingly critical. He portrayed citizens as relatively uninformed, often disinterested, and usually haphazard in their views. Opinions emerge only in time of crisis, and then fade quickly. Many people do not participate at all. Lippmann extended his harsh judgment to political leaders who skillfully manipulate public opinion. To soften his criticisms, Lippmann pointed to what he believed to be the fallacy behind public opinion: "It is bad for a fat man to try to be a ballet dancer." To expect more of the public, Lippmann felt, was an unrealistic and self-defeating illusion.*

THE PRIVATE CITIZEN today has come to feel rather like a deaf spectator in the back row, who ought to keep his mind on the mystery off there, but cannot quite manage to keep awake. He knows he is somehow affected by what is going on. Rules and regulations continually, taxes annually and wars occasionally remind him that he is being swept along by great drifts of circumstance.

Yet these public affairs are in no convincing way his affairs. They are for the most part invisible. They are managed, if they are managed at all, at distant centers, from behind the scenes, by unnamed powers. As a private person he does not know for certain what is going on, or who is doing it, or where he is being carried. No newspaper reports his environment so that he can grasp it; no school has taught him how to imagine it; his ideals, often, do not fit with it; listening to speeches, uttering opinions and voting do not, he finds, enable him to govern it. He lives in a world which he cannot see, does not understand and is unable to direct.

In the cold light of experience he knows that his sovereignty is a fiction. He reigns in theory, but in fact he does not govern. . . .

There is then nothing particularly new in the disenchantment which the private citizen expresses by not voting at all, by voting only for the head of the ticket, by staying away from the primaries, by not reading speeches and documents, by the whole list of sins of omission for which he is denounced. I shall not denounce him further. My sympathies are with him, for I believe that he has been saddled with an impossible task and that he is asked to practice an unattainable ideal. I find it so myself for, although public business is my main interest and I give most of my time to watching it, I cannot find time to do what is expected of me in the theory of democracy; that is, to know what is going on and to have an opinion worth expressing on every question which confronts a self-governing community. And I have not happened to meet anybody, from a President of the United States to a professor of political science, who came anywhere near to embodying the accepted ideal of the sovereign and omnicompetent citizen. . . .

[Today's theories] assume that either the voters are inherently competent to direct the course of affairs or that they are making progress toward such an ideal. I think it is a false ideal. I do not mean an undesirable ideal. I mean an unattainable ideal, bad only in the sense that it is bad for a fat man to try to be a ballet dancer. An ideal should express the true possibilities of its subject. When it does not it perverts the true possibilities. The ideal of the omnicompetent, sovereign citizen is, in my opinion, such a false ideal. It is unattainable. The pursuit of it is misleading. The failure to achieve it has produced the current disenchantment.

The individual man does not have opinions on all public affairs. He does not know how to direct public affairs. He does not know what is happening, why it is happening, what ought to happen. I cannot imagine how he could know, and there is not the least reason for thinking, as mystical democrats have thought, that the compounding of individual ignorances in masses of people can produce a continuous directing force in public affairs. . . .

The need in the Great Society not only for publicity but for uninterrupted publicity is indisputable. But we shall misunderstand the need seriously if we imagine that the purpose of the publication can possibly be the informing of every voter. We live at the mere beginnings of public accounting. Yet the facts far exceed our curiosity. . . . A few executives here and there . . . read them. The rest of us ignore them for the good and sufficient reason that we have other things to do. . . .

Specific opinions give rise to immediate executive acts; to take a job, to do a particular piece of work, to hire or fire, to buy or sell, to stay here or go there, to accept or refuse, to command or obey. General opinions give rise to delegated, indirect, symbolic, intangible results: to a vote, to a resolution, to applause, to criticism, to praise or dispraise, to audiences, circulations, followings, contentment or discontent. The specific opinion may lead to a decision to act within the area where a man has personal jurisdiction, that is, within the limits set by law and custom, his personal power and his personal desire. But general opinions lead only to some sort of expression, such as voting, and do not result in executive acts except in coöperation with the general opinions of large numbers of other persons.

Since the general opinions of large numbers of persons are almost certain to be a vague and confusing medley, action cannot be taken until these opinions have been factored down, canalized, compressed and made uniform. . . . The making of one general will out of a multitude of general wishes . . . consists essentially in the use of symbols which assemble emotions after they have been detached from their ideas. Because feelings are much less specific than ideas, and yet more poignant, the leader is able to make a homogeneous will out of a heterogeneous mass of desires. The process, therefore, by which general opinions are brought to cooperation consists of an intensification of feeling and a degradation of significance. Before a mass of general opinions can eventuate in executive action, the choice is narrowed down to a few alternatives. The victorious alternative is executed not by the mass but by individuals in control of its energy. . . .

. . . We must assume, then, that the members of a public will not possess an insider's knowledge of events or share his point of view. They cannot, therefore, construe intent, or appraise the exact circumstances, enter intimately into the minds of the actors or into the details of the argument. They can watch only for coarse signs indicating where their sympathies ought to turn.

We must assume that the members of a public will not anticipate a problem much before its crisis has become obvious, nor stay with the problem long after its crisis is past. They will not know the antecedent events, will not have seen the issue as it developed, will not have thought out or willed a program, and will not be able to predict the consequences of acting on that program. We must assume as a theoretically fixed premise of popular government that normally men as members of a public will not be well informed, continuously interested, nonpartisan, creative or executive. We must assume that a public is inexpert in its curiosity, intermittent, that it discerns only gross distinctions, is slow to be aroused and quickly diverted; that, since it acts by aligning itself, it personalizes whatever it considers, and is interested only when events have been melodramatized as a conflict.

The public will arrive in the middle of the third act and will leave before the last curtain, having stayed just long enough perhaps to decide who is the hero and who the villain of the piece. Yet usually that judgment will necessarily be made apart from the intrinsic merits, on the basis of a sample of behavior, an aspect of a situation, by very rough external evidence. . . .

. . . The ideal of public opinion is to align men during the crisis of a problem in such a way as to favor the action of those individuals who may be able to compose the crisis. The power to discern those individuals is the end of the effort to educate public opinion. . . .

Public opinion, in this theory, is a reserve of force brought into action during a crisis in public affairs. Though it is itself an irrational force, under favorable institutions, sound leadership and decent training the power of public opinion might be placed at the disposal of those who stood for workable law as against brute assertion. In this theory, public opinion does not make the law. But by canceling lawless power it may establish the condition under which law can be made. It does not reason, investigate, invent, persuade, bargain or settle. But, by holding the aggressive party in check, it may liberate intelligence. Public opinion in its highest ideal will defend those who are prepared to act on their reason against the interrupting force of those who merely assert their will.

That, I think, is the utmost that public opinion can effectively do. With the substance of the problem it can do nothing usually but meddle ignorantly or tyrannically. . . .

For when public opinion attempts to govern directly it is either a failure or a tyranny. It is not able to master the problem intellectually, nor to deal with it except by wholesale impact. The theory of democracy has not recognized this truth because it has identified the functioning of government with the will of the people. This is a fiction. The intricate business of framing laws and of administering them through several hundred thousand public officials is in no sense the act of the voters nor a translation of their will. . . .

Therefore, instead of describing government as an expression of the people's will, it would seem better to say that government consists of a body of officials, some elected, some appointed, who handle professionally, and in the first instance, problems which come to public opinion spasmodically and on appeal. Where the parties directly responsible do not work out an adjustment, public officials intervene. When the officials fail, public opinion is brought to bear on the issue. . . .

This, then, is the ideal of public action which our inquiry suggests. Those who happen in any question to constitute the public should attempt only to create an equilibrium in which settlements can be reached directly and by consent. The burden of carrying on the work of the world, of inventing, creating, executing, of attempting justice, formulating laws and moral codes, of dealing with the technic and the substance, lies not upon public opinion and not upon government but on those who are responsibly concerned as agents in the affair. Where problems arise, the ideal is a settlement by the particular interests involved. They alone know what the trouble really is. No decision by public officials or by commuters reading headlines in the train can usually and in the long run be so good as settlement by consent among the parties at interest. No moral code, no political theory can usually and in the long run be imposed from the heights of public opinion, which will fit a case so well as direct agreement reached where arbitrary power has been disarmed.

It is the function of public opinion to check the use of force in a crisis, so that men, driven to make terms, may live and let live.

49

V. O. KEY

From *Public Opinion and American Democracy*

Professor V. O. Key was a pioneer in the study of many facets of modern American politics, including elections, political parties, and public opinion. His detailed study of public opinion attempted to explain the relationship between the people's opinions and the political leadership's opinions. Key's analysis is complicated but clear in its recognition of both elite and mass influence. A particularly useful concept is Key's "opinion dike." He believed that the public's opinion keeps leaders from straying too far outside the parameters acceptable to the people in the making of policy. Most important, Key lifted the blame for "indecision, decay, and disaster" from the shoulders of the public onto the leadership stratum where, he alleged, it really belongs.

THE EXPLORATION of public attitudes is a pursuit of endless fascination—and frustration. Depiction of the distribution of opinions within the public, identification of the qualities of opinion, isolation of the odd and of the obvious correlates of opinion, and ascertainment of the modes of opinion formation are pursuits that excite human curiosity. Yet these endeavors are bootless unless the findings about the preferences, aspirations, and prejudices of the public can be connected with the workings of the governmental system. The nature of that connection has been suggested by the examination of the channels by which governments become aware of public sentiment and the institutions through which opinion finds more or less formal expression.

When all these linkages are treated, the place of public opinion in government has still not been adequately portrayed. The problem of opinion and government needs to be viewed in an even broader context. Consideration of the role of public opinion drives the observer to the more fundamental question of how it is that democratic governments manage to operate at all. Despite endless speculation on that problem, perplexities still exist about what critical circumstances, beliefs, outlooks, faiths, and conditions are conducive to the maintenance of regimes under which public opinion is controlling, at least in principle, and is, in fact, highly influential. . . . Though the preceding analyses did not uncover the secret of the conditions precedent to the practice of democratic politics, they pointed to a major piece of the puzzle that was missing as we sought to assemble the elements that go into the construction of a democratic regime. The significance of that missing piece may be made apparent in an indirect manner. In an earlier day public opinion seemed to be pictured as a mysterious vapor that emanated from the undifferentiated citizenry and in some way or another enveloped the apparatus of government to bring it into conformity with the public will. These weird conceptions, some of which were mentioned in our introductory chapter, passed out of style as the technique of the sample survey permitted the determination, with some accuracy, of the distribution of opinions within the population. Vast areas of ignorance remain in our information about people's opinions and aspirations; nevertheless, a far more revealing map of the gross topography of public opinion can now be drawn than could have been a quarter of a century ago.

Despite their power as instruments for the observation of mass opinion, sampling procedures do not bring within their range elements of the political system basic for the understanding of the role of mass opinion within the system. Repeatedly, as we have sought to explain particular distributions, movements, and qualities of mass opinion, we have had to go beyond the survey data and make assumptions and estimates about the role and behavior of that thin stratum of persons referred to variously as the political elite, the political activists, the leadership echelons, or the influentials. In the normal operation of surveys designed to obtain tests of mass sentiment, so few persons from this activist stratum fall into the sample that they cannot well be differentiated, even in a static description, from those persons less involved politically. The data tell us almost nothing about the dynamic relations between the upper layer of activists and mass opinion. The missing piece of our puzzle is this elite element of the opinion system. . . .

While the ruling classes of a democratic order are in a way invisible because of the vagueness of the lines defining the influentials and the relative ease of entry to their ranks, it is plain that the modal norms and standards of a democratic elite have their peculiarities. Not all persons in leadership echelons have precisely the same basic beliefs; some may even regard the people as a beast. Yet a fairly high concentration prevails around the modal beliefs, even though the definition of those beliefs must be imprecise. Fundamental is a regard for public opinion, a belief that in some way or another it should prevail. Even those who cynically humbug the people make a great show of deference to the populace. The basic doctrine goes further to include a sense of trusteeship for the people generally and an adherence to the basic doctrine that collective efforts should be dedicated to the promotion of mass gains rather than of narrow class advantage; elite elements tethered to narrow group interest have no slack for maneuver to accommodate themselves to mass aspirations. Ultimate expression of these faiths comes in the willingness to abide by the outcome of popular elections. The growth of leadership structures with beliefs including these broad articles of faith is probably accomplished only over a considerable period of time, and then only under auspicious circumstances.

If an elite is not to monopolize power and thereby to bring an end to democratic practices, its rules of the game must include restraints in the exploitation of public opinion. Dimly perceptible are rules of etiquette that limit the kinds of appeals to public opinion that may be properly made. If it is assumed that the public is manipulable at the hands of unscrupulous leadership (as it is under some conditions), the maintenance of a democratic order requires the inculcation in leadership elements of a taboo against appeals that would endanger the existence of democratic practices. Inflammation of the sentiments of a sector of the public disposed to exert the tyranny of an intolerant majority (or minority) would be a means of destruction of a democratic order. Or by the exploitation of latent differences and conflicts within the citizenry it may at times be possible to paralyze a regime as intense hatreds among classes of people come to dominate public affairs. Or by encouraging unrealistic expectations among the people a clique of politicians may rise to power, a position to be kept by repression as disillusionment sets in. In an experienced democracy such tactics may be "unfair" competition among members of the politically active class. In short, certain restraints on political competition help keep competition within tolerable limits. The observation of a few American political campaigns might lead one to the conclusion that there are no restraints on politicians as they attempt to humbug the people. Even so, admonitions ever recur against arousing class against class, against stirring the animosities of religious groups, and against demagoguery in its more extreme forms. American politicians manifest considerable restraint in this regard when they are tested against the standards of behavior of politicians of most of those regimes that have failed in the attempt to establish or maintain democratic practices. . . .

. . . Certain broad structural or organizational characteristics may need to be maintained among the activists of a democratic order if they are to perform their functions in the system. Fundamental is the absence of sufficient cohesion among the activists to unite them into a single group dedicated to the management of public affairs and public opinion. Solidification of the elite by definition forecloses opportunity for public choice among alternative governing groups and also destroys the mechanism for the unfettered expression of public opinion or of the opinions of the many subpublics. . . .

. . . Competitive segments of the leadership echelons normally have their roots in interests or opinion blocs within society. A degree of social diversity thus may be, if not a prerequisite, at least helpful in the construction of a leadership appropriate for a democratic regime. A series of independent social bases provide the foundations for a political elite difficult to bring to the state of unification that either prevents the rise of democratic processes or converts them into sham rituals. . . .

Another characteristic may be mentioned as one that, if not a prerequisite to government by public opinion, may profoundly affect the nature of a democratic order. This is the distribution through the social structure of those persons highly active in politics. By various analyses, none founded on completely satisfactory data, we have shown that in the United States the political activists—if we define the term broadly—are scattered through the socio-economic hierarchy. The upper-income and occupational groups, to be sure, contribute disproportionately; nevertheless, individuals of high political participation are sprinkled throughout the lesser occupational strata. Contrast the circumstances when the highly active political stratum coincides with the high socioeconomic stratum. Conceivably the winning of consent and the creation of a sense of political participation and of sharing in public affairs may be far simpler when political activists of some degree are spread through all social strata. . . .

Allied with these questions is the matter of access to the wider circles of political leadership and of the recruitment and indoctrination of these political activists. Relative ease of access to the arena of active politics may be a preventive of the rise of intransigent blocs of opinion managed by those denied participation in the regularized processes of politics. In a sense, ease of access is a necessary consequence of the existence of a somewhat fragmented stratum of political activists. . . .

This discussion in terms of leadership echelons, political activists, or elites falls painfully on the ears of democratic romantics. The mystique of democracy has in it no place for ruling classes. As perhaps with all powerful systems of faith, it is vague on the operating details. Yet by their nature governing systems, be they democratic or not, involve a division of social labor. Once that axiom is accepted, the comprehension of democratic practices requires a search for the peculiar characteristics of the political influentials in such an order, for the special conditions under which they work, and for the means by which the people keep them in check. The vagueness of the mystique of democracy is matched by the intricacy of its operating practices. If it is true that those who rule tend sooner or later to prove themselves enemies of the rights of man—and there is something to be said for the validity of this proposition—then any system that restrains that tendency however slightly can excite only awe. . . .

Analytically it is useful to conceive of the structure of a democratic order as consisting of the political activists and the mass of people. Yet this differentiation becomes deceptive unless it is kept in mind that the democratic activists consist of people arranged along a spectrum of political participation and involvement, ranging from those in the highest posts of official leadership to the amateurs who become sufficiently interested to try to round up a few votes for their favorite in the presidential campaign. . . . It is in the dynamics of the system, the interactions between these strata, that the import of public opinion in democratic orders becomes manifest. Between the activists and the mass there exists a system of communication and interplay so complex as to defy simple description; yet identification of a few major features of that system may aid in our construction of a general conception of democratic processes.

Opinion Dikes

In the interactions between democratic leadership echelons and the mass of people some insight comes from the conception of public opinion as a system of dikes which channel public action or which fix a range of discretion within which government may act or within which debate at official levels may proceed. This conception avoids the error of personifying "public opinion" as an entity that exercises initiative and in some way functions as an operating organism to translate its purposes into governmental action.

In one of their aspects the dikes of opinion have a substantive nature in that they define areas within which day-to-day debate about the course of specific action may occur. Some types of legislative proposals, given the content of general opinion, can scarcely expect to attract serious attention. They depart too far from the general understandings of what is proper. A scheme for public ownership of the automobile industry, for example, would probably be regarded as so far outside the area of legitimate public action that not even the industry would become greatly concerned. On the other hand, other types of questions arise within areas of what we have called permissive consensus. A widespread, if not a unanimous, sentiment prevails that supports action toward some general objective, such as the care of the ill or the mitigation of the economic hazards of the individual. Probably quite commonly mass opinion of a permissive character tends to develop in advance of governmental action in many areas of domestic policy. That opinion grows out of public discussion against the background of the modal aspirations and values of people generally. As it takes shape, the time becomes ripe for action that will be generally acceptable or may even arouse popular acclaim for its authors. . . .

The idea of public opinion as forming a system of dikes which channel action yields a different conception of the place of public opinion than does the notion of a government by public opinion as one in which by some mysterious means a referendum occurs on very major issue. In the former conception the articulation between government and opinion is relatively loose. Parallelism between action and opinion tends not to be precise in matters of detail; it prevails rather with respect to broad purpose. And in the correlation of purpose and action time lags may occur between the crystallization of a sense of mass purpose and its fulfillment in public action. Yet in the long run majority purpose and public action tend to be brought into harmony. . . .

The argument amounts essentially to the position that the masses do not corrupt themselves; if they are corrupt, they have been corrupted. If this hypothesis has a substantial strain of validity, the critical element for the health of a democratic order consists in the beliefs, standards, and competence of those who constitute the influentials, the opinion-leaders, the political activists in the order. That group, as has been made plain, refuses to define itself with great clarity in the American system; yet analysis after analysis points to its existence. If a democracy tends toward indecision, decay, and disaster, the responsibility rests here, not in the mass of the people.

50

DANIEL YANKELOVICH

From *Coming to Public Judgment*

Refining the concept of public opinion is the task of professional poll expert Daniel Yankelovich. Yankelovich makes an important distinction between two ideas that are normally thought of as one: mass opinion and public judgment. Mass opinion tends to be uninformed and fickle, while public judgment is well-thought-out and lasting. Yankelovich develops the concept of public judgment more fully by comparing it to expert opinion. Both represent knowledge but different kinds of knowledge. In making political decisions, the public's judgment is often more valid than the expert's view.

THERE ARE TWO great advantages to defining the quality of public opinion in terms of responsibility for consequences, firmness, and consistency. The first is that the definition leads directly to an objective method for ascertaining quality so that all can agree that a particular specimen of public opinion is either of poor quality or good quality, whether or not one happens to like or disapprove of it. The second and more far-reaching advantage is that the definition enables us to understand how and why public opinion has distinctive value and is not merely a second-rate reflection of expert opinion. Each form of opinion—expert and public—has its own excellences and its own failings. But public opinion is not, as is generally assumed, simply less well-informed expert opinion. It has its own integrity, and different standards of quality apply to it. It is only when we understand the differences between public and expert opinion that we have insight into the special nature of public opinion and the role it plays in democratic society.

To see the first advantage clearly—the value of an objective definition—it is useful to formalize a distinction implicit in the discussion thus far. In what follows, I will use the term *mass opinion* to refer to poor-quality public opinion as defined by the defects of inconsistency, volatility, and nonresponsibility. (People's failure to take the consequences of their views into account is mostly *non*responsible rather than *ir*responsible, which implies a willfulness that is usually absent. The term *nonresponsible* is meant to show that the public is not usually at fault for its failure to take responsibility. Most of the time the public is not given an opportunity to undertake the form of responsibility I am discussing.) I will use the term "public judgment" to refer to good-quality public opinion in the sense of opinion that is stable, consistent, and responsible.

To say that public judgment has been reached on an issue does not imply that people comprehend all of the relevant facts or that they agree with the views of elites. It does imply that people have struggled with the issue, thought about it in their own terms, and formed a judgment they are willing to stand by. It also means that if leaders understand the public's judgments, they have a stable context to work in—either to offer solutions that fit within the public's tolerances, or if they disagree with the public's judgment, to take their case forcefully to the public with full awareness that the public's view will not change easily.

Unfortunately, the umbrella term "public opinion" obscures the distinction between mass opinion and public judgment. It is almost as if we were to use the word *bread* to refer both to the baked loaf one buys from the bakery or supermarket and also to an unbaked or half-baked lump of dough. If consumers were to use the word *bread* for both objects, they would never know when they were buying the baked loaf or the half-baked one. Just so, when we refer to public opinion, we do not know whether we are referring to half-baked mass opinion or to fully developed public judgment.

Words reveal a great deal about a culture. The Eskimos have many words for *snow.* The French have a fabulous vocabulary for food. The fact that our culture has no generally accepted vocabulary to distinguish between raw mass opinion and mature public judgment reveals a blind spot in the way Americans think about this subject. . . .

We come now to the most significant advantage of the concept of public judgment. By focusing on public judgment we can crawl out from under the quality-as-information trap. We can begin to shape a concept of public opinion in which quality is defined by evidence that the public has faced up to the consequences of its convictions.

This conception gives public opinion the *gravitās** that theorists of democracy have long recognized to be a prerequisite for genuine citizenship. We begin to understand why public opinion need not be taken seriously when it manifests itself in the form of mass opinion but must be taken quite seriously when it appears as public judgment, even when it is not as well informed as journalists and political philosophers would

**Gravitās* is the Latin word for seriousness, authority, dignity.—EDS.

like. In short, we can begin to develop an alternative to the ideal of the attentive well-informed citizen, so favored by tradition. . . .

One major difficulty in developing an alternative model of quality in public opinion is that being well informed *is* the proper defining characteristic of scientific and expert opinion. We should not apply the same criteria to expert opinion as to public opinion. Generally, for expert opinion we do not have to worry about the same things as for public opinion. Well-educated and trained experts are expected to be well informed; they are rarely self-contradictory or fickle in their views, and the kinds of questions on which we consult experts—questions of fact—do not enmesh them as readily in the value conflicts that beset public opinion. Of course, experts, being human, cannot always set aside their personal feelings; but mainly we judge them on their records on being correct in their special fields of expertise.

At first glance, differentiating public opinion from expert opinion may seem unnecessary. The general view is "Everyone knows the difference between experts and the public. We do not expect the public to be experts, just reasonably informed." But familiarity with the way public opinion is judged makes it plain that a clear-cut distinction between expert opinion and public opinion is sorely needed.

Suppose an engineering expert on bridges is asked whether a particular bridge is safe for heavy traffic. The engineer's opinion, especially after studying the bridge and conducting tests on it, carries more weight than that of the citizens who live in the community. When it comes to questions of bridge safety, we consult the expert, not public opinion.

Here, quality of opinion is clearly defined in terms of knowledge and information. The bridge expert has far more knowledge about bridges than the public. But engineering knowledge may not be sufficient for the expert to know with certainty that the bridge will be safe in the future. Asked the question, "Can this bridge safely carry an anticipated 20 percent increased traffic load over the next five years?" the engineer might reasonably respond, "I do not know the answer to that question." Whereupon the question will almost surely be asked, "Well, can you give us your opinion? Is it your opinion that the bridge will safely carry the increased traffic?" Usually, the expert will then offer an opinion. ("In my opinion, this bridge is not safe. I wouldn't let my family cross it in rush hour conditions.")

In this hypothetical exchange, the expert holds firmly held convictions, but correctly and responsibly refuses to characterize them as knowledge. Part of the expert's expertise is the ability to distinguish personal opinions from knowledge. Conventional standards of what constitutes quality apply quite well to this situation. The trouble comes when we apply this same standard of quality to public opinion, which we always do for the simple reason that we have no other. . . .

Why, we might ask, is public opinion judged by standards appropriate to expert opinion rather than by its own special standards? The most obvious answer relates to the meaning of opinion in our culture. Opinion is generally defined in opposition to knowledge. We fall back on opinion when knowledge is lacking.

Using opinion as a substitute for knowledge is a common practice, and this practice gives the word *opinion* its principal meaning. The first meaning of opinion in *Webster's International Dictionary* is a belief that is "less strong than positive knowledge . . . a belief . . . based only on opinion." In this sense of opinion, the more knowledge and information the person holding the opinion has, the better that opinion is deemed to be—and rightly so.

Knowledge in the modern era has come to have a special, almost technical meaning. Knowledge is linked to validation. One *knows* that the earth is round rather than flat because this discovery has been scientifically validated: it has been proven through well-accepted empirical methods. Validated knowledge does not have to be scientific. We validate a small part of our stock of knowledge every day. Suppose you are asked, "Are you wearing your black shoes or your brown ones?" You remember putting on your black shoes, but the chances are that you will glance down before answering. Having done so, you now "know" you are wearing your black shoes because you have validated that knowledge with methods suitable for the occasion. In daily life—whether that of the expert on bridges or the person wearing black shoes—the distinction between knowledge and opinion is largely a matter of validation. The validation is carried out by empirical methods, more or less casual or scientific depending on the occasion.

In our complex society, the pool of validated knowledge is tiny compared to our need to know. We could not survive without depending on opinion—based on information—as a substitute for validated knowledge. A large proportion of our national resources are devoted to educating and training specialists on whose opinions we depend because of the excellence of their information and their skill in interpreting it. The opinions of the general public never count as much as those of the experts when it is expert-type opinion that is needed.

The reason our society judges all opinion by the standards appropriate to expert opinion is that both the dictionary definition and custom support the meaning of opinion as a substitute for knowledge. Therefore, the closer one comes to meeting the standards of knowledge, the better the quality of the opinion is deemed to be. In practice, therefore, expert opinion and public opinion are judged by a single criterion. . . .

The confusions created by these contradictions persist to the present. Public opinion is regarded with profound ambivalence. Among the general public, respect for public opinion is high. The public holds itself and its powers and privileges in great esteem. Healthy respect for public opinion is also found in those members of the business community who cater to consumers and among members of those branches of the legal profession with everyday experience with the public as jurors. In subcultures that lack daily contact with the public, public opinion often seems remote, mysterious, and abstract. For university professors, laboratory scientists, the foreign policy community, the high civil service, and the upper reaches of the press, public opinion appears fickle, impulsive, disorganized, ill-informed, and unreliable. These elites may be sincerely devoted to the principles of democracy, but their outlook is, simply stated, elitist. They think they know better than the public because they are well educated and articulate. They have superior knowledge, and because they do, they assume in the great classic tradition that they are, therefore, endowed with superior moral virtue. . . .

There *is* a logical way to resolve the conflicting traditions surrounding the status and quality of public opinion. Implicit in the discussion to this point is a fundamental distinction between public opinion and expert opinion. Both are "opinion" in the negative sense that they are not validated knowledge—in the same sense that a book on ancient Greek philosophy and contemporary sports bloopers are both categorized as nonfiction. But they differ radically from one another in their positive relation to validated knowledge. Expert opinion relates to knowledge in the conventional dictionary sense: it is a substitute for it. We fall back on expert opinion when validated knowledge is lacking. In principle, expert opinion should be capable of being validated. It should take the form of an empirical proposition. If it does not, it is not "expert opinion." The expert on bridge safety could have said, "We can test the safety of the bridge by letting the traffic build and seeing whether it collapses or not. Then we will know." Opinions are frequently elicited from experts precisely to avoid the undesirable consequences of this type of pragmatic validation.

What we want above all from expert opinion is that it be correct. The best criterion for judging the quality of expert opinion is whether it proves to be right or wrong. ("In my opinion the Democrats will continue to choose losing presidential candidates.") It will take time to validate this opinion, but, in principle, it is capable of being proven or disproven.

Because being correct is so central to the experts' mission, experts generally accept the same constraints that scientists accept in their pursuit of knowledge. Modern knowledge is empirically based. Information is its lifeblood. As we will discuss later, there are other modes of knowing than the scientific. But so great is the prestige of science that knowledge in our day has come to be virtually synonymous with scientific knowledge. In addition, and this is more controversial, scientific or expert knowledge presents itself as value-free. Experts accept the ethos of giving an "objective opinion" whether or not they personally approve of it. If experts are smokers and also research scientists studying the impact of smoking on heart disease and lung cancer, and if they are paid by a tobacco company, their self-respect as experts requires them to give an objective opinion that implicates smoking, even though it may offend their employers, ruin their careers at the tobacco company, and be dissonant with their own personal habits and values. Others may be skeptical about the experts' ability to retain objectivity under such strong cross pressures. But if they let personal bias or career concerns color their opinions, they will have violated their vocations as experts and scientists.

When we contrast public opinion with expert opinion, we see that it has a different relationship to knowledge. Unlike expert opinion, most instances of public opinion cannot be scientifically validated, even in principle, because they do not take the form of empirical propositions. Consider the typical form that expert opinion takes: "It is my opinion that smoking can cause heart disease." "It is my opinion that this bridge cannot safely absorb a 20 percent increase in traffic." "It is my opinion that this man was not legally sane on the night he shot his wife." These are empirical propositions. Most instances of public opinion do not assume this form. Their most typical form is that of a value judgment. Instead of deliberately avoiding values, they focus directly on them: "In my opinion flag burners should be put in jail, whatever the Supreme Court says." "In my opinion, doctors with AIDS should not practice medicine." Expressions of values such as these are like matters of taste: there are canons of good taste and bad taste. So, too, there are good values and bad values. But whatever the method of differentiating them may be, it is not the same as the method of validation that applies to empirical knowledge and expert opinion. . . .

The startling conclusion we draw . . . is that there are potentially as many varieties of knowing as there are human purposes and interests. The idea of varieties of knowledge linked to purpose is radical and unfamiliar. It has many implications. It means that there are modes of knowing not yet discovered or codified. It means that in the rush over the past two centuries to acquire scientific knowledge as rapidly as we can, we may have mindlessly shoved aside older authentic modes of knowing, thereby losing access to important truths. It means that we cannot judge one mode of knowing by the rules that apply to another. We cannot assume, for example, that scientific knowledge is canonical and that all other forms of knowledge are to be evaluated by whether they meet the standards of "scientific proof," as science defines it.

In this light, we are ready to examine the claim that public judgment is a genuine form of knowledge. In practice, what does this claim mean? It is a radical claim and one should be fully aware of how far-reaching its implications are. It means, in practice, that for certain purposes, public judgment should carry more weight than expert opinion—and not simply because the majority may have more political power than the individual expert but because the public's claim to *know* is actually stronger than the expert's. It means that the judgment of the general public can, under some conditions, be equal or superior in quality to the judgment of experts and elites who possess far more information, education, and ability to articulate their views. . . .

Another concept supporting the vision is [the] insight that it is disastrous to divorce human reason from the world of ordinary life—the struggle to make a living, raise families, and live peacefully as a community. When experts . . . conceive reason as something separate and apart from everyday life—the property of a trained class of specialists, scientists, and other elites—then the deepest ideals of the founding fathers of the nation are betrayed. Reason is *not* the exclusive property of a class of experts whose training and credentials certify the possession of a special endowment. Reason is a more humble, more universal, more democratic gift.

51

THOMAS CRONIN

From *Direct Democracy*

Although the United States is a representative—republican—system of government, elements of direct democracy have been introduced on the state and local levels over time, especially in the early twentieth century during the Progressive era. Initiative, referendum, and recall give citizens an immediate and direct voice in their government, beyond just electing officials.

Professor Thomas Cronin explains these instruments of direct democracy and cites California's 1978 tax-cutting Proposition 13 as a leading example of an important statewide ballot question. Controversy swirls over the wisdom of such exercises in direct democracy. Cronin weighs the advantages against the potential problems of allowing voters to have a direct say in policy-making. His conclusion is that initiative, referendum, and recall will neither destroy American government nor save it. Yet in the 1990s, with voters' openly-expressed distrust of public officials, direct democracy will surely become more and more a part of the state and local political scene.

FOR ABOUT A hundred years Americans have been saying that voting occasionally for public officials is not enough. Political reformers contend that more democracy is needed and that the American people are mature enough and deserve the right to vote on critical issues facing their states and the nation. During the twentieth century, American voters in many parts of the country have indeed won the right to write new laws and repeal old ones through the initiative and referendum. They have also thrown hundreds of state and local officials out of office in recall elections.

Although the framers of the Constitution deliberately designed a republic, or indirect democracy, the practice of direct democracy and the debate over its desirability are as old as English settlements in America. Public debate and popular voting on issues go back to early seventeenth-century town assemblies and persist today in New England town meetings.

Populist democracy in America has produced conspicuous assets and conspicuous liabilities. It has won the support and admiration of many enthusiasts, yet it is also fraught with disturbing implications. Its most important contributions came early in this century in the form of the initiative, referendum, and recall, as a reaction to corrupt and unresponsive state legislatures throughout the country. Most of us would not recognize what then passed for representative government. "Bills that the machine and its backers do not desire are smothered in committee; measures which they do desire are brought out and hurried through their passage," said Governor Woodrow Wilson at the time. "It happens again and again that great groups of such bills are rushed through in the hurried hours that mark the close of the legislative sessions, when everyone is withheld from vigilance by fatigue and when it is possible to do secret things." The threat, if not the reality, of the initiative, referendum, and recall helped to encourage a more responsible, civic-minded breed of state legislator. These measures were not intended to subvert or alter the basic character of American government. "Their intention," as Wilson saw it, was "to restore, not to destroy, representative government."

The *initiative* allows voters to propose a legislative measure (statutory initiative) or a constitutional amendment (constitutional initiative) by filing a petition bearing a required number of valid citizen signatures.

The *referendum* refers a proposed or existing law or statute to voters for their approval or rejection. Some state constitutions require referenda; in other states, the legislature may decide to refer a measure to the voters. Measures referred by legislatures (statutes, constitutional amendments, bonds, or advisory questions) are the most common ballot propositions. A *popular* or *petition referendum* (a less frequently used device) refers an already enacted measure to the voters before it can go into effect. States allowing the petition referendum require a minimum number of valid citizen signatures within a specified time. There is confusion about the difference between the initiative and referendum because *referendum* is frequently used in a casual or generic way to describe all ballot measures.

The *recall* allows voters to remove or discharge a public official from office by filing a petition bearing a specified number of valid signatures demanding a vote on the official's continued tenure in office. Recall procedures typically require that the petition be signed by 25 percent of those who voted in the last election, after which a special election is almost always required. The recall differs from impeachment in that the people, not the legislature, initiate the election and determine the outcome with their votes. It is a purely political and not even a semijudicial process.

American voters today admire and respect the virtues of representative government, yet most of them also yearn for an even greater voice in how their laws are made. They understand the defects of both representative and direct democracy and prefer, on balance, to have a mixture of the two. Sensible or sound democracy is their aspiration.

Although Americans cannot cast votes on critical national issues, voters in twenty-six states, the District of Columbia, and hundreds of localities do have the right to put measures on their ballots. Legislatures can also refer measures to the public for a general vote. And constitutional changes in every state except Delaware must be approved by voters before becoming law. Voters in fifteen states and the District of Columbia can also recall elected state officials, and thirty-six states permit the recall of various local officials.

When Americans think of their right to vote, they think primarily of their right to nominate and elect legislators, members of school boards and of city councils, and the American president. Yet California's famous Proposition 13 in June 1978 focused nationwide attention on the public's right to participate in controversial tax decision making, as Californians voted to cut their property taxes by at least half. More voters participated in this issue contest than in the same day's gubernatorial primaries.

California's Proposition 13 had two additional effects. It triggered similar tax-slashing measures (both as bills and as direct legislation by the people) in numerous other states, and it encouraged conservative interest groups to use the initiative and referendum processes to achieve some of their goals. In the past decade conservative interests have placed on state and local ballots scores of measures favoring the death penalty, victims' rights, English-only regulations, and prayer in schools, and opposing taxation or spending, pornography, abortion, and homosexuality. Several states have regularly conducted referenda on issues ranging from a nuclear freeze to seat-belt laws. Citizens are now voting on hundreds of initiatives and referenda at state and local levels. . . .

Skeptics, however, worry about tyranny by the majority and fear voters are seldom well enough informed to cast votes on complicated, technical national laws. People also worry, and justifiably, about the way well-financed special interest groups might use these procedures. Corruption at the state level is much less common today than it was early in the century, but special interests are surely just as involved as ever. The power of campaign contributions is clear. The advantages to those who can afford campaign and political consultants, direct mail firms, and widespread television and media appeals are very real. Although in theory Americans are politically equal, in practice there remain enormous disparities in individuals' and groups' capacities to influence the direction of government. And although the direct democracy devices of the initiative, referendum, and recall type are widely available, the evidence suggests it is generally the organized interests that can afford to put them to use. The idealistic notion that populist democracy devices can make every citizen a citizen-legislator and move us closer to political and egalitarian democracy is plainly an unrealized aspiration.

The initiative, referendum, and recall were born in an era of real grievances. They made for a different kind of democracy in those areas that permitted them. At the very least, they signaled the unacceptability of some of the most corrupt and irresponsible political practices of that earlier era. It is fashionable among political analysts today to say that although they have rarely lived up to their promises, neither have they resulted in the dire outcomes feared by critics. Yet they have had both good and questionable consequences. . . .

By examining direct democracy practices we can learn about the strengths and weaknesses of a neglected aspect of American politics, as well as the workings of representative democracy. We seek to understand it so we can improve it, and to improve it so it can better supplement rather than replace our institutions of representative government. . . .

A populist impulse, incorporating notions of "power to the people" and skepticism about the system has always existed in America. Americans seldom abide quietly the failings and deficiencies of capitalism, the welfare state, or the political decision rules by which we live. We are, as historian Richard Hofstadter wrote, "forever restlessly pitting ourselves against them, demanding changes, improvements, remedies." Demand for more democracy occurs when there is growing distrust of legislative bodies and when there is a growing suspicion that privileged interests exert far greater influences on the typical politician than does the common voter.

Direct democracy, especially as embodied in the referendum, initiative, and recall, is sometimes viewed as a typically American political response to perceived abuses of the public trust. Voters periodically become frustrated with taxes, regulations, inefficiency in government programs, the inequalities or injustices of the system, the arms race, environmental hazards, and countless other irritations. This frustration arises in part because more public policy decisions are now made in distant capitals, by remote agencies or private yet unaccountable entities—such as regulatory bodies, the Federal Reserve Board, foreign governments, multinational alliances, or foreign trading combines—instead of at the local or county level as once was the case, or as perhaps we like to remember.

Champions of populist democracy claim many benefits will accrue from their reforms. Here are some:

- Citizen initiatives will promote government responsiveness and accountability. If officials ignore the voice of the people, the people will have an available means to make needed law.
- Initiatives are freer from special interest domination than the legislative branches of most states, and so provide a desirable safeguard that can be called into use when legislators are corrupt, irresponsible, or dominated by privileged special interests.
- The initiative and referendum will produce open, educational debate on critical issues that otherwise might be inadequately discussed.
- Referendum, initiative, and recall are nonviolent means of political participation that fulfill a citizen's right to petition the government for redress of grievances.
- Direct democracy increases voter interest and election-day turnout. Perhaps, too, giving the citizen more of a role in governmental processes might lessen alienation and apathy.

• Finally (although this hardly exhausts the claims), citizen initiatives are needed because legislators often evade the tough issues. Fearing to be ahead of their time, they frequently adopt a zero-risk mentality. Concern with staying in office often makes them timid and perhaps too wedded to the status quo. One result is that controversial social issues frequently have to be resolved in the judicial branch. But who elected the judges?

For every claim put forward on behalf of direct democracy, however, there is an almost equally compelling criticism. Many opponents believe the ordinary citizen usually is not well enough informed about complicated matters to arrive at sound public policy judgments. They also fear the influence of slick television advertisements or bumper sticker messages.

Some critics of direct democracy contend the best way to restore faith in representative institutions is to find better people to run for office. They prefer the deliberations and the collective judgment of elected representatives who have the time to study complicated public policy matters, matters that should be decided within the give-and-take process of politics. That process, they say, takes better account of civil liberties.

Critics also contend that in normal times initiative and referendum voter turnout is often a small proportion of the general population and so the results are unduly influenced by special interests: big money will win eight out of ten times.

A paradox runs throughout this debate. As the United States has aged, we have extended the suffrage in an impressive way. The older the country, the more we have preached the gospel of civic participation. Yet we also have experienced centralization of power in the national government and the development of the professional politician. The citizen-politician has become an endangered species.

Representative government is always in the process of development and decay. Its fortunes rise and fall depending upon various factors, not least the quality of people involved and the resources devoted to making it work effectively. When the slumps come, proposals that would reform and change the character of representative government soon follow. Direct democracy notions have never been entirely foreign to our country—countless proponents from Benjamin Franklin to Jesse Jackson, Jack Kemp, and Richard Gephardt have urged us to listen more to the common citizen. . . .

The American experience with direct democracy has fulfilled neither the dreams and expectations of its proponents nor the fears of its opponents.

The initiative and referendum have not undermined or weakened representative government. The initiative, referendum, and recall have been no more of a threat to the representative principle than has judicial review or the executive veto. Tools of neither the "lunatic fringe" nor the rich, direct democracy devices have become a permanent feature of American politics, especially in the West.

The initiative, referendum, and recall have not been used as often as their advocates would have wished, in part because state legislatures have steadily improved. Better-educated members, more-professional staff, better media coverage of legislative proceedings, and longer sessions have transformed the legislative process at the state level, mostly for the better. Interest groups once denied access to secret sessions now regularly attend, testify, and participate in a variety of ways in the legislative process. Although individuals and some groups remain frustrated, the level and intensity of that frustration appear to be lower than the discontent that prompted the popular democracy movements around the turn of the century.

Still, hundreds of measures have found their way onto ballots in states across the country, and 35 to 40 percent of the more than 1,500 citizen-initiated ballot measures considered since 1904 have won voter approval. About half of these have been on our ballots since World War II. A few thousand legislatively referred measures have also been placed on the ballot, and at least 60 percent of these regularly win voter approval. Popular, or petition, referenda, placed on the ballot by citizens seeking a voter veto of laws already passed by state legislatures, have been used infrequently. . . . Recall, used mainly at the local and county level, is seldom used against state officials. The marvel is that all these devices of popular democracy, so vulnerable to apathy, ignorance, and prejudice, not only have worked but also have generally been used in a reasonable and constructive manner. Voters have been cautious and have almost always rejected extreme proposals. Most studies suggest that voters, despite the complexity of measures and the deceptions of some campaigns, exercise shrewd judgment, and most students of direct democracy believe most American voters take this responsibility seriously. Just as in candidate campaigns, when they give the benefit of the doubt to the incumbent and the burden of proof is on the challenger to give reasons why he or she should be voted into office, so in issue elections the voter needs to be persuaded that change is needed. In the absence of a convincing case that change is better, the electorate traditionally sticks with the status quo.

Few radical measures pass. Few measures that are discriminatory or would have diminished the rights of minorities win voter approval, and most of the exceptions are ruled unconstitutional by the courts. On balance, the voters at large are no more prone to be small-minded, racist, or sexist than are legislators or courts.

A case can be made that elected officials are more tolerant, more educated, and more sophisticated than the average voter. "Learning the arguments for freedom and tolerance formulated by notables such as Jefferson, Madison, Mill, or the more libertarian justices of the Supreme Court is no simple task," one study concludes. "Many of those arguments are subtle, esoteric, and difficult to grasp. Intelligence, awareness, and education are required to appreciate them fully." Yet on the occasional issues affecting civil liberties and civil rights that have come to the ballot, voters have generally acted in an enlightened way. This is in part the case because enlightened elites help shape public opinion on such occasions through endorsements, news editorials, talk-show discussions, public debates, and legislative and executive commentary. Further, those voting on state and local ballot measures are usually among the top 30 or 40 percent in educational and information levels.

The civic and educational value of direct democracy upon the electorate has been significant, but this aspect of the promise of direct democracy was plainly overstated from the start. Most voters make up their minds on ballot issues or recall elections in the last few days, or even hours, before they vote. The technical and ambiguous language of many of these measures is still an invitation to confusion, and about a quarter of those voting in these elections tell pollsters they could have used more information in making their decisions on these types of election choices.

Like any other democratic institution, the initiative, referendum, and recall have their shortcomings. Voters are sometimes confused. On occasion an ill-considered or undesirable measure wins approval. Large, organized groups and those who can raise vast sums of money are in a better position either to win, or especially to block, approval of ballot measures. Sometimes a recall campaign is mounted for unfair reasons, and recall campaigns can stir up unnecessary and undesirable conflict in a community. Most of these criticisms can also be leveled at our more traditional institutions. Courts sometimes err, as in the *Dred Scott* decision and in *Plessy v. Ferguson* or *Korematsu*. Presidents surely make mistakes (FDR's attempt to pack the Supreme Court, 1937; Kennedy's Bay of Pigs fiasco, 1961; Nixon's involvement in the Watergate break-in and subsequent coverup, 1972–1974; Reagan's involvement in the Iran-contra arms deal, 1986). And legislatures not only make mistakes about policy from time to time but wind up spending nearly a third of their time amending, changing, and correcting past legislation that proved inadequate or wrong. In short, we pay a price for believing in and practicing democracy—whatever the form.

Whatever the shortcomings of direct democracy, and there are several, they do not justify the elimination of the populist devices from those state constitutions permitting them. Moreover, any suggestion to repeal the initiative, referendum, and recall would be defeated by the voters. Public opinion strongly supports retaining these devices where they are allowed. . . .

In sum, direct democracy devices have not been a cure-all for most political, social, or economic ills, yet they have been an occasional remedy, and generally a moderate remedy, for legislative lethargy and the misuse and nonuse of legislative power. It was long feared that these devices would dull legislators' sense of responsibility without in fact quickening the people to the exercise of any real control in public affairs. Little evidence exists for those fears today. When popular demands for reasonable change are repeatedly ignored by elected officials and when legislators or other officials ignore valid interests and criticism, the initiative, referendum, and recall can be a means by which the people may protect themselves in the grand tradition of self-government.

PART TEN

Interest Groups

52

ALEXIS DE TOCQUEVILLE

From *Democracy in America*

Interest-group politics remains a big part of U.S. government today—for good and bad. But it is not as new a part as it may seem. Young French aristocrat Alexis de Tocqueville, visiting in 1831, observed how naturally Americans formed "associations." Just like today, groups were formed "to promote the public safety, commerce, industry, morality, and religion." In a country that emphasized individuality, Tocqueville felt, group allegiances gave people the power to work together to reach shared goals. American interest groups were out in the open, meeting freely to advance their viewpoints. Tocqueville, whose earlier selection from Democracy in America *opened this book, placed great faith in interest groups as a way that minorities could protect themselves from "tyranny of the majority." Today, one wonders how he would suggest that the nation protect itself from the tyranny of interest groups.*

IN NO COUNTRY IN the world has the principle of association been more successfully used, or more unsparingly applied to a multitude of different objects, than in America. Besides the permanent associations, which are established by law under the names of townships, cities, and counties, a vast number of others are formed and maintained by the agency of private individuals.

The citizen of the United States is taught from his earliest infancy to rely upon his own exertions, in order to resist the evils and the difficulties of life; he looks upon the social authority with an eye of mistrust and anxiety, and he only claims its assistance when he is quite unable to shift without it. This habit may even be traced in the schools of the rising generation, where the children in their games are wont to submit to rules which they have themselves established, and to punish misdemeanors which they have themselves defined. The same spirit pervades every act of social life. If a stoppage occurs in a thoroughfare, and the circulation of the public is hindered, the neighbors immediately constitute a deliberative body; and this extemporaneous assembly gives rise to an executive power, which remedies the inconvenience, before anybody has thought of recurring to an authority superior to that of the persons immediately concerned. If the public pleasures are concerned, an association is formed to provide for the splendor and the regularity of the entertainment. Societies are formed to resist enemies which are exclusively of a moral nature, and to diminish the vice of intemperance: in the United States associations are established to promote public order, commerce, industry, morality, and religion, for there is no end which the human will seconded by the collective exertions of individuals, despairs of attaining. . . .

An association consists simply in the public assent which a number of individuals give to certain doctrines; and in the engagement which they contract to promote the spread of those doctrines by their exertions. The right of associating with such views is very analogous to the liberty of unlicensed writing; but societies thus formed possess more authority than the press. When an opinion is represented by a society, it necessarily assumes a more exact and explicit form. It numbers its partisans, and compromises their welfare in its cause: they, on the other hand, become acquainted with each other, and their zeal is increased by their number. An association unites the efforts of minds which have a tendency to diverge in one single channel, and urges them vigorously towards the one single end which it points out.

The second degree in the right of association is the power of meeting. When an association is allowed to establish centres of action at certain important points in the country, its activity is increased, and its influence extended. Men have the opportunity of seeing each other; means of execution are more readily combined; and opinions are maintained with a warmth and energy which written language cannot approach.

Lastly, in the exercise of the right of political association, there is a third degree: the partisans of an opinion may unite in electoral bodies, and choose delegates to represent them in a central assembly. This is, properly speaking, the application of the representative system to a party.

Thus, in the first instance, a society is formed between individuals professing the same opinion, and the tie which keeps it together is of a purely intellectual nature: in the second case, small assemblies are formed which only represent a faction of the party. Lastly, in the third case, they constitute a separate nation in the midst of the nation, a government within the Government. . . .

It cannot be denied that the unrestrained liberty of association for political purposes is the privilege which a people is longest in learning how to exercise. If it does not throw the nation into anarchy, it perpetually augments the chances of that calamity. On one point, however, this perilous liberty offers a security against dangers of another kind; in countries where associations are free, secret societies are unknown. In America, there are numerous factions, but no conspiracies. . . .

The most natural privilege of man, next to the right of acting for himself, is that of combining his exertions with those of his fellow-creatures, and of acting in common with them. I am therefore led to conclude that the right of association is almost as inalienable as the right of personal liberty. . . .

53

E. E. SCHATTSCHNEIDER

From *The Semisovereign People*

The late 1950s and early 1960s was a time when political scientists placed their focus on the interest group theory of American politics. Although hardly a new idea, interest group politics was studied intensely, sometimes to be idealized as the perfect model of government and other times critiqued as the downfall of democracy. Scholar E. E. Schattschneider's much-cited book explored the "pressure system" in American politics, dominated by "organized" (as opposed to informal), "special-interest" (not public-interest) groups. Schattschneider's conclusion was that "the pressure system has an upper-class bias." Decades later, political scientists might not use the exact same language as Schattschneider, who relied on the concept of class in his analysis. Today, vastly different degrees of organization, financial resources, and intensity separate interest group claimants in the competition for getting their issues heard by the government.

MORE THAN any other system American politics provides the raw materials for testing the organizational assumptions of two contrasting kinds of politics, *pressure politics* and *party politics*. The concepts that underlie these forms of politics constitute the raw stuff of a general theory of political action. The basic issue between the two patterns of organization is one of size and scope of conflict; pressure groups are small-scale organizations while political parties are very large-scale organizations. One need not be surprised, therefore, that the partisans of large-scale and small-scale organizations differ passionately, because the outcome of the political game depends on the scale on which it is played.

To understand the controversy about the scale of political organization it is necessary first to take a look at some theories about interest-group politics. Pressure groups have played a remarkable role in American politics, but they have played an even more remarkable role in American political theory. Considering the political condition of the country in the first third of the twentieth century, it was probably inevitable that the discussion of special interest pressure groups should lead to development of "group" theories of politics in which an attempt is made to explain everything in terms of group activity, i.e., an attempt to formulate a universal group theory. Since one of the best ways to test an idea is to ride it into the ground, political theory has unquestionably been improved by the heroic attempt to create a political universe revolving about the group. Now that we have a number of drastic statements of the group theory of politics pushed to a great extreme, we ought to be able to see what the limitations of the idea are. . . .

One difficulty running through the literature of the subject results from the attempt to explain *everything* in terms of the group theory. On general grounds it would be remarkable indeed if a single hypothesis explained everything about so complex a subject as American politics. Other difficulties have grown out of the fact that group concepts have been stated in terms so universal that the subject seems to have no shape or form.

The question is: Are pressure groups the universal basic ingredient of all political situations, and do they explain everything? To answer this question it is necessary to review a bit of rudimentary political theory.

Two modest reservations might be made merely to test the group dogma. We might clarify our ideas if (1) we explore more fully the possibility of making a distinction between public interest groups and special-interest groups and (2) if we distinguished between organized and unorganized groups. . . .

As a matter of fact, the distinction between *public* and *private* interests is a thoroughly respectable one; it is one of the oldest known to political theory. In the literature of the subject the public interest refers to general or common interests shared by all or by substantially all members of the community. Presumably no community exists unless there is some kind of community of interests, just as there is no nation without some notion of national interests. If it is really impossible to distinguish between private and public interests the group theorists have produced a revolution in political thought so great that it is impossible to foresee its consequences. For this reason the distinction ought to be explored with great care.

At a time when nationalism is described as one of the most dynamic forces in the world, it should not be difficult to understand that national interests actually do exist. It is necessary only to consider the proportion of the American budget devoted to national defense to realize that the common interest in national survival is a great one. Measured in dollars this interest is one of the biggest things in the world. Moreover, it is difficult to describe this interest as special. The diet on which the American leviathan feeds is something more than a jungle of disparate special interests. In the literature of democratic theory the body of common agreement found in the community is known as the "consensus" without which it is believed that no democratic system can survive.

The reality of the common interest is suggested by demonstrated capacity of the community to survive. There must be something that holds people together.

In contrast with the common interests are the special interests. The implication of this term is that these are interests shared by only a few people or a fraction of the community; they *exclude* others and may be *adverse* to them. A special interest is exclusive in about the same way as private property is exclusive. In a complex society it is not surprising that there are some interests that are shared by all or substantially all members of the community and some interests that are not shared so widely. The distinction is useful precisely because conflicting claims are made by people about the nature of their interests in controversial matters. . . .

Is it possible to distinguish between the "interests" of the members of the National Association of Manufacturers and the members of the American League to Abolish Capital Punishment? The facts in the two cases are not identical. First, *the members of the A.L.A.C.P. obviously do not expect to be hanged.* The membership of the A.L.A.C.P. is not restricted to persons under indictment for murder or in jeopardy of the extreme penalty. *Anybody* can join A.L.A.C.P. Its members oppose capital punishment although they are not personally likely to benefit by the policy they advocate. The inference is therefore that the interest of the A.L.A.C.P. is not adverse, exclusive or special. It is not like the interest of the Petroleum Institute in depletion allowances. . . .

We can now examine the second distinction, the distinction between organized and unorganized groups. The question here is not whether the distinction can be made but whether or not it is worth making. Organization has been described as "merely a stage or degree of interaction" in the development of a group.

The proposition is a good one, but what conclusions do we draw from it? We do not dispose of the matter by calling the distinction between organized and unorganized groups a "mere" difference of degree because some of the greatest differences in the world are differences of degree. As far as special-interest politics is concerned the implication to be avoided is that a few workmen who habitually stop at a corner saloon for a glass of beer are essentially the same as the United States Army because the difference between them is merely one of degree. At this point we have a distinction that makes a difference. . . .

If we are able, therefore, to distinguish between public and private interests and between organized and unorganized groups we have marked out the major boundaries of the subject; *we have given the subject shape and scope.* We are now in a position to attempt to define the area we want to explore. Having cut the pie into four pieces, we can now appropriate the piece we want and leave the rest to someone else. For a multitude of reasons *the most likely field of study is that of the organized, special-interest groups.* The advantage of concentrating on organized groups is that they are known, identifiable and recognizable. The advantage of concentrating on special-interest groups is that they have one important characteristic in common: they are all exclusive. This piece of the pie (the organized special-interest groups) we shall call the *pressure system.* The pressure system has boundaries we can define; we can fix its scope and make an attempt to estimate its bias. . . .

The organized groups listed in the various directories (such as *National Associations of the United States*, published at intervals by the United States Department of Commerce) and specialty yearbooks, registers, etc., and the *Lobby Index*, published by the United States House of Representatives, probably include the bulk of the organizations in the pressure system. All compilations are incomplete, but these are extensive enough to provide us with some basis for estimating the scope of the system. . . .

When lists of these organizations are examined, the fact that strikes the student most forcibly is that *the system is very small.* The range of organized, identifiable, known groups is amazingly narrow; there is nothing remotely universal about it. There is a tendency on the part of the publishers of directories of associations to place an undue emphasis on business organizations, an emphasis that is almost inevitable because the business community is by a wide margin the most highly organized segment of society. Publishers doubtless tend also to reflect public demand for information. Nevertheless, the dominance of business groups in the pressure system is so marked that it probably cannot be explained away as an accident of the publishing industry. . . .

The business or upper-class bias of the pressure system shows up everywhere. Businessmen are four or five times as likely to write to their congressmen as manual laborers are. College graduates are far more apt to write to their congressmen than people in the lowest educational category are. . . .

Broadly, the pressure system has an upper-class bias. There is overwhelming evidence that participation in voluntary organizations is related to upper social and economic status; the rate of participation is much higher in the upper strata than it is elsewhere. . . .

The bias of the system is shown by the fact that *even nonbusiness organizations reflect an upper-class tendency*. . . .

The class bias of associational activity gives meaning to the limited scope of the pressure system, because *scope and bias are aspects of the same tendency.* The data raise a serious question about the validity of the proposition that special-interest groups are a universal form of political organization reflecting *all* interests. As a matter of fact, to suppose that everyone participates in pressure-group activity and that all interests get themselves organized in the pressure system is to destroy the meaning of this form of politics. The pressure system makes sense only as the political instrument of a segment of the community. It gets results by being selective and biased; *if everybody got into the act the unique advantages of this form of organization would be destroyed, for it is possible that if all interests could be mobilized the result would be a stalemate.*

Special-interest organizations are most easily formed when they deal with small numbers of individuals who are acutely aware of their exclusive interests. To describe the conditions of pressure-group organization in this way is, however, to say that it is primarily a business phenomenon. Aside from a few very large organizations (the churches, organized labor, farm organizations, and veterans' organizations) the residue is a small segment of the population. *Pressure politics is essentially the politics of small groups.*

The vice of the groupist theory is that it conceals the most significant aspects of the system. The flaw in the pluralist heaven is that the heavenly chorus sings with a strong upper-class accent. Probably about 90 percent of the people cannot get into the pressure system.

The notion that the pressure system is automatically representative of the whole community is a myth fostered by the universalizing tendency of modern group theories. *Pressure politics is a selective process* ill designed to serve diffuse interests. The system is skewed, loaded and unbalanced in favor of a fraction of a minority. . . .

The competing claims of pressure groups and political parties for the loyalty of the American public revolve about the difference between the results likely to be achieved by small-scale and large-scale political organization. Inevitably, the outcome of pressure politics and party politics will be vastly different.

54

THEODORE LOWI

From *The End of Liberalism*

No assessment of the importance of interest groups in American politics would be complete without this classic work by Theodore Lowi. Lowi presents a ground-breaking criticism of interest-group politics, which he calls "interest-group liberalism" and "pluralism." Look for his arguments about the supposed-balance among groups. Note Lowi's view about government's role in perpetuating interest-group politics. His questioning of the actual definition of an interest group is important. Lowi then considers how interest-group politics treats the American people as a whole: "The public is shut out." His final argument is stunning: interest groups resist change; they become institutionalized, with government approval, and in the end are really conservative.

THE MOST clinically accurate term to capture the American variant . . . is *interest-group liberalism.* It is liberalism because it is optimistic about government, expects to use government in a positive and expansive role, is motivated by the highest sentiments, and possesses a strong faith that what is good for government is good for the society. It is interest-group liberalism because it sees as both necessary and good a policy agenda that is accessible to all organized interests and makes no independent judgment of their claims. It is interest-group liberalism because it defines the public interest as a result of the amalgamation of various claims. A brief sketch of the working model of interest-group liberalism turns out to be a vulgarized version of the pluralist model of modern political science: (1) Organized interests are homogeneous and easy to define. Any duly elected representative of any interest is taken as an accurate representative of each and every member. (2) Organized interests emerge in every sector of our lives and adequately represent most of those sectors, so that one organized group can be found effectively answering and checking some other organized group as it seeks to prosecute its claims against society. And (3) the role of government is one of insuring access to the most effectively organized, and of ratifying the agreements and adjustments worked out among the competing leaders.

This last assumption is supposed to be a statement of how a democracy works and how it ought to work. Taken together, these assumptions amount to little more than the appropriation of the Adam Smith "hidden hand" model for politics, where the group is the entrepreneur and the equilibrium is not lowest price but the public interest. . . .

. . . Interest-group liberalism . . . had the approval of political scientists because it could deal with so many of the realities of power. It was further appealing because large interest groups and large memberships could be taken virtually as popular rule in modern dress. . . . And it fit the needs of corporate leaders, union leaders, and government officials desperately searching for support as they were losing communal attachments to their constituencies. . . .

A[n] . . . increasingly important positive appeal of interest-group liberalism is that it helps create the sense that power need not be power at all, control need not be control, and government need not be coercive. If sovereignty is parceled out among groups, then who is out anything? As a major *Fortune* editor enthusiastically put it, government power, group power, and individual power may go up simultaneously. If the groups to be controlled control the controls, then "to administer does not always mean to rule." The inequality of power and the awesome coerciveness of government are always gnawing problems in a democratic culture. . . .

In sum, leaders in modern, consensual democracies are ambivalent about government. Government is obviously the most efficacious way of achieving good purposes, but alas, it is efficacious because it is coercive. To live with that ambivalence, modern policy-makers have fallen prey to the belief that public policy involves merely the identification of the problems toward which government ought to be aimed. It pretends that through "pluralism," "countervailing power," "creative federalism," "partnership," and "participatory democracy" the unsentimental business of coercion need not be involved and that unsentimental decisions about how to employ coercion need not really be made at all. Stated in the extreme, the policies of interest-group liberalism are end-oriented but ultimately self-defeating. Few standards of implementation, if any, accompany delegations of power. The requirement of standards has been replaced by the requirement of participation. The requirement of law has been replaced by the requirement of contingency. As a result, the ends of interest-group liberalism are nothing more than sentiments and therefore not really ends at all. . . .

. . . Interest-group liberals have the pluralist paradigm in common and its influence on the policies of the modern state has been very large and very consistent. Practices of government are likely to change only if there is a serious reexamination of the theoretical components of the public philosophy and if that reexamination reveals basic flaws in the theory. Because they guide so much of the analysis of succeeding chapters, contentions about the fundamental flaws in the theory underlying interest-group liberals ought to be made explicit here at the outset. Among the many charges to be made against pluralism, the following three probably best anticipate the analysis to come.

1. The pluralist component has badly served liberalism by propagating the faith that a system built primarily upon groups and bargaining is self-corrective. Some parts of this faith are false, some have never been tested one way or the other, and others can be confirmed only under very special conditions. For example, there is the faulty assumption that groups have other groups to confront in some kind of competition. Another very weak assumption is that people have more than one salient group, that their multiple or overlapping memberships will insure competition, and at the same time will keep competition from becoming too intense. This concept of overlapping membership is also supposed to prove the voluntary character of groups, since it reassures us that even though one group may be highly undemocratic, people can vote with their feet by moving over to some other group to represent their interests. Another assumption that has become an important liberal myth is that when competition between or among groups takes place the results yield a public interest or some other ideal result. As has already been observed, this assumption was borrowed from laissez-faire economists and has even less probability of being borne out in the political system. One of the major Keynesian* criticisms of market theory is that even if pure competition among factors of supply and demand did yield an equilibrium, the equilibrium could be at something far less than the ideal of full employment at reasonable prices. Pure pluralist competition, similarly, might produce political equilibrium, but the experience of recent years shows that it occurs at something far below an acceptable level of legitimacy, or access, or equality, or innovation, or any other valued political commodity.

2. Pluralist theory is also comparable to laissez-faire economics in the extent to which it is unable to come to terms with the problem of imperfect competition. When a program is set up in a specialized agency, the number of organized interest groups surrounding it tends to be re-

*Keynesians are economists who subscribe to the ideas of Englishman John Maynard Keynes. Keynes provided the economic basis for President Franklin Roosevelt's New Deal in the 1930s by advocating government intervention in the economy to "prime the pump" during the Depression. Keynesians opposed pure market theory in which the economy would balance itself by competition. Instead, they believed that government must create jobs by spending money it borrowed, in order to stimulate employment and consumption, thereby eventually building the economy back to prosperity.—EDS.

duced, reduced precisely to those groups and factions to whom the specialization is most salient. That almost immediately transforms the situation from one of potential competition to one of potential oligopoly. As in the economic marketplace, political groups surrounding an agency ultimately learn that direct confrontation leads to net loss for all the competitors. Rather than countervailing power there is more likely to be accommodating power. Most observers and practitioners continue to hold on to the notion of group competition despite their own recognition that it is far from a natural state. [Economist John Kenneth] Galbraith was early to recognize this but is by no means alone is his position that "the support of countervailing power has become in modern times perhaps the major peace-time function of the Federal government." Group competition in Congress and around agencies is not much of a theory if it requires constant central government support.

3. The pluralist paradigm depends upon an idealized conception of the group. Laissez-faire economics may have idealized the enterprise and the entrepreneur but never more than the degree to which the pluralist sentimentalizes the group, the group member, and the interests. We have already noted the contrast between the traditional American or Madisonian definition of the group as adverse to the aggregate interests of the community with the modern view that groups are basically good things unless they break the law or the rules of the game. To the Madisonian, groups were a necessary evil much in need of regulation. To the modern pluralist, groups are good, requiring only accommodation. Madison went beyond his definition of the group to a position that "the regulation of these various interfering interests forms the principal task of modern legislation." This is a far cry from the sentimentality behind such notions as "supportive countervailing power," "group representation in the interior processes of . . . ," and "maximum feasible participation." . . .

The problems of pluralist theory are of more than academic interest. They are directly and indirectly responsible for some of the most costly attributes of modern government: (1) the atrophy of institutions of popular control; (2) the maintenance of old and the creation of new structures of privilege; and (3) conservatism in several senses of the word. These three hypotheses do not exhaust the possibilities but are best suited to introduce the analysis of policies and programs in the next six chapters.

1. In *The Public Philosophy*, Walter Lippmann was rightfully concerned over the "derangement of power" whereby modern democracies tend first toward unchecked elective leadership and then toward drainage of public authority from elective leaders down into the constituencies. However, Lippmann erred if he thought of constituents as only voting constitu-

encies. Drainage has tended toward "support-group constituencies," and with special consequences. Parceling out policy-making power to the most interested parties tends strongly to destroy political responsibility. A program split off with a special imperium to govern itself is not merely an administrative unit. It is a structure of power with impressive capacities to resist central political control.

When conflict of interest is made a principle of government rather than a criminal act, programs based upon such a principle cut out all of that part of the mass of people who are not specifically organized around values salient to the goals of that program. The people are shut out at the most creative phase of policy-making—where the problem is first defined. The public is shut out also at the phase of accountability because in theory there is enough accountability to the immediate surrounding interests. In fact, presidents and congressional committees are most likely to investigate an agency when a complaint is brought to them by one of the most interested organizations. As a further consequence, the accountability we do get is functional rather than substantive; and this involves questions of equity, balance, and equilibrium, to the exclusion of questions of the overall social policy and whether or not the program should be maintained at all. It also means accountability to experts first and amateurs last; and an expert is a person trained and skilled in the mysteries and technologies of that particular program.

Finally, in addition to the natural tendencies, there tends also to be a self-conscious conspiracy to shut out the public. One meaningful illustration, precisely because it is such an absurd extreme, is found in the French system of interest representation in the Fourth Republic. As the Communist-controlled union, the Confédération Générale du Travail (CGT), intensified its participation in postwar French government, it was able to influence representatives of interests other than employees. In a desperate effort to insure that the interests represented on the various boards were separated and competitive, the government issued a decree that "each member of the board must be *independent of the interests he is not representing*."

2. Programs following the principles of interest-group liberalism tend to create and maintain privilege; and it is a type of privilege particularly hard to bear or combat because it is touched with a symbolism of the state. Interest-group liberalism is not merely pluralism but is *sponsored* pluralism. Pluralists ease our consciences about the privileges of organized groups by characterizing them as representative and by responding to their "iron law of oligarchy" by arguing that oligarchy is simply a negative name for organization. Our consciences were already supposed to be

partly reassured by the notion of "overlapping memberships." But however true it may be that overlapping memberships exist and that oligarchy is simply a way of leading people efficiently toward their interests, the value of these characteristics changes entirely when they are taken from the context of politics and put into the context of pluralistic government. The American Farm Bureau Federation is no "voluntary association" if it is a legitimate functionary within the extension system. Such tightly knit corporate groups as the National Association of Home Builders (NAHB), the National Association of Real Estate Boards (NAREB), the National Association for the Advancement of Colored People (NAACP), or the National Association of Manufacturers (NAM) or American Federation of Labor-Congress of Industrial Organizations (AFL-CIO) are no ordinary lobbies after they become part of the "interior processes" of policy formation. Even in the War on Poverty, one can only appreciate the effort to organize the poor by going back and pondering the story and characters in *The Three Penny Opera*. The "Peachum factor" in public affairs may be best personified in Sargent Shriver and his strenuous efforts to get the poor housed in some kind of group before their representation was to begin. . . .

The more clear and legitimized the representation of a group or its leaders in policy formation, the less voluntary its membership in that group and the more necessary is loyalty to its leadership for people who share the interests in question. And, the more widespread the policies of recognizing and sponsoring organized interest, the more hierarchy is introduced into our society. It is a well-recognized and widely appreciated function of formal groups in modern society to provide much of the necessary everyday social control. However, when the very thought processes behind public policy are geared toward these groups they are bound to take on the involuntary character of *public* control.

3. The conservative tendencies of interest-group liberalism can already be seen in the two foregoing objections: weakening of popular control and support of privilege. A third dimension of conservatism, stressed here separately, is the simple conservatism of resistance to change. David Truman, who has certainly not been a strong critic of self-government by interest groups, has, all the the same, provided about the best statement of the general tendency of established agency-group relationships to be "highly resistant to disturbance":

> New and expanded functions are easily accommodated, provided they develop and operate through existing channels of influence and do not tend to alter the relative importance of those influences. Disturbing changes are those that modify either the content or the relative strength of the component forces operating

through an administrative agency. In the face of such changes, or the threat of them, the "old line" agency is highly inflexible.

If this already is a tendency in a pluralistic system, then agency-group relationships must be all the more inflexible to the extent that the relationship is official and legitimate.

Innumerable illustrations will crop up throughout the book. They will be found in new areas of so-called social policy, such as the practice early in the War on Poverty to co-opt neighborhood leaders, thereby creating more privilege than alleviating poverty. . . . Old and established groups doing good works naturally look fearfully upon the emergence of competing, perhaps hostile, new groups. That is an acceptable and healthy part of the political game—until the competition between them is a question of "who shall be the government?" At that point conservatism becomes a matter of survival for each group, and a direct threat to the public interest. Ultimately this threat will be recognized.

55

JEFFREY BIRNBAUM

From *The Lobbyists*

Journalist Jeffrey Birnbaum takes readers back to 1990, when Republican President Bush and the Democratic Congress took on the budget bill. From the start, the complex negotiations were fertile territory for Washington's corporate lobbyists. Lobbying is not a much-loved or well-respected activity. It epitomizes life "inside the Beltway." This excerpt from Birnbaum's fascinating account focuses on Wayne Thevenot, one of the many lobbyists who got involved in 1990's behind-the-scenes budget maneuverings. Thevenot, of Concord Associates (whose most important client was the National Realty Committee) was a Washington veteran who began as a congressional aide decades ago. Interest groups and lobbying, as James Madison anticipated, are inevitable in a large, diverse nation. Still, K Street, where many lobbying firms have their offices, might not have been exactly what Madison had in mind.

"Okay," the President says. "Let's talk."

IT IS THE BRIGHT, clear morning of Tuesday, June 26, 1990, and President George Bush is meeting in the White House with his economic advisers and the congressional leaders of both parties. Together, over steaming coffee in the private quarters, they face a crisis. The federal budget deficit is careening out of control, and efforts to negotiate a solution are getting nowhere. At around 8:30 A.M., after an hour of fruitless talk, the Democrats finally assert that the President has run out of choices. He must renounce his "no new taxes" pledge—the oath that was instrumental in getting him elected. He must make a public statement, they say, about the need to raise taxes.

The room grows silent.

Then the President utters those fateful words.

Not long thereafter, a short statement is quietly tacked on to a bulletin in the White House press room. "It is clear to me that both the size of the deficit problem and the need for a package that can be enacted require all of the following," it reads, including the real shocker: "tax revenue increases."

The announcement hits Washington like an explosion. . .

Later that morning in another part of town, the phones start ringing at Concord Associates, a small lobbyists-for-hire company that overlooks the Treasury Department in the Willard Office Building. Wayne Thevenot, a balding former staffer in the Senate, gets a call from his wife, Laura, who is also a lobbyist. And James Rock, a bearded former aide in the House, hears from his wife, Sue, who works inside the government on the staff of the Senate's budget committee. Both women bring the same news about the President's announcement, and both men confess embarrassment. "How could I not have known?" they each wonder. As lobbyists, they are no longer part of the government, but they know enough high officials in Washington to hear about most significant things before they are announced.

This time, as usual, they had plenty of opportunity to know in advance. Four days earlier, Rock had attended a lobbyists' breakfast where Robert C. Byrd, the powerful chairman of the Senate Appropriations Committee, was the featured speaker. And just the day before, Thevenot had been among a small group of lobbyists who paid Senate Minority Leader Robert Dole to have lunch with them at the 116 Club, an exclusive haunt for lobbyists on Capitol Hill. If anyone in Washington had known what the President was going to do, these two would have. But apparently they knew nothing; neither had breathed a word about the momentous change.

Thevenot and Rock are surprised about the turn of events, but they are not disappointed. Far from it. This is just the kind of news lobbyists love; it gives them something to act on. As a result, their expensively decorated offices now hum with excitement. Unlike [American Trucking

Association lobbyist Thomas] Donohue and [his aide, Kenneth] Simonson, who work only for the truckers, Thevenot and Rock are freelance lobbyists. They sell their services to almost anyone who is willing to pay their fees. That means that bad news for corporate America is good news for them. Crisis is their stock-in-trade, and that is precisely what the President's statement has created. His words have greatly enhanced the prospect for a big tax increase and that probably will mean more clients for Thevenot and Rock—if they are able to act quickly. So Rock parks himself in a chair across from Thevenot, who sits behind his oversized partner's desk, and they begin to plot and plan. They decide to contact the liquor distributors with whom they had once met; surely they will fear a tax increase now and will want to hire more lobbyists. Maybe there is reason to talk to securities firms too, they speculate; and some extra retainers from the real estate industry ought to be easy to find. "It's time to go to work," Rock concludes. "Now!" . . .

Washington has become a club in which the line between those inside and those outside the government is not clearly drawn. Corporate lobbyists have so suffused the culture of the city that at times they seem to be part of the government itself. One result is that corporate America, once a perennial sacrificial lamb when it came to government crackdowns, has become something of a sacred cow. Not only are lawmakers and policymakers reluctant to make changes that would hurt businesses, they even have a tendency to try to help them, as long as budgetary pressures do not interfere. In 1990, Congress passed, and President Bush signed, the biggest deficit-reduction bill ever. But of its approximately $140 billion in tax increases over five years, only 11 percent came from corporations. The rest came from individual, taxpaying families.

Most people outside of Washington see the world of corporate lobbyists in caricature: fat, cigar-smoking men who wine and dine the nation's lawmakers while shoving dollar bills into their pockets. If lobbyists were always so crass, surely they would be easier to understand. If they were so blatant, they would not be nearly as effective as they often are. And they are effective, at least on the margins. But it is there, in relatively small changes to larger pieces of legislation, that big money is made and lost. Careful investment in a Washington lobbyist can yield enormous returns in the form of taxes avoided or regulations curbed—an odd, negative sort of calculation, but one that forms the basis of the economics of lobbying.

The lobbyists' trade bears close similarity to the ancient board game Go, the object of which is to surround the enemy completely, cut him off from any avenue of escape, and thus defeat him. Blocking the decision-maker at every turn is the object of any successful lobbying campaign. Equally important is not to allow the decision-maker to know that he or she is being entrapped. That makes lobbying both high-powered and discreet, a dangerous combination.

Over time, the sheer pervasiveness of corporate lobbyists has had a major impact on government policy, beyond just the lucrative margin of legislation. The fact that lobbyists are everywhere, all the time, has led official Washington to become increasingly sympathetic to the corporate cause. This is true among Democrats as well as among Republicans.

Lawmakers' workdays are filled with meetings with lobbyists, many of whom represent giant corporations. And their weekends are stocked with similar encounters. When lawmakers travel to give speeches, they rarely address groups of poor people. The big-money lobbies often pick up the tab, and their representative fill the audiences, ask the questions, and occupy the luncheon tables and throng the cocktail parties that accompany such events. "That's the bigger issue," contends one congressional aide. "Who do these guys hang out with? Rich people. If you spend your time with millionaires, you begin to think like them." Lobbyists provide the prism through which government officials often make their decisions. . . .

Every lawmaker's chief interest is getting reelected. So lobbyists see it as their job to persuade lawmakers that voters are on the lobbyists' side. To that end, Washington has become a major marketing center, in which issues are created by interest groups and then sold like toothpaste to voters from Portland, Maine, to Portland, Oregon. Thanks to Washington-based direct-mail and telemarketing wizardry, corporations can solicit letters and phone calls from voters in any district in the nation. And clever Washington-based lobbyists know that the best way to guarantee that their point of view will be heard is to take constituents with them when they go to speak to members of Congress.

Lobbyists also function as unpaid staff to the decision-makers, who often don't have enough people on their own payrolls. Lobbyists contribute the money that lawmakers need to get reelected. And, more important, lobbyists provide information about both policy and process that government officials often cannot get from their own, often underfunded government agencies. Lobbyists are the foot soldiers and the friends of the people who run the government.

Sometimes corporate lobbyists are adversaries of the men and women who wield the federal government's enormous power. In every battle, there are winners and losers. And, sometimes, the lobbyists are the losers. Lobbyists also fight among themselves, because the corporate world is far from monolithic. As in any industry, there are also plenty of bad lobbyists. Money is wasted; campaigns can be sloppy and ham-handed. Sometimes corporate lobbyists seem to succeed despite themselves. They are the gang that couldn't shoot straight, but they manage to hit their target often enough to make a difference.

Despite their key role in the world of government, lobbyists are almost always the junior players, because, ultimately, they do not make the decisions. Taken as a group, they are a kind of underclass in the nation's capital, a lower caste that is highly compensated, in part, to make up for their relatively low stature in the city's severely stratified culture. At the top of the hierarchy are members of Congress and Cabinet secretaries. Next come congressional and Cabinet staffs. And then, at the bottom, come lobbyists. Lobbyists chafe at this. But their status is readily apparent. Frequently they suffer the indignity of standing in hallways or reception areas for hours at a time. Theirs are the first appointments canceled or postponed when other business calls. They do not even like to be called "lobbyists." They prefer "consultants" or "lawyers." They also use euphemisms like "When I left the Hill . . . " to describe the moment they left the congressional payroll to take a lobbying job.

One lobbyist put his predicament succinctly: "My mother has never introduced me to her friends as 'my son, the lobbyist.' My son, the Washington representative, maybe. Or the legislative consultant. Or the government-relations counsel. But never as the lobbyist. I can't say I blame her. Being a lobbyist has long been synonymous in the minds of many Americans with being a glorified pimp." . . .

The Main Street of lobbying is K Street, a short stretch through the heart of the sleek downtown. Spanking-new office buildings, filled with law firms, lobbying firms, and the allied services of the influence industry, sprang up everywhere in the city, eventually forming an almost unbroken corridor that stretched from Georgetown at one end of the city to Capitol Hill at the other. When even more office space was needed, metal and stone edifices were built on the Virginia side of the Potomac River. By the 1990s, Washington was home to about eighty thousand lobbyists of one kind or another, and the number was still growing. . . .

Thevenot could ingratiate himself with the best of them, and often did. He once declared at a lobbyists' Christmas party that he wished one day to be the "kissee rather than the kisser." But he was not cloying in his demeanor. He could be full of country charm and bawdy wit, with a hail-fellow manner to match. Yet he carried himself with the broad-shouldered confidence of the weight lifter he once was. He drove big cars and worked for big money. But more than that, he was a big man in Washington, a member in good standing of the political fraternity there. He might have been just a lobbyist, but in some circles he was a near equal of the lawmakers whose votes he worked to influence. He had been around for so long, he said, that to many lawmakers he was "as familiar as an old shoe." And he liked it that way.

At age fifty-four, Thevenot was sometimes bored by the repetitiveness of the legislative process. Other times he was frustrated by his inability to get things done. And having come of age in the Washington of the 1960s and early 1970s, he was forever bemoaning the "bullshitters and hurrah merchants" who were calling themselves politicians in the 1980s. But he still had not lost his touch or enthusiasm. He said he was "barnacle-encrusted," and deep down, still found fun—and, more important, profit—in playing the insider's game.

Thevenot was an access man. He survived on his ability to be accepted and trusted by the people with clout in Congress; his reputation rose and fell on having his telephone calls returned. He was not a technician. When he lobbied for changes in the tax code, for instance, he usually was versed only in the basic facts of the matter. For answers to deeper questions, he brought along an expert. But almost no one considered his need for backup a deficiency. Thevenot's job was more about strategy than details. He had to know whom to ask, when to ask, and how to ask for help, none of which was a simple question in the Byzantine world of Washington.

The secret of Thevenot's entrée was buried deep in the bayous and cotton fields of rural Louisiana. The third-oldest of eight children, Thevenot was the son of a failed farmer. "We built a house, started a farm, and proceeded to get poor," Thevenot recalled. "We also were the only ones who spoke clear English" in a region where Cajun patois was more the norm. His skill with language and his interest in government had brought him to where he was.

In the early 1960s, Thevenot worked as a television reporter for the NBC affiliate in Baton Rouge, and was part of the gang that covered the antics of the colorful governor, Earl Long. In 1963, Thevenot went over to the other side and became campaign manager for Gillis Long, a cousin of Russell's, who was waging an uphill fight for the U.S. House of Representatives against a two-term incumbent. Thevenot did a tremendous volume of work: everything from hiring hillbilly bands to trying to keep the candidate's driver out of jail. And when Gillis Long won, Thevenot's ticket to Washington had been punched.

The only problem was that the headstrong Thevenot was not interested in working for the even more headstrong Gillis Long. Thevenot told

Long that he would be his friend forever, but never again his employee. So Gillis Long telephoned Russell Long, then a U.S. senator, and asked him to find Thevenot a job. The one he found turned out to be as an elevator operator, but, in the hands of the resourceful Thevenot, it became a job with possibilities.

Between trips, Thevenot wrote speeches for his Senate patron. Soon, he moved out of the elevator and into more responsible positions on the staffs of committees that were run by Russell Long. These included panels with jurisdiction over small-business and post-office legislation. No matter what his title was officially, Thevenot always functioned as a top aide to Russell Long, who went on to become one of the most powerful men in Washington as chairman of the Senate Finance Committee.

When Russell Long had been drinking and was bruising for a brawl, Thevenot was there to spirit him away. He was also confidant to the mighty and friend to those who would become that way. He knew "Johnny" Breaux when he was a fellow staffer on Capitol Hill; Breaux went on to become a U.S. senator—in the seat vacated by Russell Long. Thevenot knew "Tommy" Boggs when he was the chubby teenage son of House Majority Leader Hale Boggs of Louisiana; in 1989 Boggs was running one of the biggest lobbying law firms in Washington. In short, Thevenot belonged to Washington's tight-knit Louisiana mafia, which like the Tabasco sauce from back home, wielded a fiery punch even in small quantities. "Thevenot's a piece of work," Senator Breaux explained. "He adds color to an otherwise bland city."

When Thevenot first left the Hill in 1975, he worked briefly for an investment-banking firm. But he soon realized that his life was too closely tied to Congress to abandon the Hill completely. Besides, he thought, becoming a lobbyist would get him faster to what was then his goal: making lots of money. "I decided that there was a point of diminished returns to being a staffer. I got to a point where I just sort of ran out of good ideas," he said. "I also had a family and financial obligations. I was making thirty-five thousand dollars a year, with four kids who had to go to college eventually. It was just not enough. So after nearly thirteen years it was just time to get out and cash in.

"I gave up the idea of changing the world. I set about to get rich."

With two friends, Thevenot set up the lobbying firm of Thevenot, Murray and Scheer. They represented a variety of business interests, but Thevenot was most drawn to real estate. After a few years, he left the partnership to become president and chief lobbyist for the National Realty Committee, one of the burgeoning new trade associations that represented specialized industry factions. The business world had grown too complex and too fragmented for huge umbrella organizations, such as the U.S. Chamber of Commerce and the National Association of Manufacturers, to represent adequately. So in 1969 the biggest real estate developers banded together to form an elite group. In the early 1980s, Thevenot became its most successful and best-known mouthpiece, and helped lead it to many victories on Capitol Hill.

The National Realty Committee's most sweeping win came in 1981, when real estate was lavished with new tax breaks at the prodding of President Reagan. That caused a spurt in development around the country, which redefined the skylines of the nation's cities and filled the pockets of Thevenot's clients with gold. Projects were planned not so much for the rent that they would bring in as for the tax benefits. The boom, however, was so excessive that it was not long before the tax goodies were taken away. "See-through skyscrapers" with no occupants to speak of were becoming a national embarrassment, and there was nothing that Thevenot could do about it. The Tax Reform Act of 1986 made real estate one of its biggest victims. Not only were the 1981 benefits excised, but some tax breaks of older vintage were trimmed away as well. It was a bloodbath for the industry. But, in typical form, Thevenot expressed his chagrin with a smile. "At least our people have nice big buildings of their own to jump from," he said.

Thevenot was not blamed for the disaster. Lobbyists rarely are when the industries they represent lose a legislative fight. He could have stayed with the National Realty Committee forever; indeed, he was on retainer to the group through 1989, at $7,500 a month plus expenses, and continued to function as its top lobbyist. But he wanted a change, and a chance to make more money. So he decided to leave the full-time employ of the real estate industry and go out on his own. He affiliated with William Boardman, a tax lawyer and lobbyist for the engineering and construction industries, who had rented some fancy new office space (at about $45 a square foot) in the Willard Office Building, which had been renovated with the help of Thevenot's early 1980s tax breaks. The two men called themselves Concord Associates, a reference to Boardman's Boston-area roots; on the elegantly papered walls they hung drawings of Revolutionary War scenes from battles around Concord.

In appearance, Thevenot was an odd mixture that mirrored the competing demands of his vocation—one part soft, another part hard as nails. He had the cherubic face of a Kewpie doll, and only slightly more hair. But he also had the beefy hands and swagger of the roughneck he was during the hardworking summers of his youth in sweltering Morgan City, Louisiana. Thevenot had come a long way since then. When Congress reconvened in January 1989, he had been an invited guest at some of the fanciest gatherings in the nation's capital, and he spent most of his time hopping from one private party to another. Senator Charles Robb of Virginia had held a bash for three thousand people at Union Station to celebrate his election. But thanks to the National Realty Committee checks that Thevenot had delivered to Robb's campaigns in the past, Thevenot had been invited to a far smaller, more intimate party in the new senator's office.

What Thevenot did there was collect information, which for him was no insignificant task. He explained, "We're talking to everybody we can about what the general mood of the Congress is. What issues are they going to deem important? How are the members lining up? How strongly they feel, for example, about new taxes to deal with the deficit problem. That is what we do, it's a network, it's a game. All the people that we know, and we've done favors for, gotten jobs for, sent them business, are part of it. What you know and your ability to interpret it—your ability to understand what's important and what's not—is what it's all about."

56

WILLIAM GREIDER

From *Who Will Tell the People*

Almost every excerpt in this section is a criticism of interest groups. Students of American government need to know the problems inherent in group-based politics. Journalist William Greider, whose approach to writing about government is undeniably counter-culture, provides a story both tragic and uplifting. He details the politicization of Washington, D.C. janitors from powerless working-poor laborers, into the "Justice for Janitors" organization. Greider's account of the janitors' "rude and crude" tactics is both sad and shocking. The lesson to be drawn from the janitors' strategy, however, is depressing. Think about Greider's janitors as you sit in college classrooms or the professional offices college graduates occupy. How do they get cleaned and neatened for us each morning?

THE QUALITY OF democracy is not measured in the contentment of the affluent, but in how the political system regards those who lack personal advantages. Such people have never stood in the front ranks of politics, of course, but a generation ago, they had a real presence, at least more than they have now. The challenging conditions they face in their daily lives were once part of the general equation that the political system took into account when it decided the largest economic questions. Now these citizens are absent from politics—both as participants and as the subjects of consideration.

These citizens are not the idle poor, though many hover on the edge of official poverty and virtually all exist in a perpetual condition of economic insecurity. These are working people—the many millions of Americans who fill the society's least glamorous yet essential jobs and rank at the bottom of the ladder in terms of compensation. A large segment of working-class Americans has effectively become invisible to the political debate among governing elites. They are neither seen nor heard nor talked about.

Their absence is a crucial element in the general democratic failure of modern politics. . . .

Like other citizens who have lost power, the humblest working folk have figured out how politics works in the modern age. They know that their only hope is "rude and crude" confrontation. To illustrate this reality, we turn to a group of citizens in Washington, D.C., who are utterly remote from power—the janitors who clean the handsome office buildings in the nation's capital. In a sense, they clean up each night after the very people and organizations that have displaced people like themselves from the political debate. While they work for wages that keep them on the edge of poverty, their political grievances are not heard through the regular channels of politics.

Like other frustrated citizens, the janitors have taken their politics, quite literally, into the streets of the nation's capital.

In late afternoon on a warm June day, while the people in suits and ties were streaming out of downtown office buildings and heading home, a group of fourteen black and Hispanic citizens gathered on the sidewalk in front of 1150 Seventeenth Street Northwest and formed a loose picket line. They were the janitors who cleaned this building every night and, though hardly anyone noticed or cared, they were declaring themselves "on strike" against poverty wages.

"Fire me? Don't bother me one bit. Can't do worse than this," Lucille Morris, a middle-aged black woman with two daughters, said. She was passing out picket signs to hesitant coworkers, most of them women. "Hold 'em up!" she exhorted the others. "Let 'em know you're tired of this mess."

Others grinned nervously at her bravado. An older Hispanic woman dressed in work clothes started into the building and was intercepted by one of the strikers. "She says she's just going in to use the bathroom," Leila Williams reported, "but she's coming back out." Williams, a sweet-faced grandmother who lives with her sixteen-year-old grandson in one of the poorest wards of southeast Washington, was wearing a bright red union tee-shirt that proclaimed: "Squeeze Me Real Hard—I'm Good Under Pressure."

"No one is working—this building isn't going to get cleaned tonight," the organizer from the Services Employees International Union announced with satisfaction. "And nobody's going to get fired," Jay Hessey reassured. "The company can't find enough people to do these jobs at this pay."

"I've been here eleven years and I still get the same pay the newcomers get—$4.75 an hour," Lucille Morris said. "We be doing like two people's work for four hours a night. We don't get nothing in the way of benefits. You get sick, you sick. You stay out too long, they fire you."

"One lady been here for fourteen years and she still get five dollars an hour for doing the bathrooms," Leila Williams added. "They give you another quarter an hour for doing the toilets. When we pass inspections, you know, they always treat us. They give us pizza or doughnuts, like that. We don't want no treats. We want the money."

The SEIU, a union that mainly represents people who do society's elementary chores, launched its "Justice for Janitors" strategy nationwide in 1987 and has staged scores of similar strikes in downtown Washington as well as other major cities. Because of the way federal government now regulates the workers' right to organize for collective action, regular union-organizing tactics have been rendered impotent. So the workers mostly stage symbolic one-night walkouts to grab attention.

The real organizing tactic is public shame—theatrical confrontations intended to harass and embarrass the owners and tenants of the buildings. The janitors will crash the owner's dinner parties and leaflet his neighborhood with accusatory handbills. They will confront the building's tenants at social events and demand help in pressuring the owners.

They, for instance, targeted Mortimer Zuckerman, the real-estate developer who owns *The Atlantic* magazine and *U.S. News & World Report*, with a nasty flier that declared: "Mort Zuckerman might like to be seen as a public citizen, responsible editor, intellectual and all-around good guy. To the janitors who clean his buildings, he is just another greedy real-estate operator." They hounded Zuckerman at important banquets and even in the Long Island Hamptons at celebrity softball games, in which he is a pitcher.

The owners and managers of some five hundred office buildings in Washington have developed an efficient system that insulates them from both unions and higher wages. Each owner hires an independent contractor to service the building and the competitive bidding for contracts is naturally won by the firm that pays the least to the janitors. About six thousand workers—most of them black or Hispanic—are left without any practical leverage over the arrangement. When the union signs up workers and demands its legal right to bargain for a contract in their behalf, the building owner promptly fires the unionized cleaning contractor and hires a new one who is nonunion. Old janitors are fired, new ones are recruited and the treadmill continues.

This management device keeps janitors like Lucille Morris stuck permanently at the same wage level year after year, hovering just above the legal minimum required by law, a wage level that provides less than $10,000 a year at full-time hours.

But these janitors do not even get full-time work from their employers. By doubling the size of the crews, the contractors can hold the workers to a four-hour shift each night and, thus, legally exclude the janitors from all of the employee benefits the firms provide to full-time employees—health insurance, pensions, paid vacations, paid sick leave. The law protects this practice too.

In order to survive, these women and men typically shuttle each day between two or three similar low-wage jobs, all of which lack basic benefits and other protections. Some of the janitors, those who are supporting families, qualify as officially poor and are eligible for food stamps, public housing or other forms of government aid. In effect, the general taxpayers are subsidizing these low-wage employers—the gleaming office buildings of Washington and their tenants—by providing welfare benefits to people who do work that is necessary to the daily functioning of the capital's commerce.

In another era, this arrangement might have been called by its right name—exploitation of the weak by the strong—but in the contemporary political landscape that sort of language is considered passé. Exploitative labor practices are subsumed under the general principle of economic efficiency and the consequences are never mentioned in the political debates on the great social problems afflicting American cities. The government may authorize welfare for the indigent, but it will not address the wages and working conditions that impoverish these people. . . .

For the city of Washington, the political neglect constitutes a social irony, for many of these janitors live in the same troubled neighborhoods where the vicious street combat over drugs occurs. The community is naturally horrified by the violence among the young drug merchants and, without much success, has deployed both police and National Guard to suppress it. Yet the city is oblivious to the plight of the janitors—the people who are working for a living, trying to be self-supporting citizens and must live in the midst of the dangerous social deterioration.

Economists might not see any connection between these two social problems, but any teenager who lives in one of the blighted neighborhoods can grasp it. One group of poor people, mostly young and daring, chooses a life of risk and enterprise with the promise of quick and luxurious returns. Another group of poor people, mostly older men and women, patiently rides the bus downtown each night, and in exchange for poverty wages, they clean the handsome office buildings where the lawyers and lobbyists work. When the janitors stage their occasional strikes, they are harassing the very people who have helped block them out of governing issues—the policy thinkers, the lawyers and lobbyists and other high-priced talent who have surrounded the government in order to influence its decisions.

By coincidence, one of the tenants at 1150 Seventeenth Street, where they were picketing, was the American Enterprise Institute, the conservative think tank that produces policy prescriptions for the political debates of Washington. When the service-employees union organizers approached AEI for support, their request was brushed off, but AEI has had quite a lot to say about minimum-wage laws and their supposedly deleterious effects. In recent years, AEI has published at least nine different scholarly reports arguing against the minimum wage. This position faithfully represents the interests of AEI's sponsoring patrons—the largest banks and corporations in America.

But the SEIU organizers insisted they were not trying to make an ideological point by picking on AEI. The real target was the building owner, which operated a dozen downtown buildings in a similar manner. Besides, they explained, most of the ostensibly liberal policy groups in Washington are no different, from the janitors' point of view.

Indeed, the next strike was planned against another building, also owned by the Charles E. Smith Management Company, which served as the home of the Urban Institute, a liberal think tank that specializes in studying the afflictions of the urban poor. The Urban Institute, though presumably more sympathetic to the working poor, has also published scholarly pamphlets questioning the wisdom of laws to improve their wages.

The Urban Institute scholars are regarded as a liberal counterpoise to such conservative institutions as AEI but, in fact, the liberals are financed, albeit less generously, by the same business and financial interests that pay for the conservative thinkers—Aetna Insurance, $75,000; Chase Manhattan Bank, $15,000; Exxon, $75,000; General Electric, $35,000; Southwestern Bell, $50,000 and so on. The commonly held illusion in Washington politics is that supposedly disinterested experts contend with each other over defining the "public good" from different viewpoints. Yet many of them get their money from the same sources—business and financial interests.

Like other tenants, officials at the Urban Institute insisted the janitors' pay was not their problem. It was a dispute for the cleaning contractor or the building owner to resolve. The SEIU organizers were twice turned down in their efforts to meet with the Urban Institute's officers, so they went out to picket their private homes and tried to crash the institute's banquet for its board of directors.

"Isn't it the same kind of issue any time you pass someone on the street who's homeless?" asked Isabel V. Sawhill, a senior fellow at the institute who is an authority on the "underclass" and related social questions. "It's hard to get involved as an individual in all these microdecisions to change the system. It can't be done at that level. Laws and policies have to be changed."

But these weren't exactly distant strangers one passed on the street. They were the very people who cleaned the office each night, carried out the trash, vacuumed the carpet and scrubbed the sinks and toilets.

"Actually, we never see them," Sawhill allowed. "I do sometimes see them, I admit, because I hang around late, but most people don't."

The janitors, it is true, were mostly invisible. Despite several years of flamboyant efforts, the janitors' campaign had gained very little presence in the civic consciousness of Washington. Public shame is not a terribly reliable lever of political power. For one thing, it only works if widely communicated, and the major media, including *The Washington Post*, had largely ignored the fractious little dramas staged by the janitors.

"People are yawning at them," said Richard Thompson, president of General Maintenance Service, Inc., the largest employer of low-wage janitors. "If there were really a justice question, people in this city would react. There are a lot of government and city government folks who wouldn't stand for it."

The janitors thought they would embarrass both local politicians and congressional Democrats when they targeted a strike at the new shopping complex in Union Station, which is owned by the federal government. Instead, the janitors were fired and commerce continued without interference from the government. Though the Democratic party is ostensibly sympathetic to people like the janitors, Democrats also rely on the real-estate industry as a major source of campaign money.

After an hour or so of picketing on Seventeenth Street, the janitors got into vans and drove over to a museum at New York Avenue and Thirteenth Street where a local charity was holding its annual fund-raising gala. The strikers had no quarrel with the charity, but they did wish to embarrass David Bruce Smith, a young man who is an officer in his grandfather's real-estate company and was serving as chairman of the benefit dinner.

The women in red tee-shirts and the union organizers spread out along the sidewalk and began giving handbills to any who would take them. "Talk with David Bruce Smith," the leaflet asked. "The Janitors Deserve Some Benefits Too!"

The encounter resembled a sidewalk parody of class conflict. As people began arriving for the event, an awkward game of dodging and ducking ensued between the black janitors and the white dinner guests in evening dress. Women from the charity dinner stationed themselves at curbside and, as cars pulled up for the valet parking, they warned the arriving guests about what awaited them. The black women came forward offering their leaflets, but were mostly spurned, as people proceeded swiftly to the door.

"Look, we are a charitable organization and this is political," a man complained bitterly to the union organizers. "People are going to see this and say, what? Are you trying to embarrass me? They're coming here to enjoy themselves."

Jay Hessey reminded him of the constitutional right to petition for redress of grievances. Three D.C. police cars were on hand in the event the janitors violated the law by blocking the doorway or waving placards. It's unfair, the official sputtered, to target an organization that is devoted to charitable activities. It was unfair, the janitors agreed, but then so is life itself. Some people get valet parking. Some people get an extra quarter for cleaning the toilets.

As tempers rose, Hessey stood toe-to-toe with the angry officials and rebuffed them with an expression of utter indifference to their distress. Hessey's colloquial term for the janitor's rude theater—"In your face"—was the essence of their politics. Cut off from the legitimate avenues of political remedy, the janitors had settled on what was left. Like it or not, fair or unfair, people were going to consider, at least for a few uncomfortable moments, the reality known to these janitors.

Most of the guests followed instructions and darted past the demonstrators to the door, but this greatly amused Lucille Morris and Leila Williams and their companions. It had taken considerable courage for these black and Hispanic cleaning women to stand on a sidewalk in downtown Washington and confront well-to-do white people from the other side of town. Once they were there, the women found themselves enjoying the encounter.

It was the white people who turned grim and anxious. Without much success, the black women followed couples to the doorway, urging them to read the handbills. An elegantly dressed woman in silk turned on them and snapped: "You know what? For three hundred dollars, you should be able to enjoy your evening!"

When a mother and daughter streaked past Leila Williams, refusing her handbill, she called after them: "All right, ladies. But you might be standing out here yourself sometime."

"That's right," another janitor exclaimed. "The Lord gave it all, the Lord can take it away."

Their exercise in public shame was perhaps not entirely futile. The elegant woman in silk evidently thought better of her harsh words to the black women because, a few minutes later, she returned outside and discreetly asked them for a copy of their leaflet. She mumbled an expression of sympathy and promised to help, then returned to the banquet.

The janitors may lack formal educations and sophisticated experience with finance but they understand the economic situation well enough.

They know, for instance, that unionized janitors in New York City or Philadelphia will earn two or three times more for doing the very same work. They know that in Washington the federal government and some major private employers, like *The Washington Post* and George Washington University, pay nearly twice as much to janitors and also provide full employee benefits. They know, because the union has explained it for them, that janitorial services represent a very small fraction of a building's overall costs and that even dramatic pay increases would not wreck the balance sheets of either the owners or the tenants.

The problem, as they see it, is not economics. Their problem is power and no one has to tell the janitors that they don't have any. Collective action is the only plausible means by which they can hope to change things. But even the opportunity for collective action has been gravely weakened for people such as these.

The janitors' predicament provides a melodramatic metaphor for a much larger group of Americans—perhaps 20 million or more—who have also lost whatever meager political presence they once had. These are not idlers on welfare or drug addicts, though they often live among them. These are working people, doing necessary jobs and trying to live on inadequate incomes.

These Americans have been orphaned by the political system. They work in the less exalted occupations, especially in the service sector, making more than the minimum wage but less than a comfortable middle-class income. Most have better jobs and higher wages than the Washington janitors—office clerks, hospital attendants, retail salespeople—but are trapped by similar circumstances. Among health-care workers, for instance, one third earn less than $13,000 a year. Some occupations that used to be much higher on the wage scale—airline stewardesses or supermarket clerks—have been pushed closer to the low end by the brutal giveback contracts that labor unions were compelled to accept during the 1980s.

The incomes of the group I'm describing range roughly upward from the poverty line (around $10,000 for a family of three) to somewhere just short of the median household income of around $35,000. "Working poor" does not accurately describe most of them but then neither does "middle class." The poor still suffer more in their daily lives, of course, but even the poor are represented in politics by an elaborate network of civic organizations.

If one asks—Who are the biggest losers in the contemporary alignment of governing power?—it is these people who are economically insecure but not officially poor. During the last generation and especially the last decade, they have been effectively stripped of political protections against exploitation in the workplace. Neither party talks about them or has a serious plan to address their grievances. In the power coordinates that govern large national questions, these people literally do not exist. . . .

After many weeks of pressure and rude confrontations, the D.C. janitors found that some people do respond to the tactics of public embarrassment. After twice rebuffing them, officials at the Urban Institute agreed to support the janitors' plea for better wages. Mortimer Zuckerman also evidently had a change of heart, for his real-estate company abruptly agreed to bargain with the union for contracts at three buildings. The Charles E. Smith Company retreated too after the expressions of community concern generated by the janitors' appearance at the charity dinner.

These breakthroughs for "Justice for Janitors" might be taken as heart-warming evidence that "the system works," as Washington political columnists like to say. But the real meaning was the contrary. The janitors' union, like others, has figured out that the way politics gets done nowadays is not by electing people to office or passing bills in Congress. Politics gets done by confronting power directly, as persistently and rudely as seems necessary.

For all its weaknesses, the irregular methodology exemplified by "Justice for Janitors" has become the "new politics" of the democratic breakdown. Other labor unions, large and small, have adopted similar strategies designed to "shame" corporations into accepting decent labor relations. They confront prominent shareholders at public gatherings or testify against the companies at zoning hearings and before government agencies. They assemble critical dossiers on a corporation's environmental record that will shock the public and drive off consumers. These and other corporate-campaign strategies are sometimes effective in forcing a company to respond to its workers. Like the "Justice for Janitors" campaign, however, the tactics are driven by the worker's essential weakness, not the potential power that lies in their collective strength. In the present circumstances, what else works?

57

ROBERTO SURO

From *Strangers Among Us*

This selection offers insights on how one Hispanic activist group developed. Author Roberto Suro first takes readers into the Los Angeles Flats to watch las madres, *the unofficial protectors of this Hispanic immigrant neighborhood. From their role in stopping street gang violence,* las madres *has grown into a grassroots political organization with broader goals. This group represents an important part of a large and growing new political constituency. Among its concerns are immigration, citizenship, and California's Proposition 187 that removed many benefits from illegal immigrants. The process of absorbing new citizens remains a real challenge for America, Suro notes, but one that cannot and should not be ignored.*

DOWN IN THE FLATS [east of the Los Angeles River] in the evenings, a third group roams the street, moving through the shadows between the day people and the night people. They are *las madres* (the mothers). Dressed in blue jeans or simple cotton dresses, they make sandwiches for the laborers, and then many nights, especially on weekends, they set out to street corners where there might be trouble among the thirteen street gangs that inhabit the Flats. The mothers are immigrants and natives, Spanish speakers, English speakers, and bilinguals. Most have big families in poor households, and most of them work—sewing in sweatshops, cleaning other people's homes and offices. "*Caminadas de amor*" (strolls for love) are what they call their forays. Carrying snacks and soft drinks, they go to the corners, sometimes as many as twenty of them at a time, and encircle their heavily armed progeny.

"They wait for us. They know we are coming and they wait for us because they like it," said Paula Hernández, one of the stalwarts of the group. "All we ever ask of them is to show respect for others. That, and we pray for them and listen to them. They are always having problems with other gangs and the police, and if we listen to them and treat them in a serious way, we can tell them they cannot solve their problems without showing respect for others."

The mothers deal with the police through a neighborhood watch organization, run clothing drives, operate a day-care center, and help support an alternative school for dropouts. With the Jesuits at the Dolores Mission, they also help run a shelter for battered women and a bakery to provide jobs for neighborhood boys. Considering how bad things are, *las madres* are not going to redeem the Flats anytime soon. But, amid the bougainvillea and the bungalows, beneath the freeway overpasses, they try to maintain order. At the heart of a sophisticated metropolis and within sight of office towers housing international banks, the mothers are the most coherent civilizing force in their community, more potent than the police, more consistent than any government agency, more respected than the schools. They represent yet another form of identity that is growing in the barrios. The mothers are a voice of resistance against life at the bottom of a stratified society. They echo the protests of the civil rights era, but in immigrant tones. They use Spanish words to master the downtown bureaucracies of public housing and Medicaid. *Las madres* represent a form of Latino identity that is as pragmatic as it is cultural and that remains proudly ethnic even as it seeks to engage America.

"Of course we are scared, and we get tired because we work all day and then come back to this," said Mrs. Hernández, gesturing down a dark alley where young male voices could be heard cackling.

Sheltered in the orange glare of a streetlight, the mothers formed a tight circle. They are bound together by more than civic spirit. Like most Latinos, *las madres* emerge from a culture that places little stock in institutions. They are at most a generation or two removed from countries where governments are more feared than trusted.

They've grown up believing that *compadrazgo* is the strongest bond outside the family. When the parents of a newborn child ask another couple to serve as the baby's godparents, the four become *compadres*, and it is understood that thenceforth their friendship is a bond for life that can be relied on for practical and emotional support even when relatives fail to heed the call. The baptism ceremony celebrates the ties among the adults as much as the arrival of an infant. And *compadrazgo* is just a formal expression of the kind of networking that begins with kinship and that usually goes much further in Latino cultures, especially in small towns and rural areas.

So there is something very Mexican about six women standing under a streetlight, looking out for their families and for one another, just as there was something very Mayan about how Juan Chanax and his *compadres* helped one another find work. But in places like the Flats, those linkages are finding new expressions and are being put to new purposes as these communities contend with the twin challenges of urban decay and steady immigration.

The mothers of the Dolores Mission are allied with an umbrella group called Las Madres de East L.A. It became one of the best-known community organizations in the city after it won a long battle to keep a prison out of the barrio, and then it won national fame by enlisting middle-class Anglo environmental groups to help it defeat plans to build a toxic-waste incinerator nearby. These battles in the 1980s helped promote a new civil rights cause, environmental racism, which alleges that environmental hazards have been inordinately, even intentionally, concentrated in poor and minority communities.

With little coordination or hierarchy, the mothers in the Flats and all across East L.A. also form a powerful grassroots political force. They helped elect Gloria Molina as the first Hispanic on the Los Angeles County Commission, and they have given important backing to several other insurgent political campaigns. When Proposition 187, the anti–illegal immigration initiative, held a huge lead in the polls, they went door-to-door to make sure that at least barrio voters would reject it.*

And this is not just a Los Angeles phenomenon. In the late 1980s and during the 1990s, barrio community organizations helped elect candidates, most of them women, to top offices in El Paso, Houston, Miami, and New York. In defiance of well-established Latino political bosses, many of these *madres* became the fresh faces and surprise winners when the ballots were counted.

"Sometimes someone says they wish things could be like they are in

*Proposition 187 would prohibit illegal immigrants from receiving social or welfare services, ban them from public schools and universities, and prevent them from receiving publicly funded health care except in emergencies.—EDS.

Mexico," Paula Hernández said. "They think women don't have to worry about their families so much there. Well, it is true women have to do more here. We are away from the children more because we work more, and that makes problems. But it is here that we have learned to get over our fear of saying what we think. It is here we have learned to work together as mothers. That happened because we were here."

Whether they are in Congress or out in the streets pacifying gang bangers, all this activism by Hispanic women reflects two political developments that are fundamentally American: the increasing prominence of women in electoral politics and the growing dynamism of community-action groups that coalesce on specific issues at the neighborhood level. These are national trends that cut across regions, economic classes, and racial or ethnic groups, and there is nothing distinctly Latino or immigrant about them. Indeed, outside the United States, Latino political culture remains male-dominated despite significant changes in the status of women over the past thirty years.

Using minority-group status to get leverage on institutions, electing female politicians, creating community-based organizations to funnel government funds into their neighborhoods—on all these many fronts Latino immigrants are adapting to the United States and learning to use American tools to fix their problems. But at the end of the day as they walk in the dark, traveling between the day people and the night people, making a community out of both, they are *comadres*, creating a sisterhood just as their mothers and grandmothers and generations of Latinas did before them in places far away. The *madres* are neither American nor Mexican. They are creating something new in the barrios out of the old ways they brought from the south and the tools they discovered on American terrain.

Down in the Flats when it started getting late, the mothers had gone home, and the night people dispersed to make their rounds. Cars screeched away. As one big black-and-red sedan pulled out, four or five firecrackers flew from the windows in a kind of mock drive-by. Some of the remaining lads flinched, their hands reaching to their pockets.

At the mission door, the day people started filing in, giving their number to a man with a clipboard. They rolled themselves in olive drab blankets, propped bundled clothes under their heads, and read *fotonovelas*, which are comic books with photos of actors instead of drawings and with soap-opera plots instead of superhero fantasies.

"Los Angeles ya es Latino," Los Angeles is already Latino. The sentence was spoken by a man in white painter pants and a faded work shirt as he smoked a last cigarette before going in to stretch out on his pew. Earlier,

he had entertained me and several other of the laborers with stories of how he had crossed the border so many times that he no longer used a *coyote*, a guide. He told tales of escaping from police who pursued him unjustly in Mexico and of eluding immigration agents in the United States. It was a migrant's *corrido* sung by a nicotine campfire. The mission door was about to close, and now the man was talking about California's [then] governor, Pete Wilson, who had been much in the news those days with his plans to balance the state government's budget by shutting down the border.

"Los Angeles is already Latino. It is too late for Wilson. What is he going to do? Deport us and all the Chicanos, too? If he wants to send two million people to Mexico, okay, let him do it; Mexico will send six million back. Then all of California will be Latino."

Two young laborers, teenagers by their looks, were terribly amused by this and so the older man indulged them. He was a natural-born ham, and before he had finished his cigarette, he had them in stitches.

"If he tries to send all the Latinos out of Los Angeles, all the *blancos* will go crazy in their dirty houses and all the *koreanos* with no one to work for them will go crazy, too. And so they will invite us—yes, *invite* us—to build a subway from Tijuana to Los Angeles that goes right under the border and under the noses of *la migra* [the immigration authorities]."

One of the boys tried to put icing on the joke as they walked into the church. "Yeah, we will get on the subway in Tijuana and they will serve us steaks at tables with napkins, and by the time we are finished eating, we will be here at Union Station."

"*Los Angeles ya es Latino*." . . .

In old downtown Los Angeles on land not far from where the Spanish monks built their mission, an odd sight developed during the winter of 1994–1995. Crowds of Latinos began forming on the sidewalks in the chilly predawn hours. They lined up and waited for the offices of the Immigration and Naturalization Services to open so that they could apply for citizenship. In Los Angeles and then in every major city across the country, immigrants suddenly rushed to seek naturalized status in such numbers that they quickly overwhelmed the bureaucracy. It started shortly after the election that produced Proposition 187 and the Republican majority in Congress, and it occurred spontaneously, with little direction or encouragement from political leaders or advocacy groups. As months and then years passed and the number of Latinos seeking citizenship remained at flood stage, it became apparent that something fundamental had changed in the mentality of the barrio.

Prior to this boom in naturalization, conventional wisdom held that immigrants in the United States acquired citizenship in proportion to the distance they had traveled to get here. So, Asians and Europeans routinely naturalized almost as soon as they became eligible, usually after five years as permanent legal immigrants. By contrast, Canadians and Mexicans rarely would become citizens even after living in the United States for decades. Along with immigrants from the Caribbean and Central America, they retained intense ties to their homelands and often lived with the dream of returning.

As a result, every barrio had a huge supply of potential citizens. That reservoir had swelled when the immigrants who came in the surge of the 1980s reached eligibility, and then it grew even larger as the nearly 3 million beneficiaries of the 1986 amnesty became eligible. In 1995, applications for citizenship topped a million nationwide, nearly twice as many as the year before. By 1997, the INS was expecting close to 2 million citizenship applications.

The long lines of Latinos seeking U.S. citizenship marked a turning point. Like the Dominicans in Washington Heights after the 1992 riots, Latino newcomers all around the country were shocked out of their sojourner mentality by the anti-immigrant backlash. Legal immigrants realized that even though they paid taxes like everyone else, they could still lose access to a social safety net that citizens took for granted. The backlash, however, did not generate the kind of counterreaction typical of minority-group politics. Latinos did not protest or march to demand recognition of their rights. They did not mobilize as a group, nor did they generate a telegenic leader who spoke for their interests. The rush to naturalization was a simple act of self-defense, in part because citizenship offered some protection from the loss of benefits. More important, however, it was a declaration by people who had long lived between two lands that they had begun to consider the United States their permanent home.

Latino immigrants will become citizens with the same quiet relentlessness they showed in entering the country, creating communities, and getting jobs. They are also becoming voters. Together with native-born Latinos, they already make up a significant slice of the electorate in New York, Chicago, Los Angeles, and a number of smaller cities. As with the Irish and the Jews early in this century, the Latinos' political importance will be magnified because they are concentrated in a few highly visible places and because they may be able to swing key states in very close races. Southern California has the potential to become a Latino political bastion in the next twenty years even with no further immigration. More than half of all the youths in Los Angeles County are Latinos, and by the year 2010 Latinos will considerably outnumber Anglos in the entire L.A. metropolitan area. All those kids who carried Mexican flags to protest Proposition 187 have only to grow up and the politics of California and the nation will change for a generation or more. Despite the mathematical inexorability of this change, its direction is not clear. There is always the chance Latinos might fail to translate their numbers into real clout. With the exception of the Miami Cubans, Latino voters have gone Democratic so predictably and by such large margins in the past that the new citizens might suffer the fate of African-Americans, who are often taken for granted because Democrats know they have nowhere else to go. Or if the new Latinos fail to articulate a distinct political identity for themselves, they might eventually resemble the Puerto Ricans and become secondary players who are constantly struggling to make themselves heard.

Initially the leaders and candidates will emerge from the ranks of Mexican-American and Puerto Rican activists who are steeped in minority-group politics, but over time, as immigrants and the children of immigrants enter the arena, it seems likely that Latinos will develop a broader political identity. Their attitudes and agendas will necessarily evolve as a reaction to their experiences with American public institutions, everything from the neighborhood school to Congress. This is perhaps the greatest source of uncertainty about the future, because Latinos are becoming American citizens at a time when America is at best ambivalent about their presence. After the backlash embodied in Proposition 187 and the restrictionist proposals in Washington, many politicians reversed field. The 1996 election produced intimations of how fast the Latino vote was growing, and leaders of both parties grew apprehensive about seeming blatantly anti-immigrant. So, elderly immigrants were not kicked out of nursing homes, and in 1997 a few provisions of immigration law were modified to soften punitive actions against Central Americans who had overstayed temporary permits and illegals in the process of fixing their status. But all that amounted to mollification at a time when a continued economic expansion generated demand for new workers and temporarily relieved some of the nation's anti-immigrant anxiety. Even with sinking welfare rolls and a shrinking budget deficit, new immigrants are still denied access to America's social safety net. Immigration is widely regarded as convenient, even desirable in good economic times, but that is not a commitment to ensuring the successful integration of a large number of newcomers, especially those who most need help from their hosts. The potential for a renewed backlash remains very real, and so it is likely that today's Latino immigrants will establish their political identity in a nation that oscillates between uneasy acceptance and fearful rejection of them.

For the first time since the Voting Rights Act of 1965 opened polling places in the Deep South to blacks, the United States is enfranchising a large new group of people who have been marked as outsiders. This is not primarily a political process or a matter that can be settled with legislation and policy directives. Latino immigrants are on the brink of taking important steps that will define their place in American society for generations to come. Latino newcomers are well along in this process, but much of what they have accomplished thus far has been done quietly. Most Americans hardly noticed the barrios until they grew large. Now the key tasks ahead can only be accomplished loudly and in the public arena. Immigrants must establish links with the United States as vibrant as those they have maintained with their home countries. The barrios must be converted from self-enclosed enclaves into organic American communities intimately connected with the cities around them. Businesses and neighborhood organizations created primarily to facilitate migration and settlement must now turn to long-term goals. And the United States must stop looking at recently arrived immigrants as appendages that can be disposed of when they are unwanted. That means reaching a new understanding of how American society cares for and absorbs people who come from abroad, work hard, remain poor, and fill their homes with children. In the early part of the next century, the new Latino immigrants will become part of the American nation. They are here already. They are not going to leave. It will happen, but the process of integration is never easy or peaceful. There is conflict on the horizon, but beyond the conflict, there may be signs of hope.

58

DAN BALZ AND RONALD BROWNSTEIN

From *Storming the Gates*

Dan Balz and Ronald Brownstein bring readers into a National Rifle Association leadership meeting. The NRA is one of the most powerful interest groups in the United States. While gun ownership is the group's main focus, its broader mission is to resist what members see as the ever-

increasing power of the national government. Other groups, based on their own particular issues, share the NRA's basic distrust of Washington.

WHAT BOTHERS JOHN COLLINS is not so much the new gun-control laws—he expected as much from Bill Clinton and the Democrats in Congress—as the video cameras on the highways in his hometown of Las Vegas. The progression worries him, the small steps, the imperceptible advances. Remember, at first, they were supposed to keep an eye on traffic? Now the cameras are being used to give out traffic tickets. What's next? Monitoring where people drive? Cataloguing license plates? "Little by little," he said ominously, letting the thought trail off in a haze of cigarette smoke.

Tanned and leathery, Collins delivered this warning while standing outside a ballroom in a downtown Phoenix hotel one sizzling afternoon in May 1995. Inside, leaders of the National Rifle Association (NRA), at once perhaps the most powerful and embattled lobby in the country, were handing out awards at a gala luncheon. Collins was one of some twenty thousand gun enthusiasts who had gathered for the NRA's annual convention. A few blocks away, in the Phoenix Convention Center, dozens of manufacturers had set up booths, displaying the latest in shotguns and handguns and telescopic sights. There were hunting bows, crafted as carefully as sculptures, and camouflage outfits and leather jackets with the names of gun manufacturers emblazoned across the back like baseball teams.

Browsing through the stacks of merchandise (down to infant-sized NRA T-shirts that read "Protecting your right to keep and bear arms, for now and for the future") was one of the two principal activities at the convention. The other was talking politics. Stephen Donnell, an NRA board member who has been with the organization for fifty years, waited until Collins had finished his disquisition on highway cameras before offering his own opinion on the state of the nation. "The real issue isn't gun control," he said. "The question is whether we are going to be subjects of the government or whether we are going to be citizens and the government is going to be subject to us." Donnell suggested digging up old newsreels of Hitler and Mussolini to gain an understanding of where Clinton was trying to take the country. What was the connection? "The similarity," John Collins jumped in, "is in the direction they are going."

Not far from Collins and Donnell, David Dutton, a slim, bearded psychologist from the small town of Coarsegold, California, was sitting on a bench, wearing a T-shirt with pictures of Bill and Hillary Clinton above the inscription "Dual Airbags." Friendly but passionate, Dutton picked up where Collins and Donnell left off. "The federal government has become a hydra-headed monster," Dutton said. "Almost any federal agency they want to cut, I would be in favor of. It's grown out of hand. It's a malignant cancer." People used to be free in America, he said almost wistfully. "Now if you pump leaded gas in your car, it's a federal offense."

Not everyone who gathered at the NRA convention was so angry at government. But most were. Like Collins, they had grievances that extended well beyond guns and gun control. Indeed, few of them said they had suffered any personal inconvenience from either the ban on semi-automatic assault weapons or the waiting period for handgun purchases Congress had approved over the previous two years. To most of them, gun control had ascended from the practical to the symbolic. Gun control was just the means to the end of enlarging government and giving Washington more power to control the lives of its citizens. Washington was taking away guns to clear the path for taking away other rights: This was the article of faith. One man from Colorado raged at being required to give his fingerprints to obtain a driver's license. Another complained about federal environmental regulations that favored turtles over farmers and snails over ranchers. Another said government welfare programs were undermining traditional moral values. Speed limits, restraints on the use of public lands, all the infringements on liberty that society demands to uphold order seemed to them an intolerable web of rules and regulations too thick to evade or even comprehend.

What made these sentiments all the more remarkable was their source. The NRA convention had a small-town, blue-collar flavor, and the men who pored over shotguns and swapped hunting stories seemed like the sort who might have broken up antiwar demonstrations with their fists twenty-five years ago. Now they sounded like the Weathermen themselves, branding the government as corrupt, voracious, malevolent. "We're going into a situation where there is a police state mentality," one man said. Another man added: "I'm not saying there is any definite, immediate conspiracy to turn America into a tyranny. But as a matter of principle, people should be afraid of their government."

At their most extreme, these beliefs bordered on the antigovernment paranoia expressed by the two men accused of blowing up a federal office building in Oklahoma City just a month before the NRA meeting. Yet they usually stopped short. Everyone in Phoenix condemned the violence, and if there was any sympathy for the bombers it was kept well hidden.

Still, the intensity of the alienation from government was palpable. When these men talked about Washington, many of them conjured up images of revolution—peaceful or political, but revolution nonetheless. In the same way they once might have spoken of Moscow as a threat to their freedom, now they pointed at their own capital. "I consider the federal government to be the greatest threat to our liberty today," Dutton said. "We've defeated communism. We've defeated Nazism. The last threat is inside the Beltway."

These angry white men are one legion in a grassroots movement that has rewritten the political equation of the 1990s, and in the process helped to transform the Republican Party. With social movements on the left like labor unions and civil rights organizations diminished in power, an army of conservative grassroots groups has mobilized middle-class discontent with government into a militant political force, reaching for an idealized past with the tools of the onrushing future: fax machines, computer bulletin boards, and the shrill buzz of talk radio. They have forged alliances with the Gingrich generation of conservatives and strengthened their hand as the dominant voice within the GOP family. Like a boulder in a highway, the conservative populist movement has become an enormous, often impassable obstacle in the path of President Clinton. No single factor in the Republican revival after Bush's defeat has been more important than the party's success at reconnecting with and invigorating the profusion of anti-Washington and antigovernment movements sprouting in every state.

These movements exist in concentric circles of alienation from government. At the farthest edge are extremist tax protesters, survivalists, and elements of the militia movement so alienated from society that they can imagine taking up arms against it. But most of the energy has been contained within the boundaries of mainstream politics. Probably not in this century have so many distinct groups, with such a broad range of grievances, simultaneously targeted the government in Washington as their enemy. The conservative, or antigovernment, populist coalition operates on at least half a dozen fronts: gun owners led by the 3.5-million-member NRA; Christian conservatives organized primarily through televangelist Marion G. (Pat) Robertson's Christian Coalition, which now counts 1.7 million members in seventeen hundred local chapters; the movement to impose term limits on members of Congress; the network of more than eight hundred state and local antitax organizations; small-business owners spearheaded by the six-hundred-thousand-member National Federation of Independent Business (NFIB), which has surpassed more conciliatory big business organizations as a legislative force in Washington; the Perot movement; and the "wise use" and property rights movements that have amalgamated ranchers, farmers, off-road enthusiasts, loggers, and miners—as well as multinational mining and timber companies—into a coalition demanding the rollback of environmental regulations, increased access to public lands, and government compensation for environmental rules that prevent landowners from developing their property.

Even this list doesn't encompass the entire range of populist right-of-center uprisings through the early 1990s, from the movements that opposed the North American Free Trade Agreement (NAFTA) and the world trade treaty known as GATT to the anti-immigration and anti-affirmative action movements that began in California and have spread elsewhere over time. "There is a synergy," said conservative political consultant Craig Shirley. "It is feeding on itself. It is keeping itself in motion."

These movements sort largely into two camps. In one are the Christian Coalition and other groups drawn to politics primarily by fears of cultural decline and the breakdown of the family. In the other are the secular organizations—like the National Federation of Independent Business, the followers of Ross Perot, the term limits and property rights movements, and the NRA—motivated mostly by opposition to the expansion of government spending and regulation. There are significant differences between and even within these camps, but the conservative populist coalition is more demographically and ideologically coherent than many on the left assume. To a striking degree, Americans in these groups express common attitudes and exhibit similar lifestyles. Gun ownership is considerably more common among groups within the antigovernment coalition than among the population as a whole. Nearly half of small-business owners consider themselves born-again Christians. Gun owners, Christian conservatives, and small-business owners are all heavy listeners to talk radio. In many states, small-business owners, antitax advocates, and Perot activists provided the foundation of support for the term limits movement. The 1995 term limits ballot initiative in Mississippi, for example, was directed by Mike Crook, a field organizer for the Christian Coalition who was also a member of the NRA. "The links are all there," Crook says. "They are all interrelated. All of these grassroots organizations . . . amount to taking back our country for the people."

PART ELEVEN

Voting and Elections

59

FRANK SORAUF

From *Inside Campaign Finance*

Since the major reform of political campaign finance law in 1974, many new concepts have entered the vocabulary of money in politics. The 1974 changes gave the Federal Election Commission (FEC) the responsibility to monitor how much money donors give to campaigns. Limits were fixed for individual and group—political action committee (PAC)—contributions. PACs had to be listed with the FEC, and they had to follow guidelines in raising money. All FEC reports were opened for public scrutiny. Political scientist Frank Sorauf is one of the nation's leading authorities on campaign finance. Here he touches on the FEC, PACs, "independent spending," individual donors, and "soft money." Regulating campaign spending, Sorauf concludes, is an imperfect art. Would a new wave of campaign finance reform solve the problem?

AMERICANS HAVE TWO contradictory reactions to the way they finance political campaigns. They remain deeply suspicious of wealth as a campaign resource. The impression persists that campaign money can buy elections and that it can similarly buy public officials. Many Americans believe that monied interests do in fact make the purchases, and commentary about campaign finance repeatedly turns to clichés like "war chests" and "the best Congress money can buy." Yet at the same time, millions of Americans, perhaps as many as 20 million in an election year, contribute willingly, even virtuously, the cash that makes the funding of American campaigns so feared and despised. Thus Americans both nurture and distrust a system of campaign finance, a system that they reject, even scorn, while making it the most broadly based in the world. Perhaps the major result of these paradoxes and anomalies is our collective inability to agree on the reality of American campaign finance and its consequences. It is hard enough to grasp the details of so technical a subject, especially in sorting out the routes and magnitudes of so much campaign money, but it is even harder to pierce the myths that surround the money's impact and consequences.

If there is any constant in the confusions about American campaign finance in the twentieth century, it is in the repeated attempts to reform it to rely on the small sums of ordinary citizens. The history of those attempts is not a happy one, and yet we have not given up. American optimism about the efficacy of reform, ironically, has run as deep as American distrust of the cash we have tried vainly to reform. So the reformers have persisted throughout the century, their efforts often limited to half-measures and just as often greeted with knowing winks. . . .

In the voluntary, private support for American campaigning, all money originates with individuals, but their money flows in different channels. To take the $471.2 million raised by all congressional candidates in 1989–90 as an example, $249.4 million, or 53 percent, went directly from individual contributors to the candidates' committees. Another 32 percent ($150.6 million) was PAC [political action committee] money raised from individuals; although sponsoring organizations such as corporations or labor unions may pay the overhead expenses of their PACs, they cannot divert funds for such political expenditures from their assets or treasuries. Another sliver, $4.3 million or 1 percent, came in contributions from party committees. The candidates themselves contributed $37.9 million (8 percent) to their campaigns in loans and cash contributions. These four main sources make up only 94 percent of the $471.2 million the candidates raised; loans from other sources and interest earned on money in the campaign treasury accounted for most of the remaining 6 percent. . . .

Money from individuals feeds the expenditure totals of the campaign in two additional ways. First, either an individual or a group (PACs or other groups) may make expenditures in a campaign to urge the election or defeat of a candidate, provided that they are made without the cooperation or knowledge of the candidate they aim to help. These "independent" expenditures totaled $4.7 million in the 1990 congressional campaigns, virtually all of that in PAC funds and thus ultimately received as individual contributions. Second, party committees may spend "on behalf of" candidates; specialists often refer to these sums as "coordinated" expenditures because they may indeed be made with the full knowledge of the candidates who benefit. In 1990 they came to $19.3 million, a figure four and a half times greater than the sum the party committees spent in direct dollar contributions to candidates. . . .

As for PACs, there is no limit on aggregate contributions in a year or a cycle—none comparable to the $25,000 per annum limit on individuals. The largest PACs can and do give millions in an election cycle to candidates for the Congress. The writers of the FECA amendments in 1974 worried largely about individual fat cats. With no aggregate limits to restrain them, PACs some time ago broke the million-dollar barrier, and in the 1990 campaign 21 different PACs gave a million dollars or more to candidates for the Congress. The Realtors Political Action Committee topped the list with total contributions of $3,094,228. . . .

That there should be these four sources of money for congressional campaigns—individuals, PACs, parties, and the candidates themselves—is neither intrinsic to the business of campaigning nor inherent in the ways of American politics. The four of them are simply the creation of the 1974 amendments to the Federal Elections Campaign Act. So too are all the statutory limits to their affluence and generosity. However important and confining, or even wise, they may be, neither the sources of the money nor the limits on them are "natural" or inevitable. They result from congressional decisions.

In defining the system of 1974, Congress created one in harmony with contemporary American politics. It was to be candidate-centered: it dealt with money going to candidates, money spent by candidates, and money spent to support or oppose candidates. . . . With the major exception of individuals making contributions, all of the other contributors, recipients, and spenders of money in the campaign were compelled to report their transactions in painful detail to the Federal Election Commission. . . .

Nothing symbolizes the post-1974 regime in campaign finance more vividly than political action committees. They dominate the media-born images of campaign funding and embody most of the public fears about a campaign finance that relies on voluntary private largesse. For some political activists they represent both the opportunities and the fruits of collective action under the new regime. They are, in short, its most conspicuous icons.

In passing the critical amendments to the FECA in 1974 the Congress did not intend to empower organized giving or fund-raising. It wanted primarily to end the power of the individual fat cats in presidential and congressional politics. In their place the reformers clearly hoped for, perhaps even anticipated, a system of campaign finance of almost naive simplicity and pristine motives: a flood of small individual contributions surging up from the political grass roots of the nation. That hope died quickly, a victim of the unplanned incentives for collective action in the new FECA and an irresistible move to group-based organization in all of American politics. The number of PACs multiplied; and less visibly, candidates, especially the incumbents, also discovered the power of organization, most notably in the revival of legislative party organizations. Brokers emerged anew to organize individual contributions in an increasingly national marketplace. So, more or less simultaneously, both contributors and candidates rediscovered one of the immutable laws of political action: organized, aggregated activity achieves more political goals more effectively.

With the instruments of political organization increasingly available, American politics entered an age of concerted action—whether in neighborhood action groups, in a flourishing Washington representation, or in the funding of campaigns. A heightened pluralism came to all of American politics, but it came to campaign finance almost for the first time in the 1970s and 1980s. With it came all the questions of the consequences of organized politics. At least as long ago as James Madison's authorship of the 10th and 51st papers of *The Federalist*, the notion of organized factions and their ability to exert countervailing limits on each other has been central to the American political tradition. Madison and his followers introduce a great paradox: that in organization there is both strength and weakness. Organization leads to a flourishing, if somewhat disorderly, representation of interests, but in the strivings of these organizations to affect the making of policy, they check, oppose, and offset, however fortuitously, the aims and influence of each other. The ultimate result, the pluralists maintain, is to prevent dangerous concentrations of political influence. The paradox within the paradox is that the greater the number of organizations and the greater their particular strength, the greater the limiting and countervailing consequences of their political activity. . . .

PACs that operate in federal elections—campaigns for the two houses of the Congress and campaigns for president—are closely regulated by the Federal Election Campaign Act of 1974. It requires that all PACs register with the FEC and report their finances and political activity to it periodically. PACs that meet the statute's standards for a "multicandidate committee"—raising money from at least 50 donors and spending it on at least five candidates for federal office—may contribute $5,000 per candidate per election. Virtually all PACs so qualify, else they would be bound to the individual contribution limit of $1,000. The statutes also decide from whom PACs may solicit funds. Corporate PACs, for example, are free to solicit stockholders and management personnel, and labor PACs may solicit only their members; each may solicit the other's clientele under limited circumstances, but they rarely do. . . .

Of all of the attempts to breach the regulatory structures in post-1974 campaign finance, none has been more publicized, even more notorious, than the raising of soft money. A term of epic imprecision, it most usefully refers to money raised outside of the restrictions of federal law (and often to circumvent those restrictions) with the intention, nonetheless, of influencing the outcome of a federal election, directly or indirectly.

That definition, however, omits the agent or actor, and it is often the agent, the recruiter of the soft money, who is the point of contention. The agents are candidates, even presidential candidates, or PACs or party committees, themselves subject to the limits and requirements of the FECA. Hard money, on the contrary, is money that meets all of the litmus tests of the FECA and is thus available for spending in the campaigns governed by the FECA.

It is a capacious definition—the jargon of campaign finance is no more exact than that of the rest of American politics—and one most easily grasps it by illustration. Suppose that the officers of a large corporation, knowing that direct corporate contributions violate federal law, give $50,000 to the Republican state committee in California, where such contributions are legal, with the hope that by strengthening the party they may help the Republican candidate for the U.S. Senate to victory. Soft money? Perhaps, but probably not: both a purposeful agent and a plan for the money's federal impact are missing. But had the money been steered to California by the National Republican Senatorial Committee, even kept in its soft-money accounts, and then allocated to California as a part of a soft-money campaign to build party organization and improve Republican chances of recapturing the Senate, the case is classic. The difference, of course, is an agent with a purpose, and so we return once more to the issue of intermediaries and brokers, if in a somewhat altered guise. . . .

The conventional wisdom is right at last: the regulatory vessel is in fact leaking. Important activity and individuals escape its requirements for reporting, and money flows outside of its controls in swelling torrents. One need only tick off the specifics: bundling, soft money, brokers, independent spending, fund-raisers netting six-figure totals in America's urban centers. However one may wish to describe the structural flaws—as "leaks" or "loopholes"—the integrity of the post-1974 regulatory structure is at grave risk.

60

LANI GUINIER

From *The Tyranny of the Majority*

Law professor Lani Guinier was withdrawn from consideration for the position of assistant attorney general for civil rights in the Justice Department, early in the Clinton administration, because of the storm of controversy over her views on representation in American elections. Critics called her the "quota queen." Professor Guinier explains here that she never advocated quotas, but rather, along with James Madison, she is resisting "the tyranny of the majority." In a diverse society, Guinier believes, winner-take-all elections shut the minority out from having any input at all. Through ideas such as cumulative voting, minorities could elect representatives without damaging the majority's voice. Guinier never received the Senate Judiciary Committee hearing she wished for in order to defend her views, but her ideas remain interesting ones.

I HAVE ALWAYS wanted to be a civil rights lawyer. This lifelong ambition is based on a deep-seated commitment to democratic fair play—to playing by the rules as long as the rules are fair. When the rules seem unfair, I have worked to change them, not subvert them. When I was eight years old, I was a Brownie. I was especially proud of my uniform, which represented a commitment to good citizenship and good deeds. But one day, when my Brownie group staged a hatmaking contest, I realized that uniforms are only as honorable as the people who wear them. The contest was rigged. The winner was assisted by her milliner mother, who actually made the winning entry in full view of all the participants. At the time, I was too young to be able to change the rules, but I was old enough to resign, which I promptly did.

To me, fair play means that the rules encourage everyone to play. They should reward those who win, but they must be acceptable to those who lose. The central theme of my academic writing is that not all rules lead to elemental fair play. Some even commonplace rules work against it.

The professional milliner competing with amateur Brownies stands as an example of rules that are patently rigged or patently subverted. Yet, sometimes, even when rules are perfectly fair in form, they serve in practice to exclude particular groups from meaningful participation. When they do not encourage everyone to play, or when, over the long haul, they do not make the losers feel as good about the outcomes as the winners, they can seem as unfair as the milliner who makes the winning hat for her daughter.

Sometimes, too, we construct rules that force us to be divided into winners and losers when we might have otherwise joined together. This idea was cogently expressed by my son, Nikolas, when he was four years old, far exceeding the thoughtfulness of his mother when she was an eight-year-old Brownie. While I was writing one of my law journal articles, Nikolas and I had a conversation about voting prompted by a

Sesame Street Magazine exercise. The magazine pictured six children: four children had raised their hands because they wanted to play tag; two had their hands down because they wanted to play hide-and-seek. The magazine asked its readers to count the number of children whose hands were raised and then decide what game the children would play.

Nikolas quite realistically replied, "They will play both. First they will play tag. Then they will play hide-and-seek." Despite the magazine's "rules," he was right. To children, it is natural to take turns. The winner may get to play first or more often, but even the "loser" gets something. His was a positive-sum solution that many adult rule-makers ignore.

The traditional answer to the magazine's problem would have been a zero-sum solution: "The children—all the children—will play tag, and only tag." As a zero-sum solution, everything is seen in terms of "I win; you lose." The conventional answer relies on winner-take-all majority rule, in which the tag players, as the majority, win the right to decide for all the children what game to play. The hide-and-seek preference becomes irrelevant. The numerically more powerful majority choice simply subsumes minority preferences.

In the conventional case, the majority that rules gains all the power and the minority that loses gets none. For example, two years ago Brother Rice High School in Chicago held two senior proms. It was not planned that way. The prom committee at Brother Rice, a boys' Catholic high school, expected just one prom when it hired a disc jockey, picked a rock band, and selected music for the prom by consulting student preferences. Each senior was asked to list his three favorite songs, and the band would play the songs that appeared most frequently on the lists.

Seems attractively democratic. But Brother Rice is predominantly white, and the prom committee was all white. That's how they got two proms. The black seniors at Brother Rice felt so shut out by the "democratic process" that they organized their own prom. As one black student put it: "For every vote we had, there were eight votes for what they wanted. . . . [W]ith us being in the minority we're always outvoted. It's as if we don't count."

Some embittered white seniors saw things differently. They complained that the black students should have gone along with the majority: "The majority makes a decision. That's the way it works."

In a way, both groups were right. From the white students' perspective, this was ordinary decisionmaking. To the black students, majority rule sent the message: "we don't count" is the "way it works" for minorities. In a racially divided society, majority rule may be perceived as majority tyranny.

That is a large claim, and I do not rest my case for it solely on the actions of the prom committee in one Chicago high school. To expand the range of the argument, I first consider the ideal of majority rule itself, particularly as reflected in the writings of James Madison and other founding members of our Republic. These early democrats explored the relationship between majority rule and democracy. James Madison warned, "If a majority be united by a common interest, the rights of the minority will be insecure." The tyranny of the majority, according to Madison, requires safeguards to protect "one part of the society against the injustice of the other part."

For Madison, majority tyranny represented the great danger to our early constitutional democracy. Although the American revolution was fought against the tyranny of the British monarch, it soon became clear that there was another tyranny to be avoided. The accumulations of all powers in the same hands, Madison warned, "whether of one, a few, or many, and whether hereditary, self-appointed, or elective, may justly be pronounced the very definition of tyranny."

As another colonist suggested in papers published in Philadelphia, "We have been so long habituated to a jealousy of tyranny from monarchy and aristocracy, that we have yet to learn the dangers of it from democracy." Despotism had to be opposed "whether it came from Kings, Lords or the people."

The debate about majority tyranny reflected Madison's concern that the majority may not represent the whole. In a homogeneous society, the interest of the majority would likely be that of the minority also. But in a heterogeneous community, the majority may not represent all competing interests. The majority is likely to be self-interested and ignorant or indifferent to the concerns of the minority. In such case, Madison observed, the assumption that the majority represents the minority is "altogether fictitious."

Yet even a self-interested majority can govern fairly if it cooperates with the minority. One reason for such cooperation is that the self-interested majority values the principle of reciprocity. The self-interested majority worries that the minority may attract defectors from the majority and become the next governing majority. The Golden Rule principle of reciprocity functions to check the tendency of a self-interested majority to act tyrannically.

So the argument for the majority principle connects it with the value of reciprocity: You cooperate when you lose in part because members of the current majority will cooperate when they lose. The conventional case for the fairness of majority rule is that it is not really the rule of a fixed group—The Majority—on all issues; instead it is the rule of shifting majorities, as the losers at one time or on one issue join with others and become part of the governing coalition at another time or on another issue. The result will be a fair system of mutually beneficial cooperation. I call a majority that rules but does not dominate a Madisonian Majority.

The problem of majority tyranny arises, however, when the self-interested majority does not need to worry about defectors. When the majority is fixed and permanent, there are no checks on its ability to be overbearing. A majority that does not worry about defectors is a majority with total power. . . .

But if a group is unfairly treated, for example, when it forms a racial minority, *and* if the problems of unfairness are not cured by conventional assumptions about majority rule, then what is to be done? The answer is that we may need an *alternative* to winner-take-all majoritarianism. In this book, a collection of my law review articles, I describe the alternative, which, with Nikolas's help, I now call the "principle of taking turns." In a racially divided society, this principle does better than simple majority rule if it accommodates the values of self-government, fairness, deliberation, compromise, and consensus that lie at the heart of the democratic ideal.

In my legal writing, I follow the caveat of James Madison and other early American democrats. I explore decisionmaking rules that might work in a multi-racial society to ensure that majority rule does not become majority tyranny. I pursue voting systems that might disaggregate The Majority so that it does not exercise power unfairly or tyrannically. I aspire to a more cooperative political style of decisionmaking to enable all of the students at Brother Rice to feel comfortable attending the same prom. In looking to create Madisonian Majorities, I pursue a positive-sum, taking-turns solution.

Structuring decisionmaking to allow the minority "a turn" may be necessary to restore the reciprocity ideal when a fixed majority refuses to cooperate with the minority. If the fixed majority loses its incentive to follow the Golden Rule principle of shifting majorities, the minority never gets to take a turn. Giving the minority a turn does not mean the minority gets to rule; what it does mean is that the minority gets to influence decisionmaking and the majority rules more legitimately.

Instead of automatically rewarding the preferences of the monolithic majority, a taking-turns approach anticipates that the majority rules, but is not overbearing. Because those with 51 percent of the votes are not assured 100 percent of the power, the majority cooperates with, or at least does not tyrannize, the minority. . . .

In the end, I do not believe that democracy should encourage rule by the powerful—even a powerful majority. Instead, the ideal of democracy promises a fair discussion among self-defined equals about how to achieve our common aspirations. To redeem that promise, we need to put the idea of taking turns and disaggregating the majority at the center of our conception of representation. Particularly as we move into the twenty-first century as a more highly diversified citizenry, it is essential that we consider the ways in which voting and representational systems succeed or fail at encouraging Madisonian Majorities.

To use Nikolas's terminology, "it is no fair" if a fixed, tyrannical majority excludes or alienates the minority. It is no fair if a fixed, tyrannical majority monopolizes all the power all the time. It is no fair if we engage in the periodic ritual of elections, but only the permanent majority gets to choose who is elected. Where we have tyranny by The Majority, we do not have genuine democracy.

My life's work, with the essential assistance of people like Nikolas, has been to try to find the rules that can best bring us together as a democratic society. Some of my ideas about democratic fair play were grossly mischaracterized in the controversy over my nomination to be Assistant Attorney General for Civil Rights. Trying to find rules to encourage fundamental fairness inevitably raises the question posed by Harvard Professor Randall Kennedy in a summary of this controversy: "What is required to create political institutions that address the needs and aspirations of all Americans, not simply whites, who have long enjoyed racial privilege, but people of color who have long suffered racial exclusion from policy-making forums?" My answer, as Professor Kennedy suggests, varies by situation. But I have a predisposition, reflected in my son's yearning for a positive-sum solution, to seek an integrated body politic in which all perspectives are represented and in which all people work together to find common ground. I advocate empowering voters and their representatives in ways that give even minority voters a chance to influence legislative outcomes. . . .

Concern over majority tyranny has typically focused on the need to monitor and constrain the substantive policy outputs of the decisionmaking process. In my articles, however, I look at the *procedural* rules by which preferences are identified and counted. Procedural rules govern the process by which outcomes are decided. They are the rules by which the game is played.

I have been roundly, and falsely, criticized for focusing on outcomes. Outcomes are indeed relevant, but *not* because I seek to advance particular ends, such as whether the children play tag or hide-and-seek, or whether the band at Brother Rice plays rock music or rap. Rather, I look to outcomes as *evidence* of whether all the children—or all the high school seniors—feel that their choice is represented and considered. The purpose is not to guarantee "equal legislative outcomes"; equal opportunity to *influence* legisative outcomes regardless of race is more like it.

For these reasons, I sometimes explore alternatives to simple, winner-take-all majority rule. I do not advocate any one procedural rule as a universal panacea for unfairness. Nor do I propose these remedies primarily as judicial solutions. They can be adopted only in the context of litigation after the court first finds a legal violation.

Outside of litigation, I propose these approaches as political solutions if, depending on the local context, they better approximate the goals of democratic fair play. One such decisionmaking alternative is called cumulative voting, which could give all the students at Brother Rice multiple votes and allow them to distribute their votes in any combination of their choice. If each student could vote for ten songs, the students could plump or aggregate their votes to reflect the intensity of their preferences. They could put ten votes on one song; they could put five votes on two songs. If a tenth of the students opted to "cumulate" or plump all their votes for one song, they would be able to select one of every ten or so songs played at the prom. The black seniors could have done this if they chose to, but so could any other cohesive group of sufficient size. In this way, the songs preferred by a majority would be played most often, but the songs the minority enjoyed would also show up on the play list.

Under cumulative voting, voters get the same number of votes as there are seats or options to vote for, and they can then distribute their votes in any combination to reflect their preferences. Like-minded voters can vote as a solid bloc or, instead, form strategic, cross-racial coalitions to gain mutual benefits. This system is emphatically not racially based; it allows voters to organize themselves on whatever basis they wish.

Corporations use this system to ensure representation of minority shareholders on corporate boards of directors. Similarly, some local municipal and county governments have adopted cumulative voting to ensure representation of minority voters. Instead of awarding political power to geographic units called districts, cumulative voting allows voters to cast ballots based on what they think rather than where they live.

Cumulative voting is based on the principle of one person–one vote because each voter gets the same total number of votes. Everyone's preferences are counted equally. It is not a particularly radical idea; thirty states either require or permit corporations to use this election system.

Cumulative voting is certainly not antidemocratic because it emphasizes the importance of voter choice in selecting public or social policy. And it is neither liberal nor conservative. Both the Reagan and Bush administrations approved cumulative voting schemes pursuant to the Voting Rights Act to protect the rights of racial- and language-minority voters.

But, as in Chilton County, Alabama, which now uses cumulative voting to elect both the school board and the county commission, any politically cohesive group can vote strategically to win representation. Groups of voters win representation depending on the exclusion threshold, meaning the percentage of votes needed to win one seat or have the band play one song. That threshold can be set case by case, jurisdiction by jurisdiction, based on the size of minority groups that make compelling claims for representation.

Normally the exclusion threshold in a head-to-head contest is 50 percent, which means that only groups that can organize a majority can get elected. But if multiple seats (or multiple songs) are considered simultaneously, the exclusion threshold is considerably reduced. For example, in Chilton County, with seven seats elected simultaneously on each governing body, the threshold of exclusion is now one-eighth. Any group with the solid support of one-eighth the voting population cannot be denied representation. This is because any self-identified minority can plump or cumulate all its votes for one candidate. Again, minorities are not defined solely in racial terms.

As it turned out in Chilton County, both blacks and Republicans benefited from this new system. The school board and commission now each have three white Democrats, three white Republicans, and one black Democrat. Previously, when each seat was decided in a head-to-head contest, the majority not only ruled but monopolized. Only white Democrats were elected at every prior election during this century.

Similarly, if the black and white students at Brother Rice have very different musical taste, cumulative voting permits a positive-sum solution to enable both groups to enjoy one prom. The majority's preferences would be respected in that their songs would be played most often, but the black students could express the intensity of their preferences too. If the black students chose to plump all their votes on a few songs, their minority preferences would be recognized and played. Essentially, cumulative voting structures the band's repertoire to enable the students to take turns.

As a solution that permits voters to self-select their identities, cumulative voting also encourages cross-racial coalition building. No one is locked into a minority identity. Nor is anyone necessarily isolated by the identity they choose. Voters can strengthen their influence by forming coalitions to elect more than one representative or to select a range of music more compatible with the entire student body's preferences.

Women too can use cumulative voting to gain greater representation. Indeed, in other countries with similar, alternative voting systems, women are more likely to be represented in the national legislature. For example, in some Western European democracies, the national legislatures have as many as 37 percent female members compared to a little more than 5 percent in our Congress.

There is a final benefit from cumulative voting. It eliminates gerrymandering. By denying protected incumbents safe seats in gerrymandered districts, cumulative voting might encourage more voter participation. With greater interest-based electoral competition, cumulative voting could promote the political turnover sought by advocates of term limits. In this way, cumulative voting serves many of the same ends as periodic elections or rotation in office, a solution that Madison and others advocated as a means of protecting against permanent majority factions. . . .

My nomination became an unfortunate metaphor for the state of race relations in America. My nomination suggested that as a country, we are in a state of denial about issues of race and racism. The censorship imposed against me points to a denial of serious public debate or discussion about racial fairness and justice in a true democracy. For many politicians and policymakers, the remedy for racism is simply to stop talking about race.

Sentences, words, even phrases separated by paragraphs in my law review articles were served up to demonstrate that I was violating the rules. Because I talked openly about existing racial divisions, I was branded "race obsessed." Because I explored innovative ways to remedy racism, I was branded "antidemocratic." It did not matter that I had suggested race-neutral election rules, such as cumulative voting, as an alternative to remedy racial discrimination. It did not matter that I never advocated quotas. I became the Quota Queen.

The vision behind my by-now-notorious law review articles and my less-well-known professional commitments has always been that of a fair and just society, a society in which even adversely affected parties believe in the system because they believe the process is fair and the process is inclusive. My vision of fairness and justice imagines a full and effective voice for all citizens. I may have failed to locate some of my ideas in the specific factual contexts from which they are derived. But always I have tried to show that democracy in a heterogeneous society is incompatible with rule by a racial monopoly of any color.

By publishing these law journal articles as a collection, I hope to spark the debate that was denied in the context of my nomination. We will have lost more than any one individual's opportunity for public service if we fail to pursue the public thirst for information about, and positive-sum solutions to, the issues at the heart of this controversy. The twentieth-century problem—the problem of the color line, according to W. E. B. Du Bois—will soon become a twenty-first-century problem if we allow opposing viewpoints to be silenced on issues of race and racism.

I hope that we can learn three positive lessons from my experience. The first lesson is that those who stand for principles may lose in the short run, but they cannot be suppressed in the long run. The second lesson is that public dialogue is critical to represent all perspectives; no one viewpoint should be permitted to monopolize, distort, caricature, or shape public debate. The tyranny of The Majority is just as much a problem of silencing minority viewpoints as it is of excluding minority representatives or preferences. We cannot all talk at once, but that does not mean only one group should get to speak. We can take turns. Third, we need consensus and positive-sum solutions. We need a broad public conversation about issues of racial justice in which we seek win-win solutions to real-life problems. If we include blacks and whites, and women and men, and Republicans and Democrats, and even people with new ideas, we will all be better off.

61

KATHLEEN HALL JAMIESON

From *Dirty Politics*

One of the most memorable campaign ads from a presidential election is the famous—or infamous—1988 Willie Horton ad. The original ad came from a political action committee (PAC) independent of President Bush's campaign. Political scientist Kathleen Hall Jamieson describes the content of the anti-Dukakis message. It showed William Horton, whom the ad referred to as "Willie," a convicted murderer, who had been given a weekend furlough while Michael Dukakis was governor of Massachusetts. The ad tells viewers that during this furlough, Horton kidnapped a couple and stabbed the man and raped the woman. Jamieson examines the Bush campaign's follow-up spot and reveals how the Willie Horton story became like a drama, filled with dangerous misinterpretations and untrue implications about the crime. William Horton was black. The couple was white. The Republicans had successfully played the "race card," with fear being a winning issue in the 1988 presidential election.

Almost three years after George Bush decisively defeated Democrat Michael Dukakis to become the president of the United States, a group of voters in Pineville, Louisiana, was asked, "Can you tell me what you remember as being important in the 1988 presidential campaign?" The individuals in the group responded.

Hmm.

I'm trying to think.

1988?

Leader: '88.

That's the last one.

Dukakis.

That was Dukakis.

It's about time for another one isn't it?

That time again. It was Dukakis wasn't it?

I just knew I couldn't vote for him.

Seems like the Democratic man that ran, he had a lot of problems. His wife and so forth.

A lot of that didn't come out 'til after the election, though.

That's right.

A lot of us didn't know of her personal problems. They hid . . . that was pretty well hid. She admitted that was . . . I don't know that was a . . .

I think the big thing against him was that, wasn't his criminal . . . I mean not his criminal record, but his . . . the handling of, um . . .

The handling of his state programs.

His state programs. I think that influenced a lot of people, how they voted.

And again, it was still a social aspect of dealing with social issues. And, uh, Bush was more international and people developing things for themselves. Giving them an opportunity to do their own thing and that will support our country. By that I mean build up business and the taxes then, and the income from growth and everything will take care of our country. I saw those as two distinct things.

Focus Group Leader: You had just mentioned how he handled state issues. Can you think of any specific issues?

Well, I think right off the . . . the one I'm thinking about was his . . . his handling of a criminal, um, and I can't right now . . .

What do you mean, a pardon of someone who has . . .

Willie Horton.

Yeah. A pardon.

Pardon.

Yeah. He pardoned that guy that went out and killed someone.

Afterwards. You know, he released this known . . . I guess he was a murderer wasn't he? Originally. And they released him anyway and he went out and killed . . .

Immediately and killed people again.

Right after getting out.

And this was brought out that he was releasing people really without seemingly too much thought. I think that had a lot to do with it.

William Horton and Michael Dukakis are now twinned in our memory. The fact that the memories are factually inaccurate does not diminish their power. Dukakis did not pardon Horton nor did the furloughed convict kill.

Although it does recount the facts of the Horton case, this chapter is not one more rehash of who did what to whom in the 1988 campaign. Instead, it sets a context for the book by examining how voters and reporters came to know what they know of politics. It argues that, in politics as in life, what is known is not necessarily what is believed, what is shown is not necessarily what is seen, and what is said is not necessarily what is heard. It then examines how in the Horton case consultants exploited the psychological quirks that characterize humans.

These quirks include a pack-ratlike tendency to gather up and interrelate information from various places, a disposition to weigh accessible, dramatic data more heavily than abstract statistical information, and a predilection for letting fears shape perception of what constitutes "fact."

At the same time, we have conventionalized journalistic norms that reward messages that are dramatic, personal, concise, visual, and take the form of narrative. In 1988, the psychological dispositions of the public coupled with the news norms to produce an environment in which an atypical but dramatic personification of deep-seated fears would displace other issues and dominate the discourse of the campaign. That dramatic, visual, personalized narrative told the "story" of William Horton.

The role that ads, Bush rhetoric, news, and audience psychology played in transforming William Horton's name for some into a symbol of the terrors of crime and for others of the exploitation of racist fears shows the powerful ways in which messages interact and the varying responses they evoke in individuals. Like pack rats, voters gather bits and pieces of political information and store them in a single place. Lost in the storage is a clear recall of where this or that "fact" came from. Information obtained from news mixes with that from ads, for example.

Although Bush had been telling the tale on the stump since June, in the second week in September 1988, the Horton story broke into prime time in the form of a National Security Political Action Committee

(NSPAC) ad. The ad tied Michael Dukakis to a convicted murderer who had jumped furlough and gone on to rape a Maryland woman and assault her fiancé. The convict was black, the couple white.*

The ad opens with side-by-side pictures of Dukakis and Bush. Dukakis's hair is unkempt, the photo dark. Bush, by contrast, is smiling and bathed in light. As the pictures appear, an announcer says "Bush and Dukakis on crime." A picture of Bush flashes on the screen. "Bush supports the death penalty for first-degree murderers." A picture of Dukakis. "Dukakis not only opposes the death penalty, he allowed first degree murderers to have weekend passes from prison." A close-up mug shot of Horton flashes onto the screen. "One was Willie Horton, who murdered a boy in a robbery, stabbing him nineteen times." A blurry black-and-white photo of Horton apparently being arrested appears. "Despite a life sentence, Horton received ten weekend passes from prison." The words "kidnapping," "stabbing," and "raping" appear on the screen with Horton's picture as the announcer adds, "Horton fled, kidnapping a young couple, stabbing the man and repeatedly raping his girlfriend." The final photo again shows Michael Dukakis. The announcer notes "Weekend prison passes. Dukakis on crime."

When the Bush campaign's "revolving door" ad began to air on October 5, viewers read Horton from the PAC ad into the furlough ad. This stark black-and-white Bush ad opened with bleak prison scenes. It then cut to a procession of convicts circling through a revolving gate and marching toward the nation's living rooms. By carefully juxtaposing words and pictures, the ad invited the false inference that 268 first-degree murderers were furloughed by Dukakis to rape and kidnap. As the bleak visuals appeared, the announcer said that Dukakis had vetoed the death penalty and given furloughs to "first-degree murderers not eligible for parole. While out, many committed other crimes like kidnapping and rape."

The furlough ad contains three false statements and invites one illegitimate inference. The structure of the ad prompts listeners to hear "first-degree murderers not eligible for parole" as the antecedent referent for "many." Many of whom committed crimes? First-degree murderers not eligible for parole. Many of whom went on to commit crimes like kidnapping and rape? First-degree murderers not eligible for parole.

*In his article "The Road to Here," included in Larry Sabato's *Toward the Millennium: The Elections of 1996,* journalist Tom Rosenstiel points out that much negative campaigning ironically originates in the primaries among fellow party members. It was fellow Democrat Al Gore who first unearthed the Willie Horton incident regarding Democrat Michael Dukakis during the presidential primaries in 1988.—EDS.

But many unparoleable first-degree murderers did not escape. Of the 268 furloughed convicts who jumped furlough during Dukakis's first two terms, only four had ever been convicted first-degree murderers not eligible for parole. Of those four not "many" but one went on to kidnap and rape. That one was William Horton. By flashing "268 escaped" on the screen as the announcer speaks of "many first-degree murderers," the ad invites the false inference that 268 murderers jumped furlough to rape and kidnap. Again, the single individual who fits this description is Horton. Finally, the actual number who were more than four hours late in returning from furlough during Dukakis's two and a half terms was not 268 but 275. In Dukakis's first two terms, 268 escapes were made by the 11,497 individuals who were given a total of 67,378 furloughs. In the ten-year period encompassing his two completed terms and the first two years of his third term (1987–88), 275 of 76,455 furloughs resulted in escape.

This figure of 275 in ten years compares with 269 who escaped in the three years in which the program was run by Dukakis's Republican predecessor, who created the furlough program.

Still the battle of drama against data continued. After the Bush campaign's furlough ad had been on the air for two and a half weeks, in the third week of October, PAC ads featuring the victims of Horton began airing. One showed the man whose fiancée had been raped by the furloughed Horton. "Mike Dukakis and Willie Horton changed our lives forever," said Cliff Barnes, speaking in tight close-up. "He was serving a life term, without the possibility of a parole, when Governor Dukakis gave him a few days off. Horton broke into our home. For twelve hours, I was beaten, slashed, and terrorized. My wife, Angie, was brutally raped. When his liberal experiment failed, Dukakis simply looked away. He also vetoed the death penalty bill. Regardless of the election, we are worried people don't know enough about Mike Dukakis."

The second ad was narrated by the sister of the teenager killed by Horton. "Governor Dukakis's liberal furlough experiments failed. We are all victims. First, Dukakis let killers out of prison. He also vetoed the death penalty. Willie Horton stabbed my teenage brother nineteen times. Joey died. Horton was sentenced to life without parole, but Dukakis gave him a furlough. He never returned. Horton went on to rape and torture others. I worry that people here don't know enough about Dukakis's record." The words that recur in the two ads are: "liberal," "experiment", "rape," worry that "people don't know enough about Dukakis," "vetoed the death penalty."

Taken together the ads created a coherent narrative. Dukakis furloughed Horton (PAC ads), just as he had furloughed 267 other escapees (Bush revolving door ad). Horton raped a woman and stabbed her fiancé (crime-quiz and victim PAC ads). Viewers could infer what must have happened to the victims of the other 267 escapees. . . .

The Horton narrative fit the requirements of news. Unlike the "soft" news found in feature stories of the sort pioneered by Charles Kuralt on television, hard news is about an event that treats an issue of ongoing concern. Because violent crime is dramatic, conflict ridden, evokes intense emotions, disrupts the social order, threatens the community, and can be verified by such official sources as police, it is "newsworthy." If one believed Bush's version of the facts, a convicted murderer who should have been executed had been furloughed to rape, torture, and murder again. In newscasts, the villain Horton appeared incarnated in a menacing mug shot. To personalize and dramatize, the news camera showed him in close-up; the less inflammatory visuals in the controversial PAC ad were shot mid-screen. Appearing in tight close-ups both in news and in the ads, the sister of the teenager Horton allegedly killed and the fiancé and now husband of the woman he raped told of their torment and urged a vote against the second villain in the story, Michael Dukakis. . . .

Helping propel the false generalizations from the isolated case of Horton to hordes of others who presumably did what he had done were complex and unspoken references to race. "'Crime' became a shorthand signal," note Thomas and Mary Edsall, "to a crucial group of white voters, for broader issues of social disorder, evoking powerful ideas about authority, status, morality, self-control, and race." "Any reference to capital punishment," argues political scientist Murray Edelman, "is also a reference to the need to restrain blacks and the poor from violence. The liberal argument that poor people and blacks are disproportionately targeted by capital punishment laws doubtless fuels this fear in a part of the public. That the association is subtle makes it all the more potent, for 'capital punishment,' like all condensation symbols, draws its intensity from the associations it represses." Without actually voicing the repressed associations, the image of Horton on the screen as the announcer notes that Dukakis opposes the death penalty serves to raise them. "'Weekend Passes' [which I have called the Horton ad] is not about Willie Horton," says NSPAC's Floyd Brown. "It's about the death penalty. George Bush stood on the side of the majority. Michael Dukakis stood on the side of the minority. The death penalty is where we win our audience."

The 1990 General Social Survey of Racial Stereotyping among White Americans demonstrates that racial prejudice correlates with support for capital punishment. According to Kinder and Mendelberg, "white Americans who regard blacks as inferior are quite a bit more likely to favor the death penalty for convicted murderers."

In the last week of October 1988, ninety-three members of ten focus groups demonstrated the power of the Horton narrative to elicit racially based fear. "If you saw an ad on prison furloughs with scenes in a prison," these voters were asked, "remember as best you can" the "race or ethnic identity" of the "people you saw in the ad. . . . " Of those who did recall the ad, nearly 60 percent (59.9 percent, 43 individuals) reported that most of the men were black. In fact, only two of the "prisoners" are identifiably black. One of them is the only one in the ad to ever look directly into the camera.

When asked to write out everything "you know about William Horton," all but five of the focus group respondents included the fact that Horton is black in their description. All but twelve wrote that the woman raped was white. One-third of the respondents indicated Horton's race twice in their descriptions. And one focus group respondent referred to Horton throughout his description as "this Black Man." Twenty-eight percent of those in the focus groups indicated that he had committed murder while on furlough. . . .

All narrative capitalizes on the human capacity and disposition to construct stories. A compelling narrative such as the Horton saga controls our interpretation of data by offering a plausible, internally coherent story that resonates with the audience while accounting causally for otherwise discordant or fragmentary information.

When news and ads trace the trauma and drama of a kidnapping and rape by a convicted murderer on furlough, the repetition and the story structure give it added power in memory. Visceral, visual identifications and appositions are better able to be retrieved than statistical abstractions.

Repeatedly aired oppositional material carries an additional power. Material aired again and again is more likely to stay fresh in our minds. The same is true for attacks.

Cognitive accessibility is upped by those message traits that characterize the Republicans' use of Horton: the dramatic, the personally relevant, the frequently repeated topic or claim—the menacing mug shot, circling convicts, empathic victims—and seemingly uncaring perpetrator—the Massachusetts governor.

When it came to William Horton, our quirks as consumers of political information worked for the Republicans and against the Democrats. In our psychic equations, something nasty has greater power and influence than something nice. When evaluating "social stimuli," negative information carries more weight than positive information. Additionally, negative information seems better able than positive to alter existing impressions and is easier to recall. Televised images that elicit negative emotion result in better recall than those that evoke positive ones. As a result, attacks are better remembered than positive reasons for voting for a candidate. And dissatisfied, disapproving voters are more likely to appear at their polling place than their more satisfied neighbors.

Messages that induce fear dampen our disposition to scrutinize them for gaps in logic. When the message is fear arousing, personal involvement and interest in it minimize systematic evaluation. In the language of cognitive psychology, "[L]arge levels of negative affect such as fear may override cognitive processing."

The Horton story magnifies fear of crime, identifies that fear with Dukakis, and offers a surefire way of alleviating the anxiety—vote for Bush. . . .

The power of the Horton mini-series was magnified as it unfolded soap-opera-like in news and ads; broadcasts that focused on the tale's strategic intent and effect couldn't effectively challenge its typicality. And since statistics don't displace stories nor data, drama, the native language of Dukakis didn't summon persuasive visions of the cops he had put on the street or the murders and rapes that hadn't been committed in a state whose crime rate was down. Abetted by news reports, amplified by Republican ads, assimilated through the cognitive quirks of audiences, William Horton came to incarnate liberalism's failures and voters' fears.

62

LARRY SABATO AND GLENN SIMPSON

From *Dirty Little Secrets*

Among the many "dirty little secrets" that taint American politics today, Larry Sabato and Glenn Simpson focus here on the technique of push-polling, a new and ugly campaign tactic. While seeming to be a candidate poll seeking voter opinion, the push-poll is really a device to communicate innuendoes that smear the opponent. Sabato and Simpson go on to explain the sophisticated telephone technology that makes techniques like push-polling possible. In case students don't fully grasp the impact of these messages, Sabato and Simpson close with an example—an actual script from Florida's 1994 gubernatorial campaign.

Oh, the telephone is now a very evil technique.

—Republican pollster Frank Luntz, November 1994

The one thing I see repeatedly is the total abuse of the phone. It's really running rampant and getting worse.

—Democratic consultant Joe Trippi, August 1995

PERKS, AND THE ABUSE OF THEM, are both as old as Congress, although the nature of the abuse has evolved considerably. But both major political parties make use of new technology, too, and not just in developing sophisticated direct-mail operations. Computerized telephone banks, made available to the candidates by the professional beneficiaries of big-money politics—the for-hire campaign consultants—have begun to make their mark. While consultants have a separate profit motive, they share with candidates a steely determination to do whatever it takes to win.

During every campaign season, a great deal of attention is properly devoted to condemning misleading television advertisements and nasty direct-mail letters. But "push-polling" has largely been ignored, even though it has become the rage in American campaigns, to the detriment of both civility and the truth. It was a factor most recently in Iowa during the 1996 Republican Caucus, when candidate Steve Forbes accused the Bob Dole campaign of tactics akin to those discussed [here]. Unless aggressive action is taken, this difficult-to-catch form of political sleaze threatens to drag our already debased electioneering even lower.

The push-poll operates under the guise of legitimate survey research to spread lies, rumors, and innuendo about candidates. Hundreds of thousands, probably millions, of voters were telephoned and push-polled during the 1994 elections. This effort dramatically increased the degree of negativity in American politics. Many voters and observers were disgusted and enraged by the tactic, but sleaze telephoning can work efficiently and effectively—and so, unless exposed and checked, it is bound to become standard ammunition in campaign arsenals across the United States. . . .

. . . *A push-poll is a survey instrument containing questions which attempt to change the opinion of contacted voters*, generally by divulging negative information about the opponent which is designed to *push* the voter away from him or her and *pull* the voter toward the candidate paying for the polling. In other words, push-polling is *campaigning under the guise of research.* This operational definition parallels the push-poll used by businesses, "sugging"—*s*elling *u*nder the *g*uise of a telephone research poll products or publications. But the push-poll is actually several forms of public opinion surveying and targeted voter contact, some legitimate and others dismaying.

The most common and defensible type is an adjunct to "opposition research," a campaigner's effort to learn about the opponents' record and discover what might reduce public support for them. Commonly, a pollster working for a candidate will pre-test positive and negative campaign themes in a random-sample public opinion survey by telephone early in the campaign season. Voters will be asked for their reactions to the virtues and the vices of the major-party candidates, including some blemishes that may not yet be publicly known. For instance, in a standard research push-poll, a respondent (that is, a citizen called by the pollster) is often read a relatively fair, paragraph-long biographical description of each candidate and asked which contender he or she supports. Then additional information is added, question by question, to test the voter's commitment, and to assess what issues might "push" a voter away from his or her initial choice. For example,

> If you learned that [Candidate A] has voted for six tax increases in the state legislature, would this make you more or less likely to support her?

> If you learned that [Candidate B] opposes a woman's right to choose an abortion, would this make you more or less likely to support him?

Some push-polls give voters several choices for answers: "Would this make you a great deal *more* likely to support him, somewhat *more* likely, somewhat *less* likely, a great deal *less* likely, or would it not make any difference to you?" In this way, a campaign can prepare itself by determining which assaults actually move opinion. Naturally, the candidate wants to know what will work or whether his ammunition is mostly blanks. One well-known national political pollster, Frederick/Schneiders, Inc. (FSI), even advertises its "extensive use" of this type of push-poll in a promotional brochure given to prospective clients: "Every poll is a mini campaign. Respondents are exposed to candidate information during a poll the same way they will be during the campaign. By testing which set of information 'stimuli' best produces a maximum vote for the client, FSI polls provide a clear picture of where a race is going and how to get there, not just where it stands today."

The information contained in research-oriented push-polls is fact-based and essentially true (even if presented in a blunt and exaggerated partisan style). The primary goal of this type of push-poll is to obtain the unbiased views of voters, not necessarily to turn the respondents off to the opponent. The respondents are "pushed" to determine what the campaign may need to do to change the image of the opponent, and the negative issues being tested in the survey will probably be ones easily transferable to public, on-the-record attacks made during the campaign (using television advertising, direct mail, or simple stump speeches). . . .

But even this "legitimate" manifestation of push-polling can be troubling. Such a survey may reach 400 to 1,500 respondents in a relatively small geographic area (say, a compact congressional district), and negative personal information about a freely discussed candidate with this many people can quickly become fodder for a districtwide gossip mill. Professional pollsters may object to this characterization. If a survey asks questions about issues or character that portray both candidates in a negative light, they reason that the research poll does no harm. However, they evaluate questions on the basis of their professional perspective—here, the goal is questionnaire balance and unbiased survey results. The trouble is that even balanced surveys yielding unbiased responses will disseminate negative information. This adversely affects the tenor and character of the campaign, and adds to the rampant negativism of modern politics.

Such information is still more worrisome if it is exaggerated or outright false, as is frequently the case with a second type of push-poll, the so-called agenda-driven survey, also known as deliberative polling. Here the pollster is still conducting a random-sample telephone survey with a representative group of voters, but the goal has changed. The agenda is to produce a favorable horse race result for the client-candidate, so that potential contributors and the press can be apprised of the candidate's "impending victory." The technique does not always work, but donors want to give hard-earned dollars to a likely winner, and the news media love to publish and air horse race polls. With a little luck, such a poll could create a bandwagon effect for the leading candidate. A good example of this "agenda-driven" push-poll can be found in Missouri's Fifth Congressional District race in 1994. A loaded survey taken in September by Republican pollster Frank Luntz for GOP nominee Ron Freeman produced an eight percentage point lead for Freeman over Democratic nominee Karen McCarthy for an open seat. Yet on election day McCarthy won easily (56.6 percent to 43.4 percent), despite the overall GOP tide. There may actually be little or no real "bandwagon effect," but politicians and consultants *believe* there is such a thing and strive to create it by looking like a winner.

They do so by providing the respondents with loads of derogatory background on the opponent. Before respondents are asked how they will vote, they may be read biographical sketches heavily biased against the opponent. The client may be portrayed as Mother Teresa and the opponent painted as one step away from the sheriff's manacles. Sometimes the poll asks a series of questions incorporating damaging assertions about the opponent. Often the worst is saved for last, culminating in the classic horse race question, "If the election were held today, would you vote for [Candidate A] or [Candidate B]?" Not surprisingly, at this point a sizable plurality tends to favor the unsullied client. The "good news" numbers are triumphantly released, with no mention of the poll format or non–horse race questions. And gullible contributors open their wallets; undiscerning journalists, usually the more inexperienced press persons, write the desired headlines; and the hundreds of voter-respondents may talk to family and friends about the shocking (though perhaps false) information they have learned about a prominent politician. Thus, the ripple effects can be far-reaching. . . .

The first two types of push-polls seem almost harmless when compared with the third form, called "negative persuasive" or "advocacy phoning." This push-poll is not really a poll at all, but a form of targeted voter contact and canvassing, since no random sample of the population is selected. Instead, the emphasis is on volume: as many voters in a target population as possible (union members, gun owners, conservative Christians, or whatever) are contacted with a highly negative message that is short—even a minute or less—and asks no demographical background information on the respondents. First, respondents are asked which candidate they favor. If the client-candidate is chosen, the respondent is thanked and placed on the get-out-the-vote (GOTV) list for election day. But if the respondent picks the opponent or says she is undecided, then a torrent of negativity is unleashed: "Would you still support this if you learned that he [is a tax-evader, a baby-killer, or shoots newborn puppies for sport]?" As one frank push-pollster put it on background, "What you're trying to do is mobilize voters *against* a candidate. . . . You're taking a specific audience and literally telling them why they shouldn't be voting for somebody."

The target audience can be voters in swing districts, or even voters in the opponent's areas of greatest strength. In both cases, push-pollsters are attempting to persuade voters that the opponent is not worthy of their backing and thereby *suppressing* his turnout. This "suppression phoning" is the reverse of a form of GOTV called "positive persuasive phoning," which delivers favorable information about the candidate-client to any respondent who is undecided. Obviously, this positive phoning is far preferable ethically to the negative variety, but this once-dominant kind of GOTV is being supplanted in many areas by attack push-polling. But like GOTV, it is done largely in the final weeks or days of a campaign—when the rush of events makes it least likely to be detected or exposed by the opposition or the press. Naturally, the harshest and most untruthful messages are saved for election eve or the weekend prior to Election Day, according to several telephone-bank consultants we interviewed. And, of course, the beauty of this ugly technique is stealth. Unless, by some wild circumstance, a respondent has his phone fitted with a recording device and has the presence of mind to turn on the tape as the interview begins, or someone on the inside talks, there is no way to find fingerprints and fix blame. . . .

The scale and telephone technology of push-polling are new; the concept itself, and the depths to which it can descend, are unfortunately not. It will surprise few to learn that Richard Nixon, whose lack of an ethical compass eventually resulted in his presidency's destruction, was one of push-polling's pioneers. In his very first campaign, a successful 1946 run for the U.S. House against Democratic incumbent Jerry Voorhis, Democratic voters throughout his district reported receiving telephone calls that began, "This is a friend of yours, but I can't tell you who I am. Did you know that Jerry Voorhis is a Communist?" at which point the caller hung up. While no firsthand evidence was produced to link the Nixon campaign directly with the calls, at least one individual has come forward admitting that she worked for Nixon at $9 a day, in a telephone-bank room where the attack calls were made. The technique, according to distinguished Nixon biographer Stephen E. Ambrose, was well-suited to the "vicious, snarling . . . dirty" Nixon campaign, which "was full of half-truths, full lies, and innuendoes, hurled at such a pace that Voorhis could never catch up with them."

Nixon was not alone in his use of gutter tactics, of course, but for decades this kind of negativity was regularly and roundly condemned by the press and most political professionals. It may be a commentary on our times that this is no longer so. In fact, candidates, parties, and consultants sometimes brag openly about their excursions into sleaze, once the campaign is over. In 1986, for example, the Democrats and their allies in the labor unions undertook massive negative persuasive phoning just before the midterm congressional elections that saw a Democratic majority in the U.S. Senate restored after six years of GOP rule. The telephone message centered upon the Reagan administration's supposed plans to undermine and reduce funding for Social Security—a highly suspect allegation that nonetheless appeared to do the trick, according to strategists for both parties. This episode has been repeatedly cited by Democrats as a clever tactic to employ in the years since. Perhaps not incidentally, the Social Security push-poll against Republicans has continued to be a mainstay of Democratic "outreach" to senior citizens until the present day. Many of the 1994 Republican congressional candidates we interviewed complained about it.

Over a hundred political consulting firms specializing in persuasive phoning have sprung up over the past two decades. For example, 154 telephone firms offering political "direct contact" services were listed by *Campaigns and Elections* magazine, a well-known trade journal for consultants and aspiring officeholders, in a publication released in February 1995. The new technology of computer-aided telephoning and target selection has made the process of political and commercial marketing by phone vastly easier and more efficient. A single operator can make 80 to 100 *completed* calls with a short message *each evening hour,* at a cost (depending on message length and company) of $0.45 to $1.30 per call. In other words, a quarter million targeted calls can be made for $112,000 to $325,000—arguably a solid investment for a multimillion-dollar statewide campaign that is probably spending many times that on diffuse television advertising. . . .

The proliferation of telephone marketing technology and the firms that sell it not only fills a campaign need but creates one. The firms' aggressive entrepreneurs—another variety of the ubiquitous political consultants that specialize in attack politics—advertise the technology's availability, and also ignite the latent fear in every campaign manager that the other side may be employing the technique already. (This same psychology once fueled the superpowers' arms race.)

Take Mac Hansbrough, the pleasant and forthcoming president of Washington, D.C.–based National Telecommunications Services, whose clients have included the Democratic National Committee, abortion-rights groups, and various Democratic candidates. Hansbrough wrote a remarkably candid 1992 article, "Dial N for Negative," in *Campaigns and Elections*. Calling negative phoning "the single most important and cost-effective communications tool a campaign can employ" and predicting its widespread use in the 1990s, Hansbrough correctly suggested that the technique would "take its place beside negative television, radio, and direct mail as a necessary tool in the . . . consultant's arsenal." And he cited the "lack of spill-over" as one vital reason why:

One can deliver different messages to multiple groups of voters with little chance that one group will receive the other's message or that the larger constituency of uncalled voters will receive any of the messages. This is a major advantage when controversial issues are being discussed, and it is an advantage that TV and radio cannot offer. . . .

Negative phoning leaves few footprints. TV and radio ads can be heard by anyone and are often reported in the newspaper. Direct mail is available to find its way into anyone's hands and has the lasting effect that goes with all printed matter. Phone calls, of course, are verbal. Scripts are tightly controlled and rarely get out to the press, general public, or opponents. Phone calls are the true communications stealth technology of the future.

In follow-up interviews, Hansbrough told us that in his experience, negative phoning was most likely to occur in a close campaign, where a desperate candidate is hard-pressed and increasingly willing to do whatever it takes to win: "You use a negative approach only when you have to, and in my opinion, you only have to when you are very sure or reasonably sure that you may be losing the election." Even in these cases, though, candidates—fearing a backlash or a damaging news story—usually desire a buffer between their campaigns and the telephoning. So the sponsorship is passed to the national or state party committee, or a friendly allied group (say, a labor union for a Democratic nominee or a conservative organization for a Republican nominee). In some cases, a separate front vehicle is actually invented, such as "Citizens for Tax Fairness" or a neutral-sounding polling research company. (See the negative persuasion phoning scripts . . . which have been used in a recent campaign by Hansbrough clients.) However, Hansbrough stressed that whatever the sponsorship, the campaign controls the message, and the final scripting normally is approved by it. Hansbrough freely admits that most of the calling occurs at the election's last minute, and that there is much hand-wringing about the practice in many campaigns. But if the race is tight enough, the doubts are usually resolved *in favor* of negative phoning. Adds Hansbrough: "There's another good reason for doing it late: . . . negative campaigning is controversial [so] don't stir it up until you have to," or until it is likely the press will not pick up on the tactic until the election is over.

Two examples of these negative persuasion phoning scripts are reproduced [here]. These scripts were used by the campaign of Florida Democratic Governor Lawton Chiles, a Hansbrough client, in his successful 1994 reelection bid against Republican Jeb Bush, son of former President George Bush. After the election, Republicans claimed that Chiles's narrow victory (65,000 votes out of 4.2 million cast) was due to these negative telephone scripts, read to tens of thousands of Floridians shortly before the election.

NEGATIVE PERSUASION PHONING: TWO EXAMPLES

SCRIPT 1

Hello, this is [interviewer's name] calling on behalf of the Florida Association of Senior Citizens.
We are calling to let you know that [Republican nominee for governor] Jeb Bush is no friend of seniors.
Bush's running mate has advocated the abolition of Social Security and called Medicare a welfare program that should be cut.
We just can't trust Jeb Bush and [lieutenant governor nominee] Tom Feeney.
Thank you and have a good day/evening.

SCRIPT 2

Hello, my name is [interviewer's name] calling from the Citizens for Tax Fairness.
I am calling to remind you that unlike thousands of your fellow citizens, Jeb Bush failed to pay local and state taxes and he has profited at the taxpayers' expense from business deals involving failed savings and loan properties. Mr. Bush doesn't play by the same rules like the rest of us and we want to make sure you are aware of this before you cast your vote on Tuesday.
Thank you and have a good day/evening.

Source: Scripts were provided by Mac Hansbrough. The campaigns using them were not identified by Hansbrough. But a year after the November 1994 election, these scripts became the center of controversy in Florida, where Republicans claimed they unfairly attacked Jeb Bush and helped to reelect Democratic Governor Lawton Chiles.

Negative phoning is just the latest, and perhaps nastiest, extension of the harsh tone of modern American politics. The technique "is effective because voters are much more prepared today to believe negative things about candidates than they once were. Negative TV ads, radio, direct mail, and news coverage have really paved the way" for negative phoning, asserts Hansbrough. Sleaze and cynicism do indeed feast at each other's table, as push-polling is proving anew.

63

STEPHEN ANSOLABEHERE AND SHANTO IYENGAR

From *Going Negative*

The weakening of political parties, growing voter cynicism, and negative campaign advertising: Political scientists Stephen Ansolabehere and Shanto Iyengar interrelate these complex developments in American politics. Illustrating their thesis with some memorable election campaign attack ads, the authors contend that a vicious cycle has developed. Middle-of-the-road, independent-minded voters are increasingly alienated by negative campaigns, with the result that politics becomes more and more the province of those on the ideological extremes.

ONCE UPON A TIME, this country divided itself neatly along party lines. Most people voted; those who did not tended to be poorer, less well-educated, and more apathetic, but still party loyal. The line between participants and nonparticipants was a fault line of sorts, but it was not terribly worrisome. Civic duty ideally would involve everyone, but, even falling short of the ideal, we were at least expressing our national will in our elections. Television has changed all that. Now, we are split by a new division: between loyalists and apathetics. On the one hand, media propaganda can often shore up loyalists to vote for their traditional party; on the other hand, that same propaganda is increasingly peeling off a band of citizens who turn from independence to apathy, even antipathy, toward our political institutions.

Pollsters and political scientists first noticed this new fault line in 1964. The number of people who proclaimed themselves independent of traditional party labels rose sharply in the mid-1960s. At the same time, candidates embraced television as a new means of independent communication with the voters. Politicians no longer needed the legions of party workers to get their messages across; they could effectively establish personal connections with their constituents using television advertising. In addition, there arose a new class of campaign manager—the media consultant, who typically had worked on Madison Avenue and viewed selling politics much like selling any other product. By the end of the 1960s, media consultants had filled the shoes left vacant by the then-extinct ward healers and precinct captains. Within the political parties, chaos reigned. The old-style politicos in both the Democratic and Republican parties battled and lost to a new regime of populists and progressives, who opened up the parties' nominating process to all comers. By most accounts, these reforms did even greater harm to the parties, shamelessly opening schisms that in earlier years were smoothed over behind closed doors.

At the time many observers mistakenly saw in the combination of televised political advertising and the nonpartisan voter the advent of a new age in America. Television advertising was to have produced a new kind of independent politician, not beholden to special interests and not part of the problems that voters increasingly associated with Washington. That day has not dawned. To be sure, the ranks of Independent voters have swollen since 1964, and television advertising is now the mainstay of contemporary political campaigns. The political parties, however, remain ascendent in elections and in government. Despite an occasional Independent candidacy and the rise of the personal electoral followings of many candidates, electoral competition is still between Republicans and Democrats. What is more, government, especially Congress, has become even more polarized and partisan than ever. The parties in Congress represent two increasingly cohesive and extreme positions.

The electorate has reacted with frustration and anger. In recent years, the political pulsetakers have registered record lows in political participation, record highs in public cynicism and alienation, and record rates of disapproval of the House of Representatives, the institution designed to represent the public will.

The single biggest cause of the new, ugly regime is the proliferation of negative political advertising on TV. Our argument is that a new synthesis in American politics has failed to emerge precisely because of the ways that partisans and nonpartisans react to televised political messages. Like product advertising, successful political advertising reflects people's beliefs, experiences, and preferences. One consequence of this simple axiom is that political campaigns reinforce the loyalties of partisans. Nonpartisans, by contrast, usually tune out political advertising. They find politicians, politics, and government distasteful; political advertising simply sounds like more of the same. Only negative messages resonate with such attitudes. As political campaigns have become more hostile over the last two decades, nonpartisans have heard plenty to reinforce their low opinions of politics. Unfortunately, negative campaigning only reinforces the nonpartisans' disillusionment and convinces them not to participate in a tainted process. As a result, nonpartisans have not become the electoral force that they might have. Instead, political advertising has produced a party renaissance, even though partisans are an increasingly unrepresentative segment of the public. . . .

The electorate has grown weary of the nastiness and negativity of campaigns. They are mad at the candidates, mad at the parties, mad at the media, and mad at anyone else who steps into the electoral arena. Many people now choose to stay home on election day; others openly express their dissatisfaction with the candidates and the parties among which they must choose. People no longer feel that they vote *for*, only against. If venom isn't really what the public is after, why do candidates insist on going negative?

Politicians and campaign consultants are, by and large, not mean-spirited people who conspire to scare voters away from the polls. The reality is more complex. The negative tenor of campaigns can be traced to the competitive nature of political advertising, to the activities of organized interests, and, last but not least, to the ways in which reporters cover the campaign. Politicians, interest groups, and journalists all act in ways that serve their own best interests. Few of these players really want to produce highly negative campaigns, but the interplay among them produces the kind of campaigns that voters have come to loathe.

"Politics," Lloyd Bentsen reflected after the 1988 election, "is a contact sport." The main event is the head-to-head competition between the candidates. This, above all else, drives candidates to assail one another with thirty-second spot ads. Put bluntly, candidates attack out of fear: fear that the opposition will throw the first punch, fear that they will appear weak if they don't respond in kind. In politics, the best defense is a strong offense, and negative advertising is the most expedient way to fend off the opposition's attacks.

In addition, candidates attack to expand the scope of the political conflict, to drag organized interests and the media into the fray. Political campaigns have about them the same excitement as a prize fight. The more intense the conflict, the more people are drawn to it. Political campaigns, however, are not nearly as orderly as professional boxing matches. No ropes keep the audience from joining in. The more a candidate attacks, the more she makes news; the more conflict there is, and stories about the conflict, the more likely the candidate's proponents are to join the fray. Corporations, professional associations, unions, and other organizations have large stakes in the outcomes of elections, and they don't remain on the sidelines long. These organizations put up millions of dollars to underwrite the candidate's campaign activities; they also aggressively publicize their support of and opposition to politicians independent of the candidate's own campaigning. Through unrestrained independent advertising, interest groups can and do influence the tone, the issues, and even the outcome of elections.

The media are less partisan, but have an equally important effect on the tenor of campaigns. Journalists report the campaign with the verve of sportswriters covering a title fight. Their job, after all, is to sell papers and attract viewers, and elections are full of great material—the mistakes and weaknesses of the candidates, the twists and turns of public opinion, and the jabs and hooks of political debate. Campaign commercials, especially the negative ones, are ideally suited to the dictates of a good news story. They pack a sensational story with good visuals and good sound into thirty brief seconds. Nothing grabs the public's attention like the smell of a scandal or the prospect of a political upset. Such stories make for entertaining reading, but they don't instill confidence in the political system. . . .

. . . [M]ost consultants subscribe to Roger Ailes's first dictum of politics: "If you get punched, punch back." The best way to defuse an attack is typically to counterattack. Here are examples of three common tactics.

---

1. DEFEND AGAINST THE CHARGES

Attack by Representative Wayne Dowdy against Senator Trent Lott, Mississippi U.S. Senate race, 1988.

SCENE: A stretch limousine barrels through a small town.

ANNOUNCER: Trent Lott says he needs to keep his taxpayer-paid, $50,000-a-year chauffeur in Washington. You can vote for a party politician who looks at life through tinted windows. Or you can vote for a Senator who sees Mississippi through the eyes of its people.

Response by Trent Lott.

GEORGE AWKWARD [Lott's African-American bodyguard, speaking directly into the camera, with the American flag in the background]: I've been a detective in a security police force in Washington, D.C., for 27 years. Wayne Dowdy calls me a chauffeur. He offends every law enforcement officer who puts his life on the line every day. Mr. Dowdy, I'm nobody's chauffeur. [pause] Got it?

---

2. Counterattack on the Same Question or on Issues that are of Greater Concern to Voters

Attack by Bruce Herschensohn on Barbara Boxer, California Senate race, 1992.

HERSCHENSOHN [speaking directly into the camera]: Ya know. A hundred and forty-three bounced checks. Wow, that's . . . that's . . . a lot. That's really a lot. That's what my opponent did. It added up to more than what most Californians make in well over a year. Forty-one thousand dollars in bounced checks. Boy. I Mean, do you want her trying to balance your budget? Our government's budget? Gee.

ANNOUNCER: Fight back with Herschensohn.

Boxer's response.

HERSCHENSOHN [newsclips]: "What I want is the repeal of *Roe v. Wade*" . . . "We need more offshore oil drilling and nuclear power plants" . . . "Demolish the Department of Energy and Education" . . . "I oppose any cuts in defense."

ANNOUNCER: That's what Bruce Herschensohn wants. Is that what you want?

---

3. Assail the Opposition's Credibility

Attack by Russell Feingold on Senator Robert Kasten, Wisconsin U.S. Senate race, 1992.

FEINGOLD [holding newspaper with headline about Senator Robert Kasten's negative campaign tactics]: If things are going to change around here, this man must be defeated in November. Not much has been written about Russ Feingold to attack. So the only option is to make something up.

FEINGOLD [holding up mock tabloid endorsement by Elvis Presley]: You voters know better than to believe everything you read.

Senator Robert Kasten's counterattack.

ELVIS IMPERSONATOR [sitting in pink Cadillac with 1950s music blaring, looking at cardboard cutout of Feingold holding mock tabloid]: I don't make many appearances. But when I heard that he was telling tales how I endorsed him, I had to come forward. You know that

Russ has been in politics for more than a decade. Feingold plans to raise our taxes over $300 billion. Well, the King would never support that. Take it from the King, this Russ Feingold record has got me all shook up.

Feingold's parting shot.

FEINGOLD [close up]: A while ago, I warned you about my opponent's history of making things up. I figured when he started distorting the truth about me, you'd take it with a grain of salt.

[Feingold picks up a jar of salt and starts pouring it on the ground. The camera zooms in on the growing pile.]

FEINGOLD: Well, get ready, because now he's telling you I have a plan to raise thousands of dollars of taxes on the middle class. Not true. Senator Kasten knows I haven't proposed any such tax increases. Period. The truth is the Senator has made up something so big that a few grains of salt won't be enough. A shovelful would be more like it.

[Camera pulls back to show Feingold holding a shovel.]

Tit-for-tat. And so it goes with many campaigns today. A negative advertisement triggers a negative response and, in turn, a negative reply. Increasingly, even positive commercials provoke attacks. Candidates who promote a particular ideology or program seem especially susceptible to criticism. Stick your neck out and get your head chopped off. . . .

Whatever its causes, negative politics generates disillusionment and distrust among the public. Attack advertisements resonate with the popular beliefs that government fails, that elected officials are out of touch and quite corrupt, and that voting is a hollow act. The end result: lower turnout and lower trust in government, regardless of which party rules.

The marginal voter—the Independent—feels the pinch of negative advertisements most sharply. Attack ads produce the highest drop in political efficacy and in intentions to participate among nonpartisans. Most of these people have shed their traditional party attachments not because they feel ambivalent about which of the two parties they should support, but because they dislike politics in general. The hostile tenor of campaign advertising further reinforces their contempt for candidates, parties, and government. As a result, negative campaigning divides the American electorate into a voting public of party loyalists and a nonvoting public of apathetics.

With each election this schism widens. Though their growth has been glacial, Independents are now the single largest of the "partisan" groups in the electorate—36 percent, according to the Gallup poll. They tend not to vote, and regardless of which party is in the majority, they do not feel that the government represents their ideas and interests. Each succeeding election raises their frustration higher yet. Our evidence is that the political campaigns deserve much of the blame for the Independents' retreat from the polls. Positive campaign advertising generally fails to reach Independents. Nonpartisans do not find the typical political commercial compelling or persuasive, and they are only further angered, frustrated, and alienated by negative campaigning. The current climate of attack politics strengthens their resolve to remain Independents, but weakens their electoral voice.

As a consequence, electoral politics [is] becoming less representative. Elected officials respond mainly to the opinions of those who vote, which is increasingly a partisan and ideologically extreme crowd. Contemporary campaigning discourages nonpartisans from expressing their interests and frustrations at the polls; it thus obstructs politicians from hearing their anger.

64

CHARLES EUCHNER

From *Extraordinary Politics*

Politics does not always take the form of campaigns, elections, congressional debates, presidential orders, and court decisions. Charles Euchner examines politics by "extraordinary" means. Some political activists choose to be heard by organizing boycotts, sit-ins, petition drives, and even violent attacks. These acts fall outside the accepted politics-as-usual approaches that are thought of as part of American government. However, extraordinary political tactics have long been part of politics, Euchner contends, and they serve a crucial role in deciding what issues will become part of the accepted political agenda.

IN FEBRUARY 1990, Vaclav Havel, the president of Czechoslovakia's new democratic regime, addressed a rare joint session of the United States Congress about the recent nonviolent revolution that overthrew his country's Communist regime. Havel, a playwright and former political dissident, delivered a message with metaphysical themes unusual for debates on Capitol Hill. Havel thanked and congratulated the West for its diligent opposition to the Soviet-led eastern bloc since the end of World War II. At the same time, Havel sternly warned his audience about the dangers facing the United States and other democracies in the modern age. The warning concerned the most profound issues of morality in the modern nation-state.

Vaclav Havel was a most improbable head of state. A founding member of Charter 77, the dissident group that pushed for democratization of Czechoslovakia, Havel still seemed more an activist than a politician. Just one year before his Capitol address, Havel sat in prison for laying a wreath at the grave of Jan Palach, the anti-Communist who had burned himself in protest against the Soviet invasion of 1968. Havel was more used to meeting with other artists in wine cellars, wearing jeans and a casual sweater, than standing at the center of a national legislature wearing an expensive suit. In New York the next day, Havel linked his own cause with American protest during the 1960s. He recalled a visit to Columbia University in 1968 during the height of the antiwar and student movements: "The atmosphere of that time very much inspired me, influenced me." Now, as a result of the "velvet revolution" that peacefully overthrew the Soviet satellite state, Havel now stood before the world's oldest democratic legislature.

Havel told Congress that even the most advanced representative systems were "merely approaching democracy" and that selfish interests too often "outweigh genuinely common and global interests." The only means to move beyond narrow interests is a "revolution in the sphere of human consciousness," a revolution that could occur only with active citizen participation in public affairs. Intellectuals and others "cannot go on forever avoiding their share of responsibility for the world and hiding their distaste for politics under an alleged need to be independent," Havel said. Citizens must get involved in the messy work of politics.

In his many writings about ethics and politics, Havel has emphasized the need for individual and group resistance to the modem state. In a February 1984 essay intended for delivery at the University of Toulouse, Havel wrote:

> System, ideology, and *apparat* have deprived humans—rulers as well as the ruled—of their conscience, of their common sense and natural speech, and thereby of their actual humanity. States grow ever more machine-like, men are transformed

into statistical choruses of voters, producers, consumers, patients, tourists, or soldiers. . . . It is the total rule of a bloated, anonymously bureaucratic power, not yet irresponsible but already operating outside all conscience, a power which can rationalize anything without ever having to brush against the truth.

The only recourse against such a calculating and unresponsive power, Havel wrote, is an "anti-political politics." Such engagement—taking the forms of civil disobedience, demonstrations, boycotts, and subversive literature and art—lacks the certainty of formal public decisionmaking. But, according to Havel, such alternative forms of politics offer the only way to confront the "monstrosities" of modem life. "The warning voice of a single brave scientist, besieged somewhere in the provinces and terrorized by a goaded community, can be heard over continents and addresses the conscience of the mighty more clearly than entire brigades of hired propagandists can, though speaking to themselves." This outsider's style of politics necessarily engenders disorder. If dissidents "were to agree on a common programme," Havel argued, "it would be the saddest outcome of all: one uniform confronting another."

Havel challenged the United States to develop alternative forms of political and social engagement. He said that Western political, legal, and social structures provided worthy models for nations like Czechoslovakia emerging from dictatorship, but he noted too that those Western political systems failed to meet their own ideals for democracy and seemed incapable of meeting the demands of modern, mass society. Just like the dissidents in the old Communist bloc, Americans need to practice "anti-politics" in order to confront unresponsive government and corporate elites. Only anti-politics can make politics work.

At the time of Havel's speech, the United States was already experiencing a basic challenge to its political regime—partly through the "anti-politics" approach that Havel endorsed. On issues large and small, Americans bypassed ordinary channels of politics to demand change in both the public and private sectors. A form of action that might be called "extraordinary politics"—protest, demonstrations, boycotts, alternative institutions, neighborhood activism, international citizen alliances—had in fact transformed American politics for more than a generation. Protest and other forms of outsider politics had come to play a central role in setting the agenda for national and local politics. By the time of Havel's visit, protest was considered a legitimate and basic form of political expression and action. . . .

Ultimately, the recent prominence of extraordinary politics stems from the gap between the ideals of democracy and the way the political system actually functions—the system's failure to meet its ideals. People get frustrated with political leadership, interest-group deal-making, cynical electoral campaigns, tangled and irrational bureaucracy, and a range of corrupt behavior. These frustrations lead people to devise new ways of "doing" politics outside of ordinary channels. Extraordinary politics represents a creative and vibrant, though inadequate, response to the limitations of formal politics.

To say that the American system has "broken down" is not to say that it does everything badly or that it is beyond useful reform. On the contrary, American politics has produced some amazing success stories: a strong middle class, abundant natural resources, military and technological power, and internationally renowned higher education and research. But a growing number of Americans consider those successes to be the exception, not the rule. Americans express deep skepticism that the government represents public interests, that government programs can solve problems, that elected and unelected officials even care to do a public-spirited job.

The decline of ordinary politics in the United States is most obvious in parties and elections. Ideally, elections offer citizens the chance to participate in great debates and decisions, to deliberate on important issues and render authoritative decisions about public policy. But the modern American electoral system is the object of apathy and scorn. Campaign rhetoric is shallow, party alliances are weak, competition for offices is lopsided, and the results are inconclusive. Even when elections indicate a clear direction for policy, political parties do not possess the strength to coordinate passage and implementation of a coherent program. Fewer and fewer people consider voting to be a civic duty, and those who do often seem embarrassed by their sense of commitment. Most voters cast negative votes, selecting the "lesser of two evils."

The American electoral system is really a set of many separate, mostly uncompetitive systems. The "first-past-the-post" system of elections excludes the possibility of the system's having several political parties and causes the two parties to converge ideologically. Even in exceptional periods—such as 1994, when an ideologically conservative Republican Party won control of Congress—the parties offer a mix of rhetoric and policies designed to reach the center of the nation's ideological spectrum. Even an apparent statement of principles, such as the Republicans' 1994 campaign "Contract with America," was driven by extensive polling and focus-group data; it is a collection of appeals to special interests rather than a coherent program for governing and reform. Because of the dominance of money in electoral politics, it is almost impossible to run for office without appealing to special interests that have the ability to raise hundreds of thousands of dollars. . . .

Extraordinary politics represents a fundamentally different approach to politics than ordinary politics. Extraordinary politics aims to force the political establishment to address issues that it would rather ignore; operating outside formal institutions, extraordinary politics enjoys a latitude of movement and tactics not found in ordinary politics. But at the same time, extraordinary politics lacks the institutional structure and connections necessary for thorough deliberation.

Established structures and patterns of conduct limit the possibilities of ordinary politics. The basic rules of the system—one vote per citizen, indirect electoral control of government bodies, narrow and technical reasoning in bureaucratic and judicial bodies—restrict the ways that people can express themselves and act politically. Because just a few elites dominate the political system, ordinary people can only *react* to the choices offered them. Ordinary politics presents a series of occasional yes-or-no decisions, but extraordinary politics is more flexible. . . .

Extraordinary politics has a wider, but less authoritative, range of actions. Activists may take advantage of formal rules and institutions that work to their advantage, but they may also subvert and challenge those same institutions when it suits their purposes. Civil disobedience, demonstrations, boycotts, gang warfare, subversion of jury trials, squatting, guerrilla art, sit-ins and teach-ins and be-ins and die-ins, rent strikes, vandalizing machinery, blocking entry to buildings, overloading public bureaucracies with applications and petitions, rioting, and self-immolation—all are forms of political action that fall outside the ordinary political process. Activists, in a sense, invent their own language and rules. The difficulty for extraordinary politics lies in maintaining political pressure and getting policy reforms implemented.

Extraordinary politics often affirms the abstract values of the political system, while at the same time attacking the failure of ordinary politics to meet those values. It is not uncommon to see activists espousing civics-textbook values like equality, fairness, openness, and local control. Martin Luther King was a master at calling upon Americans to uphold the values they proclaim, as in his "I Have a Dream" speech in 1963. But many activists attempt to subvert the core values of the regime. The movements of the 1960s attacked mainstream attitudes about race, gender, family, higher education, corporate life, and the military. The defiance of protest movements is expressed most clearly in the gay rights movement's slogan "We're queer, we're here, get used to it." . . .

Extraordinary politics blurs the lines separating the public and private spheres—a matter of profound importance since it involves the basic question of what issues are "political." Housing activists, for example, confront not only government officials but also landlords and banks. Protesters concerned about animal rights may lobby the government to offer disincentives for wearing furs, but they are more effective when they target private interests, ranging from furriers to fur-wearers on streets. Because protesters tend to have fewer resources and political options, they adopt the approach of aggressive lawyers: Go after everybody. This take-no-prisoners approach produces mixed results.

Blurring the lines between public and private realms can be liberating. By overcoming established definitions of "the political," protesters can break free of constraints on their own thinking and identity. The movements of the 1960s changed people's understanding of what was possible in politics and personal life. James Miller wrote:

> By exploring its vision of participatory democracy, a generation discovered (and eventually became addicted to) what one young radical called "breakaway experiences"—*political and cultural moments when boundaries melted away and it seemed as if anything could happen*. Such moments did, in fact, occur. They arose in the thick of passionate debate, during sit-ins, in marches, at violent confrontations—at times when people, discovering their discontents and ideas and desires in common, sensed, often for the first time and sometimes in the teeth of danger, that together they could change the world.

The basic goal of changing public consciousness necessarily requires challenging traditional public-private distinctions.

Disrespect for a traditional public-private distinction can be destructive. All political regimes need a separate and distinct arena for debate and action. Without some kind of agreement about where the arena begins and ends, politics can be unruly and destructive. Maintaining unclear political boundaries might help protesters raise hell, but it could also hurt many of their causes in the long run. Establishment figures can exploit the unsettled community for their own benefit by appealing to a public desire for "order." If activists desire lasting reform, they need a coherent political system that can implement their ideas.

Without a formal political system capable of deliberating on issues and developing workable policies, extraordinary politics falls short of democratic ideals. Daniel Yankelovich has spoken of the need to "work through" public-policy alternatives and public issues to produce a mature "public judgment" of major issues. This requires an honest, open, realistic discussion of the ramifications of different arrangements that may be imagined as responses to perceived problems. But what extraordinary politics seems to lack above all else is a structure or process for such deliberation. Extraordinary politics can put important issues on the agenda, but it often fails to produce viable and lasting reform. The ultimate legacy of extraordinary politics, in fact, might be a fractured process of public debate and deliberation.

In the final analysis, the most important consequence of extraordinary politics might be the development of a new consciousness. The change is most dramatic for the people involved in organizing. Activism can be understood as a school for politics, which teaches its pupils about history, civics, social problems, economics, and cooperation. It also teaches something about identity and the common ground that citizens share on a variety of problems. The "students" of protest politics extend far beyond the ranks of protest groups and participants in demonstrations.

When northern college students went to Mississippi from 1961 to 1964 to register black voters in rural areas, a dramatic transformation of consciousness resulted. Activists encountered a population that had been utterly intimidated by the entrenched white ruling class. Black sharecroppers were so intimidated that they were originally afraid to be in the company of whites, especially as equals. They avoided acts that could be construed as direct challenges to the ruling elite. They feared economic and violent reprisals. Because they knew nothing else, they shared in the cultural belief that whites were superior and that their own security depended on a system of segregation. They blamed themselves for their misfortunes. But when the students came to teach them how to register, this attitude began to change. Organizers set up Freedom Schools that taught them how to read and how to interpret passages of complex documents.

Fannie Lou Hamer was one of the poor rural blacks who developed a new identity and confidence during the voter registration drives. She eventually became an important organizer for the movement, and was one of the members of the insurgent Mississippi Freedom Democratic Party that demanded to be seated at the Democratic National Convention in 1964. Miss Hamer remembers how young white student activists broke through the rigid barriers that excluded blacks from the public life of the South:

> Nobody never come out into the country and talked to real farmers and things. . . . And it was these kids what broke a lot of this down. They treated us like we were special and we loved 'em. . . . We didn't feel uneasy about our language might not be right or something. We just felt like we could talk to 'em. We trusted 'em, and I can tell the whole world these kids done their share in Mississippi.

Miss Hamer's transformative experiences in the civil rights movements of the 1960s were shared by a wide range of groups in the three decades after Freedom Summer. Ethnic minorities, women, handicapped people, gays, workers, tenants, community and religious activists, and environmentalists—all entered the American political process through dissent and protest. Their engagement with the political system not only changed some of the basic laws and practices of the country but also changed the very consciousness of the nation and its diverse groups.

If Vaclav Havel's appeal for a greater conscience in politics is to be taken seriously, such a transformation of consciousness is absolutely essential to the restoration of a vibrant democratic politics in the U.S.—necessary, but not sufficient. Development of a vibrant democracy—an American *glasnost* and *perestroika*—will hinge on whether formal political institutions take up the issues that outsiders define for them. Outsiders can point out the system's shortcomings and inattentiveness, and they can suggest ways to reform the system.

Ultimately, though, people working with some authority must conduct deliberations, bargain, compromise, and look beyond the immediate issues to the long-range fortunes of the nation. Politics requires challenge, but it also requires governmental action that is considered legitimate by the community as a whole. Protest is essential, but it is not enough.

PART TWELVE

Political Parties

65

WALTER DEAN BURNHAM

From *Critical Elections and the Mainsprings of American Politics*

Political science can offer few clear-cut theories of how politics works. Because of the variable of human nature as well as the impossibility of measuring and predicting political events with exactness, political science is often less a "science" and more an "art." A few attempts at developing major theories to explain and predict politics have been made, however. One is the theory of "critical realignments." Professor Walter Dean Burnham was one of the first to try to explain why certain presidential elections throughout American history mark significant long-term changes in the social and economic direction of the nation. Citing 1800, 1828, 1860, 1896, and 1932, Burnham describes the characteristics of a critical or realigning election, the most dramatic being its supposed "uniform periodicity." They occur at roughly equal intervals apart in time.

FOR MANY DECADES it has been generally recognized that American electoral politics is not quite "all of a piece" despite its apparent diverse uniformity. Some elections have more important long-range consequences for the political system as a whole than others, and seem to "decide" substantive issues in a more clear-cut way. There has long been agreement among historians that the elections of those of 1800, 1828, 1860, 1896, and 1932, for example, were fundamental turning points in the course of American electoral politics.

Since the appearance in 1955 of V. O. Key's seminal article, "A Theory of Critical Elections," political scientists have moved to give this concept quantitative depth and meaning. . . .

It now seems time to attempt at least an interim assessment of the structure, function, and implications of critical realignments for the American political process. Such an effort is motivated in particular by the author's view that critical realignments are of fundamental importance not only to the system of political action called "the American political process" but also to the clarifications of some aspects of its operation. It seems particularly important in a period of obvious political upheaval not only to identify these phenomena and place them in time, but to integrate them into a larger (if still very modest) theory of movement in American politics.

Such a theory must inevitably emphasize the elements of stress and abrupt transformation in our political life at the expense of the consensual, gradualist perspectives which have until recently dominated the scholar's vision of American political processes and behavior. For the realignment phenomenon focuses our attention on "the dark side of the moon." It reminds us that politics as usual in the United States is not politics as always; that there are discrete types of voting behavior and quite different levels of voter response to political stimuli, depending on what those stimuli are and at what point in time they occur; and that American political institutions and leadership, once defined (or redefined) in a "normal phase" of our politics, seem to become part of the very conditions that threaten to overthrow them. . . .

In its "ideal-typical" form, the critical realignment differs from stable alignments eras, secular [gradual] realignments, and deviating elections in the following basic ways.

1. The critical realignment is characteristically associated with short-lived but very intense disruptions of traditional patterns of voting behavior. Majority parties become minorities; politics which was once competitive becomes noncompetitive or, alternatively, hitherto one-party areas now become arenas of intense partisan competition; and large blocks of the active electorate—minorities, to be sure, but perhaps involving as much as a fifth to a third of the voters—shift their partisan allegiance.

2. Critical elections are characterized by abnormally high intensity as well.

a. This intensity typically spills over into the party nominating and platform-writing machinery during the upheaval and results in major shifts in convention behavior from the integrative "norm" as well as in transformations in the internal loci of power in the major party most heavily affected by the pressures of realignment. Ordinarily accepted "rules of the game" are flouted; the party's processes, instead of performing their usual integrative functions, themselves contribute to polarization.

b. The rise in intensity is associated with a considerable increase in ideological polarizations, at first within one or more of the major parties and then between them. Issue distances between the parties are markedly increased, and elections tend to involve highly salient issue-clusters, often with strongly emotional and symbolic overtones, far more than is customary in American electoral politics. One curious property of established leadership as it drifts into the stress of realignment seems to be a tendency to become more rigid and dogmatic, which itself contributes greatly to the explosive "bursting stress" of realignment. . . .

c. The rise in intensity is also normally to be found in abnormally heavy voter participation for the time. . . .

3. Historically speaking, at least, national critical realignments have not occurred at random. Instead, there has been a remarkably uniform periodicity in their appearance. . . .

4. It has been argued, with much truth, that American political parties are essentially constituent parties. That is to say, the political-party subsystem is sited in a socioeconomic system of very great heterogeneity and diversity. . . .

Critical realignments emerge directly from the dynamics of this constituent-function supremacy in American politics. . . . In other words, realignments are themselves constituent acts: they arise from emergent tensions in society which, not adequately controlled by the organization or outputs of party politics as usual, escalate to a flash point; they are issue-oriented phenomena, centrally associated with these tensions and more or less leading to resolution adjustments; they result in significant transformations in the general shape of policy; and they have relatively profound aftereffects on the roles played by institutional elites. They are involved with redefinitions of the universe of voters, political parties, and the broad boundaries of the politically possible.

To recapitulate, then, eras of critical realignment are marked by short, sharp reorganizations of the mass coalitional bases of the major parties which occur at periodic intervals on the national level; are often preceded by major third-party revolts which reveal the incapacity of "politics as usual" to integrate, much less aggregate, emergent political demand; are closely associated with abnormal stress in the socioeconomic system; are marked by ideological polarizations and issue-distances between the major parties which are exceptionally large by normal standards; and have durable consequences as constituent acts which determine the outer boundaries of policy in general, though not necessarily of policies in detail. . . . There is much evidence . . . that realignments do recur with rather remarkable regularity approximately once a generation, or every thirty to thirty-eight years.

The precise timing of the conditions which conduce to realignment is conditioned heavily by circumstance, of course: the intrusion of major crises in society and economy with which "politics as usual" in the United States cannot adequately cope, and the precise quality and bias of leadership decisions in a period of high political tension, cannot be predicted in specific time with any accuracy. Yet a broadly repetitive pattern of oscillation between the normal inertia of mass electoral politics and the ruptures of the normal which realignments bring about is clearly evident from the data. So evident is this pattern that one is led to suspect that the truly "normal" structure of American electoral politics at the mass base is precisely this dynamic, even dialectic polarization between long-term inertia and concentrated bursts of change in this open system of action. It may well be that American political institutions, including the major political parties, are so organized that they have a chronic, cumulative tendency toward underproduction of other than currently "normal" policy outputs. They may tend persistently to ignore, and hence not to aggregate, emergent political demand of a mass character until a boiling point of some kind is reached.

In this context, the rise of third-party protests as what might be called protorealignment phenomena would be associated with the repeated emergence of a rising gap between perceived expectations of the political process and its perceived realities over time, diffused among a constantly increasing portion of the active electorate and perhaps mobilizing many hitherto inactive voters. . . .

The periodic rhythm of American electoral politics, the cycle of oscillation between the normal and the disruptive, corresponds precisely to the existence of largely unfettered developmental change in the socioeconomic system and its absence in the country's political institutions. Indeed, it is a prime quantitative measure of the interaction between the two. The socioeconomic system develops but the institutions of electoral politics and policy formation remain essentially unchanged. Moreover, they do not have much capacity to adjust incrementally to demand arising from socioeconomic dislocations. Dysfunctions centrally related to this process become more and more visible, until finally entire classes, regions, or other major sectors of the population are directly injured or come to see themselves as threatened by imminent danger. Then the triggering event occurs, critical realignments follow, and the universe of policy and of electoral coalitions is broadly redefined. It is at such moments that the constitution-making role of the American voter becomes most visible, and his behavior, one suspects, least resembles the normal pattern. . . .

In this context, then, critical realignment emerges as decisively important in the study of the dynamics of American politics. It is as symptomatic of political nonevolution in this country as are the archaic and increasingly rudimentary structures of the political parties themselves. But even more importantly, critical realignment may well be defined as the chief tension-management device available to so peculiar a political system. Historically it has been the chief means through which an underdeveloped political system can be recurrently brought once again into some balanced relationship with the changing socioeconomic system, permitting a restabilization of our politics. . . . Granted the relative inability of our political institutions to make gradual adjustments along vectors of *emergent* political demand, critical realignments have been as inevitable as they have been necessary to the normal workings of American politics. Thus once again there is a paradox: the conditions which decree that coalitional negotiation, bargaining, and incremental, unplanned, and gradual policy change become the dominant characteristic of American politics in its normal state also decree that it give way to abrupt, disruptive change with considerable potential for violence. . . .

Such a dynamically oriented frame of reference presupposes a holistic view of American politics which is radically different from that which until very recently has tended to dominate the professional literature. The models of American political life and political processes with which we are most familiar emphasize the well-known attributes of pluralist democracy. There are not stable policy majorities. Intense and focused minorities with well-defined interests exert influence on legislation and administrative rule making out of all proportion to their size. The process involves gradual, incremental change secured after bargaining has been completed among a wide array of interested groups who are prepared to accept the conditions of bargaining. It is true that such descriptions apply to a "politics as usual" which is an important fragment of political reality in the United States, but to describe this fragment as the whole of that reality is to assume an essentially ideological posture whose credibility can be maintained only by ignoring the complementary dynamics of American politics as a whole. . . .

The reality of this process taken as a whole seems quite different from the pluralist vision. It is one shot through with escalating tensions, periodic electoral upheavals, and repeated redefinitions of the rules and outcomes-in-general of the political game, as well as redefinitions—by no means always broadening ones—of those who are in fact permitted to play it. One very basic characteristic of American party politics which emerges from a contemplation of critical realignments is a profound incapacity of established political leadership to adapt itself sequentially—or even incrementally?—to emergent political demand generated by the losers in our stormy socioeconomic transformations. American political parties are not action instrumentalities of definable and broad social collectivities; as organizations they are, consequently, interested in control of offices but not of government in the broader sense of which we have been speaking.

It follows from this that once successful routines are established or reestablished for winning office, there is no motivation among party leaders to disturb the routines of the game. These routines are disturbed not by adaptive change within the party-policy system, but by the application of overwhelming external force.

66

DAVID BRODER

From *The Party's Over*

As his book title cleverly implies, journalist David Broder acknowledges the decline of American political parties. Writing in the early 1970s, he mourns their weakening and holds out hope for a reinvigorated party system. Broder attributes many of America's governmental problems to the parties' problems, and he pleads for stronger party unity in Congress and an expanded role for parties in the campaign process. Turning to voters, Broder asks for less ticket-splitting and more partisan allegiance. As the decades have passed, Broder's observations about the decline of the parties—dealignment, as scholars term it—have been borne out. His hopes for the rejuvenation of American political parties have proved less promising. Among most voters and even many office-holders, the Democratic and Republican parties are no longer the heart of the American political process.

My view is that American politics is at an impasse, that we have been spinning our wheels for a long, long time; and that we are going to dig ourselves ever deeper into trouble, unless we find a way to develop some political traction and move again. I believe we can get that traction, we can make government responsible and responsive again, only when we begin to use the political parties as they are meant to be used. And that is the thesis of this book.

It is called *The Party's Over*, not in prophecy, but in alarm. I am not predicting the demise of the Republicans or the Democrats. Party loyalties have been seriously eroded, the Democratic and Republican organizations weakened by years of neglect. But our parties are not yet dead. What happens to them is up to us to decide. If we allow them to wither, we will pay a high price in the continued frustration of government. But, even if we seek their renewal, the cost of repairing the effects of decades of governmental inaction will be heavy. The process will be painful and expensive. Whatever the fate of our political parties, for America the party *is* over. . . .

. . . The reason we have suffered governmental stalemate is that we have not used the one instrument available to us for disciplining government to meet our needs. That instrument is the political party.

Political parties in America have a peculiar status and history. They are not part of our written Constitution. The Founding Fathers, in fact, were determined to do all they could to see they did not arise. Washington devoted much of his Farewell Address to warning his countrymen against "the dangers of party in the state." And yet parties arose in the first generation of the nation, and have persisted ever since. Their very durability argues that they fill a need. That need is for some institution that will sort out, weigh, and, to the extent possible, reconcile the myriad conflicting needs and demands of individuals, groups, interests, communities and regions in this diverse continental Republic, organize them for the contest for public office; and then serve as a link between the constituencies and the men chosen to govern. When the parties fill their mission well, they tend to serve both a unifying and a clarifying function for the country. Competitive forces draw them to the center, and force them to seek agreement on issues too intense to be settled satisfactorily by simple majority referendum. On the other hand, as grand coalitions, they are capable of taking a need felt strongly by some minority of the population and making it part of a program endorsed by a majority.

When they do not function well, things go badly for America. The coming of the Civil War was marked by a failure of the reconciling function of the existing parties. Long periods of stagnation, too, can be caused by the failure of the parties to bring emerging public questions to the point of electoral decision. When the parties fail, individual citizens feel they have lost control of what is happening in politics and in government. They find themselves powerless to influence the course of events. Voting seems futile and politics a pointless charade. . . .

The governmental system is not working because the political parties are not working. The parties have been weakened by their failure to adapt to some of the social and technological changes taking place in America. But, even more, they are suffering from simple neglect: neglect by Presidents and public officials, but, particularly, neglect by the voters. It is to remind us that the parties can be used for positive purposes that this book is written.

Some students of government who share this view of the importance of political parties in American government nonetheless think it futile to exhort readers on their behalf. Such political scientists as James L. Sundquist and Walter Dean Burnham, whose knowledge of American political history is far deeper than my own, believe we are simply in the wrong stage of the political cycle to expect anything but confused signals and weak responses from the parties.

The last major party realignment, it is generally agreed, took place in 1932, and set the stage for the New Deal policies of government intervention in the economy and the development of the welfare state. We are, these scholars argue, perhaps overdue for another realignment, but until an issue emerges which will produce one, an issue as powerful as the Great Depression, it is futile to complain that party lines are muddled and governmental action is all but paralyzed. Their judgment may be correct, but I do not find it comforting. The cyclical theory of party realignment is an easy rationalization for throwing up our hands and doing nothing. But we do not know when the realignment will take place. Some scholars have thought there was a thirty-six-year cycle, with 1896 and 1932 as the last "critical elections." But 1968, the scheduled date, on this theory, for another "critical election," has come and gone, and our drift continues. . . .

. . . Basically, I believe that our guarantee of self-government is no stronger than our exercise of self-government; and today the central instruments of self-government, the political parties, are being neglected or abused. We must somehow rescue them if we are to rescue ourselves. . . .

. . . Popular dissatisfaction with the two-party system is manifested in many ways: by the decline in voting; by the rise in the number of voters who refuse to identify themselves with either party; by the increase in ticket splitting, a device for denying either party responsibility for government; and by the increased use of third parties or ad hoc political coalitions to pressure for change. . . . Is there not a better way to resolve our differences, to move ahead on our common problems? I believe there is. . . . The instrument that is available to us . . . is the instrument of responsible party government. The alternative to making policy in the streets is to make it in the voting booth. . . .

But, if that is to be more than a cliché answer, there must be real choices presented at election time—choices involving more than a selection between two sincere-sounding, photogenic graduates of some campaign consultant's academy of political and dramatic arts. The candidates must come to the voters with programs that are comprehensible and relevant to our problems; and they must have the kind of backing that makes it possible for them to act on their pledges once in office.

The instrument, the only instrument I know of, that can nominate such candidates, commit them to a program and give them the leverage and alliances in government that can enable them to keep their promises, is the political party. . . .

. . . Where do we turn? To ourselves. Obviously, that must be the answer. There is no solution for America except what we Americans devise. I believe that we have the instrument at hand, in the party system, that can break the long and costly impasse in our government. But it is up to us to decide whether to use it.

What would it entail on our part if we determined to attempt responsible party government? First, it would mean giving strong public support to those reform efforts which in the recent past have been carried on entirely by a small group of concerned political insiders, aimed at strengthening the machinery of political parties and government.

We should seek to strengthen the liaison between the presidency and Congress, on a mutual basis, and between the presidency and the heads of state and local government. We should elect the President in the same way we elect all other officials, by direct vote of his constituents, with high man winning.

We should expand the role and responsibilities of the party caucuses and the party leaders in Congress. The caucus should choose the floor leaders and policy committee members, the legislative committee chairmen and committee members, not on the basis of seniority but on the basis of ability and commitment to the party program. That leadership ought to be held accountable for bringing legislation to which the party is committed to a floor vote in orderly and timely fashion, with adequate opportunity for debate and particularly for consideration of opposition party alternatives. But procedures for due consideration should not justify devices like the filibuster, which prevent the majority party from bringing its measures to a final vote. . . .

We need to take every possible measure to strengthen the presidential nominating convention as the key device for making the parties responsible. The current effort to open the Democratic delegate-selection process to wider public participation is a promising start, and its emphasis on the congressional-district nominating convention offers corollary benefits for integrating congressional and presidential constituencies. Both parties should experiment with devices for putting heavier emphasis on the platform-writing phase of the convention's work, including the possibility of a separate convention, following the nomination, where the party's officeholders and candidates debate the program on which they pledge themselves to run and to act if elected.

Most important of all the structural reforms, we need to follow through the effort to discipline the use of money in politics, not only by setting realistic limits on campaign spending and by publicizing individual and organizational gifts, but also by channeling much more of the money (including, in my view, all general election spending) through the respective party committees, rather than through individual candidates' treasuries.

We need to strengthen the party organizations and their staffs, and recapture for them the campaign management functions that have been parceled out to independent firms which tend to operate with a fine disdain for the role of party and policy in government. We need to devise ways to make television—the prime medium of political communication—somewhat more sensitive to the claims of the parties to be a regular part of the political dialogue, and to protect the vital institution of the nominating convention from being distorted by the demands of the television cameras.

All these reforms would help, I believe, but they would not accomplish the invigoration of responsible party government unless they were accompanied by a genuine increase in the participation by the public in party affairs. The cure for the ills of democracy truly is more democracy; our parties are weak principally because we do not use them. To be strong and responsible, our parties must be representative; and they can be no more representative than our participation allows. Millions more of us need to get into partisan political activity.

We need also to become somewhat more reflective about what we do with our votes. We need to ask ourselves what it is that we want government to accomplish, and which candidate, which party comes closest to espousing that set of goals. That may sound so rationalistic as to be unrealistic. But this nation has more education, more communication, more leisure available to it than ever before. In the nineteenth century, James Bryce wrote of us, "The ordinary citizens are interested in politics, and watch them with intelligence, the same kind of intelligence (though a smaller quantity of it) as they apply to their own business. . . . They think their own competence equal to that of their representatives and office-bearers; and they are not far wrong." Are we to think less of ourselves today?

Finally, we need to examine some of our habits. It seems to me we should ask, before splitting a ticket, what it is we hope to accomplish by dividing between the parties the responsibility for government of our country, our state or our community. Do we think there is no difference between the parties? Do we distrust them both so thoroughly that we wish to set them against each other? Do we think one man so superior in virtue and wisdom that he must be put in office, no matter who accompanies him there? Why are we splitting our tickets? My guess is that, if we asked those questions, we would more often be inclined to give a temporary grant of power to one party at a time, rather than dividing responsibility so skillfully between the parties that neither can govern. If we were willing to risk this strategy, knowing that we would be able to throw the rascals out if they failed, we might even discover to our amazement that they are not always rascals.

67

XANDRA KAYDEN AND EDDIE MAHE

From *The Party Goes On*

No student of American politics can doubt that political parties have weakened. Xandra Kayden and Eddie Mahe are both political party consultants—Democratic and Republican, respectively—and they admit that old-style party activism is a thing of the past. Campaigning is increasingly professionalized; envelope-lickers, doorbell-ringers, and sign-holders are relics of a bygone time. Yet Kayden and Mahe envision a new era in which party organizers capitalize on the changed political climate. Those people who will rebuild the parties to succeed in the future will utilize technological tools suitable to the times. Test the Kayden and Mahe prediction of how a political "party goes on" against the following events: Bill Clinton's 1992 victory over President Bush; Ross Perot's winning 19 percent of the vote in 1992; the Republicans' 1994 House and Senate victories led by former Speaker Newt Gingrich and the "Contract with America"; and the 1996 and 2000 presidential and congressional contests.

IN MANY RESPECTS, the party of the future is here; it is the gap in perception of this fact that binds us to the past. If a new animal is lurking in the guise of a dead system, it will emerge sooner or later, and there may not be anything to be done about it at all. We think it is important to know what has happened and to consider the possibilities for the future, partly because it is our system of government and something we must responsibly cherish, and partly because we still seem intent on "ironing out the wrinkles" in the political system. The spirit of reform has not entirely died. The potential for leadership to improve upon or undermine growth always exists. . . .

The political elite—the tiny percentage of the population that actively participates in electoral politics—used to organize campaigns, and fill the posts of party office from election district captains to party chairpersons. Committee membership led from precinct, to ward, to city, county, state, and national levels. There were other committees as well on rules, issues, and so on. There were honorary groups within the parties for large donors who could gain access to high elected officials and special perks at party conventions in return for their contributions. The honorary groups did not necessarily give anything more than money to the party, but they did make their power felt as they sought to influence public policy. . . .

The political hacks, whether paid or unpaid, still hang about, but their role is severely curtailed. There used to be what might be referred to as "The Savior of the Week" syndrome, wherein every campaign could rely on someone dropping by the headquarters, willing to tell the staff just what was required to turn the campaign around because he or she was "in touch with The People" (having talked to a cab driver on the way over). If the Savior was sufficiently esteemed by the staff and willing to take a hand in trying out the new tactic, it might be added to the repertoire. More typically, the staff would try to ignore the interruption and continue the battle of sorting out the power structure within the campaign organization. Polling has helped to eliminate much of the uncertainty about what people are thinking and what is likely to motivate them to vote.

Today, campaigns are run by professionals (and even volunteers) who are trained in their tasks and who rely on advice and assistance from the national and state parties and the private consulting firms they employ to do their advertising, fund raising, and general campaigning. There is less room for ad hoc campaign strategy and there are definite restraints on unplanned expenditures. Storefronts may still exist, but they are not the seat of campaign decision making. In fact, they tend to do very little at all but pass out literature or house phone banks. And even the phone banks tend to be run by professional callers who can be trained and relied upon to complete their assigned tasks.

Case work was another function of local parties in the days of yore. When people needed help in coping with the public (or even private) authorities, they could turn to the party to mediate on their behalf. As local parties become less visible, that function has fallen more and more to elected officials who typically hire a staff of one or two to provide that service. Little city halls and local congressional offices are recent phenomena and represent the shift of functions.

What then is left for the new volunteer, and how will the party continue to perform that integrating function of linking private citizens with public roles and responsibilities? . . .

Finding volunteers for voter registration, canvassing, and getting out the vote remain a vehicle for participation, although it is not as essential as it once was. Campaigns used to be far more labor-intensive operations, but that is no longer the case. Bodies can still be used to stand on busy intersections holding signs during rush hour, but many of the traditional tasks have been taken over by machines or by professionals in today's more centralized campaign organizations.

One critical question the parties and their campaign organizations must resolve is how to motivate support, and once motivated, how to apply it in a meaningful way for both the participant and the organization. It goes back to the question of incentives and rewards, which is the basis of all organizations. It goes back to the constant theme of would-be party leaders that they want to "rebuild the grassroots."

It is our contention that the part of motivation dependent upon communication—upon reaching the minds (and maybe hearts) of party supporters—is very much within the sphere of party control. If anything, it has improved in quality and in quantity. Some of that communication has been in the form of direct mail solicitations which provide the recipient the opportunity to act on it, and as many fund raisers know, commitment tends to follow money: once you invest money in a cause, you come to believe in it more strongly. In that regard, then, it is likely that millions of Americans have a more firmly rooted commitment to their party.

But what of those who want to come out and contribute their spare time and energy? One reality everyone must face (including those who would like to contribute their time) is that there is less of it around these days. Seventy percent of the women under thirty-five work. Both women and men want to spend more time with their families and more time in health-related activities. The question is What can an organization do with individuals who want to make a contribution but have limited time and, usually, little to offer beyond their enthusiasm?

There will undoubtedly be many efforts made by both parties to find satisfying useful tasks. The probability remains, however, that the only elections to rely entirely on that sort of grassroots efforts will be local elections. Even state legislative races have become more expensive and more dependent on the sophisticated campaign technologies available, as PAC money moves increasingly in that direction.

Politics appears to be becoming a more passive activity, but it should be borne in mind that the percentage of the population who used to be active was always small and not always representative of the population as a whole. The legitimacy and acceptance of the entire system depended and continues to depend not on this small elite but on the proportion of the population who vote. They are being reached; they are better informed, they may be more committed in the future. More of them are contributing money to the parties, and they may feel that their participation is anything but passive, given that it was more than they did before, and they are engaged in more communication with the party as a result of their donation. . . .

By the end of the 1980s, both parties will probably have their own cable networks reaching out to the party faithful, educating them to the party's principles and the skills required for running campaigns. The lists of registered voters maintained by the parties and their affiliates will be more extensive, and the communication between the party and the voters will increase accordingly in the mails, by telephone, probably even by computer. More people will have access to more information than ever before and that, we believe, will lead to an increase in partisan intensity. The capacity to communicate so much so easily will make our politics much less labor-intensive, not unlike many of the activities in the rest of our lives.

The increased communication may mean that politics becomes more passive because so much of the former activity had to do with reaching out to voters. Certainly many of the old tasks are no longer relevant, and the campaign finance law has added to the passivity by requiring a centralization of the process in order to keep track of the income and expenditures. The general election of the president makes that point most dramatically because it is the one most likely to generate the greatest amount of enthusiasm. But the public financing prohibits contributions directly to the campaigns, and the spending limitations (combined with the uncertain relations between the presidential campaign staff and state and local parties) encourage even more centralization. It is a time when many people want to do more and find that there is less to do. The fact that there is less for the volunteer to do and the fact that, presidential elections aside, there are fewer volunteers is both cause and effect of the new circumstances. . . .

The professionalization of politics has its strengths and its weaknesses. It is part and parcel of the new system, however, and it brings us back to the focus of this book. We have been writing principally about the people who actively participate: the party structure and the individuals who make it work. It has been our view that the parties lost ground with the voters because they did not mean very much. One reason they lost control of their destiny was because most of the reforms in this century effectively weakened the structure—the ability of party leaders to make their organizations do very much at all. The strength of the new party system rests on the capability of these new professionals to make decisions about candidates and issues, and to reach out to the citizenry and make those decisions known. . . .

In some respects the parties seem like giant amoeba covering the political environment. Everything falls under them, but they are formless. Political observers talk about party decline, or even party resurgence, but the parties seem to shift only slightly, shuddering perhaps in the South as realignment takes place. They are hard to grasp intellectually; they are certainly not easy to grasp in the day-to-day practice of politics by political leaders. If parties are about power, then those who participate in them want power and they are loath to give it away to someone else. What is required of party leadership is a reshifting of the power structure to emphasize some things and move away from others. It is one reason the parties move slowly: it is not an organization with easy measures for success or failure. Elections can be won and lost for so many reasons, most of them having to do with the personalities of the candidates and the specific choices voters make between candidates.

Many people working together—sometimes working at odds with each other—have brought about dramatic changes in both major parties in the last few years. The effort seems herculean when viewed in retrospect, but it inched along with many seeming backward steps at the time. Even with all of that effort, to most observers and to most voters, the parties seem to be not very different. They still appear to be as inefficient and amoebalike as ever. Part of leadership is bringing about change, and part of it is raising our expectations. We would argue that things have changed; we are only awaiting someone to point that out and lift our spirits about what can be.

This is not to say that we have not had political leadership during this time, but rather to suggest that the leaders we have had brought new generations into the parties and that it is to those new participants we must look for evidence of the style and substance of the changes that are taking place. . . .

There are similarities between the new activists in both parties: They are more professional; they think of themselves as being more pragmatic; they tend to be more inclusive in their decision-making style than exclusive or elitist. They are concerned about the organizational structure of the parties and they have paid attention to rebuilding. David Broder . . . described the new participants in *The Changing of the Guard*, published in 1980. Both he and Xandra Kayden, writing in 1974, characterized the new people as "organizers." Broder said of them "The next ones who will take power—the babies born between 1930 and 1955—were shaped in a very different time. Theirs has been a time of affluence and inflation, of extraordinary educational advance, and of wrenching social change and domestic discord." Their objective is to change the system, not to destroy it. Their style is cool, in keeping with a television age. They contrast themselves with earlier generations who were either less educated or more elitist, and with the radicals of their own years who lost faith with the society.

This new generation, which itself will be replaced someday, has a quiet technocratic quality to it. If it were not that the individuals involved were forged out of the turmoil of the 1960s and 70s, they might seem rather boring. They can and have transformed the party structure, but they have yet to transform the public mind. It might be that we need to await another kind of personality with the capacity to mold the imagination as well as the organization. . . .

It is our view that the voters will not become strong partisans until imaginative leadership binds their hopes to the structure. The intensity of today's politics of morality and frustration may be part of that process, but we would hope for something more positive in the long run. We would hope that tolerance and a generosity of spirit enter the equation lest the partisanship become not a vehicle for structuring political thought but the front lines of battle.

The parties go on partly because the political system depends on them, even if the citizenry feels their inadequacy from time to time. They go on despite our rather feckless attitude toward them. It is our view that the parties have responded to the caring attention that those who love them have bestowed and have emerged in the 1980s as strong institutions capable of recapturing their innate functions, capable of having meaning to the voters. We expect that partisanship will increase in the 1990s if nothing cataclysmic interferes to alter our political structure.

The parties have changed because the old structures no longer worked and a new generation fought for and won the mantle of leadership. The new organization reflects the values of those leaders and the circumstances of today's society: incredibly rapid and intense communication; varied, private lifestyles; a certain cynicism or caution about all our institutions and the people who lead them.

68

E. J. DIONNE

From *They Only* Look *Dead*

The "Anxious Middle" is journalist E. J. Dionne's description of the critical segment of voters who determine the outcome of American elections. Courted at election time by politicians of the left and the right, the Anxious Middle is less interested in ideological purity than in finding solutions that are practical and workable. At various times in the 1990s, they have looked to Bill Clinton, Ross Perot, and the Republican Party for answers. Where they will look next, Dionne opines, can change quickly and unpredictably. It all depends on how well the Anxious Middle feels government is handling their problems.

THERE COULD NOT, it would seem, be two elections more different than those of 1992 and 1994. The first was a Republican debacle, the second a Democratic disaster. The first seemed to herald a new wave of government activism and the end of a conservative era. The second was widely interpreted as marking the resurrection of conservatism and perhaps more: the birth of a more hard-edged, anti-government political alignment with commitments going well beyond the soothing verities of Ronald Reagan's American morning. The first election suggested potential Democratic strength everywhere in the country, even in the staunchest Republican bastions of the South and West. The second suggested that 1992 was an aberration, that the steady march of Republicanism through the states of the Old Confederacy and the Rocky Mountains would continue and affect every level of government.

What the two elections demonstrated above all was the instability of the American body politic in the 1990s, the intense impatience of the electorate and its vague but powerful sense of crisis and unraveling. The large swings back and forth between 1984 and 1994—and especially the enormous shifts in just the two years after 1992—can be traced to the emergence of a large new group at the heart of the electorate that has abandoned traditional ideological and partisan loyalties. This group feels pressed by economic change and worries that the country is experiencing a moral and social breakdown. Its members are angry at government but uneasy over the workings of the economic system. They crave self-reliance—and honor this virtue in others—but fear that both the government and the economy are blocking their own paths to self-sufficiency. *Newsweek* columnist Joe Klein has referred to "the Radical Middle," a group that includes many of these voters but may also go beyond it. Labor Secretary Robert Reich has spoken specifically of these hard-pressed Americans as "the anxious class." Marrying aspects of both formulations, one might refer to the Anxious Middle as the group that holds the future of American politics in its hands.

The Anxious Middle set the terms for the 1992 and 1994 elections. It destroyed a Republican presidential coalition that had seemed invulnerable only a few years earlier. It made Ross Perot possible, ended George Bush's political career, sent Bill Clinton to the White House—and then rebuked Clinton and helped make Newt Gingrich one of the central figures of American politics. Perot spoke instinctively for the Anxious Middle. Bush never understood it. Clinton saw it coming long before most politicians, shaped his campaign to respond to its concerns—and then confronted its ire after only two years in office. Gingrich sought his own radical language to speak to its anxieties. . . .

The Anxious Middle first found its power in 1992, reducing a Republican president's share of the vote to a little more than a third and giving Democrats full control of the elected part of the federal government for the first time in twelve years. The Democrats, moreover, seemed ready to lead. In Bill Clinton, they had a candidate who had thought through the causes of the party's earlier failures and catastrophes. He understood the weaknesses of the party's liberal wing and accepted the need for a substantial renovation of the Democrats' public philosophy. Yet he was uncompromisingly a Democrat in a way Jimmy Carter had never been. He spoke of a new party, but was at home with its old constituencies. He understood, in principle, that if the Democratic Party did not deliver for the more threatened part of the middle class, it would not survive. Thus, a hymn to "the forgotten middle class" became his electoral anthem. Clinton knew that the middle class was torn—between hope for what government might do and skepticism over whether (and how) it would do it; between acceptance of many recent social changes and a strong streak of traditionalism. The middle class did not want to outlaw abortion, yet most of its members lived family-centered lives and respected Ronald Reagan's famous trilogy of "family, work and neighborhood."

Clinton and those who gathered around him seemed determined to end a period in which, it was said, all the ideas were on the right. Clinton offered voters a host of specific programs. He proposed welfare reform, offering recipients new training and education programs but requiring them to take jobs after two years on the rolls. He promised a Kennedyesque national service program, under which those who sought to go to college could earn tuition aid by serving their country—a harkening back to the GI Bill, one of the most successful programs for upward mobility in the country's history. He suggested a mix of tax increases on the rich and tax reductions for middle-class families with children. He had a plan for national health insurance, proposals to help high-tech companies, ideas for expanding enterprise in the inner city, suggestions for improving the public schools, youth apprenticeship programs to help young people find their footing in a new economy. All these initiatives were united under a rubric few could argue with: opportunity, responsibility, community. It sounded like a very activist program—and it was—but Clinton insisted it was "neither liberal nor conservative," but new and better. "No more something for nothing" was a constant Clinton refrain that surely did not remind people of their worst fears of liberalism.

The core political problem Clinton sought to solve was the defection of white voters of moderate incomes from Democratic ranks. Since Richard Nixon, Republicans had won by making heavy inroads in this group, which included the overlapping constituencies of blue-collar and lower-middle-class voters, northern Catholics and southern evangelicals. In a broad sense, being a "New Democrat" meant being a Democrat who would be more acceptable to these voters than, say, George McGovern or Michael Dukakis. . . .

The fog cleared with remarkable speed. Just two years after their disaster, the Republicans stood astride Washington, confining the Democrats to what looked like a White House bunker. The Republicans not only recaptured the Senate, which they had controlled as recently as 1986, but also seized control of the House of Representatives. The parallels with 1992 were striking—and dispiriting for Democrats, who now seemed to be caught in an issueless fog of their own. The Republican campaign was relentlessly negative against Clinton, of course, but the Democrats had hardly been kind to George Bush two years earlier. What made 1994 so different was the extent to which the intellectual energy had again shifted back to the right. The Republicans, and particularly Newt Gingrich, tossed off ideas as if the Bush experience had never happened.

The House Republicans' "Contract with America" was a carefully drawn document aimed at putting together the pieces of a Republican majority while also giving the party a platform from which to govern. As Ronald Brownstein of the *Los Angeles Times* put it, the Republicans' contract and overall strategy was one part Reagan, one part Perot and one part William Bennett. It combined Reagan's overall anti-government, anti-tax message with Perot's anti-system, anti-Congress appeal and Bennett's call for a revival of traditional morality.

For Perot's partisans, there were term limits, congressional reform and a balanced budget amendment. For average families, the Republicans offered a tax credit for parents with children, an idea that Clinton embraced in 1992, cast aside when he assembled his first budget and then came back to, albeit only after the Republican triumph. The children's tax credit not only had general appeal, but spoke specifically to cultural conservatives who wanted government policy to be pro-family. The Republicans' contract had other goodies for traditionalists, including an end to the "marriage penalty" in the tax code, tougher enforcement of child support decrees on absent fathers, adoption assistance, and new penalties against sexual offenses and child pornography. For another kind of social conservative, the Republicans put together a draconian welfare reform program and a series of very tough-sounding anti-crime measures. For the wealthy, there was a cut in the capital gains tax. For business, there were other tax breaks and a reform of the product liability laws that would weaken the ability of consumers to bring suit. This was part of what the Republicans called the "Common Sense Legal Reforms Act," a series of measures directed against lawyers—always a good political target—and designed to reduce the number of lawsuits. For hawkish nationalists, the Republicans promised to ban the use of American troops in multinational forces under foreign command. For senior citizens, there was a repeal of the tax on higher-income Social Security recipients passed in 1993, and a lifting of the ceiling on what seniors could earn without losing their Social Security benefits.

To a remarkable extent, the Republican program was a political mirror image of Clinton's 1992 program. In effect, the Republicans were trying to recapture both the electoral and the intellectual ground they had lost to Clinton (and Perot) two years earlier. Clinton had proposed a "new" welfare system based on the "old" values of work, family and personal responsibility. But Clinton failed to get welfare reform passed. The Republicans jumped to his right by embracing the same values but arguing that they would be best achieved by a smaller and cheaper welfare system. Clinton profited from Bush's decision to break his "read my lips" pledge not to raise taxes. He sought to trump Bush by proposing a middle-class tax cut aimed at families with children. But here again, Clinton failed to act—he abandoned his own pledge in his first budget—and the Republicans again jumped to his right with their own tax package. Clinton had promised political reform and failed to deliver. Republicans first made sure through obstruction that the outgoing Democratic Congress did not have reform achievements to bring to the voters. (The Democrats . . . made this easy by delaying the reform package until the end of the congressional session.) Then the Republicans offered their own political reforms, including many on Clinton's list plus some harder-edged stuff such as term limits.

In a sense, both the 1992 Clinton program and the 1994 Republican program were aimed at the same broad group of voters—those who were unhappy about the performance of government, doubtful that government actually operated in their interest and concerned that the country was in moral decline. And the Republicans' 1994 program worked as well as Clinton's had two years earlier.

The breadth of the Republican gains was staggering. The Republicans picked up eight seats in the Senate, a remarkable accomplishment since just thirty-five seats were being contested. . . .

But even more remarkable than the Republicans' capture of the Senate was their success in taking over the House. The Republicans picked up fifty-two seats. Their gains were national in scope, and the ranks of the defeated Democrats included representatives of every wing and style in the party. . . .

The Republicans' gains were particularly dramatic in the South, and these are likely to be their most enduring. The year 1994 was the one when the Republicans' fifty-year campaign to break the Democratic "Solid South," so successful in presidential contests, came to fruition at the congressional level. For the first time since Reconstruction, the Republicans enjoyed a majority of the congressional seats in the states that had made up the Old Confederacy. . . .

The results in the South reflected a true nationalization of American politics. In the recent past, Democrats had held on to Congress despite repeated Republican presidential victories because so many voters split their tickets. Many voters backed congressional Democrats either out of loyalty to individual politicians or as a sign of their residual faithfulness to the Democratic Party itself. What made it likely that the congressional Republicans would hold many of their 1994 southern gains over the long term was the fact that most of them came from districts that had recently voted Republican for president. This meant that their victory in the South was not a one-shot protest, but a confirmation of long-term trends. . . .

The 1994 elections might be seen as the natural result of the voters' unrequited rebellion of 1992. The angriest constituencies were the quickest to move away from George Bush, the most likely to embrace Ross Perot and the most eager to punish Bill Clinton. By the end of George Bush's presidency, voters had decided that Republicans were disengaged from their problems. A large majority rejected Bush, and a majority of those who did so were prepared to listen to Democratic arguments that active government could work. When they decided that the Democrats' version of active government had not done the job, enough of the angry voters were prepared to give the Republicans a chance to prove their claim that *less* government would work better. The edgy, pragmatic voters willing to punish politicians quickly and shift allegiances suddenly constitute the Anxious Middle. . . .

The Anxious Middle is as peculiar a political formation as its name implies. It is radical in its disaffection with the status quo, in the depth of its worries about the future, in its desire for far-reaching change, and in its critique of current political and economic arrangements. It is "middle" because it lacks the rigid definition usually associated with the words "left" and "right," "liberal" and "conservative." It is also "middle" because its longings are not utopian. The Anxious Middle does not expect a New Jerusalem, a world without sin, pain, conflict or injustice. It hopes simply for a return to the sort of economic growth that characterized the twenty-five years after World War II. It looks to greater fairness, a modicum of job security, a sense that hard work will be rewarded, and that violent crime will be punished. The fact that such demands can be seen as radical in the context of our current uncertainties is a sign of how disorderly the world of the 1990s has become.

The Anxious Middle is "middle" in another sense: It tends to be quite moderate or pragmatic on the issues that so excite liberals and conservatives. On questions of culture and morality, the Anxious Middle is neither repressive nor permissive. It senses the moral crisis, but is inclined to see both its cultural and economic sides. Its attitude toward the power of government is contingent on how effectively the government performs. On economics, the Anxious Middle is in favor of what works. It is in love neither with the market nor with government. It trusts the market and the government only so far.

69

DAN BALZ AND RONALD BROWNSTEIN

From *Storming the Gates*

For a century after the Civil War, the American South was solidly Democratic. The Republican Party, President Abraham Lincoln's party, found little support there. Today, political allegiances in the South have changed dramatically. Authors Dan Balz and Ronald Brownstein describe the variety of factors that have gradually brought many southern voters into the Republican Party; race is a central issue. Not only have conservative southern voters significantly influenced recent elections, but they have also remade the Republican Party into an increasingly conservative force.

IN 1994, THE REPUBLICAN PARTY captured the South, and the South captured the Republican Party. Both sides of this transformation will change American politics into the foreseeable future. In a geographical shift of seismic proportions, the 994 elections affirmed the South, the largest prize of all the political regions in the country, as the new Republican heartland. Republicans made significant—in some cases startling—advances throughout the region, significantly raising the strength of the Dixie accent in a party that had its origins in opposition to southern slave owners. While the differences that separate southern and northern Republicans may be far smaller than those that historically divided southern and northern Democrats, Republicans who sprouted from southern soil remain culturally and philosophically distinct from those in the North. Added to the GOP's long-standing western base, the expansion of Republican power in the South deepens all the conservative tendencies of the party, from opposition to new taxes and support for higher defense spending to a more central role for social issues such as abortion and school prayer. "Southern Republicans tend to be more conservative, they tend to be more philosophically committed, and they tend to be more confrontational," said Texas Senator Phil Gramm, whose career is the walking embodiment of all three.

Few stories in modern American politics are as rich or as enduring as the partisan transformation of the South. Over the past half century, politicians, political scientists, historians, journalists, and others have chronicled the breakup of the southern Democratic Party and the steady erosion of the one-party South. The current state of this evolution to two-party politics makes it easy to forget how far and how fast the Republicans actually have traveled. . . .

After a century as the smallest of minorities, the Republican Party now stands as a vibrant force throughout the South—in some states the dominant force—with little on the horizon likely to reverse trends that have been increasing the party's strength for a generation. . . .

The elections of 1994 represented not just another step forward for the Republicans, but the kind of quantum change that has the power to remake the politics of a region—and by implication the entire nation—for a generation. For the first time in this century, southern Republicans emerged from an election in control of a majority of the governorships, a majority of the seats in the U.S. Senate, and, most significant of all, a majority of the seats in the U.S. House. Republicans also gained 119 southern state legislative seats and captured control of three state legislative chambers, the Florida Senate, North Carolina House, and the South Carolina House. For the first time since Reconstruction, Republicans elected the Speakers of two southern legislatures. . . .

Given the inexorable trends in presidential elections over the past four decades, the changes may not seem startling, but few people anticipated that the Republican force would hit the South with such a pounding fury in November 1994. Despite the defection problems in presidential elections, Democratic candidates in the South long assumed that they could insulate themselves from what southern voters regarded as the most unappealing aspects of the national party. The 1994 elections robbed them of that illusion, perhaps for good, in large part because white southern voters rebelled against one of their own in the White House. Several factors combined to produce the earthquake, from the "rising tide lifts all boats" nature of national voting patterns, to the impact of redistricting on boundaries that long had favored Democrats, to the evolutionary nature of the changes that had been under way in the region. But Clinton's presidency became a solidifying force for Republican voters in the South that southern Democratic candidates could not overcome, and southern Republican leaders like Gingrich and party chairman Haley Barbour, intuitively recognizing the possibility for a historical transformation in their region, made the South a special focus in their election strategy. . . .

As important as the 1994 elections were in transforming the political balance in the South, they were equally significant in affecting the balance of power with the Republican Party. Those changes will shape the style, culture, and priorities of the GOP into the next century. The elections solidified Sun Belt preeminence within a party long accustomed to dominance by the Northeast and Midwest. Compared to the last time Republicans held the House, the geographic conversion appears stunning. The South and West now control more than 55 percent of Republican seats in the House, where forty years ago, the Northeast and Midwest held roughly 75 percent. In 1955, Republicans held just 10 of 120 southern congressional districts; at the end of 1995 they controlled 78 of 137, and during that same period, their strength in the Senate went from none of the 26 seats to 16 today.

White southerners, whose long memories of the Civil War made them among the most loyal of Democratic constituencies, now identify with the Republican Party in roughly the same percentages as northern Protestants, upon whose shoulders the GOP was founded. In practical terms, these white southerners, drawn over the years to the GOP's brand of economic and cultural conservatism, now represent the most loyal of all conservative constituencies—and are more likely to shape the future than their northern brethren. . . .

Like the rise of the Gingrich generation within the Republican Party, the geographic transformation of American politics did nor occur suddenly, nor was it the result of transitory currents or a few dominant personalities. Powerful forces changed the South and the political allegiances of the people there, and it has taken a generation for them to fully flower.

The most significant, of course, is race and the civil rights movement of the 1950s and 1960s, which empowered African-Americans in the South, drove white voters out of the old Democratic Party, and established a new Republican Party as their refuge. In 1994, southern Republicans received 94 percent of their votes from whites and just 2 percent from African-Americans. The Voting Rights Act of 1965 enfranchised millions of black voters in the decade after its passage by Congress, and allowed blacks who had long been excluded from the political process not only to vote but to play increasingly powerful roles within the Democratic Party. But those changes also had the effect of driving many white voters out of the Democratic Party toward the Republicans. Ironically, the Republicans then used that same legislation as the legal centerpiece of a redistricting strategy after the 1990 census that was designed to maximize the number of legislative and congressional districts with black or Hispanic majorities and, as a consequence, diminish Democratic chances of winning the adjacent, increasingly white districts. Thus, the civil rights revolution constructed the pilings of the modern Republican Party in the South and the movement's legal legacy topped off the GOP's new southern mansion with their victories in 1994. It would be a gross oversimplification to say that the racial politics of the 1960s primarily produced the results of the 1994 elections. But Republicans struggling to move beyond race deny reality when they attempt to wipe away their party's use of racial prejudice and paranoia to erode the strength of the Democratic Party and cement their relationship with a generation of white voters.

Nearly as powerful as race in transforming southern politics was the region's economic conversion throughout the post–World War II era. Long the nation's most impoverished region, the South over this period rose closer to national standards. The decline of the agrarian South and the rise of a modern economy grounded in manufacturing, defense, tourism, services, and technology has been, by anyone's measure, one of the great success stories of the late twentieth century—but in creating a more diversified society, the South's economic transformation made it difficult for Democrats to speak for the interests of all, as they once claimed to do. And the absence of labor unions robbed the Democrats in the South of a key organizing tool available in the white ethnic wards of the North. . . .

The third great current of change was population growth, fueled by the influx of northern migrants drawn by the South's expanding economic opportunities, warm weather, cheaper living standards, and more relaxed lifestyle. (Immigration from abroad reinforced the population growth, particularly in Texas and Florida.) Over a forty-year span, the population of the South grew by 81 percent, faster than the nation as a whole, and in states like Florida (366 percent) and Texas (120 percent), exploded at a breathtaking pace. Not every state, of course, shared equally in this growth. North Carolina and Georgia gained significantly; Mississippi and Alabama, long impoverished, did not. The Outer South, or Peripheral South, gained far more than the states of the Deep South, but as a whole, the region was transformed by the flood of new arrivals.

In concert with the economic changes, in-migration from the North and the swell of refugees from the farms to the cities and the imposition of court-ordered busing gave rise to a suburban South where one had never existed. Around cities like Dallas and Houston, Atlanta, Birmingham, Orlando, Raleigh, Richmond, Charlotte, and Greenville, suburbs sprouted relentlessly. Between 1980 and 1990, the South could boast of thirteen of the twenty-five fastest-growing congressional districts in the country (seven of the other twelve were in California alone), while only four of the twenty-five slowest-growing were southern based (and three of them were majority-black districts). A wave of blue-collar migration hit during the early 1980s, when hard times humbled the Rust Belt, but for the most part the migration brought middle-class, middle-income families to the corporations establishing operations in the South. Almost every new housing development rising in the suburban and exurban counties of the South represented another potential Republican enclave and a further nail in the Democrats' coffin.

These great forces transformed southern life in fundamental ways, but they did not dislodge the region's most salient political characteristic, its abiding conservatism. "Conservatism occupies an exalted position in the South," wrote brothers Earl Black and Merle Black, two political scientists who study southern politics. "Although the region has sometimes been portrayed as ripe for the construction of successful biracial coalitions of have-littles and have-nots, the growth of the urban middle class and the popularity of middle-class beliefs among southern white workers have worked against explicit class politics and in favor of conservative politics generally."

Southern conservatism remains a unique blend of patriotism, religion, faith in free markets, and distrust of outsiders. Through the enduring prism of the Civil War, the South long saw itself besieged by the moneyed interests and hostile values of the North, creating a sense of beleaguerment that made the region more protective of its own culture and cohesive in its conservatism. The arrival of millions of northern immigrants somewhat diluted this sense of embattlement, but it has not made the South significantly less conservative. No region is more resolute in its support for a strong defense, and no region has so benefited from defense spending. The network of military bases and installations across the South testifies to the tenacity of southern power brokers, from Richard Russell to Sam Nunn. But despite its dependence on federal largesse, the South long has viewed government suspiciously, and its legislatures have been far more protective of the economic elites and major industries than of using government to redistribute wealth to the impoverished masses. Southern states have historically provided the least generous benefits to welfare recipients, for example, while providing the most attractive incentives to local industries or to lure corporations to their states, although, to be fair, the mostly impoverished southern states had fewer resources to redistribute. Like the culture of the military, religion is woven more deeply into the daily life of the South than it is in any other region. The conservative values of the pulpit spill regularly into the public arena, and on a wide variety of social and cultural issues, the South is the country's most conservative section. . . .

The hardening of racial lines between the two parties represents the most troubling aspect of southern political trends. The Republicans may aspire to become the nation's majority party, but can a political institution that derives 94 percent of its vote in the South from whites ever pretend to offer credible representation to African-Americans? Most southern politicians, Republicans and Democrats, have long since abandoned overtly racial campaign appeals, but Republicans still struggle to escape their own history in the South. Younger Republicans, those who came of age with or in the aftermath of the civil rights movement, have tried to move beyond race-based campaigning. "The southern strategy, in my opinion, has been very destructive for the Republican Party," said Bob Inglis, a second-term House member from South Carolina. "You can't be a majority party if you write off 30 percent of the vote. You can't hold on. You've got to prove that conservative doesn't equal racist."

Colin Powell's decision to become an active member of the party represents an enormous boost for the GOP. But at a time when Republicans seek dramatic reforms in welfare programs that many blacks see as punitive, and when leading Republican officials press to eliminate affirmative action programs, the burden of proof on the party remains enormously high, as Powell himself has said. Who can forget the 1990 Senate race in North Carolina, in which Jesse Helms played the race card in the final month of the campaign to defeat Harvey Gantt, the black former mayor of Charlotte? Helms aired a television commercial that showed a pair of white hands holding a letter saying the recipient had been rejected for a job in favor of a minority applicant with fewer qualifications. Democrats mistake these purely racial appeals as the principal reason for their decline in the South. In reality, Republicans have gained much more in recent elections by identifying themselves with less government, fiscal conservatism, and lower taxes than by race-based arguments. But the current agenda in Washington, coupled with the desire by many prominent Republicans to end affirmative action programs, hinders the GOP's ability to reach out to black voters. Some Republican strategists posit a future in which GOP candidates routinely receive 15–20 percent of the black vote in the South, built upon the emerging black middle class. Some candidates have achieved those numbers, but not many: The party as a whole remains suspect to the most significant minority in the region, and the current agenda nationally likely will prevent the GOP from reaching those targets. . . .

The wreckage of the Democrats, increasingly divided between its liberal-minority wing and its shrinking moderate wing, lies strewn across the region. The movement of conservative voters into the GOP ensures that the liberal wing of the Democratic Party increasingly will dominate primary elections in the South, making the party's nominees less electable in general elections. The safest Democratic seats (other than those held by longtime white incumbents) belong to some of the most liberal members of the Democratic caucus, many of them African-Americans in newly created majority-minority districts. Moderate-to-conservative Democrats have become an endangered species. Of forty-two white southern Democrats in the House in 1995, twenty-eight were elected before 1990, while forty-four of seventy-seven white southern Republicans arrived after the 1990 elections. The process of generational replacement augurs well for the Republicans, for increasingly, white voters see the GOP as the party that will protect their interests. The 1994 elections, rather than strengthening the hand of moderates within the party, nearly decimated the wing symbolized by the Democratic Leadership Council, the organization founded largely by southern Democrats after the 1984 election to push the party toward the center, and the party switches and retirements in 1995—most notably Senator Sam Nunn of Georgia—underscored the sense of gloom now pervasive among Democrats in the South. "The only conservative Democrats who can survive in the South are those known as conservatives, not Democrats," Merle Black said. "In the minds of white voters, a conservative Democrat is an unreliable conservative." Unless Democrats find some new way to reverse these trends, the old-fashioned conservative Democrat could soon face extinction, as a young generation of white politicians looks to the Republicans to fulfill their ambitions. The one hope for Democrats may lie in their ability to attract populist voters fearful about the changes Republicans are making in Washington, a strategy that showed some potential in the 1995 elections.

While the Democrats are pulled left, southern Republicans have assembled a coalition that is more purely conservative than anywhere else in the country, with the possible exception of parts of the West. The southern GOP draws on a voter base that includes not only economic conservatives but far more religious and cultural conservatives than elsewhere as well. Exit polls from 1994 showed that a quarter of white southern voters identified themselves as Christian fundamentalists, compared to less than one in six nationally. The growing strength of this constituency, and its locus in a region that has become the party's new base of power, not only guarantees greater attention by the party to divisive issues like school prayer and abortion, but threatens to make secular conservatives and moderates think twice about their longer-term allegiance with the GOP. Comments by Republicans like Mississippi's Kirk Fordice that

America is a "Christian nation" represent a minority view even among the most religious of the GOP leadership, but they still damage the party's national image.

The new southern Republican coalition doesn't just reinforce the party's conservative tendencies, it threatens to accelerate them. No region, with the possible exception of the West, better typifies the strength of the conservative, antigovernment coalition that helped drive the Republicans to power. Exit polls showed that a quarter of white southern voters owned guns, that one in five regularly listened to talk radio, and that two in three agreed with the proposition that government should do less, not more, seven points higher than the national average. Northern moderates may rebel against some of the priorities of a party with such strength in the South, but the electoral trends suggest that over time there will be more southerners within the congressional ranks, not fewer. On a sweltering day in the summer of 1995, George W. Bush sat in his office in the Texas capitol, reflecting on the implications of the changes in his party and the strength of its new foundation in the South. "Lesson 101 in politics," he said, "is never leave your base." That lesson was lost on Bush's father, who in 1992 struggled unsuccessfully to reassemble the conservative coalition that twice powered Ronald Reagan to victory. But the younger Bush's words stand as an article of faith among the members of the new Republican majority that emerged from the landslide of 1994.

In breaking the Democrats' historic hold on the South, the Republicans not only helped secure their own future but also bound themselves to issues and constituencies that now push them ever rightward. The South stands as the Republicans' protective shield against Democratic counterattacks in the North, and as migration continues to increase the population of the South and West at the expense of the North and Midwest, the advantage will only enlarge. But this reshaping also risks propelling the party far enough to the right to threaten losses at the center of the political spectrum. Those dangers remain prospective. For now, the GOP can look around the South as an enlarging electoral fortress. The speed and breadth of the transformation startled even many who have worked to advance it—and the impact on the party is equally surprising. Sitting one day in an Austin, Texas, office piled high with computer printouts and Texas paraphernalia, Bush strategist Karl Rove summed up the transformation with a Civil War analogy. "The party of northern aggression," he said, "has become the party of southern dominance."

70

JESSE VENTURA

From *I Ain't Got Time to Bleed*

One of the biggest upsets of the 1998 elections was Reform Party candidate Jesse Ventura's victory over two accomplished politicians for the governorship of Minnesota. As he is fond of saying to his wrestling fans, radio listeners, film watchers, and anyone else who will listen, "I didn't need this job." Ventura, clearly no career politician, was able to beat his Democratic and Republican opponents by appealing particularly to two subsets of voters: first, those who were fed up with the usual brand of politics, and second, those who were new voters and who had not yet been activated. Ventura promised to give all citizens a voice and to do so honestly and forthrightly. While there has been no lack of coverage of Governor Ventura in the national press, reading about his motivation and aspirations may tell Americans even more about the Minnesota governor and the role he might play in our political system.

I DIDN'T NEED THIS JOB. I ran for governor to find out if the American dream still exists in anyone's heart other than mine. I'm happy to say that it does. I'm living proof that the myths aren't true. The candidate with the most money isn't always the one who wins. You don't have to be a career politician to serve in public office. You don't have to be well connected or propped up by special-interest groups. You don't even have to be a Democrat or a Republican. You can stand on your own two feet and speak your mind, because if people like where you're coming from, they will vote you in. The will of the people is still the most powerful force in our government. We can put whomever we choose into office, simply by exercising that will.

We're a nation of bootstrappers. We're visionaries. And we're not afraid to turn our visions into reality. That's the great thing about Americans—the word *can't* isn't part of our vocabulary We've always been a can-do people. And we still are, despite all the negative things we hear about how corrupt our government has become, and despite the fact that we've become too reliant on that same government for things it has no business providing. We might have lost sight of it a little bit, but we are still the keepers of the American dream.

How else could a guy like me have become the governor of Minnesota? Look at me: I'm no career politician—I'm a six-foot-four, 250-pound ex–Navy SEAL, pro wrestler, radio personality, and film actor. I only got into politics in the first place because I have a pretty noticeable habit of speaking my mind. But I guess a good bit of what I had to say must have made sense to people, because they elected me twice.

This book is mostly about me, about where I stand, and about where I came from. But what's happening in Minnesota right now is far bigger than me. History is being made. Like many other people across the nation, Minnesotans are fed up with the good-old-boy network that cares more about keeping itself well ensconced than it does about carrying out the voters' wishes. In 1998's gubernatorial race, I gave them an alternative.

I'm a Minneapolis native with working-class roots. My collar's indelibly blue. I belong to the private sector, and that's where I'm returning the minute my term as governor is over. I stand for the common man because I am him. That's one reason the people of Minnesota elected me: I know where they're coming from because I came from the same place.

They also voted for me, I think, because I'm not easy to ignore. I'm big, I'm loud, and I'm not afraid to say what I think. But I also got a powerful set of ethics from my parents, some serious hard-core discipline from the Navy SEALs, and some decent people skills from my careers as a professional wrestler, film actor, and radio personality. And I can talk to people without talking down to them.

But if I had to pick one reason Minnesotans voted for me, I would have to say that it is because I tell the truth. I stand tall and speak freely, even when it isn't politically expedient to do so. That, above all, is what I think Minnesotans voted for: honesty.

This book has two purposes: first, to tell you where I stand—and why—on the issues that affect us all. Anybody who offers themselves for public office owes you that; and second, to tell you the story of what made me who I am. I'm an ordinary guy who went for his dreams and made them happen. The only things I've ever been handed are extraordinary guidance and lifelong friendship, without which I could never have achieved all that I have. But I'm no golden child. I've had basically the same opportunities as most of you. And if a guy like me can become the governor, so could you. That's the way American government is supposed to work.

Unfortunately, there's an idea out there that's very destructive to the American electoral system. It's the idea that you have to cast your vote for whoever's most likely to win, because otherwise you're wasting your vote. That is simply not true. There is no such thing as a wasted vote.

Voting is not supposed to be just a popularity contest. It's not like betting on a horse race. It's our responsibility when we vote to vote for the ideas we would like to see become public policy. We have to choose our candidates by the things they stand for, not by their ratings in the polls. When we bow to the pressure of the polls, we get exactly the phenomenon we're complaining about now: career politicians who will say anything to get your vote and who don't stand for anything except what the latest poll tells them to support. Yet somehow, that's become the standard. But it doesn't have to be that way.

I understand why so many people don't vote anymore, and I sympathize with them. It can seem like a waste of time when the only candidates you see in the news are cookie-cutter copies of the ones you saw in the last election and the election before that. But these days you have to look beyond what the media tells you to think and make up your own mind about the issues. Your choices aren't limited to the party favorites who have the money and the influence to get themselves into the limelight. You can vote for anybody you want. My stand on voting is that if you don't cast your vote, you forfeit your right to whine about the government.

When I announced that I was running for governor, everybody said I couldn't win. They said my campaign was an exercise in futility. The media thought I was a joke. My opponents pretended I didn't exist. But on November 3, 1998, the people of Minnesota came out in droves and made it happen. This election had the largest voter turnout (in years without a presidential election) in Minnesota's history and almost the largest in the country's history. We shocked the world. We wasted the system with "wasted" votes.

My Democratic opponent, Attorney General Hubert H. "Skip" Humphrey III, called our victory a "wake-up call of the first order." Even my Republican opponent, Saint Paul Mayor Norm Coleman, said that we ignited a spark, even though he said he didn't have any idea what that spark was. They knew I was popular, but neither of them had any idea how I won.

How did I do it? With a secret weapon that the other two candidates didn't have: The people who put me in office were overwhelmingly people who had never participated in the system before, and a huge number of these new voters were college-age people.

The bottom line is that my opponents were boring. They were the same old brand of career politicians, the kind that comes out of the woodwork every four years, spouts the same old rhetoric about the same issues, and then disappears. People don't bother to come to the polls anymore because they don't see the point. The candidates are virtually indistinguishable from each other. Minnesotans might not have been quite sure what they were getting when they voted for me, but one thing they knew for sure: It wouldn't be business as usual!

There's a brand-new generation in Minnesota that has just come into the electoral system. They saw this election as an opportunity to be heard. They've infused Minnesota politics with new blood. And as long as we do what we have to do to keep this new generation involved, we're going to turn this system around.

My victory is important for another reason. I'm the first member of the Reform Party to win a statewide office. There's been talk recently that the Reform Party has had it. People have been saying that we're going to go the way of most other third parties: We'll show up and bark just loud enough to get the two traditional parties back in line a little, then we'll quietly disappear. But our government needs more than just a face-lift—it needs a major overhaul. The Reform Party's work is far from over. In fact, it's barely begun.

We have to build this party from the bottom up. It must be a grassroots organization, or else it's meaningless. And if you look at it that way, then no election is insignificant. No win for the party is too small. A government that is truly by the people has to be grassroots at its foundation. It has to come from the bottom up.

Think of the alternative. If the party's controlled from the top, then whose hands is it in? Career politicians. The comfortably ensconced people who are many levels removed from the working people of this country. The fact that our nation's government is controlled by people like that is at the heart of every complaint I hear about our government today.

Standard operating procedure in our political system today is that everyone's owned, either by one of the two parties or by special-interest groups. Career politicians are bought and sold. And that's how I'm different: No one owns me. I come with no strings attached. All the lobbyists in Minnesota are running scared right now because suddenly the rules of the game have changed. They have no leverage with me. They have no in.

One of the first things I did during the transition period between the election and the inauguration was to bring in thirteen citizens from across the state. These were people who were either first-time voters or who hadn't voted in five consecutive elections. I asked each of them a question: Now that you've come into the system, how do we keep you involved?

Their answers were very clear, very honest. They said, It's the same story every four years. Whenever an election's coming up, all the politicians come out and give you the same song and dance about the same issues, all the way up until they get elected. Then you don't hear any more from them until it's time for them to get elected again. We're tired of it. If you want to keep us involved, don't tell us what you think we want to hear, tell us the truth. . . .

I decided to run for governor because I got mad. In 1997, the State of Minnesota had a budget surplus of more than four billion dollars. The voters wanted that surplus returned to them because, in their opinion, they'd been overcharged. But Minnesota legislators chose to ignore the wishes of the people and instead dreamed up all kinds of pork-barrel projects to make themselves look good when reelection time came. Some of that surplus money was bonded to pay for high-profile projects that the people didn't want. As a result, our children are going to have to assume the payments on the out-of-date convention centers and sports facilities these politicians built to help themselves get reelected. Is that how we show our children we care for them? Is that the kind of public servants the voters really want?

I also saw that a lot of people had no voice in decisions affecting their taxes. For example, there's a group called the Metropolitan Council that can levy taxes in a seven-county area that makes up the Twin Cities, even though the council seats aren't filled by elections. Nowhere else in the state is there this extra layer of government. Another example is people who own lakeshore property. They are also highly taxed but receive very few municipal services and have no say in policy matters. In my book, these are both cases of taxation without representation.

I want to make government more directly accountable to the people. If I'd run for governor and lost because no one was interested in or cared about what I want to do, that would have been fine with me. It's their choice. But I wasn't going to be weeded out because the system said I couldn't win.

My campaign was anything but run-of-the-mill. My opponents were in suits. I was wearing jeans and a Minnesota Timberwolves jacket, and my campaign slogan was "Retaliate in '98." Since so many people were convinced I didn't have a chance, early on in the race the thought of voting for me was considered pointless but fun. Garrison Keillor even said voting for me was like throwing toilet paper in the trees to piss off

Dad. I became the candidate of choice for the rebellious. But I went out and made myself available to people. I listened. And I learned.

Unlike my opponents, not a penny of my campaign money came from special-interest groups. Instead, my supporters relied on Minnesota's Political Campaign Refund program, which allowed them to donate fifty dollars each to my campaign, and then get a fifty-dollar refund from the state after the election. I spent $600,000 on my campaign; my opponents together spent close to $13 million.

I knew that in order for the campaign to work, everyone in the state needed to know that Jesse Ventura was a candidate for governor. Many people are not on the Internet. Many people don't read newspapers. But nearly everyone watches TV, so that's where I focused my campaign. I got on TV and promised the people that there would be no big-money power brokers behind the scenes, yanking their governor's chain. I promised I'd be there to serve the people, not the special interests. And I promised to be honest with them.

A lot of people laughed at the idea of this big, beefy feather-boa-wearing ex–pro wrestler and film actor as the head of state. OK, so maybe it's funny. But there are precedents. Other entertainers have successfully gone into politics: Ronald Reagan. Senator Fred Thompson. Clint Eastwood. Sonny Bono. Even Gopher from *The Love Boat*, Fred Grandy. I'll let you in on a secret about being an entertainer: It's all about communicating, about being able to see things from a bunch of different perspectives. There's a lot about entertainment that translates directly to the kind of public relations that you have to do in politics. When you're serving in a public office, you have to be able to communicate extremely well. It didn't bother me all that much that people laughed. To tell the truth, it bothered me more when they stopped laughing after the election.

It's strange how before this victory, nobody took me seriously. Now, suddenly, everyone's lost their sense of humor. Yes, I now have a heavy responsibility, which I take very seriously. But I'm still the same person I always was. It reminds me of Voltaire's quote about God being "a comedian playing before an audience that can't laugh." That applies to me, too—not to put myself on God's level, but people take me as far more serious than I am. I don't know where our sense of humor has gone in this country. I'm finding out that when I talk to the media, a lot of the time I have to throw up my hands and say, "That's a JOKE!"

Politics is not my life. I have a career in radio and another career in film. I have a wife who is the sweetest person in the world and two kids who are growing up into terrific, well-rounded people. I don't need or want to spend the rest of my life in politics. When I'm finished with my term as governor, I'm going back to the life that's waiting for me in the private sector. For one thing, it pays better. And for another, none of the other careers I've had in my life has kept me trapped in my own home and under surveillance twenty-four hours a day. I'm accustomed to answering only to myself and my family. Now I have to answer to the entire state of Minnesota. But I'm taking on this responsibility, willingly and voluntarily, because I have a vision for how to make things better. And as a citizen of the greatest democracy in the world, I have a duty to do my small part.

This is all new to me, and I feel a little like the Rodney Dangerfield character in *Back to School*. But I'll adapt. I'll do what needs to be done. The responsibility doesn't scare me. I've been through SEAL training. I've faced death and lived to tell about it. Nothing that happens in the next four years can possibly be as tough as that.

You can rest assured that I have plans for the next four years. I'm here to affect policy as much as I can. But no matter how the next four years go, I've challenged the status quo and won. I've restored people's confidence in our political system. I've awakened their hope. My victory is part of a much bigger picture. It's a wake-up call. It's the beginning of a political revolution.

PART THIRTEEN

The Media

71

HARRISON SALISBURY

From *A Time of Change*

Veteran reporter Harrison Salisbury looks back on several pivotal events in American politics, as he remembers his years as a New York Times *correspondent. First, we read about the assassination of President Kennedy through the eyes of the paper's national editor. Then, Salisbury recalls the violence and turmoil of the 1968 Democratic Convention in Chicago, as Mayor Daley's police attacked anti-war protesters in the streets. Salisbury's long tenure with the* Times *qualifies him to critique that great paper's coverage of those events: "The gap between hot reality in Chicago and the cool of the air-conditioned offices in New York was wide as an ocean."*

I HAVE SPENT most of my life on the front lines of reporting, and it has often been a stormy passage. I was thrown out of the University of Minnesota as editor of the college daily for my uppity campaigns against the administration. I nearly lost my first journeyman's job for my reports on the Great Depression in my hometown of Minneapolis. Stalin and Molotov threatened to expel me from Russia in World War II. Some editors of the *New York Times* wanted to fire me for my reports from Moscow; Moscow banned me from Russia for the same reports. Birmingham entered millions of dollars in libel suits because I warned that the city was going to blow up in race violence—which it did. Lyndon Johnson and the Pentagon exploded when I went behind the enemy lines to Hanoi during Vietnam.

So it has been, and that is the way it should be. If a reporter is not a "disturber of the peace," he should go into cost accounting. I said at the time of Hanoi that, if I was getting nothing but bouquets, I must be missing part of the story—the vital part. . . .

I got to know Jack Kennedy in the Presidential campaign of 1960. I covered both Kennedy and Nixon in that year, and I was not wild about either. I often spoke of Kennedy as a "lace curtain Nixon," by which I meant I did not think there was much difference, if any, in their ideology. That was not true, but there was, I think, a nubbin of truth in my remark. Nixon was shabby in character but had a better grasp of the world. He had seen more of it and thought more. Kennedy had style; there were not many reporters he didn't charm, but he was lazy. I think that had he not been martyred, his Presidential rating would be much lower.

Most newsmen thought Kennedy loved them. That was not true. I have observed every President since Calvin Coolidge. None of them loved the press. FDR, Kennedy, and Reagan were the best at conning the reporters, Hoover and Carter the worst. One of Harry Truman's most amiable traits was his honest dislike of reporters. He put up with the marriage of his beloved Margaret to Clifton Daniel, but it was a bitter pill that Clifton was a newspaperman.

Jack Kennedy gave me a lift one evening from West Virginia, where he was campaigning against Hubert Humphrey. He was on his way to Washington. The plane was a puddle-jumper, and only the two of us were aboard. He spent the brief ride cursing "those sons-a-bitches," the newspaper men. He had a big envelope of clips which he pawed through and tossed away. Most of them seemed to be pieces about his father Joseph, and most of them, Jack felt, went out of their way to dig up the old Joe Kennedy scandals—his borderline bank manipulations, his speculative deals in Wall Street, the maneuvers that got him the Scotch whiskey franchises and the great Chicago Merchandise Mart (where in prohibition days, the building almost empty, a huge speakeasy with a 100-foot bar was the liveliest activity under its roof—I often ate my lunch there), and his role as spokesman for America First* and appeasement before FDR yanked him out of London as the U.S. ambassador. "Bastards," gritted Kennedy as he leafed through the reports. "Just a bunch of lies. They never tell the truth. Bunch of bastards." I didn't talk up the case for newspapering. It was his father, and he was a true member of the clan—the Kennedys against the world and, in this case, against the newsmen. But I had been given an insight into the true Kennedy feeling about the press. One thing was certain about the Kennedys. You were with them or against them. Totally. The press was on the other side.

I don't want to suggest that Nixon had any more love for the press. I think the feeling of the two men was mutual in this regard. But Kennedy could put on a bravado act, make a half dozen important Washington correspondents believe they were real friends (inside the clan). Nixon was a poor actor. His lies stuck out like cold sores. He was forever wrapping his anger at the press in a sleazy tangle of "I know what your problems are," or "Of course you have your job to do," "I don't mean to include you personally," and then out would come the hurt and anger. I guess

*America First was a prominent "isolationist" organization in the 1930s. The group opposed American involvement in European affairs, especially our taking sides against Hitler's Germany and its expansionist policies.—EDS.

you could say that, in his way, Nixon was the more honest man. Jack rarely let his distaste show in public. . . .

By the time Jack Kennedy was shot to death in Dallas at 12:30 P.M. of November 22, 1963, a lot had changed for me. Reluctantly I had bowed to Turner Catledge's insistence and taken on the post of national editor of the *New York Times*. (Catledge coined the title "Director of National Correspondence" so as not to hurt the feelings of Ray O'Neill, who held the title "National Editor.")

Catledge's proposal had reached me in Kabul, Afghanistan, where I was trying to persuade the authorities to let me go through the Khyber Pass. A small war was in progress. I never did get to the Khyber, going to Tashkent, Bokhara, and Mongolia instead. I had to accept Catledge's proposal—much as I preferred reporting. He had twice tried to make me an editor, and I knew I couldn't say no a third time. But I did get his pledge that once or twice a year I could abandon my desk and go off on a reporting trip. The promise was meticulously kept by Catledge and Punch Sulzberger, even after I set up the Op-Ed page and became an associate editor of the *Times*.

I had concluded before going to work for the *Times* in 1949 that the essence of journalism was reporting and writing. I wanted to find things out—particularly things which no one else had managed to dig out—and let people have the best possible evidence on which to make up their minds about policy. It was essentially a gloss on the old Scripps slogan: "Give Light and the People Will Find Their Way." I have never ceased to believe in it.

One day in November 1963 I was sitting at the long table in the third floor dining room of the Century Club, waiting for my lunch.

At that moment, just on one o'clock, the waiter having brought my purée mongole, Alfred De Liagre, the theatrical producer, elegant as always in English tweeds, rounded into the room, raised his voice over the cheerful hum of Century conversation, and said, a bit theatrically: "Gentlemen, I am sorry to interrupt, but the President has just been shot in the head . . . in Dallas." I dropped my napkin, leaped down the stairs, and ran the two and a half blocks west on 43rd Street to 229, up on the elevator, and to my national news desk just south of my old spot, the Hagerty desk which I had occupied for nine years. There I would remain almost continuously for the next several days.

I was used to violence in the South, violence in the country as a whole. It seemed to me that I had inhabited a violent world since I had come back from the deceptive quiet of the Moscow streets—violence in the slums of Brooklyn and Manhattan, a nationwide uprooting of populations, technological revolution in the farm belt, the bondage of the great cities in straitjackets of steel and concrete freeways, and now rising terror in the South.

Dallas . . . Kennedy . . . violence . . . it seemed an almost inevitable pattern, and my mind leaped instantly to the passion in Dallas that had raged since before Kennedy's election. Dallas had seemed like another country, ranting against *everything*. I knew of the threats and the hate ads that spewed out before the Kennedy visit. I had hardly gotten on the telephone to order staff to Dallas—everyone I could reach who could fly in by nightfall—than my mind spun with thoughts of a conspiracy by the radical right or even—I hardly dared formulate the thought—by some in the die-hard LBJ camp who so hated the Kennedys. What it might be I did not know. But plots, conspiracy, coups raced through my head. From the vicious anti-Kennedy propaganda, there seemed to me but one short step to a conspiracy to assassinate the President. . . .

. . . On November 27, 1963, five days after Kennedy was killed, the first moment I had time and strength to put down what I felt, I wrote a memorandum to myself. I said that in the year 2000 the Kennedy assassination would still be a matter of debate, new theories being evolved how and why it happened. The lone, crazed killer would not then—or ever—be accepted. It offended nature. For the Sun King to be struck down by a vagrant with bulging eyes—no, the concept was repugnant to our very being. For a man so noble the cause of death must lie in high conspiracy, the most powerful courtiers, the great barons, the captains of the earth. . . .

It was no surprise to me that the Warren Commission report did not halt the "revelations," the rumors, the legend making of the conspiracy theorists, now grown to a kind of carrion industry.

I did not think the Warren Commission had dug out any essential fact that the *Times* had not found in its intense coverage in the days and weeks after the assassination. The coverage had begun with classic reportage—Tom Wicker's on-the-scenes eyewitness. It could not be beat. Tom was the only *Times* man in Dallas that day. I made one contribution to Tom's beautiful story. At 5 P.M. I ordered him—no, *command* is the word—to halt reporting and start writing. No interruptions. Any new details we could put into the piece, if necessary, after it went into type about 8:30 P.M. that night. Just write every single thing you have seen and heard. Period. He did. No more magnificent piece of journalistic writing has been published in the *Times*. Through Tom's eye we lived through each minute of that fatal Friday, the terror, the pain, the horror, the mindless tragedy, elegant, blood-chilling prose.

To this day not one material fact has been added to the *New York Times* account of the assassination and the events that followed it. . . .

Ever since I arrived at the Union Station from Minneapolis on a frozen January 13, 1931, I have thought of Chicago as *my* city. . . .

Nothing that happens in Chicago really surprises me. But the 1968 Democratic National Convention was an exception. I expected trouble. I expected violence. I expected the nomination of Lyndon Baines Johnson. I was right about trouble and violence. I was wrong—but perhaps not that wrong—about Lyndon.

On the night of August 28, 1968, a Wednesday, I was sitting at my command post in the press section of the convention hall at the Chicago Stockyards. I *knew* there would be violence. It had been building up.

Robert Kennedy had been assassinated in June in Los Angeles. Martin Luther King had been killed in Memphis in [April]. The country was going up in smoke. One afternoon I was running to board an airplane in Newark when I heard a young woman ask the man she was with: "What's all that smoke?" He (and I) looked back. "Oh," he said, "It's just Newark burning down. Let's hurry." From the takeoff I could see Newark's black ghetto burning in the rage of King's murder.

That was my America in the summer of 1968. No way that Chicago, Hog Butcher Chicago, Daley's Chicago, wouldn't explode.

I had arrived on the watch for a Draft Johnson movement. I hadn't believed LBJ was sincere in his March 31 speech.

Mayor Daley didn't seem to take LBJ's "withdrawal" any more seriously than I did. Daley had backed Robert Kennedy until Robert was killed, then switched to LBJ. He prepared a monster birthday party for Lyndon at Soldier Field. It sounded like a campaign kickoff to me. By this time the White House was leaking to every visitor nasty stories about Humphrey. He was a loser. "He cries too much." There was no doubt what the White House was up to. I was not amazed when on an inspection of the Chicago Amphitheater, I stumbled into a storeroom where LBJ placards, banners, and posters were stacked to the ceiling. Everything was set for the convention to rise and sweep LBJ into the nomination.

But nothing in Chicago went according to plan. The antiwar forces—David Dellinger, Tom Hayden, and the Yippies led by Abbie Hoffman—had mustered their supporters by the thousand. Daley mobilized his forces—8,000 police, 5,000 Illinois guardsmen (some 5,000 U.S. regulars were alerted and held in reserve). The convention hall looked like Hitler's last bunker, barbed wire coils everywhere, barricades, checkpoints outside and inside the hall. American politics had never seen such security.

Confrontation quickly became the order of the day. The decibel count went up and up. The higher it rose, the faster prospects for a Johnson coup de theatre faded. The Secret Service would not guarantee his safety. He was confined to his Texas ranch, on the telephone to Daley, but the Blue Helmets washed LBJ out with their street brawls. Daley had to cancel the Soldier Field birthday party. Those tons of LBJ banners never left the stadium bins. . . .

Behind cordons of police and barbed wire the convention hall was an island of quiet. Not so the central convention hotel, the Conrad Hilton, which spanned a long block on Michigan Avenue. The police beat and hounded young people from Lincoln Park down to Grant Park opposite the Hilton.

Tony Lukas, just back from the Congo wars, was handling the street story. He knew the protesters, the gentle pacifists, the wild radicals, the eccentric Yippies. He knew them all.

On Tuesday evening Wallace Turner, the best of the *Times's* investigative reporters, was walking back to his hotel. He spotted three or four squad cars blocking a street. In a courtyard he saw a huddle of police and heard a patrolman say: "Sergeant, can I have me a hippie to beat the shit out of?"

The next evening it started.

Tom Wicker was standing at the big window of the *Times* news room on the twenty-first story of the Conrad Hilton, looking down on Michigan Avenue, when he saw the police charge past the National Guardsmen into Grant Park. Several hundred youngsters sat there singing; "God Bless America." The Daley men burst among them, beating, kicking, and dragging them by the feet to paddy wagons. "These are our children!" Wicker exclaimed. Next day he wrote a column headed: "These were our children, and the police were beating them." His colleague Ned Kenworthy rushed for the elevator, down to the street, two blocks up Michigan and over into the park. "Get out! Get Out!" he shouted to the young people. "The police are coming. You're doing no good to your cause." (They were mostly Gene McCarthy supporters.)

Times reporter John Kifner was with the young people marching down Michigan. He watched the police charge, clubs and blackjacks swinging. He watched them drive young and old back against the Hilton and through the plate-glass window, shards splintering, police tumbling into the dark, air-conditioned, panel-lined bar, beating and slugging everyone in their path.

Kifner raced to a telephone. He got Charlotte Curtis on the line. She was filling in for Sylvan Fox, a deskman who had suffered a heart attack and been sent to the hospital by ambulance. Charlotte Curtis listened a moment to Kif and then handed the telephone to Lukas. "You better take this yourself."

At the stockyards I was going crazy. A *Times* photographer had been beaten and dragged off—no one knew where—by the police. I was on the phone to the hospital, to the police, to Lukas' post at Tribune Tower, to our main news room in the Hilton and, most of all, to New York, trying to convey to the editors that the story had shifted away from the convention hall, where the slow nominating process was underway, onto the Chicago streets. It wasn't politics this night; it was a riot. The editors found it hard to grasp.

Kifner was trying to get Lukas to understand. "I've just witnessed something unbelievable," Kifner told him. "The police have charged on a lot of innocent people and driven them through the glass window in the Hilton cocktail lounge, following them in and are beating them."

"Come on, John," said Tony. "Don't get carried away. Don't give me that stuff. I don't believe it."

"I saw it with my own eyes," Kifner insisted.

"You saw them inside, beating people up?"

"I did."

So Lukas wrote it. He knew Kifner was an experienced reporter. If Kifner saw it, it happened.

Kenworthy was writing what he saw, too, the young people singing, police charges, bystanders' reactions, 1,500 or 2,000 words. But trouble arose in New York. I got on the phone again and again, telling the responsible editors, Abe Rosenthal and night editor Ted Bernstein, that Chicago had gone into orbit. They didn't believe me. They thought the reporters had gone out of control. I told the editors to look at TV. The TV cameras were beginning to focus on the streets. Finally most of Lukas' story was published, but only a couple of paragraphs of Kenworthy. "We don't want to influence the convention balloting" was the excuse.

I knew it was hard for anyone to get the feel of Chicago that night, anyone who did not smell the teargas and vomit in the Hilton halls, who did not hear the crack of walnut sticks on skulls, who did not see the blood-stained carpets, who did not witness the police frog-walking people out of the hotel and into patrol wagons, flailing unfortunate youngsters, male or female, who appeared on the scene; you had to see the face of Mayor Daley, sitting in the front row of the Convention, mouthing "you son of a bitch" as Senator Abraham Ribicoff of Connecticut tried to remonstrate from the podium against the hatred loosed on Chicago that night by Daley and his men.

The gap between hot reality in Chicago and the cool of the air conditioned offices in New York was wide as an ocean. A news analysis that Lukas wrote of the "blundering" of Daley and the "brutality of his blue-helmeted police" said Daley and his police had turned certain defeat for the young radicals into a startling victory. This language was too blunt for New York. "Blundering" became "miscalculation" and "Brutality" became "over-reaction."

Nowhere in the *Times* the next morning was the true tragedy of Chicago delineated, the hideous blow to American democracy inflicted by Daley's truculence and the abandon of the young; the tawdry tainting of the nomination so grudgingly released by LBJ to hapless Hubert Horatio Humphrey. Nor did we catch the melodrama of LBJ's last hurrah, setting the stage for the triumph of Richard Nixon. I left Chicago convinced that LBJ was a "mean man." And I felt that I and my *New York Times* had fallen far short of our capability to present to the country a sharp-edge, unshadowed picture of Chicago. . . .

The *New York Times* electrified the nation in 1871 when it exposed the financial crimes of Tammany and the Tweed ring. It dozed through the Koch* years, even sending its outraged and brutally honest columnist, Sydney Schanberg, to the showers. The press drowsed along with the government and its opulent contractors until *Challenger* blew up. Nearly twenty years ago Emma Rothschild in *The New Yorker* forecast the demise of Detroit. It took David Halberstam's book to detail the sordid story not of Japanese skill but of American sloth. The press slept.

I could go on and on. The world of electronic journalism, once sparkling with men like Edward R. Murrow and Walter Cronkite, slipped into the gray wasteland, with bottom-line barons taking it over, men whose testicles seemed to have been replaced by puffballs. . . . The press yawns. Candidate after candidate rolls out of the electronic image processors. Nobody hires Sy Hersh to see what skeletons lurk behind their gussified hairdos. I mean real scandals, not Gary Hart trifles.

And no one complains of all this. Not the public, not Congress, not the White House—heavens, no, not the White House. Not opposition parties. Not the princes of the press—with a few honorable exceptions: the *New York Times*, the *Washington Post*, the *Boston Globe*, the *Los Angeles*

*Edward Koch was the mayor of New York City from 1979 through 1989.—EDS.

Times. The others are too busy with their accountants and tax lawyers. We sleep. Oh, a few eccentrics raise a paranoid cry of Conspiracy. But nothing breaks the somnolence. We are, it seems, as Lincoln Steffens found Philadelphia, corrupt and content. . . .

There is no story—literally none—which the great electronic news media and the billion-dollar press aggregates cannot extract, be it from the Kremlin or the Pentagon, and bring to the public of America. Instead, they tinker with sitcoms and fourcolor ad pages. Priorities? Forget it.

72

LARRY SABATO

From *Feeding Frenzy*

When political scientist Larry Sabato published his 1991 book on the media's role in campaigning, he gave a term to a phenomenon others had already seen: a feeding frenzy. The press en masse attacks a wounded politician whose record—or more accurately, his or her character—has been questioned. Every network and cable station participates, often without any real evidence to back up the rumor. Sabato's list of thirty-six examples ends in 1990; knowledgeable readers will be able to update the list. Paradoxically, the spectacular success of the Washington Post's *Bob Woodward and Carl Bernstein in investigating Watergate set the stage for recent feeding frenzies. Today, just the fear of being a media target may deter many qualified people from entering public service, Sabato notes.*

IT HAS BECOME a spectacle without equal in modern American politics: the news media, print and broadcast, go after a wounded politician like sharks in a feeding frenzy. The wounds may have been self-inflicted, and the politician may richly deserve his or her fate, but the journalists now take center stage in the process, creating the news as much as reporting it, changing both the shape of election-year politics and the contours of government. Having replaced the political parties as the screening committee for candidates and officeholders, the media propel some politicians toward power and unceremoniously eliminate others. Unavoidably, this enormously influential role—and the news practices employed in exercising it—has provided rich fodder for a multitude of press critics.

These critics' charges against the press cascade down with the fury of rain in a summer squall. Public officials and many other observers see journalists as rude, arrogant, and cynical, given to exaggeration, harassment, sensationalism, and gross insensitivity. . . .

Press invasion of privacy is leading to the gradual erasure of the line protecting a public person's purely private life. This makes the price of public life enormously higher, serving as an even greater deterrent for those not absolutely obsessed with holding power—the kind of people we ought least to want in office. Rather than recognizing this unfortunate consequence, many in journalism prefer to relish their newly assumed role of "gatekeeper," which, as mentioned earlier, enables them to substitute for party leaders in deciding which characters are virtuous enough to merit consideration for high office. As ABC News correspondent Brit Hume self-critically suggests:

> We don't see ourselves institutionally, collectively anymore as a bunch of journalists out there faithfully reporting what's happening day by day. . . . We have a much grander view of ourselves: we are the Horatio at the national bridge. We are the people who want to prevent the bad characters from crossing over into public office.

Hume's veteran ABC colleague Sander Vanocur agrees, detecting "among some young reporters a quality of the avenging angel: they are going to sanitize American politics." More and more, the news media seem determined to show that would-be emperors have no clothes, and if necessary to prove the point, they personally will strip the candidates naked on the campaign trail. The sheer number of journalists participating in these public denudings guarantees riotous behavior, and the "full-court press" almost always presents itself as a snarling, unruly mob more bent on killing kings than making them. Not surprisingly potential candidates deeply fear the power of an inquisitorial press, and in deciding whether to seek office, they often consult journalists as much as party leaders, even sharing private vulnerabilities with newsmen to gauge reaction. The *Los Angeles Times's* Washington bureau chief, Jack Nelson, had such an encounter before the 1988 campaign season, when a prospective presidential candidate "literally asked me how long I thought the statute of limitations was" for marital infidelity. "I told him I didn't know, but I didn't think [the limit] had been reached in his case!" For whatever reasons, the individual chose not to run.

As the reader will see later in this volume, able members of the news corps offer impressive defenses for all the practices mentioned thus far, not the least of which is that the press has become more aggressive to combat the legions of image makers, political consultants, spin doctors, and handlers who surround modern candidates like a nearly impenetrable shield. Yet upon reflection, most news veterans recognize that press excesses are not an acceptable antidote for consultant or candidate evils. In fact, not one of the interviewed journalists even attempted to justify an increasingly frequent occurrence in news organizations: the publication of gossip and rumor *without convincing proof.* Gossip has always been the drug of choice for journalists as well as the rest of the political community, but as the threshold for publication of information about private lives has been lowered, journalists sometimes cover politics as "Entertainment Tonight" reporters cover Hollywood. A bitter Gary Hart* observed: "Rumor and gossip have become the coins of the political realm," and the *New York Times's* Michael Oreskes seemed to agree: "1988 was a pretty sorry year when the *National Enquirer* was the most important publication in American journalism." With all the stories and innuendo about personal vice, campaigns appear to be little more than a stream of talegates (or in the case of sexual misadventures, tailgates).

The sorry standard set on the campaign trail is spilling over into coverage of governmental battles. Ever since Watergate,† government scandals have paraded across the television set in a roll call so lengthy and numbing that they are inseparable in the public consciousness, all joined at the Achilles' heel. Some recent lynchings such as John Tower's failure to be confirmed as secretary of defense,‡ rival any spectacle produced by colonial Salem. At the same time more vital and revealing information is ignored or crowded off the agenda. *Real* scandals, such as the savings-and-loan heist or the influence peddling at the Department of Housing and Urban Development in the 1980s, go undetected for years. The sad conclusion is inescapable: The press has become obsessed with gossip rather than governance; it prefers to employ titillation rather than scrutiny; as a result, its political coverage produces trivialization rather than enlightenment. And the dynamic mechanism propelling and demonstrating this decline in news standards is the "feeding frenzy." . . .

*Former Senator (D-Col.) Gary Hart's 1988 presidential candidacy ended after media revelations about his extramarital relations with Donna Rice.—EDS.

†Watergate began with the 1972 break-in at the Democratic National headquarters by several men associated with President Nixon's re-election committee. Watergate ended two years later with the resignation of President Nixon. Nixon and his closest aides were implicated in the coverup of the Watergate burglary. Tapes made by President Nixon of his Oval Office conversations revealed lying and obstruction of justice at the highest levels of government.—EDS.

‡In 1989, the Senate rejected President Bush's nominee for secretary of defense, former Texas Senator John Tower. Senate hearings produced allegations that Tower was an excessive drinker and a womanizer.—EDS.

The term *frenzy* suggests some kind of disorderly, compulsive, or agitated activity that is muscular and instinctive, not cerebral and thoughtful. In the animal world, no activity is more classically frenzied than the feeding of sharks, piranhas, or bluefish when they encounter a wounded prey. These attack-fish with extraordinarily acute senses first search out weak, ill, or injured targets. On locating them, each hunter moves in quickly to gain a share of the kill, feeding not just off the victim but also off its fellow hunters' agitation. The excitement and drama of the violent encounter builds to a crescendo, sometimes overwhelming the creatures' usual inhibitions. The frenzy can spread, with the delirious attackers wildly striking any object that moves in the water, even each other. Veteran reporters will recognize more press behavior in this passage than they might wish to acknowledge. This reverse anthropomorphism can be carried too far, but the similarity of piranha in the water and press on the campaign trail can be summed up in a shared goal: If it bleeds, try to kill it.

The kingdom of politics and not of nature is the subject of this volume, so for our purposes, a feeding frenzy is defined as the press coverage attending any political event or circumstance where a critical mass of journalists leap to cover the same embarrassing or scandalous subject and pursue it intensely, often excessively, and sometimes uncontrollably. No precise number of journalists can be attached to the term *critical mass*, but in the video age, we truly know it when we see it; the forest of cameras, lights, microphones, and adrenaline-choked reporters surrounding a Gary Hart, Dan Quayle, or Geraldine Ferraro is unmistakable. [The following table] contains a list of thirty-six events that surely qualify as frenzies. They are occasions of sin for the press as well as the politicians, and thus ideal research sites that will serve as case studies for this book. A majority (twenty-one) are drawn from presidential politics, while seven examples come from the state and local levels, with the remaining eight focused on government scandals or personal peccadilloes of nationally recognized political figures. . . .

Conditions are always ripe for the spawning of a frenzy in the brave new world of omnipresent journalism. Advances in media technology have revolutionized campaign coverage. Handheld miniature cameras (minicams) and satellite broadcasting have enabled television to go live anywhere, anytime with ease. Instantaneous transmission (by broadcast and fax) to all corners of the country has dramatically increased the velocity of campaign developments today, accelerating events to their conclusion at breakneck speed. Gary Hart, for example, went from front-runner to ex-candidate in less than a week in May 1987. Continuous public-affairs programming, such as C-SPAN and CNN, helps put more

Feeding Frenzies: Case Studies Used for This Book

From Presidential Politics	
1952	Richard Nixon's "secret fund"
1968	George Romney's "brainwashing" about Vietnam
1968	Spiro Agnew's "fat Jap" flap
1969	Ted Kennedy's Chappaquiddick
1972	Edmund Muskie's New Hampshire cry
1972	Thomas Eagleton's mental health
1976	Jimmy Carter's "lust in the heart" *Playboy* interview
1976	Gerald Ford's "free Poland" gaffe
1979	Jimmy Carter's "killer rabbit"
1980	Billygate (Billy Carter and Libya)
1983	Debategate (Reagan's use of Carter's debate briefing books)
1984	Gary Hart's age, name, and signature changes
1984	Jesse Jackson's "Hymietown" remark
1984	Geraldine Ferraro's family finances
1985/86	Jack Kemp's purported homosexuality
1987	Gary Hart and Donna Rice
1987	Joseph Biden's plagiarism and Michael Dukakis's "attack video"
1987	Pat Robertson's exaggerated résumé and shotgun marriage
1988	Dukakis's mental health
1988	Dan Quayle (National Guard service, Paula Parkinson, academic record, rumors such as plagiarism and drugs)
1988	George Bush's alleged mistress
From the State and Local Levels	
1987/88	Governor Evan Mecham on the impeachment trail (Arizona)
1987/88	Chuck Robb and the cocaine parties (Virginia)
1983/90	Mayor Marion Barry's escapades (District of Columbia)
1987	Governor Dick Celeste's womanizing (Ohio)
1988	Mayor Henry Cisneros's extramarital affair (San Antonio, Texas)
1989/90	Governor Gaston Caperton's "soap opera" divorce (West Virginia)
1990	Texas governor's election: drugs, rape, and "honey hunts"
Noncampaign Examples	
1973/74	The Watergate scandals
1974	Congressman Wilbur Mills and stripper Fanne Foxe
1986/87	The Iran-Contra affair
1987	Supreme Court nominee Douglas Ginsburg's marijuana use (and campaign repercussions)
1989	John Tower's losing fight to become secretary of defense
1989	Speaker Jim Wright's fall from power
1989	Tom Foley's rocky rise to the Speakership
1989/90	Barney Frank and the male prostitute

of a politician's utterances on the record, as Senator Joseph Biden discovered to his chagrin when C-SPAN unobtrusively taped Biden's exaggeration of his résumé at a New Hampshire kaffeeklatsch in 1987. (This became a contributing piece of the frenzy that brought Biden down.) C-SPAN, CNN, and satellite broadcasting capability also contribute to the phenomenon called "the news cycle without end," which creates a voracious news appetite demanding to be fed constantly, increasing the pressure to include marginal bits of information and gossip and producing novel if distorting "angles" on the same news to differentiate one report from another. The extraordinary number of local stations covering national politics today—up to several hundred at major political events—creates an echo chamber producing seemingly endless repetitions of essentially the same news stories. This local contingent also swells the corps traveling the campaign trail. In 1988 an estimated two thousand journalists of all stripes flooded the Iowa caucuses, for instance. Reporters not infrequently outnumber participants at meetings and whistlestops. . . .

Whether on the rise or not, the unfortunate effects of pack journalism are apparent to both news reporters and news consumers: conformity, homogeneity, and formulaic reporting. Innovation is discouraged, and the checks and balances supposedly provided by competition evaporate. Press energies are devoted to finding mere variations on a theme (new angles and wiggle disclosures), while a mob psychology catches hold that allows little mercy for the frenzy victim. CNN's Frank Sesno captures the pack mood perfectly:

> I've been in that group psychology; I know what it's like. You think you're on to something, you've got somebody on the run. How dare they not come clean? How dare they not tell the full story? What are they trying to hide? Why are they hiding it? And you become a crusader for the truth. Goddammit, you're going to get the truth! . . .

Sesno's crusader spirit can be traced directly to the lingering effects of the Watergate scandal, which had the most profound impact of any modern event on the manner and substance of the press's conduct. In many respects Watergate began the press's open season on politicians in a chain reaction that today allows for scrutiny of even the most private sanctums of public officials' lives. Moreover, coupled with Vietnam and the civil rights movement, Watergate shifted the orientation of journalism away from mere description—providing an accurate account of happenings—and toward prescription—helping to set the campaign's (and society's) agendas by focusing attention on the candidates' shortcomings as well as certain social problems.

A new breed and a new generation of reporters were attracted to journalism, and particularly its investigative arm. As a group they were idealistic, though aggressively mistrustful of all authority, and they shared a contempt for "politics as usual." Critics called them do-gooders and purists who wanted the world to stand at moral attention for them. Twenty years later the Vietnam and Watergate generation dominates journalism: They and their younger cohorts hold sway over most newsrooms, with two-thirds of all reporters now under the age of thirty-six and an ever-increasing share of editors and executives drawn from the Watergate-era class. Of course, many of those who found journalism newly attractive in the wake of Watergate were not completely altruistic. The ambitious saw the happy fate of the *Washington Post's* young Watergate sleuths Bob Woodward and Carl Bernstein, who gained fame and fortune, not to mention big-screen portrayals by Robert Redford and Dustin Hoffman in the movie *All the President's Men. As U.S. News & World Report's* Steven Roberts sees it:

> A lot of reporters run around this town dreaming of the day that Dustin Hoffman and Robert Redford are going to play them in the movies. That movie had more effect on the self-image of young journalists than anything else. Christ! Robert Redford playing a journalist? It lends an air of glamour and excitement that acts as a magnet drawing young reporters to investigative reporting.

The young were attracted not just to journalism but to a particular *kind* of journalism. The role models were not respected, established reporters but two unknowns who refused to play by the rules their seniors had accepted. "Youngsters learned that deductive techniques, all guesswork, and lots of unattributed information [were] the royal road to fame, even if it wasn't being terribly responsible," says Robert Novak. After all, adds columnist Mark Shields, "Robert Redford didn't play Walter Lippmann and Dustin Hoffman didn't play Joseph Kraft." (Kraft, like Lippmann, had a long and distinguished career in journalism.) . . .

A clear consequence of Watergate and other recent historical events was the increasing emphasis placed by the press on the character of candidates. As journalists reviewed the three tragic but exceptionally capable figures who had held the presidency since 1960, they saw that the failures of Kennedy, Johnson, and Nixon were not those of intellect but of ethos. Chappaquiddick, Spiro Agnew, and the Eagleton affair reinforced that view. The party affiliations and ideology of these disappointing leaders varied, but in common they possessed defects of personality, constitution, and disposition. In the world of journalism (or academe), as few as two data points can constitute a trend; these six together constituted an irrefutable mother lode of proof. "We in the press learned from experience that character flaws could have very large costs," says David Broder, "and we couldn't afford to ignore them if we were going to meet our responsibility." . . .

[A] troubling consequence of modern media coverage for the political system has to do with the recruitment of candidates and public servants. Simply put, the price of power has been raised dramatically, far too high for many outstanding potential officeholders. An individual contemplating a run for office must now accept the possibility of almost unlimited intrusion into his or her financial and personal life. Every investment made, every affair conducted, every private sin committed from college years to the present may one day wind up in a headline or on television. For a reasonably sane and moderately sensitive person, this is a daunting realization, with potentially hurtful results not just for the candidate but for his or her immediate family and friends. To have achieved a nongovernmental position of respect and honor in one's community is a source of pride and security, and the risk that it could all be destroyed by an unremitting and distorted assault on one's faults and foibles cannot be taken lightly. American society today is losing the services of many exceptionally talented individuals who could make outstanding contributions to the commonweal, but who understandably will not subject themselves and their loved ones to abusive, intrusive press coverage. Of course, this problem stems as much from the attitudes of the public as from those of the press; the strain of moral absolutism in portions of the American people merely finds expression in the relentless press frenzies and ethicsgate hunts. . . . *New York Times* columnist Anthony Lewis is surely correct when he suggests, "If we tell people there's to be absolutely nothing private left to them, then we will tend to attract to public office only those most brazen, least sensitive personalities. Is that what we want to do?"

73

HOWARD KURTZ

From *Spin Cycle*

During much of Bill Clinton's second term, rumor and scandal dogged the president. Some Americans believed the accusations and some did not. Some thought them relevant to the running of the executive branch; others did not. The White House responded to the media barrage by trying to influence the press's coverage. That's called spin, and journalist Howard Kurtz portrays the Clinton administration as masters of spin. He introduces us to several of President Clinton's then-spinmeisters and the techniques they used. But spin has its costs and as time went on, Kurtz feels, "the damage to his presidency would never be repaired."

. . . THE PRESIDENT'S APPROVAL RATING was hovering at around 60 percent in the polls, and for all the scandalous headlines and political bumps in the road, the country finally seemed to have grown comfortable with him. [Press Secretary Mike] McCurry and his colleagues had mastered the art of manipulating the press and were reaping the dividends.

And now, just when they thought they had survived the worst of the investigations and the harshest media scrutiny, the latest sex scandal had hit them like a punch in the stomach. They were reeling, depressed, uncertain of the facts but all too certain that Clinton's days might be numbered. The irony was inescapable: The president who worried so openly about his historical legacy, who staunchly insisted that Whitewater was nothing next to Watergate, might make history by following Richard Nixon into oblivion because he could not resist a lowly intern. For now, at least, McCurry and his colleagues could not spin their way out of this one. They did not know whether Bill Clinton was telling the truth about Monica Lewinsky, and some of them suspected he was not.

The White House spin operation had plenty of experience in crisis management. A yearlong investigation into campaign fundraising abuses and influence-peddling charges had built to a dramatic crescendo in the fall of 1997. On the morning of October 3, the Clintonites were once again on the defensive. The Justice Department had just decided to expand its investigation into questionable fundraising calls by Vice President Al Gore and was moving toward a stepped-up probe as well of Bill Clinton's frenetic efforts to raise campaign cash in the 1996 election. The relentless charges that the administration had improperly vacuumed up millions of dollars by crassly selling access to the president was now reaching critical mass. *The New York Times*, not surprisingly, trumpeted the new developments as its lead story.

But there was another article vying for attention that day at the top of the *Times*'s venerable front page, one that probably resonated with many more readers than were following the twists and turns of the latest Washington scandal. Four days earlier, one of the administration's least favorite investigative reporters, Jeff Gerth, who had long been tormenting

Clinton and his wife, Hillary, over the Whitewater affair, had weighed in with a lengthy *Times* report on how federal inspections of imported food had plummeted just as scientists were finding more outbreaks of food-borne diseases. In fact, Gerth had learned that David Kessler, the former head of the Food and Drug Administration, had failed to persuade Clinton to give his agency the power to bar imported food that did not meet American standards. The story was a major embarrassment, but Clinton had a genius for stealing good ideas from his enemies, even those he most despised in the press. And so the White House promptly staged a ceremony in the picturesque Rose Garden as Clinton proposed giving the FDA new power to ban imported fruit and vegetables, the very power he had refused to grant years earlier. Mike McCurry even credited the *Times* for its role in spotlighting the problem.

"I've never seen anything like it," Kessler told Gerth. "They're terrified of you." Still, the White House had managed to neutralize the dogged Jeff Gerth, who called McCurry to thank him for the acknowledgment.

The day's dueling headlines revealed a larger truth about the Clinton White House and its turn-on-a-dime ability to reposition its battered leader. The central mystery of Bill Clinton's fifth year in office was how a president so aggressively investigated on so many fronts could remain so popular with the American people. Indeed, his approval rating was nearly as lofty as that of Ronald Reagan at the peak of his powers, and with the economy humming along at an impressive clip, bad news was failing to make much of a dent in those numbers.

To be sure, Clinton's performance had helped create the sense that the country was doing just fine on his watch. But it was a carefully honed media strategy—alternately seducing, misleading, and sometimes intimidating the press—that maintained this aura of success. No day went by without the president and his coterie laboring mightily to generate favorable headlines and deflect damaging ones, to project their preferred image on the vast screen of the media establishment.

For much of Clinton's first term, these efforts to control the message were clumsy at best. . . .

The second-term lineup was more seasoned but less adventurous. Senior adviser Rahm Emanuel assumed Stephanopoulos's role of behind-the-scenes press handler. Special counsel Lanny Davis became the chief spinmeister on the burgeoning fundraising scandal, an effort crisply supervised by deputy chief of staff John Podesta. Communications director Ann Lewis handled the substantive planning. Chief of staff Erskine Bowles presided over the entire operation like the corporate executive he was. Counselor Doug Sosnik served up political advice, joined over the summer by colorful strategist Paul Begala and former journalist Sidney Blumenthal. McCurry stayed on for a final mission, determined to broker a cease-fire between the president and a hostile press corps. He and his colleagues were engaged in a daily struggle to control the agenda, to seize the public's attention, however fleetingly, for Clinton's wide-ranging initiatives. They had to manage the news, to package the presidency in a way that people would buy the product.

The small group of journalists who shouted questions at the press secretary each day in the White House Briefing Room had a very different agenda. They were focused, almost fixated, on scandal, on the malfeasance and misfeasance and plain old embarrassments that had seemed to envelop this administration from the very start. They were interested in conflict, in drama, in behind-the-scenes maneuvering, in pulling back the curtain and exposing the Oz-like manipulations of the Clinton crowd. It was their job to report what the president said, but increasingly they saw it as their mission to explain why he said it and what seedy political purpose he was trying to accomplish along the way.

When the reporters had the upper hand, the headlines were filled with scandal news, a cascade of Watergate-style charges that drowned out nearly everything else. Indeed, they had plenty of material to work with. The Whitewater investigation, which had dragged on throughout the first term, involved the Clintons' role in a complicated Arkansas land deal, their partnership with a crooked couple, and allegations of a subsequent cover-up. The Travelgate probe involved charges that the first lady had orchestrated the ouster of seven employees of the White House travel office so the work could be given to friends of the Clintons. The Filegate inquiry involved charges that White House aides had deliberately obtained the sensitive FBI files of prominent Republicans. The Paula Jones lawsuit turned on allegations by a former Arkansas state employee that Clinton, while governor, had asked for sex in a Little Rock hotel room. And the campaign finance scandal, in its broadest form, involved an alleged conspiracy by Clinton and Gore to use the perks of high office to solicit cash from foreign operatives, Asian American donors, and garden-variety fat cats, perhaps in exchange for political favors.

Against this dark backdrop, what the White House press operatives did was to launder the news—to scrub it of dark scandal stains, remove unsightly splotches of controversy, erase greasy dabs of contradictions, and present it to the country crisp and sparkling white. The underlying garment was the same, but it was often unrecognizable.

A larger challenge loomed as well—simply put, to change the subject, and to do so without the benefit of dramatic presidential action like fighting a war or battling a recession or tackling some grave national crisis. When the White House team broke through, they secured precious column inches and airtime for Clinton's proposals on national education standards or seat-belt enforcement or funding for mammograms, efforts that the president's people felt resonated far more broadly than the inside-the-Beltway obsessions of the media. . . .

The reporters' frustrations began to boil over in the final weeks of the 1996 campaign, when allegations first surfaced that foreign funny money had been funneled to the Clinton camp and the White House seemed unable or unwilling to provide answers. McCurry, who usually insisted on steering such questions to the White House lawyers, reluctantly assumed control of the scandal defense just days before the election. Even as Clinton and his compatriots celebrated his triumphant reelection in Little Rock, McCurry knew that they had kept the lid on a pressure cooker that was ready to blow.

As the fundraising scandal gathered steam, McCurry and his new ally, Lanny Davis, bore the brunt of the hostile media inquiries. Within the White House they battled for disclosure, for getting the bad news behind them. But there were limits to how far McCurry and Davis would go, documents they would not release, questions they would not answer. They insisted day after day that Bill Clinton and Al Gore had done nothing out of the ordinary in dialing for dollars, sipping coffee with shady Chinese operatives, or renting out the Lincoln Bedroom, even when an avalanche of embarrassing documents decimated their denials. A few mistakes, they maintained, but nothing the other side didn't do in spades.

The White House partisans were convinced that the public was tuning it all out, that most Americans viewed this as the typical Beltway follies, but the journalists were filled with moral fervor, determined that readers and viewers should care and that somehow they would make them care. The Clintonites were equally determined to rout the journalistic naysayers and prove that they could govern in this scandal-charged atmosphere. Neutralizing the media had become ground zero in the struggle for supremacy, and the spin would clearly be as important as the substance. . . .

Bill Clinton, Al Gore, and Erskine Bowles were in the Treaty Room, the president's private study in the residence, where he often watched CNN, on the evening of February 12. McCurry walked in around 10:30, having just dispatched an aide to the loading dock of *The Washington Post*, six blocks north, where you could buy the bulldog edition for a quarter. Even in an age when most newspapers were on the World Wide

Web, this was still the fastest way to get the next day's *Post*, especially if your business was damage control.

There it was, the paper's lead story, an ominous-sounding Bob Woodward bombshell. McCurry knew it was coming because he had been on the phone with Woodward. The four men and a few aides, seated on chairs and sofas, sat reading the handful of copies that had just come off the presses.

It was the strangest goddamn piece: the Justice Department had uncovered evidence that representatives of the People's Republic of China tried to direct foreign contributions to the Democrats before the 1996 election. The Chinese embassy was used for the planning, according to electronic eavesdropping by federal agencies.

That was it. Who was involved? What contributions did they direct? How much money? When did it happen? The story didn't say. Just a couple of tantalizing details from Woodward's legendary sources. What the hell did it mean? The president and the vice president and the chief of staff didn't know anything about it. They chewed over the story, tried to decipher its meaning like some ancient hieroglyphics. It seemed like a work in progress.

Still, they knew all too well that any story with Woodward's byline had a certain cachet around town. The tireless reporter had helped drive Richard Nixon out of this very house two decades earlier, was one of the heroes of the movie *All the President's Men*. The assembled officials recalled the scene in which Jason Robards, playing Ben Bradlee, threw a half-baked story back at Woodward and Bernstein and barked, "You just don't have it." Perhaps, it was suggested, a *Post* editor should have delivered that line on this story.

McCurry received few press calls about the piece that night. It was almost as if the entire Washington press corps was still trying to divine its importance. Upon convening the 9:15 gaggle in his office for about thirty reporters the next morning, he said: "I'm having a hard time making heads or tails of the story." He added that Clinton was "puzzled" by it but "very concerned" about the allegation. That was about all he could say.

Helen Thomas was dissatisfied. "Every question is like pulling teeth," she said.

"I'm being very careful, and you know from recent experience I have good reason to be very careful," McCurry said. "You got a problem?"

"Yeah, the problem is trying to figure out what's going on."

"I'm not breezy on this subject," McCurry allowed.

"I forgive you," Thomas said.

Administration officials were worried that the flap would overshadow the visit later that day of Israel's prime minister, Benjamin Netanyahu. At a photo session with the Israeli leader, Clinton asked the assembled reporters not to start a "feeding frenzy." He promised to take their questions later in the day.

McCurry held the two o'clock gaggle for the cameras. The briefing room, crowded with visiting Israeli journalists, was unusually noisy. On television it looked as though he had the audience's undivided attention. In the room, journalists were whispering along the wall, stepping outside for a smoke, walking in from lunch. It took all of McCurry's concentration to focus on the seven cameras mounted along a riser at the back of the room and ignore the chatter in the aisles.

McCurry began by referring questions on the possible role of the Chinese government to Deputy Attorney General Jamie Gorelick, who, as he well knew, wasn't commenting.

Wolf Blitzer, undeterred, tried a different tack: "How concerned is the president, though, that there is a story out there that there possibly could have been some improper Chinese government activity designed to influence us—"

"The story, while puzzling to the president, was of concern to him, and he fully expects that any matters like that would be properly investigated," McCurry replied.

Helen Thomas tried to get McCurry to detail the gist of the matter. "Can you explain why it is that the president is puzzled or what in particular it is that causes him puzzlement?"

"The story."

"Yes, but what about it?"

"The story, what's reported, the news in the story."

"But what about it is puzzling?"

"It just seems puzzling, the news of the story."

McCurry wasn't about to repeat the allegations for television. Let the reporters characterize it any way they wanted. He wasn't going to serve as Woodward's press agent.

Two hours later, fielding questions with Netanyahu, Clinton tried to frame the issue in general terms. "Obviously, it would be a very serious matter for the United States if any country were to attempt to funnel funds to one of our political parties for any reason whatever," he said.

The China story was all over the networks. "In Washington tonight, there's a major buzz in the highest circles over a page-one story in today's *Washington Post* about the possible role of the Chinese government in raising funds for the Democratic National Committee," Tom Brokaw said on NBC.

Over at CBS, Rita Braver reported that "White House insiders are genuinely puzzled and concerned about this report—especially the possibility it may be another indirect result of their aggressive fundraising tactics."

McCurry barely had time to catch his breath before the press found new grist for its ever-churning mill. The next morning the administration released more than one hundred pages of National Security Council documents in an effort to bolster the nomination of outgoing White House aide Anthony Lake to head the CIA. In one document an NSC official warned that a major Democratic contributor, Johnny Chung, was a "hustler" trying to exploit the Clintons; Chung was nevertheless allowed to bring six Chinese businessmen to watch the president's Saturday radio address in March 1995. Wolf Blitzer was on the lawn within an hour, standing on a rubber mat to avoid the muddy grass. "Some of these documents do contain additional political embarrassments for the White House," he said into the camera.

The White House decided to put Lanny Davis on the talk-show circuit that weekend. The shows had been clamoring for Davis for weeks, but the White House booker, Stuart Schear, kept saying he wasn't ready, wasn't sufficiently steeped in scandal minutiae. The real reason was tactical in nature. White House officials didn't like to put Davis on the weekend shows because that would trigger another round of scandal segments. Since Davis's sole mission was to clean up after the fundraising mess, his very presence set the agenda. But a critical mass of scandal stories had been building up, and the White House needed someone to respond to the charges. Schear sent word that Davis was available.

In the space of twenty-four hours, Davis spoke to Wolf Blitzer on *Inside Politics Weekend*, to Tony Snow on *Fox News Sunday*, to Tim Russert on *Meet the Press*. Davis had clearly decided to stay on defense. "I'm not here to make news," he told Fox staffers before the show. The litany of questions was remarkably similar: The alleged Chinese involvement in Democratic fundraising. The parade of thugs and favor seekers at the White House coffees. A new *Washington Post* report that the administration had changed its policy toward Guam after a visit by Hillary Clinton prompted $900,000 in contributions to the Clinton campaign and the party. Davis listened to the questions with a slightly bemused expression and then unleashed his rapid-fire answers, trying to finish each rhetorical salvo before he was interrupted.

"The president regards these allegations as very serious," he told Blitzer.

"No governmental action ever resulted from a contribution," he told Snow.

"There's no policy affected by contributions to this president," he told Russert.

Darting from studio to studio, Davis got the names confused. He called Tony Snow "Brit." He twice referred to Congressman McIntosh as McIntyre. But the only time he really stumbled was when he had to acknowledge that, for all his assurances that contributions did not change administration policy, he had never personally discussed the question with the president. Brit Hume quickly moved in, asking how often he had met with Clinton since becoming White House special counsel.

"Several times," Davis said.

"Three? Two?"

"I don't want to go into it any further than that," Davis said. . . .

The Washington Post was hours away from publishing a story that Kenneth Starr was investigating whether Clinton had had an affair with a twenty-four-year-old former White House intern, had lied about it under oath, and had urged her to lie as well. Sue Schmidt, the hard-driving Whitewater reporter so loathed by the administration, had the goods on the supposed affair involving Monica Lewinsky. Schmidt's colleague Peter Baker was calling Podesta for comment. A new crisis was about to explode. . . .

But the White House instantly paid a price for the years of aggressive spinning, for the evasive answers that had angered so many journalists through so many scandals. Most of the reporters automatically assumed that Clinton was lying, that he had in fact been carrying on with Monica Lewinsky and was pathetically trying to cover it up. They had been through too many bimbo eruptions, heard too many of Clinton's carefully hedged denials. When a shaky-looking Clinton sat down for a previously scheduled interview that afternoon with PBS's Jim Lehrer, he said that "there is no sexual relationship" with Lewinsky. Suddenly Begala's phone was ringing off the hook: Why did Clinton use the present tense? Was he leaving open the possibility of a past affair? Was he deliberately fudging once again? . . .

There were more dangers yet to come: Lewinsky's potential testimony to Ken Starr, possible accounts of sexual episodes from other women, the Paula Jones trial itself. *The Washington Post*, which had played down the Kathleen Willey tale that McCurry worked so hard to contain, now gave her account page-one prominence, noting that she maintained that Clinton had "fondled her breast and put her hand on his genitals." And in a rude reminder that the campaign finance investigation was still going strong, Charlie Trie, Clinton's old pal, was indicted for illegal fundraising. Still, there was little joy in this dizzying blur of a scandal, even for the hard-bitten reporters, for Clinton's conduct was so breathtakingly tawdry and the consequences so sad for the country.

By now, the Clintonites had retreated to what they were calling a "hunker-down strategy." They would not answer further questions about Lewinsky, and neither would Clinton. After days of insisting that the president wanted to gather the facts and tell his story, the White House made clear that he would not, perhaps for a long time. After more than a year of talking up a policy of full disclosure, they now resorted, in Nixonian fashion, to an all-out stonewall. McCurry lamely told reporters he was "out of the loop." The press secretary no longer wanted to know. This was about survival now. The administration had made the hard political calculation that the public anger was subsiding and they could ride out the storm. If many Americans thought Clinton was lying, so be it. He was far more popular than his media adversaries, the strategists reasoned, and that was what ultimately mattered. The journalists would continue to investigate, to fill the air with sexual charges, but the president would trump them simply by insisting that he was busy with the country's work.

As Bill Clinton dug in for the long haul, one could see, at long last, the limits of spin. When it worked, the coordinated strategy of peddling a single line to the press, of browbeating some reporters and courting others, was stunningly effective. Damage could be contained, scandal minimized, bad news relegated to the fringes of the media world. But each time an administration did that, each time it beat back the negative publicity with shifting explanations and document dumps and manufactured announcements designed to change the subject, it paid a price. The journalists were more skeptical the next time around, less willing to give the Clinton spin team the benefit of the doubt. At some point, even a reelected president dogged by endless scandal can no longer defy the laws of political gravity.

As Clinton remained mum about the details of what did or did not happen with Monica Lewinsky, his aides' efforts to counter the negative publicity without knowing the facts were all too transparent. They asked Mark Penn to take a poll to assess the damage. They uncorked all the techniques that had worked so well for so long—blaming the press, denouncing their accusers, assailing right-wing enemies, blitzing the talk shows. But even the best spin cannot work if it is totally untethered from substance, and, in the absence of hard information about the president and the intern, the loyalists' spin had become surreal. The press wasn't buying it, and neither was much of the public. The journalists were caught up in a frenzy of unprecedented intensity, with all sorts of uncorroborated allegations echoing through the headlines and the newscasts. But for a president who loved to fill the public space with great torrents of words, his silence was the loudest sound of all.

As the state of siege grew deeper, it remained unclear whether this would be the scandal that forced Bill Clinton from office or whether he would manage yet again to hang on. What was all too clear was that the damage to his presidency would never be repaired. Clinton's efforts to persuade the press that he had an ambitious second-term agenda, to reach a rapprochement with his media antagonists, to rise above his slippery public image, had failed. The spinmeisters could no longer save him from himself. The president would have his place in history, but it was not the one he had imagined.

74

MICHAEL LEWIS

From *Trail Fever*

Journalist Michael Lewis covered the 1996 presidential campaign by creating a day-by-day account of his reflections, starting with the winter primaries and ending after the fall election. Disillusioned with candidates Clinton and Dole, Lewis became caught up in the activities of lesser-known politicians. Here, he meets up with Arizona senator John McCain at various points in the campaign. McCain is not the typical public official, Lewis finds. They meet at the Vietnam Veterans Memorial; Lewis tells readers about McCain's service during the Vietnam War. Two months later, they meet again, at the Republican convention. McCain then surfaces at the Democratic convention. On the night of the election, the journalist finds Senator McCain with losing candidate Dole in Kansas. Lewis has one last memorable encounter with McCain in January 1997.

IF YOU LOOK LONG AND HARD ENOUGH at ugliness, you often find real beauty in it. On a clear dawn the toxic swamps that lie between Manhattan and Newark Airport are breathtaking, the more so because you expect them to repel. The presidential campaign of 1996 had, for me, the same surprising appeal. Most of what I had seen of the process I'd witnessed from the usual mediated distance. And so I expected to find empty speeches, hollow candidates, dirty tactics, and political operatives who made their living by telling people things that were not true. But I did not expect to find passion, or heroism, or heart-stopping eloquence. . . . I did not expect to find on the campaign trail so much of American life. . . .

The viewpoint in books about presidential campaigns is usually the view from the top of the food chain: the Making of William Jefferson Clinton; the Tragedy of Bob Dole. What is astonishing is how stilted and, ultimately, uninteresting that view has become. Bravery, adventurousness, engagement, a passionate devotion to ideas and principles, seem to be handicaps in politics, if your goal is to win. The view from the bottom of the political food chain was far more edifying. The man at the bottom of the food chain launched his rockets directly at the political process; he struggled with the great issues of the day—or, at any rate, what will very likely be the great issues of tomorrow. . . . If you cared to see the heroic possibilities of American politics, you were far better off seeking out the senator that Dole did *not* chose as his running mate (John McCain). . . .

The trick, I decide, is not to give in to their terrible lot of the winner's life—pretending that black is white and white is black, avoiding risk and adventure—but to find the sort of people who can help me to find another way. Happily, I do this on a beach in Florida, where resolutions come easy. A few yards down the road from the sterile skyscraper in Bal Harbour that houses Bob Dole's condominium, I take time off and search through my notes from the past few months. I figure that somewhere on the trail there must be other people like me, who dread the prospect of watching the shadows of Clinton and Dole creep through their peculiar world for the next seven months. Surely politics cannot be useful, or even educational, unless someone is willing to take a risk, or say something that might get him in trouble.

Two weeks later I return to Washington. I pick up the phone and call Senator John McCain.

April 19 I leave my hotel earlier than I need to and walk down from the Washington Monument to the Vietnam Veterans Memorial. Even at 7:30 a.m. the Mall is nearly deserted, the Lincoln Memorial empty. The Vietnam Veterans Memorial, on the other hand, is teeming with people who appear to have been up for hours, walking slowly along the length of the black marble slab bearing the names of the dead. For the next twenty minutes I sit on a bench dodging bird droppings and waiting for McCain, who has agreed to meet me here to talk about why successful political campaigns are the way they are. In my attempts to spot him at a distance I can't help but notice how differently ordinary people behave from politicians. Maybe fifty likely candidates pass through my line of vision, and not one of them could pass for a U.S. senator at one hundred paces. They comb their hair in public, scratch themselves, hold hands.

At eight on the button McCain appears at my side, looking very senatorial except for a pair of outrageously wide black aviator sunglasses with some undignified name—Hobbie? Hippo?—stenciled on the earpiece. He takes the seat on the bench beside me, and for a brief moment I feel I am in one of those movies about Washington in which the clueless protagonist gleans some crucial piece of information from the terrified insider, who is constantly glancing over his shoulder. Except that there is no single piece of information I know enough to seek, and McCain long ago decided he was going to be seen with whomever he pleases.

The campaign has moved back to Washington at least until early summer. Except for a handful of tactical speeches and photos, the candidates will shape public opinion of themselves on the job, in the Senate and the White House. The net effect of this is to turn up the heat on Capitol Hill, and senators with nerve are going to exploit the moment. In a couple of weeks I've just learned, McCain himself plans to rise on the Senate floor and attach his campaign finance reform bill to some unrelated piece of legislation. This will embarrass just about every other senator since many of them have spent their careers calling for campaign finance reform while at the same time doing everything they can to stop it from happening. Bob Dole is a prime example of this phenomenon. Probably McCain's bill will require Dole to embarrass himself explaining why he is *for* big money in politics.

What makes this so interesting is that McCain suddenly find himself at the heart of the Dole campaign. Since he appeared at his side on the stage in South Carolina, McCain has been the Dole surrogate most demanded, both by Dole himself and by audiences who want to see someone speak out on Dole's behalf—and it's not hard to see why. Few Republicans seem to care about the differences between the two men—though they might soon care more. For the moment what matters most to the people who wish to see McCain speak for Dole is the formative experience that the two senators ostensibly share: both nearly died in a war; both endured indescribable pain and suffering. Dole's ordeal is at the hollow center of his national campaign—to some extent it is his campaign. McCain's trials are less known. On October 26, 1967, when he ejected out of his navy jet and into a North Vietnamese mob, McCain suffered two broken arms, a shattered knee and shoulder, and bayonet wounds in his ankle and groin. Robert Timberg's gripping book, *The Nightingale's Song*, depicts McCain two months later, in his first prison cell:

> McCain weighed less than one hundred pounds. His hair, flecked with gray since high school, was nearly snow-white. Clots of food clung to his face, neck, hair and beard. His cheeks were sunken, his neck chickenlike, his legs atrophied. His knee bore a fresh surgical slash, his ankle an angry scar from the bayonet wound. His right arm, little more than skin and bone, protruded like a stick. But it was McCain's eyes that riveted [his cell mate George] Day. "His eyes, I'll never forget, were just burning bright. They were bug-eyed like you see in those pictures from the Jewish concentration camps. His eyes were real pop-eyed like that. I said, 'The gooks have dumped this guy on us so they can blame us for killing him,' because I didn't think he was going to live out the day."

McCain survived in captivity without medical treatment for the next five years, enduring torture so exquisite that even to read about it causes sweat to pop out on your brow: his captors would hang him by his broken arms from dangling ropes for hours on end, for instance. But the astonishing part of McCain's experience was its voluntary aspect. McCain is the third generation of a distinguished military family. His father was an admiral during the Vietnam War. The North Vietnamese hoped that this famous prisoner of war would violate U.S. military policy, which dictated that prisoners be returned in the order they arrived. In accepting their offer of freedom McCain would testify to the demoralization of American troops. For five and a half years his captors tried to torture him into going home. For five and a half years he refused to go.

As McCain reminisces, I realize I have made a tactical mistake. I am in the wrong place at the wrong time. I had hoped to talk to McCain about how Dole might react to McCain's plans to saddle Dole with a campaign finance reform bill. I had hoped to find out why it was that a man ostensibly so brave is frightened of his own shadow when forced to appeal directly to people for their votes. But it feels obscene to talk about such things in such places. My blunder is what the financial speculator George Soros calls a fertile fallacy, however. All by himself McCain is leading the conversation in a direction well worth following, toward one of the peculiar fault lines in our culture that guides American politics, almost without our knowing it.

We walk alongside the black granite slab against the oncoming traffic, then back again. The tourists pass us, stopping to get the feel of the place and to read the names. One sign of the memorial's success is that it has followed a path similar to those it seeks to commemorate. Like the veterans themselves, it has gone from being feared and loathed to being widely revered. The Park Service says the memorial has become the second most frequently visited site in Washington, after the Capitol. McCain admits that at first he found it depressing and even faintly antagonistic. But one day he was passing through on his own—he visits often by himself—and discovered a couple of veterans running their hands across the inscribed names. Clearly the two men had never met before, but they had fallen into conversation, swapped war stories, and in a few minutes were clutching each other and weeping. "If that kind of healing goes on," says McCain, "well, then it's a good thing."

Someone once said that an explanation is where the mind comes to rest. There is a feeling about McCain—one that seems lacking in Dole—that he has somehow explained his own experience to himself. He has assimilated his trauma differently than the candidate he's behind. "This is the McCain theory—and I think it's valid," he says. "I was an adult when I was shot down—thirty-one years old. I'd had a whole life. He was nineteen. What were you like when you were nineteen? I believe that everything Bob Dole has done since the war was dictated by that experience." The Vietnam veteran has achieved the kind of equanimity that is supposed to be available only to veterans of good wars. When Clinton arrived at the White House, for instance, McCain sent him a note saying that anytime the president wished to walk down to the Vietnam Veterans Memorial the senator from Arizona would be glad to walk alongside him. Clinton sent back a nice note. . . .

August 12 In the lobby of John McCain's hotel I am nearly plowed over by Steve Forbes, who has the unnerving habit of walking straight ahead without blinking, like a blind man. On my way into the restaurant I brush against the leg of a table occupied by Norman Mailer. By the time I reach McCain, who sits chatting with a senator from Alaska, I am almost too jaded to notice. Such is life at the Republican convention, where you can hardly strike up a conversation without being charged a lecture fee.

Ever since I met him late one night in a private air terminal in South Carolina, McCain has caused me problems. I know well enough how to talk to an important person who shades the truth; they all do that. But I don't know how to interview an honest man who occupies high political office. A strange reversal occurs whenever I speak with McCain. I know I should be plumbing him for information, trying to get him to say things he shouldn't, the usual journalist thing. But the minute he opens his mouth he says something impolitic on the record, and some inner voice cries out in me: "For God's sake, don t say that! There might be a journalist around!"

Somehow, despite his alarming preference for the truth, McCain's name ended up on the shortlist of possible running mates for Dole. Along with four others he was invited to submit the nineteen-page questionnaire prepared by Dole's rented strangers. A lot of the questions clearly were designed to expose and eliminate anyone who in their lives courted risk or adventure. For example:

> Have you or your spouse ever been publicly identified, in person or as a member of an organization that was identified with a particularly controversial* national or local issue? If so, please describe. [A footnote explains the asterisk: "Reference to 'particularly controversial' is intended to focus on issues that could be used, even unfairly, against you." Fully one third of the questions come with this warning.]

When I ask McCain why Jack Kemp, whom Dole has ridiculed for years, and not he was chosen, he laughs and says, "I've lived a rich and full life, my friend. A better life than you even. And when you do that you end up with a few skeletons in your closet." This is true. He went through a messy divorce. He was charged with (then exonerated from) aiding and abetting savings and loan crook Charles Keating in exchange for campaign contributions. But mainly what he has against him, I think, is his willingness to say pretty much what's on his mind. I'd like to think that Dole secretly enjoys this quality in McCain. ("Any man who has spent five years in a box," Dole has said, "is entitled to speak his mind.") But honesty is kryptonite to the rented strangers.

That's the other reason McCain may have been passed over: Dole's most senior staffers—Scott Reed and John Buckley—once worked for Kemp. Kemp's selection is the best evidence yet that Dole has given himself over entirely to them.

Nevertheless, a couple of weeks ago the Dole campaign asked McCain to speak tonight at the convention about honor and duty. God knows what this means to the rented strangers, though McCain believes it means a lot to Dole. McCain sent in a draft of a six-minute talk that the Dole campaign revised heavily. "No words more than two syllables" is how McCain describes the revision. Every freelance magazine writer knows the feeling, I say, then immediately realize McCain's position is different. At the time of this exchange he was a leading candidate to be Dole's running mate. That he told the rented strangers to stuff it could not have helped his cause, though the minute McCain pulled his speech the strangers caved and told McCain he could say whatever he wanted.

After breakfast McCain drops me at the convention center in time to see the chairman of the Republican National Committee, Haley Barbour, open the proceedings. Barbour played an important role in Dole's coronation. During the primaries, when the rented strangers were busy hiring pollsters to spread lies about Forbes and Buchanan, Barbour covered Dole's flank by telling the others he'd put a stop to it. Now he's addressing the two thousand delegates, all of whom, interestingly, paid their own plane fare to get here. Against this is set the fifteen thousand journalists covering the event, all on corporate expense accounts. Probably the best investigative journalism to be written about the 1996 Republican convention is the search for the journalist who has the least compelling reason to be here. Compared to the meandering editors of glossy New York magazines, the TV crew from the Netherlands has the keening urgency of firefighters during a roaring blaze. ("I think I secured the Dutch vote," says McCain, after a brief interview with them.) . . .

August 29 I had been investigating what turned out to be a false rumor that the city of Chicago had renovated only the sides of the Henry Horner housing project visible from the United Center. On my way back from the ghetto, in the desolate no-man's-land created by a phalanx of police officers between the Democratic convention and the poor, I bump into John McCain. The shock of finding a Republican outside the Democratic convention is followed by a disturbingly pleasant sensation. I'm beginning to understand the war that must occur inside a fourteen-year-old boy who discovers he is more sexually attracted to boys than to girls. The longer I hang around McCain the harder it is to fight the feeling that just maybe I'm . . . Republican.

McCain has become so involved with the Dole campaign that he might as well be the candidate. His assignment for the next few days is to travel south from Chicago through Missouri and Kentucky, keeping one day ahead of the buses Clinton will ride out of town in the morning. The idea, as I understand him, is to poison the local media against the president, which sounds like fun. Tonight he's been stirring up trouble at the TV stations covering the convention; now he is headed out to a rich Chicago suburb for a big fund-raiser. Suddenly I face a choice: to go with McCain, or to stay behind and watch Al Gore's acceptance speech. No sane person would stay behind.

On the way out of town McCain shows me a small album of photographs from the Republican convention. After Morry Taylor, Pat Buchanan, and perhaps Colin Powell, I think McCain had the most interesting experience in San Diego. After he gave his speech in prime time on Monday night he assumed he was finished; but then on Tuesday night he got the call. "It's the *night* before the nominating speech," says McCain, "and my portable phone rings. A voice says, 'McCain, will you nominate me?' It's Dole. You know, what are you going to say? 'It'd be an honor,' I say. Dole says, 'Okay, we'll be in touch.' Then he hangs up."

There are any number of things that are remarkable about this anecdote. First, that in a campaign as thickly greased with hired strangers as any in American history no one thought to drum up a nominating speech. The Dole campaign plans its trips to the bathroom four days before it goes. Yet Dole waited until the day before the event to select his nominator. Second, that the speech came off better than anything the hired strangers have done when they've been given time to plan and scheme. (Is it possible that it came off so well *because* it was spontaneous? And that Dole procrastinated precisely so that the pros wouldn't get their grubby paws on it?) And finally, that Dole chose McCain, who in the early primaries backed Phil Gramm. Some would say that this is merely another illustration of Dole's willingness to do anything to increase his chances of winning, like his selection of Kemp as his running mate. I'd prefer to think not. Dole is forever being painted as vindictive, on the basis of a handful of sound bites ("Stop lying about my record"). In fact, he has shown himself in his actions over and again to be admirably free of the quality. Last year, when McCain came out for Gramm, Dole took him aside and said not to worry: "When this thing is all over, we'll be together."

After forty-five minutes on the road McCain and I find ourselves in an enormous house in a rich neighborhood. About one hundred prosperous people mingle with drinks in their hands beneath Impressionist paintings, discussing just about everything except what has brought them together. The only people who look slightly out of place are the Illinois Republican candidate for Senate, Al Salvi, in his middle-class polyester suit, and his wife. The slight tension is dispelled, however, when Salvi's wife accidentally knocks over a crystal lamp. "Hope you have liability insurance," someone shouts, and the crowd breaks out in knowing laughter: everyone understands liability insurance. Everyone has property to lose.

The exact words spoken are not nearly as interesting as the tone of the event, which is that of a private club gathered to discuss its affairs. At length, Salvi introduces McCain, who performs what is essentially a stand-up comedy routine written for an audience of people who make more than half a million dollars a year. "I want to thank Rich for hosting this event in his modest middle-income tract home," he begins. "The difference between us and President Clinton is that President Clinton believes that everyone should own a home. Rich and I believe that everyone should own a home like this." It turns out that McCain has done a lot of these events, and in his experience the folks are interested not in what Al Salvi has to offer America but in being humored. The host knows this, too. He goads McCain to give the crowd what it's after: "Tell them how Dole asked you to nominate him," he says. Politics—as opposed to McCain's celebrity—becomes immediately superfluous. "The good news is that Al Salvi has enough money to win this race," McCain concludes, gamely. "The bad news is that some of that money is still in your pockets." . . .

November 5 The mood on Election Day in Russell, Kansas, is much like the mood of the Dole campaign: on the surface, a great deal of hope and, just below it, a lot of anger. In nineteen speeches over two days Dole failed even to mention Russell or his upbringing. I first realized that Russell was being phased out of the Dole campaign, and out of Dole's life, when I asked Scott Reed how long Dole was planning to be there on Election Day. Reed made a sign with his hands of a plane touching down and taking off again, quickly. That the Dole campaign would not spend a night in town would come as news to the local motels, which the Dole campaign had reserved.

Still, I think people here really believe it when they say Dole is going to win. Bub Dawson, whose family drugstore employed Dole, talks about the "hoopla" that will overwhelm the town after the victory. But resentment is swelling in Russell—of Clinton, who only a few months ago was more laughed at here than hated, and of everything and everyone who is perceived to have helped him. After breakfast I am assaulted by a woman who accuses me of being a member of the liberal media. "He's a sleazy draft dodger!" she hollers, until finally I am forced to tell her that I didn't vote for Clinton. "You voted for Dole?" she says, incredulously. "Ralph Nader," I say. "Well, that's just stupid," she says, but the fury has gone out of her.

By 10:30 a.m. Main Street is lined on both sides with the town residents, who, curiously, seem to be either very young children or very old people. In Russell you always wonder where the parents have gone. At noon the Dole motorcade pulls up to the First Christian Church, and the Doles go inside to vote. One look at the reporters' drawn faces and I'm grateful for being non grata on the Dole plane, though of course in these situations you always wonder what might have been. Dole walks into the church, picks up his ballot from five elderly ladies, mentions that he is nervous because he's never voted for himself for president, and then vanishes behind a blue cloth curtain. There he stands at a metal shelf, steadying his ballot with a miniature limestone fence post that is, aside from Dole memorabilia, about the only souvenir you can buy in a Russell gift shop.

Until now in the campaign Dole usually has been surrounded by bigwigs. Everywhere he goes Dole is accompanied by governors and senators. But today, the final day of the campaign, the day Dole will discover that he never will be president, the governors and the senators seem to have vanished. At his side in the church there is no one but his wife and daughter. Even the rented strangers are thin on the ground. The paper today reports that Dole's former media adviser, Don Sipple, has suddenly realized that Dole shouldn't be running for president. "I don't think he would be a particularly good president," said Sipple. "There's the lack of communication skills, the indecisiveness, the obsession with self-reliance."

But just as it appears that Dole has been left by himself to carry the carpetbag of defeat I notice Senator John McCain, standing off to one side in aviator sunglasses and a baseball cap pulled down low over his brow. A few weeks ago in Phoenix I watched McCain rearrange his schedule over the protest of his staff so that he could be with Dole on Election Day. The staffers thought the senator should be back in Arizona celebrating probable victory with Republican freshman J. D. Hayworth. (Hayworth won by six hundred votes.) McCain thought he should be on the road coping with probable defeat with Dole. "I would think the time he might need a friend would be that night," he said back then. And so here he is, in Russell, Kansas, lecturing a reporter who would rather hear about the despair in the front of the plane than Bob Dole's place in American history. "I predict to you," I can hear him saying, "that Bob Dole's picture, win or lose, will one day hang in the lobby of the U.S. Senate."

I slip through the Russell police force to say hello. McCain tells me with real wonder in his voice that he's just heard that Lamar Alexander planned to be in Des Moines tomorrow to be followed by Steve Forbes on Thursday, laying the foundation for their presidential campaigns in 2000. Even before the campaign ends it is starting again, which of course means that it never ends. We talk about this and that until finally McCain says, by the by, almost apologetically, "I wouldn't be here if I thought he was going to win." . . .

January 23 I eat lunch with John McCain just a few hours before he's meant to go meet in the Oval Office with President Clinton. McCain's campaign finance reform bill, which failed to pass the last Congress, is the flavor of the month, especially with a White House plagued with campaign finance scandals. Clinton wants to be seen to support reform; and perhaps he actually does support it. But he is a very new crusader against the need for big money in politics: He himself spent a record $175 million on his reelection campaign. And he has a new reason to posture in front of McCain. When South Dakota senator Larry Pressler lost his race for reelection McCain ascended to the chairmanship of the Senate Commerce Committee. Immediately he announced his intention to hold investigative hearings into the Commerce Department. Under Clinton, we now know, the Commerce Department has been used to raise money from various shady foreigners for the Democratic Party. The smartest thing Clinton could do at this point is to court McCain.

As McCain explains how his bill—even with Clinton's support—will probably be killed, I am reminded once more that he is unlike most people who do what he does for a living in his taste for a losing or unpopular cause. I understand that this benefits him at some level in that it distinguishes him from the great mass of politicians and leads many people to admire him. I understand that he cannot push his courage too far without ending his career. Nevertheless, there is something extraordinary about the way he seeks out trouble to avoid violating his sense of who he must be. And it never fails to allay somewhat my general misgivings about democracy as currently practiced.

I have an image of McCain fixed in my mind that I can't quite shake. He is standing alone in the dark on the wrong side of a chain-link fence outside the Democratic convention. Inside, CNN is waiting to interview him, only he doesn't have a pass to get to them. The guards drop their pose of callous indifference and begin to shift uneasily. Their admiration for the senator's war record (they all know about it) exceeds their interest in their immediate authority. If McCain made the slightest issue of being blocked from entering they'd let him by. But he doesn't. He just stands there waiting, for maybe twenty minutes, with his hands shoved deep in his pockets.

And then a young woman who works for him rushes up, carrying a cell phone. McCain takes a series of calls from Arizona reporters. The mayor of Tempe has just been exposed as a homosexual. The revelation, in Arizona, could kill a politician; indeed, it might tarnish a politician too closely associated with the victim. All of the reporters are calling to see what McCain thinks, and McCain doesn't hesitate to tell them. Standing in the dark beside the chain-link fence outside the United Center he takes the phone and says, over and over, "The mayor of Tempe is a friend of mine. He is a fine man. Who the hell cares if he is gay?"

PART FOURTEEN

Civil Liberties and Civil Rights

75

ANTHONY LEWIS

From *Gideon's Trumpet*

Written in 1964, Gideon's Trumpet *is one of the most-assigned books in American government courses. The excerpt presented here touches on all the major points in the legal and personal story of Clarence Earl Gideon, the Florida prisoner whose case,* Gideon v. Wainwright *(1963), transformed American justice. As Gideon's story unfolds, notice the following elements in journalist Anthony Lewis's account of the landmark case that ensured all defendants legal counsel in state criminal cases:* in forma pauperis; *writ of certiorari;* Betts v. Brady; stare decisis; *Attorney Abe Fortas; Fourteenth Amendment; selective incorporation of the Bill of Rights; "a great marble temple"; "Oyez, oyez, oyez"; Justice Black; 9–0; court-appointed attorney Fred Turner; public defenders; not guilty; the Bay Harbor Poolroom.*

IN THE MORNING MAIL of January 8, 1962, the Supreme Court of the United States received a large envelope from Clarence Earl Gideon, prisoner No. 003826, Florida State Prison, P.O. Box 221, Raiford, Florida. Like all correspondence addressed to the Court generally rather than to any particular justice or Court employee, it went to a room at the top of the great marble steps so familiar to Washington tourists. There a secretary opened the envelope. As the return address had indicated, it was another petition by a prisoner without funds asking the Supreme Court to get him out of jail—another, in the secretary's eyes, because pleas from prisoners were so familiar a part of her work. . . .

. . . A federal statute permits persons to proceed in any federal court *in forma pauperis*, in the manner of a pauper, without following the usual forms or paying the regular costs. The only requirement in the statute is that the litigant "make affidavit that he is unable to pay such costs or give security therefor."

The Supreme Court's own rules show special concern for *in forma pauperis* cases. Rule 53 allows an impoverished person to file just one copy of a petition, instead of the forty ordinarily required, and states that the Court will make "due allowance" for technical errors so long as there is substantial compliance. In practice, the men in the Clerk's Office—a half dozen career employees, who effectively handle the Court's relations with the outside world—stretch even the rule of substantial compliance. Rule 53 also waives the general requirement that documents submitted to the Supreme Court be printed. It says that *in forma pauperis* applications should be typewritten "whenever possible," but in fact handwritten papers are accepted.

Gideon's were written in pencil. They were done in carefully formed printing, like a schoolboy's, on lined sheets evidently provided by the Florida prison. Printed at the top of each sheet, under the heading Correspondence Regulations, was a set of rules ("Only 2 letters each week . . . written on one side only . . . letters must be written in English . . . ") and the warning: MAIL WILL NOT BE DELIVERED WHICH DOES NOT CONFORM TO THESE RULES. Gideon's punctuation and spelling were full of surprises, but there was also a good deal of practiced, if archaic, legal jargon, such as "Comes now the petitioner . . . ".

Gideon was a fifty-one-year-old white man who had been in and out of prisons much of his life. He had served time for four previous felonies, and he bore the physical marks of a destitute life: a wrinkled, prematurely aged face, a voice and hands that trembled, a frail body, white hair. He had never been a professional criminal or a man of violence; he just could not seem to settle down to work, and so he had made his way by gambling and occasional thefts. Those who had known him, even the men who had arrested him and those who were now his jailers, considered Gideon a perfectly harmless human being, rather likeable, but one tossed aside by life. Anyone meeting him for the first time would be likely to regard him as the most wretched of men.

And yet a flame still burned in Clarence Earl Gideon. He had not given up caring about life or freedom; he had not lost his sense of injustice. Right now he had a passionate—some thought almost irrational—feeling of having been wronged by the State of Florida, and he had the determination to try to do something about it. Although the Clerk's Office could not be expected to remember him, this was in fact his second petition to the Supreme Court. The first had been returned for failure to include a pauper's affidavit, and the Clerk's Office had enclosed a copy of the rules and a sample affidavit to help him do better next time. Gideon persevered. . . .

Gideon's main submission was a five-page document entitled "Petition for a Writ of Certiorari Directed to the Supreme Court State of Florida." A writ of certiorari is a formal device to bring a case up to the Supreme Court from a lower court. In plain terms Gideon was asking the Supreme Court to hear his case.

What was his case? Gideon said he was serving a five-year term for "the crime of breaking and entering with the intent to commit a misdemeanor, to wit, petty larceny." He had been convicted of breaking into the Bay Harbor Poolroom in Panama City, Florida. Gideon said his conviction violated the due-process clause of the Fourteenth Amendment to the Constitution, which provides that "No state shall . . . deprive any person of life, liberty, or property, without due process of law." In what way had Gideon's trial or conviction assertedly lacked "due process of law"? For two of the petition's five pages it was impossible to tell. Then came this pregnant statement:

"When at the time of the petitioners trial he ask the lower court for the aid of counsel, the court refused this aid. Petitioner told the court that this Court made decision to the effect that all citizens tried for a felony crime should have aid of counsel. The lower court ignored this plea."

Five more times in the succeeding pages of his penciled petition Gideon spoke of the right to counsel. To try a poor man for a felony without giving him a lawyer, he said, was to deprive him of due process of law. There was only one trouble with the argument, and it was a problem Gideon did not mention. Just twenty years before, in the case of *Betts v. Brady*, the Supreme Court had rejected the contention that the due-process clause of the Fourteenth Amendment provided a flat guarantee of counsel in state criminal trials.

Betts v. Brady was a decision that surprised many persons when made and that had been a subject of dispute ever since. For a majority of six to three, Justice Owen J. Roberts said the Fourteenth Amendment provided no universal assurance of a lawyer's help in a state criminal trial. A lawyer was constitutionally required only if to be tried without one amounted to "a denial of fundamental fairness." . . .

Later cases had refined the rule of *Betts v. Brady*. To prove that he was denied "fundamental fairness" because he had no counsel, the poor man had to show that he was the victim of what the Court called "special circumstances." Those might be his own illiteracy, ignorance, youth, or mental illness, the complexity of the charge against him or the conduct of the prosecutor or judge at the trial. . . .

But Gideon did not claim any "special circumstances." His petition made not the slightest attempt to come within the sophisticated rule of *Betts v. Brady*. Indeed, there was nothing to indicate he had ever heard of the case or its principle. From the day he was tried Gideon had had one idea: That under the Constitution of the United States he, a poor man, was flatly entitled to have a lawyer provided to help in his defense. . . .

Gideon was wrong, of course. The United States Supreme Court had not said he was entitled to counsel; in *Betts v. Brady* and succeeding cases it had said quite the opposite. But that did not necessarily make Gideon's petition futile, for the Supreme Court never speaks with absolute finality when it interprets the Constitution. From time to time—with due solemnity, and after much searching of conscience—the Court has overruled its own decisions. Although he did not know it, Clarence Earl Gideon was calling for one of those great occasions in legal history. He was asking the Supreme Court to change its mind. . . .

Clarence Earl Gideon's petition for certiorari inevitably involved, for all the members of the Court, the most delicate factors of timing and strategy. The issue he presented—the right to counsel—was undeniably of first-rank importance, and it was an issue with which all of the justices were thoroughly familiar. . . .

. . . Professional comment on the Betts case, in the law reviews, had always been critical and was growing stronger, and within the Supreme Court several justices had urged its overruling. On the other hand, a majority might well draw back from so large a step. . . . At the conference of June 1, 1962, the Court had before it two jurisdictional statements asking the Court to hear appeals, twenty-six petitions for certiorari on the Appellate Docket, ten paupers' applications on the Miscellaneous Docket and three petitions for rehearing. . . .

The results of the deliberations at this conference were made known to the world shortly after ten A.M. the following Monday, June 4th, when a clerk posted on a bulletin board the mimeographed list of the Supreme Court's orders for that day. One order read:

Gideon v. Cochran 890 Misc.

The motion for leave to proceed *in forma pauperis* and the petition for writ of certiorari are granted. The case is transferred to the appellate docket. In addition to other questions presented by this case, counsel are requested to discuss the following in their briefs and oral argument:

"Should this Court's holding in *Betts v. Brady*, 316 U.S. 455, be reconsidered?" . . .

In the Circuit Court of Bay County, Florida, Clarence Earl Gideon had been unable to obtain counsel, but there was no doubt that he could have a lawyer in the Supreme Court of the United States now that it had agreed to hear his case. It is the unvarying practice of the Court to appoint a lawyer for any impoverished prisoner whose petition for review has been granted and who requests counsel.

Appointment by the Supreme Court to represent a poor man is a great honor. For the eminent practitioner who would never, otherwise, dip his fingers into the criminal law it can be an enriching experience, making him think again of the human dimensions of liberty. It may provide the first, sometimes the only, opportunity for a lawyer in some distant corner of the country to appear before the Supreme Court. It may also require great personal sacrifice. There is no monetary compensation of any kind—only the satisfaction of service. The Court pays the cost of the lawyer's transportation to Washington and home, and it prints the briefs, but there is no other provision for expenses, not even secretarial help or a hotel room. The lawyer donates that most valuable commodity, his own time. . . .

The next Monday the Court entered this order in the case of *Gideon v. Cochran:*

"The motion for appointment of counsel is granted and it is ordered that Abe Fortas, Esquire, of Washington, D.C., a member of the Bar of this Court be, and he is hereby, appointed to serve as counsel for petitioner in this case.

Abe Fortas is a high-powered example of that high-powered species, the Washington lawyer. He is the driving force in the firm of Arnold, Fortas and Porter. . . . A lawyer who has worked with him says: "Of all the men I have met he most knows why he is doing what he does. I don't like the s.o.b., but if I were in trouble I'd want him on my side. He's the most resourceful, the boldest, the most thorough lawyer I know." . . .

. . . "The real question," Fortas said, "was whether I should urge upon the Court the special-circumstances doctrine. As the record then stood, there was nothing to show that he had suffered from any special circumstances. . . .

When that transcript was read at Arnold, Fortas and Porter, there was no longer any question about the appropriateness of this case as the vehicle to challenge *Betts v. Brady.* Plainly Gideon was not mentally defective. The charge against him, and the proof, were not particularly complicated. The judge had tried to be fair; at least there was no overt bias in the courtroom. In short, Gideon had not suffered from any of the special circumstances that would have entitled him to a lawyer under the limited rule of *Betts v. Brady.* And yet it was altogether clear that a lawyer would have helped. The trial had been a rudimentary one, with a prosecution case that was fragmentary at best. Gideon had not made a single objection or pressed any of the favorable lines of defense. An Arnold, Fortas and Porter associate said later: "We knew as soon as we read that transcript that here was a perfect case to challenge the assumption of *Betts* that a man could have a fair trial without a lawyer. He did very well for a layman, he acted like a lawyer. But it was a pitiful effort really. He may have committed this crime, but it was never proved by the prosecution. A lawyer—not a great lawyer, just an ordinary, competent lawyer—could have made ashes of the case." . . .

As Abe Fortas began to think about the case in the summer of 1962, before Justice Frankfurter's retirement, it was clear to him that overruling *Betts v. Brady* would not come easily to Justice Frankfurter or others of his view. This was true not only because of their judicial philosophy in general, but because of the way they had applied it on specific matters. One of these was the question of precedent.

"In most matters it is more important that the applicable rule of law be settled than that it be settled right." Justice Brandeis thus succinctly stated the basic reason for *stare decisis*, the judicial doctrine of following precedents. . . .

Another issue . . . cut even deeper than *stare decisis*, and closer to Gideon's case. This was their attitude toward federalism—the independence of the states in our federal system of government. . . .

The Bill of Rights is the name collectively given to the first ten amendments to the Constitution, all proposed by the First Congress of the United States in 1789 and ratified in 1791. The first eight contain the guarantees of individual liberty with which we are so familiar: freedom of speech, press, religion and assembly; protection for the privacy of the home; assurance against double jeopardy and compulsory self-incrimination; the right to counsel and to trial by jury; freedom from cruel and unusual punishments. At the time of their adoption it was universally agreed that these eight amendments limited only the Federal Government and its processes. . . .

There matters stood until the Fourteenth Amendment became part of the Constitution in 1868. A product of the Civil War, it was specifically designed to prevent abuse of individuals by state governments. Section 1 provided: "No State shall make or enforce any law which shall abridge the privileges or immunities of citizens of the United States; nor shall any State deprive any person of life, liberty, or property, without due process of law; nor deny to any person within its jurisdiction the equal protection of the laws." Soon the claim was advanced that this section had been designed by its framers to *incorporate*, and apply to the states, all the provisions of the first eight amendments.

This theory of wholesale incorporation of the Bill of Rights has been adopted by one or more Supreme Court justices from time to time, but never a majority. . . .

But if wholesale incorporation has been rejected, the Supreme Court has used the Fourteenth Amendment to apply provisions of the Bill of Rights to the states *selectively.* The vehicle has been the clause assuring individuals due process of law. The Court has said that state denial of any right deemed "fundamental" by society amounts to a denial of due process and hence violates the Fourteenth Amendment. . . .

The difficult question has been which provisions of the first eight amendments to absorb. . . .

Grandiose is the word for the physical setting. The W.P.A. Guide to Washington* called the Supreme Court building a "great marble temple" which "by its august scale and mighty splendor seems to bear little relation to the functional purposes of government." Shortly before the justices moved into the building in 1935 from their old chamber across the street in the Capitol, Justice Stone wrote his sons "The place is almost bombastically pretentious, and thus it seems to me wholly inappropriate for a quiet group of old boys such as the Supreme Court." He told his friends that the justices would be "nine black beetles in the Temple of Karnak."

The visitor who climbs the marble steps and passes through the marble columns of the huge pseudo-classical facade finds himself in a cold, lofty hall, again all marble. Great bronze gates exclude him from the area of the building where the justices work in private—their offices, library and conference room. In the courtroom, which is always open to the public, the atmosphere of austere pomp is continued: there are more columns, an enormously high ceiling, red velvet hangings, friezes carved high on the walls. The ritual opening of each day's session adds to the feeling of awe. The Court Crier to the right of the bench smashes his gavel down sharply on a wooden block, everyone rises and the justices file in through the red draperies behind the bench and stand at their places as the Crier intones the traditional opening: "The honorable, the Chief Justice and the Associate Justices of the Supreme Court of the United States. Oyez, oyez, oyez. All persons having business before the honorable, the Supreme Court of the United States, are admonished to draw near and give their attention, for the Court is now sitting. God save the United States and this honorable Court."

But then, when an argument begins, all the trappings and ceremony seem to fade, and the scene takes on an extraordinary intimacy. In the most informal way, altogether without pomp, Court and counsel converse.

*The WPA, the Works Progress Administration, was started by President Franklin Roosevelt as part of the New Deal in 1935. WPA projects, designed to put people back to work during the Depression, included school and park building, theater and music performances, and map and guidebook writing.—EDS.

It is conversation—as direct, unpretentious and focused discussion as can be found anywhere in Washington. . . .

Chief Justice Warren, as is the custom, called the next case by reading aloud its full title: Number 155, Clarence Earl Gideon, petitioner, versus H. G. Cochran, Jr., director, Division of Corrections, State of Florida. . . .

The lawyer arguing a case stands at a small rostrum between the two counsel tables, facing the Chief Justice. The party that lost in the lower court goes first, and so the argument in *Gideon v. Cochran* was begun by Abe Fortas. As he stood, the Chief Justice gave him the customary greeting, "Mr. Fortas," and he made the customary opening: "Mr. Chief Justice, may it please the Court. . . . "

This case presents "a narrow question," Fortas said—the right to counsel—unencumbered by extraneous issues. . . .

"This record does not indicate that Clarence Earl Gideon was a person of low intelligence," Fortas said, "or that the judge was unfair to him. But to me this case shows the basic difficulty with Betts versus Brady. It shows that no man, however intelligent, can conduct his own defense adequately." . . .

"I believe we can confidently say that overruling Betts versus Brady at this time would be in accord with the opinion of those entitled to an opinion. That is not always true of great constitutional questions. . . . We may be comforted in this constitutional moment by the fact that what we are doing is a deliberate change after twenty years of experience—a change that has the overwhelming support of the bench, the bar and even of the states." . . .

It was only a few days later, as it happened, that *Gideon v. Wainwright* was decided. There was no prior notice; there never is. The Court gives out no advance press releases and tells no one what cases will be decided on a particular Monday, much less how they will be decided. Opinion days have a special quality. The Supreme Court is one of the last American appellate courts where decisions are announced orally. The justices, who divide on so many issues, disagree about this practice, too. Some regard it as a waste of time; others value it as an occasion for descending from the ivory tower, however briefly, and communicating with the live audience in the courtroom. . . .

Then, in the ascending order of seniority, it was Justice Black's turn. He looked at his wife, who was sitting in the box reserved for the justices' friends and families, and said: "I have for announcement the opinion and judgment of the Court in Number One fifty-five, Gideon against Wainwright."

Justice Black leaned forward and gave his words the emphasis and the drama of a great occasion. Speaking very directly to the audience in the courtroom, in an almost folksy way, he told about Clarence Earl Gideon's case and how it had reached the Supreme Court of the United States.

"It raised a fundamental question," Justice Black said, "the rightness of a case we decided twenty-one years ago, Betts against Brady. When we granted certiorari in this case, we asked the lawyers on both sides to argue to us whether we should reconsider that case. We do reconsider Betts and Brady, and we reach an opposite conclusion."

By now the page boys were passing out the opinions. There were four—by Justices Douglas, Clark and Harlan, in addition to the opinion of the Court. But none of the other three was a dissent. A quick look at the end of each showed that it concurred in the overruling of *Betts v. Brady*. On that central result, then, the Court was unanimous. . . .

That was the end of Clarence Earl Gideon's case in the Supreme Court of the United States. The opinions delivered that Monday were quickly circulated around the country by special legal services, then issued in pamphlets by the Government Printing Office. Eventually they appeared in the bound volumes of Supreme Court decisions, the United States Reports, to be cited as *Gideon v. Wainwright*, 372 U.S. 335—meaning that the case could be found beginning on page 335 of the 372nd volume of the reports.

Justice Black, talking to a friend a few weeks after the decision, said quietly: "When *Betts v. Brady* was decided, I never thought I'd live to see it overruled." . . .

The reaction of the states to *Gideon v. Wainwright* was swift and constructive. The most dramatic response came from Florida, whose rural-dominated legislature had so long refused to relieve the problem of the unrepresented indigent such as Gideon. Shortly after the decision Governor Farris Bryant called on the legislature to enact a public-defender law. . . .

Resolution of the great constitutional question in *Gideon v. Wainwright* did not decide the fate of Clarence Earl Gideon. He was now entitled to a new trial, with a lawyer. Was he guilty of breaking into the Bay Harbor Poolroom? The verdict would not set any legal precedents, but there is significance in the human beings who make constitutional-law cases as well as in the law. And in this case there was the interesting question whether the legal assistance for which Gideon had fought so hard would make any difference to him. . . .

. . . After ascertaining that Gideon had no money to hire a lawyer of his own choice, Judge McCrary asked whether there was a local lawyer whom Gideon would like to represent him. There was: W. Fred Turner.

"For the record," Judge McCrary said quickly, "I am going to appoint Mr. Fred Turner to represent this defendant, Clarence Earl Gideon." . . .

The jury went out at four-twenty P.M., after a colorless charge by the judge including the instruction—requested by Turner—that the jury must believe Gideon guilty "beyond a reasonable doubt" in order to convict him. When a half-hour had passed with no verdict, the prosecutors were less confident. At five twenty-five there was a knock on the door between the courtroom and the jury room. The jurors filed in, and the court clerk read their verdict, written on a form. It was *Not Guilty.*

"So say you all?" asked Judge McCrary, without a flicker of emotion. The jurors nodded. . . .

After nearly two years in the state penitentiary Gideon was a free man. . . . That night he would pay a last, triumphant visit to the Bay Harbor Poolroom. Could someone let him have a few dollars? Someone did.

"Do you feel like you accomplished something?" a newspaper reporter asked.

"Well I did."

76

Miranda v. Arizona

Chief Justice Earl Warren, the great liberal judge whose Court had already handed down a number of landmark rulings—among them, Brown v. Board of Education *(1954) on desegregation in public schools,* Mapp v. Ohio *(1961) on search and seizure by police, and* Gideon v. Wainwright *(1963) on the right to counsel in criminal trials in state courts—wrote the opinion in another major case,* Miranda v. Arizona *(1966). The case involved Ernesto Miranda, who had been arrested for kidnapping and rape, and who had been identified by the victim in a police lineup. Police officers then interrogated Miranda, who subsequently signed a confession at the top of which read that he had done so "with full knowledge of my legal rights, understanding that any statement I make may be used against me." During the trial, Miranda's confession was entered as evidence, and despite the officer's testimony that Miranda had not been told of his right to have an attorney present during interrogation, Miranda was found guilty. The Supreme Court of Arizona upheld the conviction on the grounds that Miranda had not specifically requested an attorney. The case went to the U.S. Supreme*

Court whose ruling resulted in what we now know as the "Miranda rights," a statement read to any suspect by law enforcement officers during an arrest.

Miranda v. Arizona
384 U.S. 436, 86 S.Ct. 1602 (1966)

Chief Justice WARREN delivered the opinion of the Court.

The cases before us raise questions which go to the roots of our concepts of American criminal jurisprudence: the restraints society must observe consistent with the Federal Constitution in prosecuting individuals for crime. More specifically, we deal with the admissibility of statements obtained from an individual who is subjected to custodial police interrogation and the necessity for procedures which assure that the individual is accorded his privilege under the Fifth Amendment to the Constitution not to be compelled to incriminate himself.

We dealt with certain phases of this problem recently in *Escobedo v. Illinois*, 378 U.S. 478 (1964). There, as in the four cases before us, law enforcement officials took the defendant into custody and interrogated him in a police station for the purpose of obtaining a confession. The police did not effectively advise him of his right to remain silent or of his right to consult with his attorney. Rather, they confronted him with an alleged accomplice who accused him of having perpetrated a murder. When the defendant denied the accusation and said "I didn't shoot Manuel, you did it," they handcuffed him and took him to an interrogation room. There, while handcuffed and standing, he was questioned for four hours until he confessed. During this interrogation, the police denied his request to speak to his attorney, and they prevented his retained attorney, who had come to the police station, from consulting with him. At his trial, the State, over his objection, introduced the confession against him. We held that the statements thus made were constitutionally inadmissible. . . . We adhere to the principles of *Escobedo* today.

Our holding will be spelled out with some specificity in the pages which follow but briefly stated it is this: the prosecution may not use statements, whether exculpatory or inculpatory, stemming from custodial interrogation of the defendant unless it demonstrates the use of procedural safeguards effective to secure the privilege against self-incrimination. By custodial interrogation, we mean questioning initiated by law enforcement officers after a person has been taken into custody or otherwise deprived of his freedom of action in any significant way. As for the procedural safeguards to be employed, unless other fully effective means are devised to inform accused persons of their right of silence and to assure a continuous opportunity to exercise it, the following measures are required. Prior to any questioning, the person must be warned that he has a right to remain silent, that any statement he does make may be used as evidence against him, and that he has a right to the presence of an attorney, either retained or appointed. The defendant may waive effectuation of these rights, provided the waiver is made voluntarily, knowingly and intelligently. If, however, he indicates in any manner and at any stage of the process that he wishes to consult with an attorney before speaking there can be no questioning. Likewise, if the individual is alone and indicates in any manner that he does not wish to be interrogated, the police may not question him. The mere fact that he may have answered some questions or volunteered some statements on his own does not deprive him of the right to refrain from answering any further inquiries until he has consulted with an attorney and thereafter consents to be questioned. . . .

The constitutional issue we decide in each of these cases [being decided today] is the admissibility of statements obtained from a defendant questioned while in custody or otherwise deprived of his freedom of action in any significant way. In each, the defendant was questioned by police officers, detectives, or a prosecuting attorney in a room in which he was cut off from the outside world. In none of these cases was the defendant given a full and effective warning of his rights at the outset of the interrogation process. In all the cases, the questioning elicited oral admissions, and in three of them, signed statements as well which were admitted at their trials. They all thus share salient features—incommunicado interrogation of individuals in a police-dominated atmosphere, resulting in self-incriminating statements without full warnings of constitutional rights. . . . We stress that the modern practice of in-custody interrogation is psychologically rather than physically oriented. . . . Interrogation still takes place in privacy. Privacy results in secrecy and this in turn results in a gap in our knowledge as to what in fact goes on in the interrogation rooms. A valuable source of information about present police practices, however, may be found in various police manuals and texts which document procedures employed with success in the past, and which recommend various other effective tactics. . . .

The officers are told by the manuals that the "principal psychological factor contributing to a successful interrogation is *privacy*—being alone with the person under interrogation." The efficacy of this tactic has been explained as follows:

> "If at all practicable, the interrogation should take place in the investigator's office or at least in a room of his own choice. The subject should be deprived of every psychological advantage." . . .

After this psychological conditioning, however, the officer is told to point out the incriminating significance of the suspect's refusal to talk:

> "Joe, you have a right to remain silent. That's your privilege and I'm the last person in the world who'll try to take it away from you. If that's the way you want to leave this, O.K. But let me ask you this. Suppose you were in my shoes and I were in yours and you called me in to ask me about this and I told you, 'I don't want to answer any of your questions.' You'd think I had something to hide, and you'd probably be right in thinking that. That's exactly what I'll have to think about you, and so will everybody else. So let's sit here and talk this whole thing over."

Few will persist in their initial refusal to talk, it is said, if this monologue is employed correctly.

In the event that the subject wishes to speak to a relative or an attorney, the following advice is tendered:

> "[T]he interrogator should respond by suggesting that the subject first tell the truth to the interrogator himself rather than get anyone else involved in the matter. If the request is for an attorney, the interrogator may suggest that the subject save himself or his family the expense of any such professional service, particularly if he is innocent of the offense under investigation. The interrogator may also add, 'Joe, I'm only looking for the truth, and if you're telling the truth, that's it. You can handle this by yourself.' " . . .

Even without employing brutality, the "third degree" or the specific stratagems described above, the very fact of custodial interrogation exacts a heavy toll on individual liberty and trades on the weakness of individuals. . . .

. . . In each of the cases [heard by the court], the defendant was thrust into an unfamiliar atmosphere and run through menacing police interrogation procedures. The potentiality for compulsion is forcefully apparent, for example, in *Miranda*, where the indigent Mexican defendant was a seriously disturbed individual with pronounced sexual fantasies, and in *Stewart*, in which the defendant was an indigent Los Angeles Negro who had dropped out of school in the sixth grade. To be sure, the records do not evince overt physical coercion or patent psychological ploys. The fact remains that in none of these cases did the officers undertake to afford appropriate safeguards at the outset of the interrogation to insure that the statements were truly the product of free choice.

It is obvious that such an interrogation environment is created for no purpose other than to subjugate the individual to the will of his examiner. This atmosphere carries its own badge of intimidation. To be sure, this is not physical intimidation, but it is equally destructive of human dignity. The current practice of incommunicado interrogation is at odds with one of our Nation's most cherished principles—that the individual may not be compelled to incriminate himself. Unless adequate protective devices are employed to dispel the compulsion inherent in custodial surroundings, no statement obtained from the defendant can truly be the product of his free choice. . . .

To summarize, we hold that when an individual is taken into custody or otherwise deprived of his freedom by the authorities in any significant way and is subjected to questioning, the privilege against self-incrimination is jeopardized. Procedural safeguards must be employed to protect the privilege, and unless other fully effective means are adopted to notify the person of his right of silence and to assure that the exercise of the right will be scrupulously honored, the following measures are required. He must be warned prior to any questioning that he has the right to remain silent, that anything he says can be used against him in a court of law, that he has the right to the presence of an attorney, and that if he cannot afford an attorney one will be appointed for him prior to any questioning if he so desires. Opportunity to exercise these rights must be afforded to him throughout the interrogation. After such warnings have been given, and such opportunity afforded him, the individual may knowingly and intelligently waive these rights and agree to answer questions or make a statement. But unless and until such warnings and waiver are demonstrated by the prosecution at trial, no evidence obtained as a result of interrogation can be used against him. . . . We turn now to these facts to consider the application to these cases of the constitutional principles discussed above. . . .

On March 13, 1963, petitioner, Ernesto Miranda, was arrested at his home and taken in custody to a Phoenix police station. He was there identified by the complaining witness. The police then took him to "Interrogation Room No. 2" of the detective bureau. There he was questioned by two police officers. The officers admitted at trial that Miranda was not advised that he had a right to have an attorney present. Two hours later, the officers emerged from the interrogation room with a written confession signed by Miranda. At the top of the statement was a typed paragraph stating that the confession was made voluntarily, without threats or promises of immunity and "with full knowledge of my legal rights, understanding any statement I make may be used against me."

At his trial before a jury, the written confession was admitted into evidence over the objection of defense counsel, and the officers testified to the prior oral confession made by Miranda during the interrogation. Miranda was found guilty of kidnapping and rape. He was sentenced to 20 to 30 years' imprisonment on each count, the sentences to run concurrently. On appeal, the Supreme Court of Arizona held that Miranda's constitutional rights were not violated in obtaining the confession and affirmed the conviction. 98 Ariz. 18, 401 P. 2d 721. In reaching its decision, the court emphasized heavily the fact that Miranda did not specifically request counsel.

We reverse. From the testimony of the officers and by the admission of respondent, it is clear that Miranda was not in any way apprised of his right to consult with an attorney and to have one present during the interrogation, nor was his right not to be compelled to incriminate himself effectively protected in any other manner. Without these warnings the statements were inadmissible.

77

RICHARD KLUGER

From *Simple Justice*

No Supreme Court case has so changed the United States as did Brown v. Board of Education of Topeka, Kansas *(1954). Volumes have been written on* Brown *and the aftermath of* Brown, *but the best place to start is with Richard Kluger's classic work. The selection here focuses on Earl Warren, the chief justice who wrote the landmark decision. The case that would reverse* Plessy v. Ferguson *(1896) and the "separate but equal" doctrine that the Court had upheld for half a century, was waiting to be heard when the death of Chief Justice Fred Vinson put Warren on the Court. Kluger quotes Justice Frankfurter as saying on hearing of Vinson's death, "This is the first indication I have ever had that there is a God." Kluger explores the intricate process Warren faced in forging a majority, and eventually unanimity, for overturning "separate but equal." While those Americans who were born after* Brown *cannot remember a time when it was not the law of the land, Kluger takes us back to that thrilling moment of change.*

IN THE TWO AND A HALF YEARS since they had last sat down to decide a major racial case, the Justices of the Supreme Court had not grown closer. Indeed, the philosophical and personal fissures in their ranks had widened since they had agreed—unanimously—to side with the Negro appellants in *Sweatt, McLaurin*, and *Henderson* in the spring of 1950. That had been a rare show of unanimity. By the 1952 Term, the Court was failing to reach a unanimous decision 81 percent of the time, nearly twice as high a percentage of disagreement as it had recorded a decade earlier. . . .

It was perhaps the most severely fractured Court in history—testament, on the face of it, to Vinson's failure as Chief Justice. Selected to lead the Court because of his skills as a conciliator, the low-key, mournful-visaged Kentuckian found that the issues before him were far different from, and far less readily negotiable than, the hard-edged problems he had faced as Franklin Roosevelt's ace economic troubleshooter and Harry Truman's Secretary of the Treasury and back-room confederate.

Fred Vinson's lot as Chief Justice . . . had not proven a happy one. . . .

What, then, could be expected of the deeply divided Vinson Court as it convened on the morning of December 13, 1952, to deliberate on the transcendent case of *Brown v. Board of Education*? The earlier racial cases—*Sweatt* and *McLaurin*—they had managed to cope with by chipping away at the edges of Jim Crow but avoiding the real question of *Plessy*'s continued validity.* The Court could no longer dodge that question, though it might continue to stall in resolving it. Hovering over the Justices were all the repressive bugaboos of the Cold War era. The civil rights of Negroes and the civil liberties of political dissenters and criminal defendants were prone to be scrambled together in the public mind, and every malcontent was a sitting target for the red tar of anti-Americanism. No sector of the nation was less hospitable to both civil-liberties and civil-rights claimants than the segregating states of the South, and it was the South with which the Justices had primarily to deal in confronting *Brown*. . . .

And so they were divided. But given the gravity of the issue, they were willing to take their time to try to reconcile their differences. They clamped a precautionary lid on all their discussions of *Brown* as the year turned and Fred Vinson swore in Dwight David Eisenhower as the thirty-

*The Supreme Court in *Plessy v. Ferguson* (1896) interpreted the equal protection clause of the Fourteenth Amendment to mean that the states could require separation of the races in public institutions if these institutions were equal (the "separate but equal doctrine"). From 1937 until 1954 the Court subjected "separate but equal" to increasingly rigorous scrutiny. In *Sweatt v. Painter* (1950) and *McLaurin v. Oklahoma State Regents* (1950), for example, the Court invalidated specific state racial segregationist practices in higher education on grounds that they did not permit truly equal access to black students. Yet, the Court had not overturned *Plessy*.—EDS.

fourth President of the United States. The Justices seemed to make little headway toward resolving the problem, but they all knew that a close vote would likely be a disaster for Court and country alike. The problem of welding the disparate views into a single one was obviously complicated by the ambivalence afflicting the Court's presiding Justice. As spring came and the end of the Court's 1952 Term neared, Fred Vinson seemed to be in increasingly disagreeable and edgy spirits. Says one of the people at the Court closest to him then: "I got the distinct impression that he was distressed over the Court's inability to find a strong, unified position on such an important case."

What evidence there is suggests that those on or close to the Court thought it was about as severely divided as it could be at this stage of its deliberations. . . .

During the last week of the term in June, the law clerks of all the Justices met in an informal luncheon session and took a two-part poll. Each clerk was asked how he would vote in the school-segregation cases and how he thought his Justice would vote. According to one of their number, a man who later became a professor of law: "The clerks were almost unanimous for overruling *Plessy* and ordering desegregation, but, according to their impressions, the Court would have been closely divided if it had announced its decision at that time. Many of the clerks were only guessing at the positions of their respective Justices, but it appeared that a majority of the Justices would not have overruled *Plessy* but would have given some relief in some of the cases on the ground that the separate facilities were not in fact equal." . . .

All such bets on the alignment of the Court ended abruptly a few days later when the single most fateful judicial event of that long summer occurred. In his Washington hotel apartment, Fred M. Vinson died of a heart attack at 3:15 in the morning of September 8 [1953]. He was sixty-three.

All the members of the Court attended Vinson's burial in Louisa, Kentucky, his ancestral home. But not all the members of the Court grieved equally at his passing. And one at least did not grieve at all. Felix Frankfurter had not much admired Fred Vinson as judge or man. And he was certain that the Chief Justice had been the chief obstacle to the Court's prospects of reaching a humanitarian and judicially defensible settlement of the monumental segregation cases. In view of Vinson's passing just before the *Brown* reargument, Frankfurter remarked to a former clerk, "This is the first indication I have ever had that there is a God." . . . Fred Vinson was not yet cold in his grave when speculation rose well above a whisper as to whom President Eisenhower would pick to heal and lead the Supreme Court as it faced one of its most momentous decisions in the segregation cases. . . .

Dwight Eisenhower's principal contribution to the civil rights of Americans would prove to be his selection of Earl Warren as Chief Justice—a decision Eisenhower would later say had been a mistake. The President was on hand, at any rate, on Monday, October 5, when just after noon the clerk of the Supreme Court read aloud the commission of the President that began, "Know ye: That reposing special trust and confidence in the wisdom, uprightness and learning of Earl Warren of California, I do appoint him Chief Justice of the United States. . . ." Warren stood up at the clerk's desk to the side of the bench and read aloud his oath of office. At the end, Clerk Harold Willey said to him, "So help you God." Warren said, "So help me God." Then he stepped quickly behind the velour curtains and re-emerged a moment later through the opening in the center to take the presiding seat. His entire worthy career to that moment would be dwarfed by what followed. . . . At the reargument, Earl Warren had said very little. The Chief Justice had put no substantive questions to any of the attorneys. Nor is it likely that he had given any indication of his views to the other Justices before they convened at the Saturday-morning conference on December 12. But then, speaking first, he made his views unmistakable.

Nearly twenty years later, he would recall, "I don't remember having any great doubts about which way it should go. It seemed to me a comparatively simple case. Just look at the various decisions that had been eroding *Plessy* for so many years. They kept chipping away at it rather than ever really facing it head-on. If you looked back—to *Gaines*, to *Sweatt*, to some of the interstate-commerce cases—you saw that the doctrine of separate-but-equal had been so eroded that only the *fact* of segregation itself remained unconsidered. On the merits, the natural, the logical, and practically the only way the case could be decided was clear. The question was *how* the decision was to be reached."

At least two sets of notes survive from the Justices' 1953 conference discussion of the segregation cases—extensive ones by Justice Burton and exceedingly scratchy and cryptic ones by Justice Frankfurter. They agree on the Chief Justice's remarks. The cases had been well argued, in his judgment, Earl Warren told the conference, and the government had been very frank in both its written and its oral presentations. He said he had of course been giving much thought to the entire question since coming to the Court, and after studying the briefs and relevant history and hearing the arguments, he could not escape the feeling that the Court had "finally arrived" at the moment when it now had to determine whether segregation was allowable in the public schools. Without saying it in so many words, the new Chief Justice was declaring that the Court's policy of delay, favored by his predecessor, could no longer be permitted.

The more he had pondered the question, Warren said, the more he had come to the conclusion that the doctrine of separate-but-equal rested upon the concept of the inferiority of the colored race. He did not see how *Plessy* and its progeny could be sustained on any other theory—and if the Court were to choose to sustain them, "we must do it on that basis," he was recorded by Burton as saying. He was concerned, to be sure, about the necessity of overruling earlier decisions and lines of reasoning, but he had concluded that segregation of Negro schoolchildren had to be ended. The law, he said in words noted by Frankfurter, "cannot in 'this day and age' set them apart." The law could not say, Burton recorded the Chief as asserting, that Negroes were "not entitled to *exactly same* treatment of all others." To do so would go against the intentions of the three Civil War amendments.

Unless any of the other four Justices who had indicated a year earlier their readiness to overturn segregation—Black, Douglas, Burton, and Minton—had since changed his mind, Warren's opening remarks meant that a majority of the Court now stood ready to strike down the practice.

But to gain a narrow majority was no cause for exultation. A sharply divided Court, no matter which way it leaned, was an indecisive one, and for Warren to force a split decision out of it would have amounted to hardly more constructive leadership on this transcendent question than Fred Vinson had managed. The new Chief Justice wanted to unite the Court in *Brown*. . . .

He recognized that a number of Court precedents of long standing would be shattered in the process of overturning *Plessy*, and he regretted that necessity. It was the sort of reassuring medicine most welcomed by Burton and Minton, the least judicially and intellectually adventurous members of the Court.

He recognized that the Court's decision would have wide repercussions, varying in intensity from state to state, and that they would all therefore have to approach the matter in as tolerant and understanding a way as possible. Implicit in this was a call for flexibility in how the Court might frame its decree.

But overarching all these cushioning comments and a tribute to both his compassion as a man and his persuasive skills as a politician was the moral stance Earl Warren took at the outset of his remarks. Segregation, he had told his new colleagues, could be justified only by belief in the inferiority of the Negro; any of them who wished to perpetuate the practice, he implied, ought in candor to be willing to acknowledge as much. These were plain words, and they did not have to be hollered. They cut across all the legal theories that had been so endlessly aired and went straight to the human tissue at the core of the controversy. . . .

The Warren opinion was "finally approved" at the May 15 conference, Burton noted in his diary. The man from California had won the support of every member of the Court.

. . . Not long before the Court's decision in *Brown* was announced, Warren told *Ebony* magazine twenty years later, he had decided to spend a few days visiting Civil War monuments in Virginia. He went by automobile with a black chauffeur.

At the end of the first day, the Chief Justice's car pulled up at a hotel, where he had made arrangements to spend the night. Warren simply assumed that his chauffeur would stay somewhere else, presumably at a less expensive place. When the Chief Justice came out of his hotel the next morning to resume his tour, he soon figured out that the chauffeur had spent the night in the car. He asked the black man why.

"Well, Mr. Chief Justice," the chauffeur began, "I just couldn't find a place—couldn't find a place to . . . "

Warren was stricken by his own thoughtlessness in bringing an employee of his to a town where lodgings were not available to the man solely because of his color. "I was embarrassed, I was ashamed," Warren recalled. "We turned back immediately. . . . "

. . . In the press room on the ground floor, reporters filing in at the tail end of the morning were advised that May 17, 1954, looked like a quiet day at the Supreme Court of the United States.

All of the opinions of the Court were announced on Mondays in that era. The ritual was simple and unvarying. The Justices convened at noon. Lawyers seeking admission to the Supreme Court bar were presented to the Court by their sponsors, greeted briefly by the Chief Justice, and sworn in by the clerk of the Court. Then, in ascending order of seniority, the Justices with opinions to deliver read them aloud, every word usually, without much effort at dramaturgy. Concurrences and dissents were read after the majority opinion. And then the next case, and then the next. There was no applause; there were no catcalls. There were no television or newsreel cameras. There were no questions from the newsmen in the audience. There was no briefing session in the press room or the Justices' chambers after Court adjourned. There were no weekly press conferences. There were no appearances on *Meet the Press* the following Sunday. There were no press releases elaborating on what the Court had said or meant or done. The opinions themselves were all there was. . . .

Down in the press room, as the first three routine opinions were distributed, it looked, as predicted, like a very quiet day at the Court. But then, as Douglas finished up, Clerk of the Court Harold Willey dispatched a pneumatic message to Banning E. Whittington, the Court's dour press officer. Whittington slipped on his suit jacket, advised the press-room contingent, "Reading of the segregation decisions is about to begin in the courtroom," added as he headed out the door that the text of the opinion would be distributed in the press room afterward, and then led the scrambling reporters in a dash up the marble stairs.

"I have for announcement," said Earl Warren, "the judgment and opinion of the Court in No. 1—*Oliver Brown et al. v. Board of Education of Topeka.*" It was 12:52 P.M. In the press room, the Associated Press wire carried the first word to the country: "Chief Justice Warren today began reading the Supreme Court's decision in the public school segregation cases. The court's ruling could not be determined immediately." The bells went off in every news room in America. The nation was listening.

It was Warren's first major opinion as Chief Justice. He read it, by all accounts, in a firm, clear, unemotional voice. If he had delivered no other opinion but this one, he would have won his place in American history.

Considering its magnitude, it was a short opinion. During its first part, no one hearing it could tell where it would come out. . . .

Without in any way becoming technical and rhetorical, Warren then proceeded to demonstrate the dynamic nature and adaptive genius of American constitutional law. . . . Having declared its essential value to the nation's civic health and vitality, he then argued for the central importance of education in the private life and aspirations of every individual. . . . That led finally to the critical question: "Does segregation of children in public schools solely on the basis of race . . . deprive the children of the minority group of equal educational opportunities?"

To this point, nearly two-thirds through the opinion, Warren had not tipped his hand. Now, in the next sentence, he showed it by answering that critical question: "We believe that it does." . . .

This finding flew directly in the face of *Plessy.* And here, finally, Warren collided with the 1896 decision. . . .

The balance of the Chief Justice's opinion consisted of just two paragraphs. The first began: "We conclude"—and here Warren departed from the printed text before him to insert the word "unanimously," which sent a sound of muffled astonishment eddying around the courtroom—"that in the field of public education the doctrine of 'separate but equal' has no place. Separate educational facilities are inherently unequal." The plaintiffs and others similarly situated—technically meaning Negro children within the segregated school districts under challenge—were therefore being deprived of the equal protection of the laws guaranteed by the Fourteenth Amendment.

The concluding paragraph of the opinion revealed Earl Warren's political adroitness both at compromise and at the ready use of the power of his office for ends he thought worthy. "Because these are class actions, because of the wide applicability of this decision, and because of the great variety of local conditions," he declared, "these cases present problems of considerable complexity. . . . In order that we may have the full assistance of the parties in formulating decrees," the Court was scheduling further argument for the term beginning the following fall. The attorneys general of the United States and all the states requiring or permitting segregation in public education were invited to participate. In a few strokes, Warren thus managed to (1) proclaim "the wide applicability" of the decision and make it plain that the Court had no intention of limiting its benefits to a handful of plaintiffs in a few outlying districts; (2) reassure the South that the Court understood the emotional wrench desegregation would cause and was therefore granting the region some time to get accustomed to the idea; and (3) invite the South to participate in the entombing of Jim Crow by joining the Court's efforts to fashion a temperate implementation decree—or to forfeit that chance by petulantly abstaining from the Court's further deliberations and thereby run the risk of having a harsh decree imposed upon it. It was such dexterous use of the power available to him and of the circumstances in which to exploit it that had established John Marshall as a judicial statesman and political tactician of the most formidable sort. The Court had not seen his like since. Earl Warren, in his first major opinion, moved now with that same sure purposefulness. . . .

It was 1:20 P.M. The wire services proclaimed the news to the nation. Within the hour, the Voice of America would begin beaming word to the world in thirty-four languages: In the United States, schoolchildren could no longer be segregated by race. The law of the land no longer recognized a separate equality. No Americans were more equal than any other Americans.

78

ELLIS COSE

From *The Rage of a Privileged Class*

"Black rage" is a term that many Americans identify with radical groups and radical acts: the Black Panthers of the 1960s perhaps, or the 1992 Los Angeles riots. Author Ellis Cose believes that black rage is just as correctly applied to the feelings of many successful upper-middle-class African Americans today. He discusses the difficulties that highly accomplished black professionals encounter in their careers. Cose exposes the negative stereotypes that adversely affect all black youngsters. African Americans who have achieved success in a white-dominated society wonder why so many obstacles still stand in their way. Cose puts their feelings bluntly: "We are tired of waiting."

JOEL DREYFUSS IS editor of *PC Magazine*, the nation's number-one publication for owners of personal computers. He is a man with a reputation for speaking his mind—a reputation that has not always served him well, in his view. His journalistic talent has landed him a host of impressive positions: reporter for the *Washington Post*, managing editor for *Black Enterprise*, New York bureau chief for *USA Today*, Tokyo bureau chief for *Fortune*. But an unfair perception of him as a racial rabble-rouser, he believes, has limited his success.

Dreyfuss, whose parents are Haitian, grew up shuttling among Haiti, Africa, and the United States, in the tow of a father attached to the United Nations. He settled in New York, more or less for good, at the age of fifteen. When he enrolled in school, he found that despite his elite prior education, he was immediately "put in a class of basketball players." Shortly thereafter, he took an exam, and a counselor told him in apparent astonishment that he had done extremely well. He found the counselor's attitude bewildering, since until then he had always been expected to do well.

The reassessment of his abilities gained him entry to an honors program whose ethnic composition left him puzzled. In a school that was roughly 90 percent black and Hispanic, the honors program was 90 percent white. To all appearances, they had "created a school for white kids within the school." He entered City College of New York in the mid-1960s, before the open admissions policy, at a time when CCNY was considered one of the best schools in the city. The white students often asked him how he had managed to get in.

With the country caught up in the throes of rebellion, his interest in journalism blossomed. In addition to seeing journalism as force for social reform, he saw it as something of a family tradition; his father, years previously, had been publisher of an English-language paper in Haiti. Dreyfuss got a job at the Associated Press, where one evening, while helping to edit copy, he saw an AP story about three black men who had been accused of a crime. He questioned whether the racial identification was appropriate, citing AP policy prohibiting the use of racial designations unless they were somehow relevant to the story. The editor, in explaining why race was in fact relevant, asked, "Aren't blacks arming themselves?"

For Dreyfuss, the incident was a turning point. "I became outraged and I remained outraged for about twenty years." At that moment he realized that when faced with issues involving race, normally intelligent whites could become "irrational" and "would violate their own rules." He found support for that view a short while later when he went to work for the New York *Post*, where an editor involved in his hiring remarked, "Your people are trying to destroy us."

Such foolishness from editors fueled Dreyfuss's desire to seek change. He pushed his bosses to hire more blacks and criticized coverage he considered particularly witless. Not surprisingly, some found his outspokenness annoying, but his journalistic gifts nonetheless made him a standout. At the *Washington Post*, where Dreyfuss worked after leaving New York, an editor was so impressed that she took him aside to tell him that he was doing a terrific job. "How do we get more blacks as good as Joel Dreyfuss?"she asked. Dreyfuss found the remark offensive, and told her as much.

As a result of his propensity for rubbing editors the wrong way with his racial consciousness-raising, Dreyfuss was denied a coveted transfer to the California bureau. Ben Bradlee, then executive editor, acknowledged his abilities but told him that he was "a pain in the ass." The Bradlee kiss-off became a footnote in the Bradlee legend and cemented Dreyfuss's reputation as a troublemaker. For years after he left the *Post*, recalls Dreyfuss, the widely reported Bradlee remark "made it difficult for me to get a job in the mainstream media."

He tried, often at great emotional price, to live his reputation down, and learned to keep his mouth shut even when events outraged him. Yet nearly two decades after that episode, "there are still a lot of people who view me as a dangerous subversive. . . . I've been told that."

For all the pain the 1960s and '70s evoke, Dreyfuss believes they allowed certain black journalists to thrive. In those days, race was major story, and blacks were essential to covering that story. As a result, a fair number of black journalists became stars. Now he believes the best reporting jobs are largely going to whites, a reflection not only of the changing nature of the news, but of the fact that most news organizations still have "a limited imagination when it comes to black people." . . .

The perceptual gulf, the contradictory findings, the flowering of resentments, the frequency of racial incidents—all lead toward an inescapable conclusion: racial discord will be with us for a long, long time. This "next generation," for all its idealism, openmindedness, and willingness to embrace equality and racial integration, is not even close to mastering the art of how to get along.

Once upon a time, of course, many thought that racial division would soon be a thing of the past, that the next generation, or perhaps the one after that, would achieve harmony where their parents could not. Martin Luther King's may have been the most famous 1960s dream, but he was not dreaming alone. Yet as today's young people come of age, many one time idealists are beginning to think that such dreams are rooted in little more than fantasy. . . .

. . . For even if racial peace is maintained, the web of stereotypes is left untouched, and those stereotypes, as already noted, are particularly destructive to blacks. They not only encourage whites to treat blacks as inferiors but also encourage blacks to see themselves as many whites would have them be.

These stereotypes spew forth from every segment of popular culture and constantly find new life in black and nonblack communities across America. Rap music, for instance, routinely portrays black men as "niggaz" and "gangstas" and black women as "bitches" and "hoes." A host of black comedians follow suit, depicting a jive-talking, foul-mouthed, illiterate stud who defines the essence of "black" for many young people. Attachment to this stereotype is so powerful that African Americans who choose not to personify it are often accused by other blacks of trying not to be black. Yet those with a sense of history know that the stud image did not spring from the black community but originated with whites searching for signs that blacks were intellectually inferior and morally degenerate—and therefore suitable for use as slaves. Today, through television, movies, and the innumerable interracial encounters that occur in an increasingly integrated society, blacks and whites in effect conspire to determine whether, and to what extent, the stereotypes can change—in short, what the place of African Americans will be.

Unlike recent immigrants, who are relatively free to define their own place in U.S. society, African Americans are more constrained. John Ogbu, an anthropologist at the University of California, Berkeley, who has studied immigrant and indigenous minorities, writes: "Immigrants generally regard themselves as foreigners, 'strangers' who come to America with expectation of certain economic, political, and social benefits. While anticipating that such benefits might come at some cost . . . the immigrants did not measure their success or failure primarily by the standards of white Americans, but by the standards of their homelands. Such minorities, at least during the first generation, did not internalize the effects of such discrimination, of cultural and intellectual denigration. . . . Even when they were restricted to manual labor, they did not consider themselves to be occupying the lowest rung of the American status system, and partly because they did not fully understand that system, and partly because they did not consider themselves as belonging to it, they saw their situation as temporary."

In contrast, Ogbu says, he has observed black and Mexican-American parents encouraging their children to do well in school while unconsciously passing on another, more demoralizing message: "Unavoidably, such minority parents discuss their problems with 'the system,' with their relatives, friends, and neighbors in the presence of their children. The result . . . is that such children become increasingly disillusioned about their ability to succeed in adult life through the mainstream strategy of schooling." The only way some of these kids feel they can succeed, he concludes, is to "repudiate their black peers, black identity, and black cultural frames of reference."

Few people of any race, of course, have the strength, desire, imagination, or appetite to abandon ideas they have been taught all their lives. Thus, Americans of all races continue to see each other through a prism of distorting colors, and to struggle with the problem of prejudice.

Joe Feagin, a University of Florida sociologist who has extensively studied the black middle class . . . believes that even the subtle displays of prejudice blacks today are more likely to encounter can be devastating. "Today white discrimination less often involves blatant door-slamming exclusion, for many blacks have been allowed in the corporate door. Modern discrimination more often takes the form of tracking, limiting or blocking promotions, harassment, and other differential treatment signalling disrespect." The result, writes Feagin, is the "restriction, isolation, and ostracism of middle-class blacks who have penetrated the traditionally white workplace" but who find that they are not part of the same networks that "link together not only white co-workers but also white supervisors and, in some situations, clients." And this more subtle form of exclusion produces repressed rage, inner conflict, and a deep sense of dissatisfaction: "Most middle-class blacks are caught between the desire for the American dream imbedded deeply in their consciousness and a recognition that the dream is white at its heart."

Derrick Bell, civil rights activist and legal scholar, has a perspective that is even more dispiriting than Feagin's. In *Faces at the Bottom of the Well*, Bell argues that America's brand of racism is permanent and that we must set aside the hopelessly idealistic notion that time and generosity will cure it. Since whites will never recognize blacks as equals, blacks must steel themselves for never-ending struggle: "African Americans must confront and conquer the otherwise deadening reality of our permanent subordinate status. Only in this way can we prevent ourselves from being dragged down by society's racial hostility."

In an epilogue titled "Beyond Despair," Bell invokes inspirational images from the time of slavery, when black people, "knowing there was no escape, no way out, . . . nonetheless continued to engage themselves. To carve out a humanity. To defy the murder of selfhood. Their lives were brutally shackled, certainly—but *not without meaning despite being imprisoned*." He argues that blacks today, in accepting their tragic fate, should take a cue from the slaves who managed to beat the odds "with absolutely nothing to help—save imagination, will, and unbelievable strength and courage."

In outlining his controversial thesis Bell throws out a challenge, declaring that the proposition of permanent inequality "will be easier to reject than refute." That is certainly true, for it is a prediction about the future, which by definition has not yet arrived and hence is impossible to describe with certainty. But that does not make Bell's gloomy prognosis correct. . . .

As Mary Curtis, the *New York Times* editor, observed, "You always want to think things are going to be better." Moreover, there is plenty of time to reach the conclusion that America is beyond redemption, and there is little harm in proceeding as if it were not. As [former New Jersey senator] Bill Bradley says, "I respect Derrick Bell a lot, but I'm not at that point yet where I think this is a permanent destructive aspect of American culture that can never be overcome. . . . This is not something that you're going to give up on because it's difficult."

Bradley, of course, is white, and as he quickly acknowledges, he has not walked in Bell's shoes or fought at the same barricades as Bell: "He's battled . . . a lot longer and in a much different way than I." Yet the argument for rejecting Bell's dismal prognosis is not dependent on color, or even on experience, but on a simple and hard-nosed approach to reality: if people are destined to spend their lives in struggle, they might as well struggle against a real evil instead of fighting merely to maintain their humanity in the face of continued disrespect. Moreover, maintaining one's humanity—indeed, even drawing strength from being battered by prejudice and rejection—need not be dependent on giving up hope that America can be better. As associate Judge Ricardo Urbina of the Superior Court of the District of Columbia observes, "The very things that made me vulnerable made me strong." . . .

At Cambridge University, in an address published in the *New York Times Magazine* in 1965, James Baldwin said, "I remember when the ex-Attorney General Mr. Robert Kennedy said it was conceivable that in forty years in America we might have a Negro President. That sounded like a very emancipated statement to white people. They were not in Harlem when this statement was first heard. They did not hear the laughter and the bitterness and scorn with which this statement was greeted. From the point of view of the man in the Harlem barber shop, Bobby Kennedy only got here yesterday and now he is already on his way to the Presidency. We were here for four hundred years and now he tells us that maybe in forty years, if you are good, we may let you become President."

If there was one sentiment that consistently came through in interview after interview with very successful black people in all walks of life, it can be summed up in one phrase: *We are tired of waiting.*

79

BRON TAYLOR

From *Affirmative Action at Work*

Former California lifeguard-turned-social science researcher Bron Taylor studied the controversial and timely issue of affirmative action by interviewing employees of the California State Department of Parks and Recreation. His case study reveals the diversity of views on affirmative action in the nation today, from hostility and fear to acceptance and advocacy. Taylor opens with a look at the classical liberal philosophy that underlies the nation's political system. The American values of individualism, the common good, equal opportunity, and distributive justice all figure in the debate over affirmative action. Using quotes and data from the parks department workers, Taylor offers readers a perspective on affirmative action from the people who are affected by the program on a daily basis.

DURING A BREAK in a training session on affirmative action, a frustrated middle-management woman asked, "What can I do to deal with this good-old-boy network? I just can't seem to break into the group." Moments later, a crusty, middle-aged, white, male manager, in a parody of the woman's statement, joked to several other white men, "What are we going to do about the good-old-boy system? Nothing, that's what we are going to do about it. We like it just the way it is!" Appreciative chuckles greeted his candid affirmation of the good-old-boy network.

A young, white, male employee, who believes he almost did not get into the California State Parks Department because of affirmative action and who has seen friends excluded because of such programs, said emphatically, "If I ever get to a place where I have any power over hiring, I will do everything I can to thwart this affirmative action bullshit."

A black male rank-and-file employee argued that if it were not for affirmative action the department would still be "lily white."

A middle-aged, white, woman manager said that at one time she was a clerical worker, without self-esteem or hopes of advancement, but affirmative action opened up possibilities for her. Some years ago, her supervisor, a white man supportive of affirmative action efforts to promote women and nonwhite men, told her that she had potential and encouraged her to go back to school to get management training. Now, although she has some negative feelings about affirmative action, she sees it as a lesser evil to the loss of talent and dignity that occurs when women and nonwhite men are not encouraged to develop their potential.

The above stories are about employees of the California State Department of Parks and Recreation, which provided the setting for this research into attitudes toward affirmative action. The stories illustrate how deeply held are the feelings that surround this issue. Affirmative action has become a critical locus of the tensions between racial groups and between men and women. From the workplace to legal, political, and philosophical literature, impassioned debates rage about the prudence and morality of affirmative action law and policy. Some politicians defend affirmative action, while others attempt to dismantle it. Given the origins of affirmative action in the civil rights movement, the rallying cry of opponents to affirmative action is a cry heavy with irony: affirmative action betrays civil rights; instead of producing new freedoms and opportunities, it has produced the tyranny of "quotas" and "reverse discrimination."

What is this phenomenon that has produced such intensity of feeling? To what extent has there been a backlash against affirmative action? Why has this backlash been so vehement in some quarters? What are the stakes involved in the affirmative action issue that contribute to the intensity of reaction, especially among those who feel directly affected by it? . . .

Given its grounding in the premises of philosophical Liberalism, affirmative action provides analysts a window through which to examine many of the critical moral dimensions of contemporary Liberal culture. Affirmative action is controversial largely because it represents and reflects several of the most critical unresolved moral conflicts within the Liberal culture. Some of these conflicts are grounded in the unresolved problems of nineteenth-century Liberalism. When I speak of Liberalism, I include conservatives, liberals, and libertarians of contemporary parlance. Despite real differences, all share the key tenets of Liberalism: rights naturally inhere in the individual, people are self-interested, acquisitive consumers (usually unchangeably so); these people compete in political and economic markets; and this competition produces at best a good society, or at least the best society people are capable of producing, and this society generally is characterized by economic growth and political freedom.

Affirmative action proponents and opponents often rest their arguments on one of Liberalism's central principles, namely, its version of distributive justice: the idea that preferred jobs and rewards ought to be distributed according to talents and qualifications (or *merit*) in a social context characterized by equality of opportunity. (This conception of distributive justice is often referred to by the terms *equal opportunity* or the *merit principle.*) It is possible, however, if the social context were to be characterized by increasing social scarcity, declining overall opportunities, and increasing conflicts over affirmative action policies, that the equal opportunity principle itself could be called into question. Since the equal opportunity version of the distributive justice principle is itself a fundamental premise of the Liberal culture, such a reevaluation could raise questions about the legitimacy of that culture. . . .

Whether or not the struggle over the principle of equal opportunity causes a reevaluation of the premises and legitimacy of Liberal market society, the affirmative action conflict remains important. It remains important because it presents the various options from contending Liberal perspectives concerning which principles of distribution—principles at issue since the beginning of Enlightenment thought—are morally warranted.

Since the Enlightenment, the type of individualism the equal opportunity principle represents has been a critical issue. Some libertarians and conservatives argue that this principle does not do enough to protect individuals, while some left-leaning liberals and leftists believe this principle is excessively individualistic and erodes the basis for social solidarity and cooperation.

Underlying this debate is the perpetual tension between concern for the general interest and concern for individual rights. Liberal thought has asserted both that individual, acquisitive, self-interested behavior is justified by its efficiency in producing collective benefits (promoting the commonweal) and that individuals have some inviolable rights against the group. But Liberalism has had problems in resolving tensions and conflicts between social welfare goals and individual rights.

Related to the basic issue here of how individual rights ought to be balanced against the commonweal are a variety of additional problems, the resolution (or nonresolution) of which will be important to the future of liberal culture. Some of these problems include: How to define terms such as *rights* and *justice, liberty* and *equality* and how these concepts are related to each other. Are individual rights absolute? Can criteria of economic efficiency be squared with principles of freedom and justice? Which of the premises from the variant forms of Liberal theory (for example, premises about human nature, market dynamics, and economic growth) hold up under analysis?

To summarize, the controversy over affirmative action is a battleground for conflicting values. The outcome of this battle may be decisive in determining which principles of distributive justice will guide public policy in America. The affirmative action controversy asks the perennial question regarding the proper relationship between individual rights and social justice, on the one hand, and the various principles of distributive justice that provide competing perspectives on rights and justice, on the other. The affirmative action issue, grounded as it is in the currently dominant equal opportunity principle, provides an appropriate window through which to examine moral meaning in our culture. . . .

My employment with the California State Department of Parks and Recreation provided the opportunity for participant observation. For fifteen years, I was a state park ocean lifeguard—a position with duties similar to that of a park ranger, with the additional responsibility for ocean rescue. I was involved in curriculum development and training for the department's affirmative action programs and with the Equal Opportunity Employment Committee (a statewide advisory committee responsible for advising and assisting the department in the creation, implementation, and evaluation of its affirmative action policies) between 1984 and 1988. The observations made while participating in these activities provided the first source of data on the views held by individuals from the various social groups.

My employment with the department gave me access to the chief of the Human Rights Office and to the director of the department, both of whom consented to the research. I entered into a research agreement with the department, which granted access for the interviews and the survey, in return for a report interpreting the results. . . .

There is an ongoing struggle within the Parks Department over the nature of its affirmative action program. The struggle is over whether or not the program should attempt to ensure "pure equal opportunity" and the hiring of the "best qualified" or to give preference to target groups. Evidence of this struggle is found throughout the department, beginning with the various ways people define the nature and purpose of affirmative action. Some say affirmative action means equal opportunity, others emphasize that affirmative action is a remedial process that temporarily gives preference to women and nonwhite men in an attempt to increase their numbers in the work force.

Periodically, there are discussions within the department's affirmative action bureaucracy (the Human Rights Office, the Equal Opportunity Employment Committee, recruiters, counselors, and so on) over whether personnel procedures should aim for equal opportunity or practice preferential treatment. For example, drafts of revised hiring procedures have been circulated that suggest adding preference points to the scores of underrepresented candidates based on the extent to which the individual's ethnic group is underrepresented. This idea was rejected, not because the pure equal opportunity version of affirmative action prevailed, but because preference could be extended without explicitly adding preference points. Many felt that preference points would engender too much controversy and hostility; some felt that preferences in general detract from the true purpose of the department's affirmative action efforts, namely, promoting pure equal opportunity. But extending preference remains the idea behind the efforts to improve the representation of women and nonwhite men in the department's work force.

Other evidence illustrating the ongoing struggle over the soul of the department's affirmative action program can be seen in the resistance by some in the department's affirmative action bureaucracy to using any language in training and in documents that characterizes affirmative action as preferential treatment. Even though certain aspects of the department's affirmative action program are clearly preferential to women and nonwhite men, some within the affirmative action bureaucracy constantly maintain that the department's program is designed to ensure that in each case the best qualified are hired and promoted. Many in the department, however, view such assertions as disingenuous. Even some employees who originally supported the department's affirmative action programs now resent them. They were told the programs were meant to ensure equal opportunity, but they became disillusioned when they saw that the programs really promoted preferential treatment.

The lack of clarity about the nature of the department's program produces tensions all the way down the line. In one recent example, a hiring panel (made up of a white man, a Hispanic woman, and a Hispanic man) scored all three white male candidates above a Hispanic candidate (the scores ranged from 79 to 93 out of 100 possible points). The Hispanic male panel member wanted to hire the Hispanic candidate, but the Hispanic female was adamantly opposed and demanded that she be shown where it is written in department policy that one minimally qualified may be hired over the best qualified. Her perspective prevailed in the discussion, and the panel recommended hiring the white male candidate. The white male district superintendent, however, although conceding that the three white male candidates were better qualified, said that meeting the minimum qualifications was sufficient. He overruled the panel's recommendation and selected the Hispanic candidate because this would help meet the department's hiring goals for Hispanics. The point to note here is that even among members of this panel, which was formed to include nonwhites sympathetic to affirmative action, there was controversy and uncertainty over what affirmative action is really supposed to be.

The overruling of the panel's recommendation was greeted by great anger among white male staff members. These men complained that such policies destroy one's incentive to improve one's skills, and also erodes the incentive of affirmative action candidates, because skill is not the criterion for hiring or advancement. Such sentiments are common in the department.

There is much hostility toward affirmative action in the Parks Department. Some of the anger toward the department's affirmative action program is related to the struggle over the nature of the program. Some employees are angered by what they think is dishonesty in how the program is presented. They say they have been told that the program promotes equal opportunity and hiring the best qualified person regardless of gender or ethnicity; however, the more they experience it, the more they realize that the program provides very strong preferences, and they feel they have little if any chance for jobs and promotions. Some are angry because they oppose preferences on principle.

Others are angry and disillusioned by the dishonesty itself. For example, one white male employee endorsed goals and hiring the "just qualified" over the "best qualified" as a way to extend a "helping hand" to people who need it, but he complained that sometimes the department is not honest. He said the department tells its people to hire the "best qualified," but they really mean hire the "adequately" qualified in order to meet the department's affirmative action hiring goals. I know of several disillusioned individuals who stopped actively supporting the program when they concluded that the department was misrepresenting its program. . . .

Some of the most outspoken critics of affirmative action believe their careers have been significantly, even irreparably, harmed by affirmative action. These people are sometimes so emotional in discussing affirmative action that their analysis of the situation becomes irrational and prone to exaggeration. For example, I heard more than once that affirmative action "quotas" preclude white men from being hired or promoted. I even heard this kind of sentiment in an entry-level ranger trainee class, where over half of the trainees were white men. In another example, a young white man came nervously into the interview carrying several sheets of notes on all the reasons affirmative action was wrong. His hands shook slightly as he explained that he did not want to forget anything. Obviously, the issue was of intense personal concern for him.

At one training session, a manager expressed a common management complaint, that the effort to meet affirmative action goals detracts from the more central mission of the department: maintaining park facilities, serving visitors, and protecting resources. A maintenance manager stated that it seemed to him that his mission (maintaining parks) and the trainer's mission (promoting affirmative action) were incompatible. When the trainer did not immediately respond to this statement, another maintenance manager, visibly agitated and with his arms folded across his chest, said loudly: "You better answer that, Buster." The intensity of this response was especially out of place given the sedate context of the training session. This manager deeply resented affirmative action. . . .

Closely related to hostility is fear about the negative consequences of affirmative action on one's career. More specifically, some interviewees feared that if their attitudes about affirmative action were to become known by certain people in the department, their careers could be ruined.

For example, one black employee, while declining to be interviewed, complained that people were always challenging him about affirmative action. He thought that a great deal of the hostility in his workplace toward affirmative action was also directed against him. He said he just tried to do his job, to do his best, but his co-workers were watching him, waiting for him to make a mistake. He was very suspicious and worried about "paybacks" if he were to state his views: "I really don't want to deal with it, it's not worth the risk, there are always repercussions. They [management] might call me in later and say 'Well, you said this. . . .'" When I explained the procedures I was using to insure confidentiality, he said he would talk to his attorney and get back to me. He never did. Another black employee, a woman, expressed fear that, with all the pressure on supervisors to meet affirmative action goals, the program had become too much of a "numbers game." She said that she was afraid of a "backlash" in response to this pressure, and she wished the pressure would be eased. . . .

In another example, I learned after conducting interviews in one location that a group of white men thought my research was not really for academic purposes but was part of a sting operation to discover who in the department was prejudiced. Some of these workers did not believe that the sampling was, in fact, random. One white man needed assurances that no personal characteristics would be mentioned in the research write-up that might make it possible for someone to identify him. He was afraid that if his views were to become known he would lose his chance for promotion.

The fears these examples illustrate may well have rational grounds. Virtually all hiring interviews in the department now include some questions designed to assess a candidate's knowledge of and level of support toward the department's affirmative action programs. Since the department is relatively small, it is not unusual for a person to know someone on the hiring panel. Therefore, it may be a rational decision to conceal one's true feelings about affirmative action.

Beyond these examples, I have often heard white men and women say that in the current climate, characterized by strong affirmative action goals, they would not encourage young white men to pursue careers in the department. One white woman, a strong supporter of affirmative action, said she would not advise her son to go into the Parks Department. It would be better for him to enter the private sector, she said, where there is not so much pressure to promote women and minorities. . . .

The overwhelming concern expressed in the interviews and observed in the workplace is that affirmative action harms the mission of the Parks Department. Some employees suggested that the huge amount of time, money, and effort spent on affirmative action makes it particularly hard for the department to fulfill its primary mission, especially in times of statewide budget cuts and increasing department responsibilities.

But by far the most commonly heard complaint about how affirmative action harms the department is that it reduces the quality of employees. Many complained that affirmative action has become a "numbers game," where qualifications are less important than meeting "quotas." Even some supporters of affirmative action thought there is too much pressure to meet hiring goals; they feared that this has led (or may lead) to the hiring of unqualified workers. Some added that affirmative action hinders individual initiative and creates a work environment where excellence is not rewarded. Still others complained that affirmative action has a negative impact on the morale of white and nonwhite employees alike, by limiting the opportunities of white men, on the one hand, while calling into question the competence of women and nonwhite men, on the other hand. Concern about the quality of employees seemed to be expressed most often by white men but was shared by many women and nonwhite men. . . .

Probably the rationale most commonly offered by those promoting affirmative action within the Parks Department is that affirmative action promotes equal opportunity. This is seen in the language used by supporters. For example, although most supporters do not think that the best qualified are being hired because of the pressure on supervisors to meet numerical hiring goals, they still use language expressing the idea that—after carefully recruiting women and nonwhites and after carefully scrutinizing the personnel procedures for bias—hiring panels should hire the best qualified.

Others argued that while the ultimate ideal is pure equal opportunity and merit hiring, affirmative action is a remedial process in response to the lack of equal opportunity. The implication, seldom stated explicitly, is that sometimes the ideal has to be temporarily set aside in order to promote long-term the ideal of equal opportunity. But nevertheless, in spite of the compromising of the ideal, the rationale for affirmative action remains, ultimately, the ideal of pure equal opportunity.

Some respondents argued that affirmative action is true to equal opportunity by asserting that it is needed for women and nonwhite men to "get their foot in the door," or to be given a "fair chance" or "equal consideration" for jobs and promotions. Several respondents pointed out that, before affirmative action, many job classifications in the department were not open to women and nonwhites, and they argued that without affirmative action such persons would never have been considered seriously. Several women asserted that white men still controlled the department and that without the pressure from affirmative action, these men would not give up their monopoly of power. Thus, those expressing sentiments in favor of affirmative action justified their views in terms of the principle of equal opportunity and believed that, at least in the long term, affirmative action promotes this principle.

Others, however, although expressing the prevailing assumption in favor of the principle of equal opportunity, made statements that seemed to qualify or make less absolute their support for the ideal of equal opportunity. For example, some endorsed the equal opportunity principle but then said that hiring a less qualified person (to meet hiring goals) would be acceptable if the qualifications were not too far apart—in other words, as long as the person could do the work. Others suggested that hiring the less qualified of the applicants was acceptable if the department then provided these persons with training so they could do the job. The interesting thing here is that while the people making these concessions expressed support for hiring the best qualified (a dominant Liberal idea), what was actually more important to them was that the employee could *do* the job. While these individuals professed allegiance to the equal opportunity principle, getting well-qualified workers was more important than insuring that the best-qualified person always got the job. For those who qualified their support for the equal opportunity principle, the consequences of affirmative action on their workplace team was more important to them than protecting in an absolute way the principle of pure equal opportunity.

Others qualified their endorsement of pure equal opportunity by supplementing the equal opportunity principle with another principle, which then was given priority. For example, one black female maintenance worker did not like preferences or the affirmative action "numbers game" and insisted that the American Dream is real: one can overcome discrimination with hard work. She also forcefully rejected preferences for non-whites and women, as well as notions of compensatory justice. But when it came down to whether she endorsed affirmative action hiring goals that helped a black woman, she said that they are fair because they benefited the woman, "giving her a job and trying to improve things" for her. This woman seemed to approve of pure equal opportunity, but when given a concrete example of a black woman who benefited from affirmative action preferences, she endorsed hiring the woman, even though she scored lower on the hiring interview. This suggests that among respondents who strongly endorsed the rhetoric of equal opportunity, some thought that perfect equal opportunity is not an inviolable principle—that there may be times when it is more important to help people in one's group. If concern for the group can sometimes override strong beliefs in individualistic notions of equal opportunity and hiring the best qualified, the question arises: How prevalent is a group-concern principle when people evaluate affirmative action?

My impression from the interviews is that all groups are heavily influenced by the equal opportunity rhetoric so pervasive in the Liberal culture. Nevertheless, it seems that women and nonwhite men, more than white men, articulate group-sensitive concerns that mitigate the influence of more individualistic equal opportunity ideals. In fact, some are suspicious of the idea of equal opportunity and hiring the best qualified based on merit. One Hispanic male ranger, for example, said, "Merit is a good principle . . . if you could somehow make an objective criteria for merit. . . . But the problem is that the people who have done the discrimination are defining merit." . . .

The strongest advocates of affirmative action were those who most self-consciously rejected the individualism of the equal opportunity principle. These strong advocates were also the most likely to endorse compensatory rationales for affirmative action. But others who expressed strong individualistic sentiments (such as individual initiative, competitiveness, and merit hiring) qualified these sentiments with strong expressions of concern for their group or for the society as a whole. Greater proportions of each ethnic and gender group were more concerned about the good of the group or the whole society than endorsed compensatory rationales for affirmative action: Of those interviewed, 15–33 percent of white men, 70 percent of blacks, 60 percent of Hispanics, 67 percent of native Americans, and 75 percent of white women gave at least qualified support for affirmative action—support grounded, at least in part, in group-sensitive sentiments.

This analysis, combined with the earlier analysis of arguments against affirmative action, suggests that there is a relationship between relative individualism in one's overall moral outlook and one's view about affirmative action: the more individualistic one's moral predisposition, the more likely one is to oppose affirmative action; the more concern one expresses for the group or the social whole, the more likely one is to approve of affirmative action. . . .

Several respondents (three white men, one white woman, one black man) pointed out that social stability has been threatened by the exclusion of nonwhites from the mainstream of society and argued that affirmative action benefits society by promoting social stability and preventing revolution. Others suggested that affirmative action benefits society by promoting harmony among ethnic and gender groups or by developing the talents of individuals from groups whose talents were usually previously denied to society. Sometimes this argument was put in the form of affirmative action success stories—how a woman or nonwhite was doing a terrific job after getting a position she or he probably would not have received in the absence of affirmative action.

Another argument asserts that affirmative action integrates the work force and thereby provides better public service. For example, an ex–inner city black employee suggested that a black ranger would have greater success in dealing with black visitors than a white ranger, whom some black visitors may distrust.

Another argument, especially among managers, concerns demographic changes that are increasing the proportion of nonwhites in California. The concern is that since groups such as Hispanics and blacks traditionally have not been exposed to or employed in nonurban parks, they may not fully appreciate their value. This argument continues that if the mission of the Parks Department is to succeed, the growing nonwhite constituency must be integrated into the department and visit the parks so that members of these groups will appreciate and support the department's mission. The overall moral argument is that affirmative action benefits both the department and society as a whole (assuming that preservation of parklands is important to society), by insuring continued public support for parks in times of great demographic change. . . .

Some opponents of affirmative action argue that discrimination in the United States is in retreat; therefore affirmative action is unnecessary, and only "protective" antidiscrimination measures are morally acceptable. However, the perceptions of the respondents, who are average working people, contradict this analysis. Perceptions about the facts, or the consequences of affirmative action, simply may be inaccurate. But certainly the perceptions of ordinary people, who observe daily their workplace realities, ought to be taken seriously, and what they report should be discounted only with good cause.

Most respondents saw discrimination as prevalent in society and in their workplace. Only white men were inconsistent on this point. They admitted to the existence of discrimination but did not think it was prevalent or affected chances within their own organizations. On this issue, where large majorities of nonwhites and women assert that prejudice was prevalent both in society and in their own workplace, I would submit that these traditionally excluded individuals are better situated than white men to evaluate the prevalence of discrimination.

Furthermore, large majorities of all groups except white men thought that without affirmative action, women and nonwhite men would not get serious consideration for jobs. And in the interviews, some respondents, particularly women, emphatically stated that white men would not willingly give up their monopoly on power. . . .

This research documents diverse attitudes toward affirmative action: hostility, fear, ambivalence, confusion, as well as strong support. Overall, the research found strong support for affirmative action among women and nonwhite men. White men, on the other hand, narrowly approved of affirmative action in the abstract and of "protective" affirmative action practices, but narrowly opposed preferential affirmative action practices. Put differently, within this particular work force, affirmative action enjoys a high level of support among women and nonwhite men, and broke even, more or less, among white men. Although many criticized the ideas behind and practices of the Parks Department's program, many of these same individuals nevertheless have hired women and nonwhite men, helping the department in its efforts to meet its affirmative action goals. Thus, the department's affirmative action program probably has enough support to succeed. At the very least, many individuals are willing to cooperate and not sabotage the program.

80

STEVEN EPSTEIN

Gay and Lesbian Movements in the United States

Steven Epstein begins by debunking a myth: There is no one unified gay and lesbian movement in the United States. Rather, the scope of gay and lesbian political activity is as wide and as diverse as is all political activity in America. Epstein introduces readers to the variety of words and terms used in the gay community, important events, people, leadership concerns of the movements, and their confrontations with hostile groups. Epstein then turns to the important issues of gays in the military and gay marriage, both central and controversial in the ongoing debate over the rights of gay and lesbian citizens of the United States.

FROM ITS MODEST and clandestine early forms in the 1950s, gay and lesbian activism has evolved into one of the most dynamic, controversial, and internally differentiated sets of social movements in the United States. My goal is to present an analytical history that shows how the general characteristics and tendencies, and the successes and failures of these movements can be understood in terms of both external and internal factors—aspects of U.S. politics and society, on one hand, and ideological and strategic tensions inside and among these movements, on the other.

My starting point is the assumption that the characteristically modern social identities known as "lesbian," "gay," "bisexual," "transgender," "queer," and so on carry with them no single or obvious political agenda. Political strategies and visions have to be developed and argued for, and they exist emphatically in the plural. Although this is no doubt true of gay and lesbian politics everywhere, it is perhaps especially evident in the United States, both because of the extent of the development of lesbian and gay communities and because of the highly diverse and multicultural character of the society as a whole. Even at a single moment in time—say, for instance, at one of the annual Lesbian and Gay Freedom Day parades held in cities across the United States, where contingents of sober-looking gay Mormons, young queer radicals, and leather-clad practitioners of sadomasochism may triumphantly march down the same route—the notion of a shared and fully articulated politics is a convenient fiction. [O]ne of the most noteworthy aspects of gay and lesbian movements in the United States is the *proliferation* of political beliefs, practices, and organizations that often *compete* with one another to be perceived as legitimate and preferred.

In fact, there is no such thing as "the U.S. gay and lesbian movement," except insofar as more particular movements claim to speak for it. While much of what I call mainstream lesbian and gay politics roots itself in the assertion that it *is* "the movement," upon inspection, each term in the phrase "the gay and lesbian movement" either dissolves into a fog of ambiguity or congeals into sharp contradictions. The word "the" suggests unity and coherence, when in fact there have been multiple movements over time—"homophile," "gay liberationist," "lesbian feminist," "gay rights," and "queer," to name only a few—with widely different self-understandings and political strategies. The term "gay and lesbian" is also problematic, for part of what is at stake in the contest that I describe is the very question of the movement's collective identity: who is the "we" on behalf of whom activists speak? Do gay men share with lesbians a cohesive identity that can generate a single political vision? If so, does it encompass the demands of bisexuals and transgendered people or of self-styled "queers" who reject the terms "gay and lesbian"? And if so many in the United States feel the tug of multiple and overlapping claims on their identities, forming organizations as black gay men, or Jewish lesbians, or south Asian queers, and rejecting the notion that these compound identities can be broken down into their constituent parts, then in what sense can we speak of a "gay and lesbian" movement? Finally, the word "movement" should not go unexamined. Though it typically refers to recognizably political projects that have as their end such tangible goals as gay rights legislation, it can also denote activities directed toward the redefinition of culture and selfhood—movements for "sexual freedom," for new family forms, for "gay spirituality." . . .

. . . [P]olitics in the 1990s was inflected by the tension between essentialist conceptions of gay identity and culture and challenges to that model. One side of this tension was manifest in the continued growth and cultural legitimation of the mainstream, quasi-ethnic form of gay identity and community. As many activists seized upon gay scientists' reports of the possible discovery of a "gay brain" or "gay gene," as direct marketers targeted the "gay consumer," and as pollsters sampled the opinions of the "gay voter," the mainstream lesbian and gay rights movement seemed tied to a homogeneous model of collective identity articulated substantially through consumption practices and the display of trinkets—gay-themed credit cards, "freedom rings," and rainbow flags. Quasi-ethnic territorialism also continued in full force. In 1997 the city of Chicago officially designated a stretch of North Halsted Street known familiarly as Boys' Town as one of the city's distinctive neighborhoods, along with Greektown and Chinatown, and constructed ceremonial towers along the street, ringed with the colors of the rainbow flag.

Yet at the same time, the extraordinary diversification of gay and lesbian movements in the 1990s belied this assumption of a uniform collective interest. This diversification was most clearly expressed in three respects: racial politics, a new debate over sexual expression and sexual mores, and the emergence of an overt Left/Right split within lesbian and gay communities.

A large number of gay, lesbian, or queer political organizations promoting the interests of people of color, including African Americans, Native Americans, Asian Americans, and Latinos, were born in the late 1980s and early 1990s. The Latino/a Lesbian and Gay Organization (LLEGO), dedicated to fighting homophobia, sexism, and discrimination, was founded in 1987 at the National March on Washington and brought hundreds of Latinas and Latinos from around the country to its annual meetings. The Black Lesbian and Gay Leadership Forum was established in 1988 with the goals of building alliances with black organizations, launching antiracism campaigns in the gay white community, and arranging conferences on the black church's attitudes toward homosexuality. Trikone (from the Sanskrit word for "triangle"), an organization of lesbian, gay, and bisexual south Asians, began marching in the San Francisco Lesbian and Gay Freedom Day Parade in 1986 and since 1993 has participated in India Day parades in the Bay Area. Activists in organizations like these were often inspired by writers, filmmakers, and artists who sought to articulate the particular dilemmas confronting gay men and lesbians of color—such as filmmaker Marlon Rigg's testimony, in his poignant and arresting 1991 film *Tongues Untied*: "In this great gay mecca, I was an invisible man."

Activists of color challenged the goals of the mainstream, pushed for the radicalization of the movement, and emphasized the importance of constructing coalitions between gay and lesbian communities and other constituencies promoting social change. Some activists, such as those working with the Audre Lorde Project in Brooklyn, sought to construct a multiracial coalition of queers of color. Others noted the specific effects of gay and lesbian immigration to the United States from other countries: in the "queer diaspora," political strategizing had to recognize that not everyone had the same relationship to the state or to institutions of citizenship. Still others analyzed the social and political consequences of racial eroticization and the perpetuation, within gay and lesbian communities, of racially based stereotypes concerning sexual dominance and submissiveness.

Sexuality, another site of internal diversity, once again became an area of political contention in the mid-1990s. In San Francisco, community members who felt that the annual Freedom Day Parade had become "too sexual" and that "outrageous" behavior gave ammunition to political opponents in the New Right established an alternative, "family-oriented" street fair held the preceding day. In New York, bitter fights broke out when a gay group calling itself Gay and Lesbian HIV Prevention Activists called for the city's health department to crack down on sex clubs, which were portrayed as contributing to the spread of HIV. In highly publicized books and opinion pieces in the mass media, Gabriel Rotello and Michelangelo Signorile, two spokespersons of this movement who had migrated rightward from earlier involvements in queer politics, repudiated what Rotello called the "the orgiastic, Dionysian vision of liberation proclaimed in the immediate aftermath of Stonewall," and they advocated "the construction of a gay culture that validates sexual moderation and restraint." Rotello pointed to lesbians as role models for gay men—ironically so, since by the 1990s the notion of lesbians as monogamous and sexually unadventurous was increasingly being rejected by lesbians themselves. In 1997 a number of activists and academics founded a new organization—Sex Panic!—to challenge these ideas as typical of the sex-negative and sex-phobic tendencies of U.S. society and to assert the centrality of sexual freedom to queer politics. Similar debates erupted in San Francisco, where activists fought calls to close the sex clubs that had sprung up after the closure of the bathhouses.

In part, the controversy over sexual blatancy revived the fights over sexuality that had marked the lesbian "sex wars" and the early years of the AIDS epidemic. But at root, the debate was not about just AIDS or sexuality but about broader conceptions of the community. What were its norms? Who spoke for it? What was its present relation to its own past history? The debate also marked another episode in a familiar story: the split over whether the social legitimation of the lesbian and gay mainstream should be achieved by sacrificing those in the community who were deemed unrespectable.

A further marker of the strategic and philosophical divides within the movement was the emergence of a visible gay Right. This included neoconservatives, who repudiated sexual radicalism and sought to reduce the gay movement's struggle to the establishment of equal rights in the public realm, as well as traditional conservatives, who denounced the "puerile posturing" and "queerthink" promoted by the "queer establishment." The Log Cabin Republican Club, a "home for mainstream gay and lesbian Americans who . . . care deeply about equality [and] hold Republican views on crime, fiscal responsibility and foreign policy," established more than fifty chapters around the country, with a national office in Washington, D.C. Though the organization proved capable of raising more than $100,000 per election cycle, it found itself in the embarrassing position of not being able to find many Republican candidates willing to accept the group's donations.

Other national lesbian and gay organizations, such as the Human Rights Campaign (with sixty full-time staff members and a budget of $2.5 million by 1997), pursued centrist strategies and relied heavily on wealthy, white male donors for their electoral fund-raising. The National Gay and Lesbian Task Force, by contrast (with twenty-two full-time staff members and a budget of $2.7 million), moved in a more leftward and populist direction. In 1990 its director, Urvashi Vaid, heckled President George Bush at his first major address on AIDS and denounced the president's lack of meaningful action on the issue. Vaid emphasized building an organized movement base at the grassroots and insisted that the political agenda move beyond civil rights to encompass a broader vision of a better society. In its position papers, NGLTF supported coalition politics and drew links between issues affecting gay men and lesbians and other hot topics of the 1990s, including welfare reform and immigration issues.

In the face of these various forms of political diversification, unity came primarily through organizing to fight the New Right, including mobilizing against its electoral and legislative initiatives. As the clash between lesbian and gay activists and the New Right unfolded, gay rights emerged, improbably, as one of the defining social issues of the 1990s. Opposition between the mainstream lesbian and gay rights movement and the New Right not only served to consolidate each group's identity but also encouraged each group to pursue the strategy of urging the broader public to "dis-identify" with the other. Gays and lesbians sought to convince racial and religious minorities that the New Right posed a general threat to freedom, while New Right groups tried to drive a wedge into this alliance by arguing that gay men and lesbians were a wealthy and privileged group that had inappropriately claimed for itself the mantle of the civil rights movement.

Unlike gay and lesbian movements in other countries, U.S. activists in the 1990s found themselves in the extraordinary and unenviable position of fighting not only the repeal of gay rights ordinances at the local level but also the passage of citywide and statewide referenda that sought to make it legally impossible for gay rights laws ever to be established. Activists in Oregon fought bitter but successful battles against such initiatives in 1992 and 1993, also dividing among themselves over whether to put forward a least-common-denominator antidiscrimination agenda or a more radical defense of queer sexualities. In Colorado 53 percent of voters supported a 1992 referendum that scrapped existing gay rights laws in the more liberal cities of Denver, Boulder, and Aspen and prohibited the establishment of any such laws in the future. National outrage on the part of lesbians and gay men prompted an organized boycott of travel to the state of Colorado, as well as a court challenge that eventually made its way to the United States Supreme Court. In 1996, in an important six-three decision for gays and lesbians from the Supreme Court, which was not known to favor them, the Court ruled that the state had no compelling interest in preemptively banning gays and lesbians from attempting to pass legislation securing their rights.

The creation of unity amid diversity was also the significant but transient result of two visible national mobilizations in the early 1990s: the third National March on Washington for Lesbian, Gay, and Bi Equal Rights and Liberation and New York City's Stonewall 25* which com-

*The Stonewall riot occurred on July 28, 1969 in New York City's Greenwich Village. When police began a raid on the Stonewall Inn gay bar that night, as they had done before, the guests decided to resist arrest and fights erupted. Trouble continued for many nights. Stonewall is considered by many as the start of the modern gay rights movement.—EDS.

memorated the twenty-fifth anniversary of the Stonewall riot. The National March drew as few as three hundred thousand and as many as one million participants, depending on who did the counting. Planners insisted on racial diversity and gender balance in all local delegations to the national steering committee that helped prepare for the march. And, as the name reflects, the march signaled a more complete inclusion of bisexuals in the political agenda, as well as a stated desire to accommodate both those who sought equal rights and those who insisted on a more radical politics of liberation. The following year, Stonewall 25 put more than one million marchers, including many international contingents, on the streets of Manhattan, with participants marching past the United Nations building, demanding respect for the human rights of lesbians, gays, and bisexuals around the world. Unlike earlier national marches, these events attracted significant attention in the mass media, but like earlier marches, these national shows of strength seemed to have little lasting impact on movement mobilization either nationally or locally.

The failure to build on these national demonstrations in any significant way was accompanied by another conspicuous lack: there were no widely recognized, charismatic leaders. As commentators had been noting for some time, gay and lesbian movements in the United States seemed to produce remarkably few such leaders. There was no shortage of popular heroes, such as the gay men and lesbians who became public figures through their legal battles against dismissal from the military. And celebrities, such as Chastity Bono (the lesbian daughter of Sonny Bono and Cher) and Candace Gingrich (the sister of right-wing politician Newt Gingrich), had become a familiar presence at marches and parades. But—perhaps because of the proliferation and diversity of movements and organizations—gay and lesbian movements seemed to have difficulty generating or sustaining leaders with the imagination and personal qualities needed to mobilize or redirect collective sentiments in powerful ways, to generate solidarity across the divisions within the movements, or to construct coalitions with movements of other kinds.

As activists waged trench warfare against the New Right in local initiatives around the United States, many held out the hope that larger successes might be won at the national level. Particularly in contrast to the overt, antigay hate mongering that marked the 1992 Republican National Convention, the stated positions of Democratic presidential candidate Bill Clinton seemed to hold open the prospect of a new political opportunity structure for gay and lesbian movements. Clinton explicitly mentioned gay people in his nomination acceptance speech at the Democratic National Convention and included openly gay people in his campaign team and, later, in his administration. However, when his attempt to make good on a campaign promise to end the persecution of gay men and lesbians in the U.S. military met with energetic political opposition, Clinton quickly backed down and proposed a regressive "compromise" that, in practice, continued to lead to the dismissal of gay men and lesbians from the military. This and subsequent actions by Clinton—on issues such as gay marriage—demonstrated that there was no political party of consequence in the U.S. political system with which lesbian and gay activists could unproblematically ally and that the U.S. two-party system provided restricted opportunities for the advancement of a gay rights agenda.

These two issues—gays in the military and gay marriage—merit additional attention for the extraordinary amount of controversy that they provoked. Given that no other country that has openly considered the issue of military service by lesbians and gay men has greeted the prospect with any great degree of panic or preoccupation, the popular hysteria surrounding the issue in the United States testified to unique aspects of the U.S. political and cultural environment. As Barry Adam notes, an explanation that points to the power of the New Right alone seems insufficient to account for the psychological charge of the debate, which raised the specter of "vulnerable" heterosexual soldiers being eyed by predatory homosexuals in shower rooms and pointed, in rather Freudian terms, to the threat that overt homosexual desire posed to sublimated male bonding and esprit de corps. Much like the targeting of homosexuals during the McCarthy era, the debate about gays in the military seemed wrapped up in concerns about the "feminization" of the state, in a country whose whole national identity in the period since the Second World War has centered on its global military might.

The debate over gay marriage was equally freighted with symbolic power for all concerned. In the 1980s and early 1990s, lesbians and gay men won substantial victories in obtaining domestic partner benefits such as health insurance for the lovers of gay men and lesbians employed by many businesses, city governments, and universities around the United States—no small matter in a country without national health care. A number of cities, such as San Francisco, had formal provisions for couples to register at City Hall as domestic partners. No one seemed quite prepared, however, when the Hawaii Supreme Court ruled in 1993, that a lower court had improperly dismissed a lawsuit challenging the state's policy of denying marriage licenses to gay or lesbian couples. The court suggested that it would most likely rule in favor of the lawsuit, and a lower court eventually did so in 1997. Meanwhile, conservatives around the country were shocked to realize that if Hawaii permitted gay marriages, then the U.S. Constitution might require every other state to recognize those marriages. Even as gay men and lesbians throughout the United States began imagining wedding-and-honeymoon trips to Hawaii, conservatives in many state legislatures began introducing measures to define marriage strictly as the union of a man and a woman. Such measures had become law in twenty-five states by mid-1997. At the same time, members of the U.S. Congress proposed a national Defense of Marriage Act, which Clinton announced in September 1996 that he would sign, effectively ensuring its passage.

The marriage debate was revealing for what it suggested about the limits of popular endorsement of the equality of gay men and lesbians. While substantial percentages of those surveyed in opinion polls disapproved of discrimination against gays and lesbians in the workplace, far fewer were able to conceive of gay marriage as anything other than an oxymoron. More than a referendum on homosexuality, the debate encapsulated American confusion about the very nature of the family and its place in late-twentieth-century society. At the same time, the marriage issue sparked passionate arguments among gay men and lesbians themselves. In the wake of the lesbian "baby boom" of the late 1980s and 1990s, the legal fights for custody and adoption of children by gay and lesbian parents, and well-publicized struggles by lesbians and gay men to be the acknowledged legal guardians of their partners in the event of medical incapacitation, many saw "family" issues as the cutting edge of movement politics; for them, gay marriage was the single most important marker of progress. To others, however, the "aping" of heterosexual marital institutions was a betrayal of radical liberationist and feminist critiques of traditional models of gender, sexuality, and the family and reflected an unfortunate desire to assimilate into the mainstream.

Somewhat similarly, debates within gay and lesbian communities about military service pitted those who saw inclusion in the military as the pivotal step in the march for equality and genuine citizenship against those who questioned gay support for a historically misogynistic, racist, and homophobic institution that acted in the interest of U.S. imperial ambition. Thus, viewed from one angle, the demand for inclusion in these two core institutions of the nation—marriage and the military—was a radical move; indeed it was more radical than queer antiassimilationism, which contented itself with denouncing those institutions from the sidelines. But from another angle, this conventional understanding of gay citizenship, which positioned sexual minorities as being "just like everyone else," surrendered the idea that lesbians, gay men, bisexuals, and transgendered people could promote meaningful political alternatives only insofar as they were *different* from the straight majority. In the debates over marriage and the military, "the U.S. lesbian and gay movement" once again was distinguished as much by its internal diversity and disagreement as it was by its ability to bring contentious social issues to center stage.

In November 1997, when President Clinton made his way to the podium at a fund-raising dinner for the Human Rights Campaign, it marked the first time that a U.S. president ever spoke at an event sponsored by a lesbian and gay civil rights organization. Given how unthinkable this would have been even twenty years earlier, it is clear that an impressive sea of change in public sentiment had occurred in the interim. At the same time, the fragility of gay rights in the United States is so apparent, the cultural climate surrounding sexuality is so repressive, and the strides toward equal citizenship are so limited in comparison to other Western countries that it becomes crucial to reflect both on the peculiarities of the United States and on the internal difficulties of U.S. gay and lesbian movements.

In 1960 no cities or states in the United States guaranteed equal rights to gay men and lesbians. Every state outlawed sodomy, and there were no openly gay elected officials anywhere in the United States. By 1997 thirty states and the District of Columbia had abolished their sodomy laws. Eleven states and dozens of cities and counties had passed laws protecting lesbians and gay men (and sometimes bisexuals and transgendered people) from various forms of discrimination based on sexual orientation, and elsewhere gubernatorial executive orders and mayoral proclamations officially banned discrimination. As a result, by the mid-1990s more than one-fifth of Americans lived in cities or counties providing legal protection. In addition, five states, including New York, now offer domestic partner benefits to gay and lesbian state employees. With the exception of Wisconsin and Minnesota, however, every state that has banned discrimination (including Hawaii) is on the Atlantic or Pacific Coast, leaving the inhabitants of the vast interior without protection. Sodomy laws remain on the books in most of the South, several western states, Michigan, and even liberal Massachusetts. And, although in 1997 the U.S. Senate came surprisingly close to passing a bill banning employment discrimination, relief is not very likely to come soon at the federal level.

At this writing, three members of the U.S. House of Representatives are openly gay—though all were closeted when first elected to that office—as are eleven other men and women in state-level governments. In late 1997, Virginia Apuzzo, a former executive director of the NGLTF, became the highest-ranking openly gay or lesbian person in government in U.S.

history when she was appointed assistant to the president for management and administration. Increasingly, large segments of the society appear ready to countenance the presence of lesbians and gay men in roles that were previously unthinkable—gay and lesbian ministers, gay and lesbian athletes, gay and lesbian characters in popular television shows and films. Newspapers that in the recent past covered homosexuality as a crime story or a titillating social problem now routinely present commentary and analysis on lesbian and gay politics, community, and identity. Television talk shows provide a forum, however constrained, for those with the most marginalized sexualities to tell their stories to a national audience. Even in the domain of organized religion, there have been significant changes. In 1997, for example, the Interfaith Alliance, a nationwide organization of more than fifty denominations, announced its support for a federal antidiscrimination law protecting lesbians and gay men in the workplace. . . .

The multiplicity of voices and goals within U.S. gay and lesbian movements, in combination with specific features of U.S. society, therefore structures not only the familiar dilemmas of social movement politics—gradualism versus provocation, assimilationism versus separatism, single-issue groups versus coalitions, centralization versus grassroots localism—but also the less commonly found tension between the politics of stable identity and the politics of instability and difference. In the struggle between different conceptions of politics, various groups have competed to lay claim to "the movement" and say what it "really is," but none has entirely succeeded in doing so. Is there an alternative model—one that will "play" in the U.S. context; that will not suppress or deny difference; and that has the potential to improve the life conditions of lesbians, gay men, bisexuals, transgendered people, and queer people while also challenging the social organization of gender and sexuality and the culture of sexual repression? This politics would take "identity as a point of departure rather than a final destination"—organizing less around identity than "sympathy and affinity," both within and between groups. The goal would be to forge alliances across gay and other social movements, not on the basis of shared history or the congruence of experience but on the ground of similarities in their relations to the dominant constellations of power in the society. But to succeed, this politics would need to promote a new vision of citizenship, articulating a model of belonging that neither embraced marginalization for its own sake nor surrendered the goal of social transformation.

81

ELLEN ALDERMAN AND CAROLINE KENNEDY

From *In Our Defense*

Two young attorneys have chosen to examine the Bill of Rights not from the perspective of landmark Supreme Court cases, but from a grassroots perspective. Ellen Alderman and Caroline Kennedy present the story behind an obscure federal case involving the First Amendment and freedom of religion. The U.S. Forest Service had decided to build a logging road through public lands in northern California. The land is sacred to the Yurok tribe, and the tribe hoped that the Constitution's First Amendment would protect them in their free exercise of religion. However, in 1987 the Supreme Court, in a close vote, decided otherwise. Alderman and Kennedy note, however, that Congress intervened, and the land was named protected wilderness in 1990. For now, the Yurok's sacred land is undisturbed, but without the Supreme Court's help.

"Congress shall make no law respecting an establishment of religion, or prohibiting the free exercise thereof . . . "

WHEN THE DOGWOOD TREE blossomed twice and a whale swam into the mouth of the Klamath River, the Yurok medicine man knew it was time for the tribe to perform the White Deer Skin Dance. He knew that these natural signs were messengers sent by the Great Spirit to tell the people things were out of balance in the world. The White Deer Skin Dance and Jump Dance are part of the World Renewal Ceremonies of the Yurok, Karok, Tolowa, and Hoopa Indian tribes of northern California. The World Renewal Ceremonies are performed to protect the earth from catastrophe and humanity from disease and to bring the physical and spiritual world back in balance. Preparations for the ceremonies begin far up in the mountains, in the wilderness known to the Indians as the sacred "high country."

According to Indian mythology, the World Renewal Ceremonies were initiated by the *woge*, spirits that inhabited the earth before the coming of man. The *woge* gave culture and all living things to humanity, and the ceremonies are held at sites along the river where these gifts were given. The *woge* then became afraid of human contamination and retreated to the mountains before ascending into a hole in the sky. Because the mountains were the *woge*'s last refuge on earth, they are the source of great spiritual power.

In recent years, there has been a quiet resurgence of traditional Indian religion in the high country. Young Indians who left to find jobs on the "other side of the mountain" are returning to their ancestral grounds. Lawrence "Tiger" O'Rourke, a thirty-two-year-old member of the Yurok tribe, worked for eight years around the state as a building contractor before returning to raise fish in the traditional Indian way.

"In the white man's world . . . you just spend all of your lifetime making money and gathering up things around you and it doesn't really have any value," Tiger says. "Here, the Spirit is still in everything—the trees, the rocks, the river . . . the different kinds of people. It's got a life spirit, so we're all connected. . . . The concrete world, it's kind of dead. It feels like something's missing and the people are afraid. . . . So this place is just right for me, I guess."

There are about five thousand others who, like Tiger, are happy to live in isolation from the "white man's world"; indeed the spiritual life of the high country depends on it. But when the U.S. Forest Service announced plans to build a logging road through the heart of the high country, many of the Yurok tribe decided they could not remain quiet any longer.

They went to court, claiming that the logging road would violate their First Amendment right to freely exercise their religion. They said it was like building a "highway through the Vatican." What the Indians wanted the courts to understand was that the salmon-filled creeks, singing pines, and mountain trails of the high country were their Vatican.

To prepare for the World Renewal Ceremony, the medicine man first notifies the dance givers that it is time. According to Indian law, only certain families are allowed to give dances and to own dance regalia. The privilege and the responsibility are passed down from generation to generation.

"In the beginning," says Tiger, a member of such a family, "the Spirit came up the river and he stayed at different people's houses. He only knocked and went in where he knew the people would take care of him. They would have a responsibility to the people, and the world, and the universe to make the ceremony, and they would always do it. It's a lot of work. You have to live a good life, you have to live with truth. Not everybody could do it."

The dance giver is also responsible for paying up all debts before the dance. Indian law puts a price on everything, and by paying the price the social balance is restored. If you insult someone, you owe that person a certain amount; if you kill a person, you must pay that person's family. Payment prevents hatred and anger from spreading to infect the community and brings the world back into harmony. . . .

The most sacred area of the high country is known as Medicine Mountain, a ridge dominated by the peaks of Doctor Rock, Peak 8, and Chimney Rock. Chimney Rock, a majestic outcropping of pinkish basalt, rises sixty-seven hundred feet above sea level. From its summit, views of receding blue waves of mountain ridges fade into the horizon in all directions. On a clear day, the shimmer of the Pacific Ocean gleams at the end of the winding silver ribbon of the Smith River below. . . .

Although only a few medicine men and Indian doctors actively use the sacred sites of the high country, the spiritual well-being of the entire tribe depends on performance of the ancient rituals. Despite more than a half century during which the government removed Indians from their villages and prohibited them from speaking their own language or practicing their religion, a few elderly Indians never left or gave up the old ways. Some young Indians, like Tiger, are returning to their homeland. And others, like Walter "Black Snake" Lara, are trying to balance the old world with the new.

Black Snake works felling trees. He says it is an honorable job in many parts of the lush California forests, but not in the high country. Of the sacred grounds he says, "The Creator fixed it that way for us. We're responsible for it."

Tiger, Black Snake, and others are struggling to maintain their fragile way of life. They are succeeding in part because the steep mountains, dense forests, and nonnavigable streams have protected their cemeteries, villages, and high country from encroachment by the "concrete" world. To them, the proposed highway was more than just a symbol of that concrete world. By the Forest Service's own estimates, each day it would bring about seventy-two diesel logging trucks and ninety other vehicles within a half mile of Chimney Rock.

Actually, the Forest Service started constructing a logging road through the Six Rivers National Forest in the 1930s. It began at either end, in the lumber-mill towns of Gasquet to the north and Orleans to the south, thus becoming known as the G-O Road. Under the Forest Service's management plan, once the road was completed, the towns would be connected and timber could be hauled to mills at either end of the forest. In the meantime, as construction inched toward Chimney Rock, new areas of timber were opened up to logging. "They snuck that road in from both sides," says Black Snake.

By the 1970s, the two segments of the seventy-five-mile road dead-ended in the forest. Black pavement simply gave way to gravel and dirt, and then the side of a mountain. The final six-mile section needed to complete the road was known as the Chimney Rock section of the G-O Road.

The Indians feared that if the road was built it would destroy the sanctity of the high country forever. As Sam Jones, a full-blooded Yurok dance giver put it. "When the medicine lady goes out there to pray, she stands on these rocks and meditates. The forest is there looking out. [She] talks to the trees and rocks, whatever is out there. After they get through praying, their answer comes from the mountain. Our people talk in their language to them and if it's all logged off and all bald there, they can't meditate at all. They have nothing to talk to."

An influx of tree fellers, logging trucks, tourists, and campers would also destroy the ability to make medicine in the high country. The consequences were grave; if the medicine man could not bring back the power for the World Renewal Ceremonies, the people's religious existence would be threatened. And because the land itself is considered holy by the Indians, they could not move their "church" to another location. "People don't understand about our place," Black Snake says, "because they can build a church and worship wherever they want."

The Indians filed a lawsuit in federal district court in San Francisco: *Northwest Indian Cemetery Protective Association v. Peterson*. (R. Max Peterson was named as defendant in his capacity as chief of the U.S. Forest Service.) They claimed that construction of the G-O Road would destroy the solitude, privacy, and undisturbed natural setting necessary to Indian religious practices, thereby violating their First Amendment right to freely exercise their religion.

By invoking the First Amendment, the Indians joined those before them who had sought religious freedom in America. After all, many colonists came to the New World to escape religious persecution in the Old, establishing colonies that reflected the varied beliefs of their inhabitants. The Puritans of Massachusetts sought to build their "City on a Hill," Lord Baltimore founded Maryland as a colony where Catholics and Protestants would live together and prosper, William Penn led the

Quakers to Philadelphia, and the Virginia planters were strong supporters of the Church of England. . . .

[Thomas] Jefferson's [1785 Virginia] statute served as one of [James] Madison's models for the First Amendment, which, as adopted and ratified, has two components: the establishment clause and the free exercise clause. In general terms, according to the Supreme Court, the "establishment of religion clause of the First Amendment means at least this: Neither a state nor the Federal Government can set up a church. Neither can pass laws which aid one religion, aid all religions, or prefer one religion over another. . . . In the words of Jefferson, the clause against establishment of religion by law was intended to erect 'a wall of separation between church and State.'" Courts have relied on the establishment clause to strike down state support for parochial schools, statutes mandating school prayer, and the erection of religious displays (for example, nativity scenes or menorahs) on public property.

In contrast, the free exercise clause forbids the government from outlawing religious belief. It also forbids the government from unduly burdening the exercise of a religious belief. However, some regulation of conduct expressing belief is permitted. If a person claims that a government action violates his right to freely exercise his religion, courts must first determine if the asserted religious belief is "sincerely held." If so, then the burden on individual worship must be balanced against the state's interest in proceeding with the challenged action. Only if the state's interest is "compelling" will it outweigh the individual's right to the free exercise of religion.

In the two hundred years since the First Amendment was ratified, the free exercise clause has protected many whose religious beliefs have differed from those of the majority. For example, the Supreme Court has held that unemployment benefits could not be denied to a Seventh-Day Adventist fired for refusing to work on Saturday, her sabbath; nor to a Jehovah's Witness who quit his job in a weapons production factory for religious reasons. Forcing these individuals to choose between receiving benefits and following their respective religious practices violated their right to the free exercise of religion.

In 1983, the Federal District Court for the Northern District of California held that completion of the G-O Road would violate the Northwest Indians' right to freely exercise their religion. The court concluded that the G-O Road would unconstitutionally burden their exercise of sincerely held religious beliefs, and the government's interest in building the road was not compelling enough to override the Indians' interest. Therefore, the court enjoined, or blocked, the Forest Service from completing the road. When the decision was announced, the group of fifty to a hundred Indians who had traveled south to attend the trial were convinced that their medicine had been successful.

The government appealed the decision to the Ninth Circuit Court of Appeals. While the case was pending, Congress passed the California Wilderness Act, which designated much of the sacred high country as a wilderness area. Thus all commercial activity, including mining or timber harvesting, was forever banned. But as part of a compromise worked out to secure passage of the act, Congress exempted a twelve-hundred-foot-wide corridor from the wilderness, just enough to complete the G-O Road. So although the surrounding area could not be destroyed, the road could still be built. That decision was left to the Forest Service. The medicine was still working, however; in July 1986, the Ninth Circuit affirmed the district court's decision and barred completion of the road.

The government then appealed the case to the U.S. Supreme Court. It filed a "petition for certiorari," a request that the Court hear the case. The Supreme Court receives thousands of these "cert" petitions each year, but accepts only about 150 for argument and decision. In order to take the case, four justices must vote to grant "cert." If they do not, the lower-court ruling stands. Because freedom of religion is so important in the constitutional scheme, and because the case involved principles affecting the management of vast tracts of federal land, *Northwest Indian Cemetery Protective Association* was one of the 150 cases accepted.

The Indians based their Supreme Court arguments on their victories in the lower courts and on a landmark 1972 Supreme Court case, *Wisconsin v. Yoder.* In *Yoder,* three Amish parents claimed that sending their children to public high school, as required by law, violated their right to free exercise of religion. They explained that the Old Order Amish religion was devoted to a simple life in harmony with nature and the soil, untainted by influence from the contemporary world. The Amish said that public schools emphasized intellectual accomplishment, individual distinction, competition, and social life. In contrast, "Amish society emphasize[d] informal learning-through-doing; a life of 'goodness,' rather than a life of intellect; wisdom, rather than technical knowledge; community welfare, rather than competition; and separation from, rather than integration with, contemporary worldly society." The Amish said that forcing their children out of the Amish community into a world undeniably at odds with their fundamental beliefs threatened their eternal salvation. Therefore, they claimed, state compulsory education laws violated their right to freely exercise their religion. The Supreme Court agreed.

If the Supreme Court could find that freedom of religion outweighed the state's interest in compulsory education, the Indians believed that the Constitution would make room for them too. After all, Chief Justice Warren Burger had written in *Yoder*, "A way of life that is odd or even erratic but interferes with no rights or interests of others is not to be condemned because it is different." The Indians argued that, like the Amish, they wanted only to be left alone to worship, as they had for thousands of years.

But the Forest Service argued that the Indians were seeking something fundamentally different from what the Amish had won. Whereas the exemption from a government program in *Yoder* affected only the Amish, and "interfere[d] with no rights or interests of others," the Indians were trying to stop the government from managing its own resources. From the government's point of view, if the courts allowed these Indians to block the G-O Road, it would open the door for other religious groups to interfere with government action on government lands everywhere. (It did not matter to the government that the Indians considered the high country to be *their* land.) The Forest Service produced a map marked to indicate sacred religious sites in California; the red markers nearly covered the state. Giving the Indians veto power over federal land management decisions was not, in the government's view, what the free exercise clause was intended to protect. As Justice William O. Douglas once wrote, "The Free Exercise Clause is written in terms of what the government cannot do to the individual, not in terms of what the individual can exact from the government."

The singing pines, soaring eagles, and endless mountain vistas of northern California are about as far from the white marble Supreme Court on Capitol Hill as it is possible to get in the United States. Yet like thousands of Americans before them, a small group of Indians came in November 1987 to watch their case argued before the highest court in the land. Though the Indians had never put much faith in any branch of the government, they had come to believe that if the justices could see the case through "brown eyes," they would finally make room in the Bill of Rights for the "first Americans."

Some did not realize that by the time a case reaches the Supreme Court, it no longer involves only those individuals whose struggle initiated it, but has enduring repercussions throughout the country. Unlike a legal code or statute that is written with specificity, "a constitution," wrote Chief Justice John Marshall, "is framed for ages to come, and is designed to approach immortality, as nearly as human institutions can approach it." When the Supreme Court decides a case based on the Bill of Rights, it enunciates principles that become the Supreme Law of the Land, and are used by lower courts across the United States to guide their decisions.

The Indians lost by one vote. "The Constitution simply does not provide a principle that could justify upholding [the Indians'] legal claims," Justice Sandra Day O'Connor wrote for the majority. "However much we wish that it were otherwise, government simply could not operate if it were required to satisfy every citizen's religious needs and desires."

The Court accepted that the G-O Road could have "devastating effects on traditional Indian religious practices." Nonetheless, it held that the G-O Road case differed from *Yoder* because here, the government was not *coercing* the Indians to act contrary to their religious beliefs. In what may prove to be an important development in the law, the Court concluded that unless the government *coerces* individuals to act in a manner that violates their religious beliefs, the free exercise clause is not implicated, and the government does not have to provide a compelling reason for its actions.

The Court also noted the broad ramifications of upholding the Indians' free exercise claim. While the Indians did not "at present" object to others using the high country, their claim was based on a need for privacy in the area. According to the Court, under the Indians' reasoning there was nothing to prevent them, or others like them, from seeking to exclude all human activity but their own from land they held sacred. "No disrespect for the [Indian] practices is implied when one notes that such beliefs could easily require *de facto* beneficial ownership of some rather spacious tracts of public property," the Court wrote.

Justice William Brennan's emotional dissent rejected the Court's reasoning and result. The religious freedom remaining to the Indians after the Supreme Court's decision, according to Justice Brennan, "amounts to nothing more than the right to believe that their religion will be destroyed . . . the safeguarding of such a hollow freedom . . . fails utterly to accord with the dictates of the First Amendment." Justice Brennan and the two justices who joined him, Thurgood Marshall and Harry Blackmun, rejected the Court's new "coercion test."

"The Court . . . concludes that even where the government uses federal land in a manner that threatens the very existence of a Native American religion, the Government is simply not 'doing' anything to the practitioners of that faith," Justice Brennan wrote. "Ultimately the Court's coercion test turns on a distinction between government actions that compel affirmative conduct inconsistent with religious belief, and those governmental actions that prevent conduct consistent with religious belief. In my view, such a distinction is without constitutional significance." The dissenters believed instead that the Indians' religion would be severely burdened, indeed made "impossible," by the government's actions, and that the government had not shown a compelling interest in completing the road.

"They might as well rewrite the Constitution. They teach us we have freedom of religion and freedom of speech, but it's not true," says Tiger O'Rourke. "This was our place first time, our home. It's still our home, but we don't have the same rights as other Americans."

Currently, the G-O Road is stalled. The Indians are challenging the Forest Service on environmental grounds and attempting to get Congress to add the G-O Road corridor to the existing, protected wilderness area.

Like many Americans, Tiger and Black Snake say they never thought much about the Constitution until it touched their lives directly. Among the tribes of northern California, defeat has fired a new fight for their way of life, spurred intertribal outreach and educational efforts, and brought a new awareness of the legal system. "We *have* to understand the Constitution now," says Tiger O'Rourke. "We still need our line of warriors, but now they've got to be legal warriors. That's the war now, and it's the only way we're going to survive."

N.B. On October 28, 1990, the last day of its session, the 101st Congress passed legislation adding the G-O Road corridor to the Siskiyou Wilderness. This legislation ensures that the logging road will not be completed; its two spurs will remain dead-ended in the forest beneath Chimney Rock. Because the area was protected to preserve the environment rather than the Indians' religion, the Indians found their victory bittersweet. "It's all right for us. We'll use the area as we always have," says Black Snake. "But we didn't accomplish what we set out to accomplish for other tribes. [We] can't win one on beliefs." But, he adds, "maybe it's the Creator's way of seeing just how sincere we are."

82

EDWARD DE GRAZIA

From *Girls Lean Back Everywhere*

In 1990 popular music provided the courts with a classic censorship dilemma when the Miami rap group 2 Live Crew sang about subjects that some Florida public officials believed were obscene. Edward de Grazia's long and detailed study of obscenity and the First Amendment includes the story of the 2 Live Crew controversy. In this excerpt he quotes various people about their personal reactions to the group's lyrics and its freedom to sing them. Journalists, Crew members, fans, jurors, scholars, and other performers each saw the issue from different points of view. Opinions vary on whether 2 Live Crew was spreading dangerous filth about women, or whether the white power structure was trying to silence the legitimate voices of American black men. In this case, the First Amendment let 2 Live Crew be "As Nasty As They Wanna Be."

IN 1957, FOR THE first time, the Supreme Court spoke to the question of whether literature dealing with sex was meant to be protected by the First Amendment; the Court said that literature was protected, but that "obscenity" was *not*. The justices defined "obscenity" much as [Federal] Judge [John M.] Woolsey had [in 1933], subjectively, in terms of its ability to arouse the "average person's" prurient interest in sex. Then, in a 1964 case involving Henry Miller's erotic novel *Tropic of Cancer*, the wise and courageous Justice William J. Brennan, Jr., produced a more objective and much more liberal rule by which the freedom of literature and other arts might be measured.

In fact, the rule that Brennan announced (referred to in this book as "the Brennan doctrine") was so generously fashioned to protect literature and art that it led to the freeing of hard-core pornography. In order to ensure freedom for valued cultural expression the Supreme Court had found it necessary to free what was "obscene" as well. It did this by effectively (although not formally) abandoning the effort to define what in a literary or artistic context was undefinable—"the obscene"—and providing an efficient, because nearly absolute, defense for expression "not utterly without" literary, artistic, scientific, or other social value. Thus the Court made it close to impossible for prosecutors to prove that targeted literary or artistic works were obscene but easy for defense lawyers to demonstrate that the works of literature or art created or disseminated by their clients were entitled to First Amendment protection.

Soon the Court's critics found in the Brennan doctrine grounds to blame the Court for the "tides of pornography" that were now "seeping into the sanctity of the home." The spread of pornography was cited as evidence not that entrepreneurial capitalism had made sex a multibillion-dollar industry, but that the Supreme Court had mocked the founding fathers' intentions with regard to freedom of the press.

In 1973, the Court's new chief justice, Warren E. Burger, redefined obscenity in a way he hoped would be more palatable to conservative opinion, and this led Brennan and three others who had served on the Warren Court (Stewart, Marshall, and Douglas) to disassociate themselves from Burger's position and move into deep dissent. At that point Brennan, disdaining Burger's effort to fashion an improved definition of "the obscene," called for the abandonment of attempts to define and suppress obscenity through law. It was plain to Brennan that people who express themselves through literature and art could not be fully safe from government control unless the Court constrained government to forgo any attempt to punish purveyors of pornography and obscenity to adults.

The wisdom of Brennan's 1973 position (which he reiterated frequently in dissent) recently was confirmed when the director of a Cincinnati art gallery, the leader of a Miami rap music group, and the owner of a Fort Lauderdale record store all found themselves arrested under the Burger Court's revised definition for showing, singing, and selling what police officials and prosecutors claimed was obscene because in their judgment it did not qualify as "serious" art, or even art. Splendid as Brennan's achievements of the sixties were, they have not dispelled fears that literature and art can subvert and even destroy deeply entrenched political and religious values. And they have by no means discouraged ambitious public officials and zealous religious leaders from invoking the law to suppress artistic expression they find repellent. . . .

In Miami, in June 1990, Luther Campbell, the leader of 2 Live Crew, was arrested for singing and playing "obscene" songs; thereafter he was acquitted by jurors who, aided by experts, felt they knew artistic expression when they heard it. But in Fort Lauderdale, record-store owner Charles Freeman, who was arrested around the same time for selling a recording of the same music—the 2 Live Crew album *As Nasty As They Wanna Be*—to an undercover sheriff, was convicted by a jury that failed to see the serious artistic and political value that many other people saw in the songs. Yet the First Amendment has for the past twenty-five years been put forward by the Supreme Court as a barrier to this sort of censorship. One had hoped the issue was settled. . . .

LIZ SMITH [Columnist]: In my time I've had a lot to say about how sticks and stones can break one's bones; but words can never hurt. . . . And this column has been an active defender of First Amendment rights and also the right of others to say anything they like about those in the public eye. I've always felt if we in the press offend, at least it is better than suffering suppression, censorship, etc.

But a July 2 column by John Leo in *U.S. News & World Report,* which I clipped and put aside before I went on vacation, has me on the ropes. . . .

JOHN LEO: The issue at the heart of the controversy over the rap group 2 Live Crew is not censorship, artistic freedom, sex or even obscene language. The real problem, I think, is this: Because of the cultural influence of one not very distinguished rap group, 10- and 12-year-old boys now walk down the street chanting about the joys of damaging a girl's vagina during sex. . . .

The popular culture is worth paying attention to. It is the air we breathe, and 2 Live Crew is a pesky new pollutant. The opinion industry's advice is generally to buy a gas mask or stop breathing. ("If you don't like their album, don't buy it," one such genius wrote.) But by monitoring, complaining, boycotting, we might actually get the 2 Live Crew Pollutants out of our air. Why should our daughters have to grow up in a culture in which musical advice on the domination and abuse of women is accepted as entertainment?

LIZ SMITH: So, is censorship the answer? The performance of 2 Live Crew—so violent, so anti-female—forces an almost involuntary yes! But once you censor, or forbid or arrest the real culprits, how do you deal with other artists who "offend"? Where do you draw the line? This is a tough one. But the average child isn't likely to encounter the kind of "art" that the National Endowment is trying to ban. Kids are not all over art galleries and theaters. But pop music assails them at every level and at every moment of their lives.

What I WOULD like to see is every responsible, influential and distinguished black activist, actor and role model—Jesse Jackson, Spike Lee, Whoopi Goldberg, Arsenio Hall, Eddie Murphy, Diana Ross, et al.—raising his or her voice to decry the horrible "message" of 2 Live Crew.

I would advise famous and caring whites to do the same, though they may be accused of racism. However, the issue goes far beyond race. Clips of 2 Live Crew in concert show that the audiences are not exclusively black by any means. What they are is young and unformed and dangerously impressionable.

DEBBIE BENNETT [2 Live Crew publicist]: It's nice to see that Liz Smith is keeping racism in America alive and kicking. She's so stupid it's unbelievable. She wrote that since kids don't go to art galleries or see shows with people like Karen Finley, obscene art is okay. But since they listen to music, 2 Live Crew should be banned. Way to pass judgment on every teenager in America.

In an account of the 2 Live Crew members' trial that appeared in The Village Voice, Lisa Jones reported what two teenaged black women, courthouse fans of Luther Campbell, had to say about the prosecution and the music:

ANTOINETTE JONES (18): They're just giving Luke a hard time because he's black. He's trying to make a living like everyone else. If someone wants to listen to his music that's their business. What do they think music is? They're acting like music is a gun.

LATONIA BROOKS (17): [Their lyrics] do have to do with sex and body parts, but when they rap, they put it all together. It's not like a man on the street saying dirty words to you. Their music makes sense. What they're saying is the truth. That's what most people do in bed. I don't, but that's what most other people do in bed.

Unlike the jury that convicted the record-store owner Charles Freeman for selling the "obscene" album, 2 Live Crew's jury was not all white; it found all three Crew members not guilty. Two of the (white) jurors told reporters why they had voted to acquit.

SUSAN VAN HEMERT (JUROR): I basically took it as comedy.

BEVERLY RESNICK (JUROR): This was their way of expressing their inner feelings; we felt it had some art in it.

The verdict came after four days of testimony during which the jurors "spent hours" listening to, and occasionally laughing at, two garbled tape recordings of a performance by the group that had been made by undercover deputies from the Broward County sheriff's office. The tapes, one of which had been enhanced by the police to eliminate background noise, were the prosecution's only evidence.

Defense lawyers Bruce Rogow and Allen Jacobi won the case by producing expert witnesses to testify about the artistic and political values in the group's songs, a strategy like the one that defense lawyers in the Cincinnati Mapplethorpe case had successfully used. One of the 2 Live Crew witnesses, *Newsday* music critic John Leland, gave an annotated history of hip-hop music. Another, Duke University professor and literary critic Henry Louis Gates, Jr, placed the music in its African-American oral and literary tradition. Gates explained the "signifying," and the use of "hyperbole" and "parody"; he described why it was the artistic works like *As Nasty As They Wanna Be* were not to be taken literally. This probably was the evidence which persuaded the jury that there was at least a reasonable doubt that the music was obscene.

Gates said that the Crew's lyrics took one of the worst stereotypes about black men—that they are oversexed animals—and blew it up until it exploded. He also suggested that the "clear and present danger" doctrine that judges still sometimes used to justify the suppression of speech was not applicable to the Crew's music.

PROFESSOR HENRY LOUIS GATES, JR.: There is no cult of violence [in this music]. There is no danger at all [from] these words . . . being sung.

The Crew's chief lyricist defended the group's music, and its success, on essentially political grounds.

MARK ROSS (AKA BROTHER MARQUIS): The bottom line is getting dollars and having your own. It's really a black thing with us. Even though people might say we're not positive role models to the black community, that if you ask us about our culture, we talk about sex, it's not really like that. I'm well aware of where I come from, I know myself as a black man. I think I'm with the program, very much so. You feel I'm doing nothing to enhance my culture, but I could be destroying my culture, I could be out there selling kids drugs.

Performers and purveyors of rap music, like curators of art galleries, are engaged in the communication of images and ideas through artistic means. Because of this, interference with their work by policemen, prosecutors, or judges violates the freedoms guaranteed under the First Amendment. No one can intelligently suggest that the country's musicians and distributors of music are not as entitled to be free in their professional activities as its writers and booksellers and museum curators are. The only constitutional limitations permissible with respect to songs are also applicable to books, paintings, photographs, films, and the other arts, as to all speech and press—which is to say, the restraints ought to be limited in their application to persons who use music intentionally to incite others to crime or violence, or who force nonconsenting or captive audiences to listen to it.

Purposeful disseminations to children of music that may be deemed "obscene" *for them* (in the constitutional sense mentioned in *Miller* v. *California*) would raise different questions. When 2 Live Crew played Fort Lauderdale, they were not arrested and charged with inviting or alluring minors to hear their sexually explicit songs, playing to "captive audiences" of persons who did not wish to hear what was played and could not escape it, or intentionally inciting the men in the room to rape or sexually abuse women. They were charged with singing lyrics that policemen, prosecutors, and lower court judges had heard about, decoded, and decided were not art, but were obscene. . . .

83

MARY ANN GLENDON

From *Rights Talk*

Individual rights lie at the heart of America's political system. Unfortunately, in the view of legal scholar Mary Ann Glendon, today's "rights talk" makes a mockery of the real meaning of rights. Legitimate, deeply-rooted rights have given way to what are nothing more than demands. Little thought is given to whether a right is basic or merely a convenience; to the effect of one person's claim of a right on others; to the weighing of rights versus responsibilities. Glendon, as a strong supporter of individual rights, asks people to return to a more common-sense, less artificial, definition of rights. Daily, in their private lives, Americans embrace a genuine and true concept of rights, not the "rights talk" of the public arena.

IN THE SPRING of 1990, men and women in East Germany and Hungary participated in the first fully free elections that had taken place in any of the East European countries since they came under Soviet control in 1945. Excitement ran high. The last people to have voted in that part of the world were now in their seventies. Some young parents, casting a ballot for the first time, brought their children with them to see the sight. Many, no doubt, will long remember the day as one marked with both festivity and solemnity. Meanwhile, in the United States, public interest in politics appears to be at an all-time low. Two months before the 1988 presidential election, polls revealed that half the voting-age public did not know the identity of the Democratic vice-presidential candidate and could not say which party had a majority in Congress. In that election, only half the eligible voters cast ballots, thirteen percent less than in 1960. Americans not only vote less than citizens of other liberal democracies, they display a remarkable degree of apathy concerning public affairs. Over a period of twenty years, daily newspaper readership has fallen from seventy-three percent of adults to a mere fifty-one percent. Nor have the readers simply become viewers, for ratings of network evening news programs have dropped by about twenty-five percent in the past ten years, and the slack has not been taken up by cable television news. Cynicism, indifference, and ignorance concerning government appear to be pervasive. By all outward indicators, the right and obligation to vote—a subject of wonder to East Europeans, and the central concern of many of us who worked in the civil rights movement in the 1960s—is now held here in rather low esteem.

Poor voter turnouts in the United States are, of course, mere symptoms of deeper problems, not least of which are the decline of broadly representative political parties, and the effect of the "sound-bite" on serious and sustained political discussion. On this deeper level lies the phenomenon with which this book is concerned: the impoverishment of our political discourse. Across the political spectrum there is a growing realization that it has become increasingly difficult even to define critical questions, let alone debate and resolve them.

Though sound-bites do not permit much airing of issues, they seem tailor-made for our strident language of rights. Rights talk itself is relatively impervious to the other more complex languages we still speak in less public contexts, but it seeps into them, carrying the rights mentality into spheres of American society where a sense of personal responsibility and of civic obligation traditionally have been nourished. An intemperate rhetoric of personal liberty in this way corrodes the social foundations on which individual freedom and security ultimately rest. While the nations of Eastern Europe are taking their first risk-laden and faltering steps toward democracy, the historic American experiment in ordered liberty is thus undergoing a less dramatic, but equally fateful, crisis of its own. It is a crisis at the very heart of the American experiment in self-government, for it concerns the state of public deliberation about the right ordering of our lives together. In the home of free speech, genuine exchange of ideas about matters of high public importance has come to a virtual standstill.

This book argues that the prominence of a certain kind of rights talk in our political discussions is both a symptom of, and a contributing factor to, this disorder in the body politic. Discourse about rights has become the principal language that we use in public settings to discuss weighty questions of right and wrong, but time and again it proves inadequate, or leads to a standoff of one right against another. The problem is not, however, as some contend, with the very notion of rights, or with our strong rights tradition. It is with a new version of rights discourse that has achieved dominance over the past thirty years.

Our current American rights talk is but one dialect in a universal language that has developed during the extraordinary era of attention to civil and human rights in the wake of World War II. It is set apart from rights discourse in other liberal democracies by its starkness and simplicity, its prodigality in bestowing the rights label, its legalistic character, its exaggerated absoluteness, its hyper-individualism, its insularity, and its silence with respect to personal, civic, and collective responsibilities.

This unique brand of rights talk often operates at cross-purposes with our venerable rights tradition. It fits perfectly within the ten-second formats currently preferred by the news media, but severely constricts opportunities for the sort of ongoing dialogue upon which a regime of ordered liberty ultimately depends. A rapidly expanding catalog of rights—extending to trees, animals, smokers, nonsmokers, consumers, and so on—not only multiplies the occasions for collisions, but it risks trivializing core democratic values. A tendency to frame nearly every social controversy in terms of a clash of rights (a woman's right to her own body vs. a fetus's right to life) impedes compromise, mutual understanding, and the discovery of common ground. A penchant for absolute formulations ("I have the right to do whatever I want with my property") promotes unrealistic expectations and ignores both social costs and the rights of others. A near-aphasia concerning responsibilities makes it seem legitimate to accept the benefits of living in a democratic social welfare republic without assuming the corresponding personal and civic obligations.

As various new rights are proclaimed or proposed, the catalog of individual liberties expands without much consideration of the ends to which they are oriented, their relationship to one another, to corresponding responsibilities, or to the general welfare. Converging with the language of psychotherapy, rights talk encourages our all-too-human tendency to place the self at the center of our moral universe. In tandem with consumerism and a normal dislike of inconvenience, it regularly promotes the short-run over the long-term, crisis intervention over preventive measures, and particular interests over the common good. Saturated with rights, political language can no longer perform the important function of facilitating public discussion of the right ordering of our lives together. Just as rights exist for us only through being articulated, other goods are not even available to be considered if they can be brought to expression only with great difficulty, or not at all.

My principal aim . . . has been to trace the evolution of our distinctive current rights dialect, and to show how it frequently works against the conditions required for the pursuit of dignified living by free women and men. With stories and examples drawn from disputes over flag-burning, Indian lands, plant closings, criminal penalties for homosexual acts, eminent domain, social welfare, child support, and other areas, I have endeavored to demonstrate how our simplistic rights talk simultaneously reflects and distorts American culture. It captures our devotion to individualism and liberty, but omits our traditions of hospitality and care for the community. In the images of America and Americans that it projects, as well as in the ideals to which it implicitly pays homage, our current rights talk is a verbal caricature of our culture—recognizably ours, but with certain traits wildly out of proportion and with some of our best features omitted.

Our rights-laden political discourse does provide a solution of sorts to the communications problems that beset a heterogeneous nation whose citizens decreasingly share a common history, literature, religion, or customs. But the "solution" has become part of the problem. The legal components of political discourse, like sorcerers' apprentices, have taken on new and mischief-making connotations when liberated from their contexts in the speech community of lawyers. (A person has no duty to come to the aid of a "stranger.") With its nonlegal tributaries rapidly dwindling, political rhetoric has grown increasingly out of touch with the more complex ways of speaking that Americans employ around the kitchen table, in their schools, workplaces, and in their various communities of memory and mutual aid.

Under these circumstances, what is needed is not the abandonment, but the renewal, of our strong rights tradition. But it is not easy to see how we might develop a public language that would be better suited in complexity and moral seriousness to the bewildering array of difficulties that presently face us as a mature democracy in an increasingly interdependent world. Nor is it readily apparent how the public forum, dominated as it is by images rather than ideas, could be reclaimed for genuine political discourse.

We cannot, nor would most of us wish to, import some other country's language of rights. Nor can we invent a new rhetoric of rights out of whole cloth. A political Esperanto* without roots in a living cultural tradition would die on the vine. . . . In many settings, employing a grammar of cooperative living, American women and men sound better and smarter than our current political discourse makes them out to be. The best resource for renewing our political discourse, therefore, may be the very heterogeneity that drives us to seek a simple, abstract, common language. The ongoing dialogue between freedom and responsibility, individualism and community, present needs and future plans, that takes place daily in a wide variety of American speech communities could help to revitalize our rights tradition as well as our political life.

*Esperanto was a language created in the late 1880s using simplified grammar and vocabulary borrowed from many languages in an attempt to create a common, universal method of communication. Esperanto was not accepted by people, however, and never achieved wide popularity.—EDS.

PART FIFTEEN

The Political Economy

84

JOHN KENNETH GALBRAITH

From *The Affluent Society*

Writing in the late 1950s as an associate of soon-to-be-president John Kennedy, eminent Economics Professor John Kenneth Galbraith made an eloquent case for liberal economics. He contrasted Americans' indulgence in private spending with the inadequacy of available public monies. "Social balance" was Galbraith's goal. His influential book touched on many facets of the American economy: the tax system, military spending, educational and urban problems. Although his plea for a bigger government role in allocating the use of the nation's wealth is undeniably out of vogue in the 1990s, Galbraith has been unwavering in his support of these principles over the years. The question open to debate today is: Did the United States follow Galbraith's economic prescription too far, or not far enough?

... WE MUST find a way to remedy the poverty which afflicts us in public services and which is in such increasingly bizarre contrast with our affluence in private goods. This is necessary to temper and, more hopefully, to eliminate the social disorders which are the counterpart of the present imbalance. It is necessary in the long run for promoting the growth of private output itself. Such balance is a matter of elementary common sense in a country in which need is becoming so exiguous that it must be cherished where it exists and nurtured where it does not. To create the demand for new automobiles, we must contrive elaborate and functionless changes each year and then subject the consumer to ruthless psychological pressures to persuade him of their importance. Were this process to falter or break down, the consequences would be disturbing. In the meantime, there are large ready-made needs for schools, hospitals, slum clearance and urban redevelopment, sanitation, parks, playgrounds, police and a thousand other things. Of these needs, almost no one must be persuaded. They exist because, as public officials of all kinds and ranks explain each day with practiced skill, the money to provide for them is unavailable. So it has come about that we get growth and increased employment along the dimension of private goods only at the price of increasingly frantic persuasion. We exploit but poorly the opportunity along the dimension of public services. The economy is geared to the least urgent set of human values. It would be far more secure if it were based on the whole range of need. . . .

. . . For a very large part of our public activity, revenues are relatively static. Although aggregate income increases, many tax systems return a comparatively fixed dollar amount. Hence new public needs, or even the increase in the requirements for old ones incident on increasing population, require affirmative steps to transfer resources to public use. There must first be a finding of need. The burden of proof lies with those who propose the expenditure. Resources do not automatically accrue to public authority for a decision as to how they may best be distributed to schools, roads, police, public housing and other claimant ends. We are startled by the thought. It would lead to waste.

But with increasing income, resources do so accrue to the private individual. Nor when he buys a new automobile out of increased income is he required to prove need. We may assume that many fewer automobiles would be purchased than at present were it necessary to make a positive case for their purchase. [Yet] such a case must be made for schools. . . . The solution is a system of taxation which automatically makes a pro rata share of increasing income available to public authority for public purposes. The task of public authority, like that of private individuals, will be to distribute this increase in accordance with relative need. Schools and roads will then no longer be at a disadvantage as compared with automobiles and television sets in having to prove absolute justification.

The practical solution would be much eased were the revenues of the federal government available for the service of social balance. These, to the extent of about four-fifths of the total, come from personal and corporation income taxes. Subject to some variations, these taxes rise rather more than proportionately with increases in private income. Unhappily they are presently preempted in large measure by the requirements (actual or claimed) of national defense and the competition of arms. . . .

Hopefully the time will come when federal revenues and the normal annual increase will not be preempted so extensively for military purposes. Conventional attitudes hold otherwise; on all prospects of mankind, there is hope for betterment save those having to do with an eventual end, without war, to the arms race. Here the hard cold voice of realism warns there is no chance. Perhaps things are not so utterly hopeless. . . .

However, even though the higher urgency of federal expenditures for social balance is conceded, there is still the problem of providing the revenue. And since it is income taxes that must here be used, the question of social balance can easily be lost sight of in the reopened argument over equality. The truce will be broken and liberals and conservatives will join battle on this issue and forget about the poverty in the public services that awaits correction and, as we shall see presently, the poverty of people which can only be corrected at increased public cost. All this—schools, hospitals, even the scientific research on which increased production depends—must wait while we debate the ancient and unresolvable question of whether the rich are too rich.

The only hope—and in the nature of things it rests primarily with liberals—is to separate the issue of equality from that of social balance. The second is by far the more important question. The fact that a tacit truce exists on the issue of inequality is proof of its comparative lack of social urgency. In the past, the liberal politician has countered the conservative proposal for reduction in top bracket income taxes with the proposal that relief be confined to the lower brackets. And he has insisted that any necessary tax increase be carried more than proportionately by the higher income brackets. The result has been to make him a co-conspirator with the conservative in reducing taxes, whatever the cost in social balance; and his insistence on making taxes an instrument of greater equality has made it difficult or impossible to increase them. Meanwhile the individuals with whom he sympathizes and whom he seeks to favor are no longer the tax-ridden poor of Bengal or the First Empire* but people who, by all historical standards, are themselves comparatively opulent citizens. In any case, they would be among the first beneficiaries of the better education, health, housing and other services which would be the fruits of improved social balance, and they would be the long-run beneficiaries of more nearly adequate investment in people.

The rational liberal, in the future, will resist tax reduction, even that which ostensibly favors the poor, if it is at the price of social balance. And, for the same reason, he will not hesitate to accept increases that are neutral as regards the distribution of income. His classical commitment to greater equality can far better be kept by attacking as a separate issue the more egregious of the loopholes in the present tax law. These loopholes . . . are strongly in conflict with traditional liberal attitudes, for this is inequality sanctioned by the state. There is work enough here for any egalitarian crusader. . . .

. . . One final observation may be made. There will be question as to what is the test of balance—at what point may we conclude that balance

*Bengal is a poverty-stricken region on the Indian subcontinent. The First Empire is probably a reference to the time of the ancient world civilizations, including Mesopotamia, Egypt, India, China, Greece, and Rome. According to the historical interpretation of Karl Marx, these early empires resulted from the oppression of certain groups by those who dominated, with slavery as the chief economic force.—Eds.

has been achieved in the satisfaction of private and public needs. The answer is that no test can be applied, for none exists. The traditional formulation is that the satisfaction returned to the community from a marginal increment of resources devoted to public purposes should be equal to the satisfaction of the same increment in private employment. These are incommensurate, partly because different people are involved, and partly because it makes the cardinal error of comparing satisfaction of wants that are systematically synthesized as part of an organic process with those that are not.

But a precise equilibrium is not very important. For another mark of an affluent society is the existence of a considerable margin for error on such matters. The present imbalance is clear, as are the forces and ideas which give the priority to private as compared with public goods. This being so, the direction in which we move to correct matters is utterly plain. We can also assume, given the power of the forces that have operated to accord a priority to private goods, that the distance to be traversed is considerable. When we arrive, the opulence of our private consumption will no longer be in contrast with the poverty of our schools, the unloveliness and congestion of our cities, our inability to get to work without struggle and the social disorder that is associated with imbalance. But the precise point of balance will never be defined. This will be of comfort only to those who believe that any failure of definition can be made to score decisively against a larger idea.

85

MILTON FRIEDMAN

From *Free to Choose*

Conservative economists are numerous today. But none can compete for style and consistency of viewpoint with Nobel Prize–winning Economics Professor Milton Friedman. Friedman has been the voice of conservative economics over the past half-century, during times when his ideas received little public acceptance. Free to Choose, *written with his wife Rose Friedman, became the basis for an informative, entertaining—and controversial—TV series. Friedman's central theme is "freedom," both in economics and in politics. He advocates that the maximum amount of economic power be left to individual citizens, to make their own choices, with the least possible control placed in the central government's province. Big government is Friedman's target. In the excerpt, Friedman mentions his heroes, classical economists*

Adam Smith and Friedrich Hayek. The name of Milton Friedman will join that list for future generations of conservatives.

THE STORY of the United States is the story of an economic miracle and a political miracle that was made possible by the translation into practice of two sets of ideas—both, by a curious coincidence, formulated in documents published in the same year, 1776.

One set of ideas was embodied in *The Wealth of Nations*, the masterpiece that established the Scotsman Adam Smith as the father of modern economics. It analyzed the way in which a market system could combine the freedom of individuals to pursue their own objectives with the extensive cooperation and collaboration needed in the economic field to produce our food, our clothing, our housing. Adam Smith's key insight was that both parties to an exchange can benefit and that, *so long as cooperation is strictly voluntary,* no exchange will take place unless both parties do benefit. No external force, no coercion, no violation of freedom is necessary to produce cooperation among individuals all of whom can benefit. That is why, as Adam Smith put it, an individual who "intends only his own gain" is "led by an invisible hand to promote an end which was no part of his intention. Nor is it always the worse for the society that it was no part of it. By pursuing his own interest he frequently promotes that of the society more effectually than when he really intends to promote it. I have never known much good done by those who affected to trade for the public good."

The second set of ideas was embodied in the Declaration of Independence, drafted by Thomas Jefferson to express the general sense of his fellow countrymen. It proclaimed a new nation, the first in history established on the principle that every person is entitled to pursue his own values: "We hold these truths to be self-evident, that all men are created equal, that they are endowed by their Creator with certain unalienable Rights; that among these are Life, Liberty, and the pursuit of Happiness." . . .

Economic freedom is an essential requisite for political freedom. By enabling people to cooperate with one another without coercion or central direction, it reduces the area over which political power is exercised. In addition, by dispersing power, the free market provides an offset to whatever concentration of political power may arise. The combination of economic and political *power* in the same hands is a sure recipe for tyranny. . . .

Ironically, the very success of economic and political freedom reduced its appeal to later thinkers. The narrowly limited government of the late nineteenth century possessed little concentrated power that endangered the ordinary man. The other side of that coin was that it possessed little power that would enable good people to do good. And in an imperfect world there were still many evils. Indeed, the very progress of society made the residual evils seem all the more objectionable. As always, people took the favorable developments for granted. They forgot the danger to freedom from a strong government. Instead, they were attracted by the good that a stronger government could achieve—if only government power were in the "right" hands. . . .

These views have dominated developments in the United States during the past half-century. They have led to a growth in government at all levels, as well as to a transfer of power from local government and local control to central government and central control. The government has increasingly undertaken the task of taking from some to give to others in the name of security and equality. . . .

These developments have been produced by good intentions with a major assist from self-interest. [Yet] even the strongest supporters of the welfare and paternal state agree that the results have been disappointing. . . .

The experience of recent years—slowing growth and declining productivity—raises a doubt whether private ingenuity can continue to overcome the deadening effects of government control if we continue to grant ever more power to government, to authorize a "new class" of civil servants to spend ever larger fractions of our income supposedly on our behalf. Sooner or later—and perhaps sooner than many of us expect—an ever bigger government would destroy both the prosperity that we owe to the free market and the human freedom proclaimed so eloquently in the Declaration of Independence.

We have not yet reached the point of no return. We are still free as a people to choose whether we shall continue speeding down the "road to serfdom," as Friedrich Hayek entitled his profound and influential book, or whether we shall set tighter limits on government and rely more heavily on voluntary cooperation among free individuals to achieve our several objectives. Will our golden age come to an end in a relapse into the tyranny and misery that has always been, and remains today, the state of most of mankind? Or shall we have the wisdom, the foresight, and the courage to change our course, to learn from experience, and to benefit from a "rebirth of freedom"? . . . If the cresting of the tide . . . is to be followed by a move toward a freer society and a more limited government rather than toward a totalitarian society, the public must not only recognize the defects of the present situation but also how it has come about and what we can do about it. Why are the results of policies so often the opposite of their ostensible objectives? Why do special interests prevail over the general interest? What devices can we use to stop and reverse the process? . . .

. . . Whenever we visit Washington, D.C., we are impressed all over again with how much power is concentrated in that city. Walk the halls of Congress, and the 435 members of the House plus the 100 senators are hard to find among their 18,000 employees—about 65 for each senator and 27 for each member of the House. In addition, the more than 15,000 registered lobbyists—often accompanied by secretaries, typists, researchers, or representatives of the special interest they represent—walk the same halls seeking to exercise influence.

And this is but the tip of the iceberg. The federal government employs close to 3 million civilians (excluding the uniformed military forces). Over 350,000 are in Washington and the surrounding metropolitan area. Countless others are indirectly employed through government contracts with nominally private organizations, or are employed by labor or business organizations or other special interest groups that maintain their headquarters, or at least an office, in Washington because it is the seat of government. . . .

. . . Both the fragmentation of power and the conflicting government policies are rooted in the political realities of a democratic system that operates by enacting detailed and specific legislation. Such a system tends to give undue political power to small groups that have highly concentrated interests, to give greater weight to obvious, direct, and immediate effects of government action than to possibly more important but concealed, indirect, and delayed effects, to set in motion a process that sacrifices the general interest to serve special interests, rather than the other way around. There is, as it were, an invisible hand in politics that operates in precisely the opposite direction to Adam Smith's invisible hand. Individuals who intend only to promote the *general interest* are led by the invisible political hand to promote a *special interest* that they had no intention to promote. . . .

The benefit an individual gets from any one program that he has a special interest in may be more than canceled by the costs to him of many programs that affect him lightly. Yet it pays him to favor the one program, and not oppose the others. He can readily recognize that he and the small group with the same special interest can afford to spend enough money and time to make a difference in respect of the one program. Not promoting that program will not prevent the others, which do him harm, from being adopted. To achieve that, he would have to be willing and able to devote as much effort to opposing each of them as he does to favoring his own. That is clearly a losing proposition. . . .

Currently in the United States, anything like effective detailed control of government by the public is limited to villages, towns, smaller cities, and suburban areas—and even there only to those matters not mandated by the state or federal government. In large cities, states, Washington, we have government of the people not by the people but by a largely faceless group of bureaucrats.

No federal legislator could conceivably even read, let alone analyze and study, all the laws on which he must vote. He must depend on his numerous aides and assistants, or outside lobbyists, or fellow legislators, or some other source for most of his decisions on how to vote. The unelected congressional bureaucracy almost surely has far more influence today in shaping the detailed laws that are passed than do our elected representatives.

The situation is even more extreme in the administration of government programs. The vast federal bureaucracy spread through the many government departments and independent agencies is literally out of control of the elected representatives of the public. Elected Presidents and senators and representatives come and go but the civil service remains. Higher-level bureaucrats are past masters at the art of using red tape to delay and defeat proposals they do not favor; of issuing rules and regulations as "interpretations" of laws that in fact subtly, or sometimes crudely, alter their thrust; of dragging their feet in administering those parts of laws of which they disapprove, while pressing on with those they favor. . . .

Bureaucrats have not usurped power They have not deliberately engaged in any kind of conspiracy to subvert the democratic process. Power has been thrust on them. . . .

The growth of the bureaucracy in size and power affects every detail of the relation between a citizen and his government. . . . Needless to say, those of us who want to halt and reverse the recent trend should oppose additional specific measures to expand further the power and scope of government, urge repeal and reform of existing measures, and try to elect legislators and executives who share that view. But that is not an effective way to reverse the growth of government. It is doomed to failure. Each of us would defend our own special privileges and try to limit government at someone else's expense. We would be fighting a many-headed hydra that would grow new heads faster than we could cut old ones off.*

*The Hydra was a mythical Greek monster that grew two heads for each one that was chopped off. It was killed by the hero Hercules.—EDS.

Our founding fathers have shown us a more promising way to proceed: by package deals, as it were. We should adopt self-denying ordinances that limit the objectives we try to pursue through political channels. We should not consider each case on its merits, but lay down broad rules limiting what government may do. . . .

We need, in our opinion, the equivalent of the First Amendment to limit government power in the economic and social area—an economic Bill of Rights to complement and reinforce the original Bill of Rights. . . .

The proposed amendments would alter the conditions under which legislators—state or federal, as the case may be—operate by limiting the total amount they are authorized to appropriate. The amendments would give the government a limited budget, specified in advance, the way each of us has a limited budget. Much special interest legislation is undesirable, but it is never clearly and unmistakably bad. On the contrary, every measure will be represented as serving a good cause. The problem is that there are an infinite number of good causes. Currently, a legislator is in a weak position to oppose a "good" cause. If he objects that it will raise taxes, he will be labeled a reactionary who is willing to sacrifice human need for base mercenary reasons—after all, this good cause will only require raising taxes by a few cents or dollars per person. The legislator is in a far better position if he can say, "Yes, yours is a good cause, but we have a fixed budget. More money for your cause means less for others. Which of these others should be cut?" The effect would be to require the special interests to compete with one another for a bigger share of a fixed pie, instead of their being able to collude with one another to make the pie bigger at the expense of the taxpayer. . . .

. . . The two ideas of human freedom and economic freedom working together came to their greatest fruition in the United States. Those ideas are still very much with us. We are all of us imbued with them. They are part of the very fabric of our being. But we have been straying from them. We have been forgetting the basic truth that the greatest threat to human freedom is the concentration of power, whether in the hands of government or anyone else. We have persuaded ourselves that it is safe to grant power, provided it is for good purposes.

Fortunately, we are waking up. . . .

Fortunately, also, we are as a people still free to choose which way we should go—whether to continue along the road we have been following to ever bigger government, or to call a halt and change direction.

86

WILLIAM WOLMAN AND ANNE COLAMOSCA

From *The Judas Economy*

The strength of the American economy has always depended on the work ethic, or so ordinary citizens have believed. Economists William Wolman and Anne Colamosca offer a very different picture of the 1990s. The value of labor, they believe, has lessened, while the value of capital has increased. Individuals and institutions who possess vast sums of money available for investment are the real winners in this economy, Wolman and Colamosca assert. Those who work for their financial rewards may think that they are prospering along with the big capitalists, but this is a misinterpretation. Notice their references to important economic matters such as unemployment, consumer debt, the stock market, Social Security, and the consumer price index. Despite the table and the numbers in this reading, be aware that the authors are presenting a point of view.

FEW OF US have had breakfast at Tiffany's, but a good number of us have gazed in wonderment at the jewelry displays in that elegant store's windows and those of its major competitors, Cartier's and van Cleef & Arpels. Each expensive piece is carefully displayed, set out on velvet cushions, set off by expensive floral arrangements or pieces of exquisite sculpture, and protected by security systems. Most of us have also walked in shopping districts that cater to the poor, passing by huge piles of cheap merchandise set out in jumbled heaps in the open air.

Behold the market. Its power is unparalleled. It cherishes that which it deems valuable and cheapens what it deems close to worthless. Therefore, as workers have become more abundant, the value of their labor has plunged—with devastating effects. The value of work in a world where each American competes with 15 workers globally is far lower than it was when he or she was but one in five in the industrialized West. As we have seen, both the market and public policy have turned against work. Wages are under pressure, pensions are being scaled back, rules to protect health and safety are attenuated, workers are being forced into early retirement. And most symbolic of the change, those supposedly "cherished" programs that were woven carefully into the fabric of society in a happier age for work, Social Security and Medicare, have come under attack.

The contrast between the treatment of work and the treatment of capital since the end of the cold war has had an impact on virtually all aspects of economic life. Begin with one of the two fundamental measures of economic well-being—income. One fact stands out about the years since 1989: There has been a sharp increase in the return to capital, compared to the earnings from work. There are many ways to measure the return on these two basic factors of production, all of them controversial. Yet the basic facts concerning how the division of income between work and capital has changed are fundamental—and incontrovertible.

For those who earn their living from work, real wages (money wages corrected for inflation) have been stagnant since 1973. . . .

. . . There is as well a strong suggestion in the data that most of the gains scored by the top 20 percent were concentrated in the relatively few workers at the very top of the income ladder, as [the table] shows. The numbers on real income show that the big gains were scored by the top 5 percent of the workforce, whose real incomes grew at a 7.1 percent annual rate between 1989 and 1994. The other members of the elite

THE RICH GET RICHER: CHANGE IN WEALTH BY WEALTH CLASS, 1983–1992 (1992 DOLLARS)

	Wealth* (000)			Percent Change**		
Wealth Class	1983	1989	1992	1983–89	1989–92	1983–92
Top Fifth	$744.1	$950.8	$893.6	27.8%	–6.0%	20.1%
Top 1%	6,176.0	8,777.0	7,925.0	42.0	–9.7	28.3
Next 4%	1,022.0	1,228.0	1,218.0	20.2	–0.8	19.2
Next 5%	444.3	516.1	503.9	16.2	–2.4	13.4
Next 10%	239.9	275.2	255.8	14.7	–7.0	6.6
Bottom Four-Fifths	$42.7	$45.7	$43.2	7.1%	–5.5%	1.2%
Fourth	115.0	129.0	122.2	12.2	–5.3	6.3
Middle	47.8	51.1	46.7	7.1	–8.6	–2.2
Bottom 40%	4.0	1.4	2.0	–65.2	44.8	–49.7
Average	$183.0	$224.8	$213.3	22.9%	–5.1%	16.6%
Median	47.0	50.8	43.2	8.1	–15.0	–8.1

*Wealth defined as net worth, equal to a household's assets less its debt.
**Change calculated from underlying unrounded data.
Data Economic Policy Institute.

either suffered falling income (the 80–90th percentile of income earners) or achieved modest gains (the 95–99th percentile). The vast majority of those who earn their living from work are in trouble.

The opposite is true for those who earn their living from capital. . . .

[I]t has been the class of large stock- and bondholders that has been the great beneficiary of the huge appreciation in the value of the financial assets that represent claims on the income of capital. Taken by themselves, the top 1 percent of the population held over 49 percent of stocks, over 62 percent of bonds, and 61 percent of business equity in 1992. By contrast, the share held by the entire bottom 90 percent of the population was under 14 percent of all stocks and under 9 percent of all bonds. The impact on wealth distribution was already visible by the end of 1992, as [the table] shows. Between 1983 and 1992, the net worth of the top 1 percent of the population increased by 28.3 percent and that of the top 20 percent by 20.1 percent. Over the same period, in the meantime, the net worth of half of the population actually declined. In the 1990s, we witnessed a concentration of wealth that is probably without historical precedent in the United States, one to which the wealth concentration that occurred in the decade that ended with the great 1929 crash was only a pallid prelude. And our data do not even cover the effects of the great stock market boom of 1995 and 1996.

Nor should there be any mistake about the major reason for larger portions of the economic pie going to people in the top brackets of income and wealth. The discrepancy has, as we have seen, little to do with the purported skills mismatch of the information age. Instead, the real explanation lies in certain people having access to the preferred position relative to the scarce factor of production in the new global economy: mobile capital. The star of the wealth inequality show is obviously the stock market itself. Between the end of the 1990–1991 recession and 1996, the stock market put on a pyrotechnical display, while the real wages of workers languished. . . .

It is time for a reality check for America. As the stock market soared and unemployment fell in 1995, 1996, and early 1997, American businesspeople and public officials alike were busily striding around the globe proclaiming victory in the great post–cold war economic battle, a victory that was readily accepted given that Europe and Japan seemed mired in economic rigidities of their own. After all, hadn't the United States of America accomplished the most successful adaptation of any of the advanced industrial countries to the new realities of the post–cold war economy? Was not America blessed by the most "flexible" labor market in the industrial world, the most technologically advanced industry, the most vigorous entrepreneurial spirit? Has not the dollar become the rising star of global currency markets in 1996 and early 1997?

With the American economy seemingly triumphant, a new sensibility had taken hold of a large part of the American public. As Americans watched the stock market catapult upward, they, in many cases, put their own wage stagnation and debt problems aside to become active cheerleaders—even at their own expense. Financial analysts repeated time and again to the media that any and all wage increases were bad for the stock market. Meanwhile, those who earn their living from work greatly outspent their incomes. Consumer debt soared to very high levels because people often thought the relentless rise in the Dow would somehow save them. And although wage gains were meager despite the strong economy, strikes began to be viewed as illogical, left-wing plots against the steady drumbeat of a victorious stock market that was raising the hopes of the boomer generation. Stocks, it seemed to many of them, could help create financial nest eggs large enough for the comfortable retirement that their scaled-back defined benefit pension plan would no longer include.

Those who earn their living from work in America certainly do have the right to be proud of the way they adapted to the needs of the new economy. They carried on despite twenty years of wage stagnation and the emergence of an economic system that has produced by far the largest rewards to the very rich. They had willingly worked longer hours. They had lived through a period when more and more members of each household had to go to work seeking to maintain their accustomed standard of living.

Yet economic insecurity continued to be a fact of life for the average American even as the success of the American economy was being celebrated in the annual January rituals of the State of the Union message, the rosy forecast of economists and stock market analysts, and the early reports of corporate profits that were running higher than expected. As the market launched its assault on 7000 in the Dow in January of 1997, big companies announced plans to lay off some 43,595 employees, according to the outplacement firm of Challenger, Gray and Christmas. That figure was below the total for January of 1996, when AT&T announced plans to shed some 40,000 workers. But it was 12 percent more than in January of 1995 and the second-largest figure in a year.

Nor were the sources of economic insecurity confined to the continued erosion of good jobs in the private sector. There were also signs in

1996 and 1997 that many key trends in government also represented a continuation of the attack on the economic position of Americans who earn their living primarily from work.

The true nature of the proposal for Social Security reform that was circulating in those months represented an excellent example of the continued assault on work. There was, to begin with, wide acceptance of the conclusion that future Social Security payments should be scaled back because the cost of living adjustments guaranteed by the program were based on a Consumer Price Index (CPI) that considerably overstated the rate of inflation in the country. A commission appointed by the Republican majority on the Senate Finance Committee, and headed by Michael J. Boskin, chairman of the Council of Economic Advisers during the Bush administration, unanimously argued that the Consumer Price Index overstates the inflation rate by some 1.1 percent per year, mainly because it fails to make adequate adjustment for the improvement in the quality of products made available to the American public. Their conclusions were widely proclaimed as accurate by Federal Reserve Chairman Alan Greenspan. Implicit in their findings was the notion that the growth of Social Security benefits could justly be scaled back without doing any great damage to the living standards of those in the program. The commission was composed of economists with impeccable credentials. Yet its final report never mentioned the fact that procedures instituted by the Bureau of Labor Statistics (BLS), the agency that is the keeper of the CPI, had already taken enough account of quality change so as to reduce the 1996 inflation rate from 4.7 percent to the 2.8 percent that was reported. In 1996, the inflation rate had already gotten a 1.9 percentage point haircut. The Boskin commission's report contains no discussion of the adjustment already made to the CPI, yet the members of the commission must be aware that an adjustment has been made. Do they really think that an additional 1.1 percent adjustment is required?

The failure of the Boskin commission to adequately report on work already done by the BLS to cut the reported inflation rate is disturbing, but equally serious is the rather easy acceptance by not only the conservative but also the liberal wing of the intellectual establishment of a scheme to reduce the federal deficit over the long run, bringing federal outlays under control by scaling back Social Security benefits. Those who earn their living from work will be financing this scheme. The intellectual establishment conveniently neglected to mention that the kind of Social Security reform it favors reduces the long-term returns to those who earn their living from work, while leaving the richest Americans, the only group whose incomes have increased rapidly since the end of the cold war, essentially unscathed. The reason that the well-to-do are let off scot-free is, of course, that their retirement incomes are only trivially dependent on Social Security benefits. And evident in the plans for Medicare reform is a similar lack of appreciation of the way in which trends in income distribution have hurt those who earn their living from work.

Americans who earn their living from work are being told that what is good for the rich is also good for them, and they have not given serious examination to whether that comforting generalization fully squares with the facts. There are no better examples of the advice to behave like the rich do than what is being said of the stock market, where the top 1 percent of the population owned 49.6 percent of stocks outstanding, and the top 5 percent owned 85.9 percent in 1992 before the great stock market boom of the mid-1990s began in earnest. . . . Americans are not only being told that they should invest their money in stocks but also that the monies of the Social Security system should be invested in stocks. By inviting a large portion of the U.S. population to participate in the stock market—even in a small way, via the Social Security system—Wall Street has managed to take the eyes of many American workers off their own self-interest—earning a livable wage that reflects the profits that corporate America has been raking in during the mid-1990s.

And with limited options available to fulfill their longer-term goals, today's workers are putting their faith in private sector money managers to help them keep afloat financially; whereas a couple of generations ago, the labor movement and company-defined benefit pension funds were the main ones vested with the responsibility for keeping American families afloat over the long haul. As the stock market raced upward through the mid-1990s, the new faith—that the mutual fund industry would take the place of wage hikes and labor pressure to give workers a quality life—seemed to be vindicated. The American middle class, it seemed, backed their new passion for stocks with money. In 1996 Americans poured $226 billion into mutual funds, by far the most popular household investing vehicle. Nearly all of that money was placed in funds that invest in the booming stock market rather than bonds or money market instruments. In comparison, just $22 billion was invested in mutual funds in 1990. And today more than 63 million people own shares in mutual funds, up from 38 million four years ago.

The big financial news of early 1997 was the merger of the investment banks Dean Witter and Morgan Stanley, creating a company that offers

306 funds with assets of $146 billion. Consumers had been well schooled to keep their money in mutual funds over the long term because the industry had promoted the belief that the long-term trend of stocks is up. Dips, they were led to believe, were buying opportunities; the market would eventually retrace its steps and keep going up.

Inherent in this promise is a kind of security blanket; the union chief is replaced with a mutual fund manager. Since there is no longer much emphasis on a long-term career at one company with ongoing benefits, workers are pinning their long-term domestic financial hopes on financial managers who are seen as capable of conjuring up some future bliss. More and more, the mutual fund manager has become a kind of "new millennium mom" who will somehow manage to come up with enough profits for millions of families to ensure college tuition payments, retirement with comfort, and a lot left over for illnesses and other family crises.

But the odds are that this confidence will prove a cruel pipe dream. Passive investors who earn their living from work and are increasingly reliant on Wall Street for their future quality of life could very well find themselves in a financial market where stocks are not galloping upward. In the six years between 1990 and 1996, when inflows into mutual funds grew from $22 billion to $226 billion, stock prices, as measured by the S&P 500 Index, essentially doubled. It may be that no one is implicitly promising a doubling of stock prices in the six years between 1996 and 2002. But those who believe that it is the pace at which new monies are being put into mutual funds that explains the rise in the stock market should realize that in order for prices to grow at a pace equivalent to that achieved between 1990 and 1996, new monies being put into funds today would have to increase by more than ten times from $226 billion to $2,321 trillion in six years. Where is that money going to come from if wages continue to be sluggish and debt continues to pile up? And as a result the mighty millennium mom in the guise of a fund manager is bound to run into some trouble trying to take care of her expectant small investors. We wish those who are relying more and more on the stock market to take care of their long-term needs good luck. But every page of history, and every fiber of our being, leads us to believe that today's small investors in the stock market are being asked to put their faith in a system that could be much more fallible than they expect.

There is indeed abroad in the land a general tendency to "explain away" the difficulties of those who earn their living from work and to pretend that the problems of average workers are easily solved. . . .

The one piece of good news for American workers in the 1990s is that there has been a decline in the unemployment rate. That is certainly a comforting fact. But American workers should realize that the primary reason that unemployment rates have fallen in the U.S. economy in the 1990s is because U.S. labor has become cheap and is being widely substituted for capital. Unemployment has fallen in the 1990s because, contrary to the prevailing mythology in an age of triumphant capital, the United States has become a more labor intensive economy.

PART SIXTEEN

Public Welfare

87

MICHAEL HARRINGTON

From *The Other America*

Poverty in the United States is not new, but it took social critic Michael Harrington's acclaimed book, published in 1962, to bring the reality of "the other America" in the midst of the "affluent society" to the nation's attention. Harrington's study of the middle class's withdrawal from the problems of poor city-dwellers marked the philosophical start of the "war on poverty," which was to begin later in the 1960s. Harrington explored the situation of people who were poor within a society of plenty. His characterization of the poor as "socially invisible" and "politically invisible" led to wide public recognition of the problem of poverty in America. In his later writings, Harrington continued his theme of poverty amidst wealth, warning of increasing class polarization, while holding out hope for a unified national effort to end economic and social inequality.

THERE IS a familiar America. It is celebrated in speeches and advertised on television and in the magazines. It has the highest mass standard of living the world has ever known.

In the 1950s this America worried about itself, yet even its anxieties were products of abundance. The title of a brilliant book was widely misinterpreted, and the familiar America began to call itself "the affluent society." There was introspection about Madison Avenue and tail fins*; there was discussion of the emotional suffering taking place in the suburbs. In all this, there was an implicit assumption that the basic grinding economic problems had been solved in the United States. In this theory the nation's problems were no longer a matter of basic human needs, of food, shelter, and clothing. Now they were seen as qualitative, a question of learning to live decently amid luxury.

While this discussion was carried on, there existed another America. In it dwelt somewhere between 40,000,000 and 50,000,000 citizens of this land. They were poor. They still are.

To be sure, the other America is not impoverished in the same sense as those poor nations where millions cling to hunger as a defense against

*Madison Avenue, in New York City, is the traditional home of the advertising industry. It is there that plans have been hatched for selling Americans products that they may not yet really know they want—like, in the 1950s, cars with tail fins.—EDS.

starvation. This country has escaped such extremes. That does not change the fact that tens of millions of Americans are, at this very moment, maimed in body and spirit, existing at levels beneath those necessary for human decency. If these people are not starving, they are hungry, and sometimes fat with hunger, for that is what cheap foods do. They are without adequate housing and education and medical care.

The Government has documented what this means to the bodies of the poor, and the figures will be cited throughout this book. But even more basic, this poverty twists and deforms the spirit. The American poor are pessimistic and defeated, and they are victimized by mental suffering to a degree unknown in Suburbia.

This book is a description of the world in which these people live; it is about the other America. Here are the unskilled workers, the migrant farm workers, the aged, the minorities, and all the others who live in the economic underworld of American life. . . .

The millions who are poor in the United States tend to become increasingly invisible. Here is a great mass of people, yet it takes an effort of the intellect and will even to see them. . . .

. . . The other America, the America of poverty, is hidden today in a way that it never was before. Its millions are socially invisible to the rest of us. No wonder that so many misinterpreted [economist John Kenneth] Galbraith's title and assumed that "the affluent society" meant that everyone had a decent standard of life. The misinterpretation was true as far as the actual day-to-day lives of two-thirds of the nation were concerned. Thus, one must begin a description of the other America by understanding why we do not see it.

There are perennial reasons that make the other America an invisible land.

Poverty is often off the beaten track. It always has been. . . .

. . . The American city has been transformed. The poor still inhabit the miserable housing in the central area, but they are increasingly isolated from contact with, or sight of, anybody else. Middle-class women coming in from Suburbia on a rare trip may catch the merest glimpse of the other America on the way to an evening at the theater, but their children are segregated in suburban schools. The business or professional man may drive along the fringes of slums in a car or bus, but it is not an important experience to him. The failures, the unskilled, the disabled, the aged, and the minorities are right there, across the tracks, where they have always been. But hardly anyone else is.

In short, the very development of the American city has removed poverty from the living, emotional experience of millions upon millions of middle-class Americans. Living out in the suburbs, it is easy to assume that ours is, indeed, an affluent society.

This new segregation of poverty is compounded by a well-meaning ignorance. A good many concerned and sympathetic Americans are aware that there is much discussion of urban renewal. Suddenly, driving through the city, they notice that a familiar slum has been torn down and that there are towering, modern buildings where once there had been tenements or hovels. There is a warm feeling of satisfaction, of pride in the way things are working out: the poor, it is obvious, are being taken care of. . . .

And finally, the poor are politically invisible. It is one of the cruelest ironies of social life in advanced countries that the dispossessed at the bottom of society are unable to speak for themselves. The people of the other America do not, by far and large, belong to unions, to fraternal organizations, or to political parties. They are without lobbies of their own; they put forward no legislative program. As a group, they are atomized. They have no face; they have no voice.

Thus, there is not even a cynical political motive for caring about the poor, as in the old days. Because the slums are no longer centers of powerful political organizations, the politicians need not really care about their inhabitants. The slums are no longer visible to the middle class, so much of the idealistic urge to fight for those who need help is gone. Only the social agencies have a really direct involvement with the other America, and they are without any great political power. . . .

Indeed, the paradox that the welfare state benefits those least who need help most is but a single instance of a persistent irony in the other America. Even when the money finally trickles down, even when a school is built in a poor neighborhood, for instance, the poor are still deprived. Their entire environment, their life, their values, do not prepare them to take advantage of the new opportunity. The parents are anxious for the children to go to work; the pupils are pent up, waiting for the moment when their education has complied with the law.

Today's poor, in short, missed the political and social gains of the thirties. They are, as Galbraith rightly points out, the first minority poor in history, the first poor not to be seen, the first poor whom the politicians could leave alone. . . .

What shall we tell the American poor, once we have seen them? Shall we say to them that they are better off than the Indian poor, the Italian poor, the Russian poor? That is one answer, but it is heartless. I should put it another way. I want to tell every well-fed and optimistic American that it is intolerable that so many millions should be maimed in body and in spirit when it is not necessary that they should be. My standard of comparison is not how much worse things used to be. It is how much better they could be if only we were stirred. . . .

First and foremost, any attempt to abolish poverty in the United States must seek to destroy the pessimism and fatalism that flourish in the other America. In part, this can be done by offering real opportunities to these people, by changing the social reality that gives rise to their sense of hopelessness. But beyond that (these fears of the poor have a life of their own and are not simply rooted in analyses of employment chances), there should be a spirit, an élan, that communicates itself to the entire society.

If the nation comes into the other America grudgingly, with the mentality of an administrator, and says, "All right, we'll help you people," then there will be gains, but they will be kept to the minimum; a dollar spent will return a dollar. But if there is an attitude that society is gaining by eradicating poverty, if there is a positive attempt to bring these millions of the poor to the point where they can make their contribution to the United States, that will make a huge difference. The spirit of a campaign against poverty does not cost a single cent. It is a matter of vision, of sensitivity. . . .

Second, this book is based upon the proposition that poverty forms a culture, an interdependent system. In case after case, it has been documented that one cannot deal with the various components of poverty in isolation, changing this or that condition but leaving the basic structure intact. Consequently, a campaign against the misery of the poor should be comprehensive. It should think, not in terms of this or that aspect of poverty, but along the lines of establishing new communities, of substituting a human environment for the inhuman one that now exists. . . .

There is only one institution in the society capable of acting to abolish poverty. That is the Federal Government. In saying this, I do not rejoice, for centralization can lead to an impersonal and bureaucratic program, one that will be lacking in the very human quality so essential in an approach to the poor. In saying this, I am only recording the facts of political and social life in the United States. . . .

[However] it is not necessary to advocate complete central control of such a campaign. Far from it. Washington is essential in a double sense: as a source of the considerable funds needed to mount a campaign against the other America, and as a place for coordination, for planning, and the establishment of national standards. The actual implementation of a program to abolish poverty can be carried out through myriad institutions, and the closer they are to the specific local area, the better the results. There are, as has been pointed out already, housing administrators, welfare workers, and city planners with dedication and vision. They are working on the local level, and their main frustration is the lack of funds. They could be trusted actually to carry through on a national program. What they lack now is money and the support of the American people. . . .

There is no point in attempting to blueprint or detail the mechanisms and institutions of a war on poverty in the United States. There is information enough for action. All that is lacking is political will. . . .

These, then, are the strangest poor in the history of mankind.

They exist within the most powerful and rich society the world has ever known. Their misery has continued while the majority of the nation talked of itself as being "affluent" and worried about neuroses in the suburbs. In this way tens of millions of human beings became invisible. They dropped out of sight and out of mind; they were without their own political voice.

Yet this need not be. The means are at hand to fulfill the age-old dream: poverty can now be abolished. How long shall we ignore this underdeveloped nation in our midst? How long shall we look the other way while our fellow human beings suffer? How long?

88

THOMAS SOWELL

From *Civil Rights: Rhetoric or Reality?*

During the mid-1980s, few black voices spoke from a conservative point of view. Almost all African Americans were liberals, supporting liberal Democratic candidates and following the lead of civil rights activists. Scholar Thomas Sowell took a different position, which placed him radically out of the mainstream of most of his colleagues. Today, Sowell's ideas are commonly heard, although they are still controversial within the minority community. He questions the reason for the differences between black and white income levels, attributing the gap to family structure and cultural norms, not to color. Sowell uses a historical assessment of African–American progress to support his arguments. Before the 1964 Civil Rights Act, he claims, black Americans were rapidly advancing in education, employment, and quality of life. After the act, progress in some areas was reversed. Sowell blames civil rights leaders who placed their own agenda above the genuine welfare of the black community.

BLACKS HAVE a history in the United States that is quite different from that of other American ethnic groups. The massive fact of slavery looms over more than half of that history. The Jim Crow laws and policies*, which not only segregated but discriminated, were still going strong in that part of the country where most blacks lived, in the middle of the twentieth century. "Lynching" meant—almost invariably—the lynching of blacks by whites. Blacks were widely believed to be genetically inferior in intelligence, both in the North and the South, long before Arthur Jensen's writings on the subject appeared. James B. Conant's 1961 book, *Slums and Suburbs*, reported a common assumption among school officials around the country that black children were not capable of learning as much as white children. . . .

Given the unique—and uniquely oppressive—history of blacks, it would follow almost inevitably from the civil rights vision that blacks would today suffer far more than other groups from low income, broken homes, and the whole litany of social pathology. But like so many things that follow from the civil rights vision, it happens not to be true in fact. Blacks do not have the lowest income, the lowest educational level, or the most broken homes among American ethnic groups. The habit of comparing blacks with "the national average" conceals the fact that there are other groups with very similar—and sometimes worse—social pathology. The national average is just one point on a wide-ranging spectrum. It is not a norm showing where most individuals or most groups are. The difference in income between Japanese Americans and Puerto Ricans is even greater than the difference between blacks and whites, though most of the factors *assumed* to cause black-white differences are not present in differences between Japanese Americans and Puerto Ricans. . . .

In short, the historical uniqueness of blacks has not translated into a contemporary uniqueness in incomes, occupations, I.Q., unemployment, female-headed households, alcoholism, or welfare dependency, however much blacks may differ from the mythical national average in these respects. All of these represent serious difficulties (sometimes calamities) for blacks, and indirectly for the larger society, but the question here is the *cause*. If

*Jim Crow laws were common throughout the South, beginning in the 1890s, as a way of enforcing legal segregation of the races in the post–Civil War period. Such laws mandated racial segregation in all public facilities, such as schools, trains, playgrounds, and even drinking fountains. Along with Jim Crow laws, black Americans were often prevented from registering to vote by poll taxes, literacy tests, and "grandfather" clauses. These forms of legal discrimination in the United States lasted until the 1950s and 1960s.—EDS.

that cause is either a unique history or a unique genetics, blacks would differ not only from the national average but also from other groups that share neither that history nor the same genetic background. . . .

Blacks and whites are not just people with different skin colors. Nor is a history of slavery the only difference between them. Like many other groups in contemporary America—and around the world and down through history—blacks and whites have different cultures that affect how they live individually and collectively. At the same time, there is sufficient overlap that some sets of blacks have a home life and family pattern very similar to those of most whites. Insofar as color is the over-riding factor in economic position, this will make relatively little difference in the incomes of such sets of blacks. Insofar as such cultural factors reflect traits that prove valuable and decisive in the marketplace, such sets of blacks should have incomes comparable to those of whites. . . .

A comparison of black and white male youths in 1969—again, before affirmative action—throws light on the role of color and culture. Harvard economist Richard Freeman compared blacks and whites whose homes included newspapers, magazines, and library cards, and who had also gone on to obtain the same number of years of schooling. There was no difference in the average income of these whites compared to these blacks. This had not always been true. In earlier periods, such cultural factors had little weight. But by 1969 it was true—during "equal opportunity" policies and before "affirmative action."

Home and family life differ in other ways between blacks and whites. Husband-wife families are more prevalent among whites than among blacks, though declining over time among both groups. About half of all black families with children are one-parent families, while more than four-fifths of all white families with children are two-parent families. But what of those black families that are two-parent families—more like the white families in this respect and perhaps in other respects as well? To the extent that racial discrimination is the crucial factor in depressing black income, there should be little difference between the incomes of these black families relative to their white counterparts than there is between the incomes of blacks and whites as a whole. But insofar as family structure reflects cultural values in general, those blacks whose family structure reflects more general norms of behavior should be more fortunate in the job market as well.

For more than a decade, young black husband-wife families outside the South have had incomes virtually identical to those of young white husband-wife families outside the South. In some years black families of this description have had incomes a few percentage points higher than their white counterparts. Today, where husbands and wives are both college-educated, and both working, black families of this description earn slightly *more* than white families of this description—nationwide and without regard to age.

The implication of all this is not, of course, that blacks as a group are doing as well as whites as a group—or are even close to doing as well. On the contrary. The average income of blacks as a group remains far behind the average income of whites as a group. What we are trying to find out is the extent to which this is due to cultural differences rather than color differences that call forth racism and discrimination. . . .

Anyone who has been privileged to live through the past generation of changes among blacks knows that there have been many changes that cannot be quantified. One need only listen to an interview with a Bill Russell or an O. J. Simpson, or many other articulate black athletes today, and compare that with interviews with black athletes of a generation ago, to appreciate just one symptom of a profound transformation that has affected a wide segment of the black population.

It may be understandable that black politicians and civil rights organizations would want to claim the lion's share of the credit for the economic improvements that black people have experienced. But despite their constant attempts to emphasize the role of the demand side of the equation, and particularly discrimination and anti-discrimination laws, the fact is that enormous changes were taking place on the supply side. Blacks were becoming a different people. More were acquiring not only literacy but higher levels of education, skills, and broader cultural exposure. The advancement of blacks was not simply a matter of whites letting down barriers.

Much has been made of the fact that the numbers of blacks in high-level occupations increased in the years following passage of the Civil Rights Act of 1964. But the number of blacks in professional, technical, and other high-level occupations more than doubled in the decade *preceding* the Civil Rights Act of 1964. In other occupations, gains by blacks were greater during the 1940s—when there was practically no civil rights legislation—than during the 1950s. In various skilled trades, the income of blacks relative to whites more than doubled between 1936 and 1959. The trend was already under way. It may well be that both the economic and the legal advances were products of powerful social transformations taking place in the black population and beginning to make themselves felt in the consciousness of whites, as well as in the competition of the marketplace.

Knowledge of the strengths of blacks has been ignored or repressed in a different way as well. Few people today are aware that the ghettos in many cities were far safer places two generations ago than they are today, both for blacks and for whites. Incredulity often greets stories by older blacks as to their habit of sleeping out on fire escapes or on rooftops or in public parks on hot summer nights. Many of those same people would not dare to walk through those same parks today in broad daylight. In the 1930s whites went regularly to Harlem at night, stayed until the wee hours of the morning, and then stood on the streets to hail cabs to take them home. Today, not only would very few whites dare to do this, very few cabs would dare to be cruising ghetto streets in the wee hours of the morning.

Why should discussion of positive achievements by blacks ever be a source of embarrassment, much less resentment, on the part of black leaders? Because many of these positive achievements occurred in ways that completely undermine the civil rights vision. If crime is a product of poverty and discrimination as they say endlessly, why was there so much less of it when poverty and discrimination were much worse than today? If massive programs are the only hope to reduce violence in the ghetto, why was there so much less violence long before anyone ever thought of these programs? Perhaps more to the point, have the philosophies and policies so much supported by black leaders contributed to the decline in community and personal standards, and in family responsibility, so painfully visible today? For many, it may be easier to ignore past achievements than to face their implications for current issues. . . .

The civil rights vision and the civil rights leadership continue pushing an approach which has proved counterproductive for the mass of disadvantaged blacks, beneficial primarily to those already advantaged, and which accumulates resentments against all blacks.

89

JOINT CENTER FOR POLITICAL STUDIES

From *Black Initiative and Governmental Responsibility*

A combination of self-help and government action is the solution advocated by the prestigious Joint Center for Political Studies, as it seeks ways of resolving the social and economic problems that plague some African Ameri-

can communities today. The Joint Center authors identify many resources intrinsic to black America—religious, social, educational, athletic, and entertainment organizations—that stand ready to attack the problems from within the black community. Yet these resources alone are not enough. The Joint Center sees a need for an active and vigorous governmental role to complement community efforts. "Black initiative" and "governmental responsibility" must be linked together to make the Joint Center's vision a reality.

BLACK AMERICANS have been at the helm of a profound social revolution. Since World War II, we have engineered the demise of a rigidly segregated society, used nonviolent action and litigation to compel the protection of basic rights, expanded the American society's conception and application of equality, made dramatic gains in political participation and leadership, and secured notable improvements in our socioeconomic status. Today, American society remains far from colorblind, and race continues to be a powerful predictor of status; but viewed against the backdrop of history, blacks and the entire society have made genuine progress.

It is precisely these achievements that make untenable the condition of the large part of the black population that remains enmeshed in a crisis of poverty. While only one-tenth of white Americans are poor today, more than one-third of blacks are trapped in poverty, many with only dim prospects for escape. No stable democracy can afford to ignore such disparities.

Most of the black poor are concentrated in badly deteriorated inner cities, are poorly educated and without the skills and experience required in today's workplace, are plagued by extremely high rates of unemployment or underemployment, and are strained by a rapidly deteriorating family structure. Many of these poor blacks are part of what a number of analysts call an "urban underclass" that is increasingly isolated from the mainstream of society and its opportunities. The condition of this large population of urban poor casts a shadow over the gains made by the rest of society and by blacks themselves. This dilemma and appropriate responses to it are the concerns of this statement.

The causes of persistent urban black poverty are uncommonly complex, but some of the contributing factors are abundantly clear. Sweeping economic and technological changes in recent years have substantially altered the character and distribution of urban and rural labor markets. Even more sweeping changes in the global economy have resulted in a decline in the relative competitiveness of major segments of the U.S.

economy, especially in well-paying jobs of modest skill that typically have brought other Americans into the middle class. Jobs that were plentiful in core cities when whites were residents have dispersed to the suburbs and outlying areas. Inadequate education and skill levels and damaged self-esteem and aspiration have often undermined the chances of poor blacks to compete successfully in the labor market. Finally, the cumulative effects of the long history of discrimination have impaired the capacity of many of the more disadvantaged to cope with a complex, rapidly changing economy and society.

These conditions of poverty have been allowed to fester for so long and are so difficult to eradicate that they will require the most determined and resourceful efforts by all who are implicated. The impacted network of economic and social problems is so novel and ferocious that it can be attacked effectively only by a judicious, concurrent, and sustained mix of *both* black self-help efforts *and* public and private assistance from the nation as a whole. Self-help can have only a limited impact on the economic environment, but it can encourage action and teach behavior that can pay handsome dividends for blacks and for the nation as a whole. However, the creation of a more robust economic environment and of greater equity in the distribution of its fruits is a public responsibility. Despite a vigorous continuing debate about the role of government in American life today, the mainstream American view remains that government should be an active agent for improving the quality of life of the people and for responding to community needs in times of crisis. Thus, even in the face of large budget cuts and huge deficits, farmers, children, veterans, immigrants, students, the elderly, small-business people, and others continue to be the focus of special attention and funding from government. The crisis of the black community deserves no less attention. . . .

The conditions associated with the profound urban poverty among blacks—declining male labor-force participation, very high rates of out-of-wedlock births and female-headed households, a high level of welfare dependency, poor educational performance, and high crime rates—inevitably prompt questions about the character and role of values in the black community. These questions have been raised in an effort both to account for current conditions and to search for the critical ingredients of a possible solution.

Blacks have always embraced the central values of the society, augmented those values in response to the unique experiences of slavery and subordination, incorporated them into a strong religious tradition, and espoused them fervently and persistently. These values—among them, the primacy of family, the importance of education, and the necessity for individual enterprise and hard work—have been fundamental to black survival. These community values have been matched by a strong set of civic values, ironic in the face of racial discrimination—espousal of the rights and responsibilities of freedom, commitment to country, and adherence to the democratic creed. Indeed, the country's democratic values defined black America's expectations of the society and formed the basis of our struggle for equality.

The value traditions of the black heritage are especially relevant to the needs of black people during this period. For example, commitment to the family historically has been one of the most powerful forces in black life. First as slaves, then as sharecroppers and farmers, and finally as urban workers, blacks always embraced a strong family ethic as central to our lives, and the great majority managed to maintain strong, intact families often in the face of enormous adversity. . . .

While all along pressing the larger society for equity and fairness, we have continually drawn upon our own resources in order to define ourselves positively and to renew our strengths. This has been true particularly at moments—as in the case of the current black experience—when complex new problems were suddenly added to older ones and when opposition appeared in powerful new forms. The most basic resource of the black community is the special value structure that has sustained black people through the darkest of hours. The leadership of the black community must more forcefully articulate, reaffirm, and reinforce the black value heritage with renewed vigor and commitment as a basis for action today.

There are countless ways to do this. From our experience and history, black people have at hand an extraordinary store of values and traditions developed and honed through earlier battles that can be adapted to secure old gains as we fight up to higher ground. We can begin by encouraging all of the black community's religious institutions, civic and social organizations, media, entertainers, educators, athletes, public officials, and other community leaders to make special efforts to emphasize black community values as a central feature of their service to the black community. . . .

The black community always has been an agent for its own advancement. Action by government in addressing social and economic needs has been important, but it has been both recent and modest. Blacks made the transition from a largely impoverished mass of former slaves to a strong, vibrant community largely through individual effort and through the work of civil rights, cultural, fraternal, religious, social, professional, and service organizations in the black community. Thus, black Americans have an unusually rich history of self-initiated contributions to our own well-being. Indeed, without our own vigorous, creative, and persistent efforts, many of our needs would not have been met at all.

In spite of this proud history, blacks are often skeptical of assessments of black community responsibility as compared with government's proper role—and no wonder. The history of black people is the history of countless unsuccessful efforts to get government to allow blacks the ordinary privileges of citizenship that were routinely a matter of right for whites. That history has been characterized by a societal racial obsession replete with the most negative stereotypic attitudes that blamed blacks for problems that arose directly from oppressive and unequal treatment by the majority. As a result, blacks have a valiant history of protest and demands for equity from which we shall not retreat. But as so often in the past, black people and their leadership, armed with confidence from long years of struggle and angry at recent years of retreat, are also calling on the internal strengths of the community.

Recent salutary expansion of the government's role in assisting those in need has pushed to the background recognition of the black community's long history and continuing efforts of progress through self-reliance and has created misconceptions about historic and existing roles of community and of government in black socioeconomic advancement. Further, the very success of our civil rights movement in reducing many barriers to education, employment, housing, and economic opportunity has created a gap in socioeconomic status between those blacks who were in the best position to seize new opportunities and those who were not, facilitating physical and economic separation. This new diversity within the black community has sometimes altered community structures, dispersed leadership, and diminished the capacity for cohesive, effective initiatives. . . .

This challenge does not underestimate the indisputable necessity of government action in addressing both the new and the lingering social and economic needs of the black community. To maximize—indeed, often to make community efforts bear fruit at all—government must play a principal role in the process. The complexity and magnitude of the task requires a judicious combination of public and private efforts and resources. At the same time, some of the problems blacks face cannot effectively be handled by government alone, as blacks know best of all. Moreover, community efforts, which have always been critical to black advancement, will be especially important today precisely because government has defaulted, failing altogether to act with the commitment or on the scale necessary to effect change. Blacks will never let government rest with its present posture of passivity and abdication. But as problems deepen, internal black community efforts must continue while we find ways to bring about the decent and committed governmental leadership we and the country deserve. . . .

. . . Neither blacks nor any other group can create jobs on the scale needed; nor can we restore the economy to include more jobs of moderate skill and decent pay that created the white middle class. This is preeminently the work of government. The black community cannot restore the deteriorated infrastructure of the cities that provides the physical framework for the ghetto and for ghetto conditions and attitudes. This too is the job of government. In addition, initiatives by the community, many already in progress, cannot be fully effective if completely unaided by government. The continuing problems blacks face will require firm, responsive, long-term commitment by government at every level, led by the federal government.

In the past, the federal government has been responsible in many ways for policies that have brought important changes to the lives of blacks and other Americans. It reversed its historic position and moved to ensure basic civil rights and remove the most blatant racial discrimination. It acted more equivocally to alleviate severe poverty and expand economic opportunity. Since 1981 it has retreated on all fronts, deepening black problems, especially in employment, health, education, and family stability. Even in more vigorous periods, the actions of the government were belated and sometimes ambivalent. Thus, severe handicaps are still experienced by a large portion of the black community as a result of prolonged subordination that was government-sanctioned and of poverty from which most Americans have long been relieved.

What we propose is a new framework for eradicating the growing disparities between blacks and whites. We urge a concentrated effort by government to invest first in models and then in programs and strategies for human development that will facilitate economic independence and encourage the poor to take charge of their own lives. . . .

Pervasive and persistent poverty has eroded but not destroyed the strong, deep, value framework that for so long has sustained black people. These values—among them, family, education, and hard work—are so deeply held that they remain and can be explicitly tapped today. The black value system, together with the wonderful variety of historic and existing self-initiated activities, can be the basis for a newly energized and expanded effort from within the black community to tackle a new variety of unusually resistant social and economic problems. But the inexcusable disparities between whites and blacks that continue today were not created by blacks, and they cannot be addressed by blacks alone. These disparities would never have arisen at all if official and societal discrimination had not denied blacks earlier access to equality and to opportunity. They can be eradicated only if the government assumes its appropriate role in a democratic, humane, and stable society—its role of coming to the assistance of a community in crisis.

90

THERESA FUNICIELLO

From *Tyranny of Kindness*

The debate in the 1990s about welfare reform can get very technical: AFDC, Food Stamps, block grants, entitlements, workfare. While the details of the reforms are important, first, Theresa Funiciello pleads, consider the plight of the women and children who receive welfare. Funiciello, a former AFDC recipient, chronicles the bureaucratic maze that a needy person must navigate to get any aid at all. She exposes the vast sums of public and private money spent on the "poverty industry." Too little of it gets to the poor. Too much of it goes into the pockets of those who claim that they're helping the poor. Welfare is an emotional issue, both to hard-working taxpayers and to recipients in dire need of assistance.

MY FIRST EXPERIENCE with Aid to Families with Dependent Children (AFDC)—welfare—was in upstate New York, three months after the birth of my daughter, on the heels of the departure of her father. It was 1973. I was twenty-six years old, nursing an infant, and alone. Welfare was humiliating on a personal level, and administratively it was nuts. But there wasn't anything I could do about it. At least that's what I thought.

In 1975 I moved to New York City. Like so many others, I was searching for opportunity. When I couldn't find paying work, I had my second encounter with welfare. It was nuts here, too.

Fortunately, in the city there were many thousands of others in the same boat. Looking for sympathetic advice, I stumbled onto a sturdy little volunteer organization of mostly welfare mothers, the Downtown Welfare Advocate Center (DWAC). The women at DWAC thought something could be done about the welfare, and they set about doing it. They helped people with problems negotiate the chaotic system and they helped change the way welfare mothers felt about themselves in relation to it. They also tried to influence the welfare bureaucracy. They said mothering was work. They said single mothers and children made up 95 percent of the entire AFDC population. They said welfare was a women's issue. I came back for more.

My third, fourth, and hundred-and-fifth encounters with the welfare system took place on behalf of other women as I, too, learned how to sort out the mess and be an "advocate." By late 1976, I was also organizing to change the way people thought about welfare—essential to changing the entire system from bottom to top. Over the next few years, DWAC sponsored a membership organization, which peaked at about six thousand members in 1981. Almost all were welfare mothers.

It was during this period that DWAC began to interact with the mega-charities on a fairly regular basis. These were agencies with millions of dollars in their coffers and nifty salaries for employees who "helped the poor." Actually, many of the social welfare professionals seemed to do little more than refer people who needed help to us and have luncheons to discuss the problem. It took many more years and many incarnations to find out what they were really about.

I moved on from DWAC to work at a small "change-oriented" (as they liked to call themselves) foundation that purported to give money to projects that poor people worked on. That was maybe ten percent true. So, in 1983, when Mario Cuomo became governor and his newly appointed commissioner of the New York State Department of Social Services (DSS) offered me a job, I was ready to take on the beast from inside the belly. Just maybe things could be changed from the inside.

At DSS, my worst nightmares became fire-breathing realities. Millions of dollars were regularly dispensed in contracts to virtually useless "non-profit" agencies. DSS was a patronage trough. Poor people were not the beneficiaries. They weren't even in on the deal.

Nevertheless, I'd learned a couple important lessons at DSS. One was that incompetence is a heavy contender with greed as prime motivator of the bureaucracy. Second, any time there's money to be had, every manner of opportunist crawls out for a piece. Combined, these fundamentals form the basis of public policy.

It didn't take too much intelligence to figure out the idiocy of paying thousands of dollars a month to "shelter" a homeless family instead of paying for a real apartment. Various layers of government blamed one another—but *they* were setting the rules, not Martians. Taxpayers were bilked and poor people were sacrificed as hundreds of millions of dollars were poured into the sinkholes of the social welfare establishment. Shelters. Soup kitchens. Name it. Nationwide, poverty is big business—as long as you are politically connected.

The consequence to poor people of this ever-expanding poverty industry has been that over the past two decades, the purchasing power of welfare benefits has fallen in every state in the country, in spite of the fact that aggregate spending on most other social programs has soared. It was not quite by accident, nor quite by design. Boosted by the unseeing but hardly innocent eye of the media, the poverty industry has become a veritable fifth estate. Acting as stand-ins for actual poor people, they mediate the politics of poverty with government officials. The fifth estate is a large and ever-growing power bloc that routinely and by whatever means necessary trades off the interests of poor people to advance its own parochial agenda. From the charities fleecing the state and the public, to the champagne fund-raisers charged off to Uncle Sam, to the corporations developing ever more ways of getting tax deductions for having their trash hauled away free of charge, the fix is in.

Charities have been powerful since they first popped on the scene during the middle of the nineteenth century. Run exclusively by men, they were originally premised solely on the negative—stopping behaviors they believed to be inbred and causally connected to poverty. They believed the problem would continue unchecked if poor people were able to resist their services and exist outside of charity-run poorhouses. The charities fought long and hard against "outdoor relief" (cash assistance) for poor families. The struggle was temporarily checked with the passage of the Social Security Act, which established AFDC in 1935. Poor mothers could live in their own homes and raise their children. The compromise wrested by the nascent social work profession was that, unlike social security insurance, wherein a check would go directly from the federal government to the recipient, AFDC would be mediated by them. Both the public welfare bureaucracy and its private extension (charities) expanded.

Almost every president since has promised some sort of reform of the welfare system. But it wasn't until the 1960s that the welfare rolls exploded, landing the issue back onto center stage. Launching the Great Society, President Johnson declared "War on Poverty" and spewed social service dollars in every direction (except into the pockets of poor people, that is). In part, the new programs would stimulate the economy, as tens of thousands of jobs were created to "help the poor." Few poor people got any of these jobs, however. Most of the decent ones went to middle-class social welfare professionals, who were perceived to be an important cog in a deteriorating Democratic party machine.

Despite the largess of the Great Society, a chain reaction of inner-city riots spanning several years soon shocked the nation. The rioting was a total enigma to most people—in the wake of all the anti-poverty legislative gifts. But poor people were neither receiving the money directly nor truly influencing how it would be spent. In addition to the generalized anomie caused by poverty, the indignities of welfare and unemployment, and long-repressed racial bitterness, the riots were an expression of grave despair over a government agenda and monies said to be *for them* that for the most part were getting nowhere near actual poor people.

As the agencies that *did* cash in grew and reinvented themselves, it became apparent that they were in an inherent conflict of interest with poor people. Welfare mothers, for instance, wanted an adequate guaranteed income, which would have rendered many of the activities of the social welfare professionals meaningless. The agencies wanted a guaranteed income, too: for themselves. With the money and power to lobby effectively, they got it.

As the misery of poor people increased, so did the cacophony of private interests competing for government contracts, foundation grants, donations by individuals and corporations, and tax advantages for the donations to "correct" their version of the problem. The only people who did not cash in, the only ones absent from the debate in any public way, as ever, were poor. It was not for lack of trying. Many poor women, myself included, attempted to reframe the debate, but the charitable opposition was too comfortable and powerful.

Over a period of nearly two decades, I went from being a homeless welfare mother to being an organizer of welfare mothers, an establishment insider at DSS, an adviser to some members of the New York state legislature, and a consultant for various prominent social welfare agencies. I have seen it from all sides now. I remain appalled.

The view from the bottom is substantially different from that of any other vantage point. Usually, you won't learn about it in books. Certainly it can't be found in classrooms, newsrooms, boardrooms, or bedrooms of the not so poor or the rich and famous. . . .

Tyranny of Kindness takes a look at social policy in the United States from the perspective of people who live with the consequences. I do not pretend to be "objective." I don't believe anyone can be. I do try to present some barely known history and facts that are often misinterpreted or kept discreetly, esoterically buried in reams of public and private documents. Judge for yourself, but judge. Perhaps we can work together to address the issue of poverty in ways that are truly meaningful. . . .

My own rude awakening came when, in my midtwenties, I became a welfare mother. I was single and had a baby whose father was better at providing fear than the necessities of life. When my daughter was three months old, I kicked him out. It had finally dawned on me that he (1) might kill me one of these days, (2) might try to hurt her, or (3) might kill us both in one of his blind drunks.

I didn't dwell on the consequences of kicking him out. I didn't even think about having to go on welfare. Even if I had thought about it, the result would have been the same. My father was dead, and my mother lived on social security. My father had been superstitious, so he had no private life insurance. In any event, without parents or other resources to fall back on, I did what I had to do. I soon became slave to what we (welfare mothers in New York) called "the welfare." It is a crude and irrational system of income distribution, usually capricious and often downright cruel. I have spent the better part of my adult life trying to figure it out. During the first four of those years, I was on and off the rolls intermittently.

The first time I applied for welfare was in early December of 1973. I was crushed when I received no welfare check until after Christmas. I experienced a profound sadness for my three-month-old daughter on Christmas Eve; her future seemed to loom so bleak. I wasn't the crying type, but every now and then I felt these tears rolling down my cheeks, almost as if they belonged to someone else.

A year and a half later, I got a summer job miles from where we lived, so I had to move. Since the job was in a resort town, I couldn't afford to live there either. We moved from one county to another, and I worked in still a third. I had a hunch that I might be entitled to some help with child-care expenses, but I didn't have anyone besides the welfare department to ask. I did that in all three counties. I was told that I didn't qualify for "day care" because *day care* meant daytime, and I worked nights. This, as it turned out, was not true, but at the time I didn't know it. What's more, though I was also entitled to other supplemental welfare benefits (of which I was equally ignorant), I never got them either. Instead, because I took the job, I was cut off welfare entirely, lost my food stamps and my medicaid. The job paid more than minimum wage. Nonetheless, I was worse off than before. First, I worked nights, like many single mothers, so that I could spend most of my daughter's waking hours with her. This meant that she was sleeping while I was awake, and I had to be awake when she was. By Labor Day, I was, to put it mildly, overtired, overweary, overstrained, overdriven, overfatigued, overspent, and worn out.

There were countless problems associated with money. In theory I had more than when we were on welfare. In practice it wasn't quite the case. On welfare, I could wear whatever passed for clothes without giving much thought to it. On my paying job, the expectations were not so lax. I had less energy for cooking items like dried beans half the day, baking bread, or fashioning nutritious soups out of assorted food scraps. I was living in a small city now, so I could not grow any food because I had no garden in which to sow seeds. I quickly discovered that the faster the food, the more it cost. I also had the expense of traveling back and forth to this job five nights a week. Not only did this extract gas dollars but my car had a seemingly endless capacity to languish at the mechanic's when I couldn't figure out how to fix it myself. Getting sick was out of the question. Not only would I go unpaid if I didn't show up at work but I could not afford a doctor for myself under any circumstances and I would have been reluctant to take my daughter to one had she gotten sick.

By far the most traumatic dilemma for both me and the baby, though, was child care. I could afford very little. Capitulating to the social pressure to be off welfare, I left my daughter at age one and a half with people who could not begin to match my parenting skills. And for what? For her? For me? For money? Or so people would stop watching what I bought at the grocery store? (When you pull out your food stamps at a checkout counter, all eyes within fifty feet—with the exception of those like you, who will be soon facing the music—run a quick tabulation and analysis of your purchases.)

When that job ended, I went to a state employment office in Albany, looking for better-paying work. Foolishly, I told the truth on my application. When the employment official found out I was a single mother who had recently been on welfare, he told me he was not allowed to refer me for a job. He explained that the department had to compete with private employment firms and that it was customary not to send single mothers out for job interviews since employers generally didn't want them, no matter what their skills were. At the time, there was a coding system at employment agencies to tell prospective interviewers in advance such things as your marital status (for women only) and the color of your skin (for nonwhites, of course). This ensured that certain undesirable "types" didn't get sent on interviews. Another staff person approached me and asked if I would like to file a lawsuit against them for the practice, saying he could get me a free lawyer. I gave it only brief consideration. My political consciousness at the time was, to say the least, limited. I also figured that if I went along with them I'd be stuck on welfare for years to come while I waited around for this lawsuit.

Instead, just after my daughter's second birthday in September of 1975,

I moved to New York City. I was convinced we'd never escape poverty if I couldn't find better-paying work, so I went stalking "opportunity" in the city. As it turned out, I was shortly looking to get back on welfare, finding no job coupled with acceptable child care screaming out for my skills, such as they were. There didn't seem to be much of a market for brains, and I couldn't type. I could only answer one phone line at a time. I had a college degree (acquired on scholarships), but it wasn't worth much in a city teeming with hundreds of thousands of other baby-boom graduates, many of whom had connections and no babies.

I went to the welfare with all my papers and baby in tow. After waiting interminable days for an appointment, I was finally told that I didn't qualify because I didn't have a place to live. I said that I didn't have any place to live because I didn't have any money with which to rent an apartment, and, if they would just help me, I could remedy that. I was sent packing.

In no time, I obtained a letter from a friend saying I lived in her apartment and went back to the welfare, only this time at another center, to avoid being recognized. (New York City had some forty-six welfare centers at the time. One out of every eleven welfare recipients in the country lives there.) I went through the same process, filling out reams of forms and waiting anxiously for my "appointment." There was a sign on the wall in this center stating, NO MATTER WHAT TIME YOUR APPOINTMENT IS, IF YOU ARE NOT HERE BY 8:30 A.M., YOU WILL NOT BE SEEN. After examining my application, the intake worker told me we were not eligible for welfare because we had no furniture. I started to panic but refrained from strangling her. She told me to go back where I had come from. But I couldn't.

When I got enough of a grip on myself to act, I realized that I needed to know what you had to *have*, not simply what you *didn't* have, to get on welfare in New York, because, though I didn't have any of it, I was willing to say I did. Of course, what they were telling me was not true, but, once again, I was not privy to that little piece of information. Even if I had known, I wouldn't have had the slightest idea what to do about it. I converted one of the few dollars I had left into dimes, got hold of a phone book, and proceeded to call organizations listed in the yellow pages. After a series of unproductive calls, it occurred to me to call New York NOW [National Organization for Women]. I had noticed, after all, that most of the people in the centers were women with kids. I'd heard from a friend who was on welfare, but with whom I was unable to get in touch, that there was some kind of welfare mothers' group in New York, and I inquired about it. They actually knew of it and gave me the number for the Downtown Welfare Advocate Center (DWAC, which whites usually pronounced phonetically and blacks pronounced with a flair I preferred: "DEE-wac").

Some weeks later, with the help of a law student, John Morken, who volunteered at the center, I received a welfare check and got a room in an apartment share for my baby and me. John and my friend Ann Phillips kept trying to convince me to come to DWAC some Sunday for meetings of welfare mothers who talked about their problems and about the notion of "welfare rights," whatever that was. Having virtually no political interests, I was disinclined. Sometime later, I finally relented. There were only a handful of women present at the meeting that first day I went. I don't remember what I expected, but it was more or less a consciousness-raising session for welfare mothers. It was 1975, and little did I know that I would be involved with this organization for more than a decade.

One woman there, Diana Voelker, was particularly impressive. She had grown up on the streets of New York, been a gang member. She, too, was a welfare mother, with a beautiful blond child about seven years old. Diana acted tough, but I was later to find out that was all cover. Throughout the meeting she, and to some extent the others, was "organizing" me, although I didn't know it at the time. Diana said things like "They try to make you feel guilty like you've done something wrong. There's nothing wrong with you; it's the system that's all screwed up. You're a mother, and that's a job and it's an important one." There was a poster on the wall that said WOMEN HOLD UP HALF THE SKY.

PART SEVENTEEN

America in the World

91

CHARLES KRAUTHAMMER

The Unipolar Moment

The demise of the Soviet Union in 1991 as a unified communist state, along with the disintegration of the Soviet-backed Eastern European alliance, transformed world politics. The events were so enormous, so sudden, and so far from United States control that their impact on America remains uncertain. Americans were used to a world based on Soviet-American conflict, with its good/bad guy "Cold War" clarity. Journalist and commentator Charles Krauthammer offers a start to reordering the world after the Cold War. He begins by debunking several myths about what to expect. Three characteristics, Krauthammer feels, will prevail. The world is in a "unipolar" time, with the United States as the single superpower. Krauthammer warns of the illusion of multilateralism, especially under the guise of the United Nations. His warning seems prescient in light of the events in Bosnia in the mid-1990s. Remaining the one superpower will be expensive for the United States, the author knows, and isolationist sentiment will abound. Krauthammer closes with dire predictions about the danger posed by small nations—"weapon states"—that possess the desire as well as the technology to cause enormous harm. The United States alone stands in their way, writes Krauthammer.

EVER SINCE it became clear that an exhausted Soviet Union was calling off the Cold War,* the quest has been on for a new American role in the world. Roles, however, are not invented in the abstract; they are a response to a perceived world structure. Accordingly, thinking about post-Cold War American foreign policy has been framed by several conventionally accepted assumptions about the shape of the post-Cold War environment.

First, it has been assumed that the old bipolar world would beget a multipolar world with power dispersed to new centers in Japan, Germany

*The Cold War refers to the hostility that existed between the United States and the Soviet Union from the end of World War II until recent times. The Cold War involved many forms of hostility: democracy versus communism; America's NATO allies versus the Soviet's Warsaw Pact military partners; the threat of nuclear war; economic competition; the dividing of Third World nations into pro-U.S. and pro-Soviet camps. With the demise of communism in Eastern Europe and the disintegration of the Soviet Union, the Cold War era has ended.—EDS.

(and/or "Europe"), China and a diminished Soviet Union/Russia. Second, that the domestic American consensus for an internationalist foreign policy, a consensus radically weakened by the experience in Vietnam, would substantially be restored now that policies and debates inspired by "an inordinate fear of communism" could be safely retired. Third, that in the new post-Soviet strategic environment the threat of war would be dramatically diminished.

All three of these assumptions are mistaken. The immediate post-Cold War world is not multipolar. It is unipolar. The center of world power is the unchallenged superpower, the United States, attended by its Western allies. Second, the internationalist consensus is under renewed assault. The assault this time comes not only from the usual pockets of post-Vietnam liberal isolationism (e.g., the churches) but from a resurgence of 1930s-style conservative isolationism. And third, the emergence of a new strategic environment, marked by the rise of small aggressive states armed with weapons of mass destruction and possessing the means to deliver them (what might be called Weapon States), makes the coming decades a time of heightened, not diminished, threat of war.

The most striking feature of the post-Cold War world is its unipolarity. No doubt, multipolarity will come in time. In perhaps another generation or so there will be great powers coequal with the United States, and the world will, in structure, resemble the pre-World War I era. But we are not there yet, nor will we be for decades. Now is the unipolar moment.

There is today no lack of second-rank powers. Germany and Japan are economic dynamos. Britain and France can deploy diplomatic and to some extent military assets. The Soviet Union possesses several elements of power—military, diplomatic and political—but all are in rapid decline. There is but one first-rate power and no prospect in the immediate future of any power to rival it.

Only a few months ago it was conventional wisdom that the new rivals, the great pillars of the new multipolar world, would be Japan and Germany (and/or Europe). How quickly a myth can explode. The notion that economic power inevitably translates into geopolitical influence is a materialist illusion. Economic power is a necessary condition for great power status. But it certainly is not sufficient, as has been made clear by the recent behavior of Germany and Japan, which have generally hidden under the table since the first shots rang out in Kuwait.* And while a

*In the summer of 1990, President Saddam Hussein of Iraq marched troops into Kuwait, a small nation on Iraq's border. With the backing of the United Nations and with congressional approval—although not with a declaration of war—President George Bush sent American forces into the area in January 1991. By March the Iraqis had been defeated, yet Hussein remained in power, and Iraq continued to be a potential trouble spot in world politics.—EDS.

unified Europe may sometime in the next century act as a single power, its initial disarray and disjointed national responses to the crisis in the Persian Gulf again illustrate that "Europe" does not yet qualify even as a player on the world stage.

Which leaves us with the true geopolitical structure of the post-Cold War world, brought sharply into focus by the gulf crisis: a single pole of world power that consists of the United States at the apex of the industrial West. Perhaps it is more accurate to say the United States and behind it the West, because where the United States does not tread, the alliance does not follow. That was true for the reflagging of Kuwaiti vessels in 1987. It has been all the more true of the world's subsequent response to the invasion of Kuwait.

American preeminence is based on the fact that it is the only country with the military, diplomatic, political and economic assets to be a decisive player in any conflict in whatever part of the world it chooses to involve itself. In the Persian Gulf, for example, it was the United States, acting unilaterally and with extraordinary speed, that in August 1990 prevented Iraq from taking effective control of the entire Arabian Peninsula.

Iraq, having inadvertently revealed the unipolar structure of today's world, cannot stop complaining about it. It looks at allied and Soviet support for American action in the gulf and speaks of a conspiracy of North against South. Although it is perverse for Iraqi leader Saddam Hussein to claim to represent the South, his analysis does contain some truth. The unipolar moment means that with the close of the century's three great Northern civil wars (World War I, World War II and the Cold War) an ideologically pacified North seeks security and order by aligning its foreign policy behind that of the United States. That is what is taking shape now in the Persian Gulf. And for the near future, it is the shape of things to come.

The Iraqis are equally acute in demystifying the much celebrated multilateralism of this new world order. They charge that the entire multilateral apparatus (United Nations resolutions, Arab troops, European Community pronouncements, and so on) established in the gulf by the United States is but a transparent cover for what is essentially an American challenge to Iraqi regional hegemony.

But of course. There is much pious talk about a new multilateral world and the promise of the United Nations as guarantor of a new post-Cold War order. But this is to mistake cause and effect, the United States and the United Nations. The United Nations is guarantor of nothing. Except in a formal sense, it can hardly be said to exist. Collective security? In the gulf, without the United States leading and prodding, bribing and blackmailing, no one would have stirred. Nothing would have been done:

no embargo, no "Desert Shield," no threat of force. The world would have written off Kuwait the way the last body pledged to collective security, the League of Nations, wrote off Abyssinia.

There is a sharp distinction to be drawn between real and apparent multilateralism. True multilateralism involves a genuine coalition of co-equal partners of comparable strength and stature—the World War II Big Three coalition, for example. What we have today is pseudo-multilateralism: a dominant great power acts essentially alone, but, embarrassed at the idea and still worshiping at the shrine of collective security, recruits a ship here, a brigade there, and blessings all around to give its unilateral actions a multilateral sheen. The gulf is no more a collective operation than was Korea, still the classic case study in pseudo-multilateralism.

Why the pretense? Because a large segment of American opinion doubts the legitimacy of unilateral American action but accepts quite readily actions undertaken by the "world community" acting in concert. Why it should matter to Americans that their actions get a Security Council nod from, say, Deng Xiaoping and the butchers of Tiananmen Square* is beyond me. But to many Americans it matters. It is largely for domestic reasons, therefore, that American political leaders make sure to dress unilateral action in multilateral clothing. The danger, of course, is that they might come to believe their own pretense.

But can America long sustain its unipolar preeminence? The spectacle of secretaries of state and treasury flying around the world rattling tin cups to support America's Persian Gulf deployment exposed the imbalance between America's geopolitical reach and its resources. Does that not imply that the theorists of American decline and "imperial overstretch" are right and that unipolarity is unsustainable?

It is, of course, true that if America succeeds in running its economy into the ground, it will not be able to retain its unipolar role for long. In which case the unipolar moment will be brief indeed (one decade, perhaps, rather than, say, three or four). But if the economy is run into the ground it will not be because of imperial overstretch, i.e., because America has overreached abroad and drained itself with geopolitical entanglements. The United States today spends 5.4 percent of its GNP on defense. Under John F. Kennedy, when the United States was at its economic and political apogee, it spent almost twice as much. Administration plans have U.S. defense spending on a trajectory down to four percent by 1995, the lowest since Pearl Harbor.

*Deng Xiaoping, the top leader of China's communist government, suppressed student protests in Beijing's Tiananmen Square in 1989. Tiananmen Square remains a symbol of the struggle for freedom and democracy in the face of brutal government repression.—EDS.

An American collapse to second-rank status will be not for foreign but for domestic reasons. This is not the place to engage in extended debate about the cause of America's economic difficulties. But the notion that we have spent ourselves into penury abroad is simply not sustainable. America's low savings rate, poor educational system, stagnant productivity, declining work habits, rising demand for welfare-state entitlements and new taste for ecological luxuries have nothing at all to do with engagement in Europe, Central America or the Middle East. Over the last thirty years, while taxes remained almost fixed (rising from 18.3 percent to 19.6 percent) and defense spending declined, domestic entitlements nearly doubled. What created an economy of debt unrivaled in American history is not foreign adventures but the low tax ideology of the 1980s, coupled with America's insatiable desire for yet higher standards of living without paying any of the cost.

One can debate whether America is in true economic decline. Its percentage of world GNP is roughly where it has been throughout the twentieth century (between 22 and 26 percent), excepting the aberration of the immediate post-World War II era when its competitors were digging out from the rubble of war. But even if one does argue that America is in economic decline, it is simply absurd to imply that the road to solvency is to, say, abandon El Salvador, evacuate the Philippines or get out of the gulf. There may be other good reasons for doing all of these. But it is nonsense to suggest doing them as a way to get at the root of America's economic problems.

It is, moreover, a mistake to view America's exertions abroad as nothing but a drain on its economy. As can be seen in the gulf, America's involvement abroad is in many ways an essential pillar of the American economy. The United States is, like Britain before it, a commercial, maritime, trading nation that needs an open, stable world environment in which to thrive. In a world of Saddams, if the United States were to shed its unique superpower role, its economy would be gravely wounded. Insecure sea lanes, impoverished trading partners, exorbitant oil prices, explosive regional instability are only the more obvious risks of an American abdication. Foreign entanglements are indeed a burden. But they are also a necessity. The cost of ensuring an open and safe world for American commerce—5.4 percent of GNP and falling—is hardly exorbitant.

Can America support its unipolar status? Yes. But *will* Americans support such unipolar status? That is a more problematic question. For a small but growing chorus of Americans this vision of a unipolar world led by a dynamic America is a nightmare. Hence the second major element of the post-Cold War reality: the revival of American isolationism.

I have great respect for American isolationism. First, because of its popular appeal and, second, because of its natural appeal. On the face of it, isolationism seems the logical, God-given foreign policy for the United States. It is not just geography that inclines us to it—we are an island continent protected by two vast oceans, bordered by two neighbors that could hardly be friendlier—but history. America was founded on the idea of cleansing itself of the intrigues and irrationalities, the dynastic squabbles and religious wars, of the Old World. One must have respect for a strain of American thinking so powerful that four months before Pearl Harbor the vote to extend draft enlistments passed the House of Representatives by a single vote.

Isolationists say rather unobjectionably that America should confine its attentions in the world to defending vital national interests. But the more extreme isolationists define vital national interests to mean the physical security of the United States, and the more elusive isolationists take care never to define them at all.

Isolationists will, of course, say that this is unfair, that they do believe in defending vital national interests beyond the physical security of the United States. We have a test case. Iraq's invasion of Kuwait and hegemonic designs on Arabia posed as clear a threat to American interests as one can imagine—a threat to America's oil-based economy, to its close allies in the region, and ultimately to American security itself. The rise of a hostile power, fueled by endless oil income, building weapons of mass destruction and the means to deliver them regionally and eventually intercontinentally (Saddam has already tested a three-stage rocket) can hardly be a matter of indifference to the United States.

If under these conditions a cadre of influential liberals and conservatives finds that upon reflection (and in contradiction to the doctrine enunciated by the most dovish president of the postwar era, Jimmy Carter) the Persian Gulf is not, after all, a vital American interest, then it is hard to see what "vital interest" can mean. If the Persian Gulf is not a vital interest, then nothing is. All that is left is preventing an invasion of the Florida Keys. And for that you need a Coast Guard—you do not need a Pentagon and you certainly do not need a State Department.

Isolationism is the most extreme expression of the American desire to return to tend its vineyards. But that desire finds expression in another far more sophisticated and serious foreign policy school: not isolationism but realism, the school that insists that American foreign policy be guided solely by interests and that generally defines these interests in a narrow and national manner.

Many of realism's practitioners were heroic in the heroic struggles against fascism and communism. Now, however, some argue that the time for heroism is passed. For example, Jeane J. Kirkpatrick wrote, to be sure before the gulf crisis, that "It is time to give up the dubious benefits of superpower status," time to give up the "unusual burdens" of the past and "return to 'normal' times." That means taking "care of pressing problems of education, family, industry and technology" at home. That means that we should not try to be the balancer of power in Europe or in Asia, nor try to shape the political evolution of the Soviet Union. We should aspire instead to be "a normal country in a normal time."

This is a rather compelling vision of American purpose. But I am not sure there is such a thing as normal times. If a normal time is a time when there is no evil world empire on the loose, when the world is in ideological repose, then even such a time is not necessarily peacetime. Saddam has made this point rather emphatically. If a normal time is a time when the world sorts itself out on its own, leaving America relatively unmolested—say, for America, the nineteenth century—then I would suggest that there are no normal times. The world does not sort itself out on its own. In the nineteenth century, for example, international stability was not achieved on its own but, in large part, as the product of Britain's unrelenting exertions on behalf of the balance of power. America tended her vineyards, but only behind two great ocean walls patrolled by the British navy. Alas, the British navy is gone.

International stability is never a given. It is never the norm. When achieved, it is the product of self-conscious action by the great powers, and most particularly of the greatest power, which now and for the foreseeable future is the United States. If America wants stability, it will have to create it. Communism is indeed finished; the last of the messianic creeds that have haunted this century is quite dead. But there will constantly be new threats disturbing our peace.

What threats? Everyone recognizes one great change in the international environment, the collapse of communism. If that were the only change, then this might be a normal time and the unipolar vision I have outlined would seem at once unnecessary and dangerous.

But there is another great change in international relations. And here we come to the third and most crucial new element in the post-Cold War world: the emergence of a new strategic environment marked by the proliferation of weapons of mass destruction. It is a certainty that in the near future there will be a dramatic increase in the number of states armed with biological, chemical and nuclear weapons and the means to deliver them anywhere on earth. "By the year 2000," estimates Defense Secretary Dick Cheney, "more than two dozen developing nations will have ballistic missiles, 15 of those countries will have the scientific skills to make their own, and half of them either have or are near to getting nuclear capability, as well. Thirty countries will have chemical weapons and ten will be able to deploy biological weapons."

It is of course banal to say that modern technology has shrunk the world. But the obvious corollary, that in a shrunken world the divide between regional superpowers and great powers is radically narrowed, is rarely drawn. Missiles shrink distance. Nuclear (or chemical or biological) devices multiply power. Both can be bought at market. Consequently the geopolitical map is irrevocably altered. Fifty years ago, Germany—centrally located, highly industrial and heavily populated—could pose a threat to world security and to the other great powers. It was inconceivable that a relatively small Middle Eastern state with an almost entirely imported industrial base could do anything more than threaten its neighbors. The central truth of the coming era is that this is no longer the case: relatively small, peripheral and backward states will be able to emerge rapidly as threats not only to regional, but to world, security.

Iraq, which (unless disarmed by Desert Storm) will likely be in possession of intercontinental missiles within the decade, is the prototype of this new strategic threat, what might be called the "Weapon State." The Weapon State is an unusual international creature marked by several characteristics:

— It is not much of a nation state. Iraq, for example, is a state of recent vintage with arbitrary borders whose ruling party explicitly denies that Iraq is a nation. (It refers to Iraq and Syria as regions, part of the larger Arab nation for which it reserves the term.)

—In the Weapon State, the state apparatus is extraordinarily well developed and completely dominates civil society. The factor that permits most Weapon States to sustain such a structure is oil. Normally a state needs some kind of tacit social contract with the civil society because ultimately the state must rely on society to support it with taxes. The oil states are in an anomalous position: they do not need a social contract because national wealth comes from oil and oil is wholly controlled by the state. Oil states are peculiarly distributive states. Government distributes goods to society rather than the other way around. It is therefore the source not only of power but of wealth. This makes possible an extraordinary degree of social control exercised by a powerful, often repressive state apparatus.

—The current Weapon States have deep grievances against the West and the world order that it has established and enforces. They are therefore subversive of the international status quo, which they see as a residue of colonialism. These resentments fuel an obsessive drive to high-tech military development as the only way to leapfrog history and to place themselves on a footing from which to challenge a Western-imposed order.

The Weapon State need not be an oil state. North Korea, hard at work on nuclear technology, is a candidate Weapon State: it has about as much legitimacy as a nation-state as the German Democratic Republic; its state apparatus totally dominates civil society by virtue not of oil but of an exquisitely developed Stalinism; its anti-Western grievances run deep.

The danger from the Weapon State is posed today by Iraq, tomorrow perhaps by North Korea or Libya. In the next century, however, the proliferation of strategic weapons will not be restricted to Weapon States. Windfall wealth allows oil states to import high-technology weapons in the absence of a mature industrial base. However, it is not hard to imagine maturer states—say, Argentina, Pakistan, Iran, South Africa—reaching the same level of weapons development by means of ordinary industrialization. (Today most of these countries are friendly, but some are unstable and potentially hostile.)

The post-Cold War era is thus perhaps better called the era of weapons of mass destruction. The proliferation of weapons of mass destruction and their means of delivery will constitute the greatest single threat to world security for the rest of our lives. That is what makes a new international order not an imperial dream or a Wilsonian fantasy but a matter of the sheerest prudence. It is slowly dawning on the West that there is a need to establish some new regime to police these weapons and those who brandish them. . . .

. . . [T]he overall strategy is clear. With the rise of the Weapon State, there is no alternative to confronting, deterring and, if necessary, disarming states that brandish and use weapons of mass destruction. And there is no one to do that but the United States, backed by as many allies as will join the endeavor.

The alternative to such robust and difficult interventionism—the alternative to unipolarity—is not a stable, static multipolar world. It is not an eighteenth-century world in which mature powers like Europe, Russia, China, America, and Japan jockey for position in the game of nations. The alternative to unipolarity is chaos. . . .

We are in for abnormal times. Our best hope for safety in such times, as in difficult times past, is in American strength and will—the strength and will to lead a unipolar world, unashamedly laying down the rules of world order and being prepared to enforce them. Compared to the task of defeating fascism and communism, averting chaos is a rather subtle call to greatness. It is not a task we are any more eager to undertake than the great twilight struggle just concluded. But it is just as noble and just as necessary.

92

ERIC ALTERMAN

From *Who Speaks for America?*

Foreign policy has usually been considered the special province of high-level experts and statesmen. Average citizens may have opinions and even input into domestic issues, but when it comes to foreign policy, only people at the highest levels, with the greatest training and knowledge, can make legitimate decisions. Journalist Eric Alterman questions this thesis in his exploration of the role of everyday citizens in the making of foreign policy. In a democracy, shouldn't the people take part in such decision-making? Expertise, the author suggests, is what gives the "foreign policy establishment" its power. Yet Alterman's counter to this is simple: "Much of the American public is indeed ignorant, but it is not stupid." With many examples from the past and present in American diplomacy, Alterman makes a strong case for a foreign policy process that is more inclusive of average citizens' views.

IN THE WINTER OF 1998, the Clinton administration was preparing to launch an attack on Iraq in retaliation for Saddam Hussein's unwillingness to comply with the United Nations inspection regime. Support for the plan, however, appeared lukewarm in the extreme. Among our erstwhile allies, only England and Canada believed the military route to be the correct one. At home, the plan seemed to raise more questions than answers among the American people. Even Tom Clancy, the right-wing technothriller novelist—and about as reliable a supporter of all forms of military action as one is likely to find anywhere—complained in the

New York Times that the president had failed to address the nation's most fundamental concerns: "Who has explained to the American people why it is necessary to send our sons and daughters into harm's way?" Clancy asked. "Who has prepared us and the world for the unpalatable consequences of even a successful attack? How likely is failure, and what would be the consequences?"

In an attempt to quell such anxieties, as it simultaneously garnered support at home and demonstrated its resolve abroad, the administration contacted top executives at CNN and arranged for a worldwide broadcast of a national "town meeting" at Ohio State University. The administration sent Secretary of State Madeleine Albright, Secretary of Defense William Cohen, and National Security Advisor Samuel "Sandy" Berger. As soon as the meeting began, the administration wished it hadn't. First came the loud protests of members of the Spartacist League, the Trotskyite splinter group. When they finally quieted down, an unending barrage of extremely tough and thoughtful questions demonstrated just how ill conceived was the plan for which the Clinton administration was seeking approval.

The problem was not, as administration officials later tried to claim, that the event was hampered by insufficient advance work or too large and unwieldy an audience. Rather, the top national security officials of the United States government were wholly unprepared to answer the kinds of questions with which Ohio citizens had armed themselves. Here are some of the questions asked by members of the audience on that cold February afternoon:

- The American administration has the might and the means to attack the Iraqi state, but does it have the moral right to attack the Iraqi nation? [Cheers, applause.]
- This administration has raised concerns about Iraq's threats to its neighbors, yet none of these neighbors seem too threatened. . . . Furthermore, the international community has been opposed to the bombings. If nobody's asking us for their help, how can you justify further U.S. aggression in the region? [Applause, shouts.]
- If push comes to shove and Saddam will not back down . . . or keep his word, are we ready and willing to send the troops in? [Cheers, applause.]
- President Carter . . . was quoted yesterday as saying that up to 100,000 innocent Iraqi civilians could be killed. Is that something, Secretary Albright, [Shouts, applause] that you think is a realistic possibility? Since we are unsure where Iraq's weapons are, how can we direct a bombing strike against them?

- Why bomb Iraq when other countries have committed similar violations? . . . For example, Turkey has bombed Kurdish citizens. Saudi Arabia has tortured political and religious dissidents. Why does the United States apply different standards of justice to these countries? [Cheers, applause.]

Good questions, every one of them. And the audience at Ohio State asked many more that were equally piercing and intelligent. Yet the gathered administration officials thought such concerns had no merit and were irrelevant to the task at hand. To the viewer at home, it appeared as if the questioners and the government officials were speaking two different languages. In response to the questioner who raised the issue of the inconsistency of the application of U.S. human rights policies, for instance, the secretary of state lectured, "I suggest, sir, that you study carefully what American foreign policy is, what we have said exactly about the cases that you have mentioned. Every one of them have been pointed out. Every one of them we have clearly stated our policy on. And if you would like, as a former professor, I would be delighted to spend fifty minutes with you describing exactly what we are doing on those subjects." But she did not offer a single sentence in response to the question that might fairly be considered an answer.

One anonymous administration official tried to blame the CNN anchors for the public relations debacle, insisting that moderators "Judy [Woodruff] and Bernie [Shaw] looked like they were deer caught in the headlights, they had no control over the management of this." But the true problem was an insurmountable clash of cultures. In the official meeting rooms and academic conferences, to say nothing of high-minded forums such as *Nightline* and *Newshour with Jim Lehrer*, foreign policy discussion is considered a matter for professionals only. When "the public" enters into the discussion, it is usually only in the context of a problem that needs to be managed or an inconvenience that must be finessed. Here was a public empowered by television cameras and a worldwide audience that would not defer and would not go away. The result was not only a genuine roadblock on the administration's road to war, but also a national demonstration of the distance between the governing and the governed when it comes to matters of foreign and military policy.

Speaking on *CBS Evening News*, Dan Rather called the meeting "unruly, disorganized and badly staged." A conservative *Time* magazine essayist complained that the event had been "worthless as a means of preparing the country for war." President Clinton tried to be more generous. He later referred to the Ohio State meeting as "a good old-fashioned American debate," but added, "I believe strongly that most Americans support our policy. They support our resolve." Clinton rushed, however, to undo the damage by throwing his support behind a last-ditch diplomatic effort to avert war by United Nations secretary-general Kofi Annan. Annan succeeded, and this time, war was avoided. The larger lessons of Ohio State, however, remained unlearned. The administration promised better advance work next time but no institutionalized methods of consultation or even mutual education between itself and the public on foreign policy issues. The media, as is its wont, soon forgot about Ohio State and moved on to the next scandal du jour. The problem itself, went away—or so the foreign policy establishment and the media that covers it would like to believe.

The democratization of American foreign policy is a problem that worries precious few people. In the United States, frequently termed "the world's leading democracy" by pundits and politicians, foreign policy has been deliberately shielded from the effects of democratic debate, with virtually no institutionalized democratic participation. True, we have elections. But elections occur too infrequently to have much of an impact on all but the highest-profile foreign policy decision, and in any case they rarely turn on foreign policy questions. Even in 1968, with an issue as central and divisive as Vietnam, the presidential candidates failed to offer the public a clear choice. During the Cold War, it may have been possible to argue that the survival of the nation itself depended upon the ability of our leaders to make immediate decisions regarding nuclear war. These effectively precluded the untidy mechanisms of the democratic process. Excluding a tiny percentage of decisions that deal with potential terrorist threats, that argument has passed into history along with the Soviet Union. Similarly, it may once have been possible to contend that many Americans were unaffected by most foreign policy decisions. But in an era where a decision to enter into a given trade accord with one nation can literally wipe out an entire industry or geographic community, where the failure to contain environmental destruction on one part of the globe can make life all but unbearable on another, where a new strain of *E. coli* bacteria found in Peruvian carrots can infect conventioneers in Minneapolis, and where tens of millions of Americans have their pension plans invested in global mutual funds, it is anachronistic to the point of willful blindness to argue that "foreign" policy exists apart and distinct from "domestic" policy. How, then, can the United States claim to be a functioning democracy when one of the most crucial aspects of public policy allows for almost no democratic participation?

Yet the issue fails to engage. According to a 1997 poll, majorities ranging from 55 to 66 percent say that events in Mexico, Western Europe, Asia, and Canada had little or no impact on them. They prefer to pay attention to those issues that do. Of the thousands of foreign policy monographs published in the past decade by various academics, mandarins, and aspiring secretaries of state, an extremely small percentage focus on the role that the public plays in determining—or even reacting to—those policies. A far greater percentage of the foreign policy community in Washington and in academia is concerned with the problem of improving other nations' democratic practices than with examining the character of our own. The same is true of the specialist's publication *Journal of Democracy*, which has published just a handful of articles even remotely concerned with the United States internal policies. Within the larger populace, and even in the informed debate of the Washington punditocracy, the issue simply does not arise.

At this point the reader might ask if I am not begging an obvious question: Can foreign policy be democratic at all, particularly in a country where most people prefer to remain ignorant of the details of their own politics and culture, much less anyone else's? Indeed, the problem is hardly unique to our time and place. No democracy, it must be admitted at the outset, deals well with this problem; not France, not Germany, not England, not Japan. The conflict may be endemic to democracy itself. Alexis de Tocqueville observed long ago that in the conduct of foreign affairs, "democratic governments do appear decidedly inferior to others." Foreign policy, he lamented, requires none of the good qualities peculiar to democracy but demands the cultivation of those sorely lacking. Democracies found it "difficult to coordinate the details of a great undertaking and to fix on some plan and carry it through with determination" and had "little capacity for combining measures in secret and waiting patiently for the result." The diplomatic historian Walter LaFeber calls this phenomenon "the Tocqueville problem in American history." How, LaFeber wonders, can a "democratic republic, whose vitality rests on the pursuit of individual interests with a minimum of central governmental direction, create the necessary national consensus for the conduct of an effective, and necessarily long-term, foreign policy?"

The problem is real, but hardly insoluble. Much of the American public is indeed ignorant, but it is not stupid. Over time, Americans have demonstrated an impressive consistency of values in foreign policy, one that is easily obscured by the polling data that focuses on immediate reactions to various crises. The public's values . . . are a good deal closer to the liberal republican values of the country's original founders than are those of the establishment that professes to represent them. The problem is not that the public does not care. Rather, it has no idea how to force the government to respond to its preferences.

Even if the American people were as incompetent as the members of the foreign policy establishment believe they are, that would be an unacceptable argument for their exclusion from the policy-formation process. In a democracy, a majority of the people have a right to be wrong. "Democracy," insisted Sidney Verba, former president of the American Political Science Association, in a 1995 address to his membership, "implies responsiveness by governing elites to the needs and preferences of the citizenry. More than that, it implies equal responsiveness." The rule of political equality forms the foundational basis of the American political system. It is expressed by our belief in the principle of "one person, one vote."

When Americans complain about the quality of our democracy, their focus is almost always close to home. Crime, drugs, taxes, and schools dominate the agenda while issues of electoral reform and "money politics" floated until recently in the background, most often raised by gadflies such as Ross Perot and Ralph Nader. Yet no nationally significant politician speaks of consulting the American people directly about the conduct of a foreign policy issue, and to my knowledge, no politically significant grassroots leader has put forth a plan to do so either. Despite all the populist anger at "elitist" Washington politicians and bureaucrats that has characterized American debate in recent decades, Americans remain meekly deferential when it comes to foreign policy. In a 1989 survey for the Carnegie Council on Ethics and International Affairs, the Wirthlin Group found that nearly 50 percent of those questioned disagreed with the statement that the "general public is qualified to participate in deciding on U.S. foreign policy."

The U.S. foreign policy establishment, made up of government officials, congressional staffers, insider academics, think-tank partisans, and the lawyers and bankers who shuttle back and forth into these jobs with each change of administration, concur wholeheartedly with this portion of the public. When I first began this study, I approached the head of a prestigious liberal foreign policy think tank in Washington about housing it. "I don't really believe there should be any democracy in foreign policy," he told me. "The people don't know what the [expletive deleted] they want." When I returned to the same think tank to give a talk on [this] subject . . . to its interns, an extremely self-satisfied young man announced that he did not "see why people who don't know anything about foreign policy should have the same say in what happens as those of us who do." . . .

To the degree that the makers of U.S. foreign policy recognize a role for the public in policy formation at all, it is usually that of the quietly attentive student. The responsibility of the president, for instance, according to former national security adviser Zbigniew Brzezinski, is not to act in accordance with the wishes of his voters but to "enlighten the public about global complexities and generate support for his policies." That Americans may not wish for their government to invade a particular country should not affect a policymaker's decision-making process, according to former Bush administration official Richard N. Haass. "Interventions tend to rise and fall on their merits. Success will create support that may not have existed beforehand—Grenada and the protection of Gulf shipping are cases in point—while failure will drain any support that might have existed." Grenada, explains Haass, referring to the tiny nutmeg-producing island invaded by U.S. forces under President Reagan, "shows that a president who has the courage to lead will win public support if he acts wisely and effectively." Some officials and former officials have gone so far as to argue that the president's powers to conduct foreign policy are akin to those of a general in the army. When Congress challenged George Bush's friendliness to the Chinese regime in the aftermath of the Tiananmen Square massacre, Secretary of State James Baker was sharply critical. "Leadership on this issue," he insisted, "should come from the president as commander-in-chief." General Maxwell Taylor gave this view added (and ominous) power when he explained to a television journalist in 1971 that "a citizen should know those things he needs to be a good citizen and to discharge his functions." Given what Taylor and his cohorts believed the American people "needed" to know about U.S. policy in Vietnam, his view would appear to contain within it the seeds of tragedy as well as deadly irony. . . .

What becomes clear to anyone who studies the problem carefully is that the American people do not accept the foreign policy establishment's definition of the nation's priorities in the world but do not know how to force a reassessment. Most Americans, unlike the members of the foreign policy establishment, do not live to conduct foreign policy; rather, they conduct foreign policy to live. They believe, by vast majorities, that "U.S. foreign policy should service the U.S. domestic agenda rather than remain focused on traditional internationalist problems." In a 1989 poll, designed explicitly to discover the "values" that underlay Americans' foreign policy attitudes, nearly 90 percent of those questioned insisted that "America has a moral responsibility to concentrate on domestic policy before concentrating on foreign policy." Seven years later, a series of focus groups undertaken by the National Issues Forum, a polling and educational organization, determined that almost all participants believed that "domestic needs have been neglected at the expense of foreign affairs." This belief is not the result of ignorance, insufficient education, stupidity, or an inability of the foreign policy establishment to reach the larger public. This is a core American value. At the National Issues Convention in Austin in January 1996, the percentage of participants who believed that the United States would be "better off if we just stayed at home and did not concern ourselves with problems in other parts of the world" increased by 25 percent to nearly one out of two people after each participant had the opportunity to consult with experts, facilitators, and one another. Seventy percent agreed that the "U.S. should shift resources back into helping its own economy now that the Cold War is over." When polled, Americans consistently choose "protecting American jobs" as their most important foreign policy priority, but the goal barely registers among business and opinion elites. Clearly, if it knew how to do so, the public would demand a foreign policy that served those interests, one that focused more on protecting jobs than promoting unfettered trade, one that eschewed far-flung adventures to concentrate on strengthening the American economy and society. Finally, and most importantly, the American people would like to see a foreign policy that ceases to operate as if foreign policy and domestic policy were somehow separate realms. And in this regard, it is the American people who share the viewpoint of the nation's founders and comprehend the world of today with greater realism and sophistication than their alleged intellectual superiors.

Foreign policy experts regard their competence as sufficient reason that they alone should determine the overall direction of U.S. foreign policy. (The day-to-day operation of that policy is unarguably beyond the capacities of any large-scale democratic system.) But the makers of U.S. foreign policy are unwilling to own up to increasing amounts of evidence that the values they believe should underlie the nation's foreign policy are at odds with those of the people in whose name they profess to act and speak.

The values of the foreign policy establishment are less reflective of the political interests of most Americans than of the transnational class of bankers, lobbyists, lawyers, and investors from which they are drawn. These "experts" are so shielded from the struggles of everyday American life that they have become, as John Dewey predicted, "a class with private interests and private knowledge." This development should hardly surprise anyone, nor is it cause for scandal. But it is a reality, and if we are to call ourselves a democracy, we must address it.

The disjunction between elite and mass values in foreign policy has been growing ever since the United States began to take on the accoutrements of empire. Beginning with the Cold War, however, these differences became contradictions, frequently antidemocratic in character. The elites demanded public sacrifice for their policies but employed deceitful means to build support for them. The exposure of these tawdry tactics has done much to destroy public confidence in virtually all American institutions. For instance, according to extensive public research done over a period of decades, the American public views the Vietnam War to have been "more than a mistake" and to have been "fundamentally wrong and immoral." Most members of the elite, committed to the idea of empire and, hence, to the means of defending it, find this view not merely simplistic and wrongheaded but personally offensive. The gulf, moreover, has increased rather than receded with time. When questioned by the National Issues Forum in 1996, members of the public could not credit U.S. foreign policy with a single significant accomplishment that improved their lives, or anyone else's for that matter. Rather, "participants felt that when it comes to foreign affairs, the public has been regularly misled by leaders from both parties for many years." . . .

Historically, the elite's method of dealing with popular disapproval of foreign policy has been simply to ignore it and to cover up evidence of unpopular policies whenever necessary. This was the case for President Franklin Roosevelt, who did so for brave and farsighted reasons between 1939 and 1941, and it remains true today. Unfortunately, Roosevelt's example has led many of his successors to equate their own political interests with the Nazi threat to civilization. Presidents now routinely defy the clearly stated values of the American people and then lie about it. In doing so, they undermine the democratic foundation of our political system. Richard Nixon and Henry Kissinger were guilty of this transgression when they secretly expanded the Vietnam War into Cambodia and then covered up the evidence. Ronald Reagan and Oliver North were equally culpable when they sold missiles to the Ayatollah and used the profits to funnel guns to the Nicaraguan contras. Both of these actions resulted in celebrated scandals, but they did not dissuade future presidents from engaging in the same practices.

Today, presidential actions that defy the unmistakable foreign policy preferences of the American people and are then covered up by their perpetrators are not even considered cause for scandal. For instance while the public was unarguably unenthusiastic about NAFTA, it did cite "stopping the inflow of illegal drugs" as a top priority in the most recent CCFR poll. During the NAFTA battle, however, according to a *New York Times* report, the Bush administration "often exaggerated the Mexican government's progress in the fight against drugs, playing down corruption and glossing over failures." John P. Waters, a senior official for international drug policy in the Bush White House, explained, "People desperately wanted drugs not to become a complicating factor for NAFTA. There was a degree of illicit activity that was just accepted." Motivated by what one former official called "the bigger picture," the Bush administration went so far as to overlook the killing by corrupt Mexican Army officers of seven U.S. DEA officers who were in hot pursuit of a smuggler's aircraft in Veracruz.

The administration's actions in this incident were not reported until almost five years after it took place. Had Americans wished to vote in 1992 on the basis of the foreign policy issue about which they professed to care most deeply, they would not have had the requisite information. Unless someone happened to be a particularly careful reader of the *New York Times*, a category that excludes more than 99 percent of all U.S. voters, he would probably never have seen or heard any mention of this policy at all. In such cases, democracy is subverted and the peoples' wishes denied.

To protect NAFTA, the U.S. government's whitewash of the involvement of high-level Mexican officials in drug smuggling has continued and even expanded on a bipartisan basis under President Clinton. As an example of conflicts between elite and public goals, it is U.S. foreign policy writ large. Presidents and their advisers understand that the public's natural deference and disinclination to question the details of official policy regarding foreign adversaries gives them enormous latitude to pursue policies in conflict with Americans' professed values and beliefs. In matters of war and peace in particular, Americans' patriotic desire to support their president usually overwhelms their natural bias against involvement in foreign wars. Politicians and members of the punditocracy exploit this phenomenon by deliberately exaggerating potential physical threats to the United States and by manipulating Americans' deep-seated racial fears and insecurities. With regard to trade policy and the protection of American jobs, the elite has managed to exploit the incantatory power of the term "free trade" in order to overcome mass objections to policies that sacrifice workers' wages and job security on the altar of economic efficiency.

To begin to map the potential contours of a new, democratically based foreign policy, we need to be cognizant of a dizzying number of historical trends, issues, and characterological developments within both America and the world at large. The idea, once again, is to identify the enduring collective values of the American people and then to translate these into workable and consistent political policies. Simply reading poll numbers is insufficient, for precious little polling has been done on values as opposed to mere attitudes and opinions. Furthermore, Americans frequently hold conflicting values with varying degrees of intensity, both within themselves as individuals and among themselves as groups. Listen to Ruben Alcala, a retired steelworker in Merrillville, Indiana, explain his feelings about the efficacy of the Clinton administration's Bosnia policy in mid-1995: "I'm not really following it that closely. I can't understand why it's going on so long, or why. It's a shame so many people are suffering. Sometimes I think maybe we should [intervene]. Then I think, no, let them take care of their own. Let someone else solve it. The U.S. is the greatest country in the world. Should we be the world's policeman? No, that's what we got the U.N. for."

Mr. Alcala seems to believe that a UN military force is an alternative to an American intervention. At the moment of his comment, however, the president and his advisers were facing the question of whether to deploy American troops as part of a UN peacekeeping force. Mr. Alcala insists that the United States is the world's "greatest country" but does not begin to define the meaning of those words. Were it to imply U.S. responsibility to help enforce a peace accord in Bosnia, Mr. Alcala immediately terms this the U.S. acting as the "world's policeman" and hence inappropriate. Though he is clearly troubled by "so many people suffering," he is divided between wishing to find some way to alleviate that suffering and simply defining the problem as one outside the realm of his nation's concerns. How, then, to craft a foreign policy that accurately reflects the values that underlie Mr. Alcala's confusing concerns, that honors the genuine pride and patriotism he feels about his country without pandering to his ignorance and fear?

93

GEORGE KENNAN

From *Around the Cragged Hill*

From his 1947 authorship of the major statement of America's Cold War containment doctrine under the pseudonym "X" to his 1993 reflections on the past and future of the nation, George Kennan has been one of the country's leading statesmen and thinkers. In this excerpt, Kennan concerns himself with the future of American foreign policy, urging politicians and citizens to place national interests in the forefront of their thinking. He criticizes the once-popular idea that the United States is a nation destined for greatness, and suggests a new kind of isolationism in foreign affairs that would allow national resources to go where they are most needed within the country. Kennan includes some warnings for his beloved State Department, the hub of foreign policymaking: the many fragmented interests that converge there must be sorted out, using the nation's interest as the only criterion of their importance. "The hour may be late, but there is nothing that says it is too late," writes Kennan. As Alexis de Tocqueville knew about the fragile democracy, America, Kennan also knows: "The challenge is to see what could be done, and then to have the heart and the resolution to attempt it."

THE PASSING OF THE Cold War, in presenting us a world which appears to be devoid of anything that could be seen as a major great-power enemy of this country, also obviously presents us with a problem for which few of us are prepared. One has to go back to the 1920s to find anything that could be even remotely regarded as a precedent for it; and even then, conditions have changed so greatly since that time that the precedent would be of very little relevance.

What presents itself, in this situation, is a demand for nothing less than a redesigning of the entire great pattern of America's interaction with the rest of the world. To treat this whole subject in a graceful and coherent form within the limits of a single chapter in a book of this nature would surpass the capacity of this writer. He can only attempt, as a starter, to sketch out what he feels should be the main thrust and balance of American policy in the remaining years of the century, and then to give at least a partial elucidation of this concept by commenting on several significant aspects of the problem, without attempting to bring all of these individual comments into one, comprehensive statement.

Anyone who sets out to design or to conduct the foreign policy of a great country has to be clear as to the interests that policy is supposed to serve. Only if the image of these interests is clear in his mind can the policy he evolves have coherence and usefulness.

Those who conduct American foreign policy have two sets of interests to bear in mind. First, there are the parochial interests of the country itself, in the most narrow and traditional sense of that term. Second, there are the interests that engage this country as a participant in the affairs of the international community as a whole. Both of these sets of interests deserve our respect and attention. But it is those of our own country, in the narrower sense, that lie closest to our hearts; and they demand our first consideration.

There is nothing wrong about this allotment of priorities. It is not the dictate of a national selfishness or disregard for others. This particular territory and these particular people, ourselves, are all that we, as a national state, have control over. The management of our society, and this in a creditable way, is for us an unavoidable responsibility as well as a privilege. Unless we meet this responsibility, no one else will; for there is none who could. And unless we meet it creditably, there will be very little that we can do for others—very little that we can do even to serve global interests. The first requirement for a successful participation by the United States in the confrontation with international environmental problems, for instance, will be success in coping even halfway creditably with the similar problems within its own territory.

But there is another reason, too, why the service to our own national interest is more than just selfishness. Our society serves, for better or for worse, as an example for much of the rest of the world. The life of no other people is so widely and closely observed, scrutinized, and sometimes imitated. So true is this that it is not too much to say that the American people have it in their power, given the requisite will and imagination, to set for the rest of the world a unique example of the way a modern, advanced society could be shaped in order to meet successfully the emerging tests of the modern and the future age.

The example, in any case, is going to be there, whether favorable or otherwise, and whether we like it or not. Our handling of our own problems is going to be carefully watched by others, no matter what we do. But if the example is only one of failure—of the evasion of challenge, of the inability to cope with our own major problems—this will be for others, aside from the loss of respect for us, a source of discouragement, a state of mind which can have far-reaching consequences, and for which we will bear a measure of responsibility. It is because no country can hope to be, over the long run, much more to others than it is to itself that we have a moral duty to put our own house in order, if we are to take our proper part in the affairs of the rest of the world.

But beyond the above, and as a background for all that follows in this chapter, I should make it clear that I am wholly and emphatically rejecting any and all messianic concepts of America's role in the world: rejecting, that is, the image of ourselves as teachers and redeemers to the rest of humanity, rejecting the illusions of unique and superior virtue on our part, the prattle about Manifest Destiny or the "American Century"—all those visions that have so richly commended themselves to Americans of all generations since, and even before, the foundation of our country. We are, for the love of God, only human beings, the descendants of human beings, the bearers, like our ancestors, of all the usual human frailties. Divine hands . . . may occasionally reach down to support us in our struggles, as individuals, with our divided nature; but no divine hand has ever reached down to make us, as a national community, anything more than what we are, or to elevate us in that capacity over the remainder of mankind. We have great military power—yes; but there is, as Reinhold Niebuhr so brilliantly and persuasively argued, no power, individual or collective, without some associated guilt. And if there were any qualities that lie within our ability to cultivate that might set us off from the rest of the world, these would be the virtues of modesty and humility; and of these we have never exhibited any exceptional abundance. The discussion that follows is predicated on the rejection of such illusions.

We saw, in the preceding chapters, some examples of the failures and unsolved problems of our society. There are others that could have been mentioned. Until these inadequacies have been overcome, the task of overcoming them will have to have first claim on our resources. Comprehensive programs of reform in several areas of our life will have to be devised, put in motion, and carried through. Until this is done, we will not know what resources we can spare for foreign policy; and those we find it imperative to continue to devote to that purpose will have to be cut to the bone. What we should want, in these circumstances, is the minimum, not the maximum, of external involvement.

All of this seems to me to call for a very modest and restrained foreign policy, directed to the curtailment of external undertakings and involvements wherever this is in any way possible, and to the avoidance of any assumption of new ones. This means a policy far less pretentious in word and deed than the ones we have been following in recent years. It means, in particular, a rejection of the tempting but fatuous assumption that we can find, in our relations with other countries or other parts of the world, relief from the painful domestic confrontation with ourselves.

There will no doubt be those who will be quick to label what has just been suggested as a policy of isolationism. The term is not very meaningful; but if it means what I think it does, I could only wish that something of that sort were possible; for most foreign involvements are burdens we should be happy to be without. But unfortunately, as will be seen shortly, whatever possibilities may exist for the curtailment of our external commitments and obligations, there will always be a goodly number that cannot be eliminated—not, at least, in any short space of time—and of which we must acquit ourselves as best we can. . . . The value of any policy purporting to reflect the national interests of the United States cannot be greater than the ability of the U.S. government to carry it out. And that will depend, in turn, on the extent to which the policymaker is free to address himself to that particular problem—the extent, that is, to which his field of vision and his energies are not preempted by competing undertakings in which the national interest is not a factor at all.

First of all, let us note the manner in which our government is at present set up for the conduct of foreign policy. In recent decades, the power to make foreign policy decisions has been scattered all over the vast panorama of Washingtonian bureaucracy. The process is theoretically under the ultimate control of the president, in the sense that anytime he decides to put in his word, that word is the controlling one. But the president is a very busy man. The time he has to devote to this sort of thing is limited. It was pointed out in an earlier chapter of this disquisition that under the American system of government, but not under many others, the president has to be both chief of state and prime minister, not to mention his responsibilities in party leadership. This puts great strain on him. The number of decisions, great and small, that enter daily into the conduct of American foreign policy are multitudinous. The State Department alone, we are told, receives, and is obliged to respond to, more than seven hundred telegrams a day. The president cannot possibly occupy himself personally with more than the tiniest fraction of such demands. The vast majority have to be delegated.

In recent years, this process of delegation has occurred in such a way that the power to take the necessary decisions has been fragmented, and is, as I say, farmed out all over the governmental pasture. In addition to the Department of State, the National Security Council, the Pentagon, the CIA, the Treasury, the Department of Commerce, and no end of legislators, legislative committees, and staffs all have their fingers in this pie. Parochial bureaucratic outlooks, interests, and competitive aspirations clash at every point. The result is, for obvious reasons, a very messy business. In this confusion, such a thing as a clear, firm, and prompt decision—and particularly one where all the relevant aspects of national interest are brought together, calmly weighed, and collectively taken into account—is rare indeed. It would do little good to have, here or there, at one place or another in the Washington scene, clear concepts of long-term national interest, so long as the power to make decisions remains thus fragmentized. As things now stand, many of the decisions taken are the results of long, labored, and tortuous compromises among endless numbers of individuals and committees, each of whom or of which has a different idea of the interests to be served. The result, not surprisingly, is everything else than a coherent, concise, thoughtfully formed, or clearly articulated foreign policy. . . .

Plainly, of course, there would always likewise be Congress to be taken into account. It, too, has its constitutional place in the designing of foreign policy. Decisions taken in the executive branch will always have to be compromised with the views and wishes of individual legislators and congressional committees. But here is where politics come in. Here, the president and the secretary of state, both political figures, are the ones whose responsibility it is to make the unavoidable decisions as to the extent to which congressional views and wishes, very often the reflection of lobbyist pressures, should be deferred to, compromised with, or defied in the designing of foreign policy.

In the days of my directorship at the State Department's Policy Planning Staff, I was sometimes urged to take into account, in our recommendations to the secretary of state, the domestic-political aspects of the recommendation in question. "Should you not warn the secretary," it would be asked of me, "of the domestic-political problems this recommendation would present, and make suggestions as to how they might be met?" I resisted firmly all such pressures. Our duty, I insisted, was to tell the president and the secretary what, in our view, was in the national interest. It was their duty, if they accepted the force of our recommendations, to see how far these could be reconciled with domestic-political realities. This was a duty that they were far better fitted to perform than were we. And if we did not give them, as a starter, a view of the national interest in its pure form, as we saw it, no one else would, and they would not be able to judge its importance relative to the domestic-political pressures by which they were confronted. . . .

In the behavior in recent decades of the American political establishment in matters of foreign policy, I see reflected a number of persistent motivations, most of them illustrated in what has been said in this chapter. I see, thus reflected, remnants of the astigmatism and the corruption of understanding that marked the Cold War period. I see the impulse to cater to the demands and desiderata of powerful special domestic-political interests. I see a great deal (some of it contradictory) of what I think of as diplomacy before the flattering mirror: the desire to appear as the gracious and high-minded lady bountiful (the many aid programs), as the thrilling military adventurer—the knight in shining armor, rushing to the aid of the threatened and the downtrodden (Vietnam, Panama, the Persian Gulf War)—and as the unbending champion of democracy and human rights. I see the addiction to established habit, and the ponderous inertia, of entrenched bureaucracies. And in all of this I see the never-ending compulsion of successive administrations to present themselves, for the popularity polls, in postures that feed the American public's favorite wish-images of itself. All this I see. What I do not see is any marked concern for the national interest in the narrow sense, on the one hand, or for the wider interests of the threatened planet, on the other.

The reader may recall the observation . . . to the effect that every political regime, in all places and all times, speaks with two voices: one for the interests of its people as a whole, the other for its own interests as one of the contenders in the inevitable domestic-political competition. And it strikes me that in the behavior of the American political establishment, as noted above, there is a decided, and undue, predominance of the second of those two voices. I am not arguing that it should not be heard at all. I know that this distortion of priorities is one of the prices we pay for the advantages of our form of government. I have no doubt that most of our politicians, confronted with this reproach, would say, "Don't you realize that in order to have the ability to act in the national interest, we first have to gain power; and that to gain that power requires precisely the sort of compromises and pretensions that you are professing to deplore?" But to this I would have to reply, "Yes, within limits. But I don't see any great difference in your behavior before and after an election. One electoral test successfully surmounted, you at once begin thinking of the next one; and the domestic-political considerations again crowd out the interests of the nation as a whole."

Still, I see this situation as the fault not so much of the individuals who command, at one time or another, the seats of power but rather of the political system that installs them in those positions. Is there not, I wonder, some serious structural defect that puts so great a premium on one sort of political motivation, and so little on the other? . . .

Is it a dark and despairing view of the human predicament that emerges? The writer's answer is no—it could not be. No one—neither this writer nor anyone else who undertakes to comment on the human scene—can profess to stand outside the subject on which he is commenting. There is no detached Archimedean platform from which the subject could be viewed. Just as the scientist's observation of an experiment affects the very material on which he is experimenting, the humanist, too, makes himself a part of the problem he examines; and he assumes thereby at least a small share of responsibility for the image he describes. His words, after all, may be expected to have *some* consequences, however trivial; otherwise, they would not be worth uttering. But the measure and quality of this effect is never predictable; and, that being the case, the responsibility of the writer is all the greater.

I cannot too strongly emphasize the seriousness of this responsibility. If the commentator's words sow despair, particularly among younger people whose ability to act upon life has not yet exhausted itself or even reached its peak, he may, by his despairing words, have given discouragement where courage was needed. He may have created hopelessness where, even if he could not himself see this, there was no reason not to hope.

And that, as I see it, would be the unpardonable sin. The hour may be late, but there is nothing that says that it is too late. There is nothing in man's plight that his vision, if he cared to cultivate it, and his will, if he dared to exercise it, could not alleviate. The challenge is to see what could be done, and then to have the heart and the resolution to attempt it. Anything in the way of a comment on the human condition that weakened that heart or undermined that resolution would be an inexcusable abuse of the responsibility of the speaker.

The observations brought forward in this book are offered, then, however severe some of them may seem, with a view to encouraging others to take heart—not to lose it. But to take heart is to act. It is the writer's hope that this book itself, in its own small way, is an action, and will be received accordingly.

PERMISSIONS ACKNOWLEDGMENTS

1. From *Democracy in America* by Alexis de Tocqueville, translated by Henry Reeve, published by Schoeken Books, 1961. Originally published in 1835.
2. From *The American Commonwealth* by James Bryce. Published by Macmillan, 1888.
3. Excerpts from *The Liberal Tradition in America: An Interpretation of American Political Thought Since the Revolution*, by Louis Hartz, copyright © 1955 and renewed 1983 by Louis Hartz, reprinted by permission of Harcourt, Inc.
4. From *American Exceptionalism: A Double-Edged Sword* by Seymour Martin Lipset. Copyright © 1996 by Seymour Martin Lipset. Reprinted by permission of W. W. Norton & Company, Inc.
5. Adapted with the permission of The Free Press, a Division of Simon & Schuster, Inc. from *The Ladd Report* by Everett Carll Ladd. Copyright © 1999 by Everett Carll Ladd.
6. From *Race Matters*, by Cornel West. Copyright © 1993 by Cornel West. Reprinted by permission of Beacon Press, Boston.
7. From *People of Paradox* by Michael Kammen. Copyright © 1972 by Michael Kammen. Reprinted by permission of Alfred A. Knopf, Inc., a Division of Random House, Inc.
8. From *Habits of the Heart* by Robert Bellah, et al. Copyright © 1985, 1996 The Regents of the University of California. Reprinted by permission of The University of California Press.
9. From *The American Political Tradition* by Richard Hofstadter. Copyright © 1948 by Alfred A. Knopf, Inc. and renewed 1976 by Beatrice Hofstadter. Reprinted by permission of Alfred A. Knopf, Inc., a Division of Random House, Inc.
10. *The Federalist* 10, by James Madison, 1787.
11. From *A Machine That Would Go of Itself* by Michael Kammen. Copyright © 1986 by Michael Kammen. Reprinted by permission of Alfred A. Knopf, Inc., a Division of Random House, Inc.
12. Excerpted from *The Power Elite* by C. Wright Mills. Copyright © 1956, by C. Wright Mills. Renewed 1984 by Yaraslave Mills. Used by permission of Oxford University Press.
13. From Richard Zweigenhaft and G. William Domhoff, *Diversity in the Power Elite*. Copyright © 1998 by Richard Zweigenhaft and G. William Domhoff. Reprinted by permission of Yale University Press.
14. From *Who Governs* by Robert Dahl. Copyright © 1961 by Yale University Press. Reprinted by permission of Yale University Press. From *A Preface to*

Democratic Theory by Robert Dahl. Copyright © 1956 by The University of Chicago Press. Reprinted by permission of The University of Chicago Press.

15. From Robert N. Roberts, and Marion T. Doss, Jr., *From Watergate to Whitewater: The Public Integrity War*. Copyright © 1997 by Praeger Publishers. Reprinted by permission of Greenwood Publishing Group, Inc.
16. *The Federalist* 51, by James Madison, 1787.
17. From *Congressional Government* by Woodrow Wilson. Published by Peter Smith publishers. Originally published 1885.
18. From *The Washington Community* by James Young, Copyright © 1966, Columbia University Press. Reprinted with permission of the Publisher.
19. From *Revolving Gridlock: Politics and Policy from Carter to Clinton* by David W. Brady and Craig Volden. Copyright © 1998 by Westview Press, Inc. Reprinted by permission of Westview Press, a member of Perseus Books , L.L.C.
20. *The Federalist* 39 and 46, by James Madison, 1787.
21. From *American Federalism: A View from the States*, 2nd Edition by Daniel J. Elazar. Copyright © 1984 by Harper & Row Publishers, Inc. Reprinted by permission of Addison-Wesley Educational Publishers, Inc.
22. From *Laboratories of Democracy*, by David Osborne, Boston, MA: 1991, excerpted from pages 5, 6, 67–73. Copyright © 1991 by the President and Fellows of Harvard College, all rights reserved. Reprinted by permission of Harvard Business School Press.
23. Excerpt from *United States v. Lopez* 115 S.Ct. 1624 (1995).
24. From *Power to the People: An American State at Work* by Tommy G. Thompson (HarperCollins, 1996). Copyright © 1996 by Thomas G. Thompson. Printed by permission of the author.
25. From *Congress: The Electoral Connection* by David Mayhew, published by Yale University Press. Copyright © 1974 by Yale University Press. Reprinted by permission of Yale University Press.
26. From *Home Style: House Members in Their Districts* by Richard F. Fenno, Jr. Copyright © 1978 by Little, Brown and Company. Reprinted by permission of Addison–Wesley Educational Publishers, Inc.
27. From *Congressional Women: Their Recruitment, Integration, and Behavior*, Second Edition, Revised and Updated by Irwin N. Gertzog. Copyright © 1995 by Praeger Publishers. Reprinted by permission of Greenwood Publishing Group, Inc.
28. From *Hispanics in Congress: A Historical and Political Survey* by Maurilio E. Vigil. Copyright © 1996 by Maurilio E. Vigil. Reprinted by permission of University Press of America, Inc.
29. "Pork: A Time-Honored Tradition Lives On" by Paul Starobin from *Congressional Quarterly Weekly Report*, Oct. 24, 1987. Copyright © 1987 by Congressional Quarterly, Inc. Reprinted by permission.
30. From "In Praise of Pork," by John Ellwood and Eric Patashnik, from *The Public Interest*, Number 110, Winter 1993, pp. 19–23, 31. © 1993 by National Affairs, Inc. Reprinted by permission of the authors and *The Public Interest*.
31. From *The Congressional Experience*, by David Price, Copyright © 1992 by Westview Press Inc. Reprinted by permission of Westview Press, a member of Perseus Books, L.L.C.
32. From *The Freshmen: What Happened to the Republican Revolution*? by Linda

Killian. Copyright © 1998 by Westview Press, Inc. Reprinted by permission of Westview Press, a member of Perseus Books, L.L.C.

33. Adapted with the permission of The Free Press, a Division of Simon & Schuster from *Presidential Power and the Modern Presidents: The Politics of Leadership from Roosevelt to Reagan* by Richard E. Neustadt. Copyright © 1990 by Richard E. Neustadt.
34. Excerpts from *The Imperial Presidency* by Arthur M. Schlesinger, Jr. Copyright © 1973 by Arthur M. Schlesinger, Jr. Reprinted by permission of Houghton Mifflin Co. All rights reserved.
35. From *The Paradoxes of the American Presidency* by Thomas E. Cronin. Copyright © 1998 by Oxford University Press, Inc. Used by permission of Oxford University Press, Inc.
36. From *The Rise of the Plebiscitary Presidency*, by Craig Rimmerman, Copyright © 1993 by Westview Press. Reprinted by permission of the author.
37. From *Impeachment: A Handbook* by Charles L. Black, Jr. Published by Yale University Press. Copyright © 1974: 1998 by Yale University Press. Reprinted by permission of Yale University Press.
38. From *A Government of Strangers* by Hugh Heclo. Copyright © 1977 by Brookings Institution. Reprinted by permission of Brookings Institution.
39. Reprinted by permission of Simon & Schuster from *Governing America* by Joseph A. Califano, Jr. Copyright © 1981 by Joseph A. Califano, Jr.
40. Selected excerpts from *Bureaucracy: What Government Agencies Do and Why They Do It* by James Q. Wilson. Copyright © 1989 by Basic Books, Inc. Reprinted by permission of Basic Books, a member of Perseus Books, L.L.C.
41. From *Reinventing Government*, by David Osborne and Ted Gaebler, © 1992 by David Osborne and Ted Gaebler. Reprinted by permission of Addison-Wesley Publishing Company, Inc.
42. *The Federalist* 78, by Alexander Hamilton, 1787.
43. "The Democratic Character of Judicial Review" by Eugene Rostow from the *Harvard Law Review*, December 1952. Copyright © 1952 by the Harvard Law Review Association. Reprinted by permission.
44. From *Storm Center: The Supreme Court in American Politics*, Third Edition, by David O'Brien, by permission of W. W. Norton & Company, Inc. Copyright © 1993 by David O'Brien. Reprinted by permission of W. W. Norton & Company, Inc.
45. From *Brennan vs. Rehnquist*, by Peter Irons. Copyright © 1994 by Peter Irons. Reprinted by permission of Alfred A. Knopf, Inc., a Division of Random House, Inc.
46. Adapted with permission from Simon & Schuster, Inc. from *The Center Holds: The Power Struggle Inside the Rehnquist Court* by James F. Simon. Copyright © 1995 by James F. Simon.
47. From *The American Commonwealth* by James Bryce. Published by Macmillan, 1888.
48. Reprinted with the permission of Simon & Schuster from *The Phantom Public* by Walter Lippmann. Copyright © 1925 and renewed 1953 by Walter Lippmann.
49. From *Public Opinion and American Democracy* by V.O. Key, published by Alfred Knopf, 1961. Permission granted by the executors of the Key Estate.

50. From *Coming to Public Judgment: Making Democracy Work in a Complex World* by Daniel Yankelovich. Copyright © 1991 by Daniel Yankelovich. Reprinted by permission of Syracuse University Press.
51. From *Direct Democracy*, by Thomas Cronin, Cambridge, Mass.: Harvard University Press, © 1989 by the Twentieth Century Fund, Inc. Reprinted by permission of Harvard University Press.
52. From *Democracy in America* by Alexis de Tocqueville, translated by Henry Reeve, published by Schoeken Books, 1961. Originally published 1835.
53. Excerpts from *The Semisovereign People*, Copyright © 1960 by E.E. Schattschneider and renewed 1988 by Frank W. Schattschneider, reprinted by permission of Harcourt, Inc.
54. From *The End of Liberalism: The Second Republic of the United States*, Second Edition, by Theodore J. Lowi. Copyright © 1979, 1969 by W. W. Norton & Company, Inc. Reprinted by permission of W. W. Norton & Company, Inc.
55. From *The Lobbyists*, by Jeffrey Birnbaum. Copyright © 1992 by Jeffrey Birnbaum. Reprinted by permission of Times Books, a division of Random House, Inc.
56. Adapted with the permission of Simon & Schuster from *Who Will Tell the People*, by William Greider. Copyright © 1992 by William Greider.
57. From *Strangers Among Us* by Roberto Suro. Copyright © 1998 by Roberto Suro. Reprinted by permission of Alfred A. Knopf, Inc., a division of Random House, Inc.
58. From *Storming the Gates: Protest Politics and the Republican Revival* by Don Balz. Copyright © 1996 by Don Balz and Ronald Brownstein. By permission of Little, Brown and Company (Inc.).
59. From *Inside Campaign Finance*, by Frank Sorauf, New Haven, CT: Yale University Press, 1992. Copyright © 1992 by Frank Sorauf. Reprinted by permission of Yale University Press.
60. Reprinted with the permission of The Free Press, a division of Simon & Schuster from *The Tyranny of the Majority: Fundamental Fairness in Representative Democracy*, by Lani Guinier. Copyright © 1994 by Lani Guinier.
61. Excerpted from *Dirty Politics, Distraction, and Democracy*, by Kathleen Hall Jamieson. Copyright © 1992 by Kathleen Hall Jamieson. Reprinted by permission of Oxford University Press, Inc.
62. From *Dirty Little Secrets* by Larry Sabato and Glenn Simpson. Copyright © 1996 by Larry Sabato and Glen Simpson. Reprinted by permission of Times Books, a division of Random House, Inc.
63. Adapted with the permission of The Free Press, a Division of Simon & Schuster, Inc. from *Going Negative: How Attack Ads Shrink and Polarize the Electorate* by Stephen Ansolabehere and Shanto Iyengar. Copyright © 1995 by Stephen Ansolabehere and Shanto Iyengar.
64. From *Extraordinary Politics: How Protest and Dissent are Changing American Democracy* by Charles C. Euchner. Copyright © 1996 by Westview Press, Inc. Reprinted by permission of Westview Press, a member of Perseus Books, L.L.C.
65. From *Critical Elections and the Mainsprings of American Politics* by Walter Dean Burnham. Copyright © 1970 by W. W. Norton & Company, Inc. Reprinted by permission of W. W. Norton & Company, Inc.

66. Excerpts (5) from *The Party's Over* by David S. Broder. Copyright © 1971, 1972 by David S. Broder. Reprinted by permission of HarperCollins Publishers, Inc.
67. Excerpts from *The Party Goes On* by Xandra Kayden and Eddie Mahe, Jr. Copyright © 1985 by Xandra Kayden and Eddie Mahe, Jr. Reprinted by permission of Basic Books, a member of Perseus Books, L.L.C.
68. Adapted with permission from Simon & Schuster, Inc. from *They Only* Look *Dead* by E. J. Dionne. Copyright © 1996 by E. J. Dionne.
69. From *Storming the Gates: Protest Politics and the Republican Revival* by Don Balz. Copyright © 1996 by Don Balz and Ronald Brownstein. By permission of Little, Brown and Company (Inc.).
70. From *I Ain't Got Time To Bleed* by Jesse Ventura. Copyright © 1999 by Jesse Ventura. Reprinted by permission of Villard Books, a division of Random House, Inc.
71. From *A Time of Change* by Harrison Salisbury, published by Harper & Row. Reprinted by permission of Curtis Brown, Ltd. Copyright © 1969 by Harrison Salisbury renewed.
72. From *Feeding Frenzy* by Larry Sabato. Copyright © 2000 by Larry Sabato. Reprinted by permission of LANAHAN PUBLISHERS, INC., Baltimore.
73. Adapted with the permission of The Free Press, a Division of Simon & Schuster, Inc. from *Spin Cycle: Inside the Clinton Propaganda Machine* by Howard Kurtz. Copyright © 1998 by Howard Kurtz.
74. From *Trail Fever* by Michael Lewis. Copyright © 1997 by Michael Lewis. Reprinted by permission of Alfred A. Knopf, a Division of Random House, Inc.
75. From *Gideon's Trumpet* by Anthony Lewis. Copyright © 1964 and renewed 1992 by Anthony Lewis. Reprinted by permission of Random House, Inc.
76. Excerpts from *Miranda v. Arizona*, 384 U.S. 436, 86 S.Ct. 1602 (1966).
77. From *Simple Justice* by Richard Kluger. Copyright © 1975 by Richard Kluger. Reprinted by permission of Alfred A. Knopf, Inc., a division of Random House Inc.
78. Selected excerpts from *The Rage of the Privileged Class*, by Ellis Cose. Copyright © 1993 by Ellis Cose. Reprinted by permission of HarperCollins Publishers, Inc.
79. From *Affirmative Action At Work: Law, Politics, and Ethics*, by Bron Taylor, © 1991 by University of Pittsburgh Press. Reprinted by permission of the University of Pittsburgh Press.
80. Excerpted and reprinted from "Gay and Lesbian Movements in the United States: Dilemmas of Identity, Diversity, and Political Strategy" by Stephen Epstein, included in *The Global Emergence of Gay and Lesbian Politics: National Imprints of a Worldwide Movement* edited by Barry D. Adam, Jan Willem Duyvendak, and Andre Krouwel, by permission of Temple University Press. © 1999 by Temple University. All Rights Reserved.
81. Eight pages from *In Our Defense* by Ellen Alderman and Caroline Kennedy. Copyright © 1991 by Ellen Alderman and Caroline Kennedy. By permission of William Morrow & Company, Inc.
82. From *Girls Lean Back Everywhere*, by Edward DeGrazia. Copyright © 1992 by Edward DeGrazia. Reprinted by permission of Random House, Inc.

83. Adapted with the permission of The Free Press, a Division of Simon & Schuster, Inc. from *Rights Talk: The Impoverishment of Political Discourse* by Mary Ann Glendon. Copyright © 1991 by Mary Ann Glendon.
84. Excerpts from *The Affluent Society* by John Kenneth Galbraith. Copyright © 1958, 1969, 1978, 1984 by John Kenneth Galbraith. Reprinted by permission of Houghton Mifflin Company. All rights reserved.
85. Excerpts from *Free to Choose: A Personal Statement*, copyright © 1980 by Milton Friedman and Rose D. Friedman, reprinted by permission of Harcourt, Inc.
86. From *The Judas Economy: The Triumph of Capital and the Betrayal of Work* by William Wolman and Anne Colamosca. Copyright © 1997 by Westview Press, Inc. Reprinted by permission of Westview Press, a member of Perseus Books, L.L.C.
87. Reprinted with the permission of Simon & Schuster from *The Other America: Poverty in the United States* by Michael Harrington. Copyright © 1962, 1969, 1981 by Michael Harrington.
88. Four pages from *Civil Rights: Rhetoric or Reality?* by Thomas Sowell. Copyright © 1984 by Thomas Sowell. By permission of William Morrow & Company, Inc.
89. "The Black Community's Values as a Basis for Action" from *Black Initiative and Governmental Responsibility*, Joint Center for Political and Economic Studies, 1987. Reprinted by permission.
90. From *Tyranny of Kindness*, by Theresa Funiciello. Copyright © 1993 by Theresa Funiciello. Used by permission of Grove/Atlantic, Inc.
91. "The Unipolar Movement" by Charles Krauthammer, from *Foreign Affairs* 1990/91. Reprinted by permission of Charles Krauthammer.
92. Reprinted from Eric Alterman: *Who Speaks for America: Why Democracy Matters in Foreign Policy*. Copyright © 1998 Eric Alterman. Used with permission of the publisher, Cornell University Press.
93. From *Around the Cragged Hill: A Personal and Political Philosophy*, by George F. Kennan. Copyright © 1993 by George F. Kennan. Reprinted by permission of the author and W. W. Norton & Company, Inc.